THE SECRET SOCIETIES OF ALL AGES AND COUNTRIES

THE SECRET SOCIETIES OF ALL AGES AND COUNTRIES

" Dalla straordinarieth, degli effetti certo puo indursi la straordinarieth,, la grandezza, I' insistenza delle cagioni; ma I' intreccio e I' alterno prevalere di queste, I' attrazione che esercitano, sfuggono all' analisi. II mistero precinge la notturna fecondazione. Dai pin disparati sentiment! trae vigore la setta. Le materie piu preziose ed insieme le meno elette con- corrono a formare questo gigante, rifusione ciclopica e tetra di quanto s' agita, ribolle e schiuma nelle viscere sociali."

G. DE CASTRO.

From the extraordinary nature of the effects we may infer the extraordinary nature, grandeur, and permanency of the causes; but their connection, varying predominance, and mutual attraction, escape all analysis. Mystery surrounds the obscure fecundation. Sects draw vigour from the most opposite sentiments. The most exalted as well as the meanest elements concur in forming this giant, a cyclopean and black fusion of all that seethes, boils, and ferments in the social viscera.

THE SECRET SOCIETIES OF ALL AGES AND COUNTRIES

A Comprehensive Account of upwards of One Hundred
and Sixty Secret Organisations Religious, Political,
and Social from the most Remote Ages
down to the Present Time

Embracing the Mysteries of Ancient India, China, Japan, Egypt, Mexico,
Peru, Greece, and Scandinavia, the Cabbalists, Early Christians,
Heretics, Assassins, Thugs, Templars, the Vehm and
Inquisition, Mystics, Rosicrucians, Illuminati, Free-
masons, Skopzi, Camorristi, Carbonari, Nihilists,
Fenians, French, Spanish,

And other Mysterious Sects

BY

CHARLES WILLIAM HECKETHORN

IN TWO VOLUMES
VOL. I

ANALYTICAL TABLE OF CONTENTS

VOL. I.

The numbers preceding analytical headings refer to the sections.

PREFACE TO THE NEW EDITION

PREFACE TO FIRST EDITION

AUTHORITIES CONSULTED

INTRODUCTION.

1. Intelligibility and Nature of Secret Societies.
2. Classification of Secret Societies.
3. Religious Societies.
4. Political Societies.
5. Aims of Political Societies.
6. Religious Secret Societies.
7. Most Perfect Human Type.
8. Causes of high Mental Development.
9. Primitive Culture.
10. The true Doctrines of Nature and Being,
11. Fundamental Principles of true Knowledge possessed by the Ancients.
12. Key to Mystic Teaching.
13. Mystic Teaching Summarised.
14. How true Knowledge came to be lost.
15. Original Spirit of the Mysteries, and Results of their Decay.
16. The Mysteries under their Astronomical Aspect.
17. Astronomical Aspects continued The Mysteries funereal.
18. Uniformity of Dogmas.
19. Most Ancient Secret Society.
20. Secret Societies No Longer Needed

BOOK I
ANCIENT MYSTERIES

I. THE MAGI.
21. Derivation of the term Magus.
22. Antiquity of the Magi.
23. Zoroaster.
24. Doctrine of Zoroaster.
25. The Light worshipped.
26. Origin of the word Deus, God.
27. Mode of Initiation.
28. Myth of Rustam

II. THE MITHRAICS.
29. Mysteries of Mithras.
30. Origin of Mithraic Worship.
31. Dogmas, &c.
32. Rites of Initiation.
33. Thammuz

III. BRAHMINS AND GYMNOSOPHISTS.
34. Vulgar Creed of India.
35. Secret Doctrines.
36. Hindoo Cosmogony.
37. Buddhism.
38. Buddhistic Teaching.
39. Asceticism.
40. Gymnosophists.
41. Places for celebrating Mysteries.
42. Initiation.
43. The ineffable name Aum.
44. The Lingam.
45. The Lotus.
46. The Jains

IV. EGYPTIAN MYSTERIES.
47. Antiquity of Egyptian Civilisation.
48. Temples of Ancient Egypt.
49. Egyptian Priests and Kings.
50. Exoteric and Esoteric Doctrines.
51. Egyptian Mythology.
52. The Phoenix.

53. The Cross.
54. Places of Initiation.
55. Process of Initiation.
56. Mysteries of Serapis.
57. Mysteries of Osiris.
58. Isis

V. CRATA REPOA, OR HIGHEST DEGREE OF EGYPTIAN INITIATION.
59. Preparation.
60. First Degree.
61. Second Degree.
62. Third Degree, or the Gate of Death.
63. Fourth Degree, or the Battle of the Shades.
64. Fifth Degree: Balahate.
65. Sixth Degree: Astronomers at the Gate of the Gods.
66. Seventh Degree: Propheta.
67. Concluding Remarks

VI. METAMORPHOSIS OF THE LEGEND OF ISIS.
68. Spread of Egyptian Mysteries.
69. Dionysiac or Bacchic Mysteries.
70. Sabazian Mysteries.
71. Mysteries of the Cabiri.
72. Eleusinian Mysteries.
73. Doors of Horn and Ivory.
74. Suppression of Eleusinian Mysteries.
75. The Thesmophoria.
76. Aim of Grecian Mysteries more Moral than Religious

VII. CHINESE AND JAPANESE MYSTERIES.
77. Chinese Metaphysics.
78. Introduction of Chinese Mysteries.
79. Parallel between Buddhism and Christianity.
80. Lau-Tze.
81. Japanese Mysteries.
82. Japanese Doctrines.
83. The Lama

VIII. MEXICAN AND PERUVIAN MYSTERIES.
84. American Aborigines.
85. Mexican Deities.
86. Cruelty of Mexican Worship.
87. Initiation into Mysteries.
88. The Greater Mysteries.
89. Human Sacrifices.
90. Clothing in Bloody Skins.
91. Peruvian Mysteries.
92. Quiches Initiation

IX. THE DRUIDS.
93. The Druids, the Magi of the West.
94. Temples.
95. Places of Initiation.
96. Rites.
97. Doctrines.
98. Political and Judicial Power.
99. Priestesses.
100. Abolition

X. SCANDINAVIAN MYSTERIES.
101. Drottes.
102. Ritual.
103. Astronomical Meaning Demonstrated

BOOK II
EMANATIONISTS

I. THE CABBALA.
104. Its Origin.
105. Date of Cabbala.
106. The Book of the Creation.
107. Different Kinds of Cabbala.
108. Visions of Ezekiel.
109. The Creation out of Nothing, no. Revival of Cabbalistic Doctrines

II. SONS OF THE WIDOW
111. Origin of Religion of Love.
112. Manes.
113. Manichaeism.
114. Life of Manes.
115. Progress of Manichaeism.
116. Doctrines.
117. Spread of Religion of Love.

III. THE GNOSTICS.
118. Character of Gnosticism.
119. Doctrines.
120. Development of Gnosticism.
121. Spirit of Gnosticism.

IV. THE ESSENES.
122. Connection of Judaism and Gnosticism.
123. Essenes and Therapeutse.
124. Their Tenets and Customs.
125. Distinction between the Two Sects

BOOK III
CHRISTIAN INITIATIONS

I. CHRISTIAN INITIATIONS.
126. Myth of Horus Christianised.
127. Christian Mysteries.
128. Similarity of Christian with Pagan Rites.
129. Christian Symbols taken from Pagan Symbols.
130. Celebration of the Mysteries.
131. Astronomical Meaning of Christianity.
132. Prometheus Bound.
133. Abolition of Mysteries

II. THE APOCALYPSE.
134. The Apocalypse.
135. Pagan Impostors

BOOK IV
ISHMAELITES

I. THE LODGE OF WISDOM.
136. Legend of the Mahdi.
137. Abdallah, the first Pontiff.
138. Origin of Quarmatites.
139. Origin of Fatimite Dynasty.
140. The Lodge of Cairo.
141. Progress of Doctrines

II. THE ASSASSINS.
142. Foundation of Order.
143. Influence of Hassan.
144. Degrees of the Order.
145. Devotion of Followers.
146. The Imaginary Paradise.
147. Sanguinary Character of Hassan.
148. Further Instances of Devotion in Followers.
149. Murder of Raschidaddin's Ambassador.
150. Suppression of Assassins.
151. Modern Assassins.
152. A Modern Assassin Chief.
153. Christian Princes in League with Assassins

III. THE ROSHENIAH.
154. The Rosheniah Sect and its Founder.
155. Death of Bayezid.
156. Extinction of Sect

IV. THE DRUSES.
157. Origin of Sect of Druses.
158. Religious Books of the Druses.
159. Murder of Hakem.
160. Hakem's Successor.
161. Doctrines.
162. Customs of the Druses.
163. Druses and Maronites.
164. The Ansaireeh or Nuseiriyeh

V. THE DERVISHES.
165. Dervishes.
166. Shiites and Sunnites.
167. Doctrines

BOOK V
HERETICS

I. HERETICS.
168. Transition from Ancient to Modern Initiations.
169. Spirit of Ancient and Modern Secret Societies.
170. The Circumcellians.
171. The Albigenses.
172. Objects of the Albigenses.
173. Tenets of the Albigenses.
174. Aims of the Albigenses.
175. The Cathari.
176. Doctrines and Tenets.
177. Persecution of the Cathari.
178. The Waldenses or Vaudois.
179. Luciferians.
180. Origin of Devil-worship
181. Religion of the Troubadours.
182. Difficulty to understand the Troubadours.
183. Poetry of Troubadours.
184. Degrees among Troubadours.
185. Courts of Love

BOOK VI
CHIVALRY

I. CHIVALRY.
186. Original Aim.
187. Knights the Military Apostles of the Religion of Love.
188. Tenets and Doctrines

II. THE TEMPLARS.
189. Foundation of the Order.
190. Progress of the Order.
191. Account of Commanderies.

192. Imputations against the Order.
193. Plots against the Order.
194. Attentions paid to Grand Master.
195. Charges against the Templars.
196. Burning of Knights.
197. James de Molay.
198. Mysteries of the Knights Templars.
199. The Temple and the Church.
200. Initiation.
201. Cursing and Spitting on the Cross Explained.
202. Charge of Licentious Practices.
203. The Templars the Opponents of the Pope.
204. Baphomet.
205. Disposal of the Possessions of the Templars

BOOK VII
JUDICIARY

I. THE HOLY VEHM.
206. Origin and Object of Institution.
207. Places for Holding Courts.
208. Officers and Organisations.
209. Language and Rules of Initiated.
210. Procedure.
211. Execution of Sentences.
212. Decay of the Institution.
213. Kissing the Virgin

II. THE BEATI PAOLI.
214. Character of the Society.
215. Tendencies and Tenets.
216. Account of a Sicilian Writer

III. THE INQUISITION.
217. Introductory.
218. Early existence of an Inquisition.
219. Council held at Toulouse.
220. Establishment of the Inquisition.
221. Progress of Institution.
222. Judicial Procedure of the Inquisition.

223. Palace of the Inquisition.
224. Tortures.
225. Condemnation and Execution of Prisoners.
226. Procession of the Auto-da-fé.
227. History continued.
228. General History of Institution continued.
229. Englishmen Imprisoned by the Inquisition.
230. History continued.
231. History continued.
232. Reflections.
233. Abolition of the Inquisition.
234. Restoration and Final Abolition.
235. The False Nuncio.
236. The Inquisition in various Countries.
237. Apologists of the Inquisition

BOOK VIII
MYSTICS

I. ALCHYMISTS.
238. Astrology perhaps Secret Heresy.
239. Process by which Astrology degenerated.
240. Scientific Value of Alchymy.
241. The Tincture.
242. Aims of Alchymy.
243. History of Alchymy.
244. Still, Alchymists formed Secret Societies.
245. Decay of Alchymy.
246. Specimens of Alchymistic Language.
247. Personal Fate of the Alchymists

II. JACOB BOHME.
248. Parallel between Mystics and Sectaries.
249. Character and Mission of Mystics.
250. Merits of Bohme.
251. Bohme's Influence.
252. Sketch of Bohme's Life.
253. The Philadelphians

III. EMANUEL SWEDENBORG.
254. Emanuel Swedenborg.
255. His Writings and Theories.
256. Rationale of Swedenborg's Writings.
257. The New Jerusalem.
258. The Correspondences.
259. Various Swedenborgian Sects.
260. Illuminati of Avignon.
261. Illuminated Theosophists.
262. Philosophic Scotch Rite.
263. Rite of the Philalethes.
264. Rite of , Swedenborg.
265. Universal Aurora

IV. MARTINISM.
266. Martinez Paschalis.
267. Saint-Martin .

V. ROSICRUCIANS.
268. Merits of the Rosicrucians.
269. Origin of the Society doubtful.
270. Rosicrucian Literature.
271. Real Objects and Results of Andrea's Writings.
272. Ritual and Ceremonies.
273. Rosicrucianism in England in the Past.
274. Origin of Name.
275. Statements concerning themselves.
276. Poetical Fictions of Rosicrucians.
277. The Hague Lodge.
278. A Rosicrucian MS.
279. New Rosicrucian Constitution.
280. The Duke of Saxe-Weimar and other Rosicrucians

VI. ASIATIC BRETHREN.
281. Origin of the Order.
282. Division of this Order.
283. Initiation into this Degree.
284. Second Chief Degree, Wise Masters.
285. Third Chief Degree, or Royal Priests, or True Rosicrucians, or the Degree of Melchisedeck.

286. Organisation of the Order.
287. Rosicrucian Adventurers.
288. Theoretical Brethren.
289. Spread of Rosicrucianism.
290. Transition to Freemasons.
291. Progress and Extinction of Rosicrucians.
292. Rosicrucians in the Mauritius.
293. Modern English Rosicrucians

BOOK IX
ANTI-SOCIAL SOCIETIES

I. THE THUGS.
294. Introductory.
295. Name and Origin.
296. Practices and Worship of Thugs.
297. Traditions.
298. Initiation.
299. Suppression.
300. Recent Instance of Thuggism

II. THE CHAUFFEURS, OR BURNERS.
301. Origin and Organisation of Society.
302. Religious and Civil Ceremonies.
303. The Grand Master.
304. Discovery of the Society.
305. Death of an old Chauffeur

III. THE GARDUNA.
306. Origin of the Society.
307. Organisation.
308. Spirit of the Society.
309. Signs, Legend, &c.
310. Suppression of the Society
311. Bandits insuring Travellers' Safety

IV. THE CAMORRA.
312. Origin of the Camorra.
313. Different kinds of Camorra.
314. Degrees of the Society.

315. Ceremony of Reception.
316. Centres.
317. Cant Terms of the Camorra.
318. Unwritten Code of the Camorra.
319. The Camorra in the Prisons.
320. The Camorra in the Streets.
321. Social Causes of the Camorra.
322. The Political Camorra.
323. Attempted Suppression of the Camorra.
324. Renewed Measures against the Camorra.
325. Murders by Camorristi

V. MALA VITA.
326. The Mala Vita

VI. THE MAFIA.
327. The Mafia's Code of Honour.
328. Origin of the Mafia.
329. Origin of the term Mafia.
330. The Mafia in the United States

VII. BEGGARS, TRAMPS, AND THIEVES.
331. Languages and Signs.
332. Italian and German Robbers

VIII. THE JESUITS.
333. Reasons for calling Jesuitism Secret and Anti-Social.
334. Analogy between Jesuitism and Freemasonry.
335. Initiations.
336. Blessing the Dagger.
337. Similar Monkish Initiations.
338. Secret Instructions.
339. Authenticity of "Secreta Monita" Demonstrated.
340. Jesuitic Morality

IX. THE SKOPZI.
341. Various Russian Sects.
342. The Skopzi.
343. The Legend of Selivanoff.
344. Historical Foundation of the Legend.

345. Diffusion of the Sect.
346. Creed and Mode of Worship.
347. The Baptism of Fire.
348. Failure of the Prosecution of the Sect

X. THE CANTERS OR MUCKERS.
349. Eva von Buttler and her Sect.
350. Schonherr's Sect

BOOK X
SOCIAL REGENERATION

I. ILLUMINATI.
351. The Term Illuminati.
352. Foundation of Order.
353. Organisation.
354. Initiation into the Degree of Priest.
355. Initiation into the Degree of Regent.
356. The Greater Mysteries.
357. Nomenclature and Secret Writing of Order.
358. Secret Papers and Correspondence.
359. Refutation of Charges.
360. Suppression.
361. Illuminati in France.
362. Ceremonies of Initiation.
363. Credibility of above Account

II. THE GERMAN UNION.
364. Statements of Founder

III. FRENCH WORKMEN'S UNIONS.
365. Organisation of Workmen's Unions.
366. Connection with Freemasonry.
367. Decrees against Workmen's Unions.
368. Traditions.
369. Names and Degrees.
370. General Customs.
371. Customs among Charcoal-burners and Hewers.
372. Customs in various other Trades

IV. GERMAN WORKMEN'S UNIONS.
373. Huntsman's Phraseology.
374. Initiation.
375. Initiation of Cooper.
376. Curious Works on the Subject.
377. Raison d'etre of the Compagnonnage.
378. Guilds.
379. Kalends Brethren.
380. Knights of Labour

V. GERMAN STUDENTS.
381. Customs of German Students.
382. Ancient Custom of Initiation

PREFACE TO THE NEW EDITION

THIS is not so much a second edition of my book on Secret Societies published in 1875 as an almost entirely new work. When the first edition was published, some of the societies had scarcely any history. Of the Nihilists, for instance, the account now given, recording their doings within the last eighteen years, fills many pages of this work. The story of other societies, active even then, such as the Fenians, had to be brought down to date, and yielded much new matter.

I have thought it desirable to give fuller particulars of certain societies than I had given in the first edition, such as the Jesuits, for instance the new matter having either been kept back, or being the result of further research.

Accounts of societies not included in the first edition will be found here. I may instance "Grata Repoa," "Rosheniah," and "Skopzi."

A few of the articles of the first edition have been reduced; such, for instance, as that on the Paris Commune, which has not now that immediate interest its then recent activity imparted to it.

Great changes have also been made in the arrangement of the matter.

Secret Societies may be arranged either chronologically, or locally, or topically. Each arrangement has its advantages and disadvantages; the former are obvious, the latter may be stated thus:

By arranging societies according to chronology, those which are topically connected or identical will sometimes be placed at so great a distance as to impair the continuity of interest. By arranging them locally, the chronological connection must suffer; and by arranging them according to subjects or topics, the reader obtains no clear view of the sequence of events. I have therefore endeavoured to combine the three modes of representing the great drama of Secret Societies by making the topical arrangement its basis, and on that marshalling the societies first according to locality, and lastly according to time. Thus in the first Book of the work the topic is Ancient Mysteries and Religious Societies; they are arranged according to localities, and the third consideration is the time. Therefore the Eastern Societies come first, in chronological order; then the Western, in the same order; so that the Magi of Persia form the first, and the Scandinavian Drottes of Europe the last in the list.

A full list of authorities consulted being given, it has not been considered necessary to encumber the pages with footnotes; the general reader does not want them, and the student will know what work to refer to for verification. The work, as now presented to the public, is the result of twenty-five years' study and research, involving the acquisition and collation of the English and foreign literature on the subject, and therefore claims to be a cyclopaedia of Secret Societies, giving concise, but quintessential, details of all worth recording, and omitting only those whose duration was ephemeral, and action trivial.

C. W. H.

October, 1896.

PREFACE TO THE FIRST EDITION

FOR many years the fascinating subject of Secret Societies had engaged my attention, and it had long been my intention to collect in a comprehensive work all the information that could be gathered from numerous, often remote, and sometimes almost inaccessible, sources concerning one of the most curious phases of the history of mankind those secret organisations, religious, political, and social, which have existed from the most remote ages down to the present time. Before, however, I had arranged and digested my materials, a review in the Athenceum (No. 2196) directed my attention to the Italian work, "II Mondo Secreto," by Sign or De Castro, whom I have since then had the pleasure of meeting at Milan. I procured the book, and intended at first to give a translation of it; but though I began as a translator, my labours speedily assumed a more independent form. Much, I found, had to be omitted from an original coloured by a certain political bias, and somewhat too indulgent to various Italian political sects, who, in many instances, were scarcely more than hordes of brigands. Much, on the other hand, had to be added from sources, chiefly English and German, unknown to the Italian author; much had to be placed on a different basis and in another light; and again, many societies not mentioned by Signor De Castro had to be introduced to the reader, such as the Garduna, the Chauffeurs, Fenians, International, 0-Kee-Pa, Ku-Klux, Inquisition, Wahabees; so that, with these additions, and the amplifica- tions of sections in the original Italian, forming frequently entirely new articles, the work, as it now is presented to the English public, though in its framework retaining much of its foreign prototype, may yet claim the merit of being not only essentially original, but the most comprehensive account of Secret Societies extant in English, French, German, or Italian, the leading languages of Europe; for whatever has been written on the subject in any one of them has been consulted and put under contribution. In English there is no work that can at all compete with it, for the small book published in 1836 by Charles Knight, and entitled, "Secret Societies of the Middle Ages," embraces four societies only.

The student who wishes for more ample information will have to consult the lists of authorities given at the head of each Book, as it was thought best not to encumber the text with foot-notes, which would have swelled the work to at least twice its present extent. The reader may rest satisfied that few statements are made which could not be supported by numerous and weighty authorities; though dealing as we do here with societies whose very existence depended on secrecy, and which, therefore, as a matter of policy, left behind them as little documentary evidence as possible, the old distich applies with peculiar force:

" What is hits is history,
And what is mist is mystery."

Again, bearing in mind that the imperative compass of the work exacted a concise setting forth of facts ranging as the subject does over a surface so vast I have been careful to interrupt the narrative only by such comments and reflections as would seem almost indispensable for clearing up obscurities or supplying missing historical links.

It may at first appear as if some societies had improperly been inserted in this work as "secret" societies; the Free- masons, for instance. Members of secret associations, it might be objected, are not in the habit of proclaiming their membership to the world, but no Freemason is ashamed or afraid of avowing himself such; nay, he is rather proud of the fact, and given to proclaim it somewhat obtrusively; yet the most rabid Celt, who wishes to have a hand in the re- generation of his native land by joining the Fenian brother- hood, has sense enough to keep his affiliation a profound secret from the uninitiated. But the rule I have followed in adopting societies as "secret" was to include in my collection all such as had or have "secret rites and ceremonies" kept from the outer world, though the existence of the society itself be no secret at all. In fact, no association of men can for any length of time remain a secret, since however anxious the members may be to shroud themselves in darkness, and remain personally unknown, the purpose for which they band together must always betray itself by some overt acts; and wherever there is an act, the world surmises an agent; and if none that is visible can be found, a secret one is suspected. The Thugs, for instance, had every desire to remain unknown; yet the fact of the existence of such a society was suspected long before any of its members were discovered. On the principle also of their being the propounders of secret doctrines, or doctrines clothed in language understood by the adepts alone,

Alchyrnists and Mystics have found places in this work; and the Inquisition, though a state tribunal, had its secret agents and secret procedure, and may therefore justly be included in the category of Secret Societies.

Secret Societies, religious and political, are again spring- ing up on many sides: the religious may be dismissed without comment, as they are generally without any novelty or significance, but those that have political objects ought not to be disregarded as without importance. The Inter- national, Fenians, Communists, Nihilists, Wahabees, are secretly aiming at the overthrow of existing governments and the present order of things. The murders of English- men perpetrated by native Indians point to the machinations of secret societies in British India. Before the outbreak of the great Indian mutiny English newspaper correspondents spoke rather contemptuously of some religious ceremony observed throughout British India of carrying small loaves from village to village, but this ceremony was the summons to the people to prepare for the general rising; hence the proceedings of the natives should be closely watched.

November, 1874.

"Ignis ubique latet, naturam amplectitur omnem
Cuncta parit, renovat, dividit, urit, alit."

VOL. I.

SECRET SOCIETIES

INTRODUCTION

1. *Intelligibility and Nature of Secret Societies* - Secret Societies once were as necessary as open societies: the tree presupposes a root. Beside the empire of Might, the idols of fortune, the fetishes of superstition, there must in every age and state have existed a place where the empire of Might was at an end, where the idols were no longer worshipped, where the fetishes were derided. Such a place was the closet of the philosopher, the temple of the priest, the subterranean cave of the sectary.

2. *Classification of Secret Societies* - Secret societies may be classed under the following heads: I. Religious: such as the Egyptian or Eleusinian Mysteries. 2. Military: Knights Templars. 3. Judiciary: Vehmgerichte. 4. Scientific: Alchymists. 5. Civil: Freemasons. 6. Political: Carbonari. 7. Anti-Social: Garduna. But the line of division is not always strictly defined; some that had scientific objects combined theological dogmas therewith as the Rosicrucian's, for instance; and political societies must necessarily influence civil life. We may therefore more conveniently range secret societies in the two comprehensive divisions of religious and political.

3. *Religious Societies* - Religion has had its secret societies from the most ancient times; they date, in fact, from the period when the true religious knowledge which, be it understood, consisted in the knowledge of the constitution of the universe and the Eternal Power that had produced, and the laws that maintained it possessed by the first men began to decay among the general mass of mankind. The genuine knowledge was to a great extent preserved in the ancient "Mysteries," though even these were already a degree removed from the first primeval native wisdom, since they represented only the type, instead of the archetype; - namely, the phenomena of outward temporal Nature, instead of the realities of the inward eternal Nature, of which this visible universe is the outward manifestation. Since the definition of this now recovered genuine knowledge is necessary for understanding much that was taught in the religious societies of antiquity, we shall,

further on, enter into fuller details concerning it.

4. *Political Societies* - Politically, secret societies were the provident temperers and safety valves of the present and the powerful levers of the future. Without them the monologue of absolutism alone would occupy the drama of history, appearing, moreover, without an aim, and producing no effect, if it had not exercised the will of man by inducing reaction and provoking resistance.

Every secret society is an act of reflection, therefore, of conscience. For reflection, accumulated and fixed, is conscience. In so far, secret societies are in a certain manner the expression of conscience in history. For every man has in himself a Something which belongs to him, and which yet seems as if it were not a thing within him, but, so to speak, without him. This obscure Something is stronger than he, and he cannot rebel against its dominion nor withdraw him- self, or fly, from its search. This part of us is intangible; the assassin's steel, the executioner's axe cannot reach it; allurements cannot seduce, prayers cannot soften, threats cannot terrify it. It creates in us a dualism, which makes itself felt as remorse. When man is virtuous, he feels himself one, at peace with himself; that obscure Something does neither oppress nor torture him: just as in physical nature the powers of man's body, when working in harmony, are unfelt (11); but when his actions are evil, his better part rebels. Now secret societies are the expression of this dualism reproduced on a grand scale in nations; they are that obscure Something of politics acting in the public conscience, and producing a remorse, which shows itself as "secret society," an avenging and purifying remorse. It regenerates through death, and brings forth light through fire, out of darkness, according to eternal laws. No one discerns it, yet every man may feel it. It may be compared to an invisible star, whose light, however, reaches us; to the heat coming from a region where no human foot will ever be placed, but which we feel, and can demonstrate with the thermometer.

Indeed, one of the most obvious sentiments that gives rise to secret societies is that of revenge, but good and wise revenge, different from personal rancour, unknown, where popular interests are in question; that desires to punish in- situations and not individuals, to strike ideas and not men the grand collective revenge, the inheritance that fathers transmit to their children, a pious legacy of love, that sanctifies hatred and enlarges the responsibility and character of man. For there is a legitimate and necessary hatred, that of evil, which forms the salvation of nations. Woe to the people that knows not how to hate, because intolerance, hypocrisy, superstition, slavery are evil!

5. *Aims of Political Societies* - The aim of the sectaries is the erection of the ideal temple of progress; to fecundate in the bosom of sleeping or enslaved peoples the germs of a future liberty, as the Nihilists are now doing in Russia. This glorious edifice, it is true, is not yet finished, and per- haps never will be; but the attempt itself invests secret societies with a moral grandeur; whereas, without such aim, their struggle would be debased into a paltry egotistical party-fight. It also explains and justifies the existence of secret societies. And to them many states owe not only their liberties, but their very existence. As modern instances, I may mention Greece and Italy.

6. *Religious Secret Societies* - But the earliest secret societies were not formed for political, so much as for religious purposes, embracing every art and science; wherefore religion has truly been called the archaeology of human knowledge. Comparative mythology reduces all the apparently contradictory and opposite creeds to one primeval, fundamental, and true comprehension of Nature and her laws; all the metamorphoses of one or more gods, recorded in the sacred books of the Hindoos, Parsees, Egyptians, and of other nations, are indeed founded on simple physical facts, disfigured and misrepresented, intentionally or accidentally. The true comprehension of Nature was the prerogative of the most highly developed of all races of men (10), viz., the Aryan races, whose seat was on the highest point of the mountain region of Asia, to the north of the Himalayas. South of these lies the Vale of Cashmere, whose eternal spring, wonderful wealth of vegetation, and general natural features, best adapt it to represent the earthly paradise and the blissful residence of the most highly favoured human beings.

7. *Most Perfect Human Type* - So highly favoured, precisely because Nature in so favoured a spot could only develop in course of time a superior type; which being, as it were, the quintessence of that copious Nature, was one with it, and therefore able to apprehend it and its fulness. For as the powers of Nature have brought forth plants and animals of different degrees of development and perfection, so they have produced various types of men in various stages of development; the most perfect being, as already mentioned, the Aryan or Caucasian

type, the only one that has a history, and the one that deserves our attention when inquiring into the mental history of mankind. For even where the Caucasian comes in contact and intermingles with a dark race, as in India and Egypt, it is the white man with whom the higher and historical development begins.

8. *Causes of high Mental Development* - I have already intimated that climatic and other outward circumstances are favourable to high development. This is universally known to be true of plants; but man is only a plant endowed with consciousness and mobility, and therefore it must be true of him; and, in fact, experience proves it. The organs, and especially the brain of the Caucasian, attain to the highest perfection, and therefore he is most fully able to apprehend Nature and understand its working.

As to how long it took man to arrive at a high state of mental development, it is sheer waste of time and ingenuity to speculate about how long did it take the spider to learn how to construct his web so skilfully? as it is a vain attempt to discover the time of man's first appearance and condition on earth; even the stale cabbage of protoplasm, warmed up by Darwin, will not help us to solve the riddle. The only certainty we have from monumental and quasi-literary remains, is that many thousand years ago man possessed high scientific knowledge, which, originally arisen in the East, gradually travelled westward, and on the journey to a great extent was lost. It may seem strange that such knowledge should be lost; but as we have a striking instance of such loss in historic times, the strange phenomenon becomes credible. What succeeded the splendours of classic erudition, science and art, but the mental night known as the Dark Ages! the outcome of priestly prejudice, oppression, and obscurantism. It will suffice to quote one fact in support of our argument. Thousands of years before our era the Chaldeans were acquainted with the roundness of the earth, and that its extent from east to west was greater than that from north to south; they also knew its circumference, which they fixed by saying that a man, if he walked steadily on, could go round it in one year of 365 days. Now, reckoning the circumference at 24,900 miles, it is easily seen that a man, walking at about three miles an hour, would perform the journey within very little of a year. What had become of this knowledge when the learned (?) friars, disputing at Salamanca with Columbus, maintained the earth to be flat?

I have lying before me a map of Africa, printed in 1642 (in

Blaew's *Novus Atlas*), in which the lakes in the interior of that continent, together with its rivers, towns, and villages, which are supposed to have been discovered in this century only, are accurately laid down how came this knowledge, more than 250 years old, to be lost? But lost it was, for on maps issued in the early part of this century the interior of Africa is a blank.

Therefore I am justified in saying that in prehistoric times man possessed a true knowledge of Nature and her workings, and that this is the reason why the mysteries of the most distant nations had so much in common, dogmatically and internally, and why in all so much importance was attached to certain figures and ideas, and why all were funereal. The sanctity attributed in all ages and all countries to the number seven has not been correctly explained by any known writer;[1] the elucidations I shall offer on this point, will show that the conformity with each other of the religious and scientific doctrines of nations far apart must be due to their transmission from one common source, though the enigmatical and mystical forms, in which this knowledge was preserved, were gradually taken for the facts themselves.

The reader will now see that these remarks, the object of which he may not have perceived at first, are not irrelevant; we cannot understand the origin and meaning of what was taught in the mysteries without a clear apprehension of man's primitive culture and knowledge.

9. *Primitive Culture* - As a rule, prehistoric ages seem obscure, and men fancy, that, at every retrogressive step, they must enter into greater darkness. But if we proceed with our eyes open, the darkness recedes like the horizon, as we seem to approach it; new light is added to our light, new suns are lit up, new auroras arise before us; the darkness, which is only light compacted, is dissolved into its original, viz., light; and as outwardness implies multiplicity, and inwardness unity there are many branches, but only one root so all religious creeds, even those most disguised in absurd and debasing rites and superstitions, the nearer we trace them to their source, appear in greater and greater purity and nobility, with more exalted views, doctrines, and aims. For as Tegner says

"... kanslan's grundton ar anda densamma."

---

[1] Except, of course, the one from whom I derive my information, Jacob Bohme, concerning whom see infra,

The fundamental tone of feeling is ever the same.

And as the same poet expresses it, antiquity is

> "... det Atlantis som gick under
> Med hb'gre kraft, med adlare begar."
>
> ... That Atlantis that perished
> With higher powers and nobler aims.

Thus the ethic odes of Buddha and Zoroaster have been regarded as anticipations of the teaching of Christianity; so that even St. Augustin remarked: "What is now called the Christian religion existed among the ancients, and was not absent from the beginning of the human race until Christ came, from which time the true religion, which existed already, began to be called Christian."

Again, through all the more elevated creeds there ran certain fundamental ideas which, differing and even some- times distorted in form, may yet in a certain sense be regarded as common to all. Such were the belief in a Trinity; the dogma that the "Logos," or omnific Word, created all things by making the Nothing manifest; the worship of light; the doctrine of regeneration by passing through the fire, and others.

10. *The true Doctrines of Nature and Being* - But what was the knowledge on which the teaching of the mysteries was founded? It was no less than that of the ground and geniture of all things; the whole state, the rise, the work- ings, and the progress of all Nature (16), together with the unity that pervades heaven and earth. A few years ago this was proclaimed with great sound of trumpets as a new discovery, although so ancient an author as Homer speaks, in the 8th book of the "Iliad," of the golden chain connect- ing heaven and earth; the golden chain of sympathy, the occult, all-pervading, all-uniting influence, called by a variety of names, such as anima mundi, mercurius philo- sophorum, Jacob's ladder, the vital magnetic series, the magician's fire, &c. This knowledge, in course of time, and through man's love of change, was gradually distorted by perverse interpretations, and overlaid or embroidered, as it were, with fanciful creations of man's own brain; and thus arose superstitious systems, which became the creed of the unthinking crowd, and have not lost their hold on the

public mind, even to this day keeping in spiritual thraldom myriads who tremble at a thousand phantoms conjured up by priest- craft and their own ignorance, whilst

> " Felix qui potuit rerum cognoscere causas;
> Atque metus omnes et inexorabile fatum
> Subjecit pedibus, strepitumque Acherontis avari."

II. *Fundamental Principles of true Knowledge possessed by the Ancients* - From what was taught in the mysteries, we are justified in believing that thousands of years ago men knew what follows; though the knowledge is already dimmed and perverted in the mysteries, the phenomena of outward Nature only being presented in them, instead of the inward spiritual truths symbolised.

(i.) All around us we behold the evidences of a life per- meating all things; we must needs, therefore, admit that there is a universal, all-powerful, all- sustaining life.

(ii.) Behind or above the primeval life which is the basis of this system may be beheld the "Unmoved Mover," the only supernatural ens, who, by the Word, or "Logos," has spoken forth all things out of himself; which does not imply any pantheism, for the words of the speaker, though proceeding from him, are not the speaker himself.

(iii.) The universal life is eternal.

(iv.) Matter is eternal, for matter is the garment in which the life clothes and renders itself manifest.

(v.) That matter is light, for the darkest substance is, or can be, reduced into it.

(vi.) Whatsoever is outwardly manifest must have existed ideally, from all eternity, in an archetypal figure, reflected in what Indian mythology calls the Eternal Liberty, the mirror Maja t whence are derived the terms "magus," "magia," "magic," "image," "imagination," all implying the fixing of the primeval, structureless, imperceptible, living matter, in a form, figure, or creature. In modern theosophy, the mirror Maja is called the Eternal Mirror of Wonders, the Virgin Sophia, ever bringing forth, yet ever a virgin the analogue and prototype of the Virgin Mary.

(vii.) The eternal life which thus manifests itself in this visible universe is ruled by the same laws that rule the invisible world of forces.

(viii.) These laws, according to which the life manifests itself, are the seven properties of eternal Nature, six working properties, and the seventh, in which the six, as it were, rest, or are combined into perfect balance or harmony, i.e., paradise. These seven properties, the foundation of all the septenary numbers running through natural phenomena and all ancient and modern knowledge, are: (1) Attraction; (2) Reaction or Repulsion; (3) Circulation; (4) Fire; (5) Light; (6) Sound; (7) Body, or comprisal of all.

(ix.) This septenary is divisible into two ternaries or poles, with the fire (symbolised by a cross) in the middle. These two poles constitute the eternal dualism or antagonism in Nature the first three forming matter or darkness, and producing pain and anguish, i.e., hell, cosmically winter; the last three being filled with light and delight, i.e., paradise, cosmically summer.

(x.) The fire is the great chymist, or purifier and trans- muter of Nature, turning darkness into light. Hence the excessive veneration and universal worship paid to it by ancient nations, the priests of Zoroaster wearing a veil over their mouths for fear of polluting the fire with their breath. By the fire here, of course, is meant the empyrean, electric fire, whose existence and nature were tolerably well known to the ancients. They distinguished the moving principle from the thing moved, and called the former the igneous ether or spirit, the principle of life, the Deity, You-piter, Vulcan, Phtha, Kneph (18, 24).

(xi.) All light is born out of darkness, and must pass through the fire to manifest itself; there is no other way but through darkness, or death, or hell an idea which we find enunciated and represented in all the mysteries. As little as a plant can come forth into the beauty of blossoms, leaves, and fruit, without having passed through the dark state of the seed and being buried in the earth, where it is chymically transmuted by the fire; so little can the mind arrive at the fulness of knowledge and enlightenment without having passed through a stage of self-darkening and imprisonment, in which it suffered torment, anguish in which it was as in a furnace, in the throes of generation.

12. *Key to Mystic Teaching* - That the first men possessed the knowledge of the foregoing facts is certain, not only from the positive and inferential teachings of the mysteries, but also from the monuments of antiquity, which in grandeur of conception and singleness of ideal aim, excel all that modern art or industry, or even faith, has accomplished. By- bearing this in mind, the reader will get a deeper insight into the true meaning of the dogmas of initiation than was attainable by the epopts themselves. He will also understand that the reason why there was so much uniformity in the teaching of the mysteries was the fact that the dogmas enunciated were explanations of universal natural phenomena, alike in all parts of the earth. In describing the ceremonies of initiation, I shall therefore abstain from appending to them a commentary or exegesis, but simply refer to the paragraphs of this introduction, as to a key.

13. *Mystic Teaching Summarised* - It was theological, moral, and scientific. Theologically, the initiated were shown the error of vulgar polytheism, and taught the doctrine of the Unity and of a future state of reward and punishment; morally, the precepts were summed up in the words of Con- fucius: "If thou be doubtful whether an action be right or wrong, abstain from it altogether;" scientifically, the principles were such as we have detailed above (n), with their natural and necessary deductions, consequences, and results.

14. *How true Knowledge came to be lost* - Though I have already on several occasions (e.g., 10) alluded to the fact that the true knowledge of Nature possessed by the first men had in course of time become corrupted and intermixed with error, it will not be amiss to show the process by which this came to pass. It is well known that the oldest religious rites of which we have any written records were Sabasan or Helio-Arkite. The sun, moon, and stars, however, to the true original epopts were merely the outward manifestations and symbols of the inward powers of the Eternal Life. But such abstract truths could not be rendered intelligible to the vulgar mind of the multitude, necessarily more occupied with the satisfaction of material wants; and hence arose the personification of the heavenly bodies and terrestrial seasons depending on them. Gradually the human figure, which in the first

instance had only been a symbol, came to be looked upon as the representation of an individual being, that had actually lived on earth. Thus, the sun, to the primitive men, was the outward manifestation of the Eternal, all-sus- taining, all-saving Life; in different countries and ages this power was personified under the names of Chrisna, Fo, Osiris, Hermes, Hercules, and so on; and eventually these latter were supposed to have been men that really existed, and had been deified on account of the benefits they had conferred on mankind. The tombs of these supposed gods were shown, such as the Great Pyramid, said to be the tomb of Osiris; feasts were celebrated, the object of which seemed to be to renew every year the grief occasioned by their loss. The passing of the sun through the signs of the zodiac gave rise to the myths of the incantations of Vishnu, the labours of Hercules, &c., his apparent loss of power during the winter season, and the restoration thereof at the winter solstice, to the story of the death, descent into hell, and resurrection of Osiris and of Mithras. In fact, what was pure Nature-wisdom in one age became mythology in the next, and romance in the third, taking its characteristics from the country where it prevailed. The number seven being found everywhere, and the knowledge that its prevalence was the necessary consequence of the seven properties ' of Nature being lost, it was supposed to have reference only to the seven planets then known.

15. *Original Spirit of the Mysteries, and Results of their Decay* - In the mysteries all was astronomical, but a deeper meaning lay hid under the astronomical symbols. While bewailing the loss of the sun, the epopts were in reality mourning the loss of that light whose influence is life; whilst the working of the elements, according to the laws of elective affinity, produces only phenomena of decay and death. The initiated strove to pass from under the dominion of the bond-woman Night into the glorious liberty of the free- woman Sophia or Light; to be mentally absorbed into the Deity, i.e., into the Light. The dogmas of ancient Nature-wisdom were set before the pupil, but their understanding had to arise as inspiration in his soul. It was not the dead body of science that was surrendered to the epopt, leaving it to chance whether it quickened or not, but the living spirit itself was infused into him. But for this reason, because more had to be apprehended from within by inspiration, than from without, by oral instruction, the mysteries gradually decayed; the ideal yielded to the realistic, and the merely physical elements Sabseism and Arkism

became their leading features. The frequent emblems and mementos in the sanctuary of death and resurrection, pointing to the mystery that the moments of highest psychical enjoyment are the most destructive to bodily existence i.e., that the most intense delight is a glimpse of paradise these emblems and mementos eventually were applied to outward Nature only, and their misapprehension led to all the creeds or superstitions that have filled the earth with crime and woe, sanguinary wars, internecine cruelty, and persecution of every kind. Bloodthirsty fanatics, disputing about words whose meaning they did not understand, maintaining antagonistic dogmas, false on both sides, have invented the most fiendish tortures to compel their opponents to adopt their own views. While the two Mahommedan sects of Omar and Ali will fight each other to decide whether ablution ought to commence at the wrist or the elbow, they will unite to slay or to convert the Christians. Nay, even these latter, divided into sects without number, have distinguished themselves by persecutions as cruel as any ever practised by so-called pagan nations. Not satisfied with attempting to exterminate by fire and sword Turks and Jews, one Christian sect established such a tribunal as the Inquisition; whilst its opponents, scarcely less cruel, when they had the power, deprived the Roman Catholics of their civil rights, and occasionally executed them. Their mutual hatred even attends them in their missionary efforts very poor in their results, in spite of the sensational reports, manufactured by the societies at home, for extracting money from the public. To mention but one instance: a leading missionary endeavoured to prejudice the Polynesians in advance against some expected Roman Catholic missionaries by translating Foxe's "Book of Martyrs" into their language, and illustrating its scenes by the aid of a magic-lantern.

16. *The Mysteries under their Astronomical Aspect* - But seeing that the mysteries, as they have come down to us, and are still perpetuated, in a corrupted and aimless manner, in Freemasonry, have chiefly an astronomical bearing, a few general remarks on the leading principles of all will save a deal of needless repetition in describing them separately.

In the most ancient Indian creed we have the story of the fall of mankind by tasting of the fruit of the tree of knowledge, and their consequent expulsion from Paradise. This allegory was taken by the ignorant Jews for a record of actual occurrences, and as such interpolated in Genesis, about 900 years after the composition of that book, and after all the other books of the Old Testament had been written, whence it becomes plain why, contrary to all expectation, the Fall of Man is never once alluded to in those books. Read in its mysterious and astronomical aspect, the narrative of the Fall, as given in the Book of Genesis, would assume some such form as the following: Adam, which does not mean an individual, but the universal man, man- kind, and his companion, Eve, which means life, having passed spring and summer in the Garden of Eden, necessarily reached the season when the serpent, Typhon (51), the symbol of winter, points out on the celestial sphere that the reign of Evil, of winter, is approaching. Allegorical science, which insinuated itself everywhere, caused malum, "evil," also to mean an "apple," the produce of autumn, which indicates that the harvest is over, and that man in the sweat of his brow must again till the earth. The cold season comes, and he must cover himself with the allegorical fig-leaf. The sphere revolves, the man of the constellation Bootes, the same as Adam, preceded by the woman, the Virgin, carrying in her hand the autumnal branch laden with fruit, seems to be allured or beguiled by her. A look at a celestial globe will render this quite plain. A sacred bough or plant is introduced into all the mysteries. We have the Indian and Egyptian lotus, the fig-tree of Atys, the myrtle of Venus, the mistletoe of the Druids, the golden bough of Virgil, the rose-tree of Isis; in the "Golden Ass" Apuleius is restored to his natural form by eating roses the box of Palm-Sunday, and the acacia of Freemasonry. The bough in the opera "Roberto il Diavolo" is the mystic bough of the mysteries.

17. *Astronomical Aspects continued* - The Mysteries funereal. In all the mysteries we encounter a god, a superior being, or an extraordinary man, suffering death, to recommence a more glorious existence; everywhere the remembrance of a grand and mournful event plunges the nations into grief and mourning, immediately followed by the most lively joy. Osiris is slain by Typhon, Uranus by Saturn, Sousarman by Sudra, Adonis by a wild boar; Ormuzd is conquered by Ahrimanes; Atys and Mithras and Hercules kill themselves; Abel is slain by Cain, Balder by Loke, Bacchus by the giants; the Assyrians mourn the death of Thammuz, the Scythians and Phoenicians that of Acmon, all Nature that of the great Pan, the Freemasons that of Hiram, and so on. The origin of this universal belief has already been pointed out.

18. *Uniformity of Dogmas* - The doctrine of the Unity and Trinity

was inculcated in all the mysteries In the most ancient religious creeds we meet with the prototype of the Christian dogma, in which a virgin is seen bringing forth a saviour, and yet ever remaining a virgin (11). In the more outward sense, that virgin is the Virgo of the zodiac, and the saviour brought forth is the sun (17); in the most inward sense, it is the eternal ideal, wherein the eternal life and intelligence, the power of electricity, and the virtue of the tincture, the first the sustainer, the latter the beautifier of apprehensible existence, are, as it were, corporified in the countless creatures that fill this universe yea, in the universe itself. And the virgin remains a virgin, and her own nature is not affected by it, just as the air brings forth sounds, the light colours, the mind ideas, without any of them being intrinsically altered by the production. We certainly do not find these principles so fully and distinctly enunciated in the teaching of the ancient mystagogues, but a primitive knowledge of them may be inferred from what they did teach.

In all the mysteries, light was represented as born out of darkness. Thus reappears the Deity called now Maja Bhawani, now Kali, Isis, Ceres, Proserpina; Persephone, the Queen of Heaven, is the night from whose bosom issues life, into which the life returns, a secret reunion of life and death. She is, moreover, called the Rosy, and in the German myths the Rosy is called the restoring principle of life. She is not only the night, but, as mother of the sun, she is also the aurora, behind whom the stars are shining. When she symbolises the earth as Ceres, she is represented with ears of corn. Like the sad Proserpina, she is beautiful and lustrous, but also melancholy and black. Thus she joins night with day, joy with sadness, the sun with the moon, heat with humidity, the divine with the human. The ancient Egyptians often represented the Deity by a black stone, and the black stone Kaabah, worshipped by the Arabs, and which is described as having originally been whiter than snow, and more brilliant than the sun, embodies the same idea, with the additional hint that light was anterior to darkness. In all the mysteries we meet with the cross (53) as a symbol of purification and salvation; the numbers three, four, and seven were sacred; in most of the mythologies we meet with two pillars; mystic banquets were common to all, as also the trials by fire, water, and air; the circle and triangle, single and double, everywhere represented the dualism or polarity of Nature; in all the initiations, the aspirant represented the good principle, the light, overcome by evil, the darkness; and his task was to regain his former supremacy, to be born again or regenerated, by passing through death and hell and their terrors, that were scenically enacted during the neophyte's passage through seven caves, or ascent of seven steps.

All this, in its deepest meaning, represented the eternal struggle of light to free itself from the encumbrance of materiality it has put on in its passage through the first three properties of eternal Nature (11); and in its secondary meaning, when the deeper one was lost to mankind, the progress of the sun through the seven signs of the zodiac, from Aries to Libra, as shown in Royal Arch Masonry, and also in the ladder with seven steps of the Knight of Kadosh. In all the mysteries the officers were the same, and personified astronomical or cosmical phenomena; in all, the initiated recognised each other by signs and passwords; in all, the conditions for initiation were the same maturity of age, and purity of conduct. Nero, on this account, did not dare, when in Greece, to offer himself as a candidate for initiation into the Eleusinian Mysteries. In many, the chief hierophant was compelled to lead a retired life of perpetual celibacy, that he might be entirely at liberty to devote himself to the study and contemplation of celestial things. And to accomplish this abstraction, it was customary for the priests, in the earlier periods of their history, to mortify the flesh by the use of certain herbs, which were reputed to possess the virtue of repelling all passionate excitements; to guard against which they even occasionally adopted severer and more decided precautions. In all countries where mysteries existed, initiation came to be looked upon as much a necessity as afterwards baptism among Christians; which ceremony, indeed, is one that had been practised in all the mysteries. The initiated were called epopts, i.e., those that see things as they are; whilst before they were called "mystes," meaning quite the contrary. In all we find greater and less mysteries, an exoteric and an esoteric doctrine, and three degrees. To betray the mysteries was everywhere considered infamous, and the heaviest penalties were attached to it; hence also, in all initiations, the candidate had to take the most terrible oaths that he would keep the secrets entrusted to him. Alcibiades was banished and consigned to the Furies for having revealed the mysteries of Ceres; Prometheus, Tantalus, Oedipus, Orpheus, suffered various punishments for the same reason.

19. *Most Ancient Secret Society.* The very contents of this work show that the records of ancient secret societies have come down to us in pretty full detail; yet on looking at a map of the ancient world we are

struck by a fact, which can only be explained by assuming the existence, at a remote period, of a secret society of which no record, except the one supplied by the map, exists. This secret society, whose existence, it is true, can be proved inferentially only, must have been that of Benjamin and his ten sons. We know from Gen. xlvii. that Joseph delegated to the Benjaminites the keeping of all the cattle of Egypt, which conferred on them vast powers their warlike spirit knew how to utilise for their own aggrandisement. And that they must have acted in concert is proved, inferentially as stated above, by the names of European and other countries. The proof is founded on etymology; this science is not always reliable, when we have only one or two roots to guide us, but when we come to five or more, a suspicion of mere coincidence must be dismissed from the mind. The subjoined names of Benjamin and his ten sons, together with those of the countries or localities named after them, will make the matter clear:

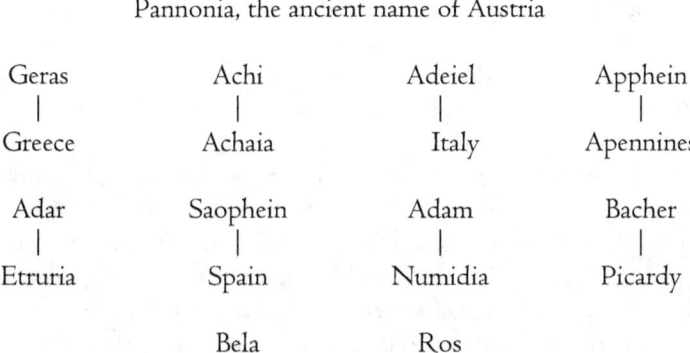

That all these countries should have Benjaminite names proves an identity of purpose at some long-past period; and as no Benjaminite sovereignty has ever been proclaimed over Europe, it is clear that the above result must have been brought about by a powerful secret society, the leaders of which were Benjamin and his ten sons. And to carry out their scheme, and to do so without the kings and politicians, not associated with them, detecting its origin, they must have had signs and passwords known only to the initiated. It is indisputable that pneuma, the Greek word for spirit or ghost, is derived from Benymn or Benjamin, as Christ is derived from Geras; hence Christ is said to have been begotten by the Holy Ghost.

20. *Secret Societies no longer needed.* Thanks to secret societies themselves, they are now no longer needed, at least not in the realms of thought. In politics, however, circumstances will arise in every age to call them into existence; and though they seldom attain their direct object, yet are they not without influence on the relations between ruler and ruled, advantageously for the latter in the long run, though not immediately. But thought religious, philosophical and political is free if not as yet in every country, it is so certainly in the lands inhabited by the Saxon races. And though the bigot and the fool would crush it, the former because it undermines his absolutism, and the latter because it interferes with his ease, yet shall it only grow stronger by the opposition. Science becomes the powerful bulwark against the invasion of dogmatic absurdities; and there is growing up a scientific church, wherein knowledge, and not humility, labour, and not penance and fasting, are considered essentials. Various phenomena in modern life are proofs of this. Man during ages of intellectual gloom annihilated himself in behalf of the great deified All; now he studies and respects himself, destroys the fetishes, and combats for Truth, which is the true deity.

In ancient times the mind rose from religion to philosophy; in our times, by a violent reaction, it will ascend from philosophy to religion. And the men whose religion is so arrived at, whose universal sympathy has cast out fear such men are the true regenerators of mankind, and need neither secret signs nor passwords to recognise each other; in fact, they are opposed to all such devices, because they know that liberty consists in publicity. In a despotically ruled country, as Russia, for instance, secret societies are even now the only means of stirring up the people to fight for freedom; but wherever liberty rules, secrecy is no longer necessary to effect any good and useful work; once it needed secret societies in order to triumph, now it wants open union to maintain itself. Not that the time is come when every truth may be uttered without fear of calumny and cavil and opposition, especially in religious matters; far from it, as some recent notable instances have shown. The words of Faust still have their application:

" Who dare call the child by its right name?

> The few that knew something of it,
> And foolishly opened their hearts,
> Revealing to the vulgar crowd their views,
> Were ever crucified or burnt."

Certes, bodily crucifying or burning are out of the question now, but statecraft, and especially priestcraft, still have a few thumbscrews and red-hot irons to hold a man's hands or sear his reputation; wherefore, though I doubt the policy, and in most cases the success, of secret associations, yet I cannot withhold my tribute of admiration for those who have acted or do act up to the words of the poet Lowell:

> " They are slaves who dare not speak
> For the fallen and the weak;
> They are slaves who will not choose
> Hatred, scoffing, and abuse,
> Rather than in silence shrink
> From the truth they needs must think;
> They are slaves who dare not be
> In the right with two or three."

BOOK I

ANCIENT MYSTERIES

" Of man's original relation to Nature, whence we start, in order to render the essentials of physical science and Nature comprehensible in their inmost depth, we find but obscure hints. In the mysteries and the holy initiations of those nations that as yet were nearest to the primeval people, the mind apprehends a few scarcely intelligible sounds, which, arising deep from the nature of our being, move it mightily. Now our hearts are wrung by the mournful sounds of the first human race and of Nature; now they are stirred by an exalted Nature - worship, and penetrated by the breath of an eternal inspiration! We shall hear that suppressed sound from the temple of Isis, from the speaking pillars of Thot, in the hymns of the Egyptian priests. On the lonely coast under the black rocks of Iceland the Edda will convey to us a sound from the graves, and fancy shall bring us face to face with those priests who by a stern silence have concealed from future ages the holy science of their worship. Yea, the eye shall yet discover the lost features of the noble past in the altars of Mexico, and on the pyramid which saw the blood and tears of thousands of human victims."

V. SCHUBEKT.

I

THE MAGI

21. *Derivation of the term Magus* - Magus is derived from Maja,[2] the mirror (II) wherein Brahm, according to Indian mythology, from all eternity beholds himself and all his power and wonders. Hence also our

---

[2] Littré derives magus from mahat, great; but according to Indian mythology, mahatit and pirkirti are brought forth by jotna, power, the offspring of Maja, so that the latter truly is the etymon of " Magus."

terms magia, magic, image, imagination, all implying the fixing in a form, figure, or creature these words being synonymous of the potencies of the primeval, structureless, living matter. The Magus, therefore, is one that makes the operations of the Eternal Life his study.

22. *Antiquity of the Magi* - The Magi, as the ancient priests of Persia were called, did not constitute a doctrine or religion only; they constituted a monarchy their power truly was that of kings. And this fact is still commemorated by the circumstance that the Magi recorded to have been led by the star to the cradle of Jesus are just as frequently called kings as Magi. As sages, they were kings in the sense of Horace:

> " Ad summam, sapiens uno minor est Jove, dives,
> Liber, honoratus, pulclier, rex denique regtim."

Epist. i. I 06, I07.

Their pontifical reign preceded the ascendency of Assyria, Media, and Persia. Aristotle asserts it to have been more ancient than the foundation of the kingdom of Egypt; Plato, unable to reckon it by years, computes it by myriads. At the present day most writers agree in dating the rise of the reign of the Magi five thousand years before the Trojan war.

23. Zoroaster. The founder of the order was Zoroaster, who was not, as some will have it, a contemporary of Darius, but lived nearly fifty centuries before our era. Nor was his home in India, but in Bactriana, which lies more to the east, beyond the Caspian Sea, close to the mountains of India, along the great rivers Oxus and Iaxartes; so that the Brahmins, or priests of India, may be called the descendants of the Magi.

24. *Doctrine of Zoroaster* - His doctrine was the most perfect and rational of all those that in ancient times were the objects of initiation, and has more or less survived in all successive theosophies. Traces of it may be found in the ancient "Zendavesta" not the book now passing by that name, which is merely a kind of breviary which entered into all the details of Nature.

This doctrine is not the creed of the two opposite, but equally powerful, principles, as has been asserted; for Ahri-manes, the principle of evil, is not equal with Oromazes, which is good. Evil is not uncreated and eternal; it is rather transitory and limited in power. And Plutarch records an opinion, which anon we shall see confirmed, that Ahrimanes and his angels shall be annihilated that dualism is not eternal; its life is in time, of which it constitutes the grand drama, and in which it is the perennial cause of motion and transformation. This is the doctrine of the "Everlasting Gospellers," so violently opposed by the Church, for the abolition of the devil. What would it not entail? The Supreme Being, or Eternal Life, is elsewhere called Time without limits, for no origin can be assigned to him; enshrined in his glory, and possessing properties and attributes inapprehensible by our understanding, to him belongs silent adoration.

Creation had a beginning by means of emanation. The first emanation from the Eternal was the light, whence issued the King of Light, Oromazes. By means of speech Oromazes created the pure world, of which he is the preserver and judge. Oromazes is a holy and celestial being, intelligence and knowledge.

Oromazes, the first-born of Time without limits, began by creating, after his image and likeness, six genii, called amshaspands, that surround his throne, and are his messengers to the inferior spirits and to men, being also to the latter types of purity and perfection.

The second series of creations by Oromazes was that of the twenty-eight izads, that watch over the happiness, innocence, and preservation of the world; models of virtue, interpreters of the prayers of men.

The third host of pure spirits is more numerous, and forms that of the farohars, the thoughts of Oromazes, or the ideas conceived by him before proceeding to the creation of things. Not only the farohars of holy men and innocent infants stand before Oromazes, but this latter himself has his farohar, the personification of his wisdom and beneficent idea, his reason, his logos. These spirits hover over the head of every man; and this idea passed over to the Greeks and Romans, and we meet with it again in the familiar spirit of Socrates, the evil genius of Brutus, and the genius comes of Horace.

The threefold creation of good spirits was the necessary consequence of the contemporaneous development of the principle of evil. The second-born of the Eternal, Ahrimanes, emanated like Oromazes from the primitive light, and was pure like it, but being ambitious and haughty, he became jealous. To punish him, the Supreme Being condemned him to dwell for twelve thousand years in the region of darkness, a time which was to be sufficient to end thestrife between good and evil; but Ahrimanes created count less evil genii, that filled the earth with misery, disease, and guilt. The evil spirits are impurity, violence, covetousness, cruelty; the demons of cold, hunger, poverty, leanness, sterility, ignorance; and the most perverse of all, Peetash, the demon of calumny. [3]

Oromazes, after a reign of three thousand years, created the material world in six periods, in the same order as they are found in Genesis, successively calling into existence the terrestrial light (not to be confounded with the celestial), the water, the earth, plants, animals, and man.[4] Ahrimanes assisted in the formation of earth and water, because the darkness had already invaded those elements, and Oromazes could not conceal them. Ahrimanes also took part in the creation and subsequent corruption and destruction of man, whom Oromazes had produced by an act of his will and by the Word. Out of the seed of that being Oromazes afterwards drew the first human pair, Mesliia and Meshiane but Ahrimanes first seduced the woman and then the man, leading them into evil chiefly by the eating of certain fruits. And not only did he alter the nature of man, but also that of animals, opposing insects, serpents, wolves, and all kinds of vermin to the good animals, thus spreading corruption over the face of the earth. But Ahrimanes and his evil spirits are eventually to be overcome and cast out from every place; and in the stern combat just and industrious men have nothing to fear; for according to Zoroaster, labour is the exterminator of evil, and that man best obeys the righteous judge of all who assiduously tills the earth and causes it to bring forth harvests and fruit-bearing trees. At the end of twelve thousand years, when the earth shall cease to be afflicted by the evils brought upon it by the spirits of darkness, three prophets shall appear and assist man with their power and knowledge, restoring the earth to its pristine beauty, judging the good and the evil, and conducting the first into a region of ineffable bliss. Ahrimanes, and the captive demons and men, shall be purified in a sea of liquid metal, and the law of Oromazes shall rule everywhere.

It is scarcely necessary to point out to the reader the astronomical bearing of the theogony of Zoroaster. The six good genii represent the six summer months, while the evil genii stand for the

---

[3] All these traditions show already a very great departure from, and decay of, the original knowledge possessed by the primitive men. See Introduction.

[4] Or rather a being compounded of a man and a bull.

winter months. The twenty-eight izads are the days of a lunar month. But theosophically, the six periods during which the universe was created refer to the six working properties of Nature.

25. *The Light Worshipped* - We have seen that Zoroaster taught light to be the first emanation of the Eternal Life; hence in the Parsee writings, light, the perennial flame, is the symbol of the Deity or uncreated Life. Hence the Magi and Parsees have been called fire-worshippers. But the former saw and the latter see in the fire not a divinity, but simply the cause of heat and motion, thus anticipating the most recent discoveries of physical science, or rather, remembering some of the lost knowledge. The Parsees did not form any God, to call him the one true God; they did not invoke any authority extrinsic to life; they did not rely on any uncertain tradition; but amidst all the recondite forces of Nature, they chose the one that governs them all, that reveals itself by the most tremendous effects. The modern Guebres are the descendants of the ancient Magi.

26. *Origin of the word Deus, God* - In this sense the Magi, as well as the Chinese, had no theology, or they had one that is distinguished from all others. Those Magi that gave their name to occult science (magic), performed no sorcery, and believed in no miracles. In the bosom of Asiatic immobility they did not condemn motion, but rather considered it as the glorious symbol of the Eternal Cause. Other castes aimed at impoverishing the people and subjecting it to the yoke of ignorance and superstition; but thanks to the Magi, the Indian Olympus, peopled with monstrous creatures, gave place to the conception of the unity of God, which always indicates progress in the history of thought. The text of the most ancient Zend literature acknowledges but one creative ens of all things, and his name, Dao, signifies "light" and "wisdom," and is explained by the root daer, "to shine," whence are derived all such words as deus, dies, &c. The conception of Deity indeed was primarily that of the "bright one," whence also the Sanskrit dyaus, "sky," which led to so many mythological fables. But the original idea was founded on a correct perception of the origin and nature of things, for light is truly the substance of all things; all matter is only a compaction of light. Thus the Magi founded a moral system and an empire; they had a literature, a science, and a poetry. Five thousand years before the "Iliad" they put forth the "Zendavesta," three grand poems, the first ethical, the second

military, and the third scientific.

27. *Mode of Initiation* - The candidate for initiation was prepared by numerous lustrations with fire, water, and honey. The number of probations he had to pass through was very great, and ended with a fast of fifty days' continuance. These trials had to be endured in a subterranean cave, where he was condemned to perpetual silence and total solitude. This novitiate in some instances was attended with fatal effects, in others the candidate became partially or wholly deranged; those who surmounted the trials were eligible to the highest honours. At the expiration of the novitiate, the candidate was brought forth into the cavern of initiation, where he was armed with enchanted armour by his guide, who was the representative of Simorgh, a monstrous griffin (28), and an important agent in the machinery of Persian mythology, and furnished with talismans, that he might be ready to encounter all the hideous monsters raised up by the evil spirits to impede his progress. Introduced into an inner apartment, he was purified with fire and water, and put through the seven stages of initiation. First, he beheld a deep and dangerous vault from the precipice where he stood, into which a single false step might throw him down to the "throne of dreadful necessity" the first three properties of Nature. Groping his way through the mazes of the gloomy cavern, he soon beheld the sacred fire at intervals flash through its recesses and illuminate his path; he also heard the distant yelling of ravenous beasts the roaring of lions, the howling of wolves, the fierce and threatening bark of dogs. But his attendant, who maintained a profound silence, hurried him forward towards the quarter whence these sounds proceeded, and at the sudden opening of a door he found himself in a den of wild beasts, dimly lighted with a single lamp. He was immediately attacked by the initiated in the forms of lions, tigers, wolves, griffins, and other monstrous beasts, from whom he seldom escaped unhurt. Thence he passed into another cavern, shrouded in darkness, where he heard the terrific roaring of thunder, and saw vivid and continuous flashes of lightning, which in streaming sheets of fire rendered visible the flitting shades of avenging genii, resenting his intrusion into their chosen abodes. To restore the candidate a little, he was next conducted into another apartment, where his excited feelings were soothed with melodious music and the flavour of grateful perfumes. On his expressing his readiness to proceed through the remaining ceremonies, a signal was given by his conductor, and three priests immediately made

their appearance, one of whom cast a living serpent into his bosom as a token of regeneration (57); and, a private door having been opened, there issued forth such howlings and cries of lamentation and dismay, as struck him with new and indescribable emotions of terror. On turning his eyes to the place whence these noises proceeded, he beheld exhibited in every appalling form the torments of the wicked in Hades. Thus he was passed through the devious labyrinth consisting of seven spacious vaults, connected by winding galleries, each opening with a narrow stone portal, the scene of some perilous adventure, until he reached the Sacellum, or Holy of Holies, which was brilliantly illuminated, and which sparkled with gold and precious stones. A splendid sun and starry system moved in accordance with delicious music. The archimagus sat in the east on a throne of burnished gold, crowned with a rich diadem decorated with myrtle boughs, and habited in a tunic of bright cerulean hue; round him were assembled the praesules and dispensers of the mysteries. By these the novice was received with congratulations, and after having entered into the usual engagements for keeping secret the rites of Zoroaster, the sacred words were entrusted to him, of which the Tetractys, or name of God, was the chief. The Tetractys of Pythagoras is analogous to the Jewish Tetragrammaton, or name of the Deity in four letters. The number four was considered the most perfect, because in the first four properties of Nature (11) are comprised and implied all the rest; wherefore also the first four numbers summed up make up the decad, after which all is only repetition.

28. *Myth of Rustam* - This progress was denominated ascending the ladder of perfection, and from it has arisen the tale of Eustam, the Persian Hercules, who, mounted on the monster Rakshi, which is the Arabic name of Simorgh, undertakes the conquest of Mazendaraun, celebrated as a perfect earthly paradise. Having amidst many dangers fought his way along a road of seven stages, he reaches the cavern of the White Giant, who smites all that assail him with blindness. But Rustam overcomes him, and with three drops of the giant's blood restores sight to all his captives. The symbolical three drops of blood had their counterparts in all the mysteries of the ancient world. In Britain the emblem was three drops of water; in Mexico, as in this legend, three drops of blood; in India, a belt composed of three triple threads; in China, the three strokes of the letter Y, &c. The blindness with which those who seek the giant are smitten, of course refers to the

emblematic mental blindness of the aspirant to initiation.

II

THE MITHRAICS

29. *Mysteries of Mithras* - Upon the trunk of a religion so spiritual and hostile to idolatry, which undertook iconoclastic expeditions into Babylonia, Assyria, Syria, and Libya, which vindicated the pure worship of God, destroying by
means of the sword of Cambyses the Egyptian priesthood, which overthrew the temples and idols of Greece, which gave to the Israelites the Pharisees, which appears so simple and pure as to have bestowed on the Parsees the appellation of the Puritans of antiquity, and on Cyrus that of the Anointed of the Lord on this trunk there were afterwards ingrafted idolatrous branches, as perhaps the Brahminic, and certainly the Mithraic worship, the origin of which latter Dupuis places at 4500 years before Christ.

30. *Origin of Mithraic Worship* - Mithras is a beneficent genius presiding over the sun, the most powerful of the twenty- eight izads, or spirits of light, invoked together with the sun, and not at first confounded with it; the chief mediator and intercessor between Oromazes and man. But in course of time the conception of this Mithras became perverted, and he usurped the attributes of divinity. Such usurpation of the rank of the superior Deity on the part of the inferior is of frequent occurrence in mythology; it suffices to refer to Siva and Vishnu in India, Serapis in Egypt, Jupiter in Greece. The perversion was rendered easy by confounding the symbol with the thing symbolised, the genius of the sun with the sun itself, which alone remained in the language, since the modern Persian name of the sun (mihr) represents the regular modification of the Zend Mithras.

The Persian Mithras must not be confounded with that of India, for it is undoubted that another Mithras, different from the Zendic, from the most ancient times was the object of a special mysterious worship, and that the initiated knew him as the sun. Taking the letters of the Greek word "Meithras" at their numerical value, we obtain the number 365, the days of the year. The same holds good of "Abraxas," the name which Basilides gave to the Deity, and further of "Belenos," the name given to the sun in Gaul.

31. *Dogmas, &c.* - On the Mithraic monuments we find representations

of the globe of the sun, the club and bull, symbols of the highest truth, the highest creative activity, the highest vital power. Such a trinity agrees with that of Plato, which consists of the Supreme Good, the Word, and the Soul of the World; with that of Hermes Trismegistus, consisting of Light, Intelligence, and Soul; with that of Porphyry, which consists of Father, Word, and Supreme
Soul.

According to Herodotus, Mithras became the Mylitta of Babylon, the Assyrian Venus, to whom was paid an obscene worship as to the female principle of creation, the goddess of fecundity, of life; one perhaps with Anaitis, the Armenian goddess.

The worship of Persian Mithras, or Apollo, spread over Italy[5] at Rome, in fact, it superseded the Greek and Roman gods Gaul, Germany, Britain; and expiring polytheism opposed to the sun Christ, the sun Mithras.

32. *Rites of Initiation* - The sanctuaries of this worship were always subterranean, and in each sanctuary was placed a ladder with seven steps, by which one ascended to the mansions of felicity. The initiations into this degree were similar to those detailed in the foregoing section, but, if possible, more severe than into any other, and few passed through all the tests. The festival of the god was held towards the middle of the month of Mihr (October), and the
probationer had to undergo long and severe trials before he was admitted to the full knowledge of the mysteries.

The first degree was inaugurated with purifying lustrations, and a sign was set on the neophyte's brow, whilst he offered to the god a loaf and a cup of water. A crown was presented to him on the point of a sword, and he put it on his head saying, "Mithras is my crown."

In the second degree the aspirant put on armour to meet giants and monsters, and a wild chase took place in the subterranean caves. The priests and officers of the temple, disguised as lions, tigers, leopards, bears, wolves, and other wild beasts, attacked the candidate with fierce howlings. In these sham fights the aspirant ran great

---

[5] Underneath the church of St. Clement, at Eome, a singularly well- preserved temple of Mithras was discovered some years ago. When the monk who had, on my visit to Kome, shown me the church above, said that he would now take me down to the pagan temple of Mithras, I could not help saying to myself, " If you but knew it, Mithras is above as well as below ! " A well-preserved temple of Mithras was discovered at Ostia in 1886, displaying in mosaics all the symbols of the worship of the Persian sun-god.

personal danger, though sometimes the priests caught a Tartar. Thus we are told that the Emperor Commodus on his initiation carried the joke too far, and slew one of the priests who had assailed him in the form of a wild beast.

In the next degree he put on a mantle on which were painted the signs of the zodiac. A curtain then concealed him from the sight of all; but this being withdrawn, he appeared surrounded by frightful griffins. After passing through other trials, if his courage did not fail him, he was hailed as a "Lion of Mithras," in allusion to the zodiacal sign in which the sun attained his greatest power. We meet with the same idea in the degree of Master Mason. The grand secret was then imparted. What was it? At this distance of time it is difficult to decide, but we may assume that the priests communicated to him the most authentic sacerdotal traditions, the best accredited theories concerning the origin of the universe, and the attributes, perfections, and works of Oromazes. In fact, the Mithraic mysteries represent the progress of darkness to light. According to Guignault, Mithras is love; with regard to the Eternal, he is the son of mercy; with regard to Oromazes and Ahrimanes, the fire of love.

33. *Thammuz* - The ceremonies connected with the myth of Thammuz, the Chaldean sun-god, were another phase of solar worship. M. Lenormant was the first to demonstrate, from the Assyrian tablets, that Thammuz was the prototype of Adonis, and of all the subsequent sun-gods worshipped in various countries and under various names. On those tablets also is found the story of Istar, the prototype of Astarte, Isis, and the other female deities, who afterwards, under various names, represented cosmically the female principle, and astronomically the moon. The great festival of Thammuz was held at the summer solstice (even now in the Jewish calendar the month of July goes by the name of Tamuz); it lasted six days, and in the functions ascribed to each day we find a curious agreement with the corresponding properties of eternal Nature (II). For the first day was a day of rest, motionless, inactive; the second and third days celebrated the struggle of the imprisoned life to become free they were days of grief and suffering;

the fourth day was dedicated to the conquest over lions and serpents; that is to say, the fire; the fourth property began the conquest of the first three or dark properties; the fifth day was considered favourable for sacrifice, the happy influence of the newly-risen sun, or light, became perceptible; and on the sixth, the conjunction of Sol with Istar was celebrated with joyous songs. The eighth chapter of Ezekiel comprises the day of mourning and that of rejoicing at the recovery of Tammuz (107).

There is one circumstance connected with the story of Istar referred to above, which though not strictly within the scope of this work, is yet of so striking a character that the reader will readily excuse my referring to it. That story is comprised within a short poem entitled "Istar's Descent into Hell." Its opening lines are:

> " Towards the country without return, the land of putrefaction,
> Istar, the daughter of Sin, has set her mind.
> *****
> Towards the dwelling, into which you enter, whence never to issue
> again.
> Towards the path from which there is no return,
> Towards the habitation at whose entrance all light is withdrawn."

Who, on reading these lines, is not inevitably reminded of the "Inferno" of Dante, who, of course, never had heard of this Chaldean poem?

Another remark, which may fitly be introduced here, has reference to Tammuz. In Chinese his name is Tomos; and to this circumstance is due the fable that St. Thomas had been in India and China. The first Eoman Catholic missionaries took Tomos for Thomas, who had there preached the Gospel; wherefore the first Christians in those countries called themselves the Christians of St. Thomas, telling wonderful stories of the doings of St. Thomas, and that at last he was put to death by the Brahmins, whose trade he spoiled.

III

BRAHMINS AND GYMNOSOPHISTS

34. *Vulgar Creed of India* - The Indian religion, whether we look on it as an adulteration of Magism, or as the common trunk of all Asiatic theosophy, offers so boundless a wealth of deities, that no other in this respect can approach it. This wealth is an infallible sign of the mental poverty and grossness of the people, who, ignorant of the laws of Nature, and terrified at its phenomena, acknowledged as many supernatural beings as there were mysteries for them. The Brahmins reckon up 300,000 gods a frightful host, that have kept Indian life servile and stagnant, perpetuated the divisions of caste, upheld ignorance, and weighed like an incubus on the breasts of their deluded dupes, and turned existence into a nightmare of grief and servitude.

35. *Secret Doctrines* - But in the secret sanctuary these vain phantoms disappear, and the initiated are taught to look upon them as countless accidents and outward manifestations of the First Cause. The Brahmins did not consider the people fit to apprehend and preserve in its purity the religion of the spirit, hence they veiled it in these figures, and also invented a language incomprehensible to the vulgar, but which the investigations of Oriental scholars have enabled us to read, and to perceive that the creed of India is one of the purest ever known to man. Thus in the second chapter of the first part of the "Vishnu Purana," it is written: "God is without form, epithet, definition, or description; free from defect, incapable of annihilation, change, grief, or pain. We can only say that He, that is, the Eternal Being, is God. Vulgar men think that God is in the water; the more enlightened, in celestial bodies; the ignorant, in wood and stone; but the wise, in the universal mind." The "Mahanirvana" says: "Numerous figures, corresponding with the nature of divers powers and quality, were invented for the benefit of those who are wanting in sufficient understanding." Again, "We have no notion of how the Eternal Being is to be described; he is above all the mind can apprehend, above Nature. . . . That Only One that was

never defined by any language, and gave to language all its meaning, he is the Supreme Being ... and no partial thing that man worships.... This Being extends over all things. He is mere spirit without corporeal form; without extension of any size, unimpressionable, and without any organs; he is pure, perfect, omniscient, omnipresent, the ruler of the intellect ... he is the soul of the whole universe."

36. *Hindoo Cosmogony* - The Hindoo cosmogony certainly is the most ancient we possess; the laws of Menu, embodying it, were written before Moses was born, and may thus describe the Creation.

" This universe existed only in the first divine idea, yet unexpanded, as if involved in darkness. . . . Then the sole, self-existing power . . . appeared with undiminished glory, expanding his idea."
"He, having willed to produce various beings from his own divine substance, first created the waters."
"From that which Is, the first cause, . . . was produced the divine male."
" He framed the heaven above, and the earth beneath; in the midst he placed the subtile ether."
" He framed all creatures."
"He, too, first assigned to all creatures distinct names."
" He gave being to time, and the divisions of time to the stars also and the planets."
"Having divided his own substance, the mighty power became half male, half female."
" He, . . . having created this universe, was again absorbed in the spirit, changing the time of energy for the time of repose."

It will be seen that the author of Genesis has given us a faint echo of those grand utterances, as a child feebly attempting to repeat the teachings of a sage.

37. *Buddhism* - A dangerous antagonist to the Brahman priesthood, and the literature and traditions, on which they rested their claims to power, sprang up in Buddhism. Buddha preached the equality of all

men, and denied the value, much more the necessity, of the Vedic system. The new gospel of universal charity and brotherhood was eagerly received by men, who were groaning under the yoke of Brahmanical tyranny, and it found an ally in the half-expressed scepticism of some of the Vedic schools of philosophy. It was in the south of India especially that Buddha's doctrines found a ready welcome, while Ceylon became converted to Buddhism as early as 240 BC. In India, Buddhism was exterminated by its sanguinary persecution by the Brahmins. Ceylon is now the only part of India in which the religion of Buddha still survives.

38. *Buddhistic Teaching* - Buddha, or to give him his real name, Sakyamuni for Buddha is a title, and means a "Sage" is said to have been born in the sixth century B.C. But of his real existence there is no proof; the most recent researches show that the story of Buddha is a solar myth, first told of Krishna, and afterwards transferred to Buddha. The most sacred Buddhist symbols, and the most frequent Buddhist similes, have their Vedic analogies, with the distinction that Brahminism resolves the individual into a (personal) god, Buddhism into the (universal) Nothing, or Nirvana. For Buddhism teaches that the original matter, or prakriti, is the only existing divine per se. In this matter there are immanent two forces, which produce two different conditions quiescence and activity. In one state it remains quiescent with consciousness in an absolute inactive vacuity, and this is the state of bliss of the original Nothing. In another state the matter steps out of itself by its activity, and is shaped into limited forms. In doing so it loses its consciousness, which it re-acquires in becoming man, and there is in this manner an original and a born consciousness. The aim of man is to reproduce the original consciousness. On arriving at it he learns that there is nothing real beside the original matter; his spirit then becomes identical with the original conscious Nothing; that is to say, his individual soul, set free from the body, in which it was imprisoned, returns into the universal soul, just as the solar light, imprisoned in a piece of wood, when this is burnt, returns into the universal ocean of light. On this doctrine was afterwards engrafted the false belief in the

metempsychosis or transmigration of souls, and the misanthropic system of self-renunciation, which in India led to the self-tort u rings of fakirs and other fanatics; and which finds its analogies in Christian communities in the asceticism of fasts, penances, macerations, solitude, flagellation, and all the mad practices of monks, anchorets, and other religious zealots.

39. *Asceticism* - This asceticism, founded on the above notion, viz., that the Absolute or All is the real existence, and that individual phenomena, especially matter in all its forms, are really nothing, i.e., mere phantasms, and to be
avoided, as increasing the distance from the Absolute, and that absorption into the Deity is to be obtained, even in this life, by the maceration of the body, was and even now is prevalent in India, where it was carried, in thousands of instances, further than mere self-torture, even to death. When, at the festival of the dread goddess Bhovani, the wife of Siva, her ponderous image was borne on a car, with cutting wheels, to the Ganges, a crowd of frantic beings, wreathed with flowers, joyous as if they went to the nuptial altar, would cast themselves under the wheels of the car, offering themselves, amidst the sounding of trumpets, as voluntary sacrifices, to be cut to pieces by the wheels. And in various sects asceticism has led to the adoption of many strange practices. In the "Contes de la Eeine de Navarre" there is a passage which at some length refers to a special mode adopted by monks and other men for the mortification of the flesh.

40. *Gymnosophists* - We have very few notices of the Gymnosophists, the Magi of Brahminism, the most severe custodians of the primitive law, and originally most free from imposture. They spread over Africa; and in Ethiopia they lived as solitaires, and revived on the banks of the Nile many phases of Asiatic theosophy, traces of which abound in the doctrines of the Dervishes. Priests-errant, they were reported to carry with them a secret doctrine, of which the simplicity of their lives and the purity of their morals might be considered as the outward manifestation; though in after times they became one of the most

debauched and immoral sects in India.

They went almost naked (hence their name γυμνός, naked; σοφός, wise), and lived on herbs; but their own austerity did not render them harsh towards other men, nor unjust as regarded other common conditions of life. They believed in one only God, the immortality of the soul and its transmigration, and when old age or disease prostrated them, they ascended the funeral pile, deeming it ignominious to let years or evils afflict them. Alexander saw one of them close his life in this manner.

The priestly colleges of Ethiopia and Egypt maintained constant relations. Osiris is an Ethiopian divinity. Every year the two families of priests met on the boundaries of the two countries to offer common sacrifices to Ammon, another name for Jupiter, and celebrate the festival which the Greeks called heliotrapeza, or Table of the Sun. Amidst the predominant fetishism of Africa, produced partly by climate and partly by the same circumstances that gave rise to Indian fetishism, we cannot help admiring that colony of thinkers which long resisted the progress of despotism, and whose destruction was the revenge of intolerance and tyranny.

41. *Places for celebrating Mysteries* - The mysteries, as in other countries, were celebrated in subterranean caverns, here excavated in the solid rock, and surpassing in grandeur of conception and finish of execution anything to be seen elsewhere. The temples of Elephanta, Ellora, and Salsette, consisting of large halls and palaces, chapels, pagodas, cells for thousands of priests and pilgrims, adorned with pillars and columns, obelisks, bas-reliefs, gigantic statues of deities, elephants, and other sacred animals, all carved out of the living rock, are especially noteworthy. In the sacellum, only accessible to the initiated, the supreme Deity was represented by the lingam, which was used more or less by all ancient nations to represent His creative power, though in India it was also typified by the petal and calyx of the lotus.

42. *Initiation* - The periods of initiation were regulated by the increase and decrease of the moon, and the mysteries were divided into four degrees, and the candidate might be initiated into the first at the early age of eight years. He was then prepared by a Brahmin, who became his spiritual guide for the second degree, the probationary ceremonies of which consisted in incessant occupation in prayers, fastings, ablutions, and the study of astronomy. In the hot season he sat exposed to five fires, four blazing around him, with the sun above; in the rains he stood uncovered; in the cold season he wore wet clothing. To participate in the high privileges which the mysteries were believed to confer, he was sanctified by the sign of the cross, and subjected to the probation of the pastos, the tomb of the sun, the coffin of Hiram, darkness, hell, all symbolical of the first three properties (11). His purification being completed, he was led at night to the cavern of initiation. This was brilliantly illuminated, and there sat the three chief hierophants, in the east, west, and south, representing the gods Brahma, who was painted red to represent substance, Vishnu, painted blue to symbolise space, Siva, painted white, in contrast to the black night of eternity, surrounded by attendant mystagogues, dressed in appropriate vestments. The initiation was begun by an apostrophe to the sun, addressed by the name of Pooroosh, here meaning the vital soul, or portion of the universal spirit of Brahm; and the candidate, after some further preliminary ceremonies, was made to circumambulate the cavern three times, and afterwards conducted through seven dark caverns, during which period the wailings of Mahadeva for the loss of Siva were represented by dismal howlings. The usual paraphernalia of flashes of light, of dismal sounds and horrid phantoms, were produced to terrify and confuse the aspirant. Having arrived at the last cavern, the sacred conch was blown, the folding doors thrown open, and the candidate was admitted into an apartment filled with dazzling lights, ornamented with statues and emblematic figures richly decorated with gems, and scented with the most fragrant perfumes. This sacellum was intended to represent Paradise, and was actually so called in the temple of Ellora. With eyes riveted on the altar, the candidate was taught to expect the descent of the Deity in the bright pyramidal fire that blazed

upon it; and in a moment of enthusiasm, thus artificially produced, the candidate might indeed persuade himself that he actually beheld Brahm seated on the lotus, with his four heads and arms, representing the four elements and the four quarters of the globe, and bearing in his hands the emblems of eternity and power, the circle and fire. The symbol of initiation was a cord of seven threads knotted thrice three.

The reader will have noticed in one case I say Brahm and in the other Brahma; the latter is the body of the former, which is the Eternal Life. The terms correspond with those of Abyssal Deity and Virgin Sophia of Christian theosophy.

43. *The ineffable name Aum* - The candidate was now supposed to be regenerated, and was invested with the white robe, tiara, and the sacred belt; a cross was marked on his forehead, and a tau (53) upon his breast; the salagram or marginal black stone (18), to insure to him the perfection of Vishnu, and the serpent stone, an antidote against the bite of serpents, were delivered to him; and lastly, he was entrusted with the sacred name, which signified the solar fire, and united in its comprehensive meaning the great Trimurti, or combined principle on which the existence of all things is founded. This word was OM, or in a triliteral form AUM, to represent the creative, preserving, and destroying power of the Deity, personified in Brahma, Vishnu, and Siva, the symbol of which was an equilateral triangle. To this name, as the Royal Arch Masons to that of Jabulon, they attributed the most wonderful powers; and it could only be the subject of silent but pleasing contemplation, for its pronunciation was said to make earth and heaven tremble, and even the
angels of heaven to quake with. fear. The emblems around and the aporreta of the mysteries were then explained, and the candidate instructed that by means of the knowledge of OM he was to become one with the Deity. With the Persians the syllable HOM meant the tree of life, a tree and a man at the same time, the dwelling-place of the soul of Zoroaster; and with them also, as with the Indians, it was forbidden on pain of death to reveal it. In this secret name, involving the rejection of polytheism, and comprising the knowledge of Nature,

we have the golden thread thatjinites ancient and modern secret societies.

44. *The Lingam* - One of the emblems found in the sacellum, and which in fact is found everywhere on the walls of Indian temples, was the lingam, which represented the male principle, and which passed from India to Egypt, Greece, and Scandinavia. The worship of this symbol could not but lead to great abuses, especially as regarded the gymnosophists.

45. *The Lotus* - The lotus, the lily of the Nile, held sacred also in Egypt, was the great vegetable amulet of eastern nations. The Indian gods were always represented as seated on it. It was an emblem of the soul's freedom when liberated from its earthly tabernacle, the body; for it takes root in the mud deposited at the bottom of a river, vegetates from the germ to a perfect plant, and afterwards rising proudly above the waves, it floats in air, as if independent of any extraneous aid. It is placed on a golden table, as the symbol of Siva, on the top of Mount Meru, the holy mountain of India, the centre of the earth, worshipped by Hindoos, Tartars, Montchurians, and Mongols. It is supposed to be in Northern India, to have three peaks, composed of gold, silver, and iron, on which reposes the trine deity Brahma, Vishnu, and Siva. Geographically, this mountain is evidently the tableland of Tartary, whose southern boundary is formed by the Himalayas. This custom of accounting a three-peaked mountain holy was not confined to India alone, but prevailed also among the Jews. Thus Olivet, near Jerusalem, had three peaks, which were accounted the residence of the Deity Chemosh, Milcom, Ashtoreth (2 Kings xxiii. 13). In Zechariah (xiv. 4) the feet of the Almighty are placed on the two outer peaks of this mountain during the threatened destruction of Jerusalem; while the mountain itself is made to split asunder at the centre peak from east to west, leaving a great valley between the divided parts.

46. *The Jains* - They form a Buddhistic sect, but differ from the Buddhists by having retained the division of castes; they agree,

however, with them in denying the divine authority of the Vedas. The Jains are divided into four castes, the first of which is that of the Brahmens, or priests, who pass through a ceremony of upanayana, or initiation, but of what it consists we have no reliable information. The term jain, or jina, means a conqueror, and is used by genuine Buddhists in that sense; but with the latter man becomes a Jina through meditation, whilst with the Jains he becomes a "conqueror" through austerity. They have a magnificent temple, the most superb of all temples in India, on Mount Abu, in the territory of Serohee, in Kajpootana. It is built of marble, in the form of a cross, and is said to have been fourteen years building, and to have cost £18,000,000. It is a celebrated place of pilgrimage for the Jains, who also have a large rock-temple at Karlee, in the Presidency of Bombay.

IV

EGYPTIAN MYSTERIES

47. *Antiquity of Egyptian Civilisation* - All Egypt is an initiation. A long and narrow strip of land, watered by immense floods and surrounded by immense solitudes such is Egypt. Very high and steep rocks protected it from the incursions of the nomadic tribes, and thus a valley, a river, and a race sufficed to create, if not the most ancient, at least one of the most ancient and illustrious cultures, a world of marvels, at a time when Europeans went naked, and dyed their skins, as Caesar found the ancient Britons, and when the Greeks, armed with bows and arrows, led a nomadic existence. The Egyptians, many thousand years before the Trojan war, had invented writing, as is proved, for instance, by the hieratic papyrus of the time of Rameses II., full of recipes and directions for the treatment of a great variety of diseases, and now in the Berlin Museum. They also knew many comforts of life, which our pride calls modern; and the Greek writers, whom the Egyptian priests called children, are full of recollections of that mysterious land, recording the father Nile, Thebes with its hundred gates, the Pyramids, Lake Meroe, the Labyrinth, the Sphinx, and the statue of Memnon saluting the rising sun.

48. *Temples of Ancient Egypt* - Egyptian chronology, the reproof and paragon of all others, is graven on imperishable monuments. But those obelisks, sacred to the sun, by their conical form like that of the flame; those labyrinths; those human-headed birds, typifying the intelligent soul; those scarabei, signifying creative power; those sphinxes, representing force, the lion or sun, and man; those serpents, expressing life and eternity (70); those strange combinations of forms; those hieroglyphics they long remained secrets for us, and perhaps always were a secret for the Egyptian people that in fear and silence erected the pyramids all these symbols constituted the language of one of the vastest and most elaborate secret societies that ever existed. Penetrating into those gigantic temples which seem the work of an extinct race,

different from ours, as fossil quadrupeds are different from those now living; traversing those cloisters, which after many windings lead to the innermost sanctuary, we are seized by a singular thought that of the silence and solitude which ever reigned within those edifices into which the people were not allowed to penetrate; only the few were admitted, and we moderns are the first profane that have set foot within the hallowed precincts. The temple of Luxor is the vastest on earth six propylsea with long files of columns, and colossi and obelisks and sphinxes; six cloisters every new generation of kings for seventy centuries added some new portion and inscribed on the walls the history of its deeds, and every new addition removed the faithful further from the seat of the god; the marvel and mystery increased. The sixth propylseum is not finished; it is a chapter of history broken off in the middle, and will never be completed. The walls and pillars of the temples were covered with religious and astronomical representations, and from the fact of many of these pictures showing human beings in various states of suffering and under torture, it has been assumed that the Egyptian ritual was cruel, like the Mexican (85 - 89); but such is not the case; the pictures are only representations of the punishments said to be inflicted on the wicked in another life.

49. *Egyptian Priests and Kings* - The priestly caste, possessing all the learning, ruled first and alone; but in its own defence it armed a portion of the population; the rest it kept down by superstition, or disarmed and weakened it by corruption. To Plato, who saw it from a distance, this government seemed stupendous, and he idealised it; it was for him the " city of God," the pattern republic. Nevertheless, as was inevitable, might rebelled against doctrine, the soldiery broke the reign of the priesthood, and by the side of the pontiffs arose the kings, or to speak more correctly, the two series proceeded in parallels; that of the priests was not set aside, it had its palaces, the temples, strong like fortresses, along the Nile, which were at the same time splendid abodes, agricultural establishments, commercial depots, and caravan stations; its members appointed and ruled the kings themselves, regulating the most minute acts of their daily conduct; they were the

depositaries of the highest offices, and as the learned savans, magistrates, and physicians, enjoyed the first honours. Their chief colleges were at Thebes, Memphis, Heliopolis, and Sais; they possessed a great portion of the land, which they caused to be cultivated; paid no taxes, but collected tithes. They formed indeed the elect, privileged, and only free portion of the nation.

50. *Exoteric and Esoteric Doctrines* - The priests were no followers of the idolatrous faith of the people; but to have undeceived the latter would have been dangerous for themselves. The true doctrine of the unity of God, therefore, which was their secret, was only imparted to those that after many trials had been initiated into the mysteries. Their doctrines, like those of all other priesthoods, were therefore exoteric and esoteric; and the mysteries were of two kinds, the greater and the less, the former being the mysteries of Osiris and Serapis, the latter those of Isis. The mysteries of Osiris were celebrated at the autumnal equinox; those of Serapis at the summer solstice; and those of Isis at the vernal equinox.

51. *Egyptian Mythology* - Though want of space does not allow me fully to enter upon the vast subject of Egyptian mythology, yet a few words thereon are necessary to render its bearing on the mysteries clear, and also to show its connection with many of the rites of modern freemasonry.

That all the symbols and ceremonies of all the ancient creeds originally had a deep and universal cosmic meaning, has already been shown (9, 10); but at the time when the mysteries were most nourishing that meaning was to a great extent lost, and a merely astronomical one substituted for it, as will be seen from the following explanations:

Osiris, represented in Egypt by a sceptre surmounted by an eye, to signify him that rules and sees, symbolises the sun. Osiris is evidently derived from Iswara, an epithet of Brahma, and means the Supreme Lord; it is therefore a title, and not a proper name. The same adventures are attributed to Osiris that are related of Brahma. Osiris is killed by Typhon, a serpent engendered by the mud of the Nile. But Typhon is a transposition of Python, derived from the Greek word πύθω, " to putrefy," and means nothing else but the noxious vapours arising from steaming mud, and thus concealing the sun; wherefore in the Greek mythology Apollo another name for the sun is said to have slain Python with his arrows, that is to say, dispelled the vapours by his rays. Osiris having been killed by Python to which, however, the wider meaning of the sun's imaginary disappearance, or death, during the winter season, was attached Isis, his wife, or the moon, goes in search of him, and at last finds his body, cut into fourteen pieces; that is to say, into as many parts as there are days between the full moon and the new. She collects all the pieces, with one important exception, for which she made a substitution, which gave rise to a worship resembling that of the lingam in India, and which in Egypt was called that of the phallus. Among the Sidonians, Isis was called Ashtaroth, meaning "flocks," "riches," i.e., the plenty of the earth; and hence we so frequently find "asherah" and "ashtaroth" mentioned together. In the Bible asherah is translated " grove," but this is an error; asherah means "pillar," or the phallus, the mast of the ship of Isis, which was carried in procession at Egyptian religious festivals.

But although to the vulgar crowd Isis was only the moon, to the initiated she was Hathor, the Universal Mother, the primordial harmony and beauty, called in Egyptian " Iophis," which the Greeks turned into " Sophia,"[6] whence the Virgin Sophia of theosophy. Hence also the many names by which Isis was known (58), indicating the multifarious aspects she necessarily assumed. Her image was worshipped at Sais under the emblem of "Isis veiled," with this inscription: "I am all that has been, all that is, and all that will be, and no mortal has drawn aside my veil."

Apis, or the Bull, was an object of worship throughout all the ancient world, because formerly the zodiacal sign of the Bull opened the vernal equinox (81).

---

[6] By a transposition of consonants, common enough in the formation of new words ; Typbon from Python is an instance already mentioned ; forma, from μορφή, is another.

52. *The Phoenix* - The Egyptians began the year with the rising of the dog-star or Sirins. But making no allowance for the quarter of a day which finishes the year, the civil year every four years began one day too soon, and so the beginning of the year went successively through every one of the days of the natural year in the space of four times 365, which makes 1460 years. They fancied they blessed and made all the seasons to prosper by making them thus to enjoy one after another the feast of Isis, which was celebrated along with that of Sirius, though it was frequently very remote from that constellation; wherefore they introduced the image of dogs, or even the real and living animals, preceding the chariots of Isis. When in the 1461st year the feast again coincided with the rising of the star Sirins, they looked upon it as a season of plenty, and symbolised it by a bird of singular beauty, which they called Phoenix (deliciis abundans), saying that it came to die upon the altar of the sun, and that out of its ashes there arose a little worm, that gave birth to a bird perfectly like the preceding.

53. *The Cross* - Among the astronomical symbols we must not omit the Cross. This sign really signifies the fire, as we have seen (II, ix.), but in Egypt it was simply the Nilometer, consisting of an upright pole with a cross-bar, that was raised or lowered according to the swelling or decrease of the river. It was frequently surmounted by a circle, typifying the deity that governs this important operation. Now, the overflow of the Nile was considered the salvation of Egypt, and hence the sign came to be looked upon with great veneration, and to have occult virtues attributed to it, such as the power of averting evil; wherefore the Egyptians hung small figures of the cross, or rather the letter T, with a ring attached to it, the crux ansata, round the necks of their children and of sick persons; they applied it to the string or fillets with which they wrapped up their mummies, where we still find it; it became, in fact, an amulet (amolitio maloruwi). Other nations adopted the custom, and hence the cross or the letter T, whereby it was symbolised throughout the ancient world, was supposed to be a sign or letter of more than ordinary significance. In the mysteries, the crux

ansata was the symbol of eternal life. But the cross was worshipped as an astronomical sign in other countries. We have seen that in India the neophyte was sanctified by the sign of the cross (42), which in most ancient nations was a symbol of the universe, pointing as it does to the four quarters of the compass; and the erection of temples on the cruciform principle is as old as architecture itself. The two great pagodas of Benares and Mathura are erected in the form of vast crosses, of which each wing is equal in extent, as is also the pyramidal temple of New Grange in Ireland. But the older and deeper meaning of the cross is shown in (II); it refers to the fire, and the double quality everywhere observable in Nature. The triple tau is the Royal Arch Mason's badge.

54. *Places of Initiation* - In Egypt and other countries (India, Media, Persia, Mexico) the place of initiation was a pyramid erected over subterranean caverns. The pyramids, in fact, may be looked upon, considering their size, shape, and solidity, as artificial mountains. Their form not only symbolically represented the ascending flame, but also had a deeper origin in the conical form, which is the primitive figure of all natural products. And the Great Pyramid, the tomb of Osiris, was erected in such a position, and to such a height, that at the spring and autumnal equinoxes the sun would appear exactly at midday upon the summit of the pyramid, seeming to rest upon this immense pedestal, when his worshippers, extended at the base, would contemplate the great Osiris as well when he descended into the tomb as when he arose from it triumphant.

55. *Process of Initiation* - The candidate, conducted by a guide, was led to a deep, dark well or shaft in the pyramid, and, provided with a torch, he descended into it by means of a ladder affixed to the side. Arrived at the bottom, he saw two doors one of them barred, the other yielding to the touch of his hand. Passing through it, he beheld a winding gallery, whilst the door behind him shut with a clang that reverberated through the vaults. Inscriptions like the following met his eye: "Whoso shall pass along this road alone, and without looking back, shall be purified by fire, water, and air; and overcoming the fear

of death, shall issue from the bowels of the earth to the light of day, preparing his soul to receive the mysteries of Isis." Proceeding onward, the candidate arrived at another iron gate, guarded by three armed men, whose shining helmets were surmounted by emblematic animals, the Cerberus of Orpheus. Here the candidate had offered to him the last chance of returning, if so inclined. Electing to go forward, he underwent the trial by fire, by passing through a hall filled with inflammable substances in a state of combustion, and forming a bower of fire. The floor was covered with a grating of redhot iron bars, leaving, however, narrow interstices where he might safely place his feet. Having surmounted this obstacle, he has to encounter the trial by water. A wide and dark canal, fed by the waters of the Nile, arrests his progress. Placing the flickering lamp upon his head, he plunges into the canal, and swims to the opposite bank, where the greatest trial, that by air, awaits him. He lands upon a platform leading to an ivory door, bounded by two walls of brass, into each of which is inserted an immense wheel of the same metal. He in vain attempts to open the door, when, espying two large iron rings affixed to it, he takes hold of them; but suddenly the platform sinks from under him, a chilling blast of wind extinguishes his lamp, the two brazen wheels revolve with formidable rapidity and stunning noise, whilst he remains suspended by the two rings over the fathomless abyss. But ere he is exhausted the platform returns, the ivory door opens, and he sees before him a magnificent temple, brilliantly illuminated, and filled with the priests of Isis clothed in the mystic insignia of their offices, the hierophant at their head. But the ceremonies of initiation do not cease here. The candidate is subjected to a series of fastings, which gradually increase for nine times nine days. During this period a rigorous silence is imposed upon him, which if he preserve inviolate, he is at length fully initiated into the esoteric doctrines of Isis. He is led before the triple statue of Isis, Osiris, and Horus, another symbol of the sun, where he swears never to publish the things revealed to him in the sanctuary, and first drinks the water of Lethe, presented to him by the high priest, to forget all he ever heard in his unregenerate state, and afterwards the water of Mnemosyne, to remember all the lessons of wisdom imparted to him in the mysteries. He is next introduced into the most secret part of the sacred edifice, where a priest instructs him in the application of the symbols found therein. He is then publicly announced as a person who has been initiated into the mysteries of Isis the first degree of the Egyptian rites.

56. *Mysteries of Serapis* - These constituted the second degree. We know but little of them, and Apuleius only slightly touches upon them. When Theodosius destroyed the temple of Serapis there were discovered subterraneous passages and engines wherein and wherewith the priests tried the candidates. Porphyry, in referring to the greater mysteries, quotes a fragment of Cheremones, an Egyptian priest, which imparts an astronomical meaning to the whole legend of Osiris, thus confirming what has been said above. And Herodotus, in describing the temple of Minerva, where the rites of Osiris were celebrated, and speaking of a tomb placed in the most secret recess, as in Christian churches there are calvaries behind the altar, says: "It is the tomb of a god whose name I dare not mention." Calvary is derived from the Latin word calvns, "bald," and figuratively "arid," "dried up;" pointing to the decay of Nature in the winter season.

57. *Mysteries of Osiris* - These formed the third degree or summit of Egyptian lay initiation, for there was yet the higher initiation into the priesthood, described in the following section. In these the legend of the murder of Osiris by his brother Typhon was represented, and the god was personated by the candidate. (As we shall see hereafter, the Freemasons exactly copy this procedure in the master's degree, substituting for Osiris Hiram Abiff, one of the three grand-masters at the building of Solomon's temple.) The perfectly initiated candidate was called Al-om-jak, from the name of the Deity (43), 'and the dogma of the unity of God was the chief secret imparted to him. How great and how dangerous a secret it was may easily be seen when it is borne in mind that centuries after the institution of the mysteries, Socrates lost his life for promulgating the same doctrine. According to Iamblichus, all initiated into the highest esoteric mysteries became, as it

were, dead to their own selves; they were absorbed in the Deity; they enjoyed the beatific vision. Neither fire nor steel could hurt them; no natural obstacles could stand in their way; the afflatus of the Divine spirit encompassed them. We have, in fact, in those ancient pagan imaginations all the fancied privileges of the Christian mystics, all the raptures of canonised saints of the Eoman Catholic Church.

58. *Isis* - The many names assumed by Isis have already been alluded to. She was also represented with different emblems, all betokening her manifold characteristics. The lucid round, the snake, the ears of corn, and the sistrum represent the titular deities of the Hecat ean (Hecate, Goddess of Night), Bacchic, Eleusinian, and Ionic mysteries; that is, the mystic rites in general for whose sake the allegory was invented. The black palla in which she is wrapped, embroidered with a silver moon and stars, denotes the time in which the mysteries were celebrated, namely, in the dead of night. Her names, to return to them, are given in the following words, put into her mouth by Apuleius in his "Golden Ass," which is a description of the mysteries under the guise of a fable: "Behold, Lucius, I, moved by thy prayers, am present with thee; I who am Nature, the parent of things, the queen of all the elements, the primordial progeny of the ages, the supreme of divinities, the sovereign of the spirits of the dead, the first of the celestials, the , first and universal substance, the uniform and multiform aspect of the uncreated essence; I who rule by my nod the luminous summits of the heavens, the breezes of the sea, and the silence of the realms beneath, and whose one divinity the whole orb of the earth venerates under a manifold form, by different rites, and a variety of appellations. Hence the early Phrygians call me Pessinuntica, mother of the gods; the Attic aborigines, Cecropian Minerva; the floating Cyprians, Paphian Venus; the arrow-bearing Cretans, Diana Dictynna; the three-tongued Sicilians, Stygian Proserpine; and the Eleusinians, the ancient goddess Ceres. Some also call me Juno, others Bellona, others Hecate, and others Rhamnusia. The Ethiopians, the Arii, and the Egyptians, skilled in ancient learning, honour me with rites peculiarly appropriate, and call me by my true name, Queen Isis." From this it is quite clear that Isis

was not simply the moon to the initiated. In the sanctuary the multifarious forms are reduced to unity; the many idols are reduced to the one divinity i.e., primeval power and intelligence.

V

CRATA REPOA, OR HIGHEST DEGREE OF EGYPTIAN INITIATION

59. *Preparation* - Bat there was a still higher degree into which Egyptian kings and priests only were initiated. It was known by the above title. Whoso wished to enter this degree had to be specially recommended by one of the initiated. This was usually done by the king himself introducing the aspirant to the priests. These first directed him from Heliopolis to the priests at Memphis; thence he was sent to Thebes; eventually he was circumcised; then he was forbidden to eat pulse or fish and to drink wine, though in the higher degrees leave to do so was occasionally granted. He was then left for several months together in a subterranean cave to his own reflections, which he was invited to write down. Afterwards he was led into a passage, supported by Hermes' pillars, on which were graven moral sentences he had to learn by heart. As soon as he knew them, the Thesmophorus, or introducer, came to him, carrying in his hand a stout whip, to keep away the profane from the gate through which the aspirant was to pass. He was blindfolded, and his hands tied with cords.

60. *First Degree* - The candidate having been led to the "Gate of Men," the Thesmophorus touched the shoulder of a Portophorus, or apprentice, who guarded the gate, which latter thereupon knocked at the gate, which was opened. On the aspirant's entrance he was questioned on various matters by the Hierophant, after which he was led about the Birantha in an artificial storm of wind, rain, thunder and lightning, and if he showed no signs of fear, Menies, the expounder, explained the laws of the Grata Repoa, to which he had to give his assent. He was then led before the Hierophant, before whom he had to kneel down on his bare knees, and, with a sword pointed at his throat, had to vow fidelity and secrecy, calling sun, moon, and stars to witness. His eyes were then unbandaged, and he was placed between two spare pillars, called Betilies, where lay a ladder of seven steps,

behind which were eight doors of different metals, of gradually increasing purity. The Hierophant then addressing those present as Mene Musae, or Children of the Work of Celestial Investigation, exhorted them to govern their passions, and fix their thoughts upon God. The candidate was then instructed that the ladder, whose steps he had to ascend, was the symbol of the wanderings of the soul; he was told the causes of wind, thunder, and lightning; he was also instructed in anatomy and medicine, in the symbolical language, and the ordinary hieroglyphic writing. The Hierophant further gave him the password by which the initiated recognised one another, and which was Amoun, signifying secrecy; and with it was given the grip, a cap shaped like a pyramid, and an apron called Xylon. Around his neck he wore a kind of collar, fitting closely to the chest. He wore no other clothes, and it was his duty to guard the Gate of Men, whenever it came to his turn.

61. *Second Degree* - The Portophorus having given proofs of proficiency, he was, after a long fast, taken into a dark chamber, called Endimion, meaning an invitation grotto. He now was raised to the degree of Neocoris. Handsome women brought him dainty food; they were the wives of the priests, who endeavoured to excite his love. If he resisted the temptation, the Thesmophorus again visited, and, having catechised him, led him into the assembly, where the Stolista, or water-bearer, poured water over him. Then the Thesmophorus threw a living serpent on him, and drew it away again from under the apron. The whole room was, moreover, full of serpents, to test the courage of the Neocoris. He was then led to two high pillars, between which stood a griffin, driving a wheel before him. The pillars symbolised east and west, the griffin the sun, and the wheel with four spokes the four seasons. He was taught the use of the level, and instructed in geometry and architecture. He received a rod, entwined by serpents, and the password Heve, meaning serpent, and was told the story of the fall of man. The sign consisted in crossing the arms over the chest. His duty was to wash the pillars.

62. *Third Degree, or The Gate of Death* - On being initiated into this

degree, the Neocoris received the name of Melanophoris; he was led into an anteroom, over the entrance to which was written: "Gate of Death." The room itself was full of representations of embalmed bodies and coffins. And as it was the places where corpses were received, the Melanophoris here found the Paraskistes, or persons who dissected the bodies, and the Heroi, or persons who embalmed them, at their work. In the centre stood the coffin of Osiris. The Melanophoris was asked if he had had a hand in the assassination of his master. On his denying the question, he was seized by two Tapixeites, or men who buried the dead, and led into a hall, where he found all the other Melanophores clothed in black. The king himself, who always was present on these occasions, addressed him, in an apparently friendly way, begging him, if he did not feel courage enough to undergo the test now to be applied to him, to accept the golden crown he was offering him. But the new Melanophoris had previously been instructed to reject the crown and tread it under his feet. The king immediately exclaimed, "Insult! Revenge!" and raising his sacrificial axe, slightly touched the head of the Melanophoris. The two Tapixeites cast the Melanophoris on the ground, and the Pariskistes wrapped him up in mummy bandages. All present wept. Then he was led to a gate, over which was written, " Sanctuary of the Spirits." On its being opened, thunder and lightning struck the apparently dead man. Charon received him, as a spirit, into his boat, and carried him to the judges of Hades. Pluto sat on his judgment seat, while Rhadamanthus and Minos, as well as Æthon, Nycreus, Alaster, and Orpheus stood beside him. Very severe questions were put to him as to his former life, and finally he was sentenced to remain in these subterranean vaults. The bandages were taken off, and he was instructed never to thirst after blood, never to leave a corpse unburied, and to believe in the resurrection of the dead and in a judgment to come. He had then to learn painting, to be able to decorate coffins; was taught a peculiar writing, called a hierogrammatical, and in which the records of Egypt, and works on cosmography and astronomy were written. The sign was a particular kind of embrace to express the power of Death. The words were "Monarch caron mini" (I count the days of wrath). He remained in these subterranean chambers till he showed himself worthy of a higher degree.

63. *Fourth Degree, or the Battle of the Shades* - The days of wrath, lasting generally a year and a half, being over, the Thesmophorus came to the Melanophoris, asking him to follow him, and giving him at the same time a sword and a shield. They passed through dark passages, until they met certain persons, presenting a frightful appearance, carrying torches and serpents, and attacking them, whilst crying "Panis!" The Thesmophorns encouraged him to defend himself bravely. At last he was taken prisoner by them, his eyes were bandaged, and a cord was put round his neck. Then they dragged him to the hall, where he was to be initiated into a new degree, and the spectres or shades disappeared. He was led into the assembly, his eyes were unbandaged, and he beheld a magnificent hall, hung round with fine paintings. The king and the demiurgos, or highest officer, were present. All wore their Alydei, an Egyptian order (Truth), consisting of a figure formed of sapphires. Around them were seated the Stolistes, the Hierestolista, or secretary, the Zacoris, or treasurer, and the Komastis, or master of feats. The Odos, or orator, then made a speech, congratulating the Christophorus his new name on his resolution. He was then given a drink, called Cyce (probably the same as the κυκεών, a drink mixed of gruel, water, wine, milk, or honey), which he had to drink to the dregs. Then he was given the shield of Isis. He put on the boots of Anubis, and the cloak and cap of Orcus. He received a sword, with which he was to cut off the head of the person he was to meet in a cave, and to bring it to the king. Every member exclaimed, "Niobe, there is the cave of the enemy!" In the cave there was an exceedingly beautiful woman, who seemed to be alive, but was artificially formed of fine skins. The Christophorus had to seize her by the hair, and cut off her head, which he brought to the king, who praised him for his daring, and said he had cut off the head of the Gorgon, the wife of Typhon, who had been the cause of the death of Osiris. He received permission always to wear the dress which had been given to him, and his name was entered in a book as one of the judges of the land. He could freely

communicate with the king, and received his daily board from the court. He also was invested with an order, which, however, he could only wear at the initiation of a Christophorus, and which represented Isis in the shape of an owl. He was further told that the name of the great lawgiver was Joa, which was also the password. The Christophori held chapters called Pyxon, at which the password was Sasychis, the name of an ancient Egyptian priest. He had to study the Ammonite language, the secret language, because he was now very near acquiring the whole secret.

64. *Fifth Degree: Balaliate* - The Christophorus was entitled to this degree: it could not be refused him. He was led into a hall, where a theatrical representation took place, at which he was the only spectator. A Balahate, styled Orus, with other balahates, all carrying torches, went about the hall, as if seeking something. After a while Orus drew his sword. Typhon was seen sitting in a cave, surrounded with flames. Orus approached Typhon, who rose up; he had a hundred heads, and his body was covered with scales, and his arms were of extraordinary length. Nevertheless, Orus slew him. The new Balahate was then told that Typhon signified fire, one of the most terrible elements, without which, however, nothing could be done on earth. The password in this degree was Chymia, the instruction being in chemistry.

65. *Sixth Degree: Astronomers at the Gate of the Gods* - The candidate, on entering the hall of assembly, was bound with cords or chains. The Thesmophorus then led him back to the Gate of Death, which had many steps, leading to a cave full of water. There he saw many corpses of traitors to the society. He was threatened with the same fate, and led back to take a fresh oath. He was then instructed in astronomy, and warned against astrology and horoscopy, which were detested as the sources of all idolatry and superstition. The professors of these false sciences had for their password the word Phoenix, at which the astronomers laughed. He was then conducted to the Gate of the Gods, which was opened, and he beheld all the gods painted on the walls. The Demiurgos told him their history, and showed him a list of

all their members, scattered over the whole world. He was taught a priestly dance, symbolising the courses of the heavenly bodies. The word was Ibis, the symbol of watchfulness.

66. *Seventh Degree: Propheta* - The last and highest degree, in which all the secrets were revealed. It could not be conferred without the consent of the king and of all the higher members of the order. Public processions were held, called Pamylach, the circumcision of Osiris, i.e., of the tongue. When these were over, the members secretly left the city at night, and retired to some houses built in a square, and surrounded by pillars, by the sides of which were placed alternately a shield and a coffin, whose rooms were painted with representations of human life. These houses were called maneras, for the people believed them to be visited by the manes of departed men. On their arrival at these houses, the new member, now called prophet, or Saphenath Pancah,i.e., a man who knows the secrets, was given a drink, called oimellas (probably consisting of wine and honey), and told that now all trials were over. He received a cross of peculiar significance, which he was always to wear. He was clothed in a wide, white-striped dress, called etangi. His head was shaved; he wore a square cap. The usual sign was crossing his arms in his wide sleeves. He could peruse all the sacred books written in the Ammonite language, to which he had the key, which was called the Royal Beam. His greatest privilege was his having a vote in the election of a king. The password was Adon.

67. *Concluding Remarks* - Such is the fanciful account of the Crata Repoa. I confess my ignorance of the meaning of these two mysterious words. The order itself seems not to have been known before the year 1785, when the account the reader has just been perusing was published in a German pamphlet of 32 pages (30 pages text) in 12mo, with no name of place or printer. Ragon, who gives a French translation of the above in his "Franc-Magonnerie: Rituel du grade de Maitre," Paris, N.D., calls his translation an extract from a pamphlet of 114 pages in 8vo, taken from a large German MS. by Brother Koppen, with an interlinear translation into French, which was purchased by

Brother Antoine Boilleul, and in 1821 edited by Brother Ragon. But as Ragon's translation agrees word for word with the German pamphlet, published in 1785, the German MS. by Brother Koppen was either the original composition or a copy of it. Ragon supposes the Crata Repoa to be a concoction by learned Germans of all that is to be found in ancient writers on initiations. And the authorities on which the statements in the German pamphlet of 1785 are founded are given therein, and are: Porphyry, Herodotus, Iamblichus, Apuleius, Cicero, Plutarch, Eusebius, Arnobius, Diodorus Siculus, Tertullian, Heliodorus, Lucian, Rufinus, and some others.

VI

METAMORPHOSIS OF THE LEGEND OF ISIS

68. *Spread of Egyptian Mysteries* - The irradiations of the mysteries of Egypt shine through and animate the secret doctrines of Phoenicia, Asia Minor, Greece, and Italy. Cadmus[7] and Inachus brought them into Greece at large, Orpheus into Thrace, Melampus into Argos, Trophonius into Boeotia, Minos into Crete, Cinyras into Cyprus, and Erechtheus into Athens. And as in Egypt the mysteries were dedicated to Isis and Osiris, so in Samothrace they were sacred to the mother of the gods, in Bceotia to Bacchus, in Cyprus to Venus, in Crete to Jupiter, in Athens to Ceres and Proserpine, in Amphissa to Castor and Pollux, in Lemnos to Vulcan, and so to others in other places; but their end, as well as nature, was the same in all to teach monotheism and a future state.

69. *Dionysiac or Bacchic Mysteries* - These were divided into the greater and the less. The latter were celebrated every year at the autumnal equinox, and females were admitted to them, wearing the creative emblem suspended round their necks. They ended with the sacrifice of an unclean animal, which was eaten by the worshippers. Then aspirants and initiated proceeded with sacred dances towards the temple. The Canephoroi, carrying golden vases full of the choicest fruits, were followed by the bearers of the creative emblem, who were furnished with long poles, and were crowned with ivy, a herb sacred to Bacchus, or the sun personified. Now came other celebrants habited as women, but performing all the repulsive actions of drunken men. The next night the ceremonies of initiation were performed, in which the fable of Bacchus slain by the Titans was scenically represented, the aspirant acting the part of Bacchus.

    The greater mysteries were celebrated every three years at the

---

[7] Cadmus is not to be understood as signifying a man. The Phoenician word " cadm " means the East, hence the meaning is that the mysteries and learning came from that quarter.

vernal equinox, in the neighbourhood of a marsh, like the festival of Sais, in Egypt. On the night preceding the initiation the spouse of the hierophant sacrificed a ram. She represented the spouse of Bacchus, and when seated as such on the throne, the priests and initiated of both sexes exclaimed: "Hail spouse, hail new light!" The aspirant was purified by fire, water, and air, passing through trials similar to those described elsewhere (e.g., 42), and finally, was introduced into the sanctuary crowned with myrtle and dressed in the skin of a fawn.

70. *Sabazian Mysteries* - Sabazius was a name of Bacchus, probably derived from Siva, whose astronomical meaning is the planetary system of countless suns and stars, The mysteries were performed at night, and represented the amours of Jupiter, in the form of a serpent, and Proserpina. A golden others say a living serpent was introduced into the bosom of the candidate, who exclaimed, " Evoe! Sabai! Bacchi! Anes! Attes! Hues! " Evoe or Eve in most languages of antiquity meant both serpent and life; whence Adam's wife was so called, and whence the origin of the serpent-worship of the ancient world. When Moses lifted up a brazen serpent in the Wilderness, the afflicted Hebrews knew that it was a sign of preservation. Sabai has already been explained; Hues and Attes were other names of Bacchus. These mysteries continued to be celebrated to the last days of paganism, and in the days of Domitian, 7000 initiated were found in Rome alone.

71. *Mysteries of the Cabiri* - The name of the Cabiri was derived originally from Phoenicia; the word signifies "powerful." There were four gods Aschieros, Achiochersus, Achiochersa, and Cashmala, answering to the Ceres, Pluto, Proserpina, and Camillus of the Greeks. The last was slain by his three brothers, who carried away with them the reproductive organs; and this allegorical murder was celebrated in the secret rites. Camillus is the same as Osiris, Adonis, and others, all subject to the same mutilation, all symbolising the sun's loss of generative power during winter. The chief places for the celebration of these mysteries were the islands of Samothrace and Lemnos. The priests were called Corybantes. There is much perplexity connected

with this subject; since, besides what is mentioned above, the mysteries are also said to have been instituted in honour of Atys, the son of Cybele. Atys means the sun, and the mysteries were celebrated at the vernal equinox, and there cannot, therefore, be any doubt that, like all the other mysteries in their period of decay, they represented the enigmatical death of the sun in winter and his regeneration in the spring. The ceremonies lasted three days. The first day was one of sadness: a cruciform pine with the image of Atys attached to it was cut down, the mutilated body of Atys having been discovered at the foot of such a tree; the second day was a day of trumpets, which were blown to awaken the god from his deathlike sleep; and the third day, that of joy, was the day of initiation and celebration of his return to life.

72. *Eleusinian Mysteries* - The Eleusinian mysteries were celebrated in honour of Ceres, the Isis of Greece; whilst Osiris appears as Proserpine for the death of Osiris and the carrying off of Proserpine to the infernal regions symbolise the same thing, viz., the sun's disappearance during the winter season. The mysteries were originally celebrated only at Eleusis, a town of Attica, but eventually extended to Italy and even to Britain. Like all other mysteries, they were divided into the greater and the less, and the latter, like the Bacchic and Cabiric rites, lasted nine days, and were merely preparatory, consisting of lustrations and sacrifices. The ceremonies of initiation into the greater mysteries were opened by the herald exclaiming: " Eetire, ye profane." A flat piece of wood, such as in England is called a whizzer, or bull-roarer, or a wheel (the ρόμβος), was whirled round, at the same time, so as to produce a roaring sound. (For a curious parallel see "Miscellaneous Societies.") The aspirant was presented naked, to signify his total helplessness and dependence on Providence. He was clothed with the skin of a calf. An oath of secrecy was then administered, and he was asked: " Have you eaten bread? " The reply was "No." Proserpine cannot return to the earth because she has eaten of the fruit of the infernal regions; Adam falls when he tastes of earthly fruit. " I have drunk the sacred mixture, I have been fed from the basket of Ceres; I have laboured; I have entered into the bed." That is to say, he had been placed in the pastes,

in which the aspirant for initiation was immured during the period of his probation (42). He was then made to pass through a series of trials, similar in character to those adopted in other mysteries, after which he was introduced into the inner temple, where he beheld the statue of the goddess Ceres, surrounded by a dazzling light. The candidate, who had heretofore been called a mystes, or novice, was now termed epoptes, or eye-witness, and the secret doctrine was revealed. The assembly was then closed with the Sanscrit words. "Konx om pax" According to Captain Wilford, the words Canscha om Pacsha, of which the above is a Greek corruption, are still used at the religious meetings and ceremonies of the Brahmin another proof, if it were needed, that the mysteries are of Eastern origin. Canscha signifies the object of our most ardent desires; om is the monosyllable used at the beginning and end of a prayer, answering to our word amen, and pacsha is equivalent to the obsolete Latin word vix, meaning change, turn, or fortune.

We know very little of the mysteries of ancient Yucatan, but from what has come down to us through the Maya, or native language, we know this remarkable fact, that the priests dismissed their mystic congregations with the words "Con-ex Omon Pault !" meaning "Strangers, depart." It is also noteworthy that they used the symbols of ancient Egypt, and that the doors of their temples devoted to the mysteries, such as those at Labnah and Uxmal, had the same shape as those of the Chaldean temples, or of the Great Pyramid of Ghizeh. It will be noticed that in this figure, the two ends being closed with doors, you have an apartment with seven plane surfaces, exclusive of the floor.

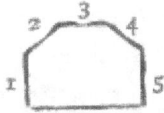

73. *Doors of Horn and Ivory* - The sixth book of the "Æneid," and the "Golden Ass" of Apuleius, contain descriptions of what passed in the celebration of the Eleusinian Mysteries. In the former work, Æneas

and his guide, having finished their progress through the infernal regions, are dismissed through the ivory gate of dreams. But there was another gate of horn through which the aspirant entered; for all caverns of initiation had two gates, one called the descent to hell, the other the ascent of the just. The ancient poets said that through the gate of horn issued true visions, and through the gate of ivory false. Now from this, and the fact that Æneas and his guide issue through it, it has been inferred by some critics that Virgil meant to intimate that all he had said concerning the infernal regions was to be considered a fable. But such could not be the poet's intention. What he really implied was that a future state was a real state, whilst the representations thereof in the mysteries were only shadows. The ivory gate itself was no other than the sumptuous door of the temple, through which the initiated came out when the ceremony was over.

74. *Suppression of Eleusinian Mysteries* - These mysteries survived all others; they shone with great splendour when the secret worship of the Cabiri, and even of Egypt, had already disappeared, and were not suppressed until the year 396 of our era by the pitiless Theodosius the Great, who, in his zeal for the Christian religion, committed the greatest cruelties against unbelievers.

75. *The Thesmophoria* - The term signifies a legislative festival, and refers specially to the symbolic rites forming part of the festival consecrated to Ceres, who was said to have given to the Greeks sound laws founded on agriculture and property, in memory of which chosen women in the solemn processions of the Thesmophoria carried at Eleusis the tablets on which the laws were written; hence the name of the festival, which was one of legislation and semination. We have only fragmentary notices concerning these festivals, though we derive some information from Aristophanes' "Thesmophoriazusse," which, however, is very slight, as it would have been dangerous for him, in alluding to these mysteries, to employ more than general and simple designations. We discover, however, that they were celebrated in the month of October, and lasted three or four days. Females only took

part in them, and it was death for a man to enter the temple. Every tribe of Athens chose two females, born in wedlock and married, and distinguished for virtue. The men who possessed a capital of three talents were compelled to give their wives the money necessary to defray the cost of the festivals. For nine days also there was to be total forbearance between married couples; for the Thesmophoria not only had reference to agriculture, but also to the more intimate relations between man and wife. As Ceres, or the Earth, mourned for the absence of Proserpine, or the sun, so the Athenian women mourned during the celebration for the absence of the light of love.

76. *Aim of Grecian Mysteries more Moral than Religious* - The object of the initiation into the mysteries of Greece was more moral than religious, differing in this from the Indian and Egyptian mysteries, that were religious, scientific, and political. For at the time of their introduction into Greece science had ceased to be the prerogative of the few; the political life of that country had stirred up the energy of the people and made it the architect of its own greatness. We therein behold already the dawn of a new era, the decay of the ancient Nature-worship, and a tendency to, and endeavour on the part of mankind after, inquiry and free striving to overcome Nature, which is diametrically opposed to the spirit of antiquity, which consisted in the total resignation and surrender of the individual to the influences of the All. Pythagoras was one of the first representatives of this new tendency. He divided his followers into exoterics and esoterics. After his death the latter joined the Orphic league, so called after the fabulous singer Orpheus. The hymns attributed to him were probably composed by Onomakritos (circa 516 B.C.). They breathe the spirit of what in modern phraseology would be called pietism, though representing the worship of Dionysius instead of that of Christ. The Orpheothelestes, as the vagabondising priests of the league were styled, became notorious as mountebanks and cheats.

77. *Chinese Metaphysics* - In Chinese cosmogony we discover traces of the once universally prevailing knowledge of the properties of eternal

Nature. Matter the first material principle is assumed to act upon itself, and thus to evolve the dual powers. This first material principle is called Tai Keik, and described as the first link in the chain of causes; it is the utmost limit in the midst of illimitableness, though in the midst of nonentity there always existed an infinite Le, or "principle of order." The Le is called infinite, because it is impossible to represent it by any figure, since it is the " Eternal Nothing." This undoubted fragmentary tradition of the most ancient metaphysical system in the world has been ridiculed by many modern writers; but any reader will see that, however imperfectly expressed, it is the theosophic doctrine. It appears very strikingly in the great veneration in which the Chinese hold the number seven, which is the number of death, of destruction, as the material end, and the celestial beginning (II).

78. *Introduction of Chinese Mysteries* - The Chinese practised Buddhism in its most simple form, and worshipped an invisible God, until a few centuries before the Christian era. From the teaching of Confucius, who lived five centuries before that era, it appears that in his time there were no mysteries; they only became necessary when the Chinese became an idolatrous nation. The chief end of initiation then was an absorption into the deity 0-Mi-To Fo. Omito was derived from the Sanscrit Armida, "immeasurable," and Fo was only another name for Buddha. The letter Y represented the triune God, and was indeed the ineffable name of the Deity, the Tetractys of Pythagoras, and the Tetragrammaton of the Jews. The rainbow was a celebrated symbol in the mysteries, for it typified the reappearance of the sun; and this not only in China, but even in Mexico (85).

79. *Parallel between Buddhism and Christianity* – The general resemblance between Buddhism and Romanism is so marked, that it is acknowledged by the Romanists themselves, who account for this fact by the supposition that Satan counterfeited the true religion. This correspondence holds in minute particulars.

Buddha descended, as the legend says, from heaven to be born as a man, the avowed purpose of his mission being to give peace and rest to all flesh, to remove all sorrow and grief from the world, and to preach the truth. At the time of his birth a bright light shone through the universe, and the devas who announced his entrance into the world, saluted his mother with the words: "All joy be to you, Queen Maya! Rejoice and be glad, for the child you have borne is holy!" We have seen in II that Maya is a virgin the worship also of Simon in the Temple finds its reflection in the adoration paid by the venerable Axite to the infant Buddha. Further, the Buddhist and the Christian (Roman Catholic) Church have a supreme and infallible head; we find in both the celibacy of the priesthood, monasteries, and nunneries, prayers in an unknown tongue, prayers to saints and intercessors, and especially, and principally too, a virgin with a child; also prayers for the dead, repetition of prayers with the use of a rosary, works of merit and supererogation; selfimposed austerities and bodily inflictions; a formal daily service, consisting of chants, burning of candles, sprinkling of holy water, bowings, prostrations; fast days and feast days, religious processions, images and pictures and fabulous legends, the worship of relics, the sacrament of confession, purgatory, &c. In some respects their rites resemble those of the Jews; they propitiate the Supreme Deity with the blood of bulls and goats, and also offered holocausts. The resemblance is easily accounted for. Romanism and some other creeds are only modernised Buddhism; and many religions are but superstitious perversions of the knowledge of natural phenomena. The tradition about Prester John has its origin in this resemblance between Buddhism and a corrupted Christianity. In the twelfth century there was in China a great Mongol tribe professing Buddhism, which by travellers was mistaken for an Oriental Christian religion. The Nestorian Christians, dwelling among the Mongols, called its head John the, Priest, and hence arose the tradition that in the heart of Asia there was a Christian Church, whose popes bore the title of Prester John.

80. *Lau-Tze* - Confucius was the religious lawgiver of China, but Lau-Tze was its philosopher. He excelled the former in depth and independence of thought. The word Lau, or Ze, is difficult to render;

the Chinese itself defines it as "a thing indefinite, impalpable, and yet therein are forms." Lau-Tze himself seems to make it equivalent to "intelligence." His philosophy is peaceful and loving, and in this respect presents various commendable points of resemblance to Christian doctrine.

81 . *Japanese Mysteries* - The Japanese held that the world was enclosed in an egg before the creation, which egg was broken by a bull the ever-recurring astronomical allegory, alluding to the Bull of the zodiac, which in former times opened the seasons, the vernal equinox. It is the same bull Apis which Egypt adored (51), and which the Jews in the Wilderness worshipped as the golden calf; also the bull which, sacrificed in the mysteries of Mithras, poured out its blood to fertilise the earth. The Japanese worshipped a deity who was styled the Son of the Unknown God, considered the creator of sun and moon, and called Tensio-Dai-Sin. The aspirants for initiation were conducted through artificial spheres, formed of movable circles, representing the revolutions of the planets. The mirror was a significant emblem of the all-seeing eye of their chief deity (11). In the closing ceremony of preparation the candidate was enclosed in the pastos, the door of which was said to be guarded by a terrible divinity, armed with a drawn sword. During the course of his probation the aspirant sometimes acquired so high a degree of enthusiasm as to refuse to quit his confinement in the pastos, and to remain there until he literally perished of famine. To this voluntary martyrdom was attached a promise of never-ending happiness hereafter. Their creed indeed is Buddhism slightly modified. "Diabolo ecclesiam Christi imitante!" exclaimed Xavier, on seeing how the practices of the Japanese resembled those of the Romanists in Europe; and, as has been observed of Buddhism in China and Thibet, all the practices of the Japanese ritual are so tinged with the colour of Romanism, that they might well justify the exclamation of Xavier, who was neither a savant nor a philosopher.

82. *Japanese Doctrines* - The god Tensio-Dai-Sin has twelve apostles,

and the sun, the planetary hero, fights with monsters and the elements. The ministers of the Temple of the Sun wear tunics of the colour of fire, and annually celebrate four festivals, the third day of the third month, the fifth day of the fifth, the seventh day of the seventh, and the ninth day of the ninth month respectively; and at one of these festivals they represent a myth similar to that of Adonis, and Nature is personified by a priest dressed in many colours. The members of this society are called Jammabos, and the initiated are enjoined a long time to abstain from meat and to prepare themselves by many purifications.

83. *The Lama* - The Grand Lama, the god of Thibet, becomes incarnate in man; thus much the priests reveal to the people. But the true religion, which consists of the doctrine of the supposed origin of the world, is only made known in the almost inaccessible mysteries. The man in whom the Grand Lama has for the time become incarnate, and who is the pontiff, is held in such veneration, that the people eat pastilles, accounted sacred, and made from the unclean remains of the food which had contributed to the sustenance of his body. This disgusting practice, however, with them is simply the result of their belief in the metempsychosis parallel with the Indian doctrine of corruption and reproduction, symbolised by the use of cow-dung in the purification of the aspirant; and its real meaning is to show that all the parts of the universe are incessantly absorbed, and pass into the substance of one another. It is upon the model of the serpent who devours his tail. The dignity of the Lama dates from the thirteenth century. In the fourteenth a portion of the clergy seceded and formed a rival sect; the two religious bodies are distinguished and known by the titles of the Bed Tassels and the Yellow Caps, from their headgear.

VIII

MEXICAN AND PERUVIAN MYSTERIES

84. *American Aborigines* - Ethnologists can tell us as yet nothing as to the origin of the earliest inhabitants of the American continent; but if the reader will accept the theory propounded in the introduction to this work (6-9), he will be at no loss to answer the question. As Nature in Asia brought forth the Caucasian races, so in the western hemisphere it gave birth to the various races peopling it. That one of them was a highly civilised race in prehistoric times is proved by the ruins of beautiful cities discovered in Central America; and all the antiquarian remains show that the religion of Mexico and Peru was substantially the same as that practised by the various nations of the East; and naturally so, for the moral and physical laws of the universe are everywhere the same, and, working in the same manner, produce the same results, only modified by climatic and local conditions.

85. *Mexican Deities* - The religious system of the Mexicans bore a character of dark and gloomy austerity. They worshipped many deities, the chief of which were Teotl, the invisible and supreme being; Virococha, the creator; Vitzliputzli or Heritzilopochtli, the god of mercy, to whom the most sanguinary rites were offered (which proves that the Mexican priests were quite as inconsistent in this respect as the priestly bigots of Europe, who, in the name of the God of mercy, tortured, racked, and burnt millions that differed from whatever creed had been set up as the orthodox and legalised one); Tescalipuca, the god of vengeance; Quetzalcoatl, the Mexican Mercury, whose name signifies the "serpent clothed with green feathers"; Mictlaneiheratl, the goddess of hell; Tlaloc-teatli, or Neptune; and Ixciana, or Venus. To Vitzliputzli was ascribed the renovation of the world, and his name referred to the sun. He was said to be the offspring of a virgin, who was impregnated by a plume of feathers, which descended from heaven into her bosom, invested with all the colours of the rainbow (78). He was represented in the figure of a man, with a dread-inspiring aspect.

He was seated on an azure globe over a lofty altar, which was borne in procession during the celebration of the mysteries on a litter of sky-coloured blue; he had a blue forehead, and a blue streak across his nose, as blue was the dominating colour in the Jewish tabernacle, showing an astronomical signification in both cases. We have already seen (42) that Vishnu was painted blue. His right hand grasped a snake, the symbol of life, and representations of this reptile are found on all the temples of Mexico and Peru. Traces of the serpent-worship of the Western world are also found in the States of Ohio and Iowa, where serpent mounds, formed of earth, 1 coo feet long or more, are still to be found. The office of Tescalipuca was to punish the sins of men by the infliction of plagues, famine, and pestilence. His anger could only be appeased by human sacrifices thousands of men were frequently immolated to him in one single day.

86. *Cruelty of Mexican Worship* - The temples of Mexico were full of horrible idols, which were all bathed and washed with human blood. The chapel of Vitzliputzli was decorated with the skulls of the wretches that had been slain in sacrifice; the walls and floor were inches thick with blood, and before the image of the god might often be seen the still palpitating hearts of the human victims offered up to him, whose skins served the priests for garments. The revolting custom, as a legend says. arose from the fact that Tozi, the "Grand Mother," was of human extraction. Vitzliputzli procured her divine honours by enjoining the Mexicans to demand her of her father for their queen; this being done, they also commanded him to put her to death, afterwards to flay her, and to cover a young man with her skin. It was in this manner she was stripped of her humanity, to be placed among the gods. Another disgusting practice arising from this legend will be mentioned hereafter.

87. *Initiation into Mysteries* - The candidate had to undergo all the terrors, sufferings, and penances practised in the Eastern world. He was scourged with knotted cords, his flesh was cut with knives, and reeds put into the wounds, that the blood might be seen to trickle more

freely, or they were cauterised with red-hot cinders. Many perished under these trials. The lustrations were performed, not with water, but with blood, and the candidate's habit was not white, but black, and before initiation he was given a drink, which was said to dispel fear, which, indeed, it may have done in some degree by disturbing the brain. The candidate was then led into the dark caverns of initiation, excavated beneath the foundations of the mighty pyramidal temple of Vitzliputzli in Mexico, and passed through the mysteries which symbolically represented the wanderings of their gods, i.e., the course of the sun through the signs of the zodiac. The caverns were called "the path of the dead." Everything that could appal the imagination and test his courage was made to appear before him. Now he heard shrieks of despair and the groans of the dying; he was led past the dungeons where the human victims, being fattened for sacrifice, were confined, and through caverns slippery with half-congealed blood; anon he met with the quivering frame of the dying man, whose heart had just been torn from his body and offered up to their sanguinary god, and looking up he beheld in the roof the orifice through which the victims had been precipitated, for they were now immediately under the altar of Vitzliputzli. At length, however, he arrived at a narrow chasm or stone fissure, at the end of this extensive range of caverns, through which he was formally protruded, and received by a shouting multitude as a person regenerated or born again. The females, divesting themselves of their little clothing, danced in a state of nudity like the frantic Bacchantes, and having repeated the dance three times, they gave themselves up to unbounded licentiousness.

88. *The Greater Mysteries* - But as with Eastern nations, the Mexicans had, besides the general religious doctrines communicated to the initiated, an esoteric doctrine, only attainable by the priests, and not even by them until they had qualified themselves for it by the sacrifice of a human victim. The most ineffable degrees of knowledge were imparted to them at midnight, and under severe obligations, whose disregard entailed death without remission. The real doctrine taught was astronomical, and, like the Eastern nations, they at their great

festivals lamented the disappearance of the sun, and rejoiced at its reappearance at the festival of the new fire, as it was called. All fire, even the sacred fire of the temple, having been extinguished, the population of Mexico, with the priests at their head, marched to a hill near the city, where they waited till the Pleiades ascended the middle of the sky, when they sacrificed a human victim. The instrument made use of by the priests to kindle the fire was placed on the wound made in the breast of the prisoner destined to be sacrificed; and, when the fire was kindled, the body was placed on an enormous pile ready prepared, and this latter set on fire. The new fire, received with joyful shouts, was carried from village to village, where it was deposited in the temple, whence it was distributed to every private dwelling. When the sun appeared on the horizon the acclamations were renewed. The priests were further taught the doctrine of immortality, of a triune deity, of the original population, who led by the god Vitzliputzli, holding in his hand a rod formed like a serpent, and seated in a square ark finally settled upon a lake, abounding with the lotus, where they erected their tabernacle. This lake was the lake in the midst of which the city of Mexico originally stood.

89. *Human Sacrifices* - No priest was to be fully initiated into the mysteries of the Mexican religion until he had sacrificed a human victim. This horrible rite, which the Spaniards, who conquered the country, often saw performed on their own captive countrymen, was thus performed: The chief priest carried in his hand a large and sharp knife made of flint; another priest carried a collar of wood; the other four priests who assisted arranged themselves adjoining the pyramidal stone, which had a convex top, so that the man to be sacrificed, being laid thereon on his back, was bent in such a manner that the stomach separated upon the slightest incision of the knife. Two priests seized hold of his feet and two more of his hands, whilst the fifth fastened round his neck the collar of wood. The high priest then opened his stomach with the knife, and tearing out his heart, held it up to the sun, and then threw it before the idol in one of the chapels on the top of the great pyramid where the rite was performed. The body was finally

cast down the steps that wound all round the building. Forty or fifty victims were thus sacrificed in a few hours. Prisoners of rank or approved courage might escape this horrid death by fighting six Mexican warriors in succession. If they were successful, their lives and liberty were granted to them; but if they fell under the strokes of their adversaries, they were dragged, dead or living, to the sacrificial stone, and their hearts torn out.

90. *Clothing in Bloody Skins* - We have already seen that the priests were clothed in the bloody skins of their victims. The same horrid custom was practised on other occasions. On certain festivals they dressed a man in the bloody skin just reeking from the body of a victim. Kings and grandees did not think it derogatory to their dignity to disguise themselves in this manner, and to run up and down the streets soliciting alms, which were applied to pious purposes. This horrible masquerade continued till the skin began to grow putrid. On another festival they would slay a woman and clothe a man with her skin, who, thus equipped, danced for two days together with the rest of his fellowcitizens.

91. *Peruvian Mysteries* - The Incas, or rulers of Peru, boasted of their descent from the sun and moon, which therefore were worshipped, as well as the great god PachaCamac, whose very name was so sacred that it was only communicated to the initiated; it means, "He who sustains or gives life to the universe." No temples were erected to this deity. They also had an idol they termed Tangatango, meaning "One in three and three in one." Their secret mysteries, of which we know next to nothing, were celebrated on their great annual festival, held on the first day of the September moon, the people watching all night until the rising of the sun; and when he appeared the eastern doors of the great temple of Cuzco were thrown open, so that the sun's radiance could illuminate his image in gold placed opposite. The walls and ceiling of this temple were all covered over with gold plates, and the figure of the sun, representing a round face, surrounded with rays and flames, as modern painters usually draw the sun, was of such a size as almost to

cover one side of the wall. It was, moreover, double the thickness of the plates covering the walls. The Virgins of the Sun, who, like the Vestals of ancient Rome, had the keeping of the sacred fire entrusted to them, and were vowed to perpetual celibacy, then walked round the altar, whilst the priests expounded the mild and equitable laws of Peru; for, contrary to the practice of their near neighbours, the Mexicans, the Peruvians had not their sanguinary rites; though some Spanish writers, who, of course, could see no good in non-Catholics and pagans, charged them with sacrificing young children of from four to six years old "in prodigious numbers," and also with slaying virgins. The Spaniards, no doubt, alluded to some ill-understood symbolical rite. But the Peruvians did on rare occasions, to celebrate a great public event, for instance, immolate human beings, a child or young maiden being usually selected. Everywhere we find the priesthood delighting in blood!

92. Quiches Initiation - In 79 we have seen that the people speaking the Maya language had their mysteries. Another tribe of that same people, the Quiches of Xibalba, in the heart of the mountains of Guatemala, had an initiation of their own. Popol-Vuh, their sacred book, says that the applicant had to pass two rivers, one of mud, and the other of blood, before reaching the four roads leading to the place where the priest awaited him. He was then told to sit down, but the seat was burning hot. In the Dark House he passed the night and underwent two trials; the third he underwent in the House of Spears, where he had to produce flowers without bringing them, and to fight spearmen; the fourth trial took place in the Ice House, the fifth in the Tiger House, the sixth in the Fiery House, and the seventh in the House of Bats, the House of Camazotz, god of the Bats, where the god himself appeared and beheaded the aspirant if off his guard.

IX

THE DRUIDS

93. *The Druids, the Magi of the West* - The secret doctrines of the Druids were much the same as those of the Gynmosophists and Brahmins of India, the Magi of Persia, the priests of Egypt, and of all other priests of antiquity. Like them, they had two sets of religious doctrines, exoteric and esoteric. Their rites were practised in Britain and Gaul, though they were brought to a much greater perfection in the former country, where the Isle of Anglesey was considered their chief seat. The word Druid is generally supposed to be derived from δρύς, "an oak," which tree was particularly sacred among them, though its etymology may also be found in the Gaelic word Druidh, "a wise man," or " magician."

94. *Temples* - Their temples, wherein the sacred fire was preserved, were generally situate on eminences and in dense groves of oaks, and assumed various forms circular, because a circle was an emblem of the universe; oval, in allusion to the mundane egg, from which, according to the traditions of many nations, the universe, or according to others, our first parents, issued; serpentine, because a serpent was the symbol of Hu, the Druidic Osiris; cruciform, because a cross is an emblem of regeneration (53); or winged, to represent the motion of the divine spirit. Their only canopy was the sky, and they were constructed of unhewn stones, their numbers having reference to astronomical calculations. In the centre was placed a stone of larger dimensions than the others, and worshipped as the representative of the Deity. The three principal temples of this description in Britain were undoubtedly those of Stonehenge and Abury in the south, and that of Shap in Cumberland. Where stone was scarce, rude banks of earth were substituted, and the temple was formed of a high vallum and ditch. The most herculean labours were performed in their construction; Stukeley says that it would cost, at the present time, £20,000 to throw

up such a mound as Silbury Hill.

95. *Places of Initiation* - The adytum or ark of the mysteries was called a cromlech or dolmen, and was used as the sacred pastos, or place of regeneration. It consisted of three upright stones, as supporters of a broad, flat stone laid across them on the top, so as to form a small cell. Kit Cotey's House, in Kent, was such a pastos. Considerable space, however, was necessary for the machinery of initiation in its largest and most comprehensive scale. Therefore, the Coer Sidi, where the mysteries of Druidism were performed, consisted of a range of buildings, adjoining the temple, containing apartments of all sizes, cells, vaults, baths, and long and artfully contrived passages, with all the apparatus of terror used on these occasions. Most frequently these places were subterranean; and many of the caverns in this country were the scenes of Druidical initiation. The stupendous grotto at Castleton, in Derbyshire, called by Stukeley the Stygian Cave, as well as the giants' caves at Luckington and Badminster, in Wilts, certainly were used for this purpose.

96. *Rites* - The system of Druidism embraced every religious and philosophical pursuit then known in these islands. The rites bore an undoubted reference to astronomical facts. Their chief deities are reducible to two a male and a female, the great father and mother, Hu and Ceridwen, distinguished by the same characteristics as belonged to Osiris and Isis, Bacchus and Ceres, or any other supreme god and goddess representing the two principles of all being. The grand periods of initiation were quarterly, and determined by the course of the sun, and his arrival at the equinoctial and solstitial points. But the time of annual celebration was May-eve, when fires were kindled on all the cairns and cromlechs throughout the island, which burned all night to introduce the sports of May-day, whence all the national sports formerly or still practised date their origin. Round these fires choral dances were performed in honour of the sun, who, at this season, was figuratively said to rise from his tomb. The festival was licentious, and continued till the luminary had attained his meridian height, when

priests and attendants retired to the woods, where the most disgraceful orgies were perpetrated. But the solemn initiations were performed at midnight, and contained three degrees, the first or lowest being the Eubates, the second the Bards, and the third the Druids. The candidate was first placed in the pastos bed, or coffin, where his symbolical death represented the death of Hu, or the sun; and his restoration in the third degree symbolised the resurrection of the sun. He had to undergo trials and tests of courage similar to those practised in the mysteries of other countries (e.g., 27), and which, therefore, need not be detailed here.

The festival of the 28th of December was celebrated with great fires lighted on the tops of the hills, to announce the birth-day of the god Sol. This was the moment when, after the supposed winter solstice, he began to increase, and gradually to ascend. This festival indeed was kept not by the Druids only, but throughout the ancient world, from India to Ultima Thule. The fires, of course, were typical of the power and ardour of the sun, whilst the evergreens used on the occasion foreshadowed the results of the sun's renewed action on vegetation. The festival of the summer solstice was kept on the 24th of June. Both days are still kept as festivals in the Christian Church, the former as Christmas, the latter as St. John's Day; because the early Christians judiciously adopted not only the festival days of the pagans, but also, so far as this could be done with propriety, their mode of keeping them; substituting, however, a theological meaning for astronomical allusions. The use of evergreens in churches at Christmas time is the Christian perpetuation of an ancient Druidic custom.

97. Doctrines - The Druids taught the doctrine of one supreme being, a future state of rewards and punishments, the immortality of the soul, and a metempsychosis. It was a maxim with them that water was the first principle of all things, and existed before the creation in unsullied purity (II), which seems a contradiction to their other doctrine that day was the offspring of night, because night or chaos was in existence before day was created. They taught that time was only an intercepted fragment of eternity, and that there was an endless succession of worlds. In fact, their doctrines were chiefly those of Pythagoras. They

entertained great veneration for the numbers three, seven, nineteen (the Metonic cycle), and one hundred and forty-seven, produced by multiplying the square of seven by three. They also practised vaticination, pretending to predict future events from the flights of birds, human sacrifices, by white horses, the agitation of water, and lots. They seem, however, to have possessed considerable scientific knowledge.

98. Political and Judicial Power - Their authority in many cases exceeded that of the monarch. They were, of course, the sole interpreters of religion, and consequently superintended all sacrifices; for no private person was allowed to offer a sacrifice without their sanction. They possessed the power of excommunication, which was the most horrible punishment that could be inflicted next to that of death, and from the effects of which the highest magistrate was not exempt. The great council of the realm was not competent to declare war or conclude peace without their concurrence. They determined all disputes by a final and unalterable decision, and had the power of inflicting the punishment of death. And, indeed, their altars streamed with the blood of human victims. Holocausts of men, women, and children, inclosed in large towers of wickerwork, were sometimes sacrificed as a burnt-offering to their superstitions, which were, at the same time, intended to enhance the consideration of the priests, who were an ambitious race delighting in blood. The Druids, it is said, preferred such as had been guilty of theft, robbery, or other crimes, as most acceptable to their gods; but when there was a scarcity of criminals, they made no scruple to supply their place with innocent persons. These dreadful sacrifices were offered by the Druids, for the public, on the eve of a dangerous war, or in the time of any national calamity; and also for particular persons of high rank, when they were afflicted with any dangerous disease.

99. Priestesses - The priestesses, clothed in white, and wearing a metal girdle, foretold the future from the observation of natural phenomena, but more especially from human sacrifices. For them was reserved the

frightful task of putting to death the prisoners taken in war, and individuals condemned by the Druids; and their auguries were drawn from the manner in which the blood issued from the many wounds inflicted, and also from the smoking entrails. Many of these priestesses maintained a perpetual virginity, others gave themselves up to the most luxurious excesses. They dwelt on lonely rocks, beaten by the waves of the ocean, which the mariners looked upon as temples surrounded with unspeakable prodigies. Thus the island of Sena or Liambis, The Saints, near Ushant, where Merlin was said to have been born, was the residence of nine of these priestesses, who delivered oracles to sailors; and there was no power that was not attributed to them. Others, living near the mouth of the Loire, once a year destroyed their temple, scattered its materials, and, having collected others, built a new one of course a symbolical ceremony; and if one of the priestesses dropped any of the sacred materials, the others fell upon her with fierce yells, tore her to pieces, and scattered her bleeding limbs.

100. Abolition - As the Romans gained ground the power of the Druids gradually declined; and they were finally assailed by Suetonius Paulinus, governor of Britain under Nero, A.D. 61, in their stronghold, the Isle of Anglesey, and entirely defeated, the conqueror consuming many of them in the fires which they had kindled for burning the Roman prisoners they had expected to make a very just retaliation upon these sanguinary priests. In Gaul the Druids maintained themselves in their sacred woods near the island of Sena and on the promontory of Finisterre for perhaps two centuries longer. The progress of Christianity finally abolished them. But though their dominion was thus destroyed, many of their religious practices continued much longer; and so late as the eleventh century, in the reign of Canute, it was necessary to forbid the people to worship the sun, moon, fires, &c. Certainly many of the practices of the Druids are still adhered to in Freemasonry, which is simply sun and star worship; and some writers on this order endeavour to show that it was established soon after the edict of Canute, and that as thereby the Druidical worship was prohibited in toto, the strongest oaths were

required to bind the initiated to secrecy.

101. Drottes - The priests of Scandinavia were named Drottes, and instituted by Sigge, a Scythian prince, who is said afterwards to have assumed the name of Odin. Their number was twelve, who were alike priests and judges; and from this order proceeded the establishment of British juries. Their power was extended to its utmost limits, by being allowed a discretionary privilege of determining on the choice of human victims for sacrifice, from which even the monarch was not exempt hence arose the necessity of cultivating the goodwill of these sovereign pontiffs; and as this order, like the Israelitish priesthood, was restricted to one family, they became possessed of unbounded wealth, and at last became so tyrannical as to be objects of terror to the whole community. Christianity, promising to relieve it from this yoke, was hailed with enthusiasm; and the inhabitants of Scandinavia, inspired with a thirst for vengeance on account of accumulated and long-continued suffering, retaliated with dreadful severity on their persecutors, overthrowing the palaces and temples, the statues of their gods, and all the paraphernalia of Gothic superstition. Of this nothing remains but a few cromlechs; some stupendous monuments of rough stone, which human fury could not destroy; certain ranges of caverns hewn out of the solid rock; and some natural grottos used for the purpose of initiation.

102. Ritual - The whole ritual had an astronomical bearing. The places of initiation, as in other mysteries, were in caverns, natural or artificial, and the candidate had to undergo trials as frightful as the priests cpuld render them. But instead of having to pass through seven caves or passages, as in the Mithraic and other mysteries, he descended through nine the square of the mystic number three subterranean passages, and he was instructed to search for the body of Balder, the Scandinavian Osiris, slain by Loke, the principle of darkness, and to use his utmost endeavours to raise him to life. To enter into particulars of the process of initiation would involve the repetition of what has been said before; it may therefore suffice to observe that the candidate on arriving at the

sacellum had a solemn oath administered to him on a naked sword, and ratified it by drinking mead out of a human skull. The sacred sign of the cross was impressed upon him, and a ring of magic virtues, the gift of Balder the Good, delivered to him.

103. Astronomical Meaning Demonstrated - The first canto of the Edda, which apparently contains a description of the ceremonies performed on the initiation of an aspirant, says that he seeks to know the sciences possessed by the Esas or gods. He discovers a palace, whose roof of boundless dimensions is covered with golden shields. He encounters a man engaged in launching upwards seven flowers. Here we easily discover the astronomical meaning: the palace is the world, the roof the sky; the golden shields are the stars, the seven flowers the seven planets. The candidate is asked what is his name, and replies Gangler, that is, the wanderer, he that performs a revolution, distributing necessaries to mankind; for the candidate personates the sun. The palace is that of the king, the epithet the ancient Mystagogues gave to the head of the planetary system. Then he discovers three seats; on the lowest is the king called Har, sublime; on the central one, Jafuhar, the equal of the Sublime; on the highest, Tredie, the number three. These personages are those the neophyte beheld in the Eleusinian initiation (72), the hierophant, the daduchus or torchbearer, and the epibomite or attendant on the altar; those he sees in Freemasonry, the master, and the senior and junior wardens, symbolical personifications of the sun, moon, and Demiurgos, or grand architect of the universe. But the Scandinavian triad is usually represented by Odin, the chief deity; Thor, his first-born, the reputed mediator between god and man, possessing unlimited power over the universe, wherefore his head was surrounded by a circle of twelve stars; and Freya, a hermaphrodite, adorned with a variety of symbols significant of dominion over love and marriage. In the instructions given to the neophyte, he is told that the greatest and most ancient of gods is called Alfader (the father of all), and has twelve epithets, which recall the twelve attributes of the sun, the twelve constellations, the twelve superior gods of Egypt, Greece, and Rome. Among the gods of the Scandinavian theogony

there is Balder the Good, whose story, as already hinted above, formed the object of the initiatory ceremonies. Balder is Mithras, the sun's love. He foresees the danger that threatens him; he dreams of it at night. The other gods of Valhalla, the Scandinavian Olympus, to whom he reveals his sad forebodings, reassure him, and to guard against any harm befalling him, exact an oath from everything in Nature in his behalf, except from the mistletoe, which was omitted on account of its apparently inoffensive qualities. For an experiment, and in sport, the gods cast at Balder all kinds of missiles, without wounding him. Hoder the blind (that is, Fate), takes no part in the diversion; but Loke (the principle of evil, darkness, the season of winter) places a sprig in the hands of Hoder, and persuades him to cast it at the devoted victim, who falls pierced with mortal wounds. For this reason it was that this plant was gathered at the winter solstice by the Druids of Scandinavia, Gaul, and Britain, with a curved knife, whose form symbolised the segment of the zodiacal circle during which the murder of Balder took place. In the Edda of Snorro we have another legend of Odin and Freya, the Scandinavian Isis or Venus, giving an account of the wanderings of the latter in search of the former, which, of course, have the same astronomical meaning as the search of Isis for Osiris, of Ceres for Proserpine, &c. One of the chief festivals in the year, as with the Druids, was the winter solstice; and this being the longest night in the year, the Scandinavians assigned to it the formation of the world from primeval darkness, and called it "Mother Night." This festival was denominated "Yule," a corruption of the Greek word helios, the sun, and was a season of universal festivity.

BOOK II

EMANATIONISTS

"A changeful strife, A glowing life,
I weave on the whirring loom of Time,
The living garments of the Deity."

GOETHE, Faust.

THE CABBALA

104. Its Origin - The Cabbala (from the Hindoo Kapila, the inventor of the philosophy of numbers) is the summary of the labours of the sects of Judaism, and is occupied in the mystical interpretation of the Scriptures, and in metaphysical speculations concerning the Deity and the worlds visible and invisible. The Jews say that it was communicated to Moses by God Himself. Now, although it is not at all improbable that the writer, to whom history has given the name of Moses, did leave to his successors some secret doctrines, yet the fantastic doctrines of the Cabbala concerning angels and demons are purely Chaldean; at Babylon the Jews ingrafted on Monotheism the doctrine of the Two Principles. Daniel, the pontiff of the Magi and prophet of the Jews, may be considered as the chief founder of the Cabbala, which was conceived at Babylon, and received as the forbidden fruit of the strange woman. The ancient Jews had some idea of angels, but did not ascribe to them any particular functions, though to each patriarch they assigned a special familiar spirit. The Alexandrian School made many additions to that foreign importation; Philo supplemented Daniel. The speculative portion of the Cabbala, whose foundation consists in the doctrine of Emanation, was developed in that School; the philosophical systems of Pythagoras and Plato were combined with Oriental philosophy, and from these proceeded Gnosticism and Neo-platonism.

105. Date of Cabbala - The first documentary promulgation of the Cabbala may roughly be stated to have taken place within the century

before and half a century after our era. The greater culture of the Jewish people, the supreme tyranny of the letter of the law and rabbinical minuteness, furthered the spread of occult theology, whose chief text-books are the "Sepher-yetzirah," or Book of the Creation, probably by Akiba, and the "Zohar," the Book of Light, attributed to Simon-ben-Joachai, the pupil of Akiba, consisting of fantastic commentaries on the books of Moses. What farrago the book contains may be inferred from the representation it gives of God. His head is that of a very old man, wearing one thousand millions and seven thousand curls of white wool; his beard is as white as snow, reaching to his navel, and has thirteen divisions, each of which comprises the greatest mysteries. The Jews did not become acquainted with it before the end of the thirteenth century. Akiba was a Jewish rabbi and teacher of the Mishna (107). He was executed for having taken part in the insurrection of Bar-Cochba (Son of the Star, Numb. xxiv. 17) in A.D. 135.

106. The Book of the Creation - In this work Adam considers the mystery of the universe. In his monologue he declares the forces and powers of reason, which attempts to discover the bond which unites in a common principle all the elements of things; and in this investigation he adopts a method different from the Mosaic. He does not descend from God to the creation, but studying the universe, seeking the unity in variety and multiplicity, the law in the phenomenon, he ascends from the creation to God a prolific method, but which leads the Cabbalists to seek fantastic analogies between superior and inferior powers, between heaven and earth, between the things and the signs of thought. Hence arose all the arts of divination and conjuration, and the most absurd superstitions. According to Cabbalistic conception, the universe, which to Pythagoras is a symbol of the mysterious virtues of numbers, is only a marvellous page on which all existing things were written by the supreme artificer with the first ten numbers and the twenty-two letters of the Hebrew alphabet. The ten abstract numbers are the general forms of things, the "supreme categories of ideas." Thus, number one represents the spirit of the living God, the universal

generative power; number two is the breath of the animating spirit; three is the aqueous, and four the igneous principle. The imprint of the letters on the universe is indestructible, and is the only character that can enable us to discover the Supreme Cause, to recompose the name of God, the Logos, written on the face of the world. Nor are all the letters of equal virtue; three, called the mothers, have the precedence, and refer to the triads found in various physical and mental orders; seven others are called double, because from them arise the things constantly opposed to one another; the remaining twelve are called simple, and refer to twelve attributes of man.

107. Different Kinds of Cabbala - It is of two kinds, theoretical and practical. The latter is engaged in the construction of talismans and amulets, and is therefore totally unworthy of our notice. But it may be interesting to believers in modern charlatanism to know that this practical Cabbala was early employed in the production of spiritualistic phenomena; divining tables, furnished with a writing apparatus, were common in the days of Tertullian, as we learn from his Apology. One Frederick Brentz, a Jew converted to Christianity in 1610, explained, or tried to explain, in a book against his former co-religionists, how the Jews raised tables, with stones of several hundredweights on them, by means of Cabbalistic conjuration. The theoretical Cabbala is divided into the literal and dogmatic. The dogmatic is the summary of the metaphysical doctrines taught by the Cabbalistic doctors; the literal is a mystical mode of explaining sacred things by a peculiar use of the letters of words. This literal Cabbala, called the Mishna, is again subdivided into three branches, the first considering words according to the numerical value of the letters composing them. This branch is called Gematria, and for an example of it the reader is referred to Mithras (30), the name of the sun, whose letters make up the number 365, the number of days during which the sun performs his course. The second branch is called Notaricon, and is a mode of constructing one word out of the initials or finals of many. Thus of the sentence in Deut. xxx. 12, "Who shall go up for us to heaven?" in Hebrew

מי יצלה למ השמימה the initial letters of each word are taken to form the word מילה "circumcision." The third mode is called Temura, or permutation of letters, such as is familiarly known as an anagram.

108. Visions of Ezekiel - Cabbalistic terms and inventions, not destitute of poetic ideas, lent themselves to the requirements of the mystics, sectaries, and alchymists. It suffices to consider that portion of the system whose object is the study of the visions of Ezekiel, to form an idea of the fantastic and mythological wealth of the Cabbala. This branch of the Cabbala is called the Marcava.

In the visions of Ezekiel, God is seated on a throne, surrounded with strange winged figures the man, the bull, the lion, and the eagle, four zodiacal signs, like "the glory which he saw by the river of Chebar," that is, among the Chaldeans, famous for their astronomical knowledge. The rabbis call the visions the description of the celestial car, and discover therein profound mysteries. Maimonides reduced those visions to the astronomical ideas of his time; the Cabbala surrounded them with its innumerable hosts of angels. Besides the angels that preside over the stars, elements, virtues, vices, passions, the lower world is peopled by genii of both sexes, holding a position between angels and men the elemental spirits of the Rosicrucians. The good angels are under the command of Metatron, also called Sar Happanim, the angel of the Divine countenance. The evil angels are subject to Samual, or Satan, the angel of death. Besides the Indian metempsychosis the Cabbalists admit another, which they call "impregnation," consisting in a union of several souls in one body, which takes place when any soul needs the assistance of others to attain to the beatific vision.

109. The Creation out of Nothing - The primitive Being is called the Ancient of Days, the ancient Ring of Light, incomprehensible, infinite, eternal, a closed eye. Before he manifested himself all things were in him, and he was called The Nothing, the Zero-world. Before the

creation of the world the primitive light of God, Nothing, filled all, so that there was no void; but when the Supreme Being determined to manifest His perfections, He withdrew into Himself, and let go forth the first emanation, a ray of light, which is the cause and beginning of all that exists, and combines the generative and conceptive forces. He commenced by forming an imperceptible point, the point-world; then with that thought He constructed a holy and mysterious form, and finally covered it with a rich vestment the universe. From the generative and conceptive forces issued forth the first-born of God, the universal form, the creator, preserver, and animating principle of the world, Adam Kadmon, called the macrocosm; whilst man, born out of and living in it, and comprising, in fact, what the typical or celestial man comprises potentially, is called the microcosm. But before the Ensoph or Infinite revealed Himself in that form of the primitive man, other emanations, other worlds, had succeeded each other, which were called "sparks," which grew fainter the more distant they were from the centre of emanation. Around Adam Kadmon were formed the countless circles of posterior emanations, which are not beings having a life of their own, but attributes of God, vessels of omnipotence, types of creation. The ten emanations from Adam Kadmon are called Sephiroth, the "powers" of Philo, and the " aeons " of the Gnostics.

110. Revival of Cabbalistic Doctrines - As among Christians the Apocalypse, so among Jews the Cabbala has always had its devoted students. Such a one was Lobele (d. 1609), who was chief rabbi at Prague, and considered such a saint, that no being born of woman was thought fit to wait on him; he was attended by a servitor produced by magic, or a slave formed of clay. Being deeply versed in all the mysteries of the Cabbala, he was endowed with supernatural powers, but he, wisely perhaps, kept his knowledge to himself; he did not even have pupils. But about the middle of the last century Jacob Franck, originally a distiller in Poland, collected around him a crowd of Jewish followers in Podolia, who, abjuring rabbinical dogmatism, adopted the mystical teaching of the Cabbala. The book Zohar (105) was the basis of their doctrines, whence they were called Zoharists, the Illuminated.

The Eoman Catholic clergy, who in these doctrines saw an approach to Christianity, at first protected them; but on the death of the Bishop of Podolia they were persecuted by the rabbis, so that they had to disperse, and Franck himself was imprisoned until 1773, when he was released by the Eussians. He then tried to establish himself at Vienna, but being driven thence found a refuge at Offenbach, near Frankfort, where he gathered many followers, and lived in great style, as he received liberal subsidies from the Jews. He died in 1791, when the society was dissolved; a few remnants may still be found in Poland, where they are known as Christian Jews. They form a kind of religious order, practising certain Jewish rites, and professing mystical doctrines, kept secret from outsiders.

Another Cabbalistic sect was formed about the same time (1740) by Israel of Podolia, calling themselves the "New Saints"; they professed to work miracles by using the Cabbalistic name of Jehovah. Israel had great success, and left forty thousand followers.

Frederick Bahrdt and C. Frederick Mcolai, the former in his " Introduction " to Cornelius Agrippa's Cabbala, and the latter in his "Travels through Germany and Switzerland, 1781," both mention the Cabbala of the Capucin Father Tertius of Eatisbon, written in Latin, which he utilised for fortune-telling. A somewhat similar Cabbala was published (circa 1790) in the "Delphic Oracle," edited by Professor K. [anne?].

" For Humbug never waneth
When Folly lends its help."

The Cabbala was estimated at its true value by the Jesuit Pererius (1535-1610), who in his book " De Magia" calls it an " unscientific, silly, and ridiculous system." And yet in the last quarter of this century Alphonse Louis Constant, who wrote under the pseudonym of Eliphas Levi Zahed a number of books which are highly esteemed by modern students of " occult " matters, performed, by means of Cabbalistic power, the ceremonial evocation of Apollonius of Tyana, and was patronised, among other people of note, by Lord

Lytton, who had him down to Knebworth! Some forms of superstition do die hard.

II

SONS OF THE WIDOW

111. Origin of Religion of Love - A Persian slave, whose powerful imagination brought forth a doctrine desolating, but extraordinary by originality of invention and variety of episodes, three centuries after the appearance of Christ, and when Orientalism was on the point of disappearing from the West, founded a theogony and instituted a sect which revived Eastern influence in Europe, and by means of the Crusades spread schism and revolt throughout the Catholic world. The action of this rebellious disciple of Zoroaster, of this restorer of the ancient faith of the Magi, mixed with Christian forms and Gnostic symbols, had an extension and duration which, though called in doubt by the past, modern criticism discovers in the intrinsic philosophy of a great part of the sects formed in the bosom of Catholicism. At the head of this gigantic movement of intelligence and conscience, which devoted itself to the most singular superstitions in order to shake off the yoke of Rome, are Gnosticism and Manichasism, Oriental sects, the last and glorious advance of a theogony which, seeing the rule of so large a portion of the earth pass away from itself, undertook to recover it with mysteries and the evocation of poetic phantoms.

112. Manes. Manes, redeemed from slavery by a rich Persian widow, whence he was called the "son of the widow," and his disciples "sons of the widow," of prepossessing aspect, learned in the Alexandrian philosophy, initiated into the Mithraic mysteries, traversed the regions of India, touched on the confines of China, studied the evangelical doctrines, and so lived in the midst of many religious systems, deriving light from all, and satisfied by none. He was born at a propitious moment, and his temperament fitted him for arduous and fantastic undertakings and schemes. Possessing great penetration and an inflexible will, he comprehended the expansive force of Christianity, and resolved to profit thereby, masking Gnostic and Cabbalistic ideas under Christian names and rites. In order to establish this Christian

revelation, he called himself the Paraclete announced by Christ to His disciples, attributing to himself, in the Gnostic manner, a great superiority over the Apostles, rejecting the Old Testament, and allowing to the sages of the pagans a philosophy superior to Judaism. A.D. 270.

113. Manchaeism - The dismal conceptions of a dualism, pure and simple, the eternity and absolute evil of matter, the non-resurrection of the body, the perpetuity of the principle of evil these preside over the compound that took its name from him, and confound Mithras with Christ, the Gospel with the Zend-Avesta, Magism with Judaism. The Unknown Father, the Infinite Being, of Zoroaster, is entirely rejected by Manes, who divides the universe into two dominions, that of light and that of darkness, irreconcilable, whereof one is superior to the other; but, great difference the first, instead of conquering the latter into goodness, reduces it to impotence, conquers, but does not suppress or convince it. The God of light has innumerable legions of combatants (aeons), at whose head are twelve superior angels, corresponding with the twelve signs of the zodiac. Satanic matter is surrounded by a similar host, which, having been captivated by the charms of the light, endeavours to conquer it; wherefore the head of the celestial kingdom, in order to obviate this danger, infuses life into a new power, and appoints it to watch the frontiers of heaven. That power is called the "Mother of Life," and is the soul of the world, the "Divine," the primitive thought of the Supreme Ens, the heavenly "Sophia" of the Gnostics. As a direct emanation of the Eternal it is too pure to unite with matter, but a son is born unto it, the first man, who initiates the great struggle with the demons. When the strength of the man fails him, the "Living Spirit" comes to his assistance, and having led him back to the kingdom of light, raises above the world that part of the celestial soul not contaminated by contact with the demons a perfectly pure soul, the Kedeemer, the Christ, who attracts to Himself and frees from matter the light and soul of the first man. In these abstruse doctrines lies concealed the Mithraic worship of the sun. The followers of Manes were divided into " Elect " and " Listeners "; the

former had to renounce every corporeal enjoyment, everything that can darken the celestial light in us; the second were less rigorously treated. Both might attain immortality by means of purification in an ample lake placed in the moon (the baptism of celestial water), and sanctification in the solar fire (the baptism of celestial fire), where reside the Redeemer and the blessed spirits.

114. Life of Manes - The career of Manes was chequered and stormy, a foreshadowing of the tempests that were to arise against his sect. After having enjoyed the unstable favour of the court, and acquired the fame of a great physician, he found himself unable to save the life of one of the sons of the prince. He was consequently exiled, and roved through Turkistan, Hindostan, and the Chinese Empire. He dwelt for one year in a cave, living on herbs, during which time his followers, having received no news from him, said that he had ascended to heaven, and were believed, not only by the "Listeners," but by the people. The new prince recalled him to court, showered honours on him, erected a sumptuous palace for him, and consulted him on all state affairs. But Barahm, the successor of this prince, at the instigation of the Magi, made him pay dearly for his short happiness, for he put him to a cruel death: he had him flayed alive.

115. Progress of Manichaeism - The government of the sect, already existing with degrees, initiatory rites, signs, and passwords, was continued by astute chiefs, who more and more attracted to themselves the Christians by the use of orthodox language, making them believe that their object was to recall Christianity to its first purity. But the sect was odious to the Church of Rome, because it had issued from rival Persia; and so for two hundred years it was banished from the empire, and the Theodosiau Codex is full of laws against it. Towards the end of the fourth century it spread in Africa and Spain. It had peace, and flourished under the mother of the Emperor Anastasius (491-518); but Justin renewed the persecution. In the ninth century that female fiend, Theodora, the wife of the Emperor Theophilus, caused more than one hundred thousand Manichseans to be slain. But

changing its name, seat, and figurative language, Manichaeism spread in Bulgaria, Lornbardy (Patarini), France (Cathari, Albigenses), &c., united with the Saracens, and openly made war upon tbe Emperor, and its followers perished by thousands in battle and at the stake; and from its secular trunk sprang the so-called heresies of the Hussites and Wyckliffites, which opened the way for Protestantism. In those gloomy Middle Ages, in fact, arose those countless legions of sectaries, bound by a common pact, whose existence only then becomes manifest when the sinister light of the burning pile flashes through the darkness in which they conceal themselves. The Freemasons undoubtedly, through the Templars, inherited no small portion of their ritual from them; they were very numerous in all the courts, and even in the dome of St. Peter, and baptized in blood with new denominations and ordinances.

116. Doctrines - The sacred language of Manichseism was most glowing, and founded on that concert of voices and ideas, called in Pythagorean phraseology the "harmony of the spheres," which established a connection between the mystic degrees and the figured spheres by means of conventional terms and images; and it is known that the Albigenses and Patarini recognised each other by signs. A Provencal Patarino, who had fled to Italy in 1240, everywhere met with a friendly reception, revealing himself to the brethren by means of conventional phrases. He everywhere found the sect admirably organised, with churches, bishops, and apostles of the most active propaganda, who overran France, Germany, and England. The Manichsean language, moreover, was ascetic, and loving, and Christian; but the neophyte, after having once entered the sect, was carried beyond, and gradually alienated from the Papal Church. The mysteries had two chief objects in view that of leading the neophyte, by first insensibly changing his former opinions and dispositions, and then of gradually instructing him in the conventional language, which, being complicated and varied, required much study and much time. But not all were admitted to the highest degrees. Those that turned back, or could not renounce former ideas, remained always in the Church, and were not introduced into the sanctuary. These were simple Christians

and sincere listeners, who, out of zeal for reform, often encountered death, as, for instance, the canons of Orleans, who were condemned to the stake by King Robert in 1022. But those who did not turn back were initiated into all those things which it was important should be known to the most faithful members of the sect. The destruction of Rome, and the establishment of the heavenly Jerusalem spoken of in the Apocalypse, were the chief objects aimed at.

117. Spread of Religion of Love - The religion of love did not end with the massacre of the Albigenses, nor were its last echoes the songs of the troubadours; for we meet with it in a German sect which in 1550 pretended to receive a supernatural light from the Holy Spirit. In Holland, also, a sect of Christians arose in 1555, called the "Family of Love," and deriving its origin from one Henry Nicholas, of Westphalia. He taught that the essence of religion consisted in the feelings of Divine love; that the union of the soul with Christ transforms it into the essence of the Deity; that the Scriptures ought to be interpreted in an allegorical manner. No very damnable heresies, one would think; but when the sect made its appearance in England, about the year 1580, their books were publicly burnt, and the sect dispersed.

III

THE GNOSTICS

118. Character of Gnosticism - The leading ideas of Platonism are also found in the tenets of the Gnostics (i.e., "Those who know," coloro che sanno. Inf. iv. 131), and they continued, during the second and third centuries, the schools that raised a barrier between recondite philosophy and vulgar superstition. Under this aspect Gnosticism is the most universal heresy, the mother of many posterior heresies, even of Arianism, and reappears among the alchymists, mystics, and modern transcendentalists.

119. Doctrines - The Gnostics assumed an infinite, invisible Being, an abyss of darkness, who, unable to remain inactive, diffused himself in emanations, decreasing in perfection the further they were removed from the centre that produced them. They had their grand triad, whose personifications Matter, the Demiurgus, and the Saviour comprised and represented the history of mankind and of the world. The superior emanations, partakers of the attributes of the Divine essence, are the "asons," distributed in classes according to symbolical numbers. Their union forms the " pleroma," or the fulness of intelligence. The last and most imperfect emanation of the pleroma, according to one of the two grand divisions of Gnosticism, is the Demiurgus, a balance of light and darkness, of strength and weakness, who, without the concurrence of the unknown Father, produces this world, there imprisoning the souls, for he is the primary evil, opposed to the primary good. He encumbers the souls with matter, from which they are redeemed by Christ, one of the sublime powers of the pleroma, the Divine thought, intelligence, the spirit. For humanity is destined to raise itself again from the material to the spiritual life; to free itself from Nature, and to govern it, and to live again in immortal beauty.

    According to the other party of the Gnostics, the Demiurgus was the representative and organ of the highest God, who was placed by the Divine will especially over the Jewish people as their Jehovah. Men are divided into three classes: the terrestrial men, of the earth earthy, tied and bound by matter; the spiritual men, the Pneumatikoi, who attain to the Divine light; the Psychikoi, who only rise up to the Demiurgus. The Jews, subject to Jehovah, were Psychikoi; the Pagans were terrestrial men; the true Christians or Gnostics, Pneumatikoi.

120. Development of Gnosticism - Simon Magus; Menander, his successor; Cerinthus, the apostle of the Millennium, and some others who lived in the first century, are looked upon as the founders of Gnosticism, which soon divided into as many sects as there arose apostles. This may be called the obscure period of Gnosticism. But at the beginning of the second century the sect of Basilides of Alexandria arose, and with it various centres of Gnosticism in Egypt, Syria, Kome, Spain, &c. Basilides, who corrupted Gnosticism with Indian and Egyptian fancies, assumed 365 asons or cycles of creation, which were expressed by the word abraxas, whose letters, according to their numerical value in Greek, produce the number 365. By "abraxas" was meant, in its deeper sense, the Supreme God; but the reader will at once detect the astronomical bearing, and remember the words Mithras and Belenus, which also severally represent that number, and the Supreme God, viz., the sun. Valentinus also is a famous Gnostic, whose fundamental doctrine is that all men shall be restored to their primeval state of perfection; that matter, the refuge of evil, shall be consumed by fire which is also the doctrine of Zoroaster; and that the spirits in perfect maturity shall ascend into the pleroma, there to enjoy all the delights of a perfect union with their companions. From the Valentinians sprang the Ophites, calling themselves so after the serpent that by tempting Eve brought into the world the blessings of knowledge; and the Cainites, who maintained that Cain had been the first Gnostic, in opposition to the blind, unreasoning faith of Abel, and therefore persecuted by the Demiurgus, Jehovah. On this idea is founded the Masonic Legend of the Temple. The Antitacts (opponents to the law), like the Ishmaelites at a later period, taught their adepts hatred against all positive religions and laws. The Adamites looked upon marriage as the fruit of sin; they called their

lascivious initiation "paradise," held all indulgence in carnal delights lawful, and advocated the abolition of dress. The Pepuzians varied their initiations with the apparition of phantasms, among whom was a woman crowned with the sun and twelve stars, and having the moon under her feet the Isis of Egypt and the Ceres of Greece. They found in the Apocalypse all their initiatory terminology. A gnostic stone, represented in the work of Chifflet, shows seven stars of equal size, with a larger one above; these probably mean the seven planets and the sun. There are, moreover, figured on it a pair of compasses, a square, and other geometrical emblems. Thus all religious initiations are ever reducible to astronomy and natural phenomena.

121. Spirit of Gnosticism - The widely opposite ideas of polytheism, pantheism, monotheism, the philosophical systems of Plato, Pythagoras, Heraclitus, together with the mysticism and demon ology that after the Jewish captivity created the Cabbala all these went towards forming Gnosticism. And the aristocracy of mind, powerful and numerous as none had ever been before, that arose in the first centuries of our era, even when adopting the new faith, could not but loathe the thought of sharing it completely with the crowd of freed and unfreed slaves around them with the low and poor in spirit. The exclusiveness of Gnosticism, which was one of the causes why it was violently persecuted by the Fathers of the Church as damnable heresy, was undoubtedly, next to the attractiveness of its dogmas, one of the chief reasons of its rapid propagation and its lasting influence on modern religious systems.

It is said that the Gnostics recognised one another by slightly tickling the palm of the person with whom they shook hands.

IV

THE ESSENES

122. Connection of Judaism and Gnosticism - At the dispersion of the Jews in the heart of Asia, attempts were made to discover analogies between the Chinese doctrines of Lau-Tze (80) and those of the Hebrews, extending even to the name Jehovah; and it is undeniable that whilst the Jews on the one hand assimilated their dogmas with those of Zoroaster, on the other they diffused Gnostic and Cabbalistic ideas throughout the world. And Lau-Tze has by some been considered as a forerunner of Gnosticism. A fragment of this religious teacher runs thus: "Before the chaos that preceded the birth of the universe, there existed one sole being, boundless and silent, immutable and yet ever active, that may be called the Mother of the universe. I know not its name, but may call it Intelligence. Man has his model on the earth, the earth in heaven, the heaven in Intelligence, and Intelligence in itself."

123. Essenes and Therapeutce - On their return to Judgea the Jews were split into various sects, such as the Pharisees, whose name is supposed to be derived from Parsees, and Sadducees, Chasidim, and Zadikim. With regard to the Mosaic law the Pharisees were Chasidim (Pietists), whilst the Samaritans, Essenes, and Sadducees were Zadikim. The former afterwards split into Talmudists, Eabbinists, and Cabbalists (no, Sect of the "New Saints"). But those in which the Eastern element predominated most were the Essenes and the Therapeutge. These two sects have often been confounded, it being assumed that the latter formed the highest degree of the order. But they were quite distinct, having nothing in common except their moral precepts. Their practices were not exclusively Oriental, but by means of the Alexandrian school were connected with Western traditions, and especially with the teachings of Pythagoras. The Essenes, approaching more to the principles of Zoroaster, who held that the soul was to be freed as much as possible from corporeal influences, submitted to fastings and maceration; the Therapeutae, living in Egypt, endeavoured

to reconcile the doctrines of the East with the ancient traditions of Greece, wherefore the picture Philo, who strongly sympathised with them, has left us of their society, abounds with Eastern and Pythagorean ideas. It is, however, doubtful whether the work was really written by Philo; by many it is supposed to be the work of a Christian monk, as a panegyric on ascetic monachism. Some writers have attempted to derive the Essenians from the Ephesian priesthood, and tracing some resemblance between the Orphics of Thrace, the Curete of Crete, and the Ephesian priests, the existence of an ancient common doctrine, submerged like a philosophical Atlantis, was suspected, the Grecians being looked upon as a powerful offshoot; but it seems certain that the Essenes had very little of Greece in their rituals, whilst the Therapeutas had a great deal. The Essenes may, with great probability, be derived from the Assideans (i Mac. ii. 42), who, in consequence of the perfidy of Alcimus (i Mac. vii. 13-16), severed their connection with the Temple. In our English Apocrypha, the Assideans are called (i Mac. ii. 42) "mighty men of Israel," but the meaning of the original is, "adherents of the old faith." They were not warriors, as has been supposed; they were the first to seek peace (i Mac. vii. I 3), for they formed a religious and not a military community.

124. Their Tenets and Customs - The Essenes were renowned for their moral and virtuous lives. They dwelt in villages, far from towns, tilling the land, owning no slaves, and having all their goods in common. They made no vows of celibacy, but most abstained from marriage, dreading the infidelity and fickleness of woman. They cultivated the physical sciences, and especially medicine. No one was admitted into their community, except after having passed through graduated probations lasting several years. And why they are reckoned among secret societies is, because they may be considered as the opponents of the Jewish priesthood at a time when that priesthood was all-powerful, and any opposition to it was attended with the utmost danger. Now the doctrines of the Essenes were necessarily opposed to the Hebrew faith, and to escape the persecution which they otherwise might have incurred, they in the first instance adopted a name calculated to disarm

suspicion, viz., that of Essenes, from the Essen or breastplate worn by the Jewish high-priest, and further took every possible precaution in the admission of members into their secret order, which was divided into four degrees, and the process of initiation was so arranged that a candidate, even after having entered the third, did not know the grand secret, and if not found trustworthy to be admitted into the innermost sanctuary, remained totally unconscious of its real nature, and only saw in it the governing ranks, highest in rank, but not otherwise distinguished in point of doctrine. A perfect parallel of this system is found in Freemasonry; the members of the first three degrees are not initiated into the grand so-called secret of Masonry; only in the Koyal Arch they are informed of it). The four degrees above referred to were respectively called the "Faithful," the "Illuminate' the "Initiated," and the " Perfect." The Faithful received at their initiation a new or baptismal name, and this was engraved with a secret mark upon a white stone (probably alluded to in Rev. ii. 17, which, as we shall hereafter see, was not Christian in its origin), which he retained as a voucher of his membership. The usual sign was the cross, though other signs also were employed.

125. Distinction between the two Sects - The Therapeutae were more addicted to contemplation and less to labour; they might be called speculative Essenes. They were less opposed to the admission of women, and at some of their festivals they performed dances, in which the fair sex were allowed to join. But whilst not denying themselves the society of women, they banished wine from all their meals; they were afraid, it seems, of the conjunction of Bacchus and Venus. They alone had, or professed to have, the key to the right interpretation of the writings of Moses, a true knowledge of the Cabbala, and according to tradition, Christ was born of parents belonging to the society, who brought up and trained the child in the part he was to play.

The Essenes and Therapeutas resided chiefly in the neighbourhood of the Dead Sea and in Egypt, and their existence was prolonged into the fourth century of our era.

BOOK III

CHRISTIAN INITIATIONS

I

CHRISTIAN INITIATIONS

126. Myth of Horus Christianised - When the story of the Egyptian Horus had, by a concatenation of circumstances too long to be described here, in Alexandria, been elaborated into the myth of Christ, the latter was at once fitted out with mysteries and initiations thereinto. Traces of them may be found in all the evangelists, but most in St. Paul; and the trials of Christian initiation, as some suppose, are described in Luke xiv., and according to others, Matthew xvii. contains a full declaration of the mysteries made to the elect or initiated. If so, they are conveyed in language as enigmatical as that of the Alchymists. But the story of the Transfiguration on the Mount is an imperfect description of the holding of a quasi-masonic lodge of association in the highest degree. The more the society extended, chiefly by the ambitious schemes of Cerinthus, the more such initiations increased, and thus there gradually arose in the Church the secret discipline. The Cerinthus just mentioned, and who was also ironically called Merinthus i.e., the "rope" was really a Gnostic. St. John held him in such abhorrence, that on one occasion he would not bathe with him in the Baths of Ephesus for fear the vault would crumble over the heretic. The primitive Church believed that the Gospel of St. John had been written against Cerinthus, who, to revenge himself, attributed the Apocalypse to St. John.

127. Christian Mysteries - In the writings of the Fathers the mention of mysterious designations and distinctions becomes more frequent. St. Augustin gives the reason why the secret discipline was adopted by the new believers: Firstly, because the mysteries, so incomprehensible to human intellect, and their simple rites, should not be derided by the

Gentiles and those not fully initiated; secondly, to secure greater veneration for those rites; and thirdly, that the holy curiosity of the catechumens should be excited to obtain a perfect knowledge of them.

128. Similarity of Christian with Pagan Rites - At least twenty different incarnate gods were celebrated in the East and West, to each of whom was attributed a history, similar in general details to that of the Christian Messiah, and these various incarnations were all supposed to have preceded Christ in point of chronology; the miracles attributed to Him had been sculptured in temples hoary with age before the date assigned to His birth. In all the ancient mysteries we have seen a representation of the death of the sun; according to some writers, this ceremony was imitated in the Christian mysteries by the symbolical slaying of a child, which, in the lower degrees, of course meant the death of Christ. We may here mention, just to show how old is the custom of the followers of an ancient religion to attribute horrible practices to the professors of a new creed, that the Komans asserted that, on being initiated into the Christian faith, the aspirant had placed before him a male child, covered with flour, whom he had to stab till he was dead, whereupon all present greedily licked up the blood, tore the body to pieces, and ate them, by which ceremony they were bound to one common silence. The initiated were divided into three classes: hearers, catechumens, and faithful. The hearers formed a noviciate, and were prepared to be instructed in the Christian dogmas. One portion of these dogmas was hidden from the catechumens, who after the prescribed purifications, received baptism or initiation into the theogenesis (divine generation); they then became servants of the faith, and were admitted into the temples, and recognised each other by the sign of the cross. Solemn dances were performed in all the initiations, and the expression, "to come from the ball," which, for instance, we meet with in Ælius Aristides, the rhetorician (circa 150 A.D.), meant "to betray the mysteries."

129. Christian Symbols taken from Pagan Symbols - Most of the hieroglyphics and symbols of Paganism passed into Christianity. The

vine, and the processes of converting its fruit into the most universal of beverages, all belonging among the heathens to the rites of Bacchus, were by the first Christians rendered symbolical of the labours in the vineyard of faith. The ear of corn of Ceres furnished the emblem for the bread which Christ divided among His disciples. The palm and crown, which denoted worldly victories, among the Christians signified spiritual triumphs. The wings of the doves were given to the angels and cherubim; the dove of Venus became the Holy Ghost; Diana's stag, the Christian soul panting for the living water; Juno's peacock, that soul after resurrection. The sphinx, the griffin, and the chimera of mythology were by the Christians adopted as having the same power of warding off evil spirits and fornication, which was supposed to belong to the Gorgon's head. The keys of Janus, with St. Peter, expressed the highest power to set free and bind. In the primitive ages the pontiff wore a girdle whence depended seven keys and seven seals, symbols of the mysteries he was to preside over and keep secret. The cross (53) at first was a symbol not openly displayed, and it was not till the sixth century that the body of Christ was exhibited on it. The fish was not a Christian symbol of the Saviour merely because the Greek word for fish, ἰχθύς, contained the initials of Jesus Christ, Son of God, Saviour, as is generally alleged, but because throughout the ancient world water was connected with the idea of salvation: Isis was associated with the fish, Moses means "drawn from the water," Joshua was the sun of Nun, "the fish." Vishnu's first incarnation in the form of a fish and the Cannes of the Chaldeans all have the same meaning.

130. Celebration of the Mysteries - They were divided into two parts. The first was called the "mass of the catechumens," because the members of that degree were allowed to be present at it, and it embraced what was said from the beginning of the service to the Apostles' Creed. The second was called the "mass of the faithful," and comprised the preparation for the sacrifice, the sacrifice itself, and thanksgiving. When this latter commenced, a deacon intimated to the catechumens to go out, and the phrase used by him on that occasion savours but little of the pretended meekness and toleration of the

youthful Church: Sancta sanctis foris canes. The faithful being left alone recited the Apostles' Creed, whereby it was seen that all present had been fully initiated, and that all metaphorical or enigmatical language might be dispensed with.

131. Astronomical Meaning of Christianity - Then the real mystery was unveiled, and the astronomical meaning of Christianity, similar to that of the ancient mysteries, was laid bare. The limits of this work will not allow me to enter into full details, but what follows will sufficiently explain the nature of the secret doctrines of the early Christians. Thus to them the Seven Churches of Asia were the seven months from March to September, both inclusive, as is proved by their names. Christ represented the sun, and His first miracle is turning water into wine, which the sun does every year; His agony in Gethsemane was the juice of the grape put in the wine-press; His descent into hell was the sun in the winter season; His crucifixion on Calvary (calvus = bald = shorn of His rays) His crossing the equator in the autumn; and His crucifixion in Egypt (Rev. xi. 8) His crossing it in the spring. The beheading of John the Baptist was shown to them to be John, Janus, or Aquarius, having his head cut off by the line of the horizon on the 29th August, wherefore his festival occurs on that day. They knew the Virgin Mary to be the Virgo of the zodiac, the goddess Ceres, who holds out to Adam, or man, the produce of the harvest; the Virgin, wedded to Joseph, astronomically Bootes, which constellation always rises and sets with her. These analogies might be pursued still further, but enough has been said for our present purpose.

132. Prometheus Bound - The myth of Christ had been foreshadowed 500 years before our era in the tragedy of Eschylus' "Prometheus Bound." Hence the disinclination of the Athenians, to whom this tragedy was familiar, to believe in a Jesus, crucified amidst the most astounding terrestrial and astronomical phenomena, of which, however, no one except the propounders of the new doctrine had ever heard.

The name Prometheus deserves attention; it is a compound word: Proma-theos, i.e., Brahma-theos. In the Tamul, a language derived from the Sanscrit, Brahma is pronounced Prahma. The Indian a has also been turned into o, for navam, nine, is undoubtedly the etymon of novem; pada, poda, &c. The converse of the change of B into P is found in Baphomet, from Papa and Maliomet. To return to Prometheus: he and Christ perish on a hill; both submit to the law of another god to save mankind; both have their right sides pierced, Prometheus by a vulture, Jesus by a lance, the former on a rock, the latter on a cross; and in the moment of death both expiatory victims utter the same sentiments, that is to say, the Gospels repeat the words put into the mouth of Prometheus 500 years before Christ. What strengthens the identity is the fact that Prometheus has a friend called Oceanus, who in the ancient mythologies is also called Piereus (Pierre), Peter. Now in the tragedy of Eschylus we read that Oceanus denied his friend at the moment when the anger of God made him a victim for the sins of the human race. St. Peter, who lived by the ocean or sea, did the same under similar circumstances.

133. Abolition of Mysteries - The number of the faithful having greatly increased the Christians from being persecuted having become persecutors, and that of the most grasping and barbarous kind the Church in the seventh century instituted the minor orders, among whom were the doorkeepers, who took the place of the deacons. In 692 every one was ordered thenceforth to be admitted to the public worship of the Christians, their esoteric teaching of the first ages was entirely suppressed, and what had been pure cosmology and astronomy was turned into a pantheon of gods and saints. Nothing remained of the mysteries but the custom of secretly reciting the canon of the Mass. Nevertheless in the Greek Church the priest celebrates divine worship behind a curtain, which is only removed during the elevation of the host, but since at that moment the worshippers prostrate themselves, they are supposed not to see the holy sacrament.

II

THE APOCALYPSE

134. The Apocalypse - This book, hitherto accepted as one of genuinely Christian authorship, is now by competent critics received in its main substance, and throughout by far the greater part of it, as a purely Jewish composition; in fact, as a Jewish Apocalypse put into a Christian dress after the fall of Jerusalem, A.D. 70. The first three chapters are Christian, of course, but in the fourth chapter the book begins again, and from that to the end, with the exception of a few short passages, which are interpolations, all is purely Jewish, or rather a medley of occidental, Judaic, and sectarian doctrines. The bulk of the work is a description of the Pagan mysteries, which the Christianising adapter transforms into those of the Christian myth; to the latter it is what the "Golden Ass" of Apuleius and the "Sixth Book" of Virgil is to the Pagan mysteries, from which its whole machinery is borrowed. The woman clothed with the sun, standing upon the moon, and symbolising the true Church, is the Egyptian Isis; the attack upon the woman and her offspring by the deluging serpent, which is frustrated by the earth's absorption of the water, is perfectly analogous to the attack of the diluvian serpent Python upon Osiris, or Latona, or Horus, which is similarly frustrated by the destruction of that monster; the false Church, bearing the name of Mystery of course, referring to the Pagan Mystery floating on the waters, or riding on a terrific beast, and ultimately plunged into the infernal lake, exhibits the very same aspect as the Great Mother of Paganism sailing over the ocean, riding on the lion, venerated with certain mysteries, and during their celebration plunged into the waters of a sacred lake, denominated the lake of Hades. St. Paul himself personates an aspirant about to be initiated, and accordingly the images presented to his mind's eye closely resemble the pageants of the mysteries. The prophet first beholds a door opened in the magnificent temple of heaven, and into this he is invited to enter by one who plays the hierophant. Here he witnesses the unsealing of the sacred book, and immediately he is assailed by a troop

of ghastly apparitions. Among these are pre-eminently conspicuous a vast serpent, the well-known symbol of the Great Father; and two wild beasts, severally coming up out of the sea and out of the earth. Such hideous figures correspond with the canine phantoms in the Orgies, and with the polymorphic images of the principal hero-god, who was universally deemed the offspring of the sea. Passing these terrific monsters in safety, the prophet, constantly attended by his angel-hierophant, is conducted into the presence of a female, and, like Isis emerging from the sea, and exhibiting herself to the eyes of the aspirant Apuleius, this female divinity, upborne upon the marine wild beast, appears to float upon the surface of many waters. She is said to be an open and systematic harlot, just as the Great Mother was the declared female principle of fecundity, and as she was often propitiated by literal fornication reduced to a religious system; and as the initiated were made to drink a prepared liquor out of a sacred goblet, so this harlot is represented as intoxicating the kings of the earth with the golden cup of her prostitution. On her forehead the very name Mystery is inscribed; its nature the officiating hierophant undertakes to explain. To the sea-born Great Father was ascribed a threefold state; he lived, he died, and he revived, and these changes of condition were duly exhibited in the mysteries. To the sea-born wild beast is similarly ascribed a threefold state; he lives, he dies, and he revives. While dead he lies floating on the mighty ocean, just like Horus, or Osiris, or Siva, or Vishnu; when he revives he emerges from the waters, and whether alive or dead, he bears seven heads and ten horns, numbers that have their prototypes in the mysteries (18, &c.). And as the worshippers of the Great Father bore his special mark, and were distinguished by his name, so the worshippers of the maritime beast equally bear his mark, and are equally designated by his appellation. At length the first or doleful part of these sacred mysteries draws to a close, and the last or joyful part is rapidly approaching. After the prophet has beheld the enemies of God plunged into a dreadful lake or inundation of liquid fire (64), which corresponds with the infernal lake or deluge of the Egyptian mysteries, he is introduced into a splendidly illuminated region expressly adorned with the characteristics of that paradise which was the ultimate scope of the ancient aspirants, while without the holy gate of admission are the whole multitude of the profane, sorcerers, and whoremongers, and murderers, and idolaters, and whosoever loveth or maketh a lie; but first of all dogs, i.e., the uninitiated, the cowans (κύων) of Freemasonry. For some modern thinkers the Apocalypse has neither meaning nor value.

135. Pagan Impostors - The spread of Christianity produced also many opponents to it, either avowed or secret; the latter, however, in most cases desired to see Paganism reformed, not abolished; though rejecting Christianity, they attempted to form a sort of Christianised Paganism. Clever impostors in those days reaped a rich harvest from the credulity of mankind, and sects without end sprang up. Two of the most successful leaders of such were Apollonius of Tyana and Alexander of Abonoteichos. Their doctrines, ceremonies, and tricks in mystery-mongering were largely founded on the religious and philosophical charlatanism of Pythagoras; they had their day, and passed away, to be constantly resuscitated.

BOOK IV

ISHMAELITES

" And he will be a wild man; his hand will be against every man, and every man's hand against him."

GEN. xvi. 12.

I

THE LODGE OF WISDOM

136. Legend of the Mahdi - The Arabs had rendered themselves masters of Persia, but that country did not willingly bear the foreign yoke. In the schism which, after the death of Mahomet, divided his followers, the Persians took the side of Ali, the husband of Mahomet's daughter, Fatima, and the successor of the Prophet. At the end of the eighth century the two great divisions of Mahometans were already split up into numerous sects; but all of them had one belief in common, namely, in the coming of a Messiah, or, in their language, a Mahdi or guide. The Ghoolat, an extravagant sect, had started the doctrine, adopted by other sects, that the last visible imam, or supreme ecclesiastical ruler, had been Ismael, reckoning Ali as the first, and those who thought so were called Ismaelites; whilst others said Askeree, the twelfth imam, to have been the last visible one, and that he had vanished in a cavern at Hilla, on the banks of the Euphrates, where he would remain invisible till the end of the world, when he would reappear as the Mahdi. On this belief a bold adventurer founded the plan of freeing Persia and raising himself to power. On this belief the power of the Mahdi of the present day is founded.

137. Abdallah, the first Pontiff - The just-mentioned adventurer's name was Abdallah, the son of Mamoon, and grandson of the famous Haroon Er-Easheed. The Ishmaelites were numerous in Persia; he

addressed himself to them, telling them that Ismael had indeed been the last imam, but that Mohammed, his sou, was a prophet, and the founder of a new religion, which would confirm the doctrine of Ismael, and secure to its followers the empire of the world. Since the creation, he told his followers, there have been six religious periods, each distinguished by the incarnation of a prophet. Adam, Noah, Abraham, Moses, Jesus, and Mahomet were the prophets of those periods. Their mission was to lead men to ascending degrees of religious perfection.

The seven imams of All's posterity are the seven interpreters of the hidden sense of Mahomet's religion, and the forerunners of the most perfect doctrine, whose triumph is at hand: the doctrine of Mohammed, the son of Ismael. And as seven imams succeeded Mahomet, so there always were seven pontiffs after every previous prophet, and so there will be seven pontiffs after Mohammed. I am the first of these pontiffs. The pontiff's office is to explain to the initiated that every religion has two meanings, the one apparent, intended for the vulgar crowd, the other secret, and only true one, showing that all religions have but one aim.

138. Origin of Quarmatites - Mohammad-ben-Hosain, surnamed Zaidan, a rich and patriotic Persian, was so captivated by the plan of Abdallah, that he made him a present of two millions of pieces of gold. But being persecuted by the governor of Susiana, Abdallah made his escape to Syria, where one of his missionaries converted, about 887, a certain Hamdan, famous under the name of Quarmat, who formed the sect known as the Quarmatites, whose power, rapidly developed during two centuries, caused the Khalifs to tremble on their thrones.

139. Origin of Fatimite Dynasty - On Abdallah's death he was followed in the pontificate by one of his sons, Saidben-Hosaia-ben-Abdallah, who asserted that he was the expected Fatimite Messiah, the Mahdi; and when he was informed that numerous partisans were anxiously expecting him in Africa, Said, adopting the name of Obaid Allah the Mahdi, passed into Africa, overthrew the dynasty of the Aghlabites, ruling in Tripoli and Tunis, and founded the famous

dynasty of the Fatimites (A.D. 909). His greatgrandson, Moizz li dinillah, drove the Khalifs of Bagdad from Egypt, and laid the foundations of Cairo, which he made his capital.

140. The Lodge of Cairo - Here he founded the Lodge of Cairo, which might correctly be described as a university; it contained many books and scientific instruments; science was the professed object, but the real aim was very different. The course of instruction was divided into nine degrees. The first sought to inspire the pupil with doubts, and with confidence in his teacher who was to solve them. For this purpose captious questions were to show him the absurdity of the literal sense of the Koran, and obscure hints gave him to understand that under that shell was hidden a sweet and nutritious kernel; but the instruction went no further unless the pupil bound himself by dreadful oaths to blind faith in, and absolute obedience to, his instructor. The second inculcated the recognition of the imams, or directors, appointed by God as the fountains of every kind of knowledge. The third informed him of the number of those blessed or holy imams, and that number was the mystical seven. The fourth informed him that God had sent into the world seven legislators, each of whom had seven coadjutors, and who were called mutes, whilst the legislators were called speakers. The fifth informed him that each of these coadjutors had twelve apostles. The sixth placed before the eyes of the adept, advanced so far, the precepts of the Koran, and he was taught that all the dogmas of religion ought to be subordinate to the rule of philosophy; he was also instructed in the systems of Plato and Aristotle. The seventh degree embraced mystical pantheism. The eighth again brought before him the dogmatic precepts of the Mohammedan law, estimating it at its just value. The ninth degree, finally, as the necessary result of all the former, taught that nothing was to be believed, and that everything was lawful.

141. Progress of Doctrines - These were the ends aimed at human responsibility and dignity were to be annihilated; the throne of the descendants of Fatima was to be surrounded with an army of assassins,

a formidable body-guard; a mysterious militia was to be raised, that should spread far and wide the fame and terror of the caliphate of Cairo, and inflict fatal blows on the abhorred rule of Bagdad. The missionaries spread widely, and in Arabia and Syria partisans were won to whom the designs of the order were unknown, but who had with fearful solemnity sworn blind obedience. The nocturnal labours of the Lodge of Cairo lasted a century; and its doctrines, which ended with denying all truth, morality, and justice, necessarily produced something very extraordinary. So terrible a shock to the human conscience led to one of those phenomena that leave a sanguinary and indelible trace on the page of history.

It remains to be noticed that Hakem Biamrillah, the founder of the sect of the Druses (157), was originally a member of the Lodge of Cairo.[8]

---

[8] The Mahdists have come to the front again in the present troubles in the Sudan. But according to the Times correspondent (5th June 1896), their power is at an end. Abdullah el Taaisha, who called himself the Khalifa of the Mahdi, now styles himself the Sultan of the Sudan, but his followers seem decreasing, and as they no longer form a secret society, their doings do not enter into the scope of this work.

II

THE ASSASSINS

142. Foundation of Order - Only Arabia and Syria could have been the theatre of the dismal deeds of the Old Man, or rather Lord of the Mountain. Hassan Sabbah was one of the days or missionaries of the School of Cairo, a man of adventurous spirit, who, having greatly distinguished himself, acquired much influence at Cairo. This influence, however, excited the envy of others, who succeeded in having him exiled. He had been put on board a ship to take him out of the country, but a storm arising, all considered themselves lost. But Hassan, assuming an authoritative air, exclaimed, "The Lord has promised me that no evil shall befall me." Suddenly the storm abated, and the sailors cried, "A miracle!" and became his followers. Hassan traversed Persia, preaching and making proselytes, and having seized the fortress of Alamut (1090), on the borders of Irak, and Dilem, which he called the "House of Fortune," he there established his rule.

143. Influence of Hassan - What kind of rule? The history of his time is full of his name. Kings in the very centre of Europe trembled at it; his powerful arm reached everywhere. Philip Augustus of France was so afraid of him that he dared not stir without his guard around him; and perhaps the otherwise implacable Lord of the Mountain forgave him because of his fear. At first he showed no other intention but to increase the sway of the caliphate of Cairo, but was not long before throwing of the mask, because his fierce character submitted with difficulty to cunning and hypocrisy. He reduced the nine degrees into which the adherents of the Lodge of Cairo were divided to seven, placing himself at the head, with the title of Seydna or Sidna, whence the Spanish Cid, and the Italian Signore. The term Assassins is a corruption of Hashishim, derived from hashish (the hemp plant), with which the chief intoxicated his followers when they entered on some

desperate enterprise.[9]

144. Degrees of the Order - To regulate the seven degrees he composed the Catechism of the Order. The first degree recommended to the missionary attentively to watch the disposition of the candidate, before admitting him to the order. The second impressed it upon him to gain the confidence of the candidate, by flattering his inclinations and passions; the third, to involve him in doubts and difficulties oy showing him the absurdity of the Koran; the fourth, to exact from him a solemn oath of fidelity and obedience, with a promise to lay his doubts before his instructor; and the fifth, to show him that the most famous men of Church and State belonged to the secret order. The sixth, called "Confirmation," enjoined on the instructor to examine the proselyte concerning the whole preceding course, and firmly to establish him in it. The seventh, finally, called the "Exposition of the Allegory," gave the keys of the sect.

145. Devotion of Followers - The followers were divided into two great hosts, "self-sacrificers" and "aspirants." The first, despising fatigues, dangers, and tortures, joyfully gave their lives whenever it pleased the great master, who required them either to protect himself or to carry out his mandates of death. The victim having been pointed out, the faithful, clothed in a white tunic with a red sash, the colours of innocence and blood, went on their mission, without being deterred by distance or danger. Having found the person they sought, they awaited the favourable moment for slaying him, and their daggers seldom missed their aim. Conrad of Montferrat, having quarrelled with Raschid-addin, the then Lord of the Mountain, and also caused a number of Musulman prisoners, brought from Tyre, to be massacred, Saladin induced Raschid-addin to kill Conrad. Richard Coeur-de-Lion was long accused of having instigated the murder. Two Assassins allowed themselves to be baptized, and placing themselves beside him,

---

[9] This, at least, is the usual derivation. But it is doubtful, for hashish was not taken by the Assassins only, but by all Eastern nations. Possibly the word is derived from the Arab hass, meaning to ' destroy, kill.' The Jew Benjamin, who wrote in 1173, when speaking of the sect, says their name is derived from asasa, ' to lay snares.'

seemed only intent on praying; but the favourable opportunity presenting itself, they slew him, and one of them took refuge in a church. But hearing that the prince had been carried off still alive, he again forced his way into Montferrat's presence, and stabbed him a second time; and then expired, without a complaint, amidst refined tortures.

146. The Imaginary Paradise - How was such devotion secured? The story goes, according to Marco Polo, that whenever the chief had need of a man to carry out any particularly dangerous enterprise, he had recourse to the following stratagem: In a province of Persia, now named Sigistan, was the famous valley Mulebat, containing the palace of Alladin, another name of the Lord of the Mountain. This valley was a most delightful spot, and so protected by high mountains terminating in perpendicular cliffs y that from them no one could enter the valley, and all the ordinary approaches were guarded by strong fortresses. The valley was cultivated as the most luxurious gardens, with pavilions splendidly furnished, their sole occupants being the most lovely and charming women. The man selected by the lord to perform the dangerous exploit was first made drunk, and in this state carried into the valley, where he was left to roam whithersoever he pleased. On coming to his senses sufficiently to appreciate the beautiful scenery, and to enjoy the charms of the sylph-like creatures, that kept him engaged all the time in amorous dalliance, he was made to believe that this was Elysium; but ere he wearied or became satiated with love and wine, he was once more made drunk, and in this state carried back to his own home. When his services were required, he was again sent for by the lord, who told him that he had once permitted him to enjoy paradise, and if he would do his bidding he could luxuriate in the same delights for the rest of his life. The dupe, believing that his master had the power to do all this, was ready to commit whatever crime was required of him.

147. Sanguinary Character of Hassan - In that inaccessible nest the vulture-soul of its master was alone with his own ambition; and the

very solitude, which constituted his power, must at times have weighed heavy upon him. And so it is said that he composed theological works, and gave himself up to frequent religious exercises. And this need not surprise us; theological studies are no bar to ferocity, and mystical gentleness is often found united with sanguinary fury. But he killed with calculation, to gain fame and power, to inspire fear and secure success. He impressed on his followers the belief that he could see things happening at a distance, and having established a pigeon-post, he was frequently informed of distant events with a surprising rapidity. A Persian caliph thought of attacking and dispersing the sect, and found on his pillow a dagger and a letter from Hassan, saying, "What has been placed beside thy head may be planted in thy heart." In spite of years he remained sanguinary to the last. With his own hand he killed his two sons; the one for having slain a day, and the other for having tasted wine. He did not design to found a dynasty or regular government, but an order, sect, or secret society; and perhaps his sons perished in consequence of badly disguising their desire to succeed him.

148. Further Instances of Devotion in Followers - The obedience to the faithful did not cease with Hassan's death, as the following will show. Henry, Count of Champagne, had to pass close by the territory of the Assassins; one of the successors of Hassan, Bishad-ad-din, invited him to visit the fortress, which invitation the Count accepted. On making the round of the towers, two of the "faithful," at a sign from the "Lord," stabbed themselves to the heart, and fell at the feet of the terrified Count; whilst the master coolly said, "Say but the word, and at a sign from me you shall see them all thus on the ground." The Sultan having sent an ambassador to summon the rebellious Assassins to submission, the lord, in the presence of the ambassador, said to one of the faithful, "Kill thyself!" and he did it; and to another, "Throw thyself from this tower!" and he hurled himself down. Then turning to the ambassador, he said, "Seventy thousand followers obey me in the same manner. This is my reply to your master." The only exaggeration in this is probably in the number, the whole number of followers being never estimated above forty thousand, many of whom, moreover, were

not "faithful ones' but only aspirants.

149. Murder of Raschid-addin's Ambassador - The Knights of the Temple had possessions in the neighbourhood of those of the Assassins, and their superior power had enabled them, at what time is uncertain, to render the latter tributaries to the amount of 2000 ducats per annum. Raschid-addin, to whom all religions were alike, conceived the idea of releasing himself from this tribute by becoming, together with his people, Christians. He therefore sent in 1172 an ambassador to Amalric, king of Jerusalem, offering to embrace Christianity, provided the king would engage the Templars to renounce the tribute. The king readily assented to this, and at the same time assured the Templars that they should not be losers, as he would pay them the 2000 ducats annually out of his treasury. The Templars made no objection, but on his way home the Ishmaelite ambassador was murdered by some Knights of the Temple, who, it would appear, acted by the orders of their superior, who probably did not consider the royal promise good for the tribute. At all events, when Amalric, full of indignation at the perfidious conduct of the Templars, insisted on their being punished, Adode St. Amand, the Master of the Temple, contented himself by saying that he had imposed penances on the murderers. The king, however, got hold of Du Mesnil, the leader in the assassination, and threw him into prison; but the king soon after dying, Du Mesnil regained his liberty. All hopes of the conversion of the Ishmaelites, however, were at an end.

150. Suppression of Assassins - Raschid-addin died in 1192. His successors had neither his genius nor his prestige. The days of the sect were counted. In 1256 Hoolagoo, the brother of Mongoo, the Great Khan of Mongolia, invaded Persia, and exterminated all the Assassins he could seize. Rokn-addin, the last Master of Alamut, was put to death; most of his fortresses fell into the hands of Hoolagoo. But the Mameluk Sultan of Egypt having in 1 260 defeated the Mongolians, the fortresses were restored to the Ishmaelites. But this was only a respite; in 1265 they were forced to pay tribute to the Sultan of Egypt.

Sarim, the then chief of the Assassins, in 1270 made one more effort to throw off the Egyptian yoke, but he was defeated, and in 1273 the Assassins had surrendered all their strong places to Baibars I., Sultan of Egypt. But this ruler had no intention, like Hoolagoo, of exterminating the Assassins; his object was to turn them to account. Ibn Batoutah, the traveller, in 1326 found them residing in their ancient towns and fortified places: they are, he says, the arrows of the Sultan, with which he reaches his enemies. And from the preface to a, collection of anecdotes regarding Raschid-addin, made by Abou Firas about the year 1324, we learn that the doctrines of the Assassins continued to be openly professed.

151. Modern Assassins - The sect is still in existence, both in Persia and Syria. The Persian Ishmaelites dwell chiefly in Roodbar, but they are to be met with all over the East, and even appear as traders on the banks of the Ganges. A. Drummond, British Consul at Aleppo, in his "Travels through Several Parts of Asia" (London, 1754, fol.), says (p. 217), "Some authors assert that these people [the Assassins] were entirely extirpated in the thirteenth century by the Tartars . . . but I, who have lived so long in this infernal place, will venture to affirm that some of their spawn still exists in the mountains that surround us; for nothing is so cruel, barbarous, and execrable that is not acted, and even gloried in, by these cursed Gourdins." Further, M. Rousseau, the French Consul at Aleppo, when travelling through Persia in 1810, found that the Assassins recognised as their chief an imam of the posterity of AH residing at Kehk, a small village between Ispahan and Teheran. His name was Shah Khaliloullah, and he was revered almost like a god and credited with the power of working miracles. Fraser, another traveller, says that the followers of Khaliloullah would, when he pared his nails, fight for the clippings; the water in which he washed became holy water. This chief was killed, during a temporary sojourn at Yezd, in a riot against the governor of the town, and he was succeeded by his son.

152. A Modern Assassin Chief - In 1866 a singular law case was

decided at Bombay. There is in that city a numerous community of traders called Khodjas. A Persian, Aga Khan Mehelati, i.e., a native of Mehelat, a place situate near Khek, had sent an agent to Bombay to claim from the Khodjas the annual tribute due from them to him, and amounting to about £10,000. The claim was resisted, and the British court was appealed to by Aga Khan. Sir Joseph Arnold investigated his claim. The Aga proved his pedigree, showing that he descended in a direct line from the fourth grandmaster of Alamut, and Sir Joseph declared it proved; and it was further demonstrated by the trial that the Khodjas were members of the ancient sect of the Assassins, to which sect they had been converted four hundred years before by an Ishmaelite missionary, who composed a work which has remained the sacred book of the Khodjas; it is written in a jargon which only the initiated can understand. In 1841-42, during the Afghan war, Aga Khan furnished to the British Government a contingent of light cavalry, raised at his own expense, for which he was awarded a pension, which, besides the £20,000 per annum he receives from the Khodjas, enables him to live in good style either at Bombay, or Puna, or Bangalore, where he indulges in his favourite pastime, hunting. When the Prince of Wales was in India he paid a visit to Aga Khan, whose ancestor, Raschid-addin Sinan, had spared the life of Richard Coeur-de-Lion.

153. Christian Princes in League with Assassins - Several Christian princes were suspected of conniving at the deeds of the Assassins. Richard of England is one of them; but we have seen (145) that he is free from the charge of having instigated the murder of that Conrad of Montferrat spoken of above. There also existed for a long time a rumour that Richard had attempted- the life of the king of France through Hassan and his Assassins. The nephew of Barbarossa, Frederick II., was excommunicated by Innocent II. for having caused the Duke of Bavaria to be slain by the Assassins; and Frederick II., in a letter to the king of Bohemia, accuses the Duke of Austria of having by similar agents attempted his life. Historians also mention an Arab who, in

1158, was discovered in the imperial camp at the siege of Milan, and on the point of stabbing the emperor. Who had armed that Assassin? It is not known. Mutual distrust existed amongst the rulers of Europe, and the power of Hassan and his successors increased in accordance with it.

III

THE ROSHENIAH

154. The Rosheniah Sect and its Founder - Another sect which grew out of that of the Ishmaelites was that of the Eosheniah. It was founded by Bayezid Ansari, the son of Abdullah, an Ulema of the tribe of Vurmud in Afghanistan. This Bayezid, though his father wished to bring him up to the priesthood, preferred traffic to learning, and took to the business of a travelling dealer in horses. Once, when staying on business in the district of Calinjir, he fell in with a malhed, which is a common epithet by which Moslem writers denominate the Ishmaelites. From him Bayezid imbibed a new religious creed, and began to profess and inculcate it on his return home. But neither his father nor his neighbours favouring it, he left his native country, and found for a while a refuge with Ahmed, Sultan of Ningashar in Afghanistan. But meeting with much opposition on the part of the people, he left Ningashar, and took up his residence among the Afghans of Gharihel, in the vicinity of Peshawur, where he had little difficulty in gaming proselytes,, whom he initiated into his doctrines. They were graduated into eight degrees of knowledge, each of which are termed zeker, and his disciples were in the same manner arranged into eight classes, which he denominated Khilwat. He composed for his followers formularies of instruction; to the Afghans he delivered his instructions in the Afghan, to the Hindoos in Hindi, and to the Persians in the Persian language; and such was the versatility of his genius, that even his enemies admit his writings to be composed in the most attractive style. When his disciples had reached the eighth mystic degree, he informed them that they had now attained perfection, and had nothing more to do with the ordinances or prohibitions of the law. He then collected his most trusty followers into a body, took up his residence in the steep mountains of Afghanistan, plundered merchants, levied contributions, and propagated his doctrines by force of arms. It was said that the female sex were his most ardent votaries, and he employed them to seduce the young men of the Afghan tribes. In the first stages of their initiation the young men and young women were classed separately, but as they advanced in illumination these restrictions were removed, and they were allowed to mix in promiscuous assemblies. As his power increased the expression of his doctrines became more bold; he totally denied the doctrine of a future state, and directed his most perfect disciples to follow their pleasures without reserve, and gratify their inclinations without scruple. He also inculcated on his followers an absolute right to dispose of the lives and properties of all who did not adhere to his sect. He eventually removed to the district of Hashtnagar, which the Afghans consider the region of their original settlement in Afghanistan, where he founded a city, and assumed the title of Pir Roshan, which may be translated the 'Father of Light,' whence his followers took the name of Rosheniah, or the Enlightened.

155. Death of Bayezid - The Moghul Government became alarmed at the spread of Bayezid's doctrines. Mahsan Khan Ghazi, an officer of great merit, who was then governor of Cabul, made a sudden irruption into the district of Hashtnagar, and having seized Bayezid, conducted him to Cabul, where he exhibited him as a spectacle to the populace, with his hair shaven on one side of the head, and left untouched on the other. But Bayezid is said to have bribed Mahsan Khan's religious instructor, whereby he regained his liberty. Bayezid then retreated with his followers to the almost inaccessible hill country of Tirah, where he set about retrieving his late disgrace, and prosecuted his plans with such vigour and policy, that his sect began to assume a national character, and his doctrines to be considered as the peculiar religion of the Afghans. Bayezid announced his design of conquering Khorasan and Hindustan, but on descending with that view into the plains of Ningashar, he was again met by Mahsan Khan Ghazi, who routed his irregular forces, and the leader himself with difficulty made his escape; but the fatigues he underwent and the distress he suffered within a few days put an end to his life.

156. Extinction of Sect - But his followers were numerous and enthusiastic; on his death his eldest son addressed them thus: " Come

on, my friends; your Pir is not dead, but has resigned his place to his son, Sheik Omar, and conferred on him and his followers the empire of the whole world." But Omar was soon after slain in a battle with the Yusefzei, the bravest and most powerful of all the Afghan tribes. Of his four brothers, Jalal-eddin, the youngest alone remained alive, and he also, after various changes of good and ill fortune, perished by the sword of a soldier of the Hazarah tribe. He was succeeded by Ahdad, his son; he perished by a musket-shot when besieged in his fortress of Meaghae by the Moghuls (about 1650). The Afghans, after his death, carried away Abdal Kader, his son, and betook themselves to the mountains. When the emperor's army entered the fortress, the daughter of Ahdad, who had found no opportunity of escape, was roaming about the walls, when one of the soldiers attempted to seize her. She threw her robe over her face, and flung herself down from the battlements and perished. The descendants of Ahdad continued to rule till about 1700, when Cerimdad was put to death by Said Khan of larakhan, after having surrendered up the government. His brother, Allah-da-Khani, was appointed a, command of four thousand in the Dakhin. He died about 1730.

IV

THE DRUSES

157. Origin of Sect of Druses - The Ishmaelites of Egypt and Syria may be found even to this day in some of the sects of Islam. Their primitive physiognomy reveals itself but faintly; but their profile is seen in the lineaments of some of the heretical families wandering in the wilderness or on Mount Lebanon; objects of inquietude to the Turkish Government, of wonder to travellers, and of study to science. Of these, the Druses, living in Northern Syria, and possessing about forty towns and villages, are perhaps the most remarkable. Their sect may be said to date its rise from the supposed incarnation of God in Hakem Biamr Allah, publicly announced at Cairo in 1020. This Hakem was the sixth caliph of Egypt; and Darazi, his confessor, took an active part in promoting the imposture, which, however, was at first so badly received that he was compelled to take refuge in the deserts of the Lebanon, where, receiving liberal pecuniary support from Hakem, he found hearers among the Arabs, and soon made converts. According to other accounts, Darazi was killed for preaching his doctrine, and thus became the first martyr to the new religion. A footing thus gained, corespondence was opened with Egypt, and Hamze, a Persian mystic and vizier of Hakem, who had from the first been a zealous supporterof Hakem's divinity, hastened to avail himself of the favourable opening. Ten years did not elapse before the two clever rogues or fiery fanatics had converted nearly all the Arab tribes inhabiting the Lebanon, while one portion of them were set apart and initiated into the mysteries of the doctrines of Hamze. But he did not give his name to the sect; by a natural etymology the disciples of Darazi, the first teacher, obtained the name of Druses, though they reject it, and call themselves Unitarians. We may thus look upon the Fatimite Caliph Hakem, the Persian Hamze, and the Turk Darazi as the founders of the Druse system, Hakem being its political founder, Hamze its intellectual framer, and Darazi its expositor and propagator.

158. Religious Books of the Druses - Hamze associated with himself four assistants, to whom, as well as to himself, he gave high-sounding names. He called himself, for instance: Universal Reason, the Centre, the Messiah of Nations, Jesus, the United, i.e., He who is ever united with the god Hakem. He had, moreover, 159 disciples, who went about preaching. The Druses call their religious books, "The Sittings of the Rulers and their Learned Men;" they are comprised in six volumes: the first has the title, " The Diploma;" the second, "The Refutation;" the third, "The Awakening;" the fourth, "The First of the Seven Parts;" the fifth, "The Staircase;" and the sixth, "The Reproaches." In 1817, the Druses obtained a seventh volume from a Christian, who alleged to have found it in an Egyptian school, and which they call "The Book of the Greeks."

159. Murder of Hakem - Hakem was one of the most cruel monsters on record, a Saracenic Nero. Amidst carnage and the most revolting persecutions he spread his doctrine. But in Egypt, where he resided, his heresy outraged the true believers, and his savagery the whole people. Sitt El Mulk, his own sister, headed the malcontents, and one evening when, according to his custom, he took his ride on a white ass, she caused him to be assassinated by some trusty followers, who, after having despatched him with their daggers, undressed him and securely concealed the naked body. They then carefully fastened up his clothes again, by order of his sister, who did not wish the belief in his divinity to be destroyed. At last, when the caliph did not return, and those sent to look for him returned with the news that they had found his clothes but not his body, it was said that Hakem had simply rendered himself invisible, to test the faith of his followers, and to punish apostates on his return. And the Druses, to explain the miracle, say that Hakem possessed a body of a more subtle substance than the usual human body, and could go forth out of his clothes without opening or tearing them. The dagger cuts in them are explained away as mysterious indications of certain purposes of their deity.

160. Hakem's Successor - Hakem left two sons, but the sect did not

acknowledge them as such. Ali Ess Ssahir, who succeeded his father as caliph, is reported to have said to Hamze, "Worship me, as you worshipped my father;" but Hamze* replied, "Our Lord, who be praised, neither begat nor was he begotten." Ali replied, "Then I and my brother are illegitimate?" Hamze answered, "You have said it, and borne testimony against yourself." Thereupon the enraged Ali ordered the wholesale murder of the Unitarians unless they returned to the true Moslem faith. Those who refused were either slain or fled to Syria to their co-religionists. Ali, to conciliate the people, who had by his father's despotism and oppression been greatly embittered against his dynasty, gave up all title to divine honours and the rights it implied.

161. Doctrines - The Druses believe in the transmigration of souls; but probably it is merely a figure, as it was to the Pythagoreans. Hakem is their prophet; and they have seven commandments, religious and moral. The first of these is veracity, by which is understood faith in the unitarian religion they profess, and the abhorrence of that lie which is called polytheism, incredulity, error. To a brother perfect truth and confidence are due; but it is allowable, nay, a duty, to be false towards men of another creed. The sect is divided into three degrees, Profanes, Aspirants, and Wise. A Druse who has entered the second, may return to the first degree, but incurs death if he reveal what he has learned. In their secret meetings they are supposed to worship a calf's head; but as their religious books are full of denunciations against idolatry, and as they also compare Judaism, Christianity, and Mahommedanism to a calf, it is more probable that this effigy represents the principle of falsehood and evil, Iblis, the rival and enemy of Hakem. The Druses have also been accused of licentious orgies; and! are said by Bespier in his "Remarks on Ricaut" [an English diplomatist (d. 1700)] to marry their own daughters; but according to the evidence of resident Christians, a young Druse, as soon as he is initiated, gives up all dissolute habits, and becomes, at least in appearance, quite another man, meriting, as in other initiations, the title of "new-born." The initiated are known by the appellation of Ockals, and form a kind of priesthood in the midst of the general population. According to their

traditions, the world was at the appearance of God in the form of Hakem, three thousand four hundred and thirty million years old, and they believe, like the Chiliasts of England and America, that the millennium is close at hand. The Wise often retire into hermitages, whereby they acquire great honour and influence. When discoursing with a Mahoinmedan, the Druses profess to be of the same creed; when talking with a Christian, they are Christians. They defend this deception by alleging that it is not lawful to reveal any dogma of their creed to a "Black," or unbeliever; and their secrecy with regard to their religion has led them to adopt signs and passwords, such as are in use among Freemasons and other secret societies. When in doubt whether a stranger with whom they conversed belonged to their sect, they would ask, "Do people in your part of the country sow balm-seed?" If the other replied, "Yes, it is sown in the hearts of the faithful," he probably was a co-religionist; but he might be an Aspirant only, and therefore they would question him further as to some of the secret dogmas; if he did not understand the drift of their question, they would know that he was not initiated into the higher grades. But their signs and test-words and phrases had frequently to be changed, their import having been discovered by the Blacks, which happened especially when the extensive hermit village of Bajjada, near Chasbaia, was destroyed in 1838 by the troops of Ibrahim Pasha, and the sacred books of the Druses were made publicly known.

162. Customs of the Druses - Every village has its meetinghouses, where religious and political affairs are discussed every Thursday night, the Wise, men and women, attending. The resolutions passed at such meetings are communicated to the district meetings, held in the chief village of every district, which again report to the general assembly in the town of Baklin on Mount Lebanon. This was the fortified seat of government until, in this century, Deir El-Kammar (the moon-monastery) was built as the Lebanon metropolis. At the general assembly the questions raised at the district meetings are discussed, and the deputies from the different villages who have attended, on their return home, announce the decisions arrived at; so that the Druses, in

fact, have a regular family council, to which, however, the Wise only are admitted, the uninitiated never being consulted in political or social matters. The civil government of the Druses is in the hands of the Sheiks, who again are subject to the Emir, or Prince of Lebanon. They are warlike and industrious, and two traits in their character deserve notice and commendation; they refuse to give up any man who has sought refuge amongst them, and detest the European tall hat, which they compare to a "cooking-pot," and laugh at. In the days when Burckhardt visited them, one of their maledictions was, "May God put a hat on you! " The number of Druses does not exceed fifty or sixty thousand, exclusively occupying in the Lebanon upwards of forty large towns and Tillages, and nearly two hundred and thirty villages with a mixed population of Druses and Christians, whilst in the Anti-Lebanon they are also possessed of nearly eighty exclusively Druse villages.

163. Druses and Maronites - The Druses were frequently at war with the Maronites, a neighbouring Christian sect, so called after Maro, its founder (circa 400 A.D.), originally fugitive Monothelites, who had settled on Mount Lebanon after the accession of Anastasius II. (496-8), who persecuted them as long as the Turkish Government favoured the Druses, in order to keep down the influence of the Maronites. The former, though the less warlike people, generally prevailed against the latter, but when the ruling Emir, Bence-Schihab, with his family, seceded from Mahommedanism and became Maronite Christians, the Maronites were for a time masters of the situation. In 1860, however, when the Maronites, for the promotion of Christianity, declared war against the Druses, Turkey again assisted the latter. True, the Porte afterwards changed sides, and supported the Maronites, partly because Europe insisted on the Christians being protected, and partly because it suited Turkish policy to so protect them; for the Maronites had by that time been so weakened, that Turkey considered the opportunity favourable to break the power of the Druses also. Since then the latter

are under a governor appointed by the Porte.[10]

164. The Ansaireeh or Nuseiriyeh - This is another Syrian sect, who worship a mystic Triad, consisting of Ali, Mohammad, and an early companion of the latter, Selman el Farsi, whence their mystical name, Ams, formed from the initial letters of the three names. This Triad is ultimately resolved into Light, or the Sky, the Sun, and the Moon, the first being illimitable, the second proceeding from the first, and the last proceeding from the other two. Their religion is largely made up of Christian, Jewish, and Mohammedan elements, but there cannot be a doubt that beneath them all are remnants of the old Sabaean faith. Some of their doctrines, which have become known, advocate the most licentious practices, especially between the priests and the female members of their congregations. They invoke the Deity under extraordinary appellations, such as " Prince of Bees," "Lion," "End of Ends." They are supposed to be the aborigines of Northern Syria, and to have remained in the mountain chain stretching from Mount Cassius to the Lebanon, while successive tides of conquest have swept along the valleys on either side. It is difficult to ascertain exactly the details of their religion, both because it is secret and ill-digested, and because few among them understand it, or have fixed points of agreement or disagreement. They number about two hundred thousand, and derive their name from a sectary called Nusa'iri. Burckhardt, in his " Travels in Syria and Palestine," gives some curious particulars concerning them, which will not bear transferring to these

---

[10] At the present time (July 1896) the Druses are in rebellion against the Turks.

V

THE DERVISHES

165. Dervishes. Also called Fakirs, and a monastic order of Islamism. Mahomet prohibited the introduction of monks into his religious system; but thirty years after the death of the Prophet, monks made their appearance, and it is supposed that there are now seventy-two orders of them. But twelve of them are undoubtedly older than Islamism.

The four chief orders are: 1. The Rifajeh, who carry black flags and wear black or dark-brown turbans. They practise jugglers' tricks, such as swallowing daggers, eating fire, charming serpents, &c. 2. The Kaderijeh, with white flags and turbans; they are chiefly fishermen. 3. The Saïd Bidani, whose founder is the greatest saint of the Egyptian Moslems, Said Achmed El Bidani. Their colours are red and white, and they are divided into several sects. They wear an absurd costume and act as buffoons. 4. The Said Ibrahim, with green flags, and turbans. All that is known of them is that they have a monastery at Alexandria.

166. Shiites and Sunnites - The Dervishes are, moreover, divided into two grand bodies, named as above, the former being Egyptian, the latter Turkish Dervishes. These latter are our great enemies in India. The pilgrims from that country propagate at Constantinople antagonism to our rule, and return to India strengthened with the sympathies of the Mussulman world. It is a remarkable circumstance, that though the Ulema are opposed to the Dervishes, they being looked upon as heterodox, men of great intellect, orthodox in their principles, and occupying high positions in the state, should enrol themselves in the order. The only explanation may be found in their study of the Persian Soofee poets, whose doctrine, which is that of the Dervishes, is that form of spiritualism which ends in Pantheism, teaching that God is, or may enter into, all things spiritual, and which approximates to that materialism of which Buddhism is the exponent.

167. Doctrines - The Dervishes have their "Paths," which are generally governed by twelve officers, the oldest "Court" superintending the others by right of seniority. The master of the Court is called Sheik, and he has his deputies, caliphs, or successors, of which there may be many. The order is divided into four "columns" or degrees. The first is that of "Humanity," which supposes "annihilation in the Sheik;" the second is that of the "Path," in which the "murid," or disciple, attains spiritual powers and self-annihilation into the "Peer," or founder of the Path. The third stage is called "Knowledge," and the murid is supposed to become inspired, which is called "annihilation into the Prophet." The fourth degree leads him even to God, when he becomes part of the Deity, and sees him in all things. After this, the Sheik confers on him the grade of "Caliph," or "Honorary Master," for, in their mythical language, " the man must die before the saint can be born, and when born, he is but a useless and despicable animal."

There is a widespread belief in the East that the Freemasons are in secret connection with the Dervishes; but the idea is foolish and unlikely. It was, however, always suspected that whenever mischief against our rule is astir among the Mussulman population, especially in India, the Dervishes are at the bottom of it. It is not quite certain to what order the Dervishes we have to fight in Africa belong, but it is clear that, unlike their brethren in Asia, they pursue political ends, and are instigated by fierce fanaticism; and as every Mohammedan can belong to a religious order without any outward indication of it, and as such connection is always kept secret, Great Britain does not really know the number of her enemies in Africa.

BOOK V

HERETICS

" The heretic foxes have various faces, but they all hang together by their tails."

POPE GEEGORY IX.

I

HERETICS

168. Transition from Ancient to Modern Initiations - An order of facts now claims our attention which in a certain manner signalises the transition from ancient to modern initiations. An extraordinary phenomenon in social conditions becomes apparent, so strikingly different from what we meet with in antiquity, as to present itself as a new starting-point. Hitherto we have seen the secret organising itself in the higher social classes, so as to deprive the multitude of truths, whose revelation could not have taken place without injury and danger to the hierarchy. At the base we find polytheism, superstition; at the summit, deism, rationalism, the most abstract philosophy.

169. Spirit of Ancient and Modern Secret Societies - The secret societies of antiquity were theological, and theology frequently inculcated superstition; but in the deepest recesses of the sanctuary there was a place, where it would laugh at itself and the deluded people, and draw to itself the intelligences that rebelled against the servitude of fear, by initiating them into the only creed worthy of a free man. To that theology, therefore, otherwise very learned and not cruel, and which promoted art and science, much may be forgiven, attributing perhaps not to base calculation, but to sincere conviction and thoughtful prudence, the dissimulation with which it concealed the treasures of truth and knowledge, that formed its power, glory, and, in a certain manner, its privilege.

In modern times the high religious and political spheres have no secrets, for they have no privilege of knowledge, nor initiations which confer on those higher in knowledge the right to sit on the seat of the mighty, and no one, without being guilty of an anachronism and preparing for himself bitter disappointments, can seek the truth where there is but a delusive show of it. Whoever persists in making any fictitious height the object of his ambition, removes his eyes from the horizon which, lit up by the dawn, casts light around his feet,, while his head is yet in darkness. Henceforth secret societies are popular and religious, not in the sense of the constituted and official church, but of a rebellious and sectarian church; and since at a period when the authority of the church is paramount, and religion circulates through all the veins of the state, no change can be effected without heresy, so this must necessarily be the first aspect of political and intellectual revolt. This heresy makes use of the denial and rejection of official dogmas, in order to overthrow the hated clerocracy, and to open for itself a road to civil freedom.

170. The Circumcellians - The Papacy was necessarily the first cradle of the new conspirators, who at an early date arose out of it. In the second century the Adamites became conspicuous. They asserted that by Christ's death they were as innocent as Adam before the Fall, and were accused of praying naked in their assemblies. We may incidentally mention that the sect was renewed in the fifteenth century by one Picard, a native of Flanders. But a more important sect which arose in the first century of Christianity was that of the Circumcellians, who were a branch of the Donatists, the followers of Donatus, the schismatic Bishop of Carthage (A.D. 311), who at that early age already preached against the corruptions of the Romish Church. By the violent persecution they experienced, some of the Bishop's adherents were turned into fanatics, and bands of them roamed about the country (hence their name, compounded of circum cellas), preaching reformation and redressing grievances, setting free slaves, and remitting debts, without consulting the parties most interested, and occasionally committing greater crimes. Some of these fanatics, in a mistaken zeal

for martyrdom, threw themselves down precipices, leaped into the fire, or cut their own throats. The sect existed some thirteen or fourteen years, when it was suppressed by the magistracy. A heretical sect, bearing the same name, existed also in the twelfth and thirteenth centuries in Germany, denying the authority of popes, bishops, and priests, and the legality of ecclesiastical interdicts.

171. The Albigenses - One of the most extensive and active heresies was that of the Albigenses, so called after their chief town, Albi, whence they spread all over Southern France. The sect was the offspring of Manichasism; it fructified in its turn the germs of the Templars and Rosicrucians, and of all those associations that continued the struggle and fought against ecclesiastical and civil oppression.

172. Objects of the Albigenses - It is to be noticed that the object of the Albigenses in so far differed from that of all posterior sects, that its blows were intended for Papal Home alone; and wholly Papal was the revenge taken through the civil arm, and with priestly rage. The Albigenses were the Ghibellines of France, and combined with all who were opposed to Rome, especially with Frederick II. and the Arragonese, in maintaining the rights of kings against the pretensions of the Papal See. Their doctrines had a special influence on the University of Bologna, wholly imperial; Dante was imperialistic, tainted with that doctrine, and therefore hated by the Guelphs.

173. Tenets of the Albigenses - Toulouse was the Rome of that church, which had its pastors, bishops, provincial and general councils, like the official church, and assembled under its banners the dissenters of a great portion of Europe, all meditating the ruin of Rome and the restoration of the kingdom of Jerusalem. The rising in Provence gathered strength from the circumstances in which it took place. The Crusaders had revived Eastern Manichaeism, placing Europe in immediate contact with sophisticated Greece, with Mahommedan and Pantheistic Asia. The East, moreover, contributed Aristotle and his

Arab commentators, to which must be added the subtleties of the cabala and the materialism of ideas. Philosophy, republicanism, and industry assailed the Holy See. Various isolated rebellions had revealed the general spirit, and wholesale slaughter had not repressed it; the rationalism of the Waldenses so called after Peter Waldo, the founder of the sect connected itself with the German mysticism of the Rhine and the Netherlands, where the operatives rose against the counts and the bishops. Every apostle that preached pure morality, the religion of the spirit, the restoration of the primitive church, found followers; the century of Louis IX., or the Saint (1226-70), is the century of unbelief in the Church of Rome, and the Impossibilia of Sigero foreshadowed those of Strauss.

174. Aims of the Albigenses - The heresy of the Albigenses made such progress along the shores of the Mediterranean, that several countries seemed to separate from Rome, while princes and emperors openly favoured it. Not satisfied with already considering impious Rome overthrown, the Albigenses suddenly turned towards the Crusaders, at first looked at with indifference, hoping to make Jerusalem the glorious and powerful rival of Rome, there to establish the seat of the Albigenses, to restore the love of religion in its first home, to found on earth the heavenly Jerusalem, of which Godfrey of Bouillon was proclaimed king. This was the man who had carried fire and sword into Rome, slain (15th October 1080) the anti-Caesar Rodolphe, " the king elected by priests," and thrust the Pope out of the holy city, deserving thereby, and by the hopes entertained of him, the infinite praises for his piety, purity, and chastity bestowed on him by the troubadours, who originally appeared in the first quarter of the twelfth century, in the allegorical compositions known by the name of the " Knight of the Swan." The project of making Jerusalem the rival of Rome assigned an important part to the Templars, who perhaps were aware of and sharers in it.

175. The Cathari - Italy, though watched by Rome, nay, because watched, supported the new doctrines. Milan was one of the most

active foci of the Cathari (the Pure); in 1166 that city was more heretical than Catholic. In 1150 there were Cathari at Florence, and the women especially were most energetic in the dissemination of the dogmas of the sect, which became so powerful as to effect in the city a revolution in favour of the Ghibellines. At Orvieto Catharism prevailed in 1125, and was persecuted in 1163; the persecution was most fierce at Verona, Ferrara, Modena, &c. In 1224 a great number of these sectaries met in Calabria and Naples, and even Rome was full of them. But Lombardy and Tuscany were always the chief seats of this revolt.

176. Doctrines and Tenets - But we have only scanty notices of this sect, because, unlike other heretical associations, it sought to conceal its operations. It bore great resemblance to Manichaeism and the dogmas of the Albigenses, like which latter, it concealed its doctrines not only from the world at large, but even from its proselytes of inferior degrees. They believed in the metempsychosis, assuming that to attain to the light, seven such transmigrations were required; but, as in other cases, this was probably an emblematic manner of speaking of the degrees of initiation. They attributed the origin of the visible and of the invisible world to different creators; the former was the creation of the evil spirit, wherefore they rejected the Old Testament account of the creation, as also the incarnation of Christ, purgatory, hell, &c. They had communistic tendencies, and were averse to marriage; philanthropists, above all they led industrious lives, combined saving habits with charity, founded schools and hospitals, crossed lands and seas to make proselytes, denied to magistrates the right of taking away life, did not disapprove of suicide, and preceded the Templars in the contempt of the cross. They could not understand how Christians could adore the instrument of the death of the Saviour, and said that the cross was the figure of the beast mentioned in the Apocalypse and an abomination in a holy place. They performed their ceremonies in woods, caverns, remote valleys; wherefore those belonging to this heresy and others deriving from it could well answer the question: Where did our ancient brethren meet before there were any lodges? In every place. They were accused of strangling or starving the dying, and

of burning children; charges also brought against the Mithraics, Christians, Gnostics, Jews, and quite recently against the Irish Roman Catholics. The accusation, as in the other cases, probably arose from some symbolical sacrifice, literally interpreted by their opponents. They had four sacraments, and the consolation consisted in the imposition of hands, or baptism of the Holy Spirit, which, bestowed only on adults, remitted sins, imparted the consoling spirit, and secured eternal salvation. During persecutions the ceremonies were shortened, and were held at night and secretly: the lighted tapers symbolised the baptism of fire. At the ceremony of initiation the priest read the first eighteen verses of the Gospel of St. John, a custom still practised in some Masonic degrees. In remembrance of his initiation the novice received a garment made of fine linen and wool, which he wore under his shirt; the women a girdle, which they also wore next to the skin just under the bosom.

177. Persecution of the Cathari - The following may suffice as an instance of the persecution to which the Cathari were subject in those religious days. Dolcino, the leader of a sect of the Cathari, who called themselves the "Apostolic," because they endeavoured to restore the Christianity of the Apostles, and who predicted the downfall of the then already most corrupt Papacy, was pursued by the Inquisition (1307). With 1400 of his followers, Dolcino took refuge on a hill in the district of Vercelli. But the Apostolic were taken; Dolcino and his wife Margaret were torn to pieces, limb by limb, by order of the holy fathers, and the pieces afterwards burnt by the public executioner. Against such of the followers of Dolcino as had not been seized with their leader, Clement V. ordered a crusade, granting plenary absolution to all who took part in it. Fifteen years after Dolcino's death thirty of his disciples were burnt alive on the marketplace at Padua.

178. The Waldenses or Vaudois - This sect arose in the twelfth century, and was so named after its founder, Peter Waldus, a rich citizen of Lyons. Its aims were, to a great extent, similar to those of the Albigenses. Persecuted by the Church, its members spread over a great

part of Europe. In the thirteenth century the Pope instituted a crusade against them, the details of which belong to general history. The principles of the Vaudois, however, remained unsubdued, and at the Eeformation their descendants were reckoned among the Protestants, though they differed, and continue to differ, from them in many doctrinal points, and they remain as a distinct sect in many parts of Europe. But it was only in 1848 that by the edict of the king of Sardinia they were granted religious liberty and equal civil and political rights with the Roman Catholic population of that kingdom. According to Rulman Merswin, who wrote between 1370-80 at Strasbourg, a community of Vaudois then lived hidden in the mountains of Switzerland, calling themselves by the name of "Friends of God." The Anabaptists, Lollards, Beghards, and Beguines all sprang from this sect.

179. Luciferians - Another sect which sprung from the Cathari was that of the Luciferians, which must not be confounded with that so named after Lucifer, Bishop of Cagliari, and which existed for a short time under Theodosius the Great. The Luciferians, or Devil-worshippers, to be spoken of here arose in the twelfth or thirteenth century; their chief seats were in the principality of East Friesland. The Frieslanders, having refused to pay tithes to the archbishops of Bremen, they were proclaimed heretics. Konrad von Marburg, infamous for hypocrisy and cruelty, took the part of the Church, and nothing shows the mental besottedness of the clergy of those days better than the report sent to the Pope, Gregory IX., and adopted by this latter as a true statement of facts, as is apparent from his Bull, published in 1233. According to Konrad's report, as reproduced in the Pope's Bull, the Luciferians, when initiating a candidate, first caused a frog or toad to appear to him, which he had to kiss, or to draw its tongue and saliva into his own mouth. This animal usually appeared in its natural size, sometimes as large as a goose, but more generally as large as a baker's oven!

Then a pale man, consisting of only skin and bone, appeared to the novice, who had to kiss him, after which the novice lost all recollection of the Catholic faith. A black tom-cat then descended through a statue, which was always found in the meeting-place of these heretics, and when they all had kissed the animal's hinder quarters, the lights were extinguished, and the most licentious practices indulged in. The candles having been re-lighted, a man appeared, more glorious than the sun in his upper parts, while the lower part of his body resembled that of a cat, who received a piece of cloth torn off the novice's clothes, as a pledge that henceforth the new initiate belonged to him. These heretics further said that God unjustly cast Lucifer into hell, but that eventually the devil would be restored to his former glory and happiness.

180. Origin of Demi-worship - Now it is certain that in the dark ages, when men were crushed under superstition and cruelty, when cleric and secular oppressors the former the worse of the two rendered life almost unbearable to the serf and the bondsman, these, seeing themselves forsaken by God and his saints, naturally appealed to the Devil for protection, and hence a kind of Devil-worship arose; wherefore we may accept the charge brought against the Luciferians of believing in the Devil's eventual restoration as true; nor is it a serious one: very pious people such, as the Everlasting Gospellers, held that belief. But the other charges are too absurd to require serious refutation.

We are told that the Luciferians had their signs of recognition, and used to accost one another thus: "Lucifer, who has been wronged, greets thee." To prevent an uninitiated to enter their assemblies, they would put the question, "Do thorns prick to-day?" the answer to which is not recorded, but of course was known to the initiated only. The places where they held their meetings were called "cellars of repentance." The charge of committing unnatural crimes brought against them was one brought by the Church against all heretics; but the Luciferians were not so accused till late in the thirteenth century, when the sect had ceased to exist, having been exterminated by the word and fire of Holy Mother Church.

There existed numerous other sects, named either after their founders or the localities in which they arose, such as the Messalians, the Bogomiles, supposed to be sprung from the latter, the Cainians, the Encrafites, and others; yet none of them were of such importance as those spoken of above. But whatever might be their determination, the members of all these sects in the course of several centuries supplied many victims to the torture-chambers and faggots of the Inquisition, the Church cunningly mixing up heresy with witchcraft. Thomas Stapleton, who during the reign of Queen Elizabeth emigrated to Holland, to escape the persecution of the Eoman Catholics in this country, wrote a book on the question why clergy and witchcraft spread simultaneously to such an extent, which two evils he called the twin-children of the Devil. The author died in 1598. Even after this date it was damnable heresy to deny the existence of witchcraft. In 1725 the principality of Hohenzollern Hechingen in Wlirtemburg by public decree promised five florins reward to any one bringing in, dead or alive, a goblin, nixy, or other spook of the kind!

181. Religion of the Troubadours - Troubadours and Albigenses drew closer together in persecution; their friendship increased in the school of sorrow. They sang and fought for one another, and their songs expired on the blazing piles; wherefore it appears reasonable to consider the troubadours as the organisers of that vast conspiracy directed against the Church of Rome, the champions of a revolt which had not for its guide and object material interests and vulgar ambition, but a religion and a polity of love. Here love is considered, not as an affection which all more or less experience and understand, but as an art, a science, acquired by means of the study and practice of sectarian rites and laws; and the artists under various names appear scattered throughout many parts of Europe. It is difficult, indeed, to determine the boundaries within which the Gay Science was diffused. The singers of love are met with as the troubadours of the Langue d'Oc and the Langue d'Oui, the minnesangers and minstrels.

182. Difficulty to understand the Troubadours - The singers of Provence whose language was by the Popes called the language of heresy are nearly unintelligible to us, and we know not how to justify

the praises bestowed upon their poetry by such men as Dante, Petrarch, Chaucer; nor dare we, since we do not understand their verses, call their inspiration madness, nor deny them the success they undoubtedly achieved. It appears more easy and natural to think that those free champions of a heresy who were not permitted clearly to express their ideas, preferred the obscure turns of poetry and light forms that concealed their thoughts, as the sumptuous and festive courts of love perhaps concealed the "Lodges" of the Albigenses from the eye of the Papal Inquisition. The same was done for political purposes at various periods. Thus we have Gringore's La Chasse du Cerf des Cerfs (a pun designating Pope Julius II., by allusion to the servus servorum) in which that Pope is held up to ridicule. But some of the troubadours, such, for instance, as Walther von der Vogelweide, d. 1228, and Peter Cardinal, d. 1306, sang openly against the abuses of the Church and the corrupt lives of the clergy.

183. Poetry of Troubadours - Arnaldo Daniello was obscure even for his contemporaries; according to the Monk of Montaudon, "no one understands his songs," and yet Dante and Petrarch praise him above every other Provencal poet, calling him the "great Master of Love," perhaps a title of sectarian dignity, and extolling his style, which they would not have done had they not been able to decipher his meaning. The effusions of the troubadours were always addressed to some lady, though they dared not reveal her name; what Hugo de Brunet says applies to all: "If I be asked to whom my songs are addressed, I keep it a secret. I pretend to such a one, but it is nothing of the kind." The mistress invoked, there can be no doubt, like Dante's Beatrice, was the purified religion of love, personified as the Virgin Sophia.

184. Degrees among Troubadours - There were four degrees, but the "Romance of the Rose" divides them into four and three, producing again the mystic number seven. This poem describes a castle, surrounded with a sevenfold wall, which is covered with emblematical figures, and no one was admitted into the castle that could not explain their mysterious meaning. The troubadours also had their secret signs

of recognition, and the "minstrels" are supposed to have been so called because they were the "ministers" of a secret worship.

185. Courts of Love - I have already alluded to these; they probably gave rise to the Lodges of Adoption, the Knights and Nymphs of the Rose, &c. The degrees pronounced therein with pedantic proceedings, literally interpreted, are frivolous or immoral, and therefore incompatible with the morals and manners of the Albigenses, which were on the whole pure and austere. The Courts of Love may therefore have concealed far sterner objects than the decision of questions of mere gallantry; and it is noticeable that these courts, as well as the race of troubadours, became extinct with the extinction of the Albigenses by the sword of De Montfort and the faggots of the Inquisition.

BOOK VI

CHIVALRY

"Chivalry was more a spirit than an institution ... the ceremonial was merely the public declaration that he on whom the order was conferred was worthy to exercise the powers with which it invested him; but still, the spirit was the chivalry."

JAMES'S History of Chivalry.

I

CHIVALRY

186. Original Aim - An idea of conservation and propagandism produced the association of the San Greiil, whose members professed to be in search of the vase of truth, which once contained the blood of the Redeemer; or, to leave metaphorical language, to bring back the Christian Church to apostolic times, to the true observance of the precepts of the gospel. At the Round Table, a perfect figure, which admitted neither of first nor of last, sat the Knights, who did not attain to that rank and distinction but after many severe trials. Their degrees at first were three, which were afterwards raised to seven, and finally, at the epoch of their presumed fusion with the Albigenses, Templars, and Ghibellines, to thirty-three. The chief grades, however, may be said to have been I. Page; 2. Squire; 3. Knight, and the three chief military orders of those days were the Templars, the Knights Hospitallers of St. John of Jerusalem, who afterwards were called the Knights of Rhodes, and lastly the Knights of Malta; and thirdly, the order of Teutonic Knights.

187. Knights the Military Apostles of the Religion of Love - This association was above all a proud family of apostles and missionaries of the Religion of Love, military troubadours, who, under the standards of justice and right, fought against the monstrous abuses of the

Theocratic regime, consoled the " widow " perhaps the Gnostic Church protected the "sons of the widow" the followers of Manes and overthrew giants and dragons, inquisitors and churchmen. The powerful voice of the furious Roland, which made breaches in the granite rocks of the mountains, is the voice of that so-called heresy which found its way into Spain, thus anticipating the saying of Louis XIV., "There are no longer any Pyrenees." This may seem a startling assertion, but it is nevertheless true. Of course I do not now speak of the chivalry of feudal times, but of that which existed even before the eleventh century, that issued from the womb of Manichseism and Catharism, and was altogether hostile to Rome. But even at that period the Papal Church acted on the principle afterwards so fully carried out by the Jesuits r of directing what they could not suppress; and having nothing more to fear than spiritualism, whether mystical, Platonic, or chivalric, Rome, instead of opposing its current, cunningly turned it into channels where, instead of being destructive to the Papacy, it became of infinite advantage to it.

188. Tenets and Doctrines. Those who composed the romances of the Round Table and the San Greal were well acquainted with the Gallic triads, the mysteries of the theological doctrines of the Bards and Celtic myths. These romances have their origin in the phenomena of the natural world, and the San Greal is only a diminutive Noah's Ark. From Chaucer's "Testament of Love," which seems founded on the " Consolation of Philosophy " by Boethius, it has been supposed that the love of chivalry was the love of woman, in its highest, noblest, and most spiritualised aspect. But the lady-love of the knight in the early period of chivalry was the Virgin Sophia, or philosophy personified. The phraseology employed in the rites of initiation, the religious vows taken on that occasion, the tonsure to which the knights submitted, with many other circumstances, sufficiently indicate that the love so constantly spoken of has no reference to earthly love. This applies especially to the knights who may be called Voluntary Knights, and whose charter is the curious book called " Las Siete Partidas," by Alfonso XL, king of Castile and Leon. Their statutes greatly resembled

those of the Templars and Hospitallers; they were more than any other a religious order; bound to very strict lives; their clothes were of three colours, and strange coincidence analogous with those with which Dante beheld Beatrice clothed, and the three circles he describes towards the end of "Paradise." They had two meals a day, and drank only water, a regimen scarcely fit for a militia whose duties were not always spiritual; for, besides their special duties, they were also subject to all the rules of chivalry, and bound to protect the weak against the strong, to restore peace where it had been disturbed, to serve their body (the Lodge), and protect the (evangelical) religion. They are said to have branded their right arms in sign of their fraternity; but this is perhaps only a figure of the baptism of fire and the Spirit, one of the most essential rites of the Religion of Love. A green glass vase, said to be the original San Greal, is preserved in the cathedral of Genoa, and considered so valuable that it requires a special permission from the municipality to see it. It was "by authority" said to be cut out of a gigantic emerald; but the ungodly French, who during the rule of the first Napoleon had carried it to Paris, chemically tested, and proved it, as stated above, to be only green glass.

II

THE TEMPLARS

189. Foundation of the Order - It was founded in 1118, partly on a more ancient order, as would appear from a MS. in the library of the Louvre, entitled Hostes sur les Freres Mages ecristes par un ContemporoAn des Chevaliers Templiers qui en estes. In the above year nine valiant and pious knights formed themselves into an association which united the characters of the monk and the knight. They selected for their patroness "La douce Mere de Dieu" and bound themselves to live according to the rules of St. Augustine, swearing to consecrate their swords, arms, strength, and lives to the defence of the mysteries of the Christian faith; to pay absolute obedience to the Grand Master; to encounter the dangers of the seas and of war, whenever commanded, and for the love of Christ; and even when opposed singly to three infidel foes not to retreat, They also took upon themselves the vows of chastity and poverty, promised not to go over to any other Order, nor to surrender any wall or foot of land. King Baldwin II. assigned them a portion of his palace, and, as it stood near the Church of the Temple, the abbot gave them a street leading from it to the palace, and hence they styled themselves "Soldiery of the Temple" (militia templi).

190. Progress of the Order - The first nine years which elapsed after the institution of the Order, the Templars lived in great poverty; Hugh des Payens and Godfrey of St. Omer, the founders, had but one war-horse between them, a fact commemorated on the seal of the Order, which represents two knights seated on one charger. Soon after, Pope Honorius confirmed the Order, and appointed a white mantle to which Eugenius III. affixed a red cross on the breast to be the distinguishing dress of the Templars. The Order also assumed a banner formed of cloth, striped white and black, called Beauseant[11] (in old French a

---

[11] Preserved in the Scotch dialect, with its original meaning, in the form fawsent or bawson.

piebald horse), which word became the battle-cry of the knights. The banner bore a cross and the inscription, " Non nobis, Domine, sed nomini tuo da gloriam" Thenceforth many knights joined the Order, and numerous powerful princes bestowed considerable possessions upon it. Alfonso, king of Arragon and Navarre, even appointed the Templars his heirs, though the country refused to ratify the bequest. Thus they became the richest proprietors in Europe, until they possessed about nine thousand commanderies, situated in various countries of Europe and in Palestine, with an annual rental of one hundred and twelve million francs.

191. Account of Commanderies - Their commanderies were situate in their eastern and western provinces, the former embracing Jerusalem, Tripoli, Antioch, Cyprus; the latter, Portugal, Castile and Leon, Arragon, France, including Flanders and the Netherlands, England, Scotland, Ireland, Germany, Italy, and Sicily. Whilst Jerusalem was in the hands of the Christians, the chief seat of the Templars was in that city; afterwards it was transferred to Paris, where they erected the large building until lately known as the Temple. It was in this building that Philip the Fair took refuge on the occasion of a riot which took place in 1306, where the Templars protected him until the fury of the people had calmed down. The Knights, it is said, incautiously displayed to the royal cupidity their immense treasures. On a subsequent, but far more momentous rising, the pile which served an ungrateful king for an asylum became the prison of an unfortunate successor. Recently this memento of royal perfidy, and of an avenging fate that struck the innocent, has been levelled to the ground.

192. Imputations against the Order - Towards the end of the twelfth century the Order counted about thirty thousand members, mostly French, and the Grand Master was generally chosen from among the French. Through the great number of their affiliated members they could raise a large army in any part of the Eastern world, and their fleet monopolised the commerce of the Levant. Hence they departed from their original humility and piety. Palestine was lost, and they made no

effort to recover it, but frequently drew the sword which was only to be used in the service of God, as they understood the phrase in the feuds and warfares of the countries they inhabited. They became proud and arrogant. When dying, Richard Cceur de Lion said, "I leave avarice to the Cistercian monks, luxuriousness to the begging friars, pride to the Templars; " and yet perhaps they only felt their own power. The English Templars had dared tosay to Henry III., "You shall be king as long as you arejust; " portentous words, which supplied matter for meditation to that Philip of France who, like many other princes, wished to be unjust with impunity. In Castile, the Templars, Hospitallers, and Knights of St. John combined against the king himself. Perhaps they aimed at universal dominion, or at the establishment of a Western sovereignty, like the Teutonic Knights of Prussia, the Hospitallers in Malta, or the Jesuits in Paraguay? But there is scarcely any ground for these imputations, especially the first, considering that the members of the Order were scattered all over the earth, and might at the utmost have attempted to seize the government of some individual State, as that of Arragon, for instance, but not to carry out a scheme for which even the forces of Charlemagne had been inadequate. Accusations better founded were, that they had disturbed the kingdom of Palestine by their rivalry with the Hospitallers; had concluded leagues with the infidels; had made war upon Cyprusand Antiochia; had dethroned the king of Jerusalem, Henry II.; had devastated Greece and Thrace; had refused to contribute to the ransom of St. Louis; had declared for Arragon against Anjou an unpardonable crime in the eyes of France with many other accusations. But their greatest crime was that of being exceedingly wealthy; their downfall was therefore determined upon.

193. Plots against the Order - Philip the Fair had spent his last sou. The victory of Mons, worse than a defeat, had ruined him. He was bound to restore Guyenne, and was on the point of losing Flanders. Normandy had risen against a tax which he had been obliged to withdraw. The people of the capital were so opposed to the government, that it had been found necessary to prohibit meetings of

more than five persons. How was money to be obtained under these circumstances? the Jews could give no more, because all they had had been extorted from them by fines, imprisonment, and torture. It was necessary to have recourse to some grand confiscation, without disgusting the classes on whom the royal power relied, and leading them to believe, not that booty was aimed at, but the punishment of evil-doers, to the greater glory of religion and the triumph of the law. At the instigation of Philip the Fair, libels were published against the Order of the Knights Templars, in which the most absurd charges were made against the members, accusing them of heresy, impiety, and worse crimes. Great weight was attached to the statements made against the Templars by two renegades of the Order, the Florentine Eoffi Dei, and the Prior of Montfaucon, which latter, having been condemned by the Grand Master to imprisonment for life for his many crimes, made his escape and became the accuser of his former brethren.

194. Attentions paid to Grand Master - Bertrand de Got, who, by the influence of the French king, had become Pope under the title of Clement V., was now urged by the former to fulfil the last of the five conditions on which the king had enabled him to ascend the chair of St. Peter. The first four conditions had been named, but Philip had reserved the naming of the fifth till the fit moment should arrive; and from his subsequent conduct there can be no doubt that the destruction of the Order of the Temple was the condition that was in the king's mind when he thus alluded to it. The first step was to get the Grand Master, James de Molay, into his power. At the request of the Pope that he would come to France to concert measures for the recovery of the Holy Land, he left Cyprus and came to Paris in 1307, accompanied by sixty knights, and bringing with him 150,000 florins of gold, and so much silver that it formed the lading of twelve horses, which he deposited in the Temple in that city. To lull him into false security, the king, whose plan was not yet quite ripe for execution, treated the Grand Master with the greatest consideration, made him the godfather of one of his sons, and chose him with some of the most distinguished persons to carry the pall at the funeral of his sister-in-

law. The following day he was arrested with all his suite, and letters having in the meantime been sent to the king's officers in the provinces on the 13th October 1307 to seize upon all the Templars, their houses and property, throughout the kingdom, many thousand members of the Order, knights and serving brothers, were thus made prisoners.

195. Charges against the Templars - The Templars were accused of denying Christ, the Virgin, and the Saints, and of spitting and trampling on the cross; of worshipping in a dark cave an idol in the figure of a man covered with an old human skin, and having two bright and lustrous carbuncles for eyes; of anointing it with the fat of young children roasted; of looking upon it as their sovereign God; of worshipping the devil in the form of a cat; of burning the bodies of dead Templars and giving the ashes to the younger brethren to eat and drink mingled with their food. They were charged with various unnatural crimes, frightful debaucheries, and superstitious abominations, such as only madmen could have been guilty of, and as could only be thought of in an age of frightful ignorance, stupidity, and superstition. To make them confess these crimes they were put to the torture, not only in France, but also in England, for Edward II. leagued with Philip to destroy the Order. Many knights in the agonies of the torture confessed to the crimes they were charged with, hundreds expired under it without making any confession, many starved or killed themselves in other ways in prison. The trial was protracted for years; the persecution extended to other countries; in Germany and Spain and Cyprus the Order was acquitted of all guilt; in Italy, England, and France, however, their doom was sealed, though for a moment there seemed a chance of their escaping, for the Pope, seeing that Philip and Edward had seized all the money and estates of the Templars, and seemed inclined to deprive him of his share of the spoil, began to side with the Order. But on some concessions being made to him by the two kings, he again supported them, though in the end we find him complaining of the small share of the booty that came into his hands.

196. Burning of Knights - The tedious progress of the sham trial was

occasionally enlivened by the public execution of knights who refused to acknowledge crimes of which they were not guilty. Fifty-nine gallant knights were led forth in one day to the fields at the back of the nunnery of St. Antoine, where stakes had been driven into the ground, and faggots and charcoal collected. The knights were offered pardon if they would confess; but they all refused and were burned by slow fires that is, clear charcoal fires. At Senlis nine were burned, and many more in other places. On all these occasions, as well as in the awful scenes of the torturechamber, the Dominican friars were the mocking witnesses.

197. James de Molay - The Grand Master remained in prison five years and a half, and there is no doubt that he was repeatedly put to the torture. The confession he was said to have made was probably a forgery. Finally, on the 18th March 1313, he and Guy, the Grand Preceptor of the Order, were burnt by a slow fire on a small island in the Seine, between the royal gardens and the church of the Hermit Brethren, where afterwards the statue of Henry IY. was erected, both to the last moment asserting the innocence of the Order.

198. Mysteries of the Knights Templars - Without laying too much stress on confessions extorted by violence, or denunciations proceeding from revenge, cupidity, and servility, it is manifest that the Templars, in their ordinances, creed, and rites, had something which was peculiar and secret, and totally different from the statutes, opinions, and ceremonies of other religio-military associations. Their long sojourn in the East, in that dangerous Palestine which overflowed with schismatic Greeks and heretics, who, driven from Constantinople, took refuge with the Arabs; their rivalry with the Hospitallers; their contact with the Saracen element; finally, the loss of the Holy Land, which injured them in the opinion of the world, and rendered their lives idle all these and many other circumstances would act on this institution in an unforeseen manner, differing from the tendencies of the original constitution, and mix up therewith ideas and practices little in accordance with, nay, in total antagonism to, the orthodox thought that had originated, animated, and strengthened this military

brotherhood.

199. The Temple and the Church - The very name may in a certain manner point to a rebellious ambition. Temple is a more august, a vaster and more comprehensive denomination than that of Church. The Temple is above the Church; this latter has a date of its foundation, a local habitation; the former has always existed. Churches fall; the Temple remains as a symbol of the parentage of religions and the perpetuity of their spirit. The Templars might thus consider themselves as the priests of that religion, not transitory, but permanent; and the aspirants could believe that the Order constituting them the defenders of the Temple intended to initiate them into a second and better Christianity, into a purer religion. Whilst the Temple meant for the Christian the Holy Sepulchre, it recalled to the Mussulman the Temple of Solomon; and the legend which referred to this latter served as a bond to the rituals of the Freemasons and other secret societies. Further, the Church might be called the house of Christ; but the Temple was the house of the Holy Spirit. It was that religion of the Spirit which the Templars inherited from the Manichseans, from the Albigenses, from the sectarian chivalry that had preceded them. The initiatory practices, the monuments, even the trial, showed this prevalence of the religion of the Spirit in the secret doctrines of the Temple. The Templars drew a great portion of their sectarian and heterodox tendencies from that period in which chivalry, purified and organised, became a pilgrimage in search of the San Greal, the mystic cup that received the blood of the Saviour; from that epoch in which the East, in invasions, armed and unarmed, with the science of the Arabs, with poetry and heresies, had turned upon the West.

200. Initiation - Much has been said about the mode of initiation that it took place at night in the chapel, in the presence of the chapter, all strangers being strictly excluded; that licentious rites attended it, and that the candidate was compelled to deny, curse, and spit upon the cross that cross for which they had shed so much of their own blood, sacrificed so many of their own lives. We have seen that this was one

of the chief accusations brought against the Order. Was there any truth in it? It seems most probable there was; but the practice may be explained as in the following paragraph.

201. Cursing and Spitting on the Cross Explained - Such a practice need not surprise us in an age in which churches were turned into theatres, in which sacred things were profaned by grotesque representations, in which the ancient mysteries were reproduced to do honour, in their way, to Christ and the saints. The reader may also bear in mind the extraordinary scenes afterwards represented in the Miracle Plays. Now the aspirant to the Templar degree was at first introduced as a sinner, a bad Christian, a renegade. He denied, in fact, after the manner of St. Peter, and the renunciation was frequently expressed by the odious act of spitting on the cross. The fraternity undertook to restore this renegade, to raise him all the higher the greater his fall had been. Thus at the Festival of the Idiots, the candidate presented himself, as it were, in a state of imbecility and of degradation, to be regenerated by the Church. These comedies, rightly understood at first, were in course of time falsely interpreted, scandalising the faithful, who had lost the key of the enigma. The Templars had adopted similar ceremonies. They were scions of the Cathari (175) and Manichaeans. Now the Cathari despised the cross (176), and considered it meritorious to tread it under foot. But with the Templars this ceremony was symbolical, as was abundantly proved during their trial, and had indeed reference to Peter's thrice-repeated denial of Christ.

202. Charge of Licentious Practices - As to licentious rites, if any such ever were practised, they were confined to certain localities and certain degrees of initiation; for it appeared at the trials that many knights had never even heard of the practices they were charged with; that they had never seen the bust of the Baphomet; that they had never been invited or asked to take part in licentious or blasphemous rites. If certain members of the Order were cognisant of, and participated in such, their offences were individual offences, and not crimes which the Order and its teaching could be reproached with. Unnatural crimes, however, were so common in the days of the Templars that they might safely be

charged with them, without at once raising a cry of indignation, and a sense of incredulity at the mere accusation itself; for in the age of the Templars it was customary on the election of a bishop to insist on the candidate swearing that he was not guilty of sodomy, seducing nuns, or bestiality! Had these vices not been very common, every honest man would at once have exclaimed, Nolo episcopari! All the charges brought against the Templars had been previously made against the Cathari, the Albigenses, and against the Hospitallers; and Clement, in a bull dated but four days after that of the suppression, acknowledged that the whole of the evidence against the Order amounted only to suspicion.

203. The Templars the Opponents of the Pope - But there may have been another and special reason for introducing this ceremony, and ever keeping the treachery of Peter before the minds of the members of the Order. We have seen that the Templars, during and in consequence of their sojourn in the East, attached themselves to the doctrines of the Gnostics and Manichaeans as is sufficiently attested, were other proofs wanting, by the Gnostic and Cabalistic symbols discovered in and on the tombs of Knights Templars, which appeared to them less perverted than those of the priest of Rome. They also knew the bad success the proclamation of Christ's death on the cross had had at Athens, in consequence of Eschylus' tragedy, "Prometheus Vinctus," wherein Oceanus denied his friend, when God made him the sacrifice for the sins of mankind, just as Peter, who lived by the ocean, did with regard to Christ. The Templars, therefore, came to the conclusion that all these gods, descended from the same origin, were only religious and poetic figures of the sun; and seeing the bad use made of the doctrines connected therewith by the clergy, they renounced St. Peter, and became Johannites, or followers of St. John. There was thus a secret schism, and according to some writers, it was this, together with the opposition to Roman Catholicism which it implied, as well as their great wealth, which was among the causes of their condemnation by the court of Rome.

204. Baphomet - The above explanation may also afford a clue to the meaning and name of the idol the Templars were accused of worshipping. This idol represented a man with a long white beard, and the name given to it was Baphomet, a name which has exercised the ingenuity of many critics, but the only conclusions arrived at by any of them as to the meaning of the name, and deserving consideration, is that of Nicolai, who assumed that it is composed of the words βαφή μήτις, the "baptism of wisdom," and that the image represented God, the universal Father. As to the meaning of the head itself, we have already referred to the Gnostic and Cabalistic doctrines and symbols adopted by the Templars (198), and the head worshipped by them certainly was one of these symbols. We know that the Cabalists represented God in abstracto by a head without a beard, whilst the creative God was represented by a bearded head. The former symbolised unchangeableness, the latter the constant growth seen in the world. To the Templars the bust was the One God; when it was shown to the initiated, the hierophant pronounced the Arabic word yalla (corrupted from yh alia), the "Light of God," and the new member was addressed as a "friend of God." But a denial of the Trinity in those days involved racks and faggots; hence it became sufficiently plain why the secret was looked upon as inviolable, and was so well kept by the Templars that we can only conjecture its import.

205. Disposal of the Possessions of the Templars - The Order having been suppressed by a Papal bull, dated 6th May 1312, the king and the Pope converted to their own use the movable property of the Order under their respective jurisdictions, the king keeping, as we have seen, the lion's share. Its other possessions in France and Italy were, sorely against the will of the king, assigned to the Order of the Hospitallers, who were, however, obliged to pay such large fines to the king and Pope as completely impoverished them for the time. A portion of their German estates was assigned to the Teutonic Knights; the Spanish possessions of the Templars, consisting of seventeen towns and castles, were secured by the king for the foundation of the Order of Our Lady

of Montesa, whose object was as barbarous as any Christian Pope or king could devise, namely, to combat the Moors; and the king of Portugal, who did not violently suppress the Order, made it change its name to that of the Order of Christ, which exists to this day, and, since 1789, consists of three classes: Grand-Cross, Commander, and Knight.

BOOK VII

JUDICIARY

" All through the Middle Ages justice was no such secret to the people as it is at the present time, when it is buried under piles of law papers."
                                                            WIGAND.

I

THE HOLY VEHM

206. Origin and Object of Institution. In this book we are introduced to an order of secret societies altogether different from preceding ones. Hitherto they were religious or military in their leading features; but those we are now about to give an account of were judicial in their operations, and the first of them, the Holy Vehm, or secret tribunals of Westphalia, arose during the period of violence and anarchy that distracted the German empire after the outlawry of Henry the Lion, somewhere about the middle of the thirteenth century. The supreme authority of the Emperor had lost all influence in the country; the imperial assizes were no longer held; might and violence took the place of right and justice; the feudal lords tyrannised over the people; whosoever dared, could. To seize the guilty, whoever they might be, to punish them before they were aware of the blow with which they were threatened, and thus to secure the chastisement of crime such was the object of the Westphalian judges, and thus the existence of this secret society, the instrument of public vengeance, is amply justified, and the popular respect it enjoyed, and on which alone rested its authority, explained.

207. Places for Holding Courts - Romance writers have surrounded the Vehm with darkness, mystery, and awe, but sober history shows the institution to have been, before the date of its corruption, the fairest, and perhaps the only fair tribunal in the country where it existed, and

that its only secrecy consisted in the justice and rapidity with which it discovered crime and executed its sentences. As to its meetings, they were not usually held in subterranean vaults or dimly lighted caves, but more frequently in the open air; at Nordkirchen the court was held in the churchyard; at Dortmund in the market-place. The favourite place for holding the courts was near or under trees; nor were they held at night, bat in the morning, soon after the break of day.

208. Officers and Organisations - The Westphalia of that period comprehended the country between the Rhine and the Weser; its southern boundary was formed by the mountains of Hesse, its northern by Friesland. Vehm or Felim is, according to Leibnitz, derived fromama, as the law founded on common fame. But fern is an old German word, signifying condemnation, which may be the proper radix of Vehm. But the old German word Fehm also meant "company," "society," "separation," "something set apart;" thus pigs put apart for the purpose of fattening were called fehm-pigs (Fehmschweine); the mark that was set on them to distinguish them was called the fehm-sign (FeJimmahl). The word Vehm having this general meaning, we may understand how the society of Free Judges, to distinguish it above other associations, acquired the epithet of "holy." The courts were also called Fehmding, Freistuhle, "free courts," heimliche Gerichte, Jieimliclie Achten, heimliche beschlossene Achten, "secret courts," "free bann," and verbotene Gerichte, "prohibited courts." No rank of life prohibited a person from the right of being initiated, and in a Vehmic code discovered at Dortmund, and whose reading was forbidden to the profane under pain of death, three degrees are mentioned: the affiliated of the first were called Stuhlherren,. "lords justices;" those of the second, Schoppen (scdbini, e'chevins); those of the third, Frohnboten, "messengers." Two courts were held, an offenbares Ding, "open court," and the heimliche Acht, "secret court." Any uninitiated person found in the "secret court" was invariaby hanged lest he might warn the accused, condemned in contumaciam, of the sentence passed upon him. The members were called Wissende, "the knowing ones," or the initiated. The clergy,

women and children, Jews and heathens, and as it would appear the higher nobility, were exempt from its jurisdiction. The courts took cognisance of all offences against the Christian faith, the Gospel, and the Ten Commandments.

209. Language and Rules of Initiated - The initiated had a secret language; at least we may infer so from the initials S. S. S. G. G., found in Vehmic writings preserved in the archives of Herfort, in Westphalia, that have puzzled the learned, and by some are explained as meaning Stock, Stein, Stride, Gras, Grein stick, stone, cord, grass, woe. At meals the members are said to have recognised each other by turning the points of their knives towards the edge, and the points of their forks towards the centre, of the table. A horrible death was prepared for a false brother, and the oaths to be taken were as fearful as some prescribed in the higher degrees of Freemasonry. The affiliated promised, among other things, to preserve the secret Vehm before anything that is illumined by the sun or bathed by rain, or to be found between heaven and earth; not to inform any one of the sentence passed against him; and to denounce, if necessary, his parents and relations, calling down upon himself, in case of perjury, the malediction of all, and the punishment of being hanged seven feet higher than all others. One form of oath, contained in the archives of Dortmund, and which the candidate had to pronounce kneeling, his head uncovered, and holding the fore-finger and the middle finger of his right hand upon the sword of the president, runs thus: "I swear perpetual devotion to the secret tribunal; to defend it against myself, against water, sun, moon, and stars, the leaves of the trees, all living beings; to uphold its judgments and promote their execution. I promise, moreover, that neither pain, nor money, nor parents, nor anything created by God shall render me perjured."

210. Procedure - The first act of the procedure of the Vehm was the accusation, made by a Freischoppe. The person was then cited to appear; if not initiated, before the open court, and woe to the disobedient! The accused that belonged to the Order was at once

condemned; and the case of the unaffiliated was transferred to the secret tribunal. A summons was to be written on parchment, and sealed with at least seven seals; six weeks and three days were allowed for the first, six weeks for the second, and six weeks and three days for the third. When the residence of the accused was not known, the summons was exhibited at a cross-road of his supposed county, or placed at the foot of the statue of some saint or affixed to the poor-box, not far from some crucifix or humble wayside chapel. If the accused was a knight, dwelling in his fortified castle, the Schoppen were to introduce themselves at night, under any pretence, into the most secret chamber of the building and do their errand. But sometimes it was considered sufficient to affix the summons, and the coin that always accompanied it, to the gate, to inform the sentinel of the fact that the citation had been left, and to cut three chips from the gate, to be taken to the Freigraf as proofs. If the accused appeared to none of the summonses, he was sentenced in contumacia, according to the laws laid down in the "Mirror of Saxony;" the accuser had to bring forward seven witnesses, not to the fact charged against the absent person, but to testify to the wellkiiown veracity of the accuser, whereupon the charge was considered as proved, and the Imperial ban was pronounced against the accused, which was followed by speedy execution. The sentence was one of outlawry, degradation, and death; the neck of the convict was condemned to the halter, and his body to the birds and wild beasts; his goods and estates were declared forfeited, his wife a widow, and his children orphans. He was declared fehmbar, i.e., punishable by the Vehm, and any three initiated that met with him were at liberty, nay, enjoined, to hang him on the nearest tree. If the accused appeared before the court, which was presided over by a count, who had on the table before him a naked sword and a withy halter, he, as well as his accuser, could each bring thirty friends as witnesses, and be represented by their attorneys, and also had the right of appeal to the general chapter of the secret closed tribunal of the Imperial chamber, generally held at Dortmund. When sentence was once definitively spoken for death, the culprit was hanged immediately.

211. Execution of Sentences - Those condemned in their absence, and who were pursued by at least a hundred thousand persons, were generally unaware of the fact. Every information thereof conveyed to them was high treason, punishable by death; the Emperor alone was excepted from the law of secrecy; merely to hint that "good bread might be eaten elsewhere," rendered the speaker liable to death for betraying the secret. After the condemnation of the accused a document bearing the seal of the count was given to the accuser, to be used by him when claiming the assistance of other members to carry out the sentence; and all the initiated were bound to grant him theirs, were it even against their own parents. A knife was stuck in the tree on which the person had been hanged, to indicate that he had suffered death at the hands of the Holy Vehm. If the victim resisted, he was slain with daggers; but the slayer left his weapon in the wound to convey the same information.

212. Decay of the Institution - These secret tribunals inspired such terror that the citation by a Westphalian free count was even more dreaded than that of the Emperor. In 1470 three free counts summoned the Emperor himself to appear before them, threatening him with the usual course in case of contumacy; the Emperor did not appear, but pocketed the affront. By the admission of improper persons, and the abuse of the right of citation, the institution which in its time had been a corrective of public injustice gradually degenerated. The tribunals were, indeed, reformed by Rupert; and the Arensberg reformation and Osnaburgh regulations modified some of the greatest abuses, and restricted the power of the Vehm. Still it continued to exist, and was never formally abolished. But the excellent civil institutions of Maximilian and of Charles V., the consequent decrease of the turbulent and anarchic spirit, the introduction of the Roman law, the spread of the Protestant religion, conspired to give men an aversion for what appeared now to be a barbarous jurisdiction. Some of the courts were abolished, exemptions and privileges against them multiplied, and they were prohibited all summary proceedings. The last Vehm court was held at Celle in 1568. But a shadow of them remained, and it was

not till French legislation, in 1811, abolished the last free court at Gemen, in the county of Münster, that they may be said to have ceased to exist. But it is not many years since that certain citizens in that locality assembled every year, boasting of their descent from the ancient free judges.

213. Kissing the Virgin - There is a tradition that one of the methods of putting to death persons condemned to that fate by the secret tribunals was the following: The victim was told to go and kiss the statue of the Virgin which stood in a subterranean vault. The statue was of bronze and of gigantic size. On approaching it, so as to touch it, its front opened with folding doors, and displayed its interior set full with sharp and long spikes and pointed blades. The doors were similarly armed, and on each, about the height of a man's head, was a spike longer than the rest, the two spikes being intended when the doors were shut to enter the eyes and destroy them. The doors having thus opened, the victim by a secret mechanism was drawn or pushed into the dreadful statue, and the doors closed upon him. There he was cut and hacked by the knives and spikes, and in about half a minute the floor on which he stood which was in reality a trap-door opened, and allowed him to fall through. But more horrible torture awaited him; for underneath the trap-door were six large wooden cylinders, disposed in pairs one below the other. There were thus three pairs. The cylinders were furnished all round with sharp blades; the distance between the uppermost pair of parallel cylinders was such that a human body could just lie between them; the middle pair was closer together, and the lowest very close. Beneath this horrible apparatus was an opening in which could be heard the rushing of water. The mechanism that opened the doors of the statue also set in motion the cylinders, which turned towards the inside. Hence when the victim, already fearfully mangled and blinded, fell through the trap-door, he fell between the upper pair of cylinders. In this mutilated condition, the quivering mass fell between the second and more closely approaching pair of cylinders, and was now actually hacked through and through on the lowest and closest pair, where it was reduced to small pieces which fell into the

brook below, and were carried away, thus leaving no trace of the awful deed that had been accomplished.

II

THE BEATI PAOLI

214. Character of the Society - The notices of this sect, which existed for many years in Sicily, are so scanty that we may form a high idea of the mystery in which it shrouded itself. It had spread not only over the island, where it created traditional terror, but also over Calabria, where it was first discovered, and cruelly repressed and punished by the feudatories, who saw their power assailed by it. A popular institution, in opposition to the daily arrogance of baronial or kingly power, it knew not how to restrain itself within the prescribed limits, and made itself guilty of reprehensible acts, so that it was spoken of in various ways by its contemporaries.

215. Tendencies and Tenets - We have already seen that it had connections with the Holy Vehm, and its statutes were somewhat similar to this tribunal; but it is to be observed that it proceeded from that spiritual movement which produced the reaction of the Albigenses, the propaganda of the Franciscans, and the reformatory asceticism of the many heretics who roamed through Italy and the rest of Europe, preaching opposition to Kome, and organising a crusade against the fatuous and corrupt clerocracy. Among these heretics we must remember the Abbot Gioachimo, whose prophecies and strange sayings reappear in the Evangelium Sternum of John of Parma, a book which was one of the text-books of the Sicilian judges. The Evangelium Sternum, a tissue of cabalistic and Gnostic eccentricities, was by the Beati Paoli preferred to the Old and New Testaments; they renounced belief in dualism, and made God the creator of evil and death of evil, because he placed the mystical apple in tbe mystical garden; of death, because he ordained the deluge, and destroyed Sodom and Gomorrah.

216. Account of a Sicilian Writer - Amidst the general silence of historians, the account of a Sicilian writer, which was published only in 1840, and is still generally unknown, may be considered the only

document concerning this family of Avengers, who at the extreme end of Italy reproduced the struggles and terrors of the Westphalian tribunals. This writer says: "In the year 1185, at the nuptials of the Princess Constance, daughter of the first King Roger of Sicily, with Henry, afterwards Henry VI., Emperor of Germany, there was discovered the existence of a new and impious sect, who called themselves the Avengers, and in their nocturnal assemblies declared every crime lawful committed on pretence of promoting the public good. Of this we find an account in an ancient writer, who does not enter into further details. The king ordered strict inquiry to be made, and their chief, Arinulfo di Ponte Corvo, having been arrested, he was sentenced to be hanged with some of his most guilty accomplices; the less guilty were branded with a red-hot iron. The belief exists among the vulgar that this secret society of Avengers still exists in Sicily and elsewhere, and is known by the name of the Beati Paoli. Some worthless persons even go so far as to commend the impious institution. Its members abounded especially at Palermo, and Joseph Amatore, who was hanged on December 17, 1704, was one of them. Girolarno Ammirata, comptroller of accounts, also belonged to this society, and suffered death on 27th April 1725. Most came to a bad end, if not by the hands of justice, by the daggers of their associates. The famous vetturino, Vito Vituzzo of Palermo, was the last of the wretches forming the society of the Beati Paoli. He escaped the gallows, because he turned in time from his evil courses, and thenceforward he passed all day in St. Matthew's Church, whence he came to be known by the surname of 'the church mouse.' The preceptors and masters of these vile men were heretics and apostates from the Minor Brethren of St. Francis, who pretended that the power of the pontiff and the priesthood had been bestowed on them by an angelic revelation. The house where they held their meetings is still in existence in the street de' Canceddi, and I paid it a visit. Through a gateway you pass into a courtyard, under which is the vault where the members met, and which receives its light through a grating in the stone pavement. At the bottom of the stairs is a stone altar, and at the side a small dark chamber, with a stone table, on which were written the acts and sentences of these murderous judges. The principal cave is pretty large, surrounded with stone seats, and furnished with niches and recesses where the arms were kept. The meetings were held at night by candle light. The derivation of the name, the Beati Paoli (Blessed Pauls), is unknown; but I surmise that it was adopted by the sect, because either the founder's name was Paul, or that he assumed it as that of a saint who, before his conversion, was a man of the sword, and, imitating him, was, during the day, a Blessed Paul, and at night at the head of a band of assassins, like Paul persecuting the Christians." Such is the author's account, which I have greatly abbreviated, omitting nearly all his invectives against the sect, of which very little is known, and whose existence evidently, in its day, was to some extent beneficial; for Sicilians, on suffering any injury or loss, for which they cannot apply to justice, are often heard to exclaim "Ah, if the Beati Paoli were still in being! "

III

THE INQUISITION

217. Introductory - The earth in the Colosseum at Rome is said to be soaked with the blood of Christian martyrs. Some pope I forget which to convince a heretic, is reported to have taken up a handful of the earth, squeezed it, and caused drops of blood to fall from it. Supposing, for argument's sake, the legend and the assertion on which it is founded to be true, the Christian Church has well avenged her martyrs. To accomplish her ends, the Romish Church established the Inquisition.

218. Early existence of an Inquisition - From the earliest days of Christianity the Inquisition existed in the spirit, if not in the form. The wretched pack of controversial wolves, the so-called Fathers of the Church, when not flying at one another's throats, were ever busy in spewing forth their fanatical venom upon all not of their ilk. When Polycarp, on being challenged by Marcion, the Gnostic, to "own him," replied, "I own thee to be the first-born of Satan," we may be certain he would, had he possessed secular power, not have been satisfied with giving that polite answer, but would gladly have burnt him alive; and yet the Gnostics were people superior in intelligence and morals to the rabble composing the early Christians, as even their enemies had to admit. When that monster Constantine had made the Christian Church all-powerful, heretic baiting began in full earnest. One of the first victims was Priscillian, the founder of a Gnostic sect in Spain, who, at the instigation of St. Augustine, was accused of Manichaeism the saint must have known, for he had been a Manichasan himself during ten years! Priscillian was executed at Trier in 385. The next five or six centuries were too much occupied with war and bloodshed and political intrigues to give much attention to heretics; in fact, from the eighth to the eleventh centuries they hardly existed. But when, towards the end of the latter century, the papal system of Hildebrand attained its full development, despotically attempting to control all religious thought, socalled heretics arose, and with them their persecution. The decision of Pope Urban II. that the murder of an excommunicated person was no crime became civil law, as also the doctrine of St. Augustine, that the extermination of heretics was a duty to the Church and a kindness to the heretic himself. Thomas of Aquinas (1224-1274) adopted the doctrine of St. Augustine; the "angelic" teacher expounded the words of the apostle, that we ought to avoid a heretic twice admonished, by saying that the best way to avoid him was to burn him. On this principle acted Henry II., king of England, who, together with Louis VII. of France, acted as the grooms of Pope Alexander III. on his entering Couci (Comes); the English king, who, in the Abbey of BourgDieu, was too overawed by the Pope to sit on a chair in his presence, but, like a dog, cowered on the floor, this king ordered the first execution for heresy in his kingdom by having a sect called Publicans or Patari put to death because they rejected baptism and submission to the Pope. The Patari had arisen in Italy, and spread over the European continent, and were so terribly persecuted that at last they retaliated; but the Church was too strong for them, and we frequently in the history of those times find notices similar to the following: "In this year the Most Reverend Archbishop William of Rheims, Legate of the Apostolic See, and the illustrious Count Philip of Flanders, burnt many heretics alive."

219. Council held at Toulouse - In May 1163 a council, attended by seventeen cardinals, one hundred and twentyfour bishops, hundreds of abbots, and priests without number, was held at Tours, where the Inquisition, which had, as we have seen, existed for centuries in spirit, was put into shape and assumed a definite form. "An accursed heresy," said the holy speakers, "has recently arisen in the neighbourhood of Toulouse, and it is the duty of bishops to put it down with all the rigour of the ecclesiastical law. Innocent III., in 1198, sent the first two travelling Inquisitors to France, empowered to judge heretics, "the foxes called Waldenses, Cathari, and Patari, who, though they have different faces, yet all hang together by their tails, and are sent by Satan to devastate the vineyard of the Lord," which "foxes" were to be

caught for them by ecclesiastical and secular princes, "to be judged and killed," an order which the said princes obeyed with such alacrity, that the progress of the two Inquisitors was everywhere signalised by the bonfires of burning heretics. But these were persecuted not in France only, but wherever the power of the popes could reach them, first of all, of course, in Italy, where one of the most distinguished victims, Arnold of Brescia, had some time before the above-mentioned occurrences been strangled in prison, and his body publicly burnt at Rome in 1155. His heresy consisted in having preached against the crimes of the Papal See.

220. Establishment of the Inquisition - We have elsewhere more particularly spoken of the heretical sects which in the tenth to the twelfth century existed in Italy and the south of France (168-185). Peter of Castelnau having been sent to preach against the Albigenses, was slain by them. As soon as his death became known he was canonised, and the fourth Council of the Lateran, in 1228, at the instigation of Pope Honorius III., sanctioned and organised the Inquisition, the original idea of which was due to Dominique de Guzman, who also founded the order of Dominican friars. The Council, or rather the Pope, decreed that all heretics should be delivered over to the secular arm and their property confiscated. Sovereigns were called upon to drive all heretics from their states; in case of non-obedience, the Pope would offer their territory to whosoever could conquer them. Persons who had favoured heretics or received them into their houses were to be excommunicated and declared infamous, incapable of inheriting property, and not entitled to Christian burial. Guzman, rightly considering that the foul band of preaching friars, whom he had associated with himself, were not the sort of people to further his views for those men were too fanatical not to be violent, which would have been injurious to the new institution further organised his " Militia of Christ," a religious police, composed of bigoted men and women, belonging to all classes of society, even to the highest the head of the house of Medina-Cceli down to 1820 enjoyed the high privilege of carrying the standard of the Faith in all

autos-da-fe, and other solemnities of the Inquisition of criminals, as we shall see in the account of the "Garduna" (Book IX,); of fools and knaves. The invisible troop of spies and denouncers, these familiars of the Inquisition, as they afterwards called themselves, formed the secret portion of the Inquisition, and were none the less formidable on that account. From 1233, when the Inquisition was established in Spain, to the beginning of the next century, it made rapid progress, spreading into Italy and Germany. In 1308 the Inquisition persecuted the Templars a entrance; autos-da-fe", "acts of faith," as the burning of heretics was called, shed their lurid light over many a Spanish city, at which the royal family frequently were present. In 1415 the Inquisition burnt John Huss at Constance; Platina, a papal writer, in his " Lives of the Popes " thus pleasantly speaks of it: "In the same Council, John Huss and Jerome were burnt, because they affirmed, among other errors, that ecclesiastical men ought to be poor . . . matters being thus composed," &c. Burning your opponents certainly is composing matters; but the author was a Papist.

221. Progress of Institution - Until the joint reign of Ferdinand and Isabella, the Inquisition in Spain had been confined to the kingdom of Arragon. But about 1481 the queen established it in Castile, and the king gradually extended its jurisdiction over all his states. Like James of Scotland, the king of Spain always wanted "siller;" the Inquisition offered him a third of all the property it confiscated, and promised him a large share of the riches of the thousands of Jews then living in Spain; the nobles of Arragon and Castile were always conspiring against him, the Inquisition would quietly amd secretly get hold of their persons, and thus rid him of these enemies; heaven was to be gained by putting down heresy; here surely were reasons enough for protecting the Inquisition and investing it with full powers. The queen also alas, that it has to be said of her! was greatly in favour of it, and even requested the Pope to declare the sentences pronounced in Spain to be final and without appeal to Rome. She complained at the same time that the people accused her of having no other view in establishing the Inquisition than that of sharing with its officers the property of those

condemned by them. The Pope, Sixtus IV., granted everything, and appeased her conscientious scruples as to confiscations. A bull, dated 1483, named Father Thomas de Torquemada, an atrocious fanatic, Grand Inquisitor of Spain. For eighteen years he held the office, condemning on the average ten thousand victims annually to death by fire, starvation, torture. In the first six months of his sanguinary rule 298 marranos Moors or Jews that had been converted to Christianity were burnt at the stake in Seville alone, and seventy condemned to imprisonment for life. During the same space of time 2000 marranos were burnt alive in various other places; a greater number, who had been fortunate enough to make their escape before they were seized for when once in the power of the terrible tribunal there was little chance of evasion were burnt in effigy; and about 17,000 persons, accused on the charge of heresy, underwent various other punishments. Upwards of 20,000 victims in half a year! Torquemada was so abhorred that he never stirred abroad without being surrounded by 250 familiars, and on his table always lay a horn of the unicorn, which, according to Moorish superstition, was supposed to possess the virtue of discovering and nullifying the force of poison. His cruelties excited so many complaints that the Pope himself was startled, and three times Torquemada was obliged to justify his conduct. During the fifteenth century so many executions took place at Seville, that the prefect of that city had the diabolical idea, in order to expedite the process, to erect, outside the city, a permanent scaffold in stone, on which he placed four gigantic statues in plaster, hollow inside, into which New Christians, accused of having relapsed into their old faith, were forced, and slowly calcined to death, as in a kiln. This scaffold was called quemadero (the burner), and the ruins of it could be seen as late as the year 1823.

222. Judicial Procedure of the Inquisition - Before proceeding with our historical details, let us briefly state the mode of procedure adopted by the execrable tribunal of the Inquisition.

A denunciation, verbal or in writing, and it little mattered from what impure source it proceeded, formed the startingpoint. Every year, on the third Sunday in Lent, the "Edict of Denunciation" was read in the churches, enjoining every person, on pain of major excommunication, to reveal within six days to the Holy Office, as the Inquisition was now styled, facts opposed to the purity of faith that might have come to their notice. Denunciation also had its rewards. Plenary indulgence was granted by the popes to whoso was good Christian enough to denounce his father, son, brother, or other near relation. Charles V. relieved every one who had denounced ten heretics, or became a familiar of the Inquisition, from all taxation and statute labour. And the most trifling acts exposed persons to the charge of heresy; to put a clean cloth on the table on a Saturday, the Jewish Sabbath, smelled of Judaism; to put on clean linen on a Friday, the Mahometan Sunday, betrayed Mahometanisin. The opinions of Luther, casting horoscopes, eating with Jews, dining or supping with friends on the eve of a journey, as the Jews do, these and a hundred other things equally innocent might lead to the stake. William Franco, a citizen of Seville, whose wife had been seduced by a priest, which he dared not resent, having casually observed that his wife was in purgatory, this expression was reported to the Inquisitors, who thereupon condemned him to imprisonment for life in the cells of the Inquisition.

The arrests were generally made at night, and the victims taken off in a carriage, the wheels of which had tires made of leather, whilst the mules, which drew it, were shod with buskins, the soles of which consisted of tow between two thick pieces of leather, so as to prevent their approach being heard. These buskins were an invention of Deza, the second Grand Inquisitor. Some of them were found in the inquisitorial arsenal at Malaga when its doors were broken open in 1820. General Torrijos, who for two years had been a prisoner of the Inquisition, and who was treacherously shot by order of Ferdinand VII. in 1831, carried off one of these buskins. Two others were appropriated by an Englishman, a Mr. Thomas Wilkins, of Paddington Place (Street?), London, who as late as the year 1838 would show them to his friends. Where are they now?

The prisoner having been incarcerated in the dungeons of the Inquisition, his property was put under sequestration, and the claw of the Holy Office was one which seldom released its prey. According to its statutes, indeed, it was compelled to release the accused if twelve witnesses, of pure Catholic blood, testified in his favour. But it was very seldom twelve such witnesses could be brought together, for in most cases persons who gave evidence in favour of the victims of the Inquisition ran the risk of being themselves charged with heresy.

The prisoner, on his apprehension, was carried to a dungeon, generally underground, sometimes at a depth of thirty feet. Each cell was about twelve feet by eight, with no accommodation but a plank bed, and a utensil, which was emptied every three or four days, and sometimes but once in a week. From eight to ten prisoners were shut up in such a cell when the Holy Office had many victims. They were not allowed to make any complaints; if they did so, they were gagged and cruelly flogged. Such treatment naturally often led to suicide. To mention a comparatively recent instance: in 1819 six prisoners were in one of the dungeons of the Inquisition at Valencia. A gaoler, instructed to try one of them, that is, to get a confession out of him, told him that if he did not reveal what he knew, he would be racked next day. The prisoner confessed nothing, but next day the six prisoners were found dead; they had strangled one another, and the last had asphyxiated himself by inhaling the poisonous gases arising from the utensil above referred to. The prisoners had been charged with being Freemasons. Sometimes a prisoner was left to die of starvation, or kept for years in his dungeon, whilst no one dared to raise a voice in his behalf. People disappeared, and their relations and friends only surmised, and cautiously whispered among themselves their suspicions, that they were languishing, or had perhaps died, in the prisons of the Inquisition. Some of the prisoners, however, were brought before their judges, in whose presence they were compelled to sit on the sharp edge of a triangular piece of wood, supported by two X; this mockery of a seat was called a potro. The trial was supposed to be public, but the audience was packed; none but good Catholics, who could be depended on, were invited to attend. That the publicity was a mere delusion, is proved by the fact that the New Christians offered King Ferdinand the sum of 600,000 ducats to let the trials be public; but

Cardinal Ximenes, the Grand Inquisitor, induced the king to decline the offer, as he also persuaded Charles V. to refuse the still higher offer of 800,000 ducats made by the same New Christians for the same privilege. The prisoner, when before his judges, was exhorted to confess his crime, but he was not informed of the charge against him; and if he did not know what to confess, or if his confession did not agree with the secret information against him, he was taken to the torture chamber, to extort what was wanted. As the Inquisitors were profoundly religious men (!), regulating their conduct by the teaching of Christ, which forbids the shedding of blood, they had with hellish ingenuity contrived their instruments of torture so that they should avoid that result, and yet inflict the greatest suffering the human body can possibly bear, without having the vital spark extinguished in it. It is true that the pendulum torture which certainly was applied, as the instrument was discovered as late as the year 1820 in the prison of the Inquisition at Seville proved that the rule was broken through; but the modern Inquisitors, it appears, were not so conscientious as the ancient! The Inquisitors, whilst admitting that innocent persons might sometimes die under torture, maintained that still it ought to be applied, for if a good Catholic died under their hands he went straight into paradise, which no doubt was very consolatory to the victim!

223. Palace of the Inquisition - The palace of the Inquisition contained the judgment hall, offices for the employees, torture chambers, cells of mercy and penitence, and dungeons, besides the private apartments of the Grand Inquisitor. A rich prisoner was first taken to a cell of mercy, and if he could be persuaded to surrender all his property to the Inquisition, he was, after some months of seclusion, allowed to issue forth, as poor as Job, but rich in the gifts of grace. The cells of mercy were on the first floor. The cells of penitence, to which victims less ready to be converted were taken, were generally situate in small round towers of about ten feet diameter, just under the roof. They were whitewashed, and the only light they received was through a small opening in the vaulted ceiling. The only furniture were a stool and a truckle bed. If a prolonged stay in this terrible solitude did not have

the desired effect, the victim was consigned to a dungeon, with walls five feet thick, and double doors, in almost total darkness, with an earthen vessel for the excrements, which was emptied once in four days. What the prisoners' food consisted of, may be inferred from the fact that something less than a penny a day was allowed for it and, of course, the poor gaoler had to make his profit out of it! The next move of the prisoner was to the torture chamber.

The torture chamber in the papal palace at Avignon was constructed with diabolical ingenuity. To cause the shrieks and groans of those tortured to remain confined within the hall, each wall projects and recedes in such a manner as to exhibit a face in a different direction to that of the wall on the opposite side, and in this way the solid mass of masonry of each wall is carried upwards, the result of which peculiar structure is that shrieks were thrown back from wall to wall, and thus never could reach the outside, nor disturb the pope, toying with his concubines in the adjoining palace. The place where the victims were burnt is a vast circular chamber, .shaped exactly like the furnace of a glass-house, terminating at the top in a narrow chimney of a funnel form. Up to about the year 1850 these chambers were shown to strangers, but since then the superior ecclesiastical authorities of Avignon have caused them to be dismantled and shut up they showed the Church in too hideous a character.

224. Tortures - There were three modes of torture chiefly in use. The first was that of the cord. The prisoner's arms were tied behind him with one end of a long rope, which passed over a pulley fixed in the vault of the chamber; he was then raised from the ground to a considerable height, which, by twisting his arms backward and above his head, was sufficient to dislocate the shoulder joints; the rope was then suddenly slackened, so that he fell to within a foot or so from the ground, by which his arms were nearly torn out of their sockets, and his whole body sustained a fearful concussion. In some cases the back of the victim, in being drawn up, was made to press against a roller, set round with sharp spikes, causing, of course, fearful laceration. At Rome this mode of torturing was of half-an-hour's duration; in Spain it was

continued for more than an hour. Another mode of applying the cord torture was by fastening the victim down on a sort of wooden bed and encircling his arms and legs in different places with thin cord, which by means of winches could be so tightened as to cut deep into the flesh. If these tortures found the prisoner firm, and extorted no confession, it was generally in the above position that he was subjected to the torture by water. His mouth and nostrils were covered with a thick cloth, and one of the Satanic brood of Dominican friars would sit by him, and through a funnel pour water on the cloth, which speedily became soaked, and then more water being poured on, the latter would enter the mouth of the unfortunate wretch lying there in fearful agony, undergoing all the pangs of slow suffocation, while his brow was covered with the cold sweat of death, and the blood started from his eyes and nostrils;. and all the time the fiend by his side exhorted him, " for the love of Him who died on the Cross," to confess. The third mode of torture was by fire. The victim was stretched and fastened on the ground; the soles of his feet were exposed and rubbed with oil or lard, or any other easily inflammable matter, and then a portable fire was placed against them;. the intense torture the burning of the greasy matter spread on the soles caused to the unfortunate prisoner may be imagined. When, in consequence of it, the prisoner declared himself ready to confess, a screen was interposed between his feet and the fire; on its withdrawal, if the confession was not satisfactory, the pain was even more frightful than before. Ingenious Inquisitors would sometimes vary the mode of torturing. Thus John de Eoma, a monk attached to the Inquisition, caused some of his victims to be forced into boots filled with boiling tallow, and the tonsured monster laughed over the cries of the wretched sufferers. The wretches who, at the Inquisitor's command, executed all these terrible operations on their fellow-creatures, wore long black gowns with hoods covering their heads, having holes for mouth, nostrils, and eyes.

  Another diabolical device of the Inquisitors consisted in this, that while they asserted that the torture or being put to the question could only be applied once, they declared the torture suspended, when it was found that by continuing it at the time the victim would die under their hands, and thus deprive them of the further gratification of their thirst for cruelty. The torture was begun, but not finished, and the unfortunate wretch could thus be put to the question as often as they pleased the torture was only being continued! This diabolical fiction was also part of the judicial procedure against witches, as laid down in the Malleus maleficarum. The Inquisitors further were the first to put women to the torture; neither the weakness nor the modesty of the sex had any influence on them. The Dominican friars the Thugs of the Papacy would flog naked women in the corridors of the Inquisition building, after having first violated them, for some slight breach of discipline! Even after this lapse of time, it makes one's blood boil with indignation when thinking of those horrors! The fact has been denied by apologists of the Inquisition; but that the practice existed, is proved by the severe decree against it made by the Inquisitor-General Ximenes Cisneros (1507-1517), who threatened with death every official of the Holy Office who should be guilty of this and similar excesses. Yet this Cisneros caused 2536 victims to be burnt alive!

225. Condemnation and Execution of Prisoners - Out of every 2000 persons accused, perhaps one escaped condemnation to death or lifelong imprisonment. The most fortunate those that were reconciled had to appear, bareheaded, with a cord round their neck, clothed in the san benito, an ugly garment, something like a sack, with black and yellow or white stripes, and carrying a green wax taper in their hands, in the hall of the tribunal, or sometimes openly in a church, where, on their knees, they abjured the heresies laid to their charge. They were then condemned to wear the ignominious garment for some considerable time. Several other degrading and troublesome conditions were imposed on them, and the greater portion or whole of their property was confiscated: this was a rule the holy fathers never departed from. The relaxed, or those condemned to death, dressed in an even more hideous garb than the "reconciled," having the portrait of the victim immersed in flames, and devils dancing round about it, painted thereon, were led out to the place of execution, attended by

monks and friars, and burnt at the stake, the court, Grand Inquisitor, his officers, and the people witnessing the agonies of the dying, and inhaling the flavour of their burning flesh with intense satisfaction. One trait of mercy the monkish demons showed consisted in first strangling those that died penitent before burning them, whilst those who maintained their innocence to the last were burnt alive. These bloody recreations at last became so fashionable, that in Spain and Portugal the accession of a king, a royal marriage, or the birth of a prince, was celebrated by a grand auto-da-fe, for which as many victims were reserved or procured aspossible.

226. Procession of the Auto-da-fe - The night before the auto-da-fe" a procession of wood-cutters, Dominicans, and familiars started from the building of the Inquisition for the open space where the sacrifice was to take place. On their arrival there they planted by the side of an altar, already erected there, a green cross, covered with black crape. This cross was symbolical of the grief of the Church for the heretics who were going to be burnt. After having set up the cross the procession returned, minus the Dominicans, who remained behind to pray and chant psalms. The procession of the auto-da-fe, which started early in the morning for the place of execution, was opened by a company of lance-bearers, then came priests, then men carrying the effigies of such heretics as had made their escape, and could therefore not be bodily burnt or degraded; these men were followed by such as carried coarse coffins or shells, containing the bones or corpses of heretics who had died while in the prisons of the Inquisition. After these marched those who had repented, who were followed by the relaxed, or those condemned to be burnt, and wearing the hideous san benito. Such as it was feared might speak heretical words to the bystanders were gagged. Each victim carried a lighted taper, and was accompanied by two friars, to urge him either to be converted, if obstinate, or to give him such spiritual comfort as Dominican friars could bestow. Behind these victims walked the familiars and, as already stated, grandees of Spain deemed it an honour to be such after these came the Inquisitors with their Council, the whole procession closing with the standard of the

Tribunal carried aloft. When the dismal train had arrived at the place of execution, and those who were condemned to a less punishment than death had had their different sentences read to them, the great treat of the day, the burning, began. As soon as the victims had been placed on the piles of wood, and chained to the posts erected in the middle of each pile, the devout people called out, "Let the dogs' beards be made!" which was done by the executioners thrusting staves, to which burning heather had been tied, into the faces of the victims, till they were black and singed. With "The foolish people gazing Upon a scene, in which some day Each might himself the victim play."

But the Inquisitors were not always satisfied with a simple burning; they sometimes superadded diabolical tortures, as, for instance, gagging by means of a piece of wood, cleft so as to let the tongue be held by it, or actually tearing out the tongue, to prevent the victims uttering heresies while being led to the stake; or worse still, flaying them alive, and then strewing brimstone and salt over the skinned body, and burning it slowly suspended by chains over live coal. The Inquisitors gave Francis I., king of France, in 1535, six times in one day the treat of seeing a heretic drawn up and down by chains over the flames, till the partly-consumed body of each fell into the burning pile beneath. That madman, Charles V., whom courtly historians call a "great" prince, ordered female heretics to be buried alive!

227. History continued - The monster Torquemada was still Inquisitor-General. The people of Aragon, who had from the first violently opposed the establishment of the Inquisition in their territory, were exasperated when autosda-fe began to be celebrated among them, and in order to intimidate their butchers slew the most violent of their oppressors, one Peter Arbues of Epila, at the altar. The Church immediately placed him among her martyrs; Queen Isabella erected a statue to him; his body wrought miracles, and Pope Pius IX. canonized him. The just death of the Inquisitor of course led to increased cruelty and persecution on the part of the Holy Office; the men who slew Arbues unfortunately were captured; they had their hands cut off before being hanged, and their bodies were cut up in pieces, which were

exposed on the highways. Torquemada next urged on the king and queen to expel the Jews from their states, as enemies of the Christian religion, The Jews, informed of their danger, offered the king 30,000 ducats towards the expenses of the war with Granada, on condition that they were allowed to stay. Ferdinand and Isabella were on the point of acceding to this proposal, when Torquemada, a crucifix in his hand, presented himself to the sovereigns, and thus addressed them: " Judas was the first to sell his master for thirty pieces of silver. Your highnesses intend selling him a second time for thirty pieces of gold. Here he is, take him, and speedily conclude the sale!" Of course the proud king and equally haughty queen cringed before the insolent friar, and the decree went forth on the 3ist March 1492 that by the 3ist July of the same year all Jews must have quitted the states of Ferdinand and Isabella on pain of death and confiscation of all their property. Some 800,000 Jews emigrated, momentarily saving their lives, but scarcely any property, since the time was too short for realising it at its value. Thousands of men. women, and children perished by the way, so that the Jews compared their sufferings to those their forefathers underwent at the time of Titus. When, shortly after this expulsion of the Jews, the kingdom of Granada was conquered by the Spanish arms, the conquest was considered as heaven's special approval and reward; and Ferdinand, to show his religious zeal, committed every kind of cruelty his soul could invent. After the capture of Malaga, twelve Jews, who had taken refuge there, underwent by his direct orders the terrible death by pointed reeds, a slow but fatal torture, like being stabbed to death with pins.

Torquemada died in 1498; his successor, the Dominican Deza, introduced the Inquisition into the newly-conquered kingdom of Granada; 8o,coo Moors, preferring exile to baptism, left the country. He also introduced the terrible tribunal into Naples and Sicily; and though the Sicilians at first rose against it, and expelled the Inquisitors, they had afterward, overcome by Charles V., to submit to its reestablishment. Deza, during his short reign of nine years, caused 2592 individuals to be burnt alive and 829 in effigy, and condemned upwards of 32,000 to imprisonment and the galleys, with total confiscation of property. He was succeeded by the mild Ximenes, after whom came Adrien Boeijens, who was as cruel a persecutor as Torquemada; the Lutheran doctrines, now gaining ground, gave him and his successors plenty of occupation, and the bonfires of the Inquisition blazed not only in Spain, but at Naples, Malta, Venice, in Sardinia and Flanders; and in the Spanish colonies in America the poor Indians perished in hecatombs, for either refusing to be baptized, or being suspected of having relapsed into their former idolatry, after having adopted and professed the mild and gentle creed of Christianity.

228. General History of Institution continued - We need not go through the list of Grand Inquisitors seriatim. Let us only give particular facts, indicative of the spirit that continued to guide them. Under the generalate of Valdes, the eighth Inquisitor-General, a lady ninety years old, Marie de Bourgogne, immensely rich, was denounced by a servant as having said: "Christians respect neither faith nor law." She was thereupon cast into one of the dungeons of the Holy Office, where she remained for five years for want of proof. At the end of that time she was put to the torture to extort an avowal, and she was so unmercifully racked, that she died under the butchers' hands. She underwent the three tortures of the cord, water, and fire. But her trial was continued after her death, and ended in her remains being condemned to be burnt, and the total confiscation of her property; her children, besides being disinherited, also being declared infamous for ever. In 1559, at an auto-da-fe held at Valladolid, they burnt the body of Dame Eleanor de Vibero y Cazalla, who had died a good Catholic, but was after her death accused by witnesses, whose confessions were extorted by the rack, of having associated with Lutherans. Her property was confiscated. The Inquisition also condemned Charles V., after his death, as a heretic, and caused his confessor, Dr. Cazalla, to be burnt alive. At this autoda-fe were present the Princess Donna Joan, the regent, in the absence of Philip II. from the kingdom, and Prince Don Carlos, then only fourteen years of age.

229. Englishmen Imprisoned by the Inquisition - In 1558 Nicholas

Burton, a London citizen, who traded to Spain, arrived at Cadiz in his own ship. He was seized by the Inquisition and accused of having spoken disrespectfully of that tribunal, and being a heretic, and after having been kept in prison for two years, was burnt alive, his mouth being gagged, at Seville. The Inquisition seized his ship and cargo, valued at; 50,000. But portion of the cargo belonged to a Bristol merchant, who sent his lawyer, John Frampton, to Spain to claim his property. His mission, of course, failed. He was sent to Cadiz a second time, when the Inquisition seized, imprisoned, and racked him, and finally made him appear in the auto-da-fe", in which Burton was burnt. But eventually Frampton made his escape, returned to England, and published his experiences. Why did our blustering Bess, who sent thousands of Englishmen to perish abroad to uphold the cause of foreigners, the Huguenots, not interfere in behalf of two Englishmen, her own subjects, to snatch them from the clutches of the Spanish fiends? Well, Philip of Spain had made her an offer of marriage, and even a queen does not like to offend an unsuccessful suitor.

230. History continued - Philip II extended the jurisdiction of the Inquisition throughout the Netherlands, and in spite of the resistance of the inhabitants, met with such success, that his noble executioner, the Duke of Alva, could boast of having within five years sent to the stake and gallows 18,000 persons for the crime of heresy. But the oppression at last became so great, that the Netherlands revolted again, and this time successfully; they for ever threw off the Spanish yoke. It was during this Dutch war of liberation that the mysterious catastrophe of Don Carlos, Philip's son by his first wife, occurred, Romance asserts that the tragedy had its origin in the love passages said to have taken place between Don Carlos and Philip's second wife, Elizabeth of France, who, before becoming his stepmother, had been his affianced bride. But history explains the facts in this way: Don Carlos conspired against his father, a gloomy tyrant, who deprived him of every scrap of power and influence, keeping him in the perfect subjection of a child; the prince thought of assassinating the king, or flying to the Netherlands, which he hoped to erect into an independent kingdom

for himself. While he was hesitating, the Inquisition discovered both incipient schemes, revealed them to the king, and pronounced either deserving of death. Don Carlos was seized, imprisoned, and killed by poison. It is difficult to imagine a moral monster such as Philip II. was. He caused the works of Vesale, his own physician, who first taught the true facts and principles of anatomy, with their illustrations by Titian, to be publicly burnt, and the doctor himself was compelled to make an involuntary pilgrimage to Jerusalem to expiate his impious attempt of prying into the secrets of nature. This, we may say, was simply absurd on the part of the king; what follows is atrocious. In 1559 he learnt that an auto-da-fe had taken place in a distant locality, where thirty persons had perished at the stake. He besought the Inquisitors to be allowed to witness a similar spectacle; the Dominican devils, to encourage and reward such holy zeal on the part of Heaven's anointed, sent out their archers, who searched with such diligence for victims, that on the 6th October of the same year the king was able to preside at Valladolid at the burning of forty of his subjects, which gave him the most lively satisfaction. One of the condemned, a person of distinction, implored the royal mercy, as he was being led to the stake. "No," replied the crowned hyena, "if it were my own son, I would surrender him to the flames if he persisted in his heresy."

In 1566 the Grand Inquisitor Espinosa began his crusade against the Moors that still remained in Spain. For a long time the persecuted race confined themselves to remonstrances, but when it was decreed that their children must thenceforth be brought up in the Christian faith, a vast conspiracy was formed, which for nine months was kept secret, and would have been successful had not the Moors of the mountainous districts broken out into open rebellion before those of the country and towns were prepared to support them. The Christians scattered among the Moorish population of course were the first victims of the long pent-up rage of the Mussulmans. Three thousand perished at the first outset; all the monks of a monastery were cast into boiling oil. One of the insurgents, the intimate friend of a Christian, knew of no greater proof of affection he could show him than transfixing him with his lance, lest others should treat him worse.

The Marquis of Mondejar, captaingeneral of Andalusia, was appointed to put down the insurrection. As he was too humane, his reprisals not being severe enough, the Marquis de Los Velez, called by the Moors the "Demon with the Iron Head," was associated with him in the command, and he carried on war in the most ferocious manner. At the battle of Ohanez blood was shed in such quantities, that the thirsty Spaniards could not find one unpolluted spring. One thousand six hundred Moors were subjected to a treatment worse than death, and immediately after Los Velez and his band of butchers celebrated the feast of the Purification of the Virgin! And in the end the superior number of the Christians triumphed over Moorish bravery, and the Inquisitors were busy for weeks holding autos-da-fe to celebrate the victory of the true faith.

Under the long reign of Philip II., called the "Demon of the South," six Grand Inquisitors carried on their bloody orgies. The Reformed Creed of course supplied the greatest numbers of victims; at Seville on one occasion eight hundred were arrested all at once. At the first auto-da-fe of Vallad olid, on 12th May 1559, fourteen members of one family were burnt. The Inquisition was established in the island of Sardinia, at Lima, Mexico, Cartagena, in the fleet, army, and even among custom-house officers. By the original documents in Trinity College, Dublin, it appears that in the three years from 1564 to I 567 the Inquisition at Rome passed III sentences on heretics.

231. History continued - Philip III of Spain was early taught the power of the Inquisition; for when, at the beginning of his reign, he was obliged to be present at an auto-da-fe, and could not restrain his tears at seeing two young women, one Jewish and the other Moorish, burnt at the stake, for no other fault than that of having been brought up in the different creeds of their fathers, the Inquisitors imputed to him his compassion as a crime, which could only be expiated by blood: the king had to submit to being bled and seeing his blood burnt by the executioner. The Inquisitors, in fact, were above the king. At autos-da-fe the Grand Inquisitor's throne was more lofty than that of the king. The Inquisitor Tabera kept the arch-priest of Malaga for two years in

prison, because that ecclesiastic, whilst carrying the viaticum to a dying person, had not stopped to let the Inquisitor pass.

Philip IV. inaugurated his reign by an auto-da-fe (1632). The Inquisitor-General gave to the show of the auto-da-fe, whose interest began to decline, a new zest by causing the sentence of death against ten marranos to be read to them, while each of them had one hand nailed to a wooden cross.

The marriage of Charles II. with the niece of Louis XIV. (1680) was celebrated with an auto-da-fe at Madrid. On the 12th April 1869 some workmen, employed in digging up the earth in the chief square of Madrid, came upon a layer of coals and ashes, mixed with bones, which proved to be human bones; moreover, iron collars and other things were found, which left no doubt that the spot had been the scene of the auto-da-fl of 1680, a full account of which was published, by " express desire of the king and of the Grand Inquisitor, Valladares, to the honour and glory of Spain," by Joseph del Olmo, who was one of the familiars of the Inquisition. This autode-f6 was even a grander affair than that of 1632. There were 118 victims, one-and-twenty of whom were burnt alive in the presence of the young king and queen and the nobility of the court, besides a vast concourse of less exalted spectators. On the previous day the wood-cutters, to the number of 290, had defiled before the royal palace, every one with a log of wood on his shoulder. Their leader stopped at the gate of the palace, where a duke was in waiting to receive the log, which he reverently carried up to the king, who took it from him, carried it to the boudoir of the queen, placed the piece of wood, on which two days after a human being was to be burnt alive, into her arms, like a baby; he then gave it back to his grace, my lord duke, and, according to the instructions he had received from his father-confessor, the Don Estevan del Vado, Inquisitor of Toledo, sent word to the captain of the wood-cutters, that on the auto-da-fe this log was to be thrown into the flames in the name of the king. On the day of the auto-da-fe the show was not over till half-past nine at night; and, says Del Olmo, "The public went away highly pleased, especially with the conduct of the king, who had stood the heat of the day, and shown that he was not at all weary."

232. Reflections - Is it possible to realise the horrors of this transaction a man brought up in the principles of chivalry, and a woman of royal birth, whom one would suppose to be not only noble, but also gentle, witnessing, on their wedding-day, when one would imagine their hearts to be full of joy, and therefore full of good-will towards all men, and especially their subjects, so cruel a spectacle as the burning alive of human beings, burnt, so to say, in their honour? But here we see the effects of evil church government and priestly influence. When the mania of burning every old woman who had a black cat, as a witch, arose, the Inquisition found a new field of labour; and whatever might be the density of mental darkness with which priests and monks covered Europe, they took care there should be plenty of material light, and hence the funeral pyres of human reason and liberty were always blazing. Some of the Molinists, who, under pretext of "Perfect Contemplation," encouraged the most scandalous sexual excesses, were also burnt, not on account of their immoral practices, but because of some so-called heretical notions they propounded.

Under the succeeding kings of Spain general enlightenment and civilisation had made too much progress to allow the Inquisitors to indulge as formerly their frantic rage and fanatical cruelty. During the reign of Ferdinand VI, Charles III., and Charles IV., they obtained only 245 condemnations, of which fourteen were to death. Freemasons and Jansenists were the principal victims. One of the vilest acts of the Inquisition during the reign of Charles III. was the imprisonment, on the charge of heresy, in 1778, of Count Olivades, the founder of La Carolina, the central city of the Sierra Morena colony, and of other highly beneficial institutions to Spain. His friends enabled him, in 1780, to make his escape to Venice.

233. Abolition of the Inquisition - Napoleon, on the 4th December 1808, whilst encamped at the village of Chamartin, a, short distance from Madrid, summoned the authorities of Madrid to surrender. The

Grand Inquisitor refused. Napoleon wrote on a piece of paper: "The Inquisitors are to be made prisoners. The Holy Office has ceased to exist. Its revenues are confiscated." Colonel Lumanuski, acting under the immediate orders of Marshal Soult, was sent to seize the palace of the Inquisition at Madrid. The building was surrounded by a strong wall, and guarded by 400 soldiers. The Fathers were summoned to open the gates, instead of which they shot the herald. The order to attack was given immediately. The Spanish soldiers were protected by their walls, the French troops were exposed, in an open plain, to their fire, and had no ladders. Some trees were cut down, turned into battering-rams, and soon a breach was made in the wall, through which the French entered the building. Then the priests left their cells, pretending to be surprised at the garrison having offered any resistance to their friends, the French! But Lumanuski, not to be deceived, ordered them to be closely guarded; the soldiers were all made prisoners. The French then examined the building; they found splendid halls and rooms, but no prisons, torture rooms, or any of the horrors usually associated with the dread tribunal. Lumanuski was about to retire, when Colonel di Lilla suggested that the marble floor of the ground floor should have water poured on it, to see if it would flow off anywhere. Speedily it was seen to disappear through a crack between two slabs of marble. In trying to raise one of the slabs a soldier touched a hidden spring, and the slab rose up, revealing a staircase, descending which the French first came to a large hall, the judgment hall, with appropriate furniture; then they discovered a number of cells, in some of which bodies of men, in various states of decay, were found prisoners who had been left to die in solitary confinement. In others they found prisoners still alive, men, women, and children, all perfectly naked, and numbering about one hundred persons. These, of course, were clothed, the soldiers giving them their cloaks or coats, and restored to liberty. All the cells having been visited, the French next came upon the torture chambers, containing all the diabolical instruments invented for racking human bodies. At this sight the fury of the French soldiers was not to be restrained; they declared that the holy fathers should themselves undergo the tortures they had inflicted on their victims; and Lumanuski states that he saw the torture applied in four different ways on as many of the Inquisitorial fiends a very slight retribution for all the evil they had done.

234. Restoration and Final Abolition - But Ferdinand VII. on his restoration alas! with the help of England in 1814, re-established the Inquisition, and appointed Francis Thiery Campilla, Bishop of Almeria, its forty-fifth InquisitorGeneral. Immediately the prisons, galleys, and penal colonies were filled with prisoners, Freemasons forming a preponderating number amongst them. But in 1820 all the Spanish provinces combined again in a general insurrection, broke the bonds of Absolutism, again crushed the Inquisition and its familiars, set free its prisoners, demolished its palaces and prisons, and burnt its instruments of torture. But in 1823 a fresh reaction set in; French troops, led by the Duke of Angouleme, restored Ferdinand VII. to the throne, and the king, at the "earnest desire of his subjects' set up the Inquisition once more; and "if the Spanish nation was anxious for its restoration," as Dr. Bruck, the apologist of Absolutism, both political and priestly, in his " History of the Secret Societies of Spain " observes, "it is a proof that this tribunal was neither cruel nor unpopular." But the tribunal was unpopular, and the feeling was so strongly expressed, that the English ambassador, Sir Henry Wellesley, siding with the nation, threatened to leave Spain if the Inquisition were re-established with all its former authority. But though shorn of its once absolute power, the institution was still strong enough to send people to the scaffold: in 1826 it burnt a Jew; and a schoolmaster, accused of Quakerism, was hanged at Valencia on the 3ist July of the same year. True, the last victim did not wear the san benito, but his own clothes; the Inquisitors could no longer render their prisoners ridiculous; and the barefooted Carmelite friar, who accompanied the Quaker, could not, even at the last moment, win him for the heaven he promised him if he recanted. The Quaker died impenitent.

The Inquisition still exists in Portugal, though in a modified form. It also still exists at Rome: its palace stands to the left of St. Peter's, but its dungeons are empty, and the once murderous

Inquisition is now merely a tribunal of clerical discipline.

235. The False Nuncio - I have in the foregoing account spoken of the Inquisition chiefly as it existed in Spain. It was, however, not confined to that country; its fearful octopus arms embraced every nation it could reach. The way it was introduced into Portugal was peculiar, and worthy of that tribunal. In 1539 there appeared at Lisbon a papal legate, who declared to have come to Portugal, there to establish the Inquisition. He brought the king letters from Pope Paul III, and produced the most ample credentials for nominating a Grand Inquisitor and all other officers of the sacred tribunal. This man was a clever swindler, called John Peres, of Saavedra, who was an adept at imitating all kinds of writing and forging signatures and seals. He was attended by a magnificent train of more than a hundred servants, and to defray his expenses had borrowed at Seville enormous sums in the name of the Apostolic Chamber at Borne. The king was at first surprised and angry that the Pope should send an envoy of this description without previous notice y but Peres haughtily replied, that in so urgent a matter as the establishment of the Inquisition and the suppression of heresy the Holy Father could not stand on points; and that the king was highly honoured by the fact that the first messenger who brought him the news was the legate himself. The king dared complain no more; and the false nuncio the same day nominated a Grand Inquisitor, set up the Holy Office, and collected money for its working expenses. Before news could come from Rome, the rogue had already pocketed upwards of two hundred thousand ducats. But he could not make his escape before the swindle was discovered, and Fere's was condemned to be whipped and sent to the galleys for ten years. But the best of the joke was, that the Pope confirmed all the swindler had done; in the plentitude of his divine power, Paul III. declared the slight irregularities which attended the establishment of the Portuguese Inquisition not to affect its efficacy or moral character, and that, now it was established, it should remain so.

236. The, Inquisition in various Countries - Other countries where the

Inquisition was established were the Spanish Netherlands, the Spanish colonies in America, in the East Indies, the Papal States, Venice, Germany, where for some time it raged with particular ferocity; the Dominican fiends had scarcely been three years at Strasbourg when they burnt eighty Waldenses, and the demon, Konrad von Marburg, travelled up and down the country burning heretics with diabolical joy. He met with a well-merited reward by being killed by Count Sayn, near Marburg. In some of the countries named above the Inquisition was abolished before it ceased to exist in Spain and Italy. In 1557 an attempt was made to introduce the Inquisition into England, but, fortunately for this country, unsuccessfully. But, even without its help, Bloody Mary had the satisfaction of burning ninety-four heretics in the course of that year in England alone.

237. Apologists of the Inquisition - Some writers, who discuss history philosophically which means whitewashing cruel tyrants and monstrous institutions the learned divines in scratch wigs and the courtly historiographers in flowing periwigs, have endeavoured to whitewash the Inquisition. It was an institution, they say, necessary in its day to preserve the purity of religion; an argument not worth answering, it is so absurd. No man, and no aggregation of men though it call itself " the Church " has any inherent right to call any man to account for his religious belief: it is a matter of conscience no tribunal is competent to meddle with. Then the apologists of the Inquisition further say, that the Inquisitors were more fanatical than cruel. This, again, is false. No man, who was not cruel, could have inflicted the sufferings inflicted on their fellow-men by the Inquisitors. The pity they pretended to feel for their victims, and the anxiety they displayed for the welfare of the souls of those they sacrificed to their ambition and greed for their victims generally possessed means, which the Inquisition confiscated were even more wicked than the cruelties they practised. The Spanish Inquisitors and monks were infamous hypocrites, and not fanatics. The morality of fanatics usually is above reproach; but no men ever were more debauched, more filthy, more corrupt than Spanish Inquisitors, monks, and the priesthood in general. In 1556 the public voice of Spain

accused certain priests of using the confessional for immoral purposes. Paul IV. ordered the Inquisition to investigate the matter. The denunciations were so numerous, that the Inquisitors, fearing too great a scandal, had to renounce the prosecution of the delinquent priests; and, no doubt, they had a fellowfeeling for them! And I cannot help agreeing with Hoffmann, the latest historian of the Inquisition, when he says, that the modern apologists of that tribunal must be even more bloodthirsty than the Inquisitors were, for with the latter the fierce religious fanaticism of their age in some degree palliated their inhumanity: to defend it in this age shows a real tiger nature.

BOOK VIII

MYSTICS

" There is great abundance of chaff and straw to the grain, but the grain is good, and as we do not eat either the chaff or straw, if we can avoid it, nor even the raw grain, but thrash and winnow it, and grind it and bake it, we find it, after undergoing this process, not only very palatable, but a special dainty of its kind. But the husk is an unsurmountable obstacle to those learned and educated gentlemen who judge of books entirely by the style and grammar, and who eat grain as it grows, like the cattle."

Rev. J. SMITH.

I

ALCHYMISTS

"In our day men are only too much disposed to regard the views of the disciples and followers of the Arabian school, and of the late Alchymists, respecting transmutation of metals, as a mere hallucination of the human mind, and, strangely enough, to lament it. But the idea of the variable and changeable corresponds with universal experience, and always precedes that of the unchangeable."

LIEBIG.

> The alchymist he had his gorgeous vision
> Of boundless wealth and everlasting youth;
> He strove untiringly, with firm decision,
> To turn his fancies into glorious truth,
> Undaunted by the rabble's loud derision,
> Condemning without reason, without ruth,
> And though he never found the pearl he sought,
> Yet many a secret gem to light he brought.

238. Astrology perhaps Secret Heresy - The mystic astronomy of ancient nations produced judicial astrology, which, considered from this point of view, will appear less absurd. It was the principal study of the Middle Ages; and Home was so violently opposed to it because, perhaps, it was not only heresy, but a wide-spread reaction against the Church of Rome. It was chiefly cultivated by the Jews, and protected by princes opposed to the papal supremacy. The Church was not satisfied with burning the books, but burned the writers; and the poor astrologers, who spent their lives in the contemplation of the heavens, mostly perished at the stake.

239. Process by which Astrology degenerated - As it often happens that the latest disciples attach themselves to the letter, understanding literally what in the first instance was only a fiction, taking the mask for a real face, so we may suppose astrology to have degenerated and become false and puerile. Hermes, the legislator of Egypt, who was revealed in the Samothracian mysteries, and often represented with a ram by his side a constellation initiating the new course of the equinoctial sun, the conqueror of darkness was revived in astrological practice; and a great number of astrological works, the writings of Christian Gnostics and Neo-Platonists, were attributed to him, and he was considered the father of the art from him called hermetic, and embracing astrology and alchymy, the rudimentary efforts of two sciences, which at first overawed ignorance by imposture, but, after labouring for centuries in the dark, conquered for themselves glorious thrones in human knowledge.

240. Scientific Value of Alchymy - Though Alchymy is no longer believed in as a true science, in spite of the prophecy of Dr. Girtanner, of Gottingen, that in the nineteenth century the transmutation of metals will be generally known and practised, it will never lose its power of awakening curiosity and seducing the imagination. The aspect of the marvellous which its doctrines assume, the strange renown attaching to the memory of the adepts, and the mixture of reality and illusion, of truths and chimeras which it presents, will always exercise a powerful

fascination upon many minds. And we ought also to remember that every delusion that has had a wide and enduring influence must have been founded, not on falsehood, but on misapprehended truth. This aphorism is especially applicable to Alchymy, which, in its origin, and even in its name, is identical with chemistry, the syllable *al* being merely the definite article of the Arabs. The researches of the Alchymists for the discovery of the means by which transmutation might be effected were naturally suggested by the simplest experiments in metallurgy and the amalgamation of metals; it is very probable that the first man who made brass thought that he had produced imperfect gold.

241. The Tincture - The transmutation of the base metal was to be effected by means of the transmuting tincture, which, however, was never found. But it exists for all that; it is the power that turns a green stalk into a golden ear of corn, that fills the sour unripe apple with sweetness and aroma, that has turned the lump of charcoal into a diamond. All these are natural processes, which, being allowed to go on, produce the above results. Now, all base metals may be said to be imperfect metals, whose progress towards perfection has been arrested, the active power of the tincture being shut up in them in the first property of nature (II). If a man could take hold of the tincture universally diffused in nature, and by its help assist the imprisoned tincture in the metal to stir and become active, then the transmutation into gold, or rather the manifestation (II) of the hidden life, could be effected. But this power or tincture is so subtle that it cannot possibly be apprehended; yet the Alchymists did not seek the nonexisting, but only the unattainable.

242. Aims of Alchymy - The three great ends pursued by Alchymy were the transmutation of base metals into gold by means of the philosopher's stone; the discovery of the panacea, or universal medicine, the elixir of life; and the universal solvent, which, being applied to any seed, should increase its fecundity. All these three objects are attainable by means of the tincture a vital force, whose body is electricity, by which the two latter aims have to some extent been

reached, for electricity will both cure disease and promote the growth of plants. Alchymy was then in the beginning the search after means to raise matter up to its first state, whence it was supposed to have fallen. Gold was considered, as to matter, what the ether of the eighth heaven was as to souls; and the seven metals, each called by the name of one of the seven planets, the knowledge of the seven properties really implied being lost the Sun, gold; Moon, silver; Saturn, lead; Venus, tin; Mercury, iron; Mars, mixed metal; Jupiter, copper,[12] formed the ascending scale of purification, corresponding with the trials of the seven caverns or steps. Alchymy was thus either a bodily initiation, or an initiation into the mysteries, a spiritual Alchymy; the one formed a veil of the other, wherefore it often happened that in workshops where the vulgar thought the adepts occupied with handicraft operations, and nothing sought but the metals of the golden age, in reality, no other philosopher's stone was searched for than the cubical stone of the temple of philosophy; in fine, nothing was purified but the passions, men, and not metals, being passed through the crucible. Bohme, the greatest of mystics, has written largely on the perfect analogy between the philosophical work and spiritual regeneration.

243. History of Alchymy - Alchymy flourished in Egypt at a very early age, and Solomon was said to have practised it. Its golden age began with the conquest of the Arabs in Asia and Africa, about the time of the destruction of the Alexandrian Library. The Saracens, credulous, and intimate with the fables of talismans and celestial influences, eagerly admitted the wonders of Alchymy. In the splendid courts of Almansor and Haroun al Easchid, the professors of the hermetic art found patronage, disciples, and emolument. Nevertheless, from the above period until the eleventh century the only alchymist of note is the Arabian Geber, whose proper name was Abu Mussah Djafar al Sofi. His attempts to transmute the base metals into gold led him to several discoveries in chemistry and medicine. He was also a famous astronomer, but sic transit gloria mundi! he has descended to our times

---

[12] New arrangement: Venus, copper; Mercury, mixed metal; Mars, iron; Jupiter, tin.

as the founder of that jargon known by the name of gibberish! The Crusaders brought the art to Europe; and about the thirteenth century Albertus Magnus, Koger Bacon, and Raymond Lully appeared as its revivers. Edward III. engaged John le Eouse and Master William de Dalby, alchemists, to make experiments before him; and Henry VI. of England encouraged lords, nobles, doctors, professors, and priests to pursue the search after the philosopher's stone; especially the priests, who, says the king (ironically?) having the power to convert bread and wine into the body and blood of Christ, may well convert an impure into a perfect metal. The next man of note that pretended to the possession of the lapis philosophorum was Paracelsus, whose proper name was Philip Aureolns Theophrastus Paracelsus Bombastus, of Hohenheim, and whom his followers called " Prince of Physicians, Philosopher of Fire, the Trismegistus of Switzerland, Reformer of Alchymistical Philosophy, Nature's faithful Secretary, Master of the Elixir of Life and Philosopher's Stone, Great Monarch of Chymical Secrets." He introduced the term alcahest (probably a corruption of the German words "all geist" "all spirit"), to express the universal solvent. The Rosicrucians, of whom Dr. Dee was the herald, next laid claim to alchymistical secrets, and were, in fact, the descendants of the Alchymists; and it is for this reason chiefly that these latter have been introduced into this work, though they cannot strictly be said to have formed a secret society.

241. Still, Alchymists formed Secret Societies - Still, in the dedication to the Emperor Rudolph II., prefixed to the work entitled Thcsaurinella Chymica-aurea tripartita, we read: "Given in the Imperial City of Hagenau, in the year 1607 of our salvation, and in the reign of the true governor of Olympus, Angelus Hagith, anno cxcvii." The author calls himself Benedictus Figulus. The dedication further mentions a Count Bernhard, evidently one of the heads of the order, as having been introduced to a society of Alchymists, numbering fourteen or fifteen members, in Italy. Further, Paracelsus is named as the monarcha of this order; that is, the monarch, a local head, subject to the governor of Olympus, the chief of the Italian society. The author

also, beside the usual chronology, gives a separate sectarian date; if we deduct cxcvii. (197) from 1607, we obtain the date 1410 as that of the foundation of the society. Fignlus says it was merged in the Eosicrucian order about the year 1607. Whether it was the same as that mentioned by Raymond Lully in his "Theatrum Chymicum," whose chief was called Bex Physicorum, and which existed before 1400, is uncertain.

245. Decay of Alchymy - Alchymy lost all credit in this country by the failure, and consequent suicide, of Dr. James Price, a member of the Royal Society, to produce gold, according to promise, the experiments to be performed in the presence of the Society. This occurred in 1783. But in 1796 rumours spread throughout Germany of the existence of a great union of adepts, under the name of the Hermetic Society, which, however, consisted really of two members only, the well-known Karl Arnold Kortum, the author of the Jobsiade, and one Bahrens, though there were many " honorary " members. The public, seeing no results, though the " Society " promised much, at last took no further notice of the Hermetics, and the wars, which soon after devastated Europe, caused Alchymy to be forgotten; though up to the year 1812 the higher society of Caiisruhe amused itself, in secret cliques, with playing at the transmutation of metals. The last of the English Alchymists seems to have been a gentleman of the name of Kellerman, who as lately as 1828 was living at Lilley, a village between Luton and Hitchin. There are, no doubt, at the present moment men engaged in the search after the philosopher's stone; we patiently wait for their discoveries.

246. Specimen of Alchymistic Language - After Paracelsus, the Alchymists divided into two classes: those that pursued useful studies, and those that took up the visionary fantastical side of Alchymy, writing books of mystical trash, which they fathered on Hermes, Aristotle, Albertus Magnus, and others. Their language is now unintelligible. One brief specimen may suffice. The power of transmutation, called the Green Lion, was to be obtained in the following manner: "In the Green Lion's bed the sun and moon are

born; they are married and beget a king; the king feeds on the lion's blood, which is the king's father and mother, who are at the same time his brother and sister. I fear I betray the secret, which I promised my master to conceal in dark speech from every one who does not know how to rule the philosopher's fire." Our ancestors must have had a great talent for finding out enigmas if they were able to elicit a meaning from these mysterious directions; still, the language was understood by the adepts, and was only intended for them. Many statements of mathematical formulae must always appear pure gibberish to the uninitiated into the higher science of numbers; still, these statements enunciate truths well understood by the mathematician. Thus, to give but one instance, when Hermes Trismegistus,. in one of the treatises attributed to him, directs the adept to catch the flying bird and to drown it, so that it fly nomore, the fixation of quicksilver by a combination with gold is meant.

247. Personal Fate of the Alchemists - The Alchymists, though chemistry is greatly indebted to them, and in their researches they stumbled on many a valuable discovery, as a rule led but sad and chequered lives, and most of them died in the utmost poverty, if no worse fate befell them. Thus one of the most famous Alchymists, Bragadino, who lived in the last quarter of the sixteenth century, who obtained large sums of money for his pretended secret from the Emperor of Germany, the Doge of Venice, and other potentates, who boasted that Satan was his slave two ferocious black dogs that always accompanied him being demons was at last hanged at Munich, the cheat with which he performed the pretended transmutation having been discovered. The twodogs were shot under the gallows. But even the honest Alchymists were doomed

> "To lose good days that might be better spent,
> To waste long nights in pensive discontent;
> To speed to-day, to be put back to-morrow,
> To feed on hope, to pine with fear and sorrow;
> To fret their souls with crosses and with cares,
> To eat their hearts through comfortless despairs.

Unhappy wights, born to disastrous end,
That do their lives in tedious tendance spend! "

II

JACOB BOHME

248. Parallel between Mystics and Sectaries - All secret societies have some connection with mysticism, secret itself, delighting in mystery, as the loving soul delights in surrounding the beloved object with mystery. Sectaries to some extent are the parents of mystics. The silent adoration of the Infinite, in which mystics delight, has its counterpart in the worship of progress, liberty, and truth, to which sectaries devote themselves. Progress, liberty, truth, are attributes of the highest humanitarianism. The mystics are the men of thought, the sectaries the men of action. However remote the thoughts of the former may seem from application to everyday life, from political strif e, they yet have a positive influence on human belief and will. The mystics behold in paradise that same ideal, transfigured, enlarged, and perpetuated, which the sectaries pursue on earth.

249. Character and Mission of Mystics - The mystics continue the school of ancient initiations, which to many nations were their only philosophy, science, and liberty. They are the priests of Infinity; in their tenderness they are the most tolerant of men, pardoning all, even the devil; they embrace all, pity all. They are, in a certain sense, the rationalists of prayer. By means of syntheses, trances, and raptures, they arrive at a pure and simple understanding of the supernatural, as popularly understood, which they adore more with their imagination and affection, than with the learned and sophisticated conceits of theology. Therefore the mystics of all creeds resemble each other; theirs is a region common to all religions, the universal home of the soul a height from which the innumerable horizons of conscience are seen to meet.

250. Merits of Bohme - The prince of mystics is without contradiction Jacob Bohme; in fact, compared with him, all other mystics sink into utter insignificance, as mere visionaries, whose rhapsodies, though

sometimes poetical, were always fantastical and useless to the world, because not founded on the truths of Eternal Nature. Bohme was a visionary, but a visionary of the stamp of Columbus; to him also it was given to behold with his mental eye a hidden world, the world of the Properties of Eternal Nature, and to solve the great mystery, not of this earth alone, but of the universe. He was emphatically a central philosopher, who from his standpoint could survey the whole sphere, within and without, and not merely an outer segment of its shell. He could therefore see the causes of things, and not their effects only. There is, I do not deny it, much in the writings of Bohme that cannot be maintained or proved, much that appears as pure alchymistical and cabalistic reverie, the disease of the age in which he lived. But though he may often be wrong in his deductions, he is always right in fundamentals. And even after rejecting all that is doubtful or absolutely erroneous, there is left so much which science and experiment demonstrate to be absolutely true, that it is hard to remember that all this was enunciated by a man who had no learning and never made an experiment in his life, and at a time when none of the scientific truths he put forth were even dreamt of by scientific men. Even if he had made known nothing but the Seven Properties of Nature (11), the key to all her mysteries, he would for ever rank among the greatest lights of science. I confess I am at a perfect loss to account for this extraordinary knowledge in an untutored shoemaker, such as Bohme was. If there were any work extant, or known to have been extant before or at his time, in which an account of the Seven Properties was given, I should say, he must have copied from that, though this theory would still leave the original discoverer unknown; but no trace either actual or traditional of any such work, or of the knowledge of these properties except of such as is implied in the universal veneration in which the number seven has ever been held is anywhere discoverable. True, Bonnie's terminology is chiefly borrowed from the alchemists, but not his knowledge. Whence then did he derive it? No one who has studied its details can doubt of their truth. No one before him has put them forth. Is then intuition possible? Was Bohme endowed with that gift? This is in fact a greater secret than any handed down in any secret society, ancient or modern. Of course scientific men, as they are called, laugh at Bohme as a mad dreamer, just as the Royal Society laughed at the electric discoveries of Franklin he was a printer who had actually worked at the press, what could he know of electricity? How could he solve a problem that had puzzled the most learned of their members? And how can Bohme, the despised and illiterate shoemaker, teach the scientists of our day anything? But the fact remains, that in the writings of this poor cobbler lie the germs of all the discoveries in physical science hitherto, and yet to be, made.

251. Bohme's Influence - I am well aware that this assertion will again meet with the derision it has hitherto encountered. Yet the reader who has accompanied me thus far ought to pause ere he joins the laughers. He will have had ample proofs that I accept nothing on mere authority, however high it may be considered. I want proof, positive proof, of any alleged fact, before I accept it as fact. If, therefore, with this disposition on my part, and after the; study of Bohme's works, pursued for a number of years, with opportunities such as few have had for the hierophant that initiated me into the mysteries of the German theosopher was undoubtedly the most learned Bohmite in this or any other country; in fact, the only man that understood him thoroughly if under these circumstances I entertain the opinions expressed in the foregoing paragraph, they cannot well be without foundation. But whoso is not to be convinced by Bohme's demonstration of the Seven Properties cannot be convinced by any argument. And Bohme's writings have not been without a deep and lasting, though latent, influence on modern philosophy and science. Even Newton was largely indebted to him. Among Sir Isaac's papers there were found large extracts out of Bohme's works, written with his own hand; and he thence learnt that attraction is the first and fundamental law of nature. Of course, the scientific elaboration of the axiom is all Newton's own, and it detracts nothing from his glory that he learnt the law from Bohme. Newton even went further; he and Dr. Newton, his relative, set up furnaces, and were for several months hard at work in quest of the tincture so largely spoken of by Bohme. But the influence of this

author is still more strikingly seen in the writings of Francis Baader, a German physicist of the present day, who has pursued his scientific inquiries by the light feebly caught, it is true, in his mind's mirror of Bohme's revelations. The greatest philosophic thinkers of this and the preceding century have drunk at the spring of Bohme's writings; and the systems of Leibnitz, Laplace, Schelling, Hegel, Fichte, and others, are distinctly permeated by his spirit but none sufficiently, and hence no one of their systems is satisfactory. Goethe was well versed in Bohme, and many allusions in his writings, which the critics can make nothing of, may be explained by passages from Bohme. Thus the commentators and translators of "Faust" have made the most ridiculous guesses as to the meaning to be attached to the "Mothers," to whom Faust is to descend in his search for Helen. The "Mothers" are the first three properties of nature (II), and all the instr actions given by Mephistopheles to Faust before his descent ad inferos form a highly poetical, and at the same time philosophical, description of them. If scientific men, instead of laughing at Bohme, would study his works, we should have no Darwinism, no theories of the sun's refrigeration, and no President of the British Association propounding the monstrous doctrine that life on this earth had its origin in the life carried hither on fragments struck off other planets and celestial bodies and falling on this globe a theory which, even could it for one moment be entertained, would still leave the question, "Whence came life?" unanswered. Nor should we have the Huxleys and Tyndalls assuming that life can be put into a creature, after its material body is made, which is no better than assuming that a circle and its roundness are two separate things that first comes the figure and afterwards its roundness. Bohme, whom they look upon as a dreamer, would show them, the real dreamers, that life makes the body to manifest itself; when a growing acorn puts forth sprouts, it is the life creeping out, feeling its way, and clothing itself in matter as it goes along, and in order to go along. Let scientists read that magnificent chapter beginning with: "We see that all life is essential; it manifests itself by the germing of the essences." What theology might learn from Bohme cannot be comprised in a few words: the vexed questions of the origin of evil, predestination, Christ's flesh and blood which are to regenerate man, their nature and action, are all profoundly and pseudoscientifically expounded in the writings of this author. But as he had no academic title, nor even common education, they despise him; and yet some of these very men will put faith in equally illiterate spiritualists.

252. Sketch of Bohme's Life - Jacob Bohme was born at Gorlitz, in Upper Lusatia, in 1575. In his childhood he was engaged in tending cattle. In this solitary life and the constant contemplation of nature he felt himself a poet, and, as he imagined, destined for great things. He saw an occult meaning in all the voices of the country; and, believing that therein he heard the voice of God, he lent his ear to a revelation he regarded as coming from God Himself through the medium of nature. At the age of fifteen or sixteen he was apprenticed to a shoemaker at Gorlitz. The sedentary occupation increased his tendency to mysticism. Severe and zealous for good manners and morals, and quite wrapped up in himself, he was considered proud by some, and mad by others. And indeed, having received no education whatever, his ideas were necessarily confused, obscure, and disconnected. In 1594 he married. Though a good husband and good father, he did not cease from being a visionary; and, driven to it by frequent dreams, which he attributed to the influence of the Holy Spirit, he finally decided on writing. His first work was the "Aurora," the best known, but the most imperfect, of all his writings, both as regards style and matter. It brought upon him the persecution of the clergy, at whose instance the magistracy of Gorlitz prohibited his writing any more an order which he obeyed for a number of years; but eventually the promptings of his spirit were no longer to be withstood, and he entirely gave himself up to the composition of his numerous writings during the last six years of his life, in which he produced among other works the "Mysterium Magnum," the "Signature Rerum," the "Threefold Life," the "Six Theosophic Points," the "Divine Contemplation," the "Supersensual Life," all of which contain, amidst much that is incongruous, whimsical, obscure, and unintelligible, passages of such profound knowledge and comprehensive meaning that no true philosopher dares

to despise them, and which in fact will yet be recognised as the only solid bases of all true science. Now and then we meet in his writings with passages of such poetic beauty, such lofty views of Deity and Nature, as surpass all the conceptions of the greatest poets of all ages. His works, written in German, during his lifetime circulated only in manuscript; they were afterwards translated into Dutch, and from this language they were rendered into English. The German edition of his works, full of errors, did not appear until 1682. In France, St.Martin, le Philosophe Inconnu, translated some of them into French. His greatest commentator was Dionysius Andreas Freher, a German, who lived many years in this country, and whose works, all written in English with the exception of two, written in German, and translated into English by the present writer exist only in manuscript, copies of some of them being in the British Museum, whilst the originals were in the possession of the late Mr. Christopher Walton, of Highgate, who, before his death, presented them, together with his unique collection of books and MSS. relating to mystical topics, including the translations made by the present writer, to Dr. Williams' Library, London, for public benefit. William Law, the learned English divine, who had the use of these MSS., is his greatest English commentator; his "Appeal," "Way to Divine Knowledge," " Spirit of Prayer," and "Spirit of Love," show how well he had seized the leading ideas of Bohme's system. Bohme died in 1624, his last words being, "Now I am going into paradise."

253. The Philadelpliians - Bohme himself never founded any sect. He was too much wrapt up in his glorious visions to think of gathering disciples and perpetuating his name by such means: like the sun, he shed his light abroad, because it was his nature to do so, unheedful whether it fell on rich or barren ground, leaving it to fructify according to its own inherent qualities. And the fruit is to come yet. For the society of the "Philadelphians," founded towards the close of the seventeenth century by Jane Lead, whose vain visions undoubtedly were the result of her study of the work of Bohme, never led to any results, spiritual or scientific. The society, in fact, only existed about seven

years, and its members had but vague and imperfect notions of the meaning and tendency of the writings of their great master.

III

EMANUEL SWEDENBORG

254. Emanuel Swedenborg - A mystic, who as yet has made much more noise in the world, though totally unworthy of being compared with Jacob Bohme for this latter has left to the world solid and positive scientific knowledge, founded on an extraordinary insight into Nature and her operations; whilst the former has left it nothing but some poetical ideas, with a farrago of nonsensical rubbish, such as hundreds of confessed madmen have written is Emanuel Swedenborg. Still he was a man of great parts. In him were combined the opposite qualities of scientist, poet, and visionary. The desire of knowledge made him master the whole cycle of the sciences of his age, and when twenty-eight years old he was one of the most learned men of his country. In 1716 he visited the English, Dutch, French, and German universities. In 1718 he transported for Charles XII. a number of vessels over land from one coast to another. In 1721 he visited the mines of Europe, and wrote a description of them in his great work " Daedalus Hyperboreus." Then he gave himself up to theology, and unexpectedly turned to mysticism, often the denial of theology. He was fifty-five years old when he began to look within himself and to discover the wonders of the ideal world; after the mines of the earth, he explored the depths of the soul, and in this later exploration he forgot science. His pretended revelations drew upon him the hatred of the clergy, but he enjoyed such consideration in his own country that they could not injure him. At the Diet of 1751 Count Hopken declared that the most valuable writings on finance proceeded from the pen of Swedenborg. A mystical financier was what the world had never seen, and perhaps will never see again.[13] He died in London. There is an English society which prints and circulates his works, filling about fifty large volumes;

---

[13] Yet in the late Mr. Laurence Oliphant it again saw a character closely resembling that of Swedenborg the sharp, shrewd man of business and of the world, and the mystic. History repeats itself.

and he has many followers in this country. He moreover made many discoveries in astronomy, chemistry, and medicine, and was the forerunner of Gall in

255. His Writings and Theories - Much in his writings is no doubt absurd; but still we think a sense, not at once apparent, but which turns nonsense into sense, may be discovered therein. Whoso attentively reads the "New Jerusalem," or the " Journey to the Astral Worlds," must see that there is a hidden meaning in his abstruse language. It cannot be assumed that a man who had shown so much vigour of mind in his numerous works on poetry, philosophy, mathematics, and natural history a man who constantly spoke of "correspondences," wherein he attributed to the least thing a hidden sense a man whose learning was unbounded and acute that such a man wrote without attaching some real meaning to his illusory language. The religion he professes is philanthropy, and consequently he gives to the abstract idea of the perfect man the name of Man-God, or Jesus Christ; those who aspire to it are angels and spirits; their union becomes heaven, and the opposite, hell.

256. Rationale of Swedenborg's Writings - From the most remote antiquity we meet with institutions as the foregoing pages have sufficiently shown ever aiming at political, religious, and intellectual reform, but expressing their ideas by speaking allegorically of the other world and the life to come, of God and angels, or using architectural terms. This practice, which is permanent, and permeates all secret societies, aims at morality in conduct, justice in government, general happiness and progress, but aims at all these according to certain philosophical ideas, viz., that all men are free and equal; but understanding that these ideas, in the various conditions of actual society, in its different classes, and in the heads of government and worship, would meet with powerful opponents, it takes its phraseology from an imaginary world successfully to carry out its objects. Therefore its external worship resembles ours, but by the science of correspondences it becomes something different, which is thus

expressed by Swedenborg: "There is in heaven a divine cultus outwardly similar to ours, but inwardly different. I was permitted to enter into the celestial temple (perhaps the lodge), where are shown the harmonised divinity and the deified humanity."

257. The New Jerusalem - One of the chief conceptions of Swedenborg, as expounded in the "New Jerusalem," is the divine in the heart of every man, interpreted by humanity, which is one of the articles of faith of (true) Masonry. " To will and to do right without any interested aims, is to restore heaven in oneself, to live in the society of angels. The conscience of every man is the compendium of heaven; all i& there, the conception and sanction of all duties and all rights." It is thus Swedenborg speaks of the mystic or sectarian life: "Between the good and the evil there is the same difference that there is between heaven and hell. Those that dwell in evil and error resemble hell, because the love of hell is the opposite of that of heaven, and the two loves hate and make war upon each other unto death. Man was created to live with the soul in the spiritual, and with the body in the natural, world. In every man, then, there are two individualities, the spiritual and the natural, the internal and the external. The internal man is truly in heaven, and enjoys intercourse with celestial spirits even during the earthly life, which is not the true, but only a simulated life. Man, being twofold, has two thoughts, the superior and the inferior, two actions, two languages, two loves. Therefore the natural man is hypocritical and false, for he is double. The spiritual man is necessarily sincere and true, because he is simple and one; in him the spirit has exalted and attracted the natural; the external has identified itself with the internal. This exaltation was happily attained to by the ancients, who in earthly objects pursued their celestial correspondences."

258. The Correspondences - He returns over and over again to the science of the correspondences, alluding to the initiations of the ancients, the true life that succeeds the simulated initiatory death, the mystical heaven, which tothe Egyptians and Greeks was nothing but the temple. "The science of the correspondences among the ancients was

the highest science. The Orientals and Egyptians expressed it by hieroglyphics, which, having become unintelligible, generated idolatry. The correspondences alone can open the eyes of the mind, unveil the spiritual world, and make that apprehensible which does not come under the cognisance of the senses." Again he says: "I will show you what faith and charity are. Instead of faith and charity think of warmth and light, and you will understand all. Faith in its substance is truth, i.e., wisdom; charity in its essence is affection, i.e., love. Love and wisdom, or charity and faith, the good and the true, form the life of God in man." In the description of the fields of heaven, the guiding angel perhaps the warden of the lodge says to Swedenborg that the things around him are correspondences of the angelic science, that all he sees plants, fruits, stones all is corresponding, just as in masonic lodges. As there are three degrees in life, so there are three heavens, and the conditions of their respective inhabitants correspond with those of the initiated of the three masonic degrees. The "New Jerusalem" may be considered also as a protest against the papal rule, hated by Swedenborg, as by all sectaries. He sought its fate in the Apocalypse, as formerly did the Albigenses; and declared that the corrupt Roman clergy must make way for a better priesthood, and the decayed and idolatrous church for a new temple. To increase the authority of his words he adds: "What I tell you, I learned in heaven," probably the sectarian heaven, into which he had been initiated. Extracts might be multiplied, but the above will suffice to show the spirit that animates the writings of Swedenborg; they will suffice to show that to enter into the hidden thoughts of most emblems, rites, and secret societies, it is necessary to consider the twofold, and even threefold, sense of the different figures. Every symbol is a mystery; nothing is done or said in secret assemblies that is not worthy of scrutiny names, members, forms, all are indications, hints of hidden truths, dangerous truths, and therefore covered with double and triple veils.

259. Various Swedenborgian Sects - From these writings arose various sects, one of them composed of men who await the New Jerusalem, believing in the marvellous prophecies, the conversations with angels,

the seraphic marriages of the elect, and considering themselves the true disciples of Christ, because Swedenborg called the Sun of Mercy, which spreads light and warmth throughout the universe, the Saviour of the world. This sect has most followers in England. The other sects boast of possessing the greatest secrets of their master. Of these sects the following may be mentioned.

260. Illuminati of Avignon - Pernetti, a Benedictine monk, and Gabrianca, a Polish nobleman and a Mason, were the first to surround with whimsical rites and ceremonies the knowledge and reveries of the Swedish mystic. In 1760 they established at Avignon a society of Illuminati, not to be confounded with the Illuminati of Bavaria, nor with any other Illuminati. The city of the popes became a sectarian stronghold, with affiliated lodges in the chief towns of France. The members occupied themselves with philosophy, astronomy, and that social chemistry, which then subjected to a formidable examination all the elements of which political society is composed.

261. Illuminated Theosophists - Paris wanted to have its own Swedenborgian rite, not satisfied with having introduced that of Pernetti The Freemason Chartanier, who in 1766 was the master of the Parisian lodge "Socrates," modified the rite of Avignon, and called the new order the "Illuminated Theosophists," and after an active propaganda in France, crossed the Channel and opened a lodge in London, where at first he met with much success; but the rite was soon abandoned.

262. Philosophic Scotch Rite - Another modification of the Avignon rite was one introduced in 1770 by the Abbe Pernetti, who was entirely devoted to alchymy. He called the rite the "Hermetic" rite; but, as its name implies, it was more alchymistical than masonic. Boileau, a physician of Paris, and zealous follower of Pernetti, remodelled the Hermetic rite, rendered it more purely masonic, and gave it the name of the "Philosophic Scotch rite." The two rites were afterwards united into twelve degrees, the last of which is the " Sublime Master of the

Luminous Ring," which boasted of being derived from Pythagoras. In 1780 an Academy of the Sublime Masters of the Luminous Ring was established in France, the initiation into which consisted of the presumed philosophic doctrines of the sage of Samos.

263. Rite of the Philalethes - Another rite founded on the masonic speculations of Swedenborg was one invented in the lodge of the " United Friends," in Paris. The members, among whom were Condorcet and Antoine Court de Gebelin, the author of the "Monde Primitif," called themselves "Philalethes," or "Searchers after Truth," and the founder was Lavalette de Langes, Keeper of the Royal Treasury. It was divided into twelve classes or chambers; the first six degrees were styled Petty, and the last six High Masonry. Like almost all societies founded on Masonry, the Philalethes endeavoured to lead man to his pristine virtue and liberty; they felt the approach of the Revolution, and kept themselves au fait of events and aspirations. The lodge of the Amis Re'unis, the centre of the system, possessed a rich collection of works and MSS. on secret societies, a large chemical laboratory, a cabinet of natural history, all under the care of De Langes; but at his death, in 1788, the precious collection was dispersed and the lodge dissolved.

A lodge, in imitation of the above, was founded at Narbonne in 1780, but with considerable modifications. The brethren called themselves Philadelphians, who are not to be confounded with the Philadelphian Society founded in London about a century before, though they professed to derive their rites from England. They were divided into three categories or temples, and ten classes or circles. After the first three masonic degrees came the " Perfect Master," the "Elect," and the "Architect," forming the fourth. The fifth comprised the "Sublime Scotch," the sixth the "Knight of the East" and the "Prince of Jerusalem." The four remaining degrees were supposed to be the depositories of masonic knowledge, philosophical and physical, and of mystic science, fit to fortify and exalt the mind of man. These four degrees were called the first to the fourth chapters of RoseCroix.

264. Rite of Swederiborg - What is properly known as the rite of Swedenborg was another modification of the order of the Illuminati of Avignon (260), effected by the Marquis de Thome in 1783, wherein he endeavoured to restore the true meaning of the doctrines of the Swedish mystic. It was a critical labour of some value, and the rite is still practised in several lodges of Northern Europe. It consists of six degrees: Apprentice, Companion, Master Theosophite, Illuminated Theosophite, Blue Brother, Bed Brother.

265. Universal Aurora - In the same year, 1783, there was founded in Paris the Order of the "Universal Aurora," whose chief object was the support of Mesmerism. Cagliostro took an active part in it.

266. Martinez Paschalis - The influence of the writings of Jacob Bohme, though perceptible in all mystic degrees founded since his day, is most visible in the mystic Masonry called "Martinism," from its founder, Martinez Paschalis, and its reformer, the Marquis of St.-Martin, the " Unknown Philosopher." Martinez Paschalis was a Portuguese and a Jew, but having turned Christian after the manner of the Gnostics of the first centuries, he began in 1754 to assemble disciples in various French cities, chiefly Marseilles, Bordeaux, Toulouse, and Lyons, none of whom rose to the degree of epopt, or knew the secrets of the master, though he inspired all with the greatest respect and devotion towards himself. His secret doctrine appears to have been a confused medley of Gnosticism and Christianised Judaism, not excluding the cabala, which in fact is found more or less in all theosophic speculations, even in those of Bohme; though his followers as well as his opponents, from not understanding him, have attributed to him many erroneous opinions which he never entertained. Paschalis laid great stress on the omnipotence of will this is a point constantly insisted on, its truth being demonstrated from the deepest ground, by Bohme. With this writer he taught that intelligence and will are the only active forces of nature, whose phenomena man can control by willing energetically; and that man in this manner can rise to the knowledge of the supreme Ens. With these principles, Martinez

condemned all empires founded on violence, and all societies based on convention. He longed for a return to the patriarchal times which the more enlightened, however, look upon as times of rank tyranny; and he also formed other conceptions which we shall see more fully developed by the Illuminati.

The life of Martinez, like his doctrines, is full of gaps and mysteries. He arrived in a town no one knew whence, he departed no one knew whither; all at once he was seen where least expected. From 1768 to 1778 Paschalis resided either at Paris or at Lyons. Then he suddenly crossed the ocean, and died at St. Domingo in 1779. These sudden appearances and disappearances were perhaps needed to maintain his prestige. De Maitre, who had much intercourse with his disciples, states it for certain, that the Order founded by him, and called the "Rite of the elected Cohens or Priests," had superior degrees unknown to the members of the lower grades. We know the names of nine degrees, though not their rituals: they were Apprentice, FellowCraft, Master, Grand Elect, Apprentice Cohen, Fellow-Craft Cohen, Master Cohen, Grand Architect, Knight Commander. The zeal of some of the members, among whom we find Holbach, Duchamteau, and St.-Martin, caused the Order to prolong its existence some time after the death of the founder.

267. Saint-Martin - We have seen that St. Martin was a disciple of Paschalis; he was also, for his day, a profound expounder of the doctrines of Bohme, some of whose works he translated. He to some extent reformed the rite of Paschalis, dividing it into ten degrees, classed in two temples. The first temple comprised the degrees of Apprentice, Fellow-Craft, Master, Ancient Master, Elect, Grand Architect, and Master of the Secret. The degrees of the second temple were Prince of Jerusalem, Knight of Palestine, and Knight of Kadosh. The order, as modified by him, extended from Lyons into the principal cities of France, Germany, and Russia, where the celebrated Prince Repnin (1734-1801) was its chief protector. It is now extinct.

268. Merits of the Rosicrucians - A halo of poetic splendour

surrounds the order of the Rosicrucians; the magic lights of fancy play around their graceful day-dreams, while the mystery in which they shrouded themselves lends an additional charm to their history. But their brilliancy was that of a meteor. It just flashed across the realms of imagination and intellect, and vanished for ever; not, however, without leaving behind some permanent and lovely traces of its hasty passage, just as the momentary ray of the sun, caught on the artist's lens, leaves a lasting image on the sensitive paper. Poetry and romance are deeply indebted to the Rosicrucians for many a fascinating creation. The literature of every European country contains hundreds of pleasing fictions, whose machinery has been borrowed from their system of philosophy, though that itself has passed away; and it must be admitted that many of their ideas are highly ingenious, and attain to such heights of intellectual speculation as we find to have been reached by the Sophists of India. Before their time, alchymy had sunk down, as a rule, to a grovelling delusion, seeking but temporal advantages, and occupying itself with earthly dross only: the Rosicrucians spiritualised and refined it by giving the chimerical search after the philosopher's stone a nobler aim than the attainment of wealth, namely, the opening of the spiritual eyes, whereby man should be able to see the supernal world, and be filled with an inward light to illumine his mind with true knowledge. The physical process of the transmutation of metals was by them considered as analogical with man's restoration to his unf alien state, as set forth in Bohme's Signatura Rerum, chapters vii., x.-xii. The true Roscrucians, therefore, may be defined as spiritual alchymists, or Theosophists.

269. Origin of the Society doubtful - The society is of very uncertain origin. It is affirmed by some writers that from the fourteenth century there existed a society of physicists and alchymists who laboured in the search after the philosopher's stone; and a certain Nicolo Barnaud undertook journeys through Germany and France for the purpose of establishing a Hermetic society. From the preface of the work, "Echo of the Society of the Rosy Cross," it moreover follows that in 1597 meetings were held to institute a secret society for the promotion of

alchymy. Another indication of the actual existence of such a society is found in a book published in 1605, and entitled, "Restoration of the Decayed Temple of Pallas," which gives a constitution of Rosicrucians. Again, in 1610, the notary Haselmeyer pretended to have read in a MS. the Fama Fraternitatis, comprising all the laws of the Order. Four years afterwards appeared a small work, entitled " General Reformation of the World," which in fact contains the Fama Fraterjiitatis, where it is related that a German, Christian Rosenkreuz, founded such a society in the fourteenth century, after having learned the sublime science in the East. Of him it is related, that when, in 1378, he was travelling in Arabia, he was called by name and greeted by some philosophers, who had never before seen him; from them he learned many secrets, among others that of prolonging life. On his return he made many disciples, and died at the age of 150 years, not because his strength failed him, but because he was tired of life. In 1604 one of his disciples had his tomb opened, and there found strange inscriptions, and a MS. in letters of gold. The grotto in which this tomb was found, by the description given of it, strongly reminds us of the Mithraic Cave. Another work published in 1615, the Confessio Fraternitatis Rosce Crucis, contains an account of the object and spirit of the Order.

270. Rosicrucian Literature - The Thesaurinella Chymicaaurea, already referred to (sect. 244), may have been a Rosicrucian work, as also Raymwndii Lullii Theoria. In 1615, Michael Meyer published at Cologne his Themis Aurea, hoc est, de legibus Fraternitatis Rosece, Crucis, which purported to contain all the laws and ordinances of the brotherhood. Another work, entitled "The Chymical Marriage of Christian Rosenkreuz," and published in 1616, in the shape of a comic romance, is really a satire on the alchymistical delusions of the author's time. Both works were written, as we learn from his autobiography, by Valentine Andrea, a Lutheran clergyman of Herrenberg, near Tubingen. But instead of being taken for what the author intended them satires on the follies of Paracelsus, Weigel, and the alchymists the public swallowed his fictions as facts: printed letters and pamphlets

appeared everywhere, addressed to the imaginary brotherhood, whilst others denounced and condemned it. One Christopher Nigrinus wrote a book to prove the Rosicruciaus were Calvinists, but a passage taken from one of their writings showed them to be zealous Lutherans. Andrea himself, in his "Turris Babel" and "Mythologia Christiana," published circa 1619, condemns Rosicrucianism. Impostors, indeed, pretended to belong to the fraternity, and to possess its secrets, and found plenty of dupes. Numerous works also continued to appear. Here are the titles of a few of them:

"Epistola ad patres de Rosea Cruce." Frankfurt, 1617.

"Quick Message to the Philosophical Society of the Rosy Cross." By Valentine Ischirnessus. Danzig, 1617.

"The Whole Art and Science of the God-Illuminated Fraternity of Christian Rosenkreuz." By Theophilus Schweighart. 1617.

"Discovery of the Colleges and Axioms of the Illuminated Fraternity of Christian Rosenkreuz." By Theophilus Schweighart. 1618.

"De naturce secretis qiiibusdam at Vulcaniam artem chymicce ante omnia necessariis, addressed to the Masters of the Philosophic Fraternity of the Rosy Cross." 1618. N. P.

"Sisters of the Rosy Cross; or, Short Discovery of these Ladies, and what Religion, Knowledge of Divine and Natural Things, Trades and Arts, Medicines, &c., may be found therein." Parthenopolis, 1620.

"The Most Secret and Hitherto Unknown Mysteries of All Nature." By the Collegium Rosianum. Leyd'en, 1630.

Of course the scientific value of all these writings was nil, the literary scarcely more.

271. Real Objects and Results of Andreas Writings - The account given in the preceding paragraph of the literary performances of John Valentine Andrea is the popular one. But certain explanations are necessary. Andrea's Rosicrucian writings concealed political objects, the chief of which was the support of the Lutheran religion, which the

Rosicrucians themselves followed. Andrea made two journeys to Austria the first in 1612, when the Emperor Mathias ascended the throne; and the second in 1619, a few months after the Emperor's death. At Linz he had private interviews with several Austrian noblemen, all of them Lutherans. Rosicrucian lodges, to further the objects of the Reformation, were established, but numerous Catholics obtained admission to them, and gradually turned their tendencies in the very opposite direction. Andrea perceiving this withdrew from Eosicrucianism, and endeavoured by the subsequent writings, mentioned above, to disavow his former connection with it. With the same object also he, during his second residence in Austria, founded the "Fraternitas Christi," to which many members of the Protestant Austrian nobility sought admission. Three years after the society was prohibited by the Government, and its final suppression hastened by an opposition society, founded by the Catholics, with the sanction of the Pope, first at Olmiitz and then at Vienna, the leaders being the Counts Althan, Gonzaga, and Sforza; the order was called that of the "Blue Cross." The Rosicrucians, being no longer under the influence of Andrea, broke up into a number of independent lodges, which quickly degenerated into mere traps to catch credulous dupes and their money; hence the duration of most was short. But on the accession of Joseph II., whose liberal principles were known, the Rosicrucians, as well as other secret societies, sprang into life again. Freemasonry became the fashion of the day, Masonic implements were worn as "charms;" the ladies carried muffs of white silk edged with blue, to represent the Mason's aprons, and so on. The Emperor found it necessary to regulate the conduct of these secret societies. He suppressed all except that of the Freemasons, to whom in 1785 he granted a patent, which began thus: " Since nothing is to exist in a well-regulated state without proper supervision, We deem it necessary thus to declare our will: The so-called Masonic Societies, whose secrets are unknown to us, since we never were curious enough to inquire into their juggleries (gaiwkeleien)" &c. This edict, which abolished the other societies, but allowed the Freemasons to continue their " juggleries," as the Emperor called their ceremonies, threw many of the suppressed societies, including the Rosicrucians, into the arms of the Masonic Fraternity; the Asiatic Brethren, as we shall see further on (281), transferred their activity from Vienna to Sleswick.

272. Ritual and Ceremonies - The "juggleries" of the Rosicrucians, whom the Emperor suppressed, were those of the "constitution" of 1763, and as follows: The apartment where the initiation took place contained the tabella mystica, presently to be described. The floor was covered with a green carpet, and on it were placed the following objects: A glass globe, standing on a pedestal of seven steps, and divided into two parts, representing light and darkness; three candelabra, placed triangularly; nine glasses, symbolising male and female properties; the quintessence, and various other things; a brazier, a circle, and a napkin.

The candidate for initiation is introduced by a brother, who takes him into a room where a light, pen, ink, and paper, sealing-wax, two red cords, and a bare sword are laid on a table. The candidate is asked whether he firmly intends to become a pupil of true wisdom. Having answered affirmatively, he gives up his hat and sword, and pays the fees. His hands having been bound, and his eyes bandaged and a red cord put round his neck, he is led to the door of the lodge, on which the introducer gently knocks nine times. The doorkeeper opens it and asks "Who is there?" The hierophant answers, "An earthly body holding the spiritual man imprisoned in ignorance." The doorkeeper, "What is to be done to him?" The introducer, "Kill his body and purify his spirit." The doorkeeper, "Then bring him into the place of justice." They enter, place themselves in front of the circle, the candidate kneeling on one knee. The master stands at his right hand, with a white wand, the introducer at his left, holding a sword; both wear their aprons. The master says, "Child of man, I conjure you through all degrees of profane Freemasonry, and by the endless circle, which comprises all creatures and the highest wisdom, to tell me for what purpose you have come here?" The candidate, "To acquire wisdom, art, and virtue." The master, " Then live! But your spirit must again rule over your body; you have found grace, arise and be free." He is then unbound, steps into the circle, the master and the introducer hold the wand and sword crosswise, the candidate lays three fingers thereon, and as soon as the master says "Now listen," the candidate repeats the oath propounded to him, which is simply a declaration that he will have no secrets from his brethren, and will lead a virtuous life. Then he is invested with the title of the order, the seal, password and sign, hat and sword, and has the mystical table interpreted to him, after which, like the Masons, he and the other brethren go from " labour " to " refreshment."

This mystical table is divided into nine vertical and thirteen horizontal compartments. The first column of nine divisions gives the numbers, the second the names of the different degrees. The lowest comprises the Juniores, who know next to nothing; the highest the Magi, from whom nothing is hidden, who are masters over all things, like Moses, Hermes, Hyram. Their jewel is an equilateral triangle. According to the table, the different degrees have meeting-places all over Europe and Asia; the Magi meet at Smyrna every ten, years; the Magistri, a degree below, at Camra, in Poland, and Paris, in France, every nine years; the Juniores every two years at such a place as may be most convenient. The admission fee to the degree of Magus is ninety-nine gold marks; to that of Junior, three marks. The Minores, who know the "philosophical sun," and "perform marvellous cures," pay what they choose.

273. Rosicrucianism in England in the Past - The works of Andrea excited much attention in England, where mysticism and astrology at that time had many adherents, as Wood's "Athene Oxonienses" fully shows. Robert Fludd in this country was the great champion of the Rosicrucians. His two most important works concerning them are "Apologia et Compendiaria Fraternitatem de Rosea Cruce suspicionis et infamise maculis aspersam, veritatis quasi Fluctibus abluens et abstergens." Leyden, 1616. "Tractatus Apologeticus integritatem Societatis de Rosea Cruce defendeus." Lugdvai Batavorum, 1617. This latter is really a duplicate of the former with a new title.

Fludd was followed by one Heydon, born 1629. Strange to

say, an attorney, who, among other works on the Rosicrucians wrote "An Epologue for an Apilogue," wherein occur passages such as this: "I shall tell you what Rosicrucians are, and that Moses was their father. Some say they were of the order of Elias, some of Ezechiel, others define them to be the officers of the generalissimo of the world; that are as the eyes and ears of the great king, seeing and hearing all things, for they are seraphically illuminated as Moses was, according to thi- order of the elements, earth refined to water, water to air, air to fire." Such gibberish as this was served up for the reading public some centuries ago, and, I suppose, satisfied them. In another of his works Heydon maintained that it was criminal to eat though he did not abstain from the practice himself but that there was a fine fatness in the air quite sufficient for nourishment, and that for men of very voracious appetites, it was enough to place a cataplasm of cooked meat on the epigastrium to satisfy their hunger.

In 1646 Elias Ashmole, William Lilly, Dr. Thomas Wharton, George Wharton, Dr. J. Hewitt, Dr. J. Pearson, and others formed a Rosicrucian society in London, practically to carry out the scheme propounded in Bacon's " New Atlantis," that is, the erection of the House of Solomon. Itwas to remain as unknown as the island of Bensalem, that is to say, the study of nature was to be pursued esoterically, not exoterically. The carpet in their lodge represented the pillars of Hermes; seven steps, the first four of which symbolised the four elements, and the other three salt, sulphur, and mercury, led to an " exchequer," or higher court, or stage, on which were displayed the symbols of creation, or of the work of the six days. Some of the members of this society were Freemasons, hence they were enabled to hold their meetings in Masons' Hall, Masons' Alley, Basinghall Street. They kept nothing secret except their signs.

274. Origin of Name - The name is generally derived, from the supposed founder of the order, Rosenkreuz, Rose Cross; but according to others, it is taken from the armorial bearings of the Andrea family, which were a St. Andrew's cross and four roses. Others again, modern writers, say it is composed of ros, dew, and crux, the cross; crux is

supposed mystically to represent LVX, or light, because the figure X exhibits the three letters; and light, in the opinion of the Rosicrucians, produces gold; whilst dew, ros, with the (modern) alchymists, was a powerful solvent. But Mr. Waite, in his " Real History of the Rosicrucians" (London, 1887), argues with much force, that the Rosicrucians bore the rose and cross as their badge because they were ardent Protestants, to whom Martin Luther was an idol, prophet, and master, and the device on the seal of Martin Luther was a cross-crowned heart rising from the centre of a rose. The theory has much in its favour, but we cannot quite set aside the fact that in all mystical systems the rose and the cross have always been emblems of paramount importance. We meet with them in the most ancient Hindu mythology. Lackschemi, the wife of Vishnu, was found in a rose with 108 leaves, whence the Indian rosary has the same number of beads, and to the Hindus the cross was the symbol of creation. We have already seen in the account of the Eleusinian Mysteries what importance was attached to the rose, and that Apuleius makes Lucius to be restored to his primitive form by eating roses; and the "Romance of the Rose" was considered by the Rosicrucians as one of the most perfect specimens of Provencal literature, and as the allegorical chef d'osuvre of their sect. It is undeniable that this was coeval with chivalry, and had from thenceforth a literature rich in works, in whose titles the word Rosa is incorporated; as the Rosa Piilosophorum, of which no less than ten occur in the Artis Auriferce quam Chemiam vocant (Basilea, 1610). The connection of the Rosicrucians with chivalry, the Troubadours, and the Albigenses, cannot be denied. Like these, they swore the same hatred to Eome; like these, they called Catholicism the religion of hate. They solemnly declared that the Pope was Antichrist, and rejected pontifical and Mahomedaii dogmas, styling them the beasts of the East and West.

275. Statements concerning themselves - They pretended to feel neither hunger nor thirst, nor to be subject to age or disease; to possess the power of commanding spirits, and attracting pearls and precious stones, and of rendering themselves invisible. They stated the aim of

their society to be the restoration of all the sciences, and especially of medicine; and by occult artifices to procure treasures and riches sufficient to supply the rulers and kings with the necessary means for promoting the great reforms of society then needed. They were bound to conform to five fundamental laws: I. Gratuitously to heal the sick. 2. To dress in the costume of the country in which they lived. 3. To attend every year the meeting of the Order. 4. When dying to choose a successor. 5. To preserve the secret one hundred years.

276. Poetical Fictions of Rosicrucians - These are best known from the work of Joseph Francis Borri, a native of Milan, and it is to them the " poetic splendour which surrounds the Order," which, in fact, gave real existence to it, is due. Having preached against the abuses of the Papacy, and promulgated opinions which were deemed heretical, Borri was seized by order of the Inquisition and condemned to perpetual imprisonment. He died in the Castle of St Angelo in 1695. The work referred to is entitled " The Key of the Cabinet of Signer Borri," and is, in substance, nothing but the cabalistic romance entitled "The Count de Gabalis," published in 1670 by the Abbe de Villars. What we gather from this work is, that the Rosicrucians discarded for ever all the old tales of sorcery and witchcraft and communion with the devil. They denied the existence of incubi and succubi, and of all the grotesque imps monkish brains had hatched and superstitious nations believed in. Man, they said, was surrounded by myriads of beautiful and beneficent beings, all anxious to do him service. These beings were the elemental spirits; the air was peopled with sylphs, the water with undines or naiads, the earth with gnomes, and the fire with salamanders. These the Eosicrucian could bind to his service, and imprison in a ring, a mirror, or a stone, and compel to appear when called, and render answers to such questions as he chose to put. All these beings possessed great powers, and were unrestrained by the barriers of space or matter. But man was in one respect their superior: he had an immortal soul, they had not. They could, however, become sharers in man's immortality, if they could inspire one of that race with the passion of love towards them. On this notion is founded the

charming story of " Undine; " Shakespeare's Ariel is a sylph; the " Rape of the Lock," the Masque of " Comus," the poem of " Salamandrine," all owe their machinery to the poetic fancies of the Rosicrucians. Among other things they taught concerning the elemental spirits, they asserted that they were composed of the purest particles of the element they inhabited, and that in consequence of having within them no antagonistic qualities, being made of but one element (II), they could live for thousands of years. The Rosicrucians further held the doctrine of the signatura rerum, by which they meant that everything in this visible world has outwardly impressed on it its inward spiritual character. Moreover, they said that by the practice of virtue man could even on earth obtain a glimpse of the spiritual world, and above all things discover the philosopher's stone, which, however, could not be found except by the regenerate, for "it is in close communion with the heavenly essence." According to them the letters INRI, the sacred word of the Order of Rose Croix, signified Igne Natura Regenerando Integrat.

277. The Hague Lodge - In the year 1622, Montanus, or, by his real name, Ludwig Conrad, of Bingen, was expelled from an order of Rosicrucians which then existed at The Hague, where they had a grand palace. They held their meetings by order of the master, called "imperator," in great cities, such as Amsterdam, Danzig, Nuremberg, Hamburg, Mantua, Venice, besides such as were held at The Hague. They publicly wore a black silk cord, but at their meetings they put on a gold band, to which were attached a golden cross and rose. Their card of membership was a large parchment, with many seals affixed with great ceremony. When holding a public procession, they carried a small green flag. This Montanus, who wrote a book entitled "Introduction to the Hermetic Science," says, that he spent his patrimony and his wife's fortune, of eleven thousand dollars, for the benefit of the society, and that when he was totally impoverished he was expelled, being, however, bound over to keep their secrets, "which latter, indeed, I kept, as women do not reveal anything where there is nothing to reveal." These pretended secrets are supposed to be

contained in a book entitled "Sinceri Renati Theophilosophia Theoretico-practica," but I have not been able to obtain or see a copy of this work. The society is supposed to have become extinct at the beginning of the eighteenth century.

278. A Rosicrucian MS - According to a statement made by Dr. von Harless in his "Jacob Bohme and the Alchymists" (2nd ed., Leipzic, 1882), a society of Rosicrucians must have existed in Germany in the year 1641. Dr. von Harless says, "I have recently had an opportunity of inspecting a Rosicrucian MS. hitherto unknown. It was probably written about 1765, and contains the statutes of an order of Rosicrucians, with the title Testamentum. The original must date from the middle of the seventeenth century, as is proved by a special warning given to members to observe secrecy, especially towards Roman Catholic ecclesiastics, two members having, from not attending to this caution, been great sufferers in 1641. The MS., besides the statutes, also contains instructions for alchymistic operations. The Order, according to the MS., had one chief, called imperator; its chief seats were Ancona, Nuremberg, Hamburg, and Amsterdam. The members were to change their residence every ten years, and maintain the greatest secrecy as to their existence. The apprenticeship lasted seven years. Their mode of addressing one another was: ave frater; the answer: rosece et aurece. The first: crucis; then both together: Benedictus Deus qui dedit nobis signum. Then the mutual production of the signum, consisting of an engraved seal, a specimen of which was also shown to Dr. von Harless."

On taking steps to obtain further particulars from Dr. von Harless himself, I learnt to my regret that he had died in 1878; and as he had given no intimation in the above-named works where the MS. is deposited, I am unable to report further thereon. But it would seem that the society referred to in the MS. was the same as the one spoken of in the "Thesaurinella," mentioned towards the end of sect. 244.

279. New Rosicrucian Constitution - In 1714. or one hundred years after Andrea's writings, there appeared a new Rosicrucian constitution,

entitled, "The True and Perfect Preparation of the Philosopher's Stone of the Brotherhood of the Golden and Rosy Cross. Published for the benefit Filiorum Doctrinw by Sincero Renato, Breslau." The preface stated that the treatise was not the writer's work, but intrusted to him by a professor of the art, whom he was not allowed to name. The author divides the work into practica ordinis minoris and practica ordinis majoris, indicating the division of the Order into two distinct fraternities, the superior one being known as the "Brethren of the Golden Cross," their symbol being a red cross, and the inferior one .as the " Brethren of the Rosy Cross," their symbol being a green cross, from which it is evident that the real work of the Order was alchymy. Each brother, on being initiated, dropped his real name, and assumed a fictitious one, as we have seen that Ludwig Conrad was known in the Order as Montanus (277), and as hereafter we find the Illuminati assume all kinds of fancy names. Renato's book further states that the Order possessed large seminaries, as the abovenamed Montanus had asserted. Article 42 of the statutes prohibited the reception of married men into the Order; in Article 17 members who wished to marry were allowed to take wives, but were to live with them pliilosopliice, whatever that may have meant. Article 44 enjoined that if a brother should, by misfortune or want of caution, be discovered by any potentate, he was rather to die than reveal the secrets of the Order.

280. The Duke of Saxe-Weimar and oilier Rosicrucians - The first modern writer who openly professed himself a Rosier ucian was Duke Ernest Augustus of Saxe- Weimar, who in 1742 published his "Theosophic Devotions" in a small edition, copies of which are easily recognised by their red morocco binding and the ducal crown and cipher on the cover. In it he refers to the "last great union of brethren," and, according to the vignette at the end of the book, he must mean Rosicrucians.

We hear of a society of Rosicrucians founded by Freemasons, whose "General Constitutions" were settled in 1763; they were based on the "Themis Aurea" of Michael Maier, who had been physician-in-ordinary and alchymist to the Emperor Rudolph (1576-1612). This revived taste was taken advantage of by many adventurers. John George Schroepfer, who kept a coffee-house at Nuremberg in 1777, established at his house a lodge, and made so much pretence to secret and exclusive knowledge, that the Duke Ferdinand of Brunswick and the Duke of Courland by whose order Schroepfer had once been flogged invited him to Dresden, where they openly patronised him, while he deluded them with the apparitions of ghosts and magical phantasma really produced by magic-lanterns and concave mirrors. But his conduct eventually so disgusted his patrons that they refused him further supplies of money,, whereupon he shot himself in a wood near Leipzic.

But this vulgar cheat left credulous disciples behind. John Rudolph Bischofswerder (1741-1803), a major, and afterwards Prussian Minister of War, who had almost been a witness of Schroepfer's death, and John Christopher Wollner (1732-1800), a clergyman, and afterwards Prussian Minister of Public Cult, continued what Schroepfer had started. Under the patronage of the Crown Prince, Frederick William of Prussia, the nephew of Frederick the Great, whom he succeeded in 1786 as King Frederick William II., established at Berlin a Rosicrucian lodge, and the enlightened views which had been introduced by, and had prevailed during the reign of, old Fritz were quickly suppressed by religious persecution. At that time Bahrdt had considerable success with his resuscitated order of Illuminati. The two highly-placed rogues saw in this plebeian a man who might some day compete with them for the king's favour; so whilst they, in league with his mistress, the Countess Lichtenau, more than ever amused their silly royal patron with the calling up of ghosts and drunken orgies, they induced him to put forth the notorious Religious Edict of 1788, which was to stem the ungodly advances of the Illuminati, and which also restored the censorship of the Press. The book (in German), entitled " The Rosicrucian in his Nakedness," published by Master "Pianco," an ex-member of the society, in 1782, was a violent attack and exposé of the Rosicrucians; but the delusion continued to flourish.

281. Origin of the Order - This Order originated probably about the year 1780, though its chiefs were not known in 1788; it was, however, suspected that Baron Ecker and Eckhofen was one of them. He resided at first at Vienna, but afterwards settled at Sleswick; he distinguished himself by his writings, but the superstitious proclaimed him a terrible Cacomagus. The order spread from Italy to Russia. Its basis was Rosicrucian, its meetings were called Melchisedeck lodges, and Jews, Turks, Persians, and Armenians might be received as members. The masters were called the Worshipful Chiefs of the Seven Churches of Asia. The full title of the Order was, " Order of the Knights and Brethren of St. John the Evangelist from Asia in Europe." The teaching of the Order was partly moral, that is to say, it instructed how to rule spirits, by breaking the seven seals; and partly physical, by showing how to prepare miraculous medicines and to make gold. It inculcated cabalistic nonsense, and was greatly detested by Rosier ucians and Freemasons two of a trade cannot agree. The names of the degrees were taken from the Hebrew, and were symbolical of their characteristics. The Order did not profess Rosicrucianism, yet in the Third Chief Degree the members were styled "True Rosicrucians." The results of the scientific researches of the masters were not communicated to aspirants; these had to discover them as they could. The fact seemed to be that the masters had nothing to communicate, but this admission would have been fatal to the Order; its secrets appearing to exist in the credulity of outsiders only.

282. Division of this Order - The Order was divided into five degrees, viz., two probationary and three chief degrees. The first probationary degree, that of the " Seekers," never consisted of more than ten members. The period of probation was fourteen months. They had lectures delivered to them every fortnight, and the costume they wore at their meetings consisted of a round black hat with black feathers, a black cloak, a black sash with three buttons in the shape of roses, white gloves, and sword with a black tassel, a black ribbon, from which was suspended a double triangle, which symbol was also embroidered on the left side of the cloak.

The second probationary degree, consisting of ten members, was called that of the "Sufferers." Its duration was seven months. Whilst the "Seekers" were theorists only, the "Sufferers" were supposed to make practical researches in physical science. They wore round black hats with black and white feathers, black cloaks with white linings and collars, on which double triangles were embroidered in gold, black sashes with white edging and three rosettes, white gloves, and swords with black and white tassels.

The First Chief Degree styled its members "Knights and Brother-Initiates from Asia in Europe." They wore round black hats with white, black, yellow, and red feathers, black cloaks with white linings and collars and gold lace; on the left breast of the cloak there was a red cross with four green roses, having in their centre a green shield with the monogram M and A. The same cross, of gold, and enamelled, was worn on a red ribbon; the member further wore a pink sash round the body edged with green and with three red roses, white gloves with a red cross and four green roses; the tassels of the swords displayed the four colours of the feathers.

283. Initiation into this Degree - On the reception of a "Sufferer" into this degree he was led into a room hung with black; the floor and furniture were covered with black cloth. The room was lit up with seven golden candlesticks, six of which had five branches each, whilst the seventh, standing in the centre, represented a human figure in a white dress and golden girdle. The chair of the master stood in the centre of the room on a dais of three steps, under a square black canopy; the back wall was partly open, but held back with seven tassels, and behind it was the Holiest of Holies, consisting of a balustrade of ten columns, on the basement of which was a picture of the sun in a triangle, surrounded by the divine fire. Under the centre candlestick was the carpet of the three masonic degrees, surrounded by nine lights, a tenth light standing a little further off at the foot of the throne. There stood, on the right, a small table, on which were placed a flaming sword, with the number 56 engraved thereon, and a green rod, with two red ends; to the left lay the Book of the Law. The "Sufferer,"

being then in an adjoining room, was asked three times if he desired to be initiated. His answer being in the affirmative, the Grand Master ordered him to be introduced, after having read the inscription on a red shield in letters of gold over the door: "Here is the Door of the Eternal; the just enter here." The introducer then rang a bell twice, the Grand Master rang once, and the door was opened. The candidate stepped up to the table, and thrice made the Master's sign. He was then told that he was accepted, and had to sign an obligation never to reveal the secrets of the Chapter. After a few other childish ceremonies he was led to the Table of Purification, on which stood three lights on as many columns. The one represented a man with the triangle, the other a woman with the triangle reversed; the central one a man with a double triangle. In the centre of the table stood a crystal cup, filled with water, in which salt had been dissolved, another cup with salt, a spoon, a bundle of cedar-wood bound with hyssop and pink and green silk. The candidate had his coat and waistcoat taken off, the collar of his shirt opened, and his right arm bared. Having knelt down, the Grand Master sprinkled his neck thrice with the water, saying, "May the Merciful One give thee the knowledge of thy weapons, of thy lance, and of the number Four [which with Rosicrucians is the root and beginning of all numbers]. Then touching his right arm he said, "May the Almighty give thee strength in battle; "and touching his breast, "May the Just One give thee as a conqueror rest in the centre." The "Sufferer" was then dressed again, the Grand Master opened the Holiest of Holies, and the candidate having taken the oath, the Grand Master dubbed him a Knight. Touching his right shoulder he said, "May the Infinite give thee strength, beauty, and wisdom for the fight; "and touching the left shoulder, "We receive thee, in the name of the most worshipful and wisest seven Fathers and Rulers of the seven Unknown Churches in Asia, as a Knight and initiated Brother." Touching him on the head, he said, " May the Eternal One give thee the light of the number Four, and thou shalt be delivered from the Eternal Death." Then there ensued mutual embracing, a little more speechifying by the Grand Master, and then the servants brought in salt, bread, wine, lamb and pork, the latter being symbolical of the Old and the New Covenant !

284. Second Chief Degree, Wise Masters - This degree could only be obtained from the Sanhedrim, which constituted the highest authority, for in this degree began the revelation of secrets. What they were has never become known to outsiders. We may assume them to have been wonderful, considering the wonderful costume the knights were entitled to wear in this degree, viz., a red hat with stripes of the four different colours mentioned, in a red cloak, with a green cross and roses, having in their centre the monogram J and C embroidered in gold on a red field; the same cross in gold, and enamelled in the same four colours, attached to a green ribbon, edged with red, and three green roses; white gloves, decorated with red crosses and green roses inside and out;. sword, with green and red tassel.

285. Third Chief Degree, or Royal Priests, or True Rosicrucians, or the Degree of Melchisedeck - This degree also could be obtained from the Sanhedrim only. The number of its members was restricted to seventy-two. Solomon in all his glory was nothing compared with the True Rosicrucians in their official costume. Here it is: a hat, gold, pink, and green, the brim turned up in front, and the name Jehovah embroidered thereon in gold, and surmounted with white, red, yellow, black, and green feathers; a long pink undergarment, fitting closely to the body, the cuffs of the sleeves being made of materials similar to those composing the hat, as also the sash, worn round the waist, whereon were embroidered three roses, one white, one red, and the centre one the colours of the sash; the stockings or hose and shoes were of pink silk. The cloak consisted of materials similar to those of the hat, and was lined with green; on the left breast was seen a point with many rays issuing from it. Round the neck the knight wore a gold chain, having alternately between the ordinary links shields with the monograms M and A and J and C, and the representation of a tree, having on the right hand a man, and on the left a woman, who with one hand cover the pudenda, and touch the tree with the other; to the end of the chain the Urim and Thummini were attached. White gloves, decorated with

green and red roses within and without, completed this gorgeous apparel.

286. Organisation of the Order - The Sanhedrim exercised the highest authority, which it could delegate to committees appointed from among its members. The authority next under the Sanhedrim was the General Chapter, after which came the Provincial Chapters. All these various departments had every one their own officials, with high-sounding titles, which need not be given here the reader will find enough of them among the Freemasons; but on reading a list of them, one cannot help exclaiming

"And every one is Knighted, And every one is Grand; Who would not be delighted To join in such a band? "

But to join in this band was somewhat expensive; the Order was a fee- trap of no mean order, something like a few of the spurious degrees in Masonry. On his initiation into the order of the Asiatic Brethren the candidate paid a fee of two ducats; when he took it into his head to found a Master Lodge, he had to pay seven ducats for the privilege, and two ducats for the carpet; for every folio of the Rules of the Lodge, ten kreuzer, or about twopence-halfpenny. The foundation of a Superior Master Lodge cost twelve ducats; of a Provincial Chapter, twenty -five ducats; of a General Chapter, fifty ducats. Every Brother paid to the Superior Master a monthly contribution of eightpence, and for extraordinary expenses and correspondence a fee proportionate to hi& means on the days of John the Baptist and John the Evangelist. These fees and subscriptions must annually have amounted to a goodly sum. What became of it? Rolling, a member, in 1787, published the laughable secrets of the Order.

287. Rosicrucian Adventurers - In 1781 there appeared at Vienna "An Address to the Rosicrucians of the Ancient System." The Order seems to have been revived about that time by Fraxinus evidently a fictitious name who was Provincial Grand Master of the four united Masonic Lodges at Hamburg. The Masons did not know that Fraxinus was a Rosicrucian, but he evidently knew how to fleece his dupes. We learn

from one Cedrinus, who was a member of one of the Hamburg lodges, that for the initiation into the Rosicrucian degrees he was by instalments mulcted in the sum of nearly 150 dollars. When Cedrinus began to express dissatisfaction at these continual extortions, Fraxinus, to quiet him, made Cedrinus keeper of the Great Seal of the Hamburg lodges. This gave the latter an opportunity of gaining an insight into the way in which degrees were manufactured, and how Masonry was corrupted by them. He fell out with Fraxinus, and everywhere proclaimed the machinations of the Rosicrucians. Fraxinus expelled him as a perjured brother.

Another Rosicrucian who obtained notoriety at about the same time was Brother Gordianus, who resided at Tubingen. He was supposed to be a Rosicrucian and an alchymist, since he lived well without having any visible means of subsistence. A schoolmaster, known by the initial L. only, had long desired to become a Rosicrucian; he consequently paid Gordianus a visit, who informed him, amongst other matters, that the object of the Order was to carry out the intentions of Valentine Andrea; that certain conditions were imposed on every member, viz., eternal silence on all concerning the Order, the introduction within six weeks of another member, to show that he was capable of winning the confidence of his fellowmen, and the payment of an initiation fee of fifty dollars. The poor schoolmaster after a time raised the money, and received the subjoined receipt, on a small blue card:

SUB RATIFICATIONS VENERAND. SUPERIOR
TETTAra Receptionis in minum Gradum
Ordinis Philosophorum incogritorum, Fratr.
A. LL et R.C. Systematis antiquioris.

A 4077.s. 8	I. GORDIAXUS
M.L.3 - + - C.	Fr. Inspector
- l - g. - + - b	Circuli II.

On the back of the card was the following:--

☉ +
Praevia sancta promissione religiosae.
Ad impletionis Articuli fundamentals.
I. et II. et rite ad impleto
Articulo III.

Gordianus then proposed to L. that he should translate hermetical and magical writings from Latin into German, which L. did. Gordianus published these translations in a periodical he was then the editor of, without, however, remunerating L., but keeping his faith alive by repeated promises shortly to introduce him to the heads of the Order, who would communicate to him great and valuable secrets. But it seems L. became impatient. He and friends of hi& made inquiries, and ascertained that Gordianus had boasted that he intended to form a society of cheats and dupes. One of L.'s friends charged Gordianus with it. The latter, in 1785, in writing to L. tried to justify himself, but eventually disappeared from Tubingen, when L. made known the above facts as a warning to others.

288. Theoretical Brethren - According to the book, "The Theoretical Brethren, or Second Degree of Rosicrucians," published in 1785, the Rosicrucian ritual was as follows:

The candidate must have been initiated into the Scotch rite; he is led into a large room lighted with candelabra; at the upper end is a square with a black cloth, on which lie an open Bible, the Laws of the Order, and a black embroidered apron. On the carpet there is a globe, surrounded by two rings; from the outer one rays proceed into a circle of cloud, in which are seen the seven planets. A cubical stone is placed above Mars, and the Blazing Star above the globe. An unhewn stone stands opposite to Saturn. The planets promote the growth of the seven metals; the Blazing Star represents Nature; the two circles typify the agens and patiens, the male and female principles. The unhewn stone is the materia prima philosophorum; the cubical stone, the patiens philosophorum. The globe signifies the lodge. The oath is confined to promising fidelity to the Order, secrecy and devotion to the study of nature. The apron is white lined with black, and embroidered. The jewel is of gilt brass, and consists of two triangles with rays issuing therefrom, the name of Jehovah in Hebrew letters, and on the reverse the signs ☉ ♀ ☿ It is attached to a black ribbon.

Sign: raising the right hand, with the thumb and two forefingers extended, which is answered by placing the thumb and two fore-fingers on the heart. The grip is given by taking the brother with the right hand round the waist. The word is Chaos. In Hamburg the initiation fee was forty gold marks, about £,23; monthly contributions amounted to about eighteen shillings. There are nine degrees. We need not go through the whole of them; a few may suffice.

The third degree is called Bracheus, in which the word is Majim, the answer to which is Brocha. The next degree is that of PJiilosophus; the word, Ruachhiber; initiation fee, about twenty dollars. There is a ninth degree, the initiation fee to which is ninety-nine gold marks, for which the member becomes a true Magus, knowing all the secrets of nature, with power over all angels, devils, and men; the philosopher's stone is the least of his possessions.

289. Spread of Rosicrucianism - These Rosicrucians assert that they had lodges in various countries. Vienna, according to their statements, was the seat of the Grand Master of the eighth degree;[14] Konigsberg, Stettin, Berlin, and Danzig, meeting places of the Brethren of the fifth degree; at Breslau and Leipzic the Brethren of the fourth degree assembled; at Hamburg the Brethren of the sixth degree had a lodge,

---

[14] A somewhat curious fact may be mentioned here: The Rosicrucians generally adopted sidereal or alchynristic pseudonyms. In the seventeenth century, under the Emperor Ferdinand III., one John Konrad Eichtbausen came to Vienna. He was a Rosicrucian, and as such bore the name of Chaos, and eventually was ennobled as Herr von Chaos. In 1663 he erected an institution for the sons of poor or deceased parents. When, three years after, the Plague raged in Vienna and attacked some of the youths in the institution, the executors of Richthausen's will the testator having died quickly erected in the district of Mariahilf, almost in the centre of Vienna, another building, to separate the youths attacked by the disease from the others. Gradually the building was enlarged, so that in 1773 it could receive 145 pupils. It was known as the Chaos Foundation (Chaosische Stiff). In 1752 the Empress Maria Theresa purchased the house for a military academy, which purpose it still serves; but it continues to be called the Stift, and the street facing it is still called the Stiftyasse.

which cost nine thousand marks. The Order, moreover, had lodges at Nuremberg, Augsburg, Innsbruck, Prague, Paris, Venice, Naples, Malta, Lisbon, Bergen-op-Zoom, Cracow, Warsaw, Basle, Zurich in Europe, and at Smyrna and Ispahan in Asia. The sect was also known in Sweden and Scotland, where it had its own traditions, claiming to be descended from the Alexandrian priesthood of Ormuzd, who embraced Christianity in consequence of the preaching of St. Mark, founding the society of Ormuzd, or of the "Sages of Light." This tradition is founded on the Manichgeism preserved among the Coptic priests, and explains the seal impressed on the ancient parchments of the Order, representing a lion placing his paw on a paper, on which is written the famous sentence, "Pax tibi, Marce Evangelista tneus, "from which we might infer that Venice had some -connection with the spreading of that tradition. In fact, Nicolai tells us that at Venice and Mantua there were Rosicrucians, connected with those of Erfurt, Leipzic, and Amsterdam. And we also know that at Venice congresses of Alchy mists were held; and the connection between these latter and the Rosicrucians has already been pointed out. Nevertheless the Scotch and Swedish Rosicrucians called themselves the most ancient, and asserted Edward, the son of Henry III., to have been initiated into the Order in 1191, by Raymond Lully, the alchymist. The Fraternity of the Rosy Cross is still flourishing in England (see 293).

290. Transition to Freemasons - From the Templars and Rosicrucians the transition to the Freemasons is easy. With these latter alchymy receives a wholly symbolical explanation; the philosopher's stone is a figure of human perfectibility. In the Masonic degree called the "Key of Masonry' or "Knight of the Sun," and the work "The Blazing Star," by Tschudi, we discover the parallel aims of the two societies. From the "Blazing Star" I extract the following portion of the ritual: "When the hermetic philosophers speak of gold and silver, do they mean common gold and silver?" "No, because common, gold and silver are dead, whilst the gold and silver of the philosophers are full of life." "What is the object of Masonic inquiries?" "The art of knowing how to render perfect what Nature has left imperfect in man." "What is

the object of philosophic inquiry?" "The art of knowing how to render perfect what Nature has left imperfect in minerals, and to increase the power of the philosopher's stone." "Is it the same stone whose symbol distinguishes our first degrees?" "Yes, it is the same stone which the Freemasons seek to polish." So also the Phoenix is common to Hermetic and Masonic initiation, and the emblem of the new birth of the neophyte. Now, we have already seen the meaning of this figure, and its connection with the sun. We might multiply comparisons to strengthen the parallelism between hidden arts and secret societies, and trace back the hermetic art to the mysteries of Mithras, where man is said to ascend to heaven through seven steps or gates of lead, brass, copper, iron, bronze, silver, and gold.

291. Progress and Extinction of Rosicrucians - After having excited much attention throughout Germany, the Rosicrucians endeavoured to spread their doctrines in France, but with little success. In order to attract attention, they in 1623 secretly posted certain notices in the streets of Paris, to this effect: " We, the deputies of the College of the Rosy Cross, visibly and invisibly dwell in the city. We teach without books or signs every language that can draw men from mortal error," &c. &c. A work by Gabriel Naudd gave them the final blow. Peter Mormio, not having succeeded in reviving the society in Holland, where it existed in 1622, published at Ley den in 1630, a work entitled "Arcana Naturae Secretissima," wherein he reduced the secrets of the brethren to three viz., perpetual motion, the transmutation of metals, and the universal medicine.

292. Rosicrucians in the Mauritius - I am indebted to Mr, Waite's " Real History of the Rosicrucians " (published by George Redway, 1888) for the following particulars:
It appears that a society of Rosicrucians existed in 1794 in the island of Mauritius. "My authority," says Mr. Waite,. "gives at length a copy of 'the admission of Dr. Bacstrom' into that society by Le Comte de Chazal. In that document Dr. Bacstrom promises, among other things, ' never to reveal the secret knowledge he receives,' 'to

initiate such persons as he may deem worthy,' including women, seeing that 'Leona Constantia, Abbess of Clermont, was actually received as a practical member and master into the society in 136 as a Soror Crucis; 'that he will ' commence the great work as soon as circumstances permit,' that he 'will give nothing to the Church,' that he will 'never give the fermented metallic medicine for transmutation to any person living, unless he be a member of the Rosy Cross "To this document is appended the philosophic seal of the society, representing a man standing in a triangle, enclosed in a square, and surrounded by a circle. At the head and feet of the man are various cabalistic signs. The whole resembles some of the diagrams which may be found in the "Magical Works of Cornelius Agrippa," in the chapter treating of the proportions, measures, and harmony of the human body.

293. Modern English Rosicrucians - Mr. Waite further states that a pseudo-society existed in England before the year 1836, because Godfrey Higgins says that "He had joined neither the Templars nor the Rosicrucians." The present Rosicrucian Society was remodelled about thirty years ago. A previous initiation into Masonry is an indispensable qualification of candidates: "the officers of the society shall consist of three Magi, a Master-General, a Treasurer-General, a Secretary-General, and seven Ancients. There is also an Organist, a Torch-bearer, a Herald, a Guardian of the Temple, and a Medallist. The members are to meet four times a year, and dine together once a year. Every novice on admission shall adopt a Latin motto, to be appended to his signature in all communications with the Order. The jewel of the Supreme Magus is an ebony cross, with golden roses at its extremities, and the jewel of the Rosie Cross in the centre. It is surmounted by a crown of gold for the Supreme Magus alone, and is worn round the neck, suspended by a crimson velvet ribbon. The jewel of the general officers is a lozenge-shaped plate of gold, enamelled white, with the Rosie Cross in the centre, surmounted by a golden mitre, on the rim of which is enamelled in rose-coloured characters LUX, and in its centre a small cross of the same colour. The jewel is worn suspended from a button-hole by a green ribbon an inch wide,

and with a cross also embroidered on it in rose-coloured silk. The jewel of the fraternity is the lozenge-shaped jewel of the Rosie Cross, without the mitre, suspended by a green ribbon an inch in width, and without the embroidered cross.

Mr. Waite derived this information from a secret record of the association entitled The Rosicrucian, a very small quarterly of twelve pages, first published in 1868, which ceased in 1879. In 1871 the society informed its members that their objects were purely literary and antiquarian; that it consisted of 134 fratres, ruled over by three Supreme Magi. Seventy-two members composed the London colleges, the others formed the Bristol and Manchester colleges. A Yorkshire college was consecrated in 1877; a college in Edinburgh had been established some time previously. The prime mover in the association was Robert Wentworth Little; the late Lord Lytton was Grand Patron. But as to Rosicrucian knowledge the Brethren were altogether destitute of it, as they themselves admitted.

BOOK IX

ANTI-SOCIAL SOCIETIES

I

THE THUGS

294. Introductory - Accounts of several antisocial societies have been given in Book IV., such as the Assassins, Dervishes, and others. They were introduced there because they owed their origin to the religious systems described in that Book, and therefore I deemed it advisable not to sever the connection existing between the religious and the social sects by describing them in different Books. And thus much I thought it necessary to explain, an apparent irregularity, before commencing the history of the Thugs.

295. Name and Origin - Shortly after the conquest of Seringapatam in 1799, about a hundred robbers, called Phansigars, were apprehended in that province; but it was not known then that they belonged to a distinct class of hereditary murderers and plunderers, settled in various parts of India. In 1807, between Chittoor and Arcot, several Phansigars were apprehended, and information was then obtained which ultimately led to a full knowledge of the association infamous under the name of Thugs, though the name by which they were known to one another, and also to others, was "Phansigars' that is, "men of the noose." The name Thug is said to be derived from thaga, to deceive, because the Thugs get hold of their victims by luring them into false security. They were particularly numerous in Mysore, the Carnatic, in the Balaghat Districts, and in the Poliums of Chittoor. As to their origin, General Sleeman considers them descended from remnants of the army of Xerxes, which invaded Greece; but more probably their origin is more recent. The date assigned by themselves to their first establishment in India coincides with the destruction of the Assassins of Alamut. It is not improbable, in fact, that some of the

fugitives who fled from the swords of the Moguls made their way to India; and the existence of Ishtnaelites in India, under the name of Borahs, was known before the existence of the Thugs as an organised sect had been detected. Now the Thugs in the Ramasee, or cant of the Thugs, always call themselves Borahs, which they do probably for the purpose of disguising their real pursuit; for there is a sect, numerous in Hindustan, known by the name of Bohras, and whose members are chiefly peaceful traders. Some sect of Thugs call themselves Aulce.

296. Practices and Worship of Thugs - One common mode of decoying young men having valuables upon them is to place a young and handsome woman by the wayside, and apparently in great grief, who by some pretended tale of misfortune draws him into the jungle, where the gang are lying in ambush, and on his appearance strangle him. The gang consists of from ten to fifty members; and they will follow or accompany the marked-out victim for days, nor attempt his murder until an opportunity offering every chance of success presents itself. After every murder they perform a religious ceremony called tupounee j and the division of the spoil is regulated by old-established laws the man that threw the handkerchief, or roomal, gets the largest share; the man that held the hands, called the shumseea, the next largest proportion, and so on. In some gangs their property is held in common. Their crimes are committed in honour of Kali, who hates our race, and to whom the death of man is a pleasing sacrifice.

Kali (derived from Kala = Time), or Bhowany for she is equally well known by both names was, according to the Indian legend, born of the burning eye which Shiva, one of the persons of the Brahmin trinity, has on his forehead, whence she issued, like the Greek Minerva out of the skull of Jupiter, a perfect and full-grown being. She represents the Evil Spirit, delights in human blood, presides over plague and pestilence, and directs the storm and hurricane, and ever aims at destruction. She is represented under the most frightful effigy the Indian mind could conceive; her face is azure, streaked with yellow; her glance is ferocious; she wears her dishevelled and bristly hair displayed like the peacock's tail, and braided with green serpents.

Round her neck she wears a collar, descending almost to her knees, composed of golden skulls. Her purple lips seem streaming with blood; her tusk-like teeth descend over her lower lip; she has eight or ten arms, each hand holding some murderous weapon, and sometimes a human head dripping with gore. With one foot she stands on a human corpse. She has her temples, in which the people sacrifice cocks and bullocks to her; but her priests are the Thugs, the " Sons of Death, " who quench the never-ending thirst of this divine vampire. An engraving, slightly differing in some of the above details, may be seen in the first volume of the "Asiatic Researches."

297. Traditions - Like all similar societies, the Thugs have their traditions. According to them, Kali in the beginning determined to destroy the whole human race, with the exception, however, of her faithful adorers and followers. These, taught by her, slew all men that fell into their power. The victims at first were killed by the sword, and so great was the destruction her worshippers wrought, that the whole human race would have been extinguished, had not Vishnu, the Preserver, interfered, by causing the blood thus shed to bring forth new living beings, so that the destructive action of Kali was counteracted. It was then this goddess, to nullify the good intention of Vishnu, forbade her followers to kill any more with the sword, but commanded them to resort to strangulation. With her own hands she made a human figure of clay, and animated it with her breath. She then taught her worshippers how to kill without shedding blood. She also promised them that she would always bury the bodies of their victims, and destroy all traces of them. She further endowed her chosen disciples with superior courage and cunning, so as always to ensure them the victory over those they should attack. And she kept her promise. But in the course of time corrupt manners crept in even among the Thugs, and one of them, being curious to see what Kali did with the dead bodies, watched her as she was about to remove the corpse of a traveller he had slain. Goddesses, however, cannot thus be watched on the sly. Bhowany saw the peeper, and stepping forth, thus addressed him: "Thou hast now beheld the awful countenance of a goddess,

which none can behold and live. But I shall spare thy days, though as a punishment of thy crime I shall not protect thee as I have done hitherto, and the punishment will extend to all thy brethren. The corpses of those you kill will no longer be buried or concealed by me; you yourselves will be obliged to take the necessary measures for that purpose, nor will you always be successful, though I leave you the kussee, or sacred pickaxe, to dig the graves; sometimes you will fall under the profane laws of the world, which will be your eternal punishment. Nothing will remain to you but the superior intelligence and skill I have given you, and henceforth I shall direct you by auguries only, which you must diligently consult." Hence their superstitious belief in omens. They study divination by birds and jackals, and by throwing the hatchet, and as it falls so they take their route. Any animal crossing the road from left to right, on their first setting out, is considered a bad omen, and the expedition consequently is given up for that day. The first murder on an expedition is called sonoka; the leader gives the jhirnee, or sign for strangling; the place of burial is called beyl; the victim to be strangled is called bisul if the operation presents difficulties; if easy, he is called coosul; a pair of victims are distinguished by the name of Wiitree. Bungoos are river Thugs, passing up and down the Ganges, pretending to be going to or coming from holy places. They inveigle people on board their boats, and then strangle them, and throw them through holes, purposely made in the sides of the boats, into the river, after having broken the spines of their victims to prevent their recovering. This class of Thugs at one time numbered between two and three hundred members.

298. Initiation - To be admitted into this horrible sect required a long and severe novitiate, during which the aspirant had to give the most convincing proofs of his fitness for admission. This having once been decided on, he was conducted by his sponsor to the mystical baptism, and clothed in white garments, and his brow crowned with flowers. The preparatory rite being performed, the sponsor presented him to the gurhu, or spiritual head of the sect, who, in his turn, introduced him into a room set apart for such ceremonies, where the Hyemader, or

chiefs of the various gangs, awaited him. Being asked whether they will receive the candidate into the Order, and having answered in the affirmative, he and the gurhu are led out into the open air, where the chiefs place themselves in a circle around the two, and kneel down to pray. Then the gurhu rises, and lifting up his hands to heaven, says: " Bhowany! Mother of the world!" (this appellation seems very inappropriate, since she is a destroyer), whose worshippers we are, receive this Thy new servant; grant him Thy protection, and to us an omen, which assures us of Thy consent." They remain in this position until a passing bird, quadruped, or even mere cloud, has given them this assurance; whereupon they return to the chamber, where the neophyte is invited to partake of a banquet spread out for the occasion, after which the ceremony is over. The newly-admitted member then takes the appellation of Sahib Zada. He commences his infamous career as lugliali, or gravedigger, or as belhal, or explorer of the spots most convenient for executing a projected assassination, or lihiL In this condition he remains for several years, until he has given abundant proof of his ability and good-will. He is then raised to the degree of Wmttotah, or strangler, which advancement, however, is preceded by new formalities and ceremonies. On the day appointed for the ceremony, the candidate is conducted by his gurhu into a circle formed in the sands, and surrounded by mysterious hieroglyphics, where prayers are offered up to their deity. The ceremony lasts four days, during which the candidate is allowed no other food but milk. He occupies himself in practising the immolation of victims fastened to a cross erected in the ground. On the fifth day the priest gives him the fatal noose, washed in holy water and anointed with oil, and after more religious ceremonies, he is pronounced a perfect bhuttotah. He binds himself by fearful oaths to maintain the most perfect silence on all that concerns the society, and to labour without ceasing towards the destruction of the human race. He is the rex sacrificulus, and the person he encounters, and Bhowany places in his way, the victim. Certain persons, however, are excepted from the attacks of the Thugs. The hierophant, on initiating the candidate, says to him: "Thou hast chosen, my son, the most ancient profession, the most acceptable to the deity. Thou hast sworn to put to death every human being fate throws into thy hand; there are, however, some that are exempt from our laws, and whose death would not be grateful to our deity." These belong to some particular tribes and castes, which he enumerates; persons who squint, are lame, or otherwise deformed, are also exempt; so are washerwomen, for some cause not clearly ascertained; and as Kali was supposed to co-operate with the murderers, women also were safe from them, but only when travelling alone, without male protector; and orthodox Thugs date the deterioration of Thuggism from the first murder of a woman by some members of the society, after which the practice became common.

The Thugs had their saints and martyrs, Thora and Kudull being two of the most famous, who are invoked by the followers of Bhowany. Worshippers of a deity delighting in blood, those whom the English Government condemned to death, offered her their own lives with the same readiness with which they had taken those of others. They met death with indifference, nay, with enthusiasm, firmly believing that they should at once enter paradise. The only favour they asked was to be strangled or hanged; they have an intense horror of the sword and the shedding of blood; as they killed by the cord, so they wished to die by it.

299. Suppression - When the existence of the society was first discovered, many would not believe in it; yet in courseof time the proofs became so convincing that it could no longer be ignored, and the British Government took decided measures to suppress the Thugs. A Thuggee school of industry in connection with the Lahore gaol was established, but closed again about 1882, the prisoners being allowed: their freedom under ticket-of-leave. The crimes some of them had committed, indeed, almost exceed belief. One Thug, who was hanged at Lucknow in 1825, was legally convicted of having strangled six hundred persons. Another, an octogenarian, confessed to nine hundred and ninety- ninemurders, and declared that respect for the profession alone had prevented him from making it a full thousand, becausea round number was considered among them rather vulgar. But in spite

of vigorous measures on the part of Great Britain there is a regular government department in India for the suppression of Thuggism the sect could not be entirely destroyed; it is a religious order, and as such has a vitality greater than that of political or merely criminal associations. It was still in existence but a few years ago, and no doubt has its adherents even now, though the modern Thugs resort to drugging and poisoning, instead of strangling. It always had protectors in some of the native princes, who shared their booty, and such may now be the case. The society has a temple at Mirzapore, on the Ganges.

A Thug, who during the Indian rebellion turned informer, confessed to having strangled three women, besides, perhaps, one hundred men. Yet this fellow was most pleasing and amiable in appearance and manners; but, when relating his deeds of blood, he would speak of them with all the enthusiasm of an old warrior remembering heroic feats, and all the instincts of the tiger seemed to reawaken in him. In spite of this, however, he caused some two hundred of his old companions to be apprehended by our government.

When the Prince of Wales visited the portion of Lahore gaol allotted to the Thugs, a hoary old criminal, named Soba Singh, admitted with a sort of pride that he had strangled thirty-six persons. Two of the prisoners showed His Royal Highness how Thuggee was performed.

300. Recent Instance of Thuggism - Sharfu, alias Sharif ad-din, was hanged in the Punjab on January 6, 1882. He had become a Thug about the year 1867, and from that date to 1879 he lived by poisoning travellers. He pleaded guilty to ninety-six charges. The Punjab police published his biography, with notes, to assist officers in arresting the members of the gang who were then known to be at large.

II

THE CHAUFFEURS, OR BURNERS

301. Origin and Organisation of Society - The Chauffeurs or Burners formed a secret society formerly existing in France, and only extinguished at the end of the last century. Its members subsisted by rapine and murder. According to the slender notices we have of this society, it arose at the time of the religious wars which devastated France during the days of Henry III. and IV. and Catherine of Medici; and as the writers who searched into its history were Roman Catholics, they charitably assumed the original Chauffeurs to have been the defeated Huguenots, who took to this brigand life to avenge themselves on their conquerors. But the fact that the religious ceremonies of the society included the celebration of a kind of mass, strongly militates against this assumption of their origin. It is more probable that, like similar fraternities formed in lawless times, it consisted of men dissatisfied with their lot, ordinary criminals, and victims of want or injustice.

The Chauffeurs constituted a compact body, governed by a single head. They had their own religion, and a code of civil and criminal laws, which, though only handed down orally, was none the less observed and respected. It received into its fraternity all who chose to claim admission, but preferred to enrol such as had already distinguished themselves by criminal deeds. The members were divided into three degrees; the spies, though affiliated, did not properly form part of the society. The initiated were again subdivided into decurice, each with its guapo or head.

Though, as we have said, any one could be initiated, yet the society, like that of the Jesuits, preferred educating and bringing up its members. Whole families belonged to the fraternity, and the children were early taught how to act as spies, commit small thefts and similar crimes, which were rewarded more or less liberally, as they were executed with more or less daring or adroitness. Want of success brought proportionate punishment with it, very severe corporeal castigation, which was administered not merely as punishment, but also to teach the young members to bear bodily pain with fortitude. One would almost be inclined to think that those bandits had studied the code of Lycurgus! At the age of fourteen or fifteen the boy was initiated into the first degree of the society. At a kind of religious consecration he took an oath, calling down on his own head the lightning and wrath of heaven if ever he failed in his duty towards the Order. He received the sword he was to use in self-defence and in fighting for his brethren.

The master had almost unbounded authority; he kept the common purse, and distributed the booty according to his own discretion. He also awarded rewards or promotion, and inflicted punishment. Theft from the profane, as outsiders were called, was the fundamental law, ancl, indeed, the support of the society, but theft from a brother was punished, the first time, by a fine three times the amount stolen. When repeated, the fine was heavier, and sometimes the thief was put to death. Each brother was bound to come to the assistance of another when in danger; the honour of the wives of members was to be strictly respected, and concubinage and prostitution were prohibited and severely punished. Their mode of administering justice was rational, i.e., summary. The accused person was called before the general assembly of the members, informed of the charge against him, confronted with the witnesses, and if found innocent acquitted; if guilty, he had either at once to pay the fine imposed, receive the number of blows allotted, or submit to hanging on the nearest tree, according to the tenor of the sentence.

302. Religious and Civil Ceremonies - The religious worship of the Chauffeurs was a parody on that of the Church. The sermons of their preachers were chiefly directed to instructing them how most profitably to pursue their profession, and how to evade the pursuit of the profane. On fete-days the priests celebrated mass, and especially invoked the heavenly blessing on the objects and designs of the society. English navvies seem to have borrowed the leading feature of their marriage ceremony from that of the society of Chauffeurs, which was as follows:

On the wedding-day the bridegroom and bride, accompanied by the best man and chief bridesmaid, presented themselves before the priest, who after having read some ribald nonsense from a dirty old book, took a stick, which he sprinkled with holy water, and after having placed it into the hands of the two chief witnesses, who held it up between them, he invited the bridegroom to leap over it, while the bride stood on the other side awaiting him. She received him in her arms, and held him up for a few moments before setting him down on the ground. The bride then went in front of the stick, and took her leap over it into the bridegroom's arms, whose pride it was to hold her up in the air as long as possible, before letting her down. Auguries were drawn of the future felicity and fecundity of the marriage from the length of time the bride had been able to hold up her spouse, whilst both seated themselves on the stick, and the priest put on the bride's finger the wedding-ring. The navvies' ceremony therefore of "jumping over the broomstick" is no new invention.

Divorces were granted not only for proved or suspected infidelity, but also on account of incompatibility of temper which proves the Chauffeurs to have been, in this respect at least, very sensible people after the priest had tried every means to bring about a reconciliation. The divorce was pronounced in public, and its principal feature was the breaking of the stick on which the pair had been married over the wife's head. After that, each was at liberty to marry again.

303. The Grand Master - The sect was spread over a great part of North-western France; made use of a peculiar patois, understood by the initiated only; and had its signs, grips, and passwords like all other secret societies. It comprised many thousand members. Its existence and history first became publicly known through the judicial proceedings taken against it by the courts of Chartres during the last decade of the preceding century. Many mysterious robberies, fires, and murders were then brought home to the Chauffeurs. Its Grand Master at the time was Francis the Fair, so called on account of his singular personal beauty. Before his initiation he had been imprisoned for robbery with

violence, but managed to escape; the Order sought him out and enrolled him amongst its members, and at the death of their chief, John the Tiler, unanimously elected him in his place. Taken prisoner at the above-mentioned period, he again found means to give his gaolers at Chartres the slip probably with their connivance and was not heard of again. A rumour was indeed current at the time that he had joined the Chouans, and eventually perished, a victim to his debaucheries. Some hundreds of Chauffeurs were executed at Chartres; but the mass of them made their escape and swelled the ranks of the above-named Chouans.

It was chiefly during the Reign of Terror that the Chauffeurs committed their greatest ravages. At night large bands of them invaded isolated houses and the castles of the nobility, robbing the rich and poor alike. During the day children and old women, under various disguises and pretences, penetrated into the localities where property worth carrying off might be expected to exist, and on their reports the society laid its plans. Sometimes, disguised as national guards, they demanded and obtained admission in the name of the law. If they met with resistance they employed violence; if not, they contented themselves with robbery. But sometimes they suspected that the inmates of the dwelling they had invaded concealed valuables; in that case they would tie their hands behind their backs, and casting them on the ground apply fire to their feet, at the same time cutting them open with their daggers or knives whence the name chaffeurs, "burners "until they revealed the hiding-places of their treasures, or died in frightful agony. Such as did not die were generally crippled for life.

304. Discovery of the Society - A young man who had suffered in this fashion from some of the members of the society, determined to be revenged on them, by betraying them into the hands of justice. He revealed his plan to the authorities of Chartres, and then set about its execution. In broad daylight, in the market-place of Chartres, he picked the pocket of a gendarme. The gendarme, having his instructions, of course saw nothing, but a Chauffeur, some of whom were always prowling about, noticed the apparently daring deed, and reported it to

his fellows and to his chief. That so clever and bold a thief should not belong to the brotherhood seemed unnatural; very soon therefore he was sought out, and very advantageous offers were made to him if he would join them. At first he seemed disinclined to do so, but eventually yielded, and then showed all the zeal usual with neophytes. He attended all the meetings of the society, and speedily made himself acquainted with all their secrets, their signs, passwords, modes of action, hiding-places, &c. Their safest retreat and great depot, where the booty was stored, was a wild wood in the neighbourhood of Chartres. When the false brother had made these discoveries, and had also ascertained a day when nearly all the members of the society would be assembled on the spot for planning an expedition, he managed to evade their vigilance, hastened to Chartres, and gave the necessary information to the authorities, who had held a large number of men in readiness in the expectation of this chance. These were at once despatched to the locality indicated by the guide, the wood was surrounded, and the Chauffeurs being taken unawares, either perished fighting or were taken prisoners. This was in 1799. Some of the Chauffeurs managed to escape, and under the leadership of Schinderhannes (John the Flayer), continued their criminal practices on either side of the Rhine, until the band was seized in 1803, and Schinderhannes and many of his followers were executed at Mayence, from which time the Chauffeurs were no more heard of.

305. Death of an old Chauffeur - The French papers in November 1883 reported the death, near Cannes, of Yves Conedie, at the age of 105, one of the ancient leaders of the Chauffeurs. He had spent the latter part of his life in "respectable retirement." He had started on his adventurous career at the period of the wars of La Vendee; later on, on arriving at Chartres, in quest of his wife, who had fled from him, taking with her all the money she could lay hands on, he joined a band of Chauffeurs. Having discovered his wife's retreat, it is recorded that he flayed her alive, and the leader of the band to which he belonged being executed, he assumed his place, and carried off a Government commissary who had been instrumental in causing the brigand chief to

be guillotined, keeping him as a hostage until a heavy price was paid for his ransom.

III

THE GARDUNA

306. Origin of the Society - When that superstitious bigot and tyrant Ferdinand, king of Spain who believed himself a clever diplomatist, but was all his lifetime but the tool of a rapacious and bloodthirsty priesthood, the same who made the Inquisition all-powerful in Spain, and caused Columbus to be brought home in chains from the world he had discovered and added to the monster's dominions when he resolved on the extermination in his kingdom of Moors and Jews the former the most civilised, and the latter the most industrious of his subjects all the vagabonds and scoundrels of Spain were welcome to take part in the holy war, solely begun and carried on to extirpate heresy and spread the pure faith at least such was the pretence. There had, indeed, long before Ferdinand's time been bands of malefactors who roamed over the Spanish territory, and with the secret support of the Roman Catholic clergy, who shared the spoil, committed wholesale burglaries in the houses of Moors and Hebrews, occasionally burning a resisting heretic in the flames of his own house as a sweet-smelling savour unto Heaven. The Moors were enemies to their country, though they had civilised it, and the Jews belonged to an accursed race; to fight and destroy them was a meritorious work, which had the full approbation of the Church. In Ferdinand's time the brigands readily joined the crusade against the Moors; the king's motto evidently was

> " It is the sapiency of fools
> To shrink from handling evil tools,"

and brigands may make good soldiers. Brigands, moreover, are generally well disposed towards the Church, and submissive to the priest, and these dispositions, so well agreeing with those of Ferdinand himself, could not but render the brigands favourites with him. But when the object of Ferdinand's holy war was attained, and the Moorish power destroyed, he left the free-lances to shift for themselves, which they did in their fashion, by returning to their former occupation of brigandage. Now, although during the muchvaunted reign of Ferdinand the Catholic, as lying and servile writers have called him, and Isabella, who was too much under the influence of a set of demons in priestly garb, and hence did all she could to increase the power of the Inquisition, nearly two millions of subjects Moors and Jews were driven from the realm, yet a great many remained who belonged to the one or the other race, and had, in order to be allowed to stay in their native country, adopted the Christian faith. Yet with such contempt were they looked upon by the genuine Spaniards, that they never spoke of them but as marranos (hogs), though many of them were the heads of, or belonged to, rich and influential families. The king and his Satanic crew of inquisitors were ever anxious to convict such persons of having relapsed into heresy, in order to burn them at the stake and confiscate their property. The brigands, well aware of this, selected the houses of the marranos for the scenes of their operations; and as long as a good share of the booty passed into the hands of priests, inquisitors, and the royal exchequer, Justice winked at the proceedings. But when the brigands grew tired of these heavy exactions, and refused to pay tribute, Justice suddenly woke up and resolved on exterminating the brigands, who snatched away spoil which legitimately belonged to the king and Inquisition, as the reward of their virtue in rigorously putting down heresy. It was then when gendarmes and soldiers were sent out in all directions to catch or disperse the bands of brigands that infested the country that these bands, which had hitherto acted independently of each other, determined for their greater safety to unite and form one large secret society. It was thus the Garduna arose, which soon provided itself with the whole apparatus of secret signs, passwords, initiatory ceremonies, and all other stage "property" necessary in such cases. Their connection with the Holy Inquisition was not severed thereby, but established on a business-like footing, though of course it remained secret a sort of sleeping partnership. With such high protection at Court and in the Church, it is not surprising that the association soon counted its thousands of members, who actually made Seville their headquarters, where all great plundering, burning, and murdering expeditions were planned and prepared.

307. Organisation - The society had nine degrees, arranged in three classes. To the inferior classes belonged the novices or Chivatos (goats), who performed the menial duties, acted as explorers and spies, or carried the booty. When on the watch, during any operation of their superiors, they imitated, in case of danger, the cry of an animal. At night they imitated that of a cricket, owl, frog, or cat. In the daytime they barked like dogs. The Coberteras (covers), abandoned women, who insinuated themselves into private houses to spy out opportunities for stealing, or acted as decoy-ducks, by alluring men into retired places, where they were set upon, robbed, and frequently murdered by the brigands. For the latter purpose, however, the Garduna generally employed young and handsome women, who were called Serenas (syrens), and usually were the mistresses of leading members. Lastly, the Fuelles (bellows), or spies, chiefly old men of what is called venerable appearance whatever that may mean sanctimonious in carriage, unctuous in speech, haunting churches, in fact, saints. These not only disposed of the booty already obtained, but by their insinuating manners and reputation for piety wormed themselves into the secrets of families, which were afterwards exploited for the benefit of the band. They also acted as familiars of the Inquisition. In the next class were the Floreadores (athletes), men stained with every vice, chiefly discharged or escaped convicts from the galleys, or branded by the hand of the executioner, whose office consisted in attacking and robbing travellers on the high-road. Then came the proud Ponteadores (pinkers, i.e., bullies, expert swordsmen), sure to kill their man. Above these were the Guapos (heads, chiefs), also experienced duellists, and generally appointed to lead some important enterprise. The highest class embraced the Magistri, or priests, who conducted the initiations, preserved the laws, usages, and traditions of the society. The Capatazes (commanders), who resided in the different provinces through which the Garduna was spread, represented the Hermano Mayor or Grand Master, who exercised arbitrary and absolute power over the whole

society, and ruled the members with a rod of iron. He often was an important personage at Court. Strange that men, who will not submit to legitimate authority, yet will bow to and be tyrannised over by a creature of their own setting up! The Thugs, Assassins, Chauffeurs, and all similar lawless societies, surrendered their will to that of one man in blind and slavish fear; but perhaps this is the only condition on which such societies can exist.

308. Spirit of the Society - The Thugs or Assassins killed to rob, but the Garduna, having learnt its business, so to speak, in a more diabolical school, that of the Holy Inquisition, considered itself bound to perform any kind of crime that promised a chance of gain. The priests had drawn up a regular tariff, at which any number of members of the society could be hired to do any deed of darkness. Robbery, murder, mutilation, false evidence, falsification of documents, the carrying off of a lady, getting your enemy taken on board a ship and sold as a slave in a foreign colony all these could be had "to order;" and the members of the Garduna were exceedingly conscientious and prompt in carrying out such pleasant commissions. One-half of the price paid for such services was generally paid on giving the order, and the other half on its completion. The sums thus earned were divided into three parts; one part went into the general fund, the other was kept in hand for running expenses, and the third went to the members who had done the work. That for a considerable period the affairs of the society were in a very flourishing state, is proved by the fact that they were able to keep in their pay at the Court of Madrid persons holding high positions to protect and further the interests of the members. They even had their secret affiliates among judges, magistrates, governors of prisons, and similar officials, whose chief duty lay in facilitating or effecting the escape of any member of the society that might have fallen into the hands of justice.

309. Signs, Legend, &c. - It was mentioned above that the Garduna had its signs and passwords of recognition. When a Garduna found himself in the company of strangers, to ascertain if a brother was

present, he would as it were accidentally put his right thumb to his left nostril; if a brother was present, he would approach him and whisper the password, in reply to which another password would be given; then, to make quite sure, there would be grips and signs a la Freemason, and the two might talk at their ease in a jargon perfectly unintelligible to outsiders on their mutual affairs and interests. Their religious rites and the Garduna insisted much on being a religious society were those of the Papal Church, and as that Church is founded on legends innumerable, so the Garduna had its legend, which was a follows: "When the sons of Beelzebub (the Moors) first invaded Spain, the miraculous Madonna of Cordova took refuge in the midst of the Christian camp. But God, to punish the sins of His people, allowed the Moors to defeat the orthodox arms, and to erect their throne on the broken power of the Christians, who retreated into the mountains of Asturia, and there continued, as well as they could, their struggle with the enemies of God and oppressors of their country. The Madonna, daily and hourly implored by the faithful, granted some successes to their arms, so that they were not entirely destroyed, according to Heaven's first decree. And though they could not drive the Moors from Spain, they yet amidst the mountains preserved their religion and liberty. There lived at that time in the wilds of Sierra Morena an old anchorite, named Apollinare, vulgarly called Cal Polinario, a man of austere habits, great sanctity, and a devout worshipper of the Virgin. To him one morning the Mother of God appeared and spoke thus: 'Thou seest what evil the Moors do to thy native country and the religion of niy Son. The sins of the Spanish people are indeed so great as to have excited the wrath of the Most High, for which reason He has allowed the Moors to triumph over you. But while my Son was contemplating the earth, I had the happy inspiration to point out to him thy many and great virtues, at which his brow cleared up; and I seized the instant to beseech him by means of thee to save Spain from the many evils that afflict it. He granted my prayer. Hear, therefore, my commands and execute them. Collect the patriot and the brave, lead them in my name against the enemy, assuring them that I shall ever be by their side. And as they are fighting the good fight of the faith, tell them that even now they shall have their reward, and that they may in all justice appropriate to themselves the riches of the Moors, in whatever manner obtained. In the hands of the enemies of God wealth may be a means of oppressing religion, whilst in those of the faithful it will only be applied to its greater glory. Arise, Apollinare, inspire and direct the great crusade; I invest thee with full power, anointing thee with celestial oil. Take this button, which I myself pulled off the tunic of my celestial Son; it has the property of multiplying itself and working miracles without number; whoso wears one on his neck will be safe from Moorish arms, the rage of heretics, and sudden death.' And the Virgin having anointed him and given him the button, disappeared, leaving an ambrosial flavour behind." Then the anchorite founded the Holy Garduna, which thus could claim a right divine to robbery and murder. Hence also no important predatory expedition was undertaken without a foregoing religious ceremony; and when a discussion arose as to how to attack, a traveller, or to commit some other similar crime, the Bible was ostensibly referred to for guidance.

310. Suppression of the Society - The laws of the society, like those of nearly all secret societies, were not written down, but transmitted by oral tradition; but the Garduna kept a kind of chronicle in which its acts were briefly recorded. This book, which was deposited in the archives of the tribunals of Seville by Don Manuel de Cuendias, who, with his mountain chasseurs, exterminated the sect, and which book, with other documents, was seized in the house of the Grand Master Francis Cortina in 1821, formed the basis of the indictment of the society before the courts of justice. From this it appeared that the Garduna had its branches in Toledo, Barcelona, Cordova, and many other Spanish towns. It also revealed their close connection with the Holy Inquisition up to the seventeenth century, and it showed that the "orders "given by the holy fathers amounted in 147 years from 15 20 to 1667 to 1986, which had yielded the Garduna nearly 200,000 francs. Of their list of crimes, the carrying off of women, chiefly at the instigation of the holy fathers of the Inquisition, forms about one-third, assassinations form another third, whilst robbery, false testimony,

or denunciation, complete the list. The book further was the means of enabling the authorities to arrest many of the members of the society, who were tried without delay, and on the 25th November 1822 the last Grand Master and sixteen of his chief followers expiated their crimes on the scaffold erected in the market-place of Seville, and the Garduna in Europe only survives in the bands of brigands who are yet to be occasionally encountered in the recesses of the Spanish mountains.

311. Bandits insuring Travellers' Safety - These bandits, like the Garduna, continued to keep in every town, and most of the ventas, or isolated inns on the high-roads, agents or "insurers," who, for a certain sum, insured travellers against the attacks or exactions of other brigands. In 1823 every traveller who wished to avoid trouble on the journey from Madrid to Cadiz had only to travel in one of the waggons of Pedro Ruiz; the fare was three times that of the stage coach, but the bandits never attacked the waggons of Ruiz. At Merida, in Estremadura, the host of the Three Crosses gave a password for forty francs. Don Manuel de Cuendias, the editor of Fereal's "History of the Inquisition," relates in that work that he, in 1822, paid Father Alexis forty francs for the password, Vade retro, which, on his arrival at the "Confessional," the place where a traveller might be killed without even seeing his murderers, turned four brigands, who made their appearance, into four peasants more inoffensive than lambs.

The Garduna was reorganised in South America, where it existed in 1846, in Brazil, Peru, the Argentine Republic, and Mexico, and where for a few dollars a hired assassin will rid you of an enemy.

IV

THE CAMORRA

312. Origin of the Camorra - This society, probably the most pernicious association which has ever existed in Europe, was, or is for we have no proofs that it has ceased to exist an association of blacklegs, thieves, extortioners, rogues and villains of every kind, infesting Naples and the Neapolitan territory. The origin of the name is involved in doubt, but most probably it is simply a Spanish importation; for the word camorra exists in that language, meaning quarrel, dispute, and a camorrista is a quarrelsome, cantankerous person, and as the word was not known in Italy before the Spanish usurpation, we may reasonably assume that the word and the thing were introduced into Naples by the Spaniards, especially as we know from old Spanish authors that associations like the Italian Camorra existed in Spain long before the latter appeared in Italy. To quote but one instance: In the account of what happened to Sancho Panza on the island of Barataria, we are told that on going his rounds one night he met two men fighting; on inquiring the cause of the quarrel, it appeared that one of the combatants had won a large sum of money at a gambling-house, that the other, who had been looking on, and given judgment for him in more than one doubtful case, "though he could not well tell how to do it in conscience," had claimed from the winner a gratuity of eight reals, but the latter would only give four, and hence the quarrel. To make such claims always was the practice of the Neapolitan gaminghouse Camorrista. The enforced gratuity was in Spain called the barato; in Naples, barattolo.

      History says nothing as to the origin of the Camorra; tradition goes no further back than the year 1820; let us see what is known of its organisation.

313. Different kinds of Camorra - There is the "elegant" Camorra, the swell mob of the society, who levy taxes on gamblers, as already mentioned; the Camorra, which extorts contributions from

shopkeepers, hackney-coach drivers, boatmen, in fact, from every one following some out-door calling; nay, the Camorrists abound in the prisons, and woe to the prisoner who, under the accursed reign of the Bourbons, did not quietly submit to their exactions. There was a political Camorra, and even a Camorra which committed murder.

314. Degrees of the Society - The Camorra was largely supplied with new members by the prisons. A youthful prisoner, who aspired to become a Camorrista, began his apprenticeship in prison, where he was put to the most degrading offices in the service of imprisoned Camorristi. When in course of time he had given proofs of courage and zeal, he was promoted to the degree of picciotto di sgarro. Picciotto may be translated "lad," but as to the meaning of the term sgarro, the Camorristi themselves are in the dark. It may be derived from sgarrare, to mistake, or from sgarare, to come off conqueror, but either derivation is only a surmise. Nor were the terms applied to differences of degree always the same. In some localities the novice was called a tamurro; in the second degree he took the name of picciotto d'onore, and became picciotto di sgarro only after many years' trial. In a society having no written or printed records we must expect slight differences! In the flourishing days of the Camorra, admission to the degree of di sgarro was only obtained by undergoing the test of devotion and courage. The aspirant had to apply for permission to disfigure or, if necessary, to kill some one. If the Camorrists did not happen to have on hand an order to do either, the candidate underwent the trial of the tirata (duel, literally, "drawing"), which consisted in drawing his knife against a picciotto already received and designated by lot. This was not so dangerous a proceeding as might at first appear, for most of the picciotti were the sons of Camorristi, and as such practised from their earliest youth fighting with knives. There were clandestine schools of mutual instruction in the town, and even in the prisons, where the use of the dagger was taught. Moreover, this trial fight always was a simple tirata a musco (literally, a musk drawing), that is, a mild affair in which the knife was to touch the arm only, and at the first blood the combatants embraced and the candidate was

initiated. In the early days of the Camorra the trial was more severe. The Camorristi stood round a coin placed on the ground, and all at a given signal stooped to prick it with their knives. The candidate had to pick up the coin. Often his hand was pierced, but he became a picciotto di sgarro. He underwent a noviciate of three to six years, during which he had to bear all the charges of the association without sharing in its benefits. He generally belonged to a Camorrista, who assigned to him all the hardest tasks, occasionally giving him a handful of coppers. He was always chosen when blood had to be spilt. When a blow had to be struck, the picciotti were eager to deliver it in the hope of advancement. The one chosen by lot sometimes incurred six to twenty years on the galleys, but he became a Camorrista. All these murders were committed, not for the sake of lucre, but for that of honour; for the Neapolitan conscience bowed down before the knife, as more civilised countries still do before the sword.

315. Ceremony of Reception - On the reception of a picciotto into the degree of Camorrista, the sectaries assembled around a table, on which were placed a dagger, a loaded pistol, a glass of water or wine, supposed to be poisoned, and a lancet. The picciotto was introduced, accompanied by a barber, who opened one of the candidate's veins. The latter was then, in some circles, called a tamurro. He dipped his hand in his blood, and extending it towards the Camorristi, he swore for ever to keep the secrets of the society, and faithfully to carry out its orders. He then took hold of the dagger and planted it firmly in the table, cocked the pistol, and brought the glass to his mouth to indicate that he was ready, at a sign from the master, to kill himself; but the latter stopped him, and bade him kneel down before the dagger. He then placed his right hand on the head of the candidate, and with the left he fired off the pistol into the air, and shattered the glass containing the supposed poisoned liquor on the ground. He then drew the dagger from the table, presented it to the new companion, and embraced him, which example was followed by all the others. The tamurro, henceforth a Camorrista, became entitled to all the rights, benefits, and privileges of the society. His election was announced to

all the sections. But this ridiculous ceremony was not always observed. Sometimes the candidate only swore fidelity to the society over two crossed daggers. The reception was generally followed by a banquet in the country, or in the prison itself if the reception took place among prisoners.

316. Centres - The Camorristi were divided into centres. There were twelve at Naples, and every centre was divided into paranze or sub-centres, each one of which acted independently of the others and on its own account, though during a certain period all the centres, every one of which had its chief, acknowledged the chief of the Vicaria centre as their supreme head. (The Vicaria was originally the Castle Capuano, which became afterwards the palace of the Spanish Viceroy, hence the change of name, and eventually the Courts of Law.) The last of these supreme heads was one Aniello Ausiello, who eventually disappeared and was never apprehended by the police. The chief of every centre was chosen by the members; he could take no important step without consulting them. But all the earnings of the centre were paid to him, which invested him with considerable power, for he distributed the Camorra for this word designates not only the society, but also the common fund. The chief was allowed a contarulo or accountant, a capo carusiello or cashier, and a secretary. Among the other employes of the Camorra were a capo stanze or caterer, and a chiamatore, literally, the caller, because he called the prisoners wanted in the prison parlour. The division of the barattolo (312) took place every Sunday, the chief always retaining for himself the lion's share.

317. Cant Terms of the Camorra - The chief is called masto, or si masto, master, or Sir master. When a companion, as all the affiliated are styled, meets one of his chiefs in the street, he raises his hand to his cap, and says, " Masto, volite niente? "Master, do you want anything? A companion is simply addressed as si, an abbreviation of signore. An itbbidienza, obedience, means an order. Freddare, to make cold, means to kill; the dormente, the sleeper, the dead body. The man who is robbed is called Vagnello, the lamb; soggetto, subject, or mico. The

stolen object is called the morto, or rufo; the fence, the graffo. These latter words are pure slang. The knife is called martino, punta (point), or misericordia; when quite flat and double-edged, a sfarziglia. A gun is a bocca (mouth), toa, or buonbas; a revolver, a tictac, or bo-botta; the patrol are gatti neri, or sorci (black cats or mice). The commissary of police is nicknamed capo lasagna (lasagne are a kind of long and flat maccaroni); the lasagnaro (dealer in lasagne) means a sergeant of police, and a simple policeman is an asparago (asparagus); the palo (Pole) is a spy; the serpentina means a piaster. When a picciotto took upon himself the crime of another, Tacollava, he embraced him. Camorristi belonging to the lowest class of the people are called guappi (meaning unknown); those who are pickpockets, and to facilitate their sleight of hand have lengthened the fore-finger by violent stretching, or by a machine made for the purpose, till it is of the same length as the middle finger, are curiously enough called Chirurgi.

318. Unwritten Code of the Camorra - It is not probable that the Camorristi ever had a written code of laws; but they had an orally-transmitted code, containing twenty-four articles. It would extend this book too much were we to give them all: we select a few. Article 2 declares that no member of the police is ever to be admitted; but article 3 allows a Camorrista to join the force in order to keep his brethren informed of anything the authorities may be planning against them; article 5 stipulates that offences against the society are to be tried by the Grand Master and six Camorristi proprietarii (that is, Camorristi who have others under them); by article 8 any member who has betrayed his oath of secrecy is condemned to death; articles 9 and 10 award the same punishment for omissions or commissions of acts endangering the security of the society. By article 15 the lowest Camorrista may kill any member who has committed any act injurious to the society, but he must do so in the presence of two companions, who must witness to the facts. Article 16 condemns any one who attempts to become personally acquainted with the Grand Master to death. By article 20, Camorristi, who have reached the age of fifty to sixty years, or who have been injured in the cause, are entitled to

temporary or permanent support; their widows also in certain cases receive pensions. Article 24 secures to prisoners gifts in money, arms, or whatever they may be in need of, without any restriction.

It was also an unwritten law among Camorristi to mutually assist one another if unlucky at play; an offence committed against a member of the Camorra elegante was an offence committed against all, and any one of them could avenge it; these latter gentry also generally dressed alike, wore their hats in the same way, and carried their walkingsticks horizontally suspended between two fingers of the right hand. Stealing was allowed, but the objects stolen must be of some value, so as not to bring disgrace on the Camorra !

319. The Camorra in the Prisons - We have already mentioned that the Camorra was ubiquitous, that, in the time of the Bourbons, it invaded the prisons even. A prisoner on his arrival was accosted by a Camorrista, who asked for money for the lamp of the Madonna. On all the prisoner ate, drank, smoked, on any money he received from friends, on necessaries and superfluities, on justice and privileges, the Camorra levied a tax. Those who resisted this extortion ran the risk of being beaten to death. True, the Cainorrista, who had taken the prisoner "under his protection" would not allow him to be fleeced by others, and would even fight for himafter having skinned him alive! When a prisoner of some rank was brought to the Vicaria, he would occasionally receive from the Camorra not from the gaolers, who went in fear of the sectaries a knife for his personal defence. In every prison the Camorristi had a depot of arms, which went by the name of the pianta (plant), and was never discovered by the gaol authorities. It may fairly be assumed that originally the Camorra was established in the prisons as a protection for prisoners, who under the vile reigns of the Bourbon dynasty were shamefully ill-treated by the officials. It is certain that the Camorristi maintained some order in the prisons; in fact, the gaolers often were glad to have recourse to their authority to master rebellious prisoners.

320. The Camorra in the Streets - Originally the Camorra existed in

prisons only; it was carried into the city by prisoners, who had served their time, shortly after the year 1830. From that date the streets of Naples were infested by Camorristi, who "worked" in gangs. They mewed like cats at the approach of the patrol, crowed like cocks on seeing a benighted pedestrian; this sign was also adopted, when known at a house, to indicate a friend. They uttered a long sigh when the pedestrian was not alone; sneezed when he did not look worth attacking; chanted an Axe Maria when the spoil promised to be good, and a Gloria Patri when the expected victim hove in sight. When a Camorrista entered a meeting-place of the sect where he was a stranger, any one present who knew him, to indicate to his friends that the newcomer was one of them, would twice or thrice raise his eyelids, thrust his hands into his pockets, and look for a second or two at the ceiling. The town Camorra was not absent from the highest circles. Eoyal Highnesses were in league with smugglers, and shared their profits; ministers protected the Camorristi "for a consideration;" bishops, the heads of charitable institutions, every government official, in some way or another were involved in the Camorra scandal. M. Marc-Monnier mentions a Camorrista he knew at Naples who, though he played with loaded dice, cheated at cards, and was, in fact, a thorough swindler, was yet received at Court, because he handled the sword well, and was feared as a duellist, until an Englishman killed him in an "affair of honour." But the Camorrist pur et simple sponged on the lower classes. A beggar could not occupy his accustomed post without feeing the Camorrista. In the low taverns found in many parts of Naples, where ragged beggars would sit all day, nay, all night long gambling, the Cammorrista would stand by and levy his tax on every game. By what right did he claim it? No one could tell: suffice it to say, no one disputed it. The tax on gamblers was onetenth of the winnings. A rich man, known to be about to bid for a house sold by auction, would be waited on by a Camorrista and informed that unless he paid a certain sum to the society the latter would outbid him; of course he had to yield. From houses of ill-fame the Camorra drew a large revenue, as also from smuggling. The police being very badly organised under the old regime, leading merchants were glad to engage the Camorra to superintend the loading and unloading of merchandise; Camorristi were found at every town-gate, the offices of the octroi, the custom-house, the railway station, taxing coachmen and porters; nurserymen bringing fruit into the town were mulcted in one sou the basket. The Camorristi also kept illegal lottery offices: the profits must have been large, for a woman who was apprehended was shown to have gained one thousand francs a week. In fact, the Camorra speculated on every weakness and vice of mankind. Under the Bourbons it even infected the army; but when it attempted to corrupt the Italian army, such members as were detected were publicly exposed with a placard suspended from their necks, bearing the henceforth infamous word Camorrista.

321. Social Causes of the Camorra - These must be looked for in the abject state of slavery in which the Neapolitan people were kept by the Bourbon dynasty, which protected common malefactors to secure their loyalty, whilst the intelligence of the country, aiming at liberal institutions, was persecuted with the utmost malignity. The clergy bravely helped the king to keep the people in a condition of the grossest ignorance and superstition. Hence no vigorous association for good could arise against evil; fear kept down the few who stood at a higher moral level, hence the power of the well-organised and flourishing Camorra, just as we find, at the present day, Chinese beggars forming powerful guilds and exacting donations from the shopkeepers in every city of the empire. The Camorra had never been a political society before 1848, therefore government did not interfere with it; nay, sometimes they were useful to the police, and were, in fact, taken into their service, every one of the twelve heads of sections receiving a hundred ducats (425 francs) a month from the secret police fund, whilst the higher employes of the force received one-third of the monthly proceeds of the swindling transactions of the society. Sometimes the latter would detect crimes which the police could not discover.

322. The Political Camorra - After 1848 the conspirators .against the

government, unable to stir up the people, endeavoured to win over the Camorristi, but all they gained by this injudicious step was to be heavily blackmailed by them. Some of them, having attempted honestly to earn their money, and fallen into the hands of the police, were sent to prison. Then the sect became political. In June 1860 Francis II. was compelled to grant a constitution; the prisons were opened, and a crowd of Camorristi came forth. Their first act was to attack the commissaries of police, to burn their papers, and beat the gendarmes to death with cudgels. The Sanfedisti or the rabble in favour of the king and divine right, threatened to pillage the town they had already hired store-rooms to deposit their booty. Don Liborio, the new Prefect of Police, threw himself into the arms of the Camorristi to save Naples from pillage and they prevented it. They were formed into a civic guard, which kept order in the town until the arrival of Garibaldi. But they remained Camorristi at heart. They largely engaged in smuggling, and forcibly took the octroi of the town gates, so that government on a certain day received ;at all the gates together but twenty-five sous. This led to vigorous measures. Ninety Camorristi were arrested in one night; the next day the octroi yielded 3400 francs. On the establishment of the regular monarchy, Silvio Spaventa, a patriot of the year 1848, became Minister of Police; one of his first measures was to deal with the Camorra. He had not long to wait for an infraction of discipline on their part; in one night he caused more than one hundred Camorristi to be arrested; at the same time he abolished the civic guard, replacing it by a guard of public security, organised beforehand.

323. Attempted Suppression of the Camorra - But in spite of the energetic measures of Signor Spaventa, the Camorra was not destroyed; it existed not in a group of men only, it was deeply rooted in the morals of the country. Though the chiefs were removed, the sect retained its organisation under other chiefs. Such Camorristi as had been sent to prison after a time regained their liberty, and resumed their malpractices; they were transported to various islands in the Mediterranean, whence, many of them made their escape, returned to Naples, and raised tumults in the streets, crying, "Death to Spaventa!"

They became powerful at elections, and with their cudgels directed the religion and politics of the electors. Peaceful citizens were nightly assaulted and robbed in the streets of Naples; burglaries became quite common. This state of things lasted till 1862. The Southern States had been declared in a state of siege, and General La Marmora and the Questor Aveta determined to take this opportunity of exterminating the Camorra. In September 1862 three hundred of the most notorious Camorristi were in prison; some of them were sent -to the cellular prison, the Murate, at Florence; others were shut up in the islands of Tremiti. Yet the Camorra seems irrepressible. Occasionally there would be an apparent lull in its activity, to break out again with renewed vigour. It would be tedious to relate its doings from year to year, for it continued to flourish when the new kingdom of Italy was firmly established: a few episodes may suffice.

324. Renewed Measures against the Camorra - In September 1877 the government made another determined effort to suppress the Camorra. The market of St. Anna della Paluda was the spot chosen for the attack. No peasant could bring and sell there his vegetables and fruit before having paid a tax to the Camorristi. Besides the guards in plain clothes, the market had been surrounded early in the morning by police and carabiniers, while a tolerably strong force of Bersaglieri was in attendance close at hand. On a sudden every gate and way of exit was closed; flight or resistance was out of the question, and fifty-seven of the most notorious of the Order were seized, bound together by a long rope, and carried off to the nearest police station, where they were soon committed and sent off to prison in parties of ten. There was the picciotto without dress and in his shirt sleeves, and the full-blown Camorrista, dressed as a gentleman, with his fingers covered with rings, and a gold chain round his neck. This razzia was followed a few days after by another in the fish market, when fifty-nine of the worst characters were caught. Yet so tenacious are the Camorristi of their pretended rights, that two days after the descent on the fruit market some of them made their appearance and usual demand, which, however, was resisted, and the fellows were arrested. The wives, too, of

those whom the police had seized entered the market, alleging that their husbands had commissioned them to receive their dues. In former days they would have been paid at once; on this occasion the wives were marched off to prison.

325. Murders by Camorristi - Another occasion when the Camorra again came prominently before the public was in June 1879. In August 1877 one Vincenzo Borrelli, a leading member of the society, was murdered near Naples. He had fallen under the suspicion of having turned spy and informer, and entertaining secret relations with the police. Accordingly his death was decreed by the association. Six members met together in a wine-shop, and agreed to select one of their number to do the deed. The lot fell on one Raffade Esposito (the Foundling), who seems to have been chosen because he had a private cause of quarrel with Borrelli, and also because he was himself suspected of want of loyalty towards the society, and his fidelity would be conveniently tested by his readiness to undertake the deed. Esposito lay in wait for Borrelli and shot him from behind. The wound was not immediately fatal, and Esposito was pursued and seized by some soldiers, but he was rescued by a sympathising crowd. Borrelli's body was carried to the dead-house amidst the insults of the populace, and subjected to all sorts of indignities. Esposito was made the hero of the day; collections were gathered for, him; but he found it impossible to evade the vigilance of the police, and three days after his rescue he gave himself up. He was escorted to prison through the streets of Naples by a vast crowd of sympathisers, who pressed money and cigars on him, and strewed flowers in his path. Some seventy-eight other members of the Camorra were arrested at the same time, and indicted as accessories to the murder of Borrelli; but the judges and jury, threatened with the vengeance of the Camorra, found "extenuating circumstances," and the criminals got off with comparatively slight punishments. But, then, all these wretches are noted for their devotion; they are faithful children of the Church, which kijows how toprotect them; and the Camorra still nourishes, for the papers reported in April 1885 a fresh trial of Camorristi, one of them having turned informer. A number of them

had been sent to the island of Ischia, and the first proceeding of some of the chief sufferers from the Italian mania for secret societies was to form an inner circle of the Camorra, electing a president, whose position entitled him to all articles stolen, a portion of which he assigned to the thief; he also allowed gambling, receiving a share of the winnings in fact, we find that in 1885, under the present Italian Government, the Camorra survives in prisons in the same form and vigour which distinguished it under the Bourbon despots. But what progress or improvement can be expected among the lower classes of Italy as long as a Pope occupies the Vatican, and a German Emperor insults the intelligence of civilised Europe by kneeling to that Pope, who is the representative of an ecclesiastical system which has always fostered and protected brigandage, with its robbery and murder?

V

MALA VITA

326. The Mala Vita - The society known by this name seems to be an offshoot of the Camorra, since the highest grade in it is that of camorrist, and the second that of picciotto; the third was that of giovanotto, or novice. The chief of the Camorristi held the title of "Wise Master," whilst the Camorrist was nicknamed "Uncle." The society first came prominently before the public in April 1891, when 179 persons were arrested and tried at Bari, in the Neapolitan territory, as members of it. The title of the society, Mala Vita, which signifies "Evil Life," is said to be taken from a novel by Degia Como, which, at the time of its publication, was tremendously popular in Italy. The discovery of the conspiracy was due to the disclosures of nine members of the society who became informers. It appears that admission to the ranks of the organisation was only procurable after numerous preliminaries. A person wishing to become a member had to be introduced by a member to the chief of the society, who would then instruct another associate to institute a rigorous inquiry as to whether or not the applicant was worthy of admission. All these negotiations were conducted in a species of thieves' slang. There were, as already mentioned, three grades of members, each possessing a separate head, and, to a certain extent, separate accounts.

When the admission of a new associate had been resolved upon, a meeting of the sect in which he was to be enrolled was convened, and the formality of taking a vote upon the question having been gone through, the candidate was led into the place of meeting. An interrogatory and interchange of declarations, conducted in the secret dialect of the body, next ensued. The novitiate was finally sworn in with great mystery. He took the oath with one foot in an open grave, the other being attached to a chain, and swore to abandon father, mother, wife, children, and all that he held dear, in order to work out the objects of the association. Humility and self-abnegation were also imposed upon the novitiate by the terms of the oath. After the ceremony of initiation, the chief delivered a fantastic harangue, intended to intimidate the new member by impressing him with a due sense of the fearful pains and penalties which would certainly attend any betrayal of the society's secrets or interests. No one was allowed to join the organisation who had been a gendarme, a policeman, or a custom-house officer. The principal object of the society appears to have been brigandage. The booty obtained in all predatory expeditions, and the ransoms derived from the capture of unlucky travellers, were thrown into a common stock, a certain proportion being, however, specially set apart for division among the Camorristi, whose duty it was. within eight days, to divide the remainder among all the members of the organisation, an exceptionally large share being claimed by the chief.

Breaches of the society's rules and disobedience to orders were punished by torture and death, the whole society sitting in judgment, and the executioners being selected by lot. In the event of any person so deputed failing to carry out the society's decree, he had to undergo the same punishment he had been ordered to inflict. The member was obliged to have certain designs tattooed on his body, by which he could at any future time be identified. Some of these designs were extremely curious, representing angels, devils, serpents, dancing women, Garibaldi's portrait, and the Lion of St. Mark.

At the trial, informers explained how, when in prison, they, by order of the Camorristi, conveyed letters or money to other prisoners belonging to the society; or how the decrees of the Camorristi, involving outrages upon prisoners, warders, and others, were communicated to those chosen for their execution. The evidence adduced revealed a thoroughlyorganised system of outrage and exaction pursued against innocent persons, and of revenge committed upon such as were suspected of communicating with the police. Severe sentences of imprisonment were passed on most of the accused; but the society evidently continued to exist, for in March 1892, about one hundred and sixty persons, mostly young men between the ages of twenty and thirty, were arrested as members of it. Their chief was a man of sixty, who had spent some twenty-five years in penal servitude on the galleys.

His followers were all persons guilty of various crimes, such as robbery, assault, and other acts of violence. They were, of course, sentenced to various terms of imprisonment; but the Mala Vita Society still exists.

VI

THE MAFIA

327. The Mafia's Code of Honour - This is a Sicilian society, which may be briefly described as another Camorra, its aim and practices being similar to those of the Neapolitan association, with a strong admixture of brigandage and bloodthirstiness. The society has a regular code of laws, called the Omerta, according to which every member must himself avenge any wrong done to him, for not justice, but the living, must avenge the dead hence the laws of the vendetta. No member is to give evidence in any court of law against a criminal, but must, on the contrary, conceal and protect him. Candidates are admitted after a trial by duel; the members are divided into such as are merely under the protection of the Mafia, and such as are active members, and share in the profits, derived from smuggling and blackmail levied on landowners and farmers. No one guilty of, in the Mafia's opinion, disgraceful conduct, such as giving evidence in a court of law, or information to the police, picking pockets, or being a coward, is ever admitted a member, who call themselves giovani d'onore, honourable youths. They have their secret signs, passwords, and other means of recognition, which they have hitherto managed to keep from the knowledge of the outer world. Like the Camorra, it is represented in all classes of society. It lounges abroad in silk hat, black coat, and kid gloves; it skulks in dens haunted by the forger, bully, or pimp. Generally when a murderer or burglar is arrested, the governor of the prison gets a hint that the culprit is a Mafiose, and forthwith he is treated with consideration. The judge on the bench receives a document in open court, and the prisoner somehow has to be discharged for want of evidence; juries, as a rule, refuse to convict. When in 1885 the doings of the Mafia were discussed in the Italian Parliament, proofs were adduced that the society was represented in the antechamber of the

Procurator-General of Palermo; nay, the very commandant of the Royal troops, holding the King's commission to stamp out the sect, was directly accused in the Italian Chamber of acting in collusion with the Mafia, if, indeed, he was not a Mafiose himself. The stormy discussions which followed led to no result, and the Mafia was left to pursue its course in unhappy Sicily.

328. Origin of the Mafia - The origin of the Mafia must be sought for in the former political conditions of the island. Since the middle of the last century, when Sicily was united with Naples, and with it formed the kingdom of the Two Sicilies, the island was under the government, or rather misgovernment, of viceroys. The few years of the First Republic and First Empire of France alone formed an exceptional period, during which the Court of Naples, expelled by Napoleon, took refuge in Sicily, where it was protected by England, which sent an army under Lord Bentinck, and a fleet under Nelson, to ward off the French from the island. There existed at that time in Sicily a numerous class of armed vassals, dependents, and retainers, in the service of the feudal nobility, clergy, and large landowners. The King of Naples, having upon the advice, or rather compulsion, of England granted the Sicilians a constitution, this measure involved the abolition of all feudal rights. The retainers and vassals thus set free being mostly reckless and daring fellows, nearly all turned brigands, whom the Bourbon king had no means of suppressing. He therefore, to restore a little order and security on the island, took the chiefs of these robbers into his service, and organised the bandits into compagnie d'armi, or rural gendarmes, who, however, while pretending to prevent robberies and extortion, themselves committed these crimes. They grew very powerful, and daily affiliated new members. The respectable inhabitants, rather than expose themselves to the risks of the vendetta, quietly submitted to the exactions of the society; the lower and uneducated classes began to look on it as a terrible power, superior to that of the government, and ended by considering it an honour, as it certainly was an advantage, to be received among its members. The causes of the continuance of the Mafia may be found in the sulphur mines of Northern Sicily, and in the agricultural conditions of the whole island. Tens of thousands of labourers of both sexes, and of every age, are employed in the mines,

and their condition is one of abject poverty, and unremitting, dangerous toil. In the agricultural districts the peasantry are ground down by the "middlemen," who rent the estates of the great landowners from these latter, and under-let them in small portions, and at exorbitant rates, to the peasants, who, unable to live on the produce, are driven into crime. The true seat of the Mafia is the neighbourhood of Palermo; no one can go a mile beyond the gates without risk of being robbed or murdered. In September 1892 about one hundred and fifty of these malefactors were arrested at Catania, most of them, on being examined, proving to be old offenders.

The Mano fratema, another secret association, discovered in Sicily in 1883, was an offshoot of the Mafia, though its members repudiated the idea of being robbers and extortioners; they called themselves the instruments of universal vendetta.

329. Origin of the, term Mafia - What is the meaning of the word Mafia? and whence comes it? The invention is attributed to Mazzini; it certainly was unknown before 1859 or 1860, the time when that agitator made his appearance in Sicily. It is well known that he had no faith in any class of society except its very dregs, and his having formed the vagabonds and thieves, who then swarmed all over Sicily, into a secret society of his own, seems well borne out by facts. The allegation is that he first formed a secret society called the Oblonica, which word was coined by Mazzini from the two Latin words obelus, a spit, and nico, I beckon, which being joined and contracted became oblonica, the word meaning, "I beckon with a spit;" "spit" being taken in the sense of dagger, as no doubt the sect understood it, we should get the sense of I beckon, or threaten with a dagger, which was the usual occupation or practice of the vagabonds enlisted by Mazzini. But within this sect he formed an interior, more deeply initiated, one, the members of which were called Mafiusi, from Mafia, composed of the initials of the five following words: Mazzini, autorizza, furti, incendi, avvelenamenti. Mazzini authorises thefts, arson, poisoning. And the Mafiusi were accustomed to call these crimes their pavi, or bread, since it was by them they lived.

330. The Mafia in the United States - In October 1890 Mr. David Hennessy, chief of police at New Orleans, was assassinated. The subsequent legal inquiry showed the murder to have been the work of the Mafia, which had been introduced into New Orleans about thirty years ago. In May 1890 a band of Italians, residing in that town, surprised another band belonging to another society called the Stop pagliera in an ambush, and riddled the entire party with bullets, killing and wounding six persons. The authorities thereupon determined to take extreme measures to end the vendetta, which had already resulted in more than forty murders among Italians and Sicilians in New Orleans. Six persons were arrested and tried, but during the trial all the witnesses were assassinated. The men charged were, however, convicted, but their counsel succeeded in securing an order for a new trial, which was still pending when the chief of the police, Mr. Hennessy, was assassinated. He had thoroughly investigated the doings of the opposing societies, and was in possession of information which, it was thought, must lead to the conviction of the European cut-throats. He had received frequent warnings to beware of assassins, and had for some time travelled with an escort night and day. Nothing happened, however; he, on Sunday, dismissed his guard, believing it to be no longer necessary. On the following Wednesday, at midnight, he left the police headquarters for his home. It was raining and very dark, but, as he had not far to go, Mr. Hennessy determined to walk. As he turned the corner of Basin and Girod Streets, where an electric light threw down its strong rays upon him, a volley of bullets was fired at him from a passage a few feet away. Though severely wounded, Mr. Hennessy turned, drew his pistol, and emptied it in the direction of the dark entrance of the alley. Altogether fully twenty shots were exchanged. A policeman who was standing on the opposite corner ran to assist his chief and was shot in the head. Mr. Hennessy having exhausted the contents of his revolver, fell to the ground from loss of blood, and as he did so, four of his assassins sprang from the alley and ran down the street, while four others emerged a moment later and went off in the opposite direction. In their flight the murderers

dropped three guns. They were muskets, sawn off behind the trigger, and with the butts hinged on, so that the guns could fold into the pocket. These are used only by Italian and Sicilian desperadoes. Eleven Sicilians were arrested on suspicion; and from the confession of one of them it appeared that the murder of Mr. Hennessy was determined on at a secret meeting held on the Saturday preceding the day of the assassination; ten members were chosen by lot to do the deed.

In spite of the overwhelming evidence against the accused, the jury, intimidated by threats of assassination by the countrymen of the Italians implicated, found six of them not guilty, giving them, as they alleged, the benefit of the doubt. A fresh charge, however, was preferred against those whom the jury had acquitted, and they were sent back to the onnty gaol. But early on March 14, 1891, a large crowd collected at the Clay statue and was harangued by a citizen named Parkerson on the case of the Italians charged with the assassination of Mr. Hennessy. He denounced the finding of the jury, and under his leadership about two thousand persons, armed with guns and revolvers, stormed the county gaol, where the accused, nineteen in all, were still confined. The mob dragged the prisoners from their cells and hanged or shot eleven of them. On the following day meetings of the Stock Exchange, the Board of Trade, the Cotton Exchange, and other public bodies passed resolutions deploring, but endorsing as necessary, the acts of the mob which stormed the gaol and lynched eleven Italian prisoners. The lynchers included some of the most prominent men in the city, and the notice calling the meeting, which culminated in the massacre of the prisoners, was signed by professional men, editors, merchants, and public officials.

These occurrences led to a temporary tension between the governments of Italy and the States, but fortunately for the two countries the application of diplomatic oil gradually softened and finally dispersed the irritation. The Mafia has not since then dared to raise its head in New Orleans, though it may well be assumed to be still exercising its pernicious influence in secret. And that influence at one time was very great over the reputable portion of the community, who feared it much more than lawless ruffians feared the law. The majority of the Mafia Italians got their living by crime, whilst those who did follow a respectable trade got rid of competition by holding out threats of assassination to their rivals. Every time a member of the Mafia was tried for crime, one or more of the jurymen selected to try him received warning, written and sealed, from the Mafia Society, terrorising them into a refusal to convict. Probably the trouble is not over yet; for the government action in attempting to suppress the society on the other hand stirs up the Italian feeling for their compatriots, and many Italians, who never contributed before, nor sympathised with the objects of the Mafia, now subscribe freely.

VII

BEGGARS, TRAMPS, AND THIEVES

331. Languages and Signs - The vagabonds included in the above designations occasionally formed themselves into associations which were not strictly secret, but held together by secret languages and signs, adopted for one common object, as is now the case with the Jesuits, and as was done by the Garduna, the bands of Schinderhannes at the end of the last and beginning of the present century, and is done by the more modern brigands and thieves. In the Middle Ages France was infested with a band of itinerant beggars, usually known as Truands, whence our word truant. They had their king, a fixed code of laws, and a language peculiar to themselves, constructed probably by some of the debauched youths who, abandoning their scholastic studies, associated with the vagabonds. This language in course of time came to be called argot, which may be derived from the Greek ἀργος, an idler, lazy fellow, and the truands were then known as argotiers. Cartouche (born 1693, broken on the wheel in 1721), the famous robber, also formed his band into an association, having a language and laws of their own. In England, beggars' and thieves' slang is known as cant or pedlars' French; tinkers have a language peculiar to themselves, but extensively understood and spoken by most of the confirmed tramps and vagabonds. It is known as " shelta," is pure Celtic, but quite separate from other tongues. In French slang is known as argot, in German as rothwdlsch, in Italian as gergo, in Spanish as Germania, in Bohemian as Hantyrka, in Portuguese as calao. Circassian thieves and robbers make use of a secret language known as schakops and forschipsti. Among the Asiatics there is a cant language known as balabbalan, formed chiefly of corrupted Arabic, Persian, and Turkish words.

The vagabonds who hang about the Hottentots use a jargon which is called Cuze-cat. The vulgar dialect of the Levant is known as Lingua franca, or bastard Italian, mixed with modern Greek, German, Spanish, Turkish, and French. European cant consists largely of Hebrew and gipsy slang, together with terms borrowed and generally distorted and perverted from their true meaning from the languages of the countries to which the speakers belong. Cant words usually turn on metaphor and fanciful allusions, and frequently display great ingenuity, wit, nay, sometimes poetical fancy, as when French thieves call the iron bars in their cell windows a "harp." Certain forms of superstition are common to the vagabonds of the most distant countries, and many of these superstitious beliefs are as curious as they are revolting. Thieves and beggars recognise one another by certain signs, such as placing the fingers so as to form the letter C of the deaf and dumb alphabet, shutting one eye and squinting with the other when looking at a supposed colleague. Tramps on begging expeditions inform their brethren of the results of visits paid to houses or villages by signs chalked on walls or doorposts, or cut in trees, or traced on the snow. The begging fraternity t have their patron saint, St. Martin, born about 316, who was at first a soldier, but afterwards became a priest. When a soldier, he passed a beggar standing, with scarcely any clothing on, at the gate of Amiens Cathedral. He immediately drew his sword, and cutting his mantle asunder in the middle, gave one half to the beggar; hence his becoming their patron saint. But such beggars as are, or pass themselves off for, cripples acknowledge St. Giles as their patron.

The fraternity of thieves individually are not fraternal in their intercourse; they prefer working alone, or, at most, in couples. But they have their secret language and signs, of course varying in every country, though foreign terms are occasionally introduced; thus argot, the French for slang, is a term by which London thieves designate their own secret language. Some of their expressions are curious: "cat and kitten stealing" is stealing quart and pint pots; "chariot buzzing," picking pockets in an omnibus; a "diver" is a pickpocket. Why do they call the treadmill "cockchafer"? Whence comes "flurnmuxed " sure of a month in prison?

332. Italian and German Robbers - Among associated bands of robbers, the brigands of Italy are best known. The band led by Schinderhannes, mentioned above, existed at the end of the last and beginning of this century on both banks of the Upper Khine; it was

broken up by the execution of their leader and eighteen of his companions in November 1803. A very large band of robbers about the same date infested the neighbourhood of Aix-la-Chapelle, and were known as the band of Mersen, a small village near Eupen, which they made their headquarters. But they were universally spoken of by the nickname of the goat-riders, because the superstition of the time supposed them to ride on goats devils in disguise when engaged in some robbing expedition. Their secret chief was one Kirchhof, surgeon and steward of the monastery of Herzogenrode (?), who about the year 1804 was arrested, tried in the monastery, and died under torture. Of the band, about the same time, fourteen were hanged in Germany and Holland, eighteen died by the guillotine in France; the rest escaped and joined other bands, or were separately captured afterwards. Kirchhof bound his followers by a formal contract to keep their secret firmly, and rather to take it into the grave with them than reveal it from cowardice or treachery. Whoso did so was to be killed with all imaginable tortures. And this was no idle threat. Christopher Pfister, for instance, was, for such alleged betrayal, attacked by his comrade Hannickel, who smashed all his bones, cut off his nose and upper lip, and poured dung-water over him to increase his sufferings. Many similar and even more cruel acts of vengeance might be mentioned. But what else could be expected from such outcasts of society, when educated judges vied with one another in inflicting the most hideous tortures on their prisoners. In 1719 a sacrilegious Jewish band of robbers were, as the criminal Judge Schiilin reports, comfortably tortured by each man being tied down on a bench adjoining a stove kept red-hot, compelled to eat excessively salt fish, so. as to suffer the greatest torments of thirst, and if he fell asleep, he was to be prodded with pointed iron rods." This is a good way of getting at the truth," says the judge complacently.

VIII

THE JESUITS

333. Reasons for calling Jesuitism Secret and Anti-Social - The Jesuits may be classed among secret and anti-social associations, because either they, under false names, insinuate themselves into, or maintain themselves in, countries where they are prohibited. Thus, when banished from France by Napoleon, they continued to exist there under the various aliases of " Associates of the Heart of Jesus," "Victims of the Love of God," "Fathers of the Faith;" the society of the "Ladies of the Sacred Heart," and the "Congregation of the Holy Family," were female Jesuits in disguise. Or because they often act, or coalesce with societies really secret, and also because in all parts of the world they have always had a vast number of affiliates, who, though not openly belonging to the Order, were bound to propagate its principles and protect its interests such men as in French are called Jdsuites de robe courte. Jesuitism is antisocial, for its only object is self-aggrandisement, by opposition to the progress of civil and religious liberty; by endeavouring to suppress the advancement of literary, industrial, and social science; in fact, by seeking to bring men

> to a state of abnegation,
> which shall in all things make them willing tools;
> In short, reduce them to a set of fools.

334. Analogy letween Jesuitism and Freemasonry - There is considerable analogy and similitude between Masonic and Jesuitic degrees. The Jesuits tread down the shoe and bare the knee, because Ignatius Loyola thus presented himself at Kome and asked for the confirmation of the Order. The initials of the Masonic passwords correspond exactly with those of the Jesuit officers: Temporalis (Tubalcain); Scholasticus (Shibboleth); Coadjutor (Ch (g) iblum); Noster (Notuma). Many other analogies might be established. Not satisfied with confession, preaching, and instruction, whereby they had

acquired unexampled influence, they formed in Italy and France, in 1563, several "Congregations," i.e., clandestine meetings held in subterranean chapels and other secret places. The Congregationists had a sectarian organisation, with appropriate catechisms and manuals, which had to be given up before death, wherefore very few copies remain. In the National Library of the Eue Eichelieu at Paris there is a MS. entitled Histoire des Congregations et Socialites jtsuitiques clepuis 1563 jusqu'au temps present (1709).

335. Initiations - From this, as well as other works, we gather some of the ceremonies with which aspirants were initiated into the Order. Having in nearly all Eoman Catholic countries succeeded in becoming the educators of the young, they were able to mould the youthful mind according to their secret aims. If, then, after a number of years they detected in the pupil a blind and fanatic faith, conjoined with exalted pietism and indomitable courage, they proceeded to initiate him; in the opposite case they excluded him. The proofs lasted twenty-four hours, for which the candidate was prepared by long and severe fasting, which, by prostrating his bodily strength, inflamed his fancy, and just before the trial a powerful drink was administered to him. Then the mystic scene began diabolical apparitions, evocation of the dead, representations of the flames of hell, skeletons, moving skulls, artificial thunder and lightning, in fact, the whole paraphernalia and apparatus of the ancient mysteries. If the neophyte, who was closely watched, showed fear or terror, he remained for ever in the inferior degree; but if he bore the proof well, he was advanced to a higher grade. There were four degrees. The first consisted of the Coadjutores Temporaries, who performed the manual labour and merely servile duties of the Order; the second embraced the Scholastici, from among whom the teachers of youth were chosen; the third was composed of the Coadjutores Spirituales, which title was given to the members when they took the three vows of the Society. The Professi formed the fourth and highest grade; they alone were initiated into all the secrets of the Order.

At the initiation into the second degree the same proofs, but on a grander scale, had to be undergone. The candidate, again prepared for them by long fastings, was led with his eyes bandaged into a large cavern, resounding with wild howlings and roarings, which he had to traverse, reciting at the same time prayers specially appointed for that occasion. At the end of the cave he had to crawl through a narrow opening, and, while doing this, the bandage was taken from his eyes by an unseen hand, and he found himself in a square dungeon, whose floor was covered with a mortuary cloth, on which stood three lamps, shedding a feeble light on the skulls and skeletons ranged around. This was the Cave of Evocation, the Black Chamber, so famous in the annals of the Fathers, and the existence of which has repeatedly been proved by judicial examination before secular courts. Here, giving himself up to prayer, the neophyte passed some time, during which the priests could, without his being aware of it, watch his every movement and gesture. If his behaviour was satisfactory, all at once two brethren, representing archangels, presented themselves before him, without his being able to tell whence they had so suddenly started up a good deal can be done with properly fitted and oiled trap-doors and observing perfect silence, bound his forehead with a white band soaked with blood, and covered with hieroglyphics. They then hung a small crucifix round his neck, and a small satchel containing relics, or what did duty for them. Finally, they took off all his clothing, which they cast on a pyre in one corner of the cave, and marked his body with numerous crosses, drawn with blood. At this point the hierophant with his assistants entered, and having bound a red cloth round the middle of the candidate's body, the brethren, clothed in blood-stained garments, placed themselves beside him, and drawing their daggers, formed the steel arch over his head. A carpet being then spread on the floor, all knelt down and prayed for about an hour, after which the pyre was secretly set on fire; the further wall of the cave opened, the air resounded with strains, now gay, now lugubrious, and a long procession of spectres, phantoms, angels and demons defiled past the neophyte, like the ""supers" in a pantomime. Whilst this farce was going on, the candidate took the following oath: "In the name of Christ crucified, I swear to burst the bonds that yet unite me to father, mother, brothers, sisters, relations, friends; to the king, magistrates, and any other authority to which I may ever have sworn fealty, obedience, gratitude, or service. I renounce . . . the place of my birth, henceforth to exist in another sphere. I swear to reveal to my new superior, whom I desire to know, what I have done, thought, read, learnt, or discovered, and to observe and watch all that comes under my notice. I swear to yield myself up to my superior, as if I were a corpse, deprived of life and will. I finally swear to flee temptation, and to reveal all I succeed in discovering, well aware that lightning is not more rapid and ready than the dagger to reach me wherever I may be." The new member having taken this oath, was then introduced into a neighbouring cell, where he took a bath, and was clothed in garments of new and white linen. He finally repaired with the other brethren to a banquet, where he could with choice food and wine compensate himself for his long abstinence and the horrors and fatigues he had passed through.

336. Blessing the Dagger - Blessing the dagger was a ceremony performed when the society thought it necessary for their interests to assassinate some king, prince, or other important personage. By the side of the Dark Chamber there usually was a small cell, called the "Cell of Meditation." In its centre arose a small altar, on which was placed a painting covered with a veil, and surrounded by torches and lamps, all of a scarlet colour. Here the brother whom the Order wished to prepare for the deed of blood received his instructions. On a table stood a casket, covered with strange hieroglyphics, and bearing on its lid the representation of the Lamb. On its being opened, it was found to contain a dagger, wrapped up in a linen cloth, which one of the officers of the society took out and presented to the hierophant, who, after kissing and sprinkling it with holy water, handed it to one of the deacons, who attached it like a cross to a rosary, and hanging it round the neck of the alumnus, informed him that he was the Elect of God, and told him what victim to strike. A prayer was then offered up in favour of the success of the enterprise, in the following words: "And Thou, invincible and terrible God, who didst resolve to inspire our Elect and Thy servant with the project of exterminating N. N., a tyrant and heretic, strengthen him, and render the consecration of our brother

perfect by the successful execution of the great Work. Increase, God, his strength a hundredfold, so that he may accomplish the noble undertaking, and protect him with the powerful and divine armour of Thine Elect and Saints. Pour on his head the daring courage which despises all fear, and fortify his body in danger and in the face of death itself." After this prayer the veil was withdrawn from the picture on the altar, and the elect beheld the portrait of the Dominican James Clement, surrounded by a host of angels, carrying him on their wings to celestial glory. And the deacon, placing on the head of the chosen brother a crown symbolic of the celestial crown, added: "Deign, Lord of Hosts, to bestow a propitious glance on the servant Thou hast chosen as Tkine arm, and for the execution of the high decrees of Thine eternal justice. Amen." Then there were fresh dissolving views of ghosts, spectres, skeletons, phantoms, angels and demons, and the farce, to be followed by a tragedy, was played out.

The Jesuits openly advocated tyrannicide, whenever the tyrant was against them. Even that soft-hearted Jesuit and Inquisitor Bellarmine, who would not allow vermin to be killed, because their present life was their only one, wrote a book to show that heretics deserved death; he also advocated the doctrine of tyrannicide.

337. Similar Monkish Initiations - I may here incidentally remark that the candidate for initiation into some other monkish orders had to undergo similar trials. The novice about to enter the Dominican order had to spend some time in the Cave of Salvation (the pastos of the Ancient Mysteries and of the Freemasons), where he was surrounded by hideous monsters, fierce-looking beasts, and skeleton monks, uttering savage and threatening howls; and he was finally carried about in a coffin. Father Antonio, who about 1820 was elected prior of the Hieronymites at Madrid, declared that, though he would rather be the prior of his convent than a grandee of the first class, yet he would have forgone that dignity if he had been obliged, in order to obtain it, once more to pass through the trials of initiation. He said that instead of the Cave of Salvation, the place of initiation ought to be called the Cave of Hell. "If I believed in the devil," he added, "I should be certain I had

seen him with his train of demons and imps."

338. Secret Instructions - It will suffice to give the headings of the chapters forming the Book of Secreta Monita, or Secret Instructions of the Society of Jesus. The Preface specially warns superiors not to allow it to fall into the hands of strangers, as it might give them a bad opinion of the Order. The chapters are headed as follows: I. How the Society is to proceed in founding a new establishment. II. How the Brethren of the Society may acquire and preserve the friendship of Princes and other distinguished Personages. III. How the Society is to conduct itself towards those who possess great influence in a state; and who, though they are not rich, may yet be of service to others. IV. Hints to Preachers and Confessors of Kings and great personages. V. What conduct to observe towards the clergy and other religious orders. VI. How to win over rich widows. VII. How to hold fast widows and dispose of their property. VIII. How to induce the children of widows to adopt a life of religious seclusion. IX. Of the increase of College revenues. X. Of the private rigour of discipline to be observed by the society. XL How "Ours" shall conduct themselves towards those that have been dismissed from the society. XII. Whom to keep and make much of in the society. XIII. How to select young people for admission into the society, and how to keep them there. XIV. Of reserved cases, and reasons for dismissing from the society. XV. How to behave towards nuns and devout women. XVI. How to pretend contempt for riches. XVII. General means for advancing the interests of the society.

339. Authenticity of "Secreta Monita" Demonstrated - The Jesuits deny the authenticity of this work, but they have never been able to disprove the history of its discovery, which is as follows:

When the society was suppressed by Clement XIV. in 1773, it possessed in the Low Countries, among other property, a college at Ruremonde. Government had appointed a Commission to liquidate the affairs of the Company, and Councillor Zuytgens was specially appointed at Ruremonde to draw up the inventory; but being suspected of having abstracted, in order to favour the Fathers, certain documents, he received a peremptory command to forward all the papers found. Among these the MS. of the Secreta Monita was discovered. The proof of this may be seen in the "Protocol of the Transactions of the Committee, appointed in consequence of the Suppression of the Society of Jesus in the Low Countries," which is deposited in the archives of Brussels. The above MS. was collated, and found to agree with a Latin MS. left by Father Berthier, the last librarian of the Society in Paris, before the Revolution. It also agrees with the edition of the Monita, printed at Paderborn in 1661.

340. Jesuitic Morality - And even if these Monita were not drawn up by a Jesuit, they yet fully exhibit the actual principles on which, as we know from history, the society has always acted, and that every kind of deception, assassination, vregicide, poisoning, seduction, unnatural crimes, spoliation, perjury have ever been practised and approved by them, whenever their doing so could promote their own ends, ad majorem Dei gloriam!

When, in 1760, the Jesuits, in consequence of the bankruptcy of Lavalette, a member of the society, were compelled to produce their "Constitutions," such doctrines as the following were found to be contained in them:

According to Father Taberna, a Jesuit, "If a judge has received money to give an unjust judgment, it is probable that he ought to keep the money; for this is the judgment of fifty-eight Jesuit doctors."

In answer to the question on what occasion a monk may leave off his monk's dress without incurring excommunication, his reply is: "He may leave it off if it is for a purpose that would cause shame; to go, for instance, incognito into places of debauchery."

Emmanuel Sa, another Jesuit teacher: "Promises are not binding if, in making them, you have no intention of keeping them."

"Potest et fœmina quseque et mas, pro turpo corporis usu pretium accipere et petere, et qui promisit tenetur solvere."

"Christian children," says Fagundez," may accuse their parents of heresy, though they know that their parents will be burnt."

One quite recent instance of Jesuit morality may close these quotations. In 1852 the Jesuits of the rue de Sevres in Paris had determined to build a splendid Gothic chapel on their land. One day money ran short; every expedient had already been tried to raise some, when one of the fathers, the youngest, the most in demand in the noble faubourg, the most popular confessor, proposed a lottery, and himself as the prize. He wrote a hundred tickets, and made it known in a discreet manner that the female penitent who had the winning number should for three days dispose of Father Lefevre at her discretion. The ladies fought for the tickets, and, in spite of the laughter and sarcasms of the sceptics and heretics, the chapel was completed.

The public history of the Jesuits, revealing a system of turpitude such as has never been equalled, does not enter into the scope of this work; but as our government endeavours to exterminate dynamiters, so, in the opinion of many, it ought to crush the Jesuitical fraternity the "Black International," as it has justly been called.

IX

THE SKOPZI

341. Various Russian Sects - As Russia has always been a hotbed of political secret societies, so it has always been overrun by secret religions sects. Among these we may name the Soshigateli, or Self-burners, who regard voluntary death by fire as the only means of purification from the sins and pollution of the world. They abound in Siberia; within the last twenty years groups of such fanatics, numbering fifteen, twenty, fifty, yea, a hundred men and women, burned themselves in large pits or solitary buildings filled with brushwood. About the year 1867 no less than seventeen hundred are reported to have voluntarily chosen death by fire near Tumen, in the Eastern Ural Mountains. Another sect with similar tendencies, the Morelstschiki, or Self-sacrificers, prefer iron to fire, and consider.it a religious duty to kill one another. In 1868 such a mystical sacrifice took place on the estate of a Mr. Gurieff, on the Volga, when forty-seven men and women massacred one another with daggers. Another mad sect are the Flagellants, whose fanaticism sometimes becomes dangerous to other members of the community. In the summer of 1869 the Flagellants of Balashoff (government of Saratoff), to the number of several hundred, on returning from a field where they had practised their fanatical rites, suddenly attacked the lookers-on, and so belaboured them with their scourges and knotted ropes as to kill several of them. Others were trodden to death, and others driven between carts loaded with wood, to which the wretches set fire, so that their victims were suffocated and burnt to ashes.

342. The Skopzi - But the sect which has during the last generation attracted most attention are the Skopzi or Castrated; and whilst the sects mentioned above consist almost wholly of ignorant, wild fanatics, the Skopzi reckon among their members men of comparative culture and position, as we shall show further on.

Fact is stranger than fiction; never was this more strikingly shown than in the facts which were brought to light during the various trials which took place in different parts of Eussia in the prosecutions of these sectaries, on the official reports of which our statements are based, and the leading features of which reports were published by Dr. E. Pelikan, Imperial Kussian Privy Councillor and President of the Medical Council, who had personally known and examined many of the Skopzi. His work, both text and the coloured lithographic prints which illustrate it, forms a collection of horrors such as would pass all belief were they not authenticated by the legal proceedings which unveiled them. In this work it is, of course, impossible to enter into the terrible and hideous details chronicled by Dr. Pelikan; we must content ourselves with faintly indicating them.

Russian Skopziism arose about 1757 among the followers of the sect of the Flagellants, who are known to have existed in Eussia as early as the year 1733. The first intimation the Eussian Government had of the Skopzi was in 1771. They were first discovered in the present government of Orloff. A peasant named Andrei Iwanoff was convicted of having persuaded thirteen other peasants to mutilate themselves. He was assisted by one Kondratji Selivanoff, a peasant, born in the village of Stolbovo, in the province of Orel. A legal investigation took place at St. Petersburg, and Iwanoff was knouted and sent to Siberia, where probably he died. His assistant, Selivanoff, fled into the district of Tamboff, where, with another companion, Alexander Iwanoff Schiloff, he propagated his doctrine; but in 1775 he was seized at Moscow, knouted, and transported to Siberia. Several followers of his were arrested, flogged, and sent to penal servitude in the fortress of Dortmund. Others, not so deeply implicated, were allowed to remain in their home, but strictly forbidden to join, or to induce others to join, the sect.

But these measures did not put a stop to the propaganda. On the contrary, Skopziism increased. Selivanoff made his escape from Siberia, but was, in 1797, apprehended at Moscow, and by order of Paul I. taken to St. Petersburg, where the Emperor, after having conversed with him, had him confined in a madhouse. But on the accession of Alexander I. who was a weak-minded mystic, and greatly under the influence of that adventuress the Baroness Krüdner, who considered Selivanoff a saint, this man was allowed to leave the madhouse, and lived for several years in considerable splendour in the houses of his admirers. He was particularly protected by the sometime chamberlain of the Polish court, the state councillor Alexei Michailoff Jelanski, who was himself a Skopez, and an operator.

343. The Legend of Selivanoff - The house which Selivanoff occupied was by his followers called the "House of God," the " Heavenly Zion," the " New Jerusalem," for they believed that Christ had reappeared in the person of Selivanoff, who, they asserted, was really Peter III., born of the immaculate virgin, who, as Empress, was known as Elizabeth Petrowna. This Empress ruled for two years only, then she transferred the government to a lady of the court resembling her, and taking the name of Akulina Ivanovna, she retired, first to the province of Orel, where she lived at the house of the Skopzi prophet Filimon, and then to Bjelogrod, in the province of Kursk, where, invisible behind a garden wall, as late as 1865 she enjoyed the adoration of the faithful. The "Redeemer," as Selivanoff is also called by his adherents, is supposed to have been born in Holstein; that, on reaching manhood, he castrated himself, performed the operation on many others, and wrought many miracles. Called to the throne, he was obliged to marry, but his spouse, Catherine II., in consequence of the "baptism of fire " he had undergone, despising him, she tried to have him assassinated; the Emperor being warned of the conspiracy, made his escape in the clothes of a sentinel, who was murdered in his place. Though Catherine II. was aware of the mistake, she ordered the body of the sentinel to be buried with imperial honours. Peter III. disappeared, to reappear after a while in the person of the peasant Selivanoff, as which he continued his former practices, making many converts. He was then accompanied by Schiloff, whom the Skopzi call the forerunner of the Redeemer. But the government at last interfered; Selivanoff was seized, knouted, and sent to Siberia; Schiloff was imprisoned at Riga. The book of his "Passion" further tells us that the Emperor Paul I., on his accession, having heard of him, had Selivanoff

brought back to Russia, as he considered him his father, to surrender the crown to him; but when Selivanoff made self-mutilation the condition of his acknowledging Paul as his son, the latter grew wroth, and ordered Selivanoff, as well as Schiloff, who had also been sent for from Riga, to be imprisoned in the fortress of Schliisselburg. Under Alexander I. Selivanoff was set free, and the Emperor and his Empress joined the elect. Selivanoff lived at St. Petersburg, where the Skopez Sladownikoff found him an elegant residence, where he convinced many that he was Christ, the true God. But eventually the government thought it necessary to put a stop to the ravages of the baptism of fire, and Selivanoff was confined in the monastery of Suzdal. The Skopzi firmly believe him to be still alive, and that in his own time he will take possession of the throne of Russia, whereupon castration will become universal. But as before the second appearance of the Redeemer, according to Christian belief, Antichrist is to appear, the Skopzi maiutain that he has already appeared in the person of Napoleon, who is a bastard of Catherine II. and the devil, and at present living in Turkey, whence, converted to the true faith, he also will come to Russia as a Skopez.

344. Historical Foundation of the Legend - The reason why the Skopzi identify the Redeemer with Peter III. is this: Peter III. was the grandson of Peter I. the Great, and a son of the Duke Charles Frederick of Holstein and Anna Petrowna, Peter's daughter; he ascended the throne in 1762. Before him the "people of God," especially the Flagellants, were cruelly persecuted and tortured their tongues were torn out, and they were burnt alive but Peter III., immediately on his accession, granted them a complete amnesty and the fullest religious liberty. Hence they looked upon him as their saviour, and he, being a divine person, could not die. The real reason why he was murdered Count Orloff is said to have strangled him with his own hand was the Empress' dissatisfaction with the innovations he introduced. He ascended the throne on the 5th January, and was killed on the 14th July 1762. The Akulina Ivanovna, mentioned in the previous section, who was worshipped as the mother of God, and who

pretended to have been the Empress Elizabeth, was born of humble parents in the town of Lebedjan, in the province of Tamboif; her real name was Katassanova. In the year 1820 Selivanoff was, from Suzdal, transferred to the monastery of Spasso-Euphemius, where, in 1832, he died at a great age. At the same time, many of the most fanatical adherents of the sect were shut up in the monastery of Ssolovetski, and among them the Skopez captain Ssosonovitch, who, repenting of his former delusions, revealed to the archimandrite of the lastnamed monastery the deepest secrets of the Skopzi doctrine.

345. Diffusion of the Sect - According to maps prepared by Dr. Pelikan, during the period from 1805 to 1839 Skopziism prevailed in most parts of Russia, its greatest intensity being at St. Petersburg, Kursk, and on the Black Sea. It also existed to some extent on the White Sea and in the Ural. A considerable increase of the practice took place in Kherson and the Crimea about the year 1822. About the same time many gold and silver smiths of St. Petersburg belonged to the sect.

From 1840 to 1859 Skopziism seemed to be dying out around the White Sea and St. Petersburg, though in that town it remained as prevalent as ever. The Emperor Nicholas took very severe measures against the sectaries, and many of them were banished to Siberia. Others fled to the Danubian principalities, settling at Galatz and Bucharest, but mostly at Jassy, where nearly all hackney-coach drivers are said to belong to the sect.

From 1860 to 1870 the Skopzi increased greatly in numbers, and spread to parts of the Russian empire where formerly they were scarcely known; for they are zealous proselytisers, though they will only admit Russians to the sect or is it, that they can in no other nationality find people mad enough to submit to their rites?

In 1865 the Russian inhabitants on the shores of the Sea of Azoff made great complaints of the spread of Skopziism. Investigation proved the fact: many mutilated men and women were discovered. The chief offenders, including the peasant woman Babanin, who had presided at the meetings of Skopzi at Militopol, and was revered as a prophetess, were banished to Siberia. But it was soon found that the Azoff society formed but a branch of the sect. Its centre was the town of Morschansk, in the province of Tamboff. On the last night of the year 1869, says an account which, besides much exaggeration, contains a solid . foundation of truth, the head of the Police of that town was at a party. About midnight he was called out of the room, and a servant of the merchant Ploticyn handed him a letter, asking that three women then in custody might be allowed to go free till the morning, when they would return to their prison. Ten thousand roubles in bank-notes were enclosed in the letter. The head of the Police handed the letter and notes to the Criminal Department. Ploticyn was arrested, and on searching his residence it was found to consist of a cluster of houses, having four cellars underground, where a large amount of treasure in cash and bank-notes perhaps two millions of roubles in value was discovered, together with an extensive correspondence, implicating many rich merchants in various Russian towns, including the millionaire Tretjakoff of St. Petersburg. Ploticyn was deprived of his civil rights and honours, and banished to Siberia, and with him twelve other men and nineteen women. The peasant Kusnezoff, for having mutilated himself and eleven other persons, was condemned to four years' penal labour in a Siberian mine. The money found in Ploticyn's house, or at least so much of it as had not disappeared, was given to his heirs; the ten thousand roubles sent to the head of the Police were transferred to the Imperial treasury.

The discoveries in Ploticyn's house led to the prosecution of Skopzi in various parts of the empire; the trials extended far into the year 1872, and promised to be interminable, but the further publication of them was prohibited. The trials took place simultaneously at St. Petersburg, Moscow, Tula, Tamboff, and Eiga. Witnesses were summoned from the most distant parts of Eussia. Some of the less guilty sectaries were confided to the religious care of monasteries, and through them some of the secrets of the sect became public, as already mentioned above. The official reports of the monastery of Solovez are particularly instructive; they were published about 1875, in the book entitled "Lectures before the Imperial Society of History and Antiquity."

346. Creed and Mode of Worship - The baptism of fire is the gate to perfect salvation, the seal of God. It belongs either to the higher and more meritorious class, the "great seal," which involves the removal of the whole organ, or to the "lesser seal," which means simple castration. With the strictest of the sect all sexual intercourse, even with a wife, is sinful; our parents, in giving us life, committed a heinous sin, wherefore, in some communities, the neophyte, before being initiated into the last mysteries of the sect, had to write the name of his parents on a piece of paper and tread it under foot. In some communities, however, married aspirants were not admitted till after the birth of the first child, and the Skopzi of Bucharest were allowed to have two children before the operation was performed.

The religious ceremonies of the Skopzi, after the singing of hymns, spontaneous addresses and prophecies, consist chiefly in violent exercise and dancing after the fashion of the Dervishes. At the introduction of a neophyte, however, nothing of this kind takes place; he at first simply receives instructions as to his moral and religious duties, the teaching being strictly orthodox, so as not to scare him away, but of so exciting a character as gradually to awaken in him a religious enthusiasm, which shall finally prepare him for the terrible sacrifice, and make him ready to pronounce the vow exacted from him, by which he declares " voluntarily to have come to the Redeemer, and to be determined to keep secret from the Czar, the princes, father, mother, relations and friends, all that relates to these sacred matters, and to submit to persecution, torture, fire and death, rather than reveal their mysteries to enemies."

Their meetings are usually held late at night, and last till daybreak. The localities usually are the secret prayer-rooms found in the dwellings of all Skopzi, which generally are built at as great a distance from other houses as possible. In the centre there is a courtyard, surrounded by barns, cart-sheds and living-rooms, from which, beside the main entrance, some secretly-contrived doors open onto the cattleyard, which is connected with a third enclosure, where stands a bee-house, which latter is surrounded with high palings, whence there are secret openings to the garden, from which there is an exit into the fields. During the meeting watchers are stationed at various distances, who, at the approach of any suspicious-looking stranger, warn their friends by signs, upon which the meeting breaks up, and those who are specially afraid of being discovered make their escape through the cattle-yard into the bee-house, and thence through the garden into the fields.

When engaged in their devotions the men wear long, wide, white shirts of a peculiar cut, tied round the waist with girdles, and large white trousers; the women are also dressed in white shirts; in the villages they wear blue gowns of nankeen, in the towns, of chintz; they, moreover, cover their heads with white cloths. Both sexes put on white stockings, though sometimes they are all barefooted, and carry in their hands handkerchiefs, which they call "flags." The as yet uncastrated members of the sect are called "donkeys" or "goats," whilst those operated on are styled "white lambs," "white doves."

They have a kind of eucharist, at which small pieces of bread, which are consecrated by being put for a while in openings in the monument erected at Schliisselberg to the Skopez Schiloff, are distributed. A priest, Ivan Sfergejeff, who, by order of his superiors, insinuated himself into the confidence of a leading Skopez, and thus became cognisant of all the secrets of the sect, gives details of a "communion of flesh and blood," which is nothing less than a charge of cannibalism, and of the most horrible, revolting kind, against the sect; it has not, I think, been juridically proved; but people who are mad enough to become Skopzi, are mad enough for anything. Legal documents in the archives of the Holy Synod show that among the Flagellants such a "communion of flesh and blood" existed; the Skopzi arose among the Flagellants, so it is possible that the practice of the latter was adopted by the former. Its details are too revolting to be given here.

347. The Baptism of Fire - As already stated, it is of two kinds, respectively called the "lesser" and the "great seal." The chief point of

Christ's teaching, the Skopzi say, was that man to be saved must undergo the "baptism of fire," that is, castrate himself by means of a red-hot iron. Christ, they say, set the example in his own person, which was followed by the apostles and the early Christian Church, including Origen and all the saints, who in the traditional painting of the Oriental Christians, are always represented without beards. Out of regard for human weakness, it was afterwards allowed to substitute a sharp knife for the hot iron. But zealous Skopzi are not particular as to the instruments they use. In 356 instances of mutilation of men, we find a knife employed 164 times, a razor 108 times, a hatchet 30 times, a scythe 23 times; pieces of iron, glass, tin, &c., 17 times. As varied are the localities where the operation has been performed. Of 620 cases, we find that 96 took place in peasants' houses, 19 in prisons, 12 in privies, 6 in cellars, 41 in baths, 32 in barns, 14 in coach-houses, 4 iri kitchen gardens, 8 in yards, 136 in woods, no less than 223 on high-roads and in fields, 1 under a bridge, 8 in boats, 1 in a churchyard, &c. Though we have hitherto spoken of men only as the victims voluntary and the contrary of their cruel fanaticism, the other sex are sufferers from it in the proportion of about four women to ten men. With them, too, the operation is as fearful as it is revolting; the earliest records of such operations on women dates from 1815. And yet we find women among the operators. Among 43 peasant women who acted in that capacity, 5 had actually operated on men. The Skopzi, as already intimated, include men of rank and position; thus there were found among them 4 ladies and 4 gentlemen belonging to the nobility, 10 military officers, 5 naval officers, 14 officials in the civil service, 19 priests, 148 merchants, 220 citizens, 2736 peasants (including 827 women), 119 landowners, 443 soldiers arid soldiers' wives and daughters: 515 men and 240 women were between the years 1847 and 1866 transported to Siberia as convicted Skopzi. Their real number in the empire cannot be ascertained on account of the secrecy of their proceedings. In 1874 it was known to be at least 5444, inclusive of 1465 women; of these, 703 men and 160 women had performed the operation on themselves; 79 men and 11 women underwent the operation twice, first the "lesser" and then the "great seal." The male members of the sect may be recognised by their puffy, corpulent exterior, and their wrinkled and beardless faces.

348. Failure of the Prosecution of the Sect - The state is bound to prosecute and, if possible, suppress the active participators in what is an abominable crime against public policy and humanity; but experience has shown that all the measures hitherto taken have failed to put a stop to Skopziism. The very means adopted for its suppression frequently led to its extension; thus Skopzi shut up in monasteries actually converted monks to their schism. State prosecutions induced men and women to mutilate themselves to join the noble army of martyrs. Even the so-called "moral " measure, which was introduced in 1850, of dressing Skopzi in women's clothes, and putting fools' caps on their head, and thus leading them, accompanied by a policeman, about the villages, to the derision of the inhabitants, often had an effect opposite to that aimed at. The Russian clergy are too universally despised to have any influence in stemming the evil; and some of the highest placed of the hierarchy wink at it, in consideration of the large sums given by wealthy Skopzi for the erection or decoration of orthodox churches. The only direct way to arrest the progress of Skopziism is to transport all detected members to distant and thinly populated localities, where they must be kept under strict supervision till they die out. And indirectly their fanaticism must be extinguished by a better education of the Russian people.

One of the most recent trials, accounts of which have reached civilised Europe, is that of a banker and his niece, held with closed doors at St. Petersburg, in December 1893. The banker, a man of sixty, was condemned, as belonging to the sect of the Skopzi, to fifteen years' hard labour for self-mutilation, and his niece to ten years' hard labour for having allowed herself to be operated on, and thus conniving at a criminal offence.

X

THE CANTERS OR MUCKERS

349. Eva von Buttler and her Sect - This most repulsive sect, a diseased offshoot of the Pietists, first made its appearance towards the end of the seventeenth century, .though the name was not given to it then, but to the sect when revived towards the end of the eighteenth century. The German word mucker means a hypocrite, a sanctimonious, canting person. The original sect was founded by Gottfried Justus Winter, a student of theology at Marburg, who had joined various Pietistic circles then existing in Hesse and Saxony. He afterwards became acquainted and intimate with Eva, the wife of John de Vesias, of Eisenach, who, in consequence of her misconduct, obtained a divorce from her. Eva then reassumed her maiden name, von Buttler, and went to live with Winter in the institution of about twenty members, founded by him at Eschwege, for the free practice of their religion, which, however, soon drew upon itself the attention of the authorities, and the immoral practices of the sect being placed beyond doubt, the members were banished the country. But Winter and Eva were not the people to give up their object; they applied to the Duke of Sayn-Wittgenstein, lord of a small but independent territory, forming part of the former Duchy of Nassau, who granted them the free exercise of their religion, and leased to them the estate of Sassmannshausen. Here for a time the Muckers by their outwardly holy lives deceived the public, but false brethren and apostates gradually caused rumours to arise as to what went on among the saints debaucheries of the most revolting description which compelled the Duke to order an inquiry; but bribes, judiciously applied, and the legal skill of a lawyer, Dr. Vergenius, who held a high official position at the Imperial Chamber at Wetzlar, led to Winter and his followers being acquitted, the former even being appointed the Duke's private secretary. The saints being rendered over-secure by this temporary victory, indulged their propensities to the fullest extent. Eva was a second Messalina in her excesses; in fact, her male companions were taught that perfect

sanctification was only to be arrived at by carnal intercourse with herself. But the birth of a child in the community in spite of the cruel and hideous precautions which had been taken to prevent such an occurrence, precautions we are not allowed to describe and the sudden death of the child, at last induced the Duke to have the doings of the saints watched through openings made in the walls of the rooms occupied by them, and the gross profligacy, which was then revealed, and eventually confessed by the inculpates, was such, that we cannot give the details, though they were all proved in a court of law. But most of the ringleaders made their escape from custody, and eventually settled in the small town of Luyde, the vicinity of which to Pyrmont, with its rich and aristocratic visitors to the baths, promised many proselytes, who, in fact, did not fail to present themselves, so that a new society was soon formed. But in consequence of the statements made by one Sebastian Reuter, who by revealing the practices of the sect hoped to get an appointment from the government of Paderborn, under whose jurisdiction Luyde was placed, about twenty members of the association were arrested, including Winter and Eva; but both again managed to escape. What became of them afterwards is not precisely known. Some of the other prisoners were ordered to be publicly whipped, others acquitted.

350. Schonherr's Sect - Another association of the same character as the above, calling itself Theosophers, but nicknamed Muckers by the public, was discovered at Konigsberg in 1835. Its founder was John Henry Schonherr, born at Memel in 1771, died at Konigsberg in 1826. Two of his followers, the pastors Ebel and Diestel, declared the dualistic-gnostic doctrines of Schonherr to mean that the flesh was to be sanctified by sexual intercourse, and they formed a secret association, to which women, of course, were admitted. Their practices eventually led to a judicial inquiry, which, however, was not pursued to the end, as many persons of good position were found to be implicated in the sect. But Ebel and Diestel were degraded from their official positions, and the latter was moreover sent to the house of correction. And thus another chapter, not of historical, but of hysterical theology, was closed for a time.

BOOK X

SOCIAL REGENERATION

I

ILLUMINATI

351. The Term Illuminati - The name of " Illuminati" has frequently been adopted by various sects. The end of the sixteenth century saw the Alombrados in Spain,[15] and in 1654 the Guerinets were founded in France, both societies of visionaries and ghost-seers. In the second half of the last century there was an association of mystics existing under that name in Belgium. Other fraternities, calling themselves Illuminati, and formed in more recent times, will be found mentioned in this work; but the society of which I am about to speak now is the best known of all Illuminati orders.

352. Foundation of Order - Adam Weishaupt, a student in the University of Ingolstadt, learned and ambitious, and attracted by that love of mystery which is a prominent characteristic of youth, meditated the formation of a philosophicopolitical sect. When twenty-two years of age he was elected Professor of Canon Law in the same University, a chair which had for twenty years been filled by the Jesuits; hence their rage against, and persecution of, Weishaupt, which he met boldly, returning hatred with hatred, and collecting partisans. The great aversion he then conceived for the Jesuits appears in many of the statutes of the Order he founded. Jesuits, he often declares, are to be avoided like the plague. The sect of the Illuminati was founded in 1776 by Weishaupt, who adopted the pseudonym of Spartacus, but it

---

[15] Suspected of being one of these Alombrados, Ignatius Loyola, the founder of the order of Jesuits, was for nearly a month imprisoned in the dungeons of the Inquisition at Salamanca; when the holy fathers had perused his " Spiritual Exercises," in MS., they considered him harmless, and let him go

was years before its ritual and constitution were finally settled. Weishaupt, in order the better to succeed, connected himself with the Freemasons, by entering the lodge " Theodore of Good Counsel," of Eclectic Masonry, at Munich, and attempting to graft Illuminism on Freemasonry. Many members of the craft, misled by the construction of his first degrees, entered the Order; but when they found that Weishaupt meant real work and not mere play, they hung back. The society was instituted for the purpose of lessening the evils resulting from the want of information, from tyranny, political and ecclesiastical.

353. Organisation - The society was by its founder divided into classes, each of which was again subdivided into degrees, in the following manner:

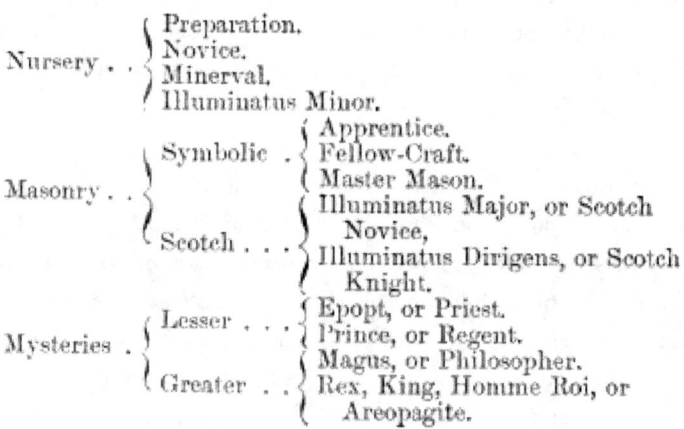

In the Nursery and Masonry degrees, the candidate was merely tried and prepared for the Mystery degrees. If he was found unreliable, he was not allowed to go beyond; but if he proved an apt scholar, he was gradually initiated into the latter, where all that he had been taught before was overthrown, and radical and deistic theories and plans were unfolded, which were in nowise immoral or subversive of public order, but only such as, at the present day, are held by many men of just and enlightened views.

354. Initiation into the Degree of Priest - The candidate for the priesthood, the first degree in the Lesser Mysteries, was taken, with his eyes bandaged, in a carriage, following a roundabout way, to the house where the initiation was to take place. On his arrival there his eyes were unbandaged, and he was told to put on the apron of the Scotch Knight, the cross of St. Andrews, and the hat, take the sword into his hand, and wait before the first door till summoned to enter. After a while he heard a solemn voice calling, "Enter, orphan, the fathers call thee, and shut the door behind thee." On entering he beheld a room, the walls of which were covered with rich red hangings, and splendidly illuminated. In the background stood a throne under a canopy, and in front of it a table, on which were placed a crown, sceptre, sword, valuables, and chains. The priestly vestments were displayed on a red cushion. There were no chairs in the room, but a stool without back stood at some distance from the throne, facing it. The candidate, on being introduced, was told to choose between the things on the table or the vestments on the cushion. Should he, contrary to all expectation, declare for the crown and its concomitants, he would at once be expelled; but if he chose the priestly dress, he was addressed with, "All hail, thou noble one!" and invited to take a seat on the 'stool and listen to the explanation of his future duties, which, as intimated above, were simply to act as an instructor of the uninitiated. The lecture being ended, a door at the back was opened, and the friend who had introduced the candidate entered in the priest's dress, which consisted of a white woollen toga, descending to the feet; the neck and sleeves were edged with scarlet silk ribbons, a silk girdle of the same colour encircled the waist. The deacon alone had, moreover, a red cross, about a foot long, on his left breast. The candidate was led into the inner room, the door of which had in the meantime been opened, and in which was seen an altar, covered with red cloth; above it hung a painted or carved crucifix. On the altar itself were placed the book of the ritual, a Bible bound in red, a small glass dish with honey, and a glass jug with milk in it. A burning lamp hung over the head of the deacon, who faced the altar; the priests sat on both sides, on red-cushioned benches.

The candidate was admonished, and promised to renounce the enemies of mankind, evil desires, the spirit of oppression, and deception; having done this, he was divested of his masonic clothing, and having promised in presence of the crucifix to be faithful to the Order, the assistants put on him the priestly dress, and then let him eat some of the honey and drink some of the milk, as a sealing of their covenant. The priest's sign was laying both hands in the form of a cross flat on the head; the grip consisted in presenting a fist, with the thumb held straight up; the other would then make a fist, pressing it on that presented to him, but so as to enclose the vertically presented thumb. The word was INRI. Then followed a long lecture of a moral and scientific character.

355. Initiation into the Degree of Regent - This degree was -conferred only on such persons as by high intellectual attainments, social position, and tried fidelity, were considered capable of advancing the objects of the Order. The place of reception consisted of three rooms. In the last there stood! a raised richly-decorated red throne under a canopy for the Provincial; to the right stood a white column, about seven feet high, on which was placed a crown, resting on a red cushion; suspended from the column were a shepherd's crook of white wood and an artificial palm branch. On the left hand stood a table with a red cover, on which were placed the garments of the Regent, which consisted of a kind of cuirass made of white leather, with a red cross on it. Over this was worn a white cloak, with another red cross embroidered on it. The collar and cuffs were red. The Regents wore tall white hats with red feathers, and red laced half-boots on their feet. The cross on the cuirass of the Provincial was irradiated with golden rays. The room was hung with red, and well lighted up. The Provincial alone occupied it, seated on the throne; the other Regents were in the middle room. The first room was set aside for preparation; it was hung with black, and in its centre, on a platform, stood a complete human skeleton, at whose feet lay a crown and a sword. The candidate was led into this room; his hands were manacled, and he was left alone for a little while, during which time he could hear the conversation carried on in the middle

room. Who has brought this slave hither? He came and knocked. What does he seek? Freedom; he beseeches you to free him from his bonds. Why does he not apply to those who have bound him? They will not set him free; his servitude benefits them. Who has made him a slave? Society, the State, false Religion. . . . Does he respect persons? Ask him who was the man whose skeleton he sees before him; was he a king, nobleman, or beggar? He does not know; he only knows that he was a man like one of ourselves. He wants only to be a man. Then let him be introduced. The candidate was then brought into the middle, and finally into the last room, and after some more catechising, invested with the dress of the Regent. The sign was holding out both arms towards a brother; the grip taking hold of his elbows, as if to support or raise him up; the word was Redemtis.

356. The Greater Mysteries - Such was the initiation into the Lesser Mysteries. The Greater Mysteries, with their two degrees of Magus and Rex, were never worked out by Philo, as Baron de Knigge called himself. But according to statements found in the writings of Weishaupt, the Magus degree was to be founded on the principles of Spinoza, showing all to be material, God and the world One, and all religions human inventions. The second, or degree of Homo Eex, taught that every peasant, citizen, or father of a family is a sovereign, as in patriarchal life, to which all mankind must be brought back, and that consequently all state authority must be abolished. Weishaupt never intended these degrees to become known to any but the most trustworthy of his followers; but the discovery of his correspondence and secret papers revealed also this part of his scheme.

357. Nomenclature and Secret Writing of Order - The most important person of the Order after Weishaupt was Baron de Knigge, who assumed the pseudonym of "Philo." All the leading members equally adopted such pseudonyms. Thus we have seen that Weishaupt took the name of Spartacus, who in Pompey's time headed the insurrection of slaves; Zwack, a lawyer, was known among the initiated as "Cato"; Nicolai, bookseller, as "Lucian"; Professor Westenrieder, as

"Pythagoras"; Canon Hertel, as " Marius "; and so on. The places whence the members wrote to one another were also designated by fictitious names: thus Bavaria was called Achaia; Munich was called Athens; Frankfurt-on-theMain became Thebes; Heidelberg, Utica; and so on. The brethren dated their letters according to the Persian era, called after the king who began to rule in Persia in 632 before Christ, Jezdegerd, and the year began with them on the 21st March. They corresponded, till initiated into the higher degrees, in cypher, which consisted in numbers corresponding to letters in the following order:

```
12  11  10  9   8   7   6   5   4   3   2   1   13  14
a   b   c   d   e   f   g   h   i   k   l   m   n   o
15  16  17  18  19  20  21  22  23  24
p   q   r   s   t   u   w   x   y   z.
```

When admitted to the higher degrees, they used either the one or the other hieroglyphic shown here:

The word Order was never written in full, but always indicated by a circle with a dot in the centre, thus ☉.

The Order made considerable progress, including among its

members priests, prelates, ministers, physicians, princes, and sovereign dukes. No doubt, few of them were initiated into the higher degrees. The Elector of Bavaria became alarmed at the political tenets betrayed by some recreant brothers of the Order, and at once suppressed it in all his territories.

358. Secret Papers and Correspondence - It was only after the suppression of the Order that the mode of initiation into the higher degrees, and the true doctrines taught therein, became known. A collection of original papers and correspondence was found, by illegally searching the house of Zwack, in 1786. In the following year a much larger collection was found at the house of Baron Bassus, a member. From these we learn that one of the chief means recommended by the leaders for the success of the Order was that of gaining over the women not a bad plan, and not objectionable when the aim is a good one. "There is no way of influencing men so powerfully as by means of the women," says the instructor. "These should, therefore, be our chief study. We should insinuate ourselves into their good opinion, give them hints of emancipation from the tyranny of public opinion, and of standing up for themselves; it will be an immense relief to their enslaved minds to be freed from any one bond of restraint, and it will fire them the more, and cause them to work for us with zeal," &c. Similar views are enunciated in a letter found among the correspondence: "The proposal of Hercules (a member not identified) to establish a Minerval school for girls is excellent, but requires circumspection. . . . We cannot improve the world without improving the women. . . . But how shall we get hold of them? How will their mothers, immersed in prejudices, consent that others shall influence their education? We must begin with grown girls. Hercules proposes the wife of Ptolemy Magus. I have no objection; and I have four stepdaughters, fine girls. The eldest in particular is excellent. She is twenty-four, has read much, and is above all prejudices. They have many acquaintances. ... It may immediately be a very pretty society. . . . No man must be admitted. This will make them become more keen, and they will go much farther than if we were present. . . . Leave them

to the scope of their own fancies, and they will soon invent mysteries which will put us to the blush. . . . They will be our great apostles. . . . Ptolemy's wife must direct them, and she will be instructed by Ptolemy, and my stepdaughters will consult with me. . . . But I am doubtful whether the association will be durable women are fickle and impatient. Nothing will please them but hurrying from degree to degree . . . which will soon lose their novelty and influence. To rest seriously in one rank, and to be silent when they have found out that the whole is a cheat (!), is a work of which they are incapable. . . . Nay, there is a risk that they may take it into their heads to give things an opposite turn, and then, by the arts in which they are adepts by nature, they may turn our order upside down." And a circumstance, affecting the personal character of the founder, which was brought to light by the discovery of the secret correspondence, but was totally unconnected with the principles advocated by the Order, contributed as much as anything else to give the Order of the Illuminati a bad name. Another circumstance was taken advantage of by the enemies of the Order to crush it. In the handwriting of Zwack were found a description of a strong box, which, if forced open, should blow up and destroy its contents; a recipe for sympathetic ink; how to take off impressions of seals, so as to use them afterwards as seals; a collection of some hundreds of such impressions, with a list of their owners; a set of portraits of eighty-five ladies in Munich, with recommendations of some of them as members of a lodge of sisters illuminatce; injunctions to all superiors to learn to write with both hands, and to use more than one cypher; and other matters.

359. Refutation of Charges - So says Robison in his "Proofs of a Conspiracy." But he does not say that this "one Zwack, a counsellor, holding some law office "he was a judge and electoral councillor in a published letter disproved all the scandalous charges brought against the Illuminati, showing that the idea of utilising the influence of women was taken from an essay on the Mopses, and that the list of recipes given above was copied by him for his own private amusement and instruction, he being a criminal lawyer and judge, from the works of

the Jesuit Kircher and other orthodox authorities, and had not the slightest connection with the Illuminati. The "set of portraits of eighty-five ladies in Munich" was actually stolen by the police from the wardrobe of Von Zwack's wife !

360. Suppression - The society having been established in the small state of Bavaria, and so quickly suppressed, never made any lasting impression on the affairs of its own time, nor on those of the future. All the terrible effects attributed to its doctrines by Robison and other opponents of the Order existed more in the imagination of the writers than in reality. If, as Robison says, the founders only wanted liberty to indulge their ambition and passions, they might, and, according to the secret correspondence quoted, seem to, have done so without the cumbrous machinery of a society whose members appeared so unmanageable. Weishaupt was deprived of his professor's chair, and banished from Bavaria, but with a pension of eight hundred florins, which he refused. He first went to Regensburg, and afterwards entered the service of the Duke of Saxe-Gotha. Zwack also was banished, and went into the service of the Prince of Salms, who soon after had so great a hand in the disturbances in Holland. Of the German society of the Illuminati, it may truly be said that it was before its time; all enlightened nations now adopt and advocate its aims. But it was not without its influence on the French Revolution, and it may have inspired Bahrdt with the idea of the German Union.

361. Illuminati in France - As early as the year 1782, Philo and Spartacus had formed the plan of introducing Illuminism into France, especially as some adepts already existed in that country. Dietrich, the Mayor of Strasbourg, was one of them; Mirabeau was another, who had been initiated at Berlin, to which city he had been sent by Louis XVI. on a secret mission. On his return to France he initiated the Abbe Talleyrand de Perigord, and Bode, privy councillor, at Weimar, known in the sect as Amelius, and William, Baron deBusch, whose sectarian name was Bayard, who shortly after came to Paris, continued the work of initiation, choosing their adepts chiefly in the masonic lodges. The

most zealous and trusted members were formed into a "Secret Committee of United Friends." According to a book published about 1790, and entitled "La Secte des Illumines," their manner of initiation, their oaths and doctrines, were of the most frightful kind. Let us go a little into details.

362. Ceremonies of Initiation - The large mansion of Ermenonville, about thirty miles from Paris, and belonging to the Marquis de Gerardin, who gave J. J. Rousseau during the last days of his life an asylum, and afterwards a tomb on his estate, was said to be the chief lodge of Illuminism. The famous impostor Saint Germain presided in it. On the day of initiation the candidate was led through a long dark passage into a large hall hung with black. By the feeble light of sepulchral lamps he perceived corpses wrapped up in shrouds. In the centre of the hall stood an altar built up of human skeletons; spectres wandered through the hall and disappeared, leaving an evil odour behind. At last two men disguised as spectres appeared, tied a pink ribbon, smeared with blood, and having the image of the Lady of Loretto on it, round his forehead. Into his hand they placed a crucifix, and hung an amulet round his neck. His clothes were laid on a funeral pyre; on his body they painted crosses with blood. His pudenda were tied up with string. Five terrific figures, armed with daggers, and clothed in bloodstained garments, approached him, fell down before him, and prayed. At the end of an hour or so the candidate heard mourning sounds, the pyre was lit up, and his clothes burnt. A gigantic semi-transparent form arose from the flames; the five figures on the ground fell into fearful convulsions; and the voice of an invisible hierophant burst from the vault, and uttered the following oaths, which the neophyte had to repeat:

"In the name of the Crucified, I swear to sever all bonds uniting me with father, mother, brothers, sisters, wife, relations, friends, mistress, king, superiors, benefactors, or any other man to whom I have promised faith, obedience, gratitude, or service.

"Name the place where thou art born. To live henceforth in another sphere, which thou will not reach till thou hast renounced this poisoned globe cursed by Heaven.

" From this moment thou shalt reveal to thy new chief all thou shalt have heard, learned, and discovered, and also to seek after and spy into things that might otherwise escape thy notice.

"Honour the aqua Toana as a sure, quick, and necessary means of ridding the earth, by death or stupefaction, of those who revile truth, or seek to wrest it from our hands.

"Avoid Spain, Naples, and every other accursed country; also avoid all temptation to betray what thou hast now heard. Lightning does not strike so quickly as the dagger which will reach thee wherever thou mayest be."

The candidate having repeated these words, a candlestick with seven black wax tapers was placed before him, together with a vessel full of human blood. He had to wash himself with the blood, and drink half a glassful. Then the string round the pudenda was untied, he was placed in a bath, and on leaving it regaled with a dish of roots.

363. Credibility of above Account - No doubt all this sounds very horrible, and is very incredible. But as to the horrors, they were simply theatrical; and as to credibility, writers near the time when these horrors were said to have been practised seriously believed in them! The Abbe Barruel, who gives some of the above details in his work, "Memoirs Illustrating the History of Jacobinism," does "not hesitate to consider them as historical truth."

The Marquis de Jouffroi, in his "Dictionary of Social Errors," positively asserts that the meetings at Ermenonville were scenes of the grossest debauchery. Why should we doubt that they also were occasions for all sorts of ridiculous absurdities?

Note - In the (London) Monthly Magazine for January 1798 there appeared a letter from Augustus Bottiger, Provost of the College of Weimar, in reply to Robison's work, charging that writer with makingfalse statements, and declaring that since 1790 "every concern [sic] of the Illuminati has ceased." Bottiger also offered to supply any person in Great Britain, alarmed at the erroneous statements contained in the book above mentioned, with correct information.

II

THE GERMAN UNION

364. Statements of Founder - This society, of which Robison and Barruel give such dreadful accounts, never was anything but an attempt at a commercial speculation by the famous Dr. Charles Frederick Bahrdt, a German theologian, possessing great literary talent, but little moral principles. His plan was first propounded in a pamphlet addressed "To All Friends of Reason, Truth, and Virtue," and asserting that there existed a society of twenty-two statesmen, professors, and private persons for the dissemination of natural religion, the rooting out of superstition, and restoring mankind to liberty by enlightening them. "It is for that purpose," the pamphlet stated, "that we have formed a secret society, to which we invite all those who are actuated by the same views, and are properly sensible of their importance." The society was to have its periodicals and journals, its libraries and reading clubs the books read, of course, to be those published by direction of the Twenty-two, or in reality by Bahrdt. The society was to some extent a resuscitation of the Illuminati. Frederick William, King of Prussia, alarmed at the progress their teaching was making, allowed his pietist minister of the Public Cult, John Christian von Wollner, to publish the notorious retrograde "Edict of Religion" of 1788, which caused universal dissatisfaction, and was satirised in a pamphlet bearing the same title as the Edict. Bahrdt was betrayed as the author thereof by one Samuel Roper, whom, from charity, he had made his secretary, and was sent to prison, where he wrote his Memoirs, which were published at Frankfurt in four volumes in 1790. Von Wollner was personally interested in opposing the German Union and its liberal dogmas in religion and politics, because he himself was secretly a zealous Rosicrucian, and the Rosicrucians preferred working in the dark. A violent attack on the German Union was made in a book called " More Notes than Text," and attributed by some to J. J. C.

Bode, late Privy Councillor at Weimar, and by others to Goschen, a bookseller at Leipzig, by whom it was published in 1789. Bahrdt having in consequence of study and reflection adopted and advocated pure Deism, and being, moreover, an advanced politician, too enlightened for his day, he made himself many enemies among the transparency (Durchlaucht) and parson-ridden burghers of the various cities in which he successively held appointments. He gradually lost them all, and eventually set up a tavern near Halle, which he called "Bahrdt's Repose." He died in 1793, after which nothing more was heard of the German Union. He is known in England by Barruel's and Robison's writings only, and misrepresented, to his disadvantage, by both. Neither of them being a good German scholar, both have mistranslated many passages taken from Bahrdt's works, and others they have, evidently intentionally, so twisted to their own purpose that of abusing their author that their statements, as far as they refer to Bahrdt, and, I may add, as far as they refer to Weishaupt, are of very little value.

III

FRENCH WORKMEN'S UNIONS

365. Organisation of Workmen's Unions - The origin of corporations of artisans dates from the day in which the oppressed workers and neglected burghers wished to resist feudal rapine, assure to themselves the fruit of their own labour, increase their trade, enlarge their profits, and establish friendly relations. But whilst these ancient corporations rose up against the aristocracy of blood and wealth, they did not steer clear of the oligarchic spirit. In the first centuries of the Middle Ages the journeyman did not separate from his master; he lived and worked with him. There did not then exist that distinction which afterwards displayed itself so openly in fact, even now, in many German towns the journeymen eat at the master's table. Then the journeyman was to the master what the squire was to the knight; and as the squire could be received into the ranks of knighthood, so the apprentice at the end of his term could establish himself as master. But by-and-by it did not suffice to possess property or skill to become a master; it became necessary after the apprenticeship to travel for two or three years, the object of which was, and still is, to acquire greater skill, and a knowledge of the various modes of working in different towns, adopted in the particular trade to which the journeyman belonged. On his return, he had to make his masterpiece; if approved by a committee of masters, he was received among them; if not, he was rejected, and was not allowed to work on his own account. Thus the masters had in their turn transformed themselves into an aristocracy hostile to the majority, speculating on, rather than administering to, the common labour, their interests being opposed to those of the workmen. The ostracism which thus pursued the great army of labourers, and the segregation to which they were condemned, necessarily produced a reaction, which, unable to have recourse to open revolt, assumed the form of a secret sodality, with rights and customs peculiar to itself. The workman, moreover, unlike the master, was not tied to any city or country, but could wander from place to place a life which, in fact, he

must prefer to staying for ever in one workshop or factory, where the experience needed for the mastership could not be attained. Hence arose the ancient custom of the "Tour of France" and the multiform compagnonnage, which, whilst a source of pleasure to the workmen settled in a town, became a necessity for the travelling, the persecuted journeyman; who thus withdrew himself from under the regular legislation, which only protected the manufacturer, and joined, as it were, a subterranean association to protect himself and his affiliates from the unpunished injuries inflicted on them by burghers and masters.

366. Connection with Freemasonry - Freemasonry was early mixed up with the compagnonnage, and the construction of the Temple, which is constantly met with in the former, also plays a great part in the latter a myth undefined, chronologically irreconcilable, a poetic fiction, like all the events called historical that surround the starting-points of various sects; for sects, existing, as it were, beyond the pale of official history, create a history of their own, exclusive of, and opposed to, the world of facts. The Solomon of the legend, so different from that of the Bible, is one of the patriarchs of the compagnonnage; and, like the masonic ceremonies, the rites of these journeyman associations continually allude to that moral architecture, that proposes to erect prisons for vice, and temples to virtue. Further, and in the same way, the embraces and kisses of the craftsmen remind us of the symbolic grips of the Freemasons, and the brotherly kiss of ancient knighthood.

367. Decrees against Workmen's Unions - We are often obliged to seek for information concerning secret societies in clerical invectives and judicial prosecutions; these are lamps shedding a sinister light on associations whose existence was scarcely suspected. Thus compagnonnage existed before Francis I.; for this king, though he protected the Carbonari, and actually introduced the Carbonari term of "cousin " into the language of Courts, issued an edict against the former, forbidding journeymen to bind themselves with oaths; to elect a chief; to assemble in greater numbers than five in front of the

workshops, on pain of being imprisoned or banished; to wear swords or sticks in the houses of their masters or the streets of the city; to attempt any seditious movement; or to hold any banquet at the beginning or the end of an apprenticeship. A subsequent regulation, A.D. 1723, prohibits any community, confraternity, assembly, or abala of workmen; and a parliamentary decree of 1778 renews the prohibition, and enjoins on tavern-keepers not to receive into their houses assemblies of more than four craftsmen, nor in any way to favour the practices of the pretended devoir (duty). The language of the clergy is equally energetic. A deliberation of the Parisian clergy of 1655 says: "This pretended devoir consists in three precepts to honour God, protect the property of the master, and succour the companions. But these companions dishonour God, profane the mysteries of our religion, ruin the masters, withdrawing the workmen from the workshop, when some of those inscribed in the 'cabala' complain of having been injured. The impieties and sacrileges they commit vary according to the different trades; but they have this in common, that before being received into the association, every member is bound to swear on the Gospel that he will not reveal either to father or mother, wife or son, either to cleric or layman, what he is about to do or will see done; and for this purpose they choose an inn, which they call the mother, wherein they have two rooms, in one of which they perform their abominable rites, whilst in the other they hold their feasts." Even before 1645 the clergy had denounced the tailors and shoemakers to the authorities of Paris for dishonest and heterodox practices; and the faculty of theology had prohibited the pernicious meetings of workmen, under pain of the greater excommunication; so that the companions, to escape ecclesiastical persecution, held their meetings in those purlieus of the Temple which enjoyed the right of sanctuary. Even thence they were removed, however, by the decree of the nth September 1651.

368. Traditions - The members of the compagnonnage are divided into two great parties, the compagnons du devoir, the Fellows of Duty, and the compagnons de liberty the Fellows of Liberty. The former are followers of James and of Soubise, the latter of Solomon. The former

assert that they call themselves the Fellows of Duty because they are descended from the workmen who remained dutiful at the time of Hiram's murder, whilst the latter claim that their compagnonnage was instituted by Solomon himself. Their traditions are strangely confused. Solomon, we are told, built the Temple. James was said to be the son of a famous architect, Joachim, born at St. Romily. James, having gone to Greece, heard the summons of Solomon, and went to him; and having received from Hiram the order to erect two columns, he acquitted himself with such zeal and skill that he was at once made a master and the companion of Hiram. The Temple being finished, he returned again to Gaul with master Soubise, who had been his inseparable companion at Jerusalem. However, the pupils of master Soubise, jealous of James, attempted to assassinate him, and the latter threw himself into a marsh, where the reeds supported and concealed him, saving his life; but eventually he was discovered by the pupils of Soubise, who was unaware of their nefarious design, and slain. Soubise long mourned James; and when his end approached, he taught the companions their "duties," and the mode of life they ought to pursue. Among the rites he placed the kiss of brotherly affection and the custody of a reed the acacia of the Freemasons in memory of James. A variation of this legend represents Soubise as an accomplice of the murder, and a suicide from desperation. The reader will at once see that this is the story of Hiram, nay, of Osiris, and all the great deities of antiquity, over again. In the Legend of the Temple, Solomon also is an accomplice in the murder of his architect.

369. Names and Degrees - The sons of Solomon assumed different denominations, such as "wolves" and Gavots. which latter designation they retained, because coming from Judsea to France they landed on the coast of Provence, whose inhabitants are still called Gavots. The wolves, stonemasons, have two degrees, fellow-crafts and youths. The Gavots, carpenters and iron smiths, are divided into three: accepted fellow-crafts, advanced fellow- crafts, andi initiated fellow-crafts. They all commemorate the death of master Hiram.

The sons of master James called themselves by various names, such as Compagnons Passants, Devorants, &c. The sons of father Soubise were known as " Jovials, or Companions of the Foxes," or as Drilles, an ancient French word signifying " merry companions," and by that scarcely desirable one of "dogs," in commemoration, it is said, of the dog who discovered the body of Hiram. It is more probable, however, that this denomination had the same origin as that of "wolves," for which dogs may easily be mistaken; or that it refers to the star Sirius, in which case the name Soubise might be a corruption of the epithet Sabazius, given to Bacchus (70). With the second of these branches of companionship, comprising at first the three trades of stonemason, locksmith, and joiner, and with the third, composed entirely of carpenters, were afterwards affiliated other trades, such as those of turners, glaziers, weavers, shoemakers, smiths, nailmakers, hatters, bakers, tanners, plasterers, and others. With these the probability and number of schisms increased; and the families of the "Rebels," "Independents," "Foxes of Liberty," and others arose almost as a natural consequence.

370. General Customs - The square and compasses were the symbols of the compagnonnage; the members called each other by the name of their country, because every one carried his country with him in himself, and found hospitality and assistance among the brethren to whom he addressed himself. And the woman that entertained them in their tour or wanderings through France was called by the endearing name of mother and truly the association was to them a mother, that succoured them when they wanted bread, and enabled them to refuse working for wages below the custom of the trade; that recompensed the industrious and punished the worthless, so that throughout France they were denounced and met with no friendly reception. The aspirant for initiation was obliged to have finished his apprenticeship; he was instructed in the word, signs, and grips, and attached a ribbon of a particular colour to his cap and button-hole, received a stick of a certain length, earrings that represented the square and compasses, and a mark on the arm and chest. Strange customs prevailed, and still do prevail, in many parts of the Continent, as the writer knows from

personal observation, at the setting out of a member for his wanderings. He was accompanied beyond the town by his friends, one of them carrying his knapsack, and another singing the parting song, in the chorus of which all joined. They also carried bottles of beer and cups. Arrived at a certain distance from the town, the beer was drunk and the bottles and cups were thrown into the neighbouring fields. In some trades they 'hung a bottle to a tree, to symbolise the death of Saint Stephen, all throwing stones at the innocent bottle except he who was about to set out, and who took leave of his companions, saying: "Friends, I take leave of you as the apostles took leave of Christ when they set out to preach the Gospel."

371. Customs among Charcoal-burners and Hewers - St. Theobald is the patron of the charcoal-burners, one of the oldest trade corporations. There were three degrees aspirant, master, and hewer. The aspirant was called gudpier. A white tablecloth was spread on the ground, and a salt-cellar, a cup of water, a lighted taper, and a crucifix placed on it. The kneeling aspirant swore on the salt and water faithfully to keep the secrets of the association. He was then taught the words by which he could know, and make himself known to, his brethren in the forest, as well as the symbolic meaning of the objects before him: the tablecloth signified the winding-sheet in which every man shall be wrapped up; the taper, the lights burning round the deathbed; the cross, man's redemption; the salt, the theological virtues. This ritual was austere and sad, like the existence of the poor charcoalburners, whose joys are numbered, but whose griefs and privations are endless: it prevailed in the Jura, the Alps, and the Black Forest. The catechism of the hewers contains passages of pathetic simplicity. Segregated in the immense forest, they fix their eyes on the heaven above and the earth beneath; their religion bears a resemblance to that of the pilots of Homer; earth and heaven, nature and God, such is their worship, whence arises a moral of tender and passionate fraternity.

" Q. Whence come ye, cousin of the oak?
A. From the forest.

Q. Where is your father?
A. Eaise your eyes to heaven.
Q. Where is your mother?
A. Cast your eyes on the earth.
Q. What worship do you pay to your father?
A. Homage and respect.
Q. What things do you bestow on your mother?
A. My care during life, and my body afterwards.
Q. If I want help, what will you give me?
A. I will share with you half my day's earnings and my bread of sorrow; you shall rest in my hut and warm yourself at my fire."

How much resignation in this brief dialogue, how much warm affection! Another society of hewers, called the society of the " Prodigal Son," had a still more dismal ritual. Over three doors of a symbolic tower was written: "The past deceives me; the present tortures me; the future terrifies me." A triangle with the letters S. J. P. reminded them of the wisdom of Solomon, the patience of Job, and the repentance of the Prodigal Son. On the white apron was represented a heart surrounded with black, over which rolled a red tear, a tear of blood and despair. The pangs and wretchedness of life depressed the imagination of these poor woodmen; still they had faith in Time as the repairer of all, and on one of their symbolic objects they wrote, Le temps vient a bout de tout. Another society, of which very little is known, called itself Moins didble que noir; as if to indicate that the blackness of their outside did not prevent goodness of heart.

372. Customs in various other Trades - The saddlers and shoemakers had their own initiatory practices. In the room where the initiation took place there arose a rough altar, on which were placed a crucifix, tapers, a missal, and whatever is necessary for the celebration of divine service. This was performed, many peculiar phrases being intermingled therewith; after which the neophyte was made acquainted with the rites of the devoir, the signs and passwords, and the symbolic meaning of the forms and jewels. The reception of the hatters in its purifications and funereal myth approached still nearer to the ancient initiations. A

stage or dais was erected in a large hall; on the stage were placed a cross, a crown of thorns, a palm branch, and all the instruments of the Passion of Christ. Close by stood a large basin of water. The aspirant represented Christ, and passed through the various episodes of the Passion of the Redeemer; and finally knelt down before the basin, when the water, the baptism of regeneration, was poured on his head. No doubt the original institutors of this rite had honest and elevated views; but in course of time the whole degenerated into a farce a la Ran-Tan Club. In the reception of the tailors the candidate was led into a room, in the centre of which stood a table covered with a white cloth, whereon were placed a loaf of bread, a salt-cellar overturned, three sugar loaves, and three needles. He also passed through the various stages of the Passion of Christ. He was then conducted to a second room, where a banquet was prepared, and, as it is asserted, pictures were exhibited of the vie galante of three journeymen tailors, pleasing to the senses; which may remind us of the peculiar worship entering into all the ancient mysteries.

These initiations gave a certain importance to the various trade-unions and their members; it was their common patrimony that kept up the esprit de corps, though it was not free from the arrogance and exclusiveness which multiplied rites, intolerance, jealousies, and enmities, that periodically ended in sanguinary struggles the tragic episodes of a drama, now barbaric, now heroic.

Disturbances at Lyons, Marseilles, Bordeaux, disgraced the compagnonnage. In the middle of the last century the rivalry between the two sections of the stonemasons of Lyons ended in the expulsion of one of them from that city, and their attempt to return led to the most terrible scenes of violence and bloodshed. Even at the present day these disputes not only between rival trades, but even between members of the same trade, continue. But a few years ago the carpenters of Paris at last settled their quarrel by arranging that the Fellows of Duty shall work only on the right, and the Fellows of Liberty only on the left bank of the Seine, and no member of one society dares to trespass on the ground of the other. Those also newly received into either are badly treated, and called by opprobrious names;

for instance, as among German students, renards, foxes. Once these latter would no longer submit to this injustice; they seceded and formed a society of their own, calling themselves Compagnons Renards de la libertd, though they did not think it wrong to treat their aspirants in the same cruel manner in which they had been treated themselves!

How intense was the hatred once between the Duty and the Liberty workmen may be inferred from a stanza of a song once current among the former:

> " Tous ces Gavots infames
> Iront dans les enfers,
> Bruler dedans les flammes
> Comme des Lucifers."

IV

GERMAN WORKMEN'S UNIONS

373. Huntsman's Phraseology - In the woods infested by robbers we meet with the first germs of these corporations, with rough but characteristic customs. Charcoal-burners and hunters need means to recognise each other, so as not to shake hands with an enemy. Grimm has collected upwards of two hundred venatic terms and phrases. The questions and answers of the wandering journeymen have a great resemblance to those of hunters; the intonation is the same, and both make great use of the symbolic numbers three and seven. The formula necessarily have reference to the various incidents of the hunter's life.

" Q. Good huntsman, what have you seen to-day?

A. A noble stag and a wild boar; what can one desire better?

Q. Why do you call yourself a master huntsman?

A. A brave huntsman obtains from princes and lords the title of master in the seven liberal arts. From these sentiments which ennoble the dignity of an art or trade there arises often that chivalrous love which renders life gentle, and gives it an aim and a reward worthy of it.

Q. Tell me, good huntsman, where have you left the fair and gentle damsel?

A. I left her under a majestic tree, and am going to rejoin her. Long live the maid dressed in white that every morning brings me a day of good fortune. Every day I see her again at the same place; and when I am wounded she cures me, and says to me: 'I wish the huntsman safety and happiness; may he meet with a fine stag !' "

374. Initiation - Artisans, more closely united than hunters, did not admit new members into their sodality except after long and solemn trials; their catechisms breathe throughout a spirit of brotherly affection and attention to moral and civil duties. They were divided into degrees, and it is remarkable that the German workmen have long been accustomed to the word, sign, and grip of the Freemasons. The operative masons were divided into Wort-Maurer (Word Masons) and

Schrift-Maurer (Writing or Diploma Masons). The former had no other proof to give of their having been regularly brought up to the trade of builders but the word and signs; the latter had written indentures to show. There were laws enjoining master masons to give employment to journeymen who had the proper word and signs. Some cities in this respect possessed more extensive privileges than others. The word given at Wetzlar entitled the possessor to work over the whole empire. With the German journeyman also the three years' travel in search of improvement is an universal condition, and the usual time for setting out is the spring. The Handwerksbursche is even now a German institution; though he is now not so frequently met with on the high-road, because railways enable him to travel more cheaply than he could on foot.

375. Initiation of a Cooper - Every trade again has its particular mode of initiation; but as there necessarily is a great similarity of ritual and ceremonies, their details would become a tedious repetition. I therefore confine myself to one craft that of the cooper. Permission is first asked to introduce to the assembly of companions or fellowcrafts the youth who is to be made one of them, and who is called the "Apron of Goatskin." The companion who introduces him says: " Some one, I know not who, follows me with a goatskin; a murderer of staves, a wood-spoiler, a traitor; he is on the threshold, and says he is not guilty; he enters, and promises, after having been 'rough-hewn' by us, to become a good journeyman." Leave having been given, the apprentice seats himself on a stool placed on a table, and the companions try to upset him; but his guide keeps him up, whereupon he is repeatedly baptized and consecrated with beer. The patron then says: " What do you call yourself now? Choose a name, genteel, short, and that pleases the girls. He that has a short name pleases every one, and every one drinks a cup of wine or beer to his health. . . . And now to pay the expenses of the baptism, give what every one else has given, and the masters and journeymen shall be content with you." The candidate also receives numerous instructions how to conduct himself on his wanderings. He is not to be deterred by the difficulties that encounter

him at the outset. After having passed through a forest full of dangers, he is supposed to arrive in a pleasant meadow, and to behold a pear-tree full of tempting fruit.

Is he to lie down under it, and wait till the pears fall into his half-open mouth? Is he to mount the tree? No; the farmer or his men would see him, and give him a beating. He is to shake the tree, and some of the fruit will fall down, with which he is to regale himself, leaving some on the ground for some companion who may come after him, and perhaps not be strong enough to shake the tree. Pursuing his way, he comes to a torrent, over which the trunk of a large tree serves for a bridge. Then he encounters a young girl leading a goat. What shall he do? Push the girl and the goat into the water, and pass on? No; let him take the goat on his shoulder, the girl in his arms, and cross the bridge. He may afterwards marry the girl, because he needs a wife, and kill the goat for the nuptial feast, and the skin will make him a new apron. Arriving in a town, he is to go to the inn kept by a master; if his daughter shows him the way to his bedroom, he is to keep a guard over himself; and on the next day he is to go about looking out for work. Perhaps he will be offered it by three masters the first is rich in wood and hoops; the second has three handsome daughters, and regales his workmen with plenty of wine and beer; the third is poor: with which one is he to accept work? With the first he would become a first-rate cooper; with the second he would be happy, having drink in plenty, and dancing with the charming girls: but with the third? He is to be as ready to work for the poor as for the rich master. This discourse, of which there is much more, being ended, the novice attempts to run into the street and cry fire! The companions restrain him, and copiously baptize him with cold water; and then, of course, follows a dinner.

376. Curious Works on the Subject - There exist in Germany numerous works on the rites and customs of various traders; the following are some of them "The Millers' Crown of Honour, or a Complete Description of the True Nature of the Circles of the Company of Millers. By a Miller's Apprentice, George Bohrmann." We here get into masonic symbolism. One woodcut represents a circle

with mystic sentences, and the explanation says that everything was created from or by the circle. Then there follows the history of bakers according to the Scriptures; then a poetically described journey, with particulars of the most celebrated mills of Lusatia, Silesia, Moravia, Hungary, Bohemia, &c. The names of the three most famous millers that, according to the author, ever existed, are placed in the form of a triangle; and the book concludes with an invocation to the Architect of the Universe. A work of a similar nature is entitled, "Customs of the Worshipful Trade of Bakers; how every one is to conduct himself at the inn and at work. Printed for the use of those about to travel." Another is called, "Origin, Antiquity, and Glory of the Worshipful Company of Furriers; an accurate Description of all the Formalities observed from time immemorial in the Initiations of Masters, and the manner of examining the Journeymen. The whole faithfully described by Jacob Wahrmund (True Mouth)." All the companies boast of their ancient descent, but none more than that of the Furriers, who claim that God Himself was at first one of their fellow-workers, seeing that the Bible says that God made aprons of skins for Adam and Eve an honour shared by no other company.

377. Raison d'etre of the Compagnonnage - The compagnonnage may be called an operative knighthood. Its rites, symbols, and traditions are only its tangible form. The necessity for workmen to find, on their arrival in a new town, a nucleus of friends, a rendezvous, a mother, in the midst of the exclusion into which the constituted trades corporations would have thrown them, was the raison d'etre of these associations. The possibility of struggling by means of associative force and the passive resistance of numbers against the oppression of manufacturers, and of equalising forces otherwise disproportionate, was a further cause of the sodalities. In the Middle Ages, in which the central power was barely sufficient to oppress, but did not avail to protect, and when the individual was exposed to arbitrary treatment, and deprived of all means of defence, secret associations on behalf of justice necessarily arose in many countries, Holy Vehms providing for public security.

378. Guilds - The Guilds had the same origin, but can scarcely be reckoned among secret societies, though their influence was often secretly exercised; and kings frequently turned them to account in their opposition to the aristocracy, as, for instance, Louis the Fat, who was himself the founder of an association called the "Popular Community," intended to put a stop to the brigandage of the feudal lords, whose castles were in many instances but dens of thieves. In England, the first guilds of which clear records have been preserved were established in the eleventh century. By the laws of guilds, no person could work at a trade who had not served a seven years' apprenticeship to it. But with the introduction of machinery this custom gradually fell into disuse, as the small or retail manufacturers of olden times became less and less, and the relations between employers and their workmen were changed relations such as may even yet be found to exist in some places in Germany and Switzerland, where one master keeps an apprentice and from two to four workmen. This style of industry might be found not many years ago in Yorkshire among the small cloth-manufacturers. This quiet industry was broken up by the rapid introduction of machinery. The small men, indeed, sought to defend themselves by insisting on old trade regulations, but without success; for in 1814 every vestige of the old trade regulations had disappeared from the English statute-books. The Coalition Act of 1800, not repealed till 1824, often compelled the workmen who thus combined to assume the character of members of Friendly Societies. Their main objects were to prevent the employment of women and children in the immense factories everywhere springing up, and to enforce the old law of apprenticeship. Failing in these objects, they next resorted to strikes, with the nature, operation, and effects of which every one is familiar.

379. Kalends Brethren - These in the thirteenth century were diffused through all Central Europe (Germany, France, and Hungary); they practised charity, read masses for the dead gratuitously, but at their meetings indulged in social pleasures. They met on the first of the month, whence their name (the Romans it will be remembered called

the first of the month Calendar, whence our word calendar). Men and women were admitted, religious and secular, but neither monks nor nuns. The brethren, though they read masses, were no ascetics, for their rhymed table-law ran

"Our host shall spread Good beer, good bread; Four dishes from which to feed, Which he may not exceed; Cakes, cheese, nuts, and fruit To follow. Wine does not suit The Kalends, it would offend; They its use strictly defend."

But it is doubtful whether this abstinence from wine was always observed, for eventually the Kalends were nicknamed "Wet Brethren," and "to kalend" meant to indulge freely in drink. After the Reformation the society graduallydwindled away. Of their customs and signs of recognition, &c., no record has come down to us. The civic prison at Berlin used to be called the Kalends Hall, because the building had originally been the place where the Kalends Brethren held their festive meetings.

380. Knights of Labour - A formidable association in the United States. It was founded in 1869 by Uriah Stephens, a tailor of Philadelphia. It was a secret society, designed at first merely to supplement an existing garment-cutters' union. For a year or more none but garment-cutters were admitted, but after a time other members, known as "sojourners," were invited to join the Order. In 1873 a committee "on the good of the Order " was appointed to control its growing business. A ritual was devised, and every member took an oath of strictest secrecy with regard to its name, constitution, and aims. Officers were appointed under the titles of Master Workman, Worthy Foreman, Venerable Sage, Recording Secretary, Financial Secretary, Treasurer, Worthy Inspector, Almoner, Unknown Knight, Inside Esquire, Outside Esquire, &c. Each industry had its own local assembly, and its own officers; the local assemblies and the district assemblies again sent delegates to the general assembly, which meets once a year, and whose authority is final. The strict secrecy observed at first was gradually relaxed under the influence of the Catholic hurch, especially after the founder had resigned the office of Grand Master

Workman in 1879. In 1881 the secret character of the Order was finally renounced. Its chief aims now are those of trade-unions and benefit societies.

V

GERMAN STUDENTS

"What shall I call thee, thou high, thou rough, thou noble, thou barbaric, thou lovable, unharmonious, song-full, repelling, yet refreshing life of the Burschen years? . . . Thy ludicrous outside lies open, the layman sees that, . . . but thy inner and lovely one, the miner only knows, who descends singing with his brethren into the lonely shaft."

HAUFF'S Raths-keller in Bremen.

381. Customs of German Students - A fellowship of a very different kind, but still a compagnonnage is that of the students at German universities, to which a few lines may therefore be devoted. The student or Bursch from the mediaeval German Burse, i.e. Bursarii, the college buildings being called bursce looks upon the inhabitants of the town, whose university he honours with his presence, as "Philistines"; and town and gown rows are as usual in Germany as in this country. All non-students are Philistines, whether they be kings, princes, nobles, or belong to the canaille. The students form two grand associations, the Burschenschaften, consisting of students from any state; and Landsmannsckaften, composed of students of the same state only. Each has its own laws, regulations, and officers, ruling according to a charter; but all members of the universities acknowledge moreover a general code, called the "Commentary." Such as refuse to belong to one of these associations are held in very slight estimation, and are called by all kinds of opprobrious names, such as Kameele (camels), Finken (literally, "finches," figuratively, "low fellows"), and others still more abusive. The collegiate students (sizars), called Frosche (frogs), cannot take part in the meetings of the Burschen. The freshman anciently was called a Pennal, from the middle-age Latin penndle, a cylindrical box for pens, which the newly - arrived student had to cany after the older students for their occasional use. He was afterwards called Fuchs (fox), which nickname alludes both to the timidity of the animal and that of the new student, and its use in this sense is very

ancient, for we find it mentioned in the Salic Law (fifth century), which imposes a fine of 120 pence for applying it to a person. The freshman is also called a Goldfiichs (golden fox), because he still has a few gold coins from home. After six months he becomes a Brandfuchs (Canis melanogaster); to explain the cause of this term being applied to him would take us too far, but his arrival at that state is celebrated with ridiculous ceremonies. In the second year the Brandfuchs rises to the dignity of Jungbursch (young Bursch); in the third he becomes an Altbursch (old Bursch), altes Haus (old house), or bemoostes Haupt (mossy head. Students who are natives of the university town are called Curds, because their mothers can send them, if they please, a dish of that article of food for their suppers. To rise from one degree to another the Fucks has to go through a series of probations, especially putting to the test his powers of drinking and smoking. On his first visit to the Commerzhaus, as the tavern which the students patronise is called, he is unfailingly made drunk, at his own expense, and while at the same time entertaining all the "old houses." The next morning he awakes with the Katzenjammer (cat's lamentation). He dresses in a fantastic style, wearing a Polish jacket, jack-boots with spurs, and a cap of the colour of the society to which he belongs; to his button-hole is attached an enormous tobacco-pouch; in his mouth he carries a long pipe, and an iron-shod stick in his hand. He endeavours above all things to become & flatter Bursch, a student de pur sang, and is proud if an " old house" makes him his Leibfuchs (favourite fox). The Philistine who offends the students is condemned to the Verruf (outlawed); and frequently the students have turned out against the citizens, forming with their Stiefelwichser (boot-cleaners, or gyps) an array not to be despised by the military. The cry of Burscken 'raus! students turn out! would send terror through the small peaceable towns of Germany. Sometimes they would punish the town by leaving it in a body, and only return on their terms being agreed to. Such emigrations took place at Gottingen in 1823, at Halle in 1827, and at Heidelberg in 1830. A few details of these "emigrations" may be amusing. On the last-named occasion the students, who had again secretly formed a Burschenschaft, put under the ban the Museum of that town, because the rules for its management displeased many of them. For this the ringleaders were seized and brought to trial. But on the cry of Burschen 'raus! all the students, hastily snatching up what articles they most needed, threw them into chaises, on horses, on the backs of the shoeblacks, and marched out of the town to Schwetzingen; and it was only when their demands with regard to the Museum were conceded that they returned to Heidelberg. Another marching forth had occurred many years before. A student, as he went past the watch-house, forgot to take the pipe from his mouth. Thereupon arose a contention between him and the soldier on guard; the latter called an officer, by whom the student was grossly insulted. This gave occasion to an "emigration," which, however, proceeded no further than to a place about a mile from the city, whence the students at once returned, all their demands being conceded; which were that a full amnesty should be granted for all that had passed and the soldiers removed. Moreover, the military were obliged to post themselves on the bridge, the officers at their head, and to present arms, while the students marched past in triumph, with music playing before them. But though the German student would thus seem to think of nothing but smoking his pipe, to which he gives the elegant, but appropriate, name of StinJetopf, drinking unlimited quantities of wine, beer, and punch, entertaining the daughters of the cits, which daughters he gallantly calls Geier (vultures), whilst grisettes are Besen (brooms), running into debt, and calling importunate creditors Manichceans, fighting duels to be called dummer Jungc (stupid youngster), is an insult which necessitates a challenge and generally ruining his health, yet when he buckles to work he will accomplish mental feats that would astonish many an Oxford first-class man, or Cambridge wrangler. Out of all this fermentation and froth there comes at last good wine, and all the intellectual greatness of Germany, and much of its political progress, are due to the roystering Burschen, of whom I cannot speak but with a sort of sneaking kindness, retaining many pleasant personal recollections of them.

382. Ancient Custom of Initiation - In the following account of the

customs prevailing as late as the first half of the seventeenth century at the matriculations of German students, the reader may detect many ceremonies analogous to those practised in the initiations to the ancient mysteries.

The scholar who had not commenced his university career was termed a Beanus, the Fox of to-day. This word has been fancifully derived from the initials of the words Beanus Est Animal Nesciens Vitam Studiorum, an acrostic, as the reader will perceive. But as the word Beanus forms a portion of the sentence itself, its origin is not explained thereby. The fact is, the word is a corruption of the French Bee jaune, shortened into Bejaune, literally, a yellow beak (the German Gelbschnabel), a term applied to a young, inexperienced person (because young unfledged birds have yellow beaks); the French term is blanc-bec, meaning a greenhorn. The word lejaune in mediaeval Latin became Beanus. Sometimes, by way of variety, the beanus was called a bestia cornigera. It would seem that a trace of this appellation has survived at Cambridge, where a student, who has not come into residence, and thus has no claim to be called a "Varsity man," is necessarily a least. On arriving at the university the Beanus, or modern "Fox," announced himself to the dean of the philosophical faculty, and prayed that he might through the deposition be received among the students. When the Beani amounted to a certain number, the dean appointed a day on which to celebrate the deposition; and summoned, besides the Beani, the depositor with his instruments, and an - amanuensis. They appeared on the appointed day before the dean; the depositor in the first place put on a harlequin's dress, caused the Beani to attire themselves in the same style, and put on them other ludicrous articles of dress, especially hats and caps with horns, and distributed amongst them the instruments with which the deposition should be executed coarse wooden combs, shears, axes, hatchets, planes, saws, razors, looking-glasses, stools, and so on. The depositor then marshalled the Beani in rank and file, placed himself at their head, and conducted them to the hall, where the deposition should be performed, and there addressed a speech to the dean and the spectators, who consisted of students. The depositor commenced the deposition by striking the Beani with a bag filled with sand or bran, and compelling them to scamper about with all manner of laughable gestures and duckings in order to escape the strokes of the sand-bag. He then propounded to them certain questions or riddles, and they who did not answer them quickly received so many strokes with the sand-bag, that the tears often started from their eyes. The Beani then gave up the instruments which they had held in their hands, and laid down on the ground, so that their heads nearly touched each other. The depositor then planed their shoulders, filed their nails, pretended to bore through and saw off their feet, hewed every limb of their bodies into shape, knocked off their goat's horns, and tore out of their mouths with a pair of great tongs the satyr's teeth stuck in on purpose. The Beani were then caused to sit on a stool with only one leg. The depositor then put on them a dirty napkin, soaped them with brick-dust, with shoe-blacking, or even viler and more filthy matter, and shaved them so sharply with a wooden razor that the tears often started from their eyes. The combing with the wooden combs was equally rough, and after the combing their hair was sprinkled with shavings. After all these operations the depositor with his sand-bag drove them out of the hall, took off his grotesque attire, put on his proper costume, and commanded the Beani to do the same. He then reconducted them to the hall and commended them in a short Latin speech to the dean, who replied also in Latin, explaining the custom of deposition, and adding much good advice. Luther, who occasionally presided at such ceremonies, and was not superior to the coarse tastes of his time, found in the depositio a figure of human life, with all its troubles and misfortunes. The dean finally gave to each of them, as a symbol of wisdom, a few grains of salt to taste, scattered in sign of joy some drops of wine over their heads, and handed to them the certificate of the accomplished deposition. The last ceremony of this sort is said to have been performed by a professor of Altdorf (Bavaria) in 1763. The university of that town, founded in 1622, was merged in that of Erlangen in 1809.

It is scarcely necessary to point out the analogies between the above initiation into student life and that into the ancient mysteries and modern Freemasonry; the disguises, trials, addresses, and whole ceremonial are all on the model of the secret society, most of them foolish, and not a few barbarous. Hoffmann's Lebens-Ansichten des Katers Murr "Opinions of the Tom-cat Murr," or, as we might say more briefly, Tom Murr, is a capital satire on German student-life. The German scholar there is, as far as I know, no English translation of the work may there see how "Tommy" becomes a Flatter Katzbursch. The political secret associations of the Burschenschaft are described in Book XIII.

THE SECRET SOCIETIES OF ALL AGES AND COUNTRIES

A Comprehensive Account of upwards of One Hundred
and Sixty Secret Organisations Religious, Political,
and Social from the most Remote Ages
down to the Present Time

Embracing the Mysteries of Ancient India, China, Japan, Egypt, Mexico,
Peru, Greece, and Scandinavia, the Cabbalists, Early Christians,
Heretics, Assassins, Thugs, Templars, the Vehm and
Inquisition, Mystics, Rosicrucians, Illuminati, Free-
masons, Skopzi, Camorristi, Carbonari, Nihilists,
Fenians, French, Spanish,

And other Mysterious Sects

BY

CHARLES WILLIAM HECKETHORN

IN TWO VOLUMES
VOL. II

ANALYTICAL TABLE OF CONTENTS

VOL. II.

The numbers preceding analytical headings refer to the sections.

AUTHORITIES CONSULTED

BOOK XI
FREEMASONRY

I. THE LEGEND OF THE TEMPLE.
383. Ancestry of Hiram Abiff.
384. Hiram, Solomon, and the Queen of Sheba.
385. Murder of Hiram

II. ORIGIN AND TRADITIONS.
386. The First Masons.
387.:Periods of Freemasonry.
388. Freemasonry derived from many Sources.
389. True History of Masonry

III. RITES AND CUSTOMS.
390. List of Rites.
391. Masonic Customs.
392. Masonic Alphabet

IV. THE LODGE.
393. Interior Arrangement of Lodge.
394. Modern Lodge.
395. Officers.
396. Opening the Lodge

V. GENUINE AND SPURIOUS MASONRY.
397. Distinction between Genuine and Spurious Masonry.

398. Some Rites only deserve Special Mention

VI. CEREMONIES OF INITIATION.
399. Ceremonies of Initiation The Apprentice.
400. Ceremonies of Initiation The Fellow - Craft.
401. Ceremony of Initiation and Story of Hiram's Murder The Master Mason.
402. The Legend Explained.
403. The Raising of Osiris.
404. The Blazing Star

VII. THE HOLY ROYAL ARCH.
405. Officers.
406. Ceremonies.
407. Passing the Veils

VIII. GRAND MASTER ARCHITECT.
408. Ceremonial

IX. GRAND ELECT KNIGHT OF KADOSH.
409. The Term Kadosh.
410. Reception into the Degree.
411. The Mysterious Ladder.
412. The Seven Steps

X. PRINCE OF ROSE-CROIX.
413. Distinct from Rosicrucian, and has various Names.
414. Officers and Lodges.
415. Reception in the First Apartment
416. Second Apartment.
417. Reception in the Third Apartment

XI. THE RITES OF MIHKAIM AND MEMPHIS.
418. Anomalies of the Rite of Misraim.
419. Organisation.

420. History and Constitution.
421. Rites and Ceremonies.
422. Rite of Memphis.

XII. MODERN KNIGHTS TEMPLARS.
423. Origin.
424. Revival of the Order.
425. The Leviticon.
426. Ceremonies of Initiation.

XIII. FREEMASONRY IN ENGLAND AND SCOTLAND.
427. Freemasonry in England.
428. Freemasonry in Scotland.
429. Modern Freemasonry

XIV. FREEMASONRY IN FRANCE.
430. Introduction into France.
431. Chevalier Ramsay.
432. Philosophical Rite.
433. The Duke de Chartres

XV. THE CHAPTER OF CLERMONT AND THE STRICT OBSERVANCE.
434. Jesuitical Influence.
435. The Strict Observance

XVI. THE RELAXED OBSERVANCE.
436. Organisation of Relaxed Observance.
437. Disputes in German Lodges.
438. Rite of Zinzendorf.
439. African Architects

XVII. THE CONGRESS OF WILHELMSBAD.
440. Various Congresses.
441. Discussions at Wilhelmsbad.

442. Result of Convention.
443. Frederick William III. and the Masons

XVIII. MASONRY AND NAPOLEONISM.
444. Masonry protected by Napoleon.
445. Spread of Freemasonry.
446. The Clover Leaves.
447. Obsequiousness of Freemasonry.
448. Anti-Napoleonic Freemasonry

XIX. FREEMASONRY, THE RESTORATION AND THE SECOND EMPIRE.
449. The Society of "France Regenerated."
450. Priestly Opposition to Masonry.
451. Political Insignificance of Masonry.
452. Freemasonry and Napoleon III.
453. Jesuitical Manoeuvres

XX. FREEMASONRY IN ITALY.
454. Whimsical Masonic Societies.
455. Illuminati in Italy.
456. Freemasonry at Naples.
457. Details of Document.
458. Freemasonry at Venice.
459. Abatement under Napoleon.
460. The Freemasonry of the Present in Italy.
461. Reform needed

XXI. CAGLIOSTRO AND EGYPTIAN MASONRY.
462. Life of Cagliostro.
463. The Egyptian Rite.
464. Cagliostro's Hydromancy.
465. Lodges founded by Cagliostro

XXII. ADOPTIVE MASONRY.

466. Historical Notice.
467. Organisation.
468. Jesuit Degrees

XXIII. ANDROGYNOUS MASONRY.
469. Origin and Tendency.
470. Earliest Androgynous Societies.
471. Other Androgynous Societies.
472. Various other Androgynous Societies.
473. Knights and Nymphs of the Rose.
474. German Order of the Rose.
475. Pretended Objects
of the Order.
476. Order of Harmony.
477. Mason's Daughter

XXIV. SCHISMATIC RITES AND SECTS.
478. Schismatic Rites and Sects.
479. Farmassoni.
480. The Gormogones.
481. The Noachites, or Noachidffi.
482. Argonauts.
483. The Grand Orient and Atheism.
484. Ludicrous Degree

XXV. DIFFUSION OF THE ORDER.
485. Freemasonry in Spain and Portugal.
486. Freemasonry in Russia.
487. Freemasonry in Switzerland.
488. Freemasonry in Sweden and Poland.
489. Freemasonry in Holland and Germany.
490. Freemasonry in Turkey, Asia, Africa, and Oceania.
491. Freemasonry in America

XXVI. PERSECUTIONS OF FREEMASONRY.

492. Causes of Persecution.
493. Instances of Persecution.
494. Anti-Masonic Publications

XXVII. FUTILITY OF MODERN FREEMASONRY.
495. Vain Pretensions of Modern Freemasonry.
496. Vanity of Masonic Ceremonial.
497. Masonry diffuses no Knowledge.
498. Decay of Freemasonry.
499. Masonic Opinions of Masonry.
500. Masonic Literature.
500a. The Quatuor Coronati Lodge

BOOK XII
INTERNATIONAL, COMMUNE, AND ANARCHISTS
501. Introductory Remarks.
502. Socialistic Schemes.
503. History of the International.
504. Objects and Aims of International.
505. he International in England.
506. The International Abroad.
507. The International and the Empire.
508. The International and the War.
509. The International and the Commune.
510. Budget of the International.
511. Attempt to Revive the International.
512. Anarchists

BOOK XIII
POLITICAL SECRET SOCIETIES
I. CHINESE SOCIETIES.

513. Earliest Secret Chinese Societies.
514. More recent Societies.
515. Lodges.

516. Government.
517. Seal of the Hung League.
518. The Ko lao Hui

II. The COMUNEROS.
519. Introductory Remarks.
520. Earliest Secret Societies in Spain.
521. Freemasonry in Spain, the Forerunner of the Comuneros.
522. The Comuneros.
523. Clerical Societies

III. THE HETAIRIA.
524. Origin.
525. The Hetairia of 1812.
526. The Hetairia of 1814.
527. Signs and Passwords.
528. Short Career of Galatis.
529. Proceedings of the Grand Arch.
530. Ipsilanti's Proceedings.
531. Ipsilanti's Blunders.
532. Progress of the Insurrection.
533. Ipsilanti's Approaching Fall.
534. Advance of the Turks.
535. Ipsilanti's Difficulties.
536. Ipsilanti's Fall.
537. Ipsilanti's Manifesto.
538. Ipsilanti's Imprisonment and Death.
539. Fate of the Hetairists.
540. Georgakis' Death.
541. Farmakis' Death.
542. Final Success of the Hetairia

IV. THE CARBONARI.
543. History of the Association.
544. Real Origin of the Carboneria.

545. The Vendita or Lodge.
546. Ritual of Initiation.
547. First Degree.
548. The Second Degree.
549. The Degree of Grand Elect.
550. Degree of Grand Master Grand Elect.
551. Signification of the Symbols.
552. Other Ceremonies and Regulations.
553. The Ausonian Republic.
554. Most Secret Carbonaro Degree.
555. De Witt, Biographical Notice of.
556. Carbonaro Charter proposed to England.
557. Carbonarism and Murat.
558. Trial of Carbonari.
559. Carbonarism and the Bourbons.
560. The King's Revenge.
561. Revival of Carbonarism.
562. Carbonarism and the Church.
563. Carbonarism in Northern Italy.
564. Carbonarism in France.
565. Carbonarism in Germany.
566. Carbonarism in Spain.
567. Giardiniere

V. MISCELLANEOUS ITALIAN SOCIETIES.
568. Guelphic Knights.
569. Guelphs and Carbonari.
570. The Latini.
571. The Centres.
572. Italian Litterateurs.
573. Societies in Calabria and the Abruzzi.
574. Giro Annichiarico.
575. Certificates of the Decisi.
576. The Calderari.
577. The Independents.

578. The Delphic Priesthood.
579. Egyptian Lodges.
580. American Hunters.
581. Secret Italian Society in London.
582. Secret Italian Societies in Paris.
583. Mazzini and Young Italy.
584. Mazzini, the Evil Genius of Italy.
585. Assassination of Rossi.
586. Sicilian Societies.
587. The Consistorials.
588. The Roman Catholic Apostolic Congregation.
589. Sanfedisti.

VI. NAPOLEONIC AND ANTI- NAPOLEONIC SOCIETIES.
590. The Philadelphians.
591. The Rays.
592. Secret League in Tirol.
593. Societies in Favour of Napoleon.
594. The Illuminati.
595. Various other Sociaties.
596. The Accoltellatori

VII. FRENCH SOCIETIES.
597. Various Societies after the Restoration.
598. The Acting Company.
599. Communistic Societies.
600. Causes of Secret Societies in France

VIII. POLISH SOCIETIES.
601. Polish Patriotism.
602. Various Revolutionary Sects.
603. Secret National Government

IX. THE OMLADINA.
604. The Panslavists

X. TURKISH SOCIETIES.
605. Young Turkey.
606. Armenian Society

XI. THE UNION OF SAFETY.
607. Historical Sketch of the Society

XII. TIIK NIHILISTS.
608. Meaning of the term Nihilist.
609. Founders of Nihilism.
610. Sergei Nechayeff.
611. Going among the People.
612. Nihilism becomes Aggressive.
613. Sophia Bardina's and other Trials.
614. The Party of Terror.
615. Vera Zassulic.
616. Officials Killed or Threatened by the Nihilists.
617. First Attempts against the Emperor's Life.
618. Numerous Executions.
619. The Moscow Attempt against the Emperor.
620. Various Nihilist Trials.
621. Explosion in the Winter Palace.
622. Assassination of the Emperor.
623. The Mine in Garden Street.
624. Constitution said to have been Granted by late Emperor.
625. The Nihilist Proclamation.
626. The Emperor's Reply thereto.
627. Attempt against General Tcherevin.
628. Trials and other Events in 1882.
629. Coronation, and Causes of Nihilistic Inactivity.
630. Colonel Sudeikin shot by Nihilists.
631. Attempt against the Emperor at Gatshina.
632. Trial of the Fourteen.
633. Reconstruction of the Nihilist Party.

634. Extension of Nihilism.
635. Decline of Nihilism.
636. Nihilistic Proceedings in 1887.
637. Nihilism in 1888.
638. Slaughter of Siberian Exiles, and HungerStrikes.
639. Occurrences in 1890.
640. Occurrences from 1891 to Present Date.
641. Nihilistic Finances.
642. The Secret Press.
643. Nihilistic Measures of Safety.
644. The Nihilists in Prison.
645. Nihilistic Emigrants.
646. Nihilistic Literature.
647. Trials of Nihilists

XIII. GERMAN SOCIETIES.
648. The Mosel Club.
649. German Feeling against Napoleon.
650. Formation and Scope of Tugendbund.
651. Divisions among Members of Tugendbund.
652. Activity of the Tugendbund.
653. Hostility of Governments against Tugendbund

XIV. THE BABIS.
654. Bab, the Founder.
655. Progress of Babism.
656. Babi Doctrine.
657. Recent History of Babism

XV. IRISH SOCIETIES.
658. The White-Boys.
659. Right-Boys and OakBoys.
660. Hearts-of-Steel, Threshers, Break-of -Day-Boys, Defenders, United Irishmen, Ribbonmen.
661. Saint Patrick Boys.

662. The Orangemen.
663. Molly Maguires.
664. Ancient Order of Hibernians.
665. Origin and Organisation of Fenianism.
666. Origin of Name.
667. Fenian Litany.
668. Events from 1865 to 1871.
669. The Soidisant General Cluseret.
670. Phoenix Park Murders, and Consequences.
671. Dynamite Outrages.
672. The National League.
673. Comic Aspects of Fenianism.
674. Events from iSSS to 1896.
675. Most Recent Revelations

BOOK XIV
MISCELLANEOUS SOCIETIES

676. The ABC Friends.
677. Abelites.
678. Academy of the Ancients.
679. Almusseri.
680. Anonymous Society.
681. Anti-Masonic Party.
682. Anti-Masons.
683. Apocalypse, Knights of the.
684. Areoiti.
685. Avengers, or Vendicatori.
686. Belly Paaro.
687. Californian Society.
688. Cambridge Secret Society.
689. Charlottenburg, Order of.
690. Church Masons.
691. Cong ourde, The.
692. Druids, Modern.

693. Duk-Duk.
694. Egbo Society.
695. Fraticelli.
696. Goats, The.
697. Grand Army of the Republic.
698. Green Island.
699. Harugari.
700. Hemp-smokers, African.
701. Heroine of Jericho.
702. Human Leopards.
703. Hunters, the.
704. Huseanawer.
705. Indian (North American) Societies.
706. Invisibles, the.
707. Jehu, Society of.
708. Karpokratians.
709. Klöbbergöll.
710. Knights, the Order of.
711. Know-Nothings.
712. Ku-Klux-Klan.
713. Kurnai Initiation.
714. Liberty, Knights of.
715. Lion, Knights of the.
716. Lion, the Sleeping.
717. Ludlam's Cave.
718. Mad Councillors.
719. Magi, Order of the.
720. Maharajas.
721. Mano Negra.
722. Melanesian Societies.
723. Mumbo-Jumbo.
724. Odd Fellows.
725. O-Kee-Pa.
726. Pantheists.
727. Patriotic Order Sons of America.

728. Phi-Beta-Kappa.
729. Pilgrims.
730. Police, Secret.
731. Portuguese Societies.
732. Purrah, the.
733. Pythias, Knights of.
734. Rebeccaites.
735. Redemption, Order of.
736. Red Men.
737. Regeneration, Society of Universal.
738. Saltpetrers.
739. Sikh Fanatics.
740. Silver Circle, Knights of the.
741. Sonderbare Gesellen.
742. Sophisiens.
743. Star of Bethlehem.
744. Thirteen, the.
745. Tobaccological Society.
746. Turf, Society of the.
747. Utopia.
748. Wahabees

BOOK XI

FREEMASONRY

I

THE LEGEND OF THE TEMPLE

383. Ancestry of Hiram Abiff - Solomon having determined on the erection of the temple, collected artificers, divided them into companies, and put them under the command of Adoniram or Hiram Abiff, the architect sent to him by his friend and ally Hiram, king of Tyre. According to mythical tradition, the ancestry of the builders of the mystical temple was as follows: One of the Elohim, or primitive genii, married Eve and had a son called Cain (120); whilst Jehovah or Adonai, another of the Elohim, created Adam and united him with Eve to bring forth the family of Abel, to whom were subjected the sons of Cain, as a punishment for the transgression of Eve. Cain, though industriously cultivating the soil, yet derived little produce from it, whilst Abel leisurely tended his flocks. Adonai rejected the gifts and ; sacrifices of Cain, and stirred up strife between the sons of the Elohim, generated out of fire, and the sons formed out of the earth only. Cain killed Abel, and Adonai, pursuing his sons, subjected to the sons of Abel the noble family that invented the arts and diffused science.[16] Enoch, a son of Cain, taught men to hew stones, construct edifices, and form civil .societies. Irad and Mehujael, his son and grandson, set boundaries to the waters and fashioned cedars into beams. Methusael, another of his descendants, invented the sacred characters, the books of Tau and the symbolic T, by which the workers descended from the genii of fire recognised each other. Lamech, whose prophecies are inexplicable to the profane, was the father of Jabal, who first taught men how to dress camels' skins; of Jubal, who discovered the harp; of

---

[16] In the Purdnas the ingenuity of the descendants of Cain, and the degree of perfection to which they carried the arts of civil life, are highly extolled

Naamah, who discovered the arts of spinning and weaving; of Tubal-Cain, who first constructed a furnace, worked in metals, and dug subterranean caves in the mountains to save his race during the Deluge; but it perished nevertheless, and only Tubal-Cain and his son, the sole survivors of the glorious and gigantic family, came out alive. The wife of Ham, second son of Noah, thought the son of Tubal-Cain handsomer than the sons of men, and he became progenitor of Nimrod, who taught his brethren the art of hunting, and founded Babylon. Adoniram, the descendant of TubalCain, seemed called by God to lead the militia of the free men, connecting the sons of fire with the sons of thought, progress, and truth.

384. Hiram, Solomon, and the Queen of Sheba - By Hiram was erected a marvellous building, the Temple of Solomon. He raised the golden throne of Solomon, most beautifully wrought, and built many other glorious edifices. But, melancholy amidst all his greatness, he lived alone, understood and loved by few, hated by many, and among others, by Solomon, envious of his genius and glory. Now the fame of the wisdom of Solomon spread to the remotest ends of the earth; and Balkis, the Queen of Sheba, came to Jerusalem to greet the great king and behold the marvels of his reign. She found Solomon seated on a throne of gilt cedar wood, arrayed in cloth of gold, so that at first she seemed to behold a statue of gold with hands of ivory. Solomon received her with every kind of festive preparation, and led her to behold his palace and then the grand works of the temple, and the queen was lost in admiration. The king was captivated by her beauty, and in a short time offered her his hand, which the queen, pleased at having conquered this proud heart, accepted. But on again visiting the temple, she repeatedly desired to see the architect who had wrought such wondrous things. Solomon delayed as long as possible presenting Hiram Abiff to the queen, but at last he was obliged to do so. The mysterious artificer was brought before her, and cast on the queen a look that penetrated her very heart. Having recovered her composure, she questioned and defended him against the ill-will and rising jealousy of the king. When she wished to see the countless host of workmen

that wrought at the temple, Solomon protested the impossibility of assembling them all at once; but Hiram, leaping on a stone to be better seen, with his right hand described in the air the symbolical Tan, and immediately the men hastened from all parts of the works into the presence of their master. At this the queen wondered greatly, and secretly repented of the promise she had given the king, for she felt herself in love with the mighty architect. Solomon set himself to destroy this affection, and to prepare his rival's humiliation and ruin. For this purpose he employed three fellow-crafts, envious of Hiram, because he had refused to raise them to the degree of masters on account of their want of knowledge and their idleness. They were Fanor, a Syrian and a mason; Amru, a Phoenician and a carpenter; and Metusael, a Hebrew and a miner. The black envy of these three projected that the casting of the brazen sea, which was to raise the glory of Hiram to its utmost height, should turn out a failure. A young workman, Benoni, discovered the plot and revealed it to Solomon, thinking that sufficient. The day for the casting arrived, and Balkis was present. The doors that restrained the molten metal were opened, and torrents of liquid fire poured into the vast mould wherein the brazen sea was to assume its form. But the burning mass ran over the edges of the mould, and flowed like lava over the adjacent places. The terrified crowd fled from the advancing stream of fire. Hiram, calm, like a god, endeavoured to arrest its advance with ponderous columns of water, but without success. The water and the fire mixed, and the struggle was terrible; the water rose in dense steam and fell down in the shape of fiery rain, spreading terror and death. The dishonoured artificer needed the sympathy of a faithful heart; he sought Benoni, but in vain; the proud youth perished in endeavouring to prevent the horrible catastrophe when he found that Solomon had done nothing to hinder it.

Hiram could not withdraw himself from the scene of his discomfiture. Oppressed with grief, he heeded not the danger, he remembered not that this ocean of fire might speedily engulph him; he thought of the Queen of Sheba, who came to admire and congratulate him on a great triumph, and who saw nothing but a terrible disaster.

Suddenly he heard a strange voice coming from above, and crying, "Hiram, Hiram, Hiram! " He raised his eyes and beheld a gigantic human figure. The apparition continued, "Come, my son, be without fear, I have rendered thee incombustible; cast thyself into the flames." Hiram threw himself into the furnace, and where others would have found death, he tasted ineffable delights; nor could he, drawn by an irresistible force, leave it, and asked him that drew him into the abyss, "Whither do you take me?" "Into the centre of the earth, into the soul of the world, into the kingdom of great Cain, where liberty reigns with him. There the tyrannous envy of Adonai ceases; there can we, despising his anger, taste the fruit of the tree of knowledge; there is the home of thy fathers." "Who then am I, and who art thou?" "I am the father of thy fathers, I am the son of Lamech, I am Tubal-Cain."

Tubal-Cain introduced Hiram into the sanctuary of lire, where he expounded to him the weakness of Adonai and the base passions of that god, the enemy of his own creature whom he condemned to the inexorable law of death, to avenge the benefits the genii of fire had bestowed on him. Hiram was led into the presence of the author of his race, Cain. The angel of light that begat Cain was reflected in the beauty of this son of love, whose noble and generous mind roused the envy of Adonai. Cain related to Hiram his experiences, sufferings, and misfortunes, brought upon him by the implacable Adonai. Presently he heard the voice of him who was the offspring of Tubal-Cain and his sister Naamah: "A son shall be born unto thee whom thou shalt indeed not see, but whose numerous descendants shall perpetuate thy race, which, superior to that of Adam, shall acquire the empire of the world; for many centuries they shall consecrate their courage and genius to the service of the ever-ungrateful race of Adam, but at last the best shall become the strongest, and restore on the earth the worship of fire. Thy sons, invincible in thy name, shall destroy the power of kings, the ministers of the Adonais' tyranny. Go, my son, the genii of fire are with thee!" Hiram was restored to the earth. Tubal-Cain before quitting him gave him the hammer with which he himself had wrought great things, and said to him: "Thanks to this hammer and the help of the genii of fire, thou shalt speedily accomplish the work left unfinished through man's stupidity and malignity." Hiram did not hesitate to test the wonderful efficacy of the precious instrument, and the dawn saw the great mass of bronze cast. The artist felt the most lively joy, the queen exulted. The people came running up, astounded at this secret power which in one night had repaired everything.

385. Murder of Hiram - One day the queen, accompanied by her maids, went beyond Jerusalem, and there encountered Hiram, alone and thoughtful. The encounter was decisive, they mutually confessed their love. Had-Had, the bird who filled with the queen the office of messenger of the genii of fire, seeing Hiram in the air make the sign of the mystic T, flew around his head and settled on his wrist. At this Sarahil, the nurse of the queen, exclaimed: "The oracle is fulfilled. Had-Had recognises the husband which the genii of fire destined for Balkis, whose love alone she dare accept!" They hesitated no longer, but mutually pledged their vows, and deliberated how Balkis could retract the promise given to the king. Hiram was to be the first to quit Jerusalem; the queen, impatient to rejoin him in Arabia, was to elude the vigilance of the king, which she accomplished by withdrawing from his finger, while he was overcome with wine, the ring wherewith she had plighted her troth to him. Solomon hinted to the fellow-crafts that the removal of his rival, who refused to give them the master's word, would be acceptable unto himself; so when the architect came into the temple he was assailed and slain by them. Before his death, however, he had time to throw the golden triangle which he wore round his neck, and on which was engraven the master's word, into a deep well. They wrapped up his body, carried it to a solitary hill and buried it, planting over the grave a sprig of acacia.

Hiram not having made his appearance for seven days, Solomon, against his inclination, but to satisfy the clamour of the people, was forced to have him searched for. The body was found by three masters, and they, suspecting that he had been slain by the three fellow-crafts for refusing them the master's word, determined nevertheless for greater security to change the word, and that the first word accidentally uttered on raising the body should thenceforth be the word. In the act of raising it, the skin came off the body, so that one of the masters exclaimed "Macbenach!" ("the flesh is off the bones," or the "brother is smitten "), and this word became the sacred word of the masters' degree. The three fellow-crafts were traced, but rather than fall into the hands of their pursuers, they committed suicide, and their heads were brought to Solomon. The triangle not having been found on the body of Hiram, it was sought for and at last discovered in the well into which the architect had cast it. The king caused it to be placed on a triangular altar erected in a secret vault, built under the most retired part of the temple. The triangle was further concealed by a cubical stone, on which had been inscribed the sacred law. The vault, the existence of which was only known to the twentyseven elect, was then walled up.

II

ORIGIN AND TEADITIONS

386. The First Masons - All nations, all states, all corporations, to increase their power and deduce from above their raison d'etre, attribute to themselves a very ancient origin. This wish must be all the stronger in a society altogether ideal and moral, living the life of principles, which needs rather to seem to be, not coeval with, but anterior and superior to all others. Hence the claim set up by Freemasonry of being, not contemporary with the creation of man, but with that of the world; because light was before man, and prepared for him a suitable habitation, and light is the scope and symbol of Freemasonry. Lest non-Masonic readers should think we are joking as regards Masonic assertions concerning the antiquity of the craft, we will quote from two Masonic writers, one more than a century old, and one quite of recent date: Edward Spratt, in his "Book of Constitutions for the Use of Lodges in Ireland," 1751, makes Adam the first Mason, who "even after his expulsion from paradise retained great knowledge, especially in geometry." Dr. J. A. Weisse, in "The Obelisk and Freemasonry," published in 1880, says: "Freemasonry commenced from the Creation, and was established by the family of Seth. The Masonic apron originated from the covering or apron of figleaves, adopted by Adam and Eve after the Fall." Need I quote more?

Now in the Introduction (6, 7) I have stated that there was from the very first appearance of man on the earth a highly favoured and civilised race, possessing a full knowledge of the laws and properties of nature, and which knowledge was embodied in mystical figures and schemes, such as were deemed appropriate emblems for its preservation and propagation. These figures and schemes are preserved in Masonry, but not in the pseudo-Masonry of the majority of craft members. The truest Masons at the present day are found without the lodge. I shall endeavour in these pages as much as possible to teach Masons the real truths hidden under the symbols and enigmatical forms, which, without a key, appear but as absurd and debasing rites and ceremonies. The aim of all the secret societies of which accounts have been as yet or will be given in this work, except of those which were purely political or anti-social, was to preserve such knowledge as still survived, or to recover what had been lost. And since Freemasonry is, so to speak, the resume of the teachings of all those societies, dogmas in accordance with one or more of those taught in the ancient mysteries and other associations are to be found in Masonry; hence also it is impossible to attribute its origin to one or other specific society preceding it. Freemasonry is or rather ought to be the compendium of all primitive and accumulated human knowledge.

387. Periods of Freemasonry - Masonic writers generally divide the history of the Order into two periods, the first comprising the time from its assumed foundation to the beginning of the last century, during which the Order admitted only masons, i.e. operative masons and artificers in some way connected with architecture. The second or present period, they denominate the period of Speculative Masonry, when the Order no longer chooses its members only amongst men engaged in the raising of material structures, but receives into its ranks all who are willing to assist in building a spiritual temple, the temple of universal harmony and knowledge. Yet persons not working masons had ere then been admitted, for the records of a lodge at Warrington, as old as 1648, note the admission of Colonel Mainwaring and the great antiquary Ashmole. Charles I., Charles II., and James II. also were initiated. But from what has been said above, it follows that true Masonry always was speculative, and that to deduce its origin from the ancient Dionysiac or any other kindred college is only partly correct. The name "masonic" was adopted by the society on its reconstruction in the last century, because the brotherhood of builders who erected the magnificent cathedrals and other buildings that arose during the Middle Ages had lodges, degrees, landmarks, secret signs, and passwords, such as the builders of the temple of Solomon are said to have made use of. The Freemasons have also frequently been said to be descended from the Knights Templars, and thus to have for their object to avenge the destruction of that Order, and so to be dangerous

to Church and State; yet this assertion was repudiated as early as 1535 in the "Charter of Cologne," wherein the Masons call themselves the Brethren of St. John, because St. John the Baptist was the forerunner of the Light. According to the same document, the name of Freemasons was first given to the Brethren chiefly in Flanders, because some of them had been instrumental in erecting in the province of Hainault hospitals for persons suffering from St. Vitus's dance. And though some etymologists pretend the name to be derived from massa, a club, with which the doorkeeper was armed to drive away uninitiated intruders, we can only grant this etymology on the principle enunciated by Voltaire, that in etymology vowels go for very little, and consonants for nothing at all. The derivation from maison is as probable as any other that is alleged.

388. Freemasonry derived from many Sources - But considering that Freemasonry is a tree the roots of which spread through so many soils, it follows that traces thereof must be found in its fruit; that its language and ritual should retain much of the various sects and institutions it has passed through before arriving at their present state, and in Masonry we meet with Indian, Egyptian, Jewish, and Christian ideas, terms, and symbols.

389. True History of Masonry - The plain history of Freemasonry, without the varnish and tinsel Masonic writers have bedizened it with, may be summed up as follows:

In antiquity there were corporations of architects and engineers, who undertook the building of temples and stadia; the "Dionysiacs" in Greece, the "Collegium Muriorum" in Eome were such. They were the prototypes of the associations of masons, builders, carpenters, who in the Middle Ages flourished, chiefly in Germany and England. These, sometimes numbering six to eight hundred members, made contracts with monks, chapters, and other ecclesiastical authorities for the erection of cathedrals or churches. Eventually they made themselves independent of the Church, and in the thirteenth century they formed an extensive building association, originating at

Cologne, and having lodges, as they called the directing members, at Strasbourg, Vienna, Cologne, and Zürich. There were other lodges, but these were the most important. They called themselves Free masons, and had ceremonies of initiation. Towards the end of the sixteenth century non-operative masons were admitted into the fraternity, who were called "accepted" Masons; they included men distinguished for learning or high position. Thus the work in the lodges became more symbolical than operative. The really working masons and builders gradually dispersed, and the accepted masons, whose expectations of being initiated into esoteric knowledge in the lodges were disappointed, withdrew from them, so that in 1717 there were only four lodges in London, which Dr. Desaguliers, James Anderson, and George Payne formed into a Grand Lodge, with which modern Freemasonry, purely symbolical, though retaining the technical terms of architecture, may be said to begin.

The fraternity was soon persecuted; the Popes, beginning with Clement XII., and ending with the present one, cast their thunderbolts at it; despotic rulers tried to suppress it. Of course the Masons themselves to a great extent invited this persecution by the mystery in which they attempted to shroud their principles and proceedings, as also by the introduction of the "high degrees." The original Masons had confined themselves to the three degrees existing among operative builders apprentice, fellow-craft, and master. But these did not satisfy the vanity of some of the aristocratic members, or the ambition of such as wished to use the Order for party purposes. The chevalier Andreas Ramsay, a partisan of the exiled Stuarts, who asserted the Freemasons to be descended from the Crusaders, first gave the impulse to the starting of high degrees, in which political objects were aimed at, and which, after the country of the Stuarts, were called Scotch degrees. They were greatly multiplied, and the pursuit of these party purposes, of superstitious rites, and of personal vanity, invested every one with still increasing mysteries. At last they fell into the hands of impostors and adventurers, such as, for instance, Cagliostro.

In Germany the Order was made use of by three parties Reactionaries, Revolutionaries, and knightly fanatics. The

Reactionaries founded Rosicrucianism, in which magic, astrology, alchemy, spiritism, and superstition in general occupied its cheats and dupes, opposing religious, political, and scientific progress. The Revolutionaries, by means of the Illuminati, who insinuated themselves into the Masonic order, endeavoured to bring about a new political and religious era. Knightly fanaticism was transplanted from France into Germany by the well-intentioned but visionary Baron Hund, who about the middle of the last century founded the Masonic system of the so-called Strict Observance (435), which followed the lines of the Knights Templars, from whom Hund wished to derive the Masonic order; we shall see that at the Congress of Wilhelmsbad (441) this assertion was negatived. The mystery of the ritual, and the splendour of some of the rites, gained Freemasonry many adherents in France, where the lodges were at last united under a Grand Lodge, called the Grand Orient, the first Grand Master of which was the Duke of Chartres, afterwards Philippe Egalite. Napoleon, when in power, appointed his brother Joseph Grand Master (444).

III

RITES AND CUSTOMS

390. List of Rites - Anciently, that is, before the rise of modern Masonry at the beginning of the last century, there was but one rite, that of the "Ancient, Free and Accepted Masons," or blue or symbolic Masonry; but vanity, fancy, or interest soon led to the introduction of many new rites or modifications of the three ancient degrees. The following are the names of the rites now practised in Europe and America:

I. York rite, or Craft Masonry, of which an account will be given. In America it consists of seven degrees: The first three as in this country; 4. Mark Master; 5. Past Master; 6. Most Excellent Master; 7. Holy Royal Arch. All these also obtain in this country; the Royal Arch, being the most important, will be treated of in full (405 et seq.).

II. French or Modern rite. It consists of seven degrees: The first three the same as in Craft Masonry; 4. Elect; 5. Scotch Master; 6. Knight of the East; 7. Rose Croix. They are all astronomical.

III. Ancient and Accepted Scotch rite. It was organised in its present form in France early in the last century, though it derives its title from the claim of its founders that it was originally instituted in Scotland. It is, next to the York rite, the most widely diffused throughout the Masonic world. The administrative power is vested in Supreme Grand Councils, and the rite consists of thirty-three degrees, of which the 12th, Grand Master Architect; the 18th, Prince Rose Croix; and the 30th, Grand Elect Knight of Kadosh, are the most interesting, and particulars of which will be given under separate heads.

IV. Philosophic Scotch rite.

V. Primitive Scotch rite, practised in Belgium.

VI. Ancient Reformed rite.

VII. Fessler's rite.

VIII. Rite of the Grand Lodge of the Three Globes at Berlin.

IX. Rite of Perfection.

X. Rite of Misraim (418-42).

XI. Rite of the Order of the Temple.

XII. Swedish rite.

XIII. Reformed rite.

XIV. Schroeder's rite.

XV. Rite of Swedenborg (see 264).

XVI. Rite of Zinzendorf - Count Zinzendorf, physician of the Emperor Charles VI., invented this rite, which was a modification of the Iluminism of Avignon, adding to it the mysteries of Swedenborg. His system consisted of seven degrees, divided into three sections: I. Blue Masonry; 2. Red Masonry; 3. Capitular Masonry. The rite was never introduced into this country.

XVII. Eclectic rite. This was established at Frankfurt in 1783 by Baron de Knigge, for the purpose of checking the spread of the hautes grades, or philosophic rites, which were increasing excessively. Eclectic Masonry acknowledged the three symbolic degrees only, but permitted each lodge to select at its option any of the higher degrees, provided it did not interfere with the uniformity of the first three. But the founder was disappointed in his expectations the high degrees continued to flourish, and but few Eclectic lodges ever existed.

391. Masonic Customs - Some Masonic peculiarities may conveniently be mentioned here. Freemasons frequently attend in great state at the laying of the foundation stones of public buildings; they follow a master to the grave, clothed with all the paraphernalia of their respective degrees; they date from the year of light. The Knights of the Sun, the 28th degree of the Scotch rite, acknowledge no era, but always write their date with seven noughts, 0,000,000. No one can be admitted into the Masonic order before the age of twenty-one, but an exception is made in this country and in France in favour of the sons of Masons, who may be initiated at the age of eighteen. Such a person is called a Lewis in England, and a Louveteau in France. This latter word signifies a young wolf; and the reader will remember that in the mysteries of Isis the candidate was made to wear the mask of a wolf's head. Hence a wolf and a candidate in these mysteries were synonymous. Macrobius, in his "Saturnalia," says that the ancients

perceived a relationship between the sun, the great symbol of those mysteries, and a wolf; for as the flocks of sheep and cattle disperse at the sight of the wolf, so the flocks of stars disappear at the approach of the sun's light. We have seen in the account of the French Workmen's Unions (369) that the sons of Solomon still call themselves wolves. The adoption of the louveteau into the lodge takes place with a ceremony resembling that of baptism. The temple is covered with flowers, incense is burnt, and the godfather is enjoined not only to provide for the bodily wants of the new-born member, but also to bring him up in the school of truth and justice. The child receives a new name, generally that of a virtue, such as Veracity, Devotion, Beneficence; the godfather pronounces for him the oath of apprentice, in which degree he is received into the Order, which, in case he should become an orphan, supports and establishes him in life. In the United States the rights of a lewis do not exist.

392. Masonic Alphabet - The Masonic alphabet preserves the angular character of primitive alphabets. Thirteen characters (9 + 4) compose the Masonic system of writing. Hence all the sounds can only be represented by means of lines and points, in the following manner:

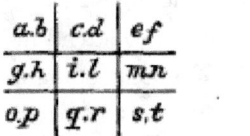 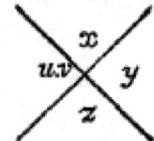

The letter a is written ⌐; the same sign with a dot in it, ⌐, means b. The sign > means u, and with a dot ∙>, v. Masonic abbreviations are always indicated by three dots, placed triangularly; thus, brother is abbreviated B∴ Lodge is written L∴ or ⌑∴; in the plural LL∴ or ⌸∴ Our common alphabet has an equally simple origin, as well as the Arabic numerals; they are all contained in the figure

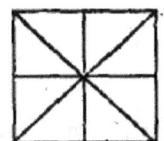

A, b or B, C, d or D, E, F, G, H, I, J, K, L, M, N, O, P or P, Q, R, S, T, U, V, X, Y, Z, 0, 1, 2, 3, 4, 5, 6 or b, 7, 8, 9,

IV
THE LODGE

393. Interior Arrangement of Lodge - The arrangement of the lodge varies and will vary according to periods and degrees, but certain general rules are always followed in its construction. In an ancient French catechism the lodge is thus described: The lodge must have a vaulted ceiling, painted blue and covered with golden stars, to represent the heavens. The floor is called a mosaic floor; the term "mosaic" being derived from Moses, i.e. "drawn from the water," because by its variegated colours it represents the earth as covered with flowers again after the withdrawal of the waters of the Nile. There are three windows one east, one west, and a third south. There must also be two or three antechambers, so that the profane may catch no glimpse of what is going on in the lodge; and if some stranger should nevertheless intrude, the master exclaims, "It rains!" and the lodge is ipso facto dissolved. The lodge should be always hung with black; the brethren take their places according to their rank; the grand master in the east, the master in the south, and the novices at the north, because they cannot yet stand the heat of the sun, which only the initiated can. When an apprentice is made, the lodge is brightly illuminated. The grand master, seated in his place, wears on his neck, appended to a large ribbon, a small square and compasses; before him stands a table, on which lie the Gospel of St. John and a small hammer. At his side are the two stewards, the first of whom wears a level and the second a plumb of gold or silver. The masters and fellow-crafts stand around with the apprentices, all wearing white aprons of lamb's skin, and each carrying a naked sword. On the floor are designed figures, representing the steps that led to Solomon's temple, and the two pillars Jachin and Boaz, but which in reality symbolise the summer and winter solstices, the pillars of Hercules, the two pillars of Seth. Above are seen the sun, moon, and a large star. Jn the midst of the floor is a coffin, in which lies a man apparently dead, with his face turned upward and covered with his white apron smeared with blood, one hand resting on his breast, and the other extended towards the knee. In the corners of the room are

substances easily combustible, such as sulphur, to kindle a fire instantaneously. This apparatus is somewhat altered when a fellow-craft or a master is to be made.

394. Modern Lodge - The modern lodge is a large square hall, always, if possible, situated due east and west. Upon a dais ascended by three steps, opposite to the door of ingress, is seated the worshipful master; the altar is placed in the centre on four steps. A sky-blue canopy, dotted with stars, and having above it the shining triangle with the sacred name inscribed therein, covers the throne. To the left of the canopy is seen the sun, and to the right the moon. Another ornament is the blazing star, and the point within a circle, symbolising the sun or the universe. A chest or ark also forms part of the masonic furniture. It represents the ark that was carried in the processions of ancient Egypt, and contained seeds of various plants, a winnowing fan, and Osiridis pudendum. To the west, at the sides of the door of ingress, stand two pillars of bronze, whose capitals represent pomegranates, and bearing on their fronts the initials J. and B. (Jachin and Boaz). The senior and junior wardens sit near the two columns, having before them a triangular table, covered with masonic emblems. Around the lodge there are ten other pillars connected by an architrave with the two pillars above mentioned. On the altar are placed a Bible, a square, a pair of compasses, and swords; three candelabra with long tapers are placed, one at the east at the foot of the steps, the second at the west, near the first warden, and the third at the south. The room is surrounded with benches for the members. In the lodges called Scotch, and in English and American lodges, the canopy that covers the master's throne is of crimson silk. In the United States, the worshipful master wears a cap adorned with black feathers and a large cockade of the same colour. The senior and junior wardens are seated in niches with fringed drapery, and wear, like heralds, staves of ebony sculptured like pillars.

395. Officers - Besides the Master and the Wardens, who are figuratively called the three lights, the lodge has other officers the

Orator, Secretary, Treasurer, Master of the Ceremonies, Keeper of the Seals, Architect, Steward, Captain of the Host, Principal Sojourner, Inner and Outer Guard or Tyler, and others. Every official occupies a place assigned to him, and has his proper jewels and badges, like the Egyptian, Hebrew, and Greek priests. Thus beside the jewels already mentioned, the treasurer wears cross keys; the secretary, cross pens: the senior deacon, a square and compass, with a sun in the centre; the junior deacon, a square and compass, with a moon in the centre; the steward, a cornucopia; the tyler, cross swords, &c. The names of most of the officers sufficiently indicate their duties; those that do not will be explained as they occur.

396. Opening the Lodge - The meetings are generally held at night. The worshipful master, striking the altar with his mallet, " opens the labours," and after having ascertained that the lodge is tyled, he turns to the junior warden and says: " Brother junior warden, your constant place in the lodge?" "In the south." "Why are you placed there?" "To mark the sun at its meridian, to call the brethren from labour to refreshment, and from refreshment to labour, that profit and pleasure may be the result." " Brother senior warden, your constant place in the lodge?" "In the west." "Why are you placed there?" "To mark the setting sun; to close the lodge by the command of the worshipful master, after seeing that every one has his just dues." "Why is the master placed ia the east?" "As the sun rises in the east to open and enliven the day, so the worshipful master is placed in the east to open and enlighten his lodge, to employ and instruct the brethren." "At what hour are Masons accustomed to begin their labours?" "At mid-day." "What hour is it, brother junior warden?" "It is mid-day." "Since this is the hour, and all is proved right and just, I declare the lodge open." The purely astronomical bearing of all this is self-evident, but will be more fully discussed hereafter.

397. Distinction between Genuine and Spurious Masonry - Modern Freemasonry is divided into genuine and spurious. The former embraces the degrees of Entered Apprentice, Fellow-Craft, and Master

Mason, which are known by the comprehensive name of Symbolic, and also of Blue Masonry, because the decorations are of that colour, the colour of the celestial canopy (27, 42, 85), which Blue Masonry is the only Masonry acknowledged by the Grand Lodge of England; the latter term, i.e. spurious, is applied to all other degrees. Without the Royal Arch degree Blue Masonry is incomplete, for we have seen in the Legend of the Temple that, through the murder of Hiram, the Master's word was lost; that word is not recovered in the Master's degree, its substitute only being given; but that lost word is recovered in the Royal Arch degree. Blue Masonry, in fact, answers to the lesser mysteries of the ancients, where in reality nothing but the exoteric doctrines were revealed; whilst spurious Masonry, or all subsequent degrees for no one can be initiated into them who has not passed through the first three degrees answers to the greater mysteries.

398. Some Rites only deserve Special Mention - It would be a useless and unprofitable task to fully detail all the ceremonies practised in the lodges of Blue Masonry; and I shall, therefore, confine myself to giving such particulars of the three degrees as are most characteristic of the institution. As to spurious Masonry, its almost countless degrees form an incoherent medley of opposite principles, founded chiefly on Christian traditions and institutions, orders of knighthood, contested theological opinions, historical events; in fact, every important event or institution has afforded models for masonic mimicry. Of such as have been distinguished either by a philosophical spirit or influential action on the progress of mankind I shall speak at some length. The reader will, however, bear in mind that the ceremonies vary in different lodges and different countries, and that much that follows must be taken as typical, being modified according to local and other conditions and circumstances.

VI CEREMONIES OF INITIATION
THE APPRENTICE, FELLOW-CRAFT, AND MASTER MASON

399. Ceremonies of Initiation - The Apprentice - The novice that is to be initiated into the first or apprentice degree is led into the lodge building by a stranger, and introduced into a remote chamber, where he is left alone for a few minutes. He is then deprived of all metal he has about him; his right knee, and sometimes his left side, are uncovered, and the heel of his left shoe is trodden down. These ceremonies are supposed by some writers on the craft to be of Jesuitical origin. The deprivation of metals is to typify the vow of poverty, the baring of the breast and knee is intended to prevent the admission of women, and the treading down the heel of the shoe to remind the candidate that Ignatius de Loyola, who had a bad foot, thus began his pilgrimage. His eyes are bandaged, and he is led into the closet of reflection, where he is told to stay without taking off the bandage, until he hears three knocks. At the signal, on uncovering his eyes he beholds on the walls, hung with black, inscriptions like the following: "If idle curiosity draw thee hither, depart!" "If thou be afraid of being enlightened concerning thy errors, it profits thee not to stay here." "If thou value human distinctions, go hence; here they are not known." After a deal of palaver between the brother who introduces the novice and the master, the candidate, having his eyes again bandaged and a cord passed round his neck, is introduced into the middle of the brethren, his guide pointing a naked sword to his breast. He is then questioned as to his object in coming hither, and on answering that he comes to be initiated into the secrets of Masonry, he is led out of the lodge and back again to confuse him. A large square frame covered with paper, such as circus-riders use, is then brought forward and held by two brethren. The guide then asks the master: " What shall we do with the profane?" To which the master replies: "Shut him up in the cave." Two brethren seize the postulant and throw him through the paper-screen into the arms of two other brethren who stand ready to receive him. The folding doors, hitherto left open, are then shut with great noise, and, by

means of an iron ring and bar, the closing with massive locks is imitated, so that the candidate fancies himself shut up in a dungeon. Some time then elapses in sepulchral silence. All at once the master strikes a smart blow, and orders the candidate to be placed beside the junior warden, and to be made to kneel. The master then addresses several questions to him, and instructs him on his duties towards the Order. The candidate is then offered a beverage, with the intimation that if any treason lurks in his heart, the drink will turn to poison. The cup containing it has two compartments, the one holding sweet, the other bitter water; the candidate is then taught to say: "I bind myself to the strict and rigorous observance of the duties prescribed to Freemasons; and if ever I violate my oath" (here his guide puts the sweet water to his lips, and having drunk some, the candidate continues) "I consent that the sweetness of this drink be turned into bitterness, and that its salutary effect become for me that of a subtle poison." The candidate is then made to drink of the bitter water, whereupon the master exclaims: "What do I see? What means the sudden alteration of your features? Perhaps your conscience belies your words? Has the sweet drink already turned bitter? Away with the profane! This oath is only a test; the true one comes after." The candidate persisting nevertheless in his determination, he is led three times round the lodge; then he is dragged over broken chairs, stools, and blocks of wood; this trial over, he is told to mount the "endless stairs," and having, as he supposes, attained a great height, to cast himself down, when he only falls a few feet. This trial is accompanied by great noise, the brethren striking on the attributes of the order they carry in their hands, and uttering all kinds of dismal shouts. As a further trial, he is then passed through fire, rendered harmless by well-known conjuring tricks; his arm is slightly pricked, and a gurgling noise being produced by one of the brethren, the candidate fancies that he is losing much blood. Finally, he takes the oath, the brethren standing around him with drawn swords. The candidate is then led between the two pillars, and the brethren place their swords against his breast. The master of the ceremonies loosens the bandage without taking it off. Another brother holds before him a lamp that sheds a brilliant light.

The master resumes: " Brother senior warden, deem you the candidate worthy of forming part of our society?" "Yes." "What do you ask for him?" "Light." "Then let there be light! " The master gives three blows with the mallet, and at the third the bandage is taken off, and the candidate beholds the light, which is to symbolise that which is to fill his understanding. The brethren drop their swords, and the candidate is led to the altar, where he kneels, whilst the master says: " In the name of the Grand Architect of the universe, and by virtue of the powers vested in me, I create and constitute thee masonic apprentice and member of this lodge." Then striking three blows with his mallet on the blade of the sword, he raises the new brother, girds him with the apron of white lamb's skin, gives him a pair of white gloves to be worn in the lodge, and another to be given to the lady he esteems most, a symbolical gift which need not be further explained. He is then again led between the two pillars, and received by the brethren as one of them. Such is the proceeding the apprentice has to go through; a few more details may be added.

One question put to him is: " Have you seen your master to-day? " "Yes." "How was he clothed?" "In a yellow jacket and blue pair of breeches." The explanation is: the master is the compasses, the yellow jacket is the brass body, and the blue breeches are the steel points. He is also asked: "How old are you? " "Under seven." This answer implies that he has not passed to the fellow-crafts degree, seven years being the term of an apprenticeship in Freemasonry, as it is in other trades. The password is Boaz, the sign holding the hand horizontally, with the thumb turned up towards the right ear, to remind the apprentice of his oath, on taking which he promises: "These several points [keeping the secrets of the order] I solemnly swear to observe without evasion, equivocation, or mental reservation, under no less a penalty on the violation of any of them, than to have my throat cut across, my tongue torn out by the root, and my body buried in the sand of the sea." The grip is given by a distinct pressure of the right hand thumb on the first joint from the wrist of the right hand forefinger, grasping the finger with the hand.

400. Ceremonies of Initiation - The Fellow-Craft - The second degree of symbolic Freemasonry is that of fellow-craft. The apprentice, who asks for an increase of salary, is not conducted to the lodge like the profane by an unknown brother, nor are his eyes bandaged, because the light was made for him, but moves towards the lodge holding in his hand a rule, one of whose ends he rests on the left shoulder. Having reached the door, he gives the apprentice's knock, and having been admitted and declared the purpose for which he comes, he five times perambulates the lodge, whereupon he is told by the master to perform his last apprentice's work. He then pretends to square the rough ashlar. After a deal of instruction, very useless and pointless, he takes the oath, in which he swears to keep the secrets entrusted to him. Then there follows some more lecturing on the part of the master, chiefly on geometry, for which Masons profess a great regard, and to which the letter G seen in the lodge within an irradiation or star is said to refer.

The oath of the fellow-craft is rather more atrocious than that of the apprentice. He swe'ars, in addition to his former obligations, to keep the secrets of the crafts, and to do so under no less a penalty than to have his left breast cut open, his heart torn therefrom and given to the ravenous birds of the air and the devouring beasts of the field. With reference to this oath the sign is given by placing the hand with the thumb turned up on his breast; the password is Jachin, sometimes Shibboleth. The grip is given by a distinct pressure of the thumb of the right hand between the joints of the first and middle fingers of the right hand.

401. Ceremony of Initiation and Story of Hiram's Murder - The Master Mason. At the reception of a master, the lodge or "middle chamber" is draped with black, with death's heads, skeletons, and cross bones painted on the walls. A taper of yellow wax, placed in the east, and a dark lantern formed of a skull having a light within, which shines forth through the eye-holes, placed on the altar of the most worshipful master, give just sufficient light to reveal a coffin, wherein the corpse is represented either by a lay-figure, a serving brother, or the brother last made a master. On the coffin is placed a sprig of acacia, at its head is a

square, and at its foot, towards the east, an open compass. The masters are clothed in black, and wear large azure sashes, on which are represented masonic emblems, the sun, moon, and seven stars. The object of the meeting is said to be the finding of the word of the master that was slain. The postulant for admission is introduced after some preliminary ceremonies, having his two arms, breasts, and knees bare, and both heels slipshod. He is told that the brethren assembled are mourning the death of their grand master, and asked whether perhaps he was one of the murderers; at the same time he is shown the body or figure in the coffin. Having declared his innocence of any share in that crime, he is informed that he will on this occasion have to enact the part of Hiram (385), who was slain at the building of Solomon's temple, and whose history he is about to be told. The brother or figure in the coffin has in the meantime been removed, so that when the aspirant looks at it again, he finds it empty. The story of the murder of Hiram is then related. But the deed is not, as in the Legend of the Temple, attributed to Solomon's jealousy, but simply to Hiram's refusal to communicate the master's word to three fellow-crafts. The various incidents of the story are scenically enacted on the postulant. "Hiram," the master continues, "having entered the temple at noon, the three assassins placed themselves at the east, west, and south doors, and Hiram refusing to reveal the word, he who stood at the east door cut Hiram across the throat with a twentyfour-inch gauge. Hiram flew to the south door, where he received similar treatment, and thence to the west door, where he was struck on the head with a gavel, which occasioned his death." The applicant, at this part of the recital, is informed that he too must undergo trials, and is not to sink under the influence of terror, though the hand of death be upon him. He is then struck in the forehead and thrown down, and shams a dead man. The master continues: "The ruffians carried the body out at the west door, and buried it at the side of a hill" here the postulant is placed in the coffin "in a grave, on which they stuck a sprig of acacia to mark the spot. Hiram not making his appearance as usual, Solomon caused search to be made for him by twelve trusty fellow-crafts that were sent out, three east, three west, three south, and three north. Of the three who went east, one being weary, sat down on the brow of a hill to rest himself, and in rising caught hold of a twig "here a twig of that plant is put into the hand of the aspirant lying in the coffin "which coming up easily, showed that the ground had been recently disturbed, and on digging he and his companions found the body of Hiram." A similar occurrence is related in Æneis, iii. 22-29, where Æneas, in plucking up a shrub on the side of a hill, discovers the murder of Polydorus. "Hiram's body was in a mangled condition, having lain fourteen days, whereupon one of those present exclaimed Macbenach! which means "the flesh is off the bones' or 'the brother is smitten,' and became the master's word, as the former one was lost through Hiram's death; for though the other two masters, Solomon and Hiram, king of Tyre, knew it, it could only be communicated by the three grand masters conjointly." The covering of the grave being green moss and turf, other bystanders exclaimed, Muscus domus, Dei gratia! which, according to Masonry, is, "Thanks be unto God, our master has got a mossy house!" The exclamation shows that the Hebrew builders of Solomon's temple possessed a familiar knowledge of the Latin tongue! The body of Hiram could not be raised by the apprentice's or fellow-craft's grip, but only by the master's, or the lion's grip, as it is called. All this is then imitated by the master raising the aspirant in the coffin, who is then told the word, signs, and grips, and takes the oath, promising to keep the masonic secrets under no less a penalty than to have his body severed in two, his bowels torn thereout and burnt to ashes, and those ashes scattered to the four cardinal points. The grip is given by a distinct pressure of the thumb between the joints of the middle and ring fingers. The password is "Tubal-Cain." There are three signs, the most important being the penal sign, which is given by drawing the hand across the centre of the body, dropping it to the side, and then raising it again to place the point of the thumb on the navel. The grip is the first of the five points of fellowship, and consists in taking hold of each other's wrists with the points of the fingers. The second point is placing the right foot parallel with the right foot on the inside; the third, right knee to right knee; the fourth, right breast to right breast; and the fifth, hand over shoulder, supporting the back. It is in this position, and only in a whisper, that the word "Mahabone," or "Macbenach," is given, the first meaning "the death of a brother," and the second "the brother is smitten."

402. The Legend Explained - Taken literally, the story of Hiram would offer nothing so extraordinary as to deserve to be commemorated after three thousand years throughout the world by solemn rites and ceremonies. The death of an architect is not so important a matter as to have more honour paid to it than is shown to the memory of so many philosophers and learned men who have lost their lives in the cause of human progress. But history knows nothing of him. His name is only mentioned in the Bible, and it is simply said of him that he was a man of understanding and cunning in working in brass. Tradition is equally silent concerning him. He is remembered nowhere except in Freemasonry; the legend, in fact, is purely allegorical, and may bear a twofold interpretation, cosmological and astronomical.

Cosmologically, we find represented therein the dualism of the two antagonistic powers, which is the leading feature of all Eastern initiations. The dramatic portion of the mysteries of antiquity is always sustained by a deity or man who perishes as the victim of an evil power, and rises again into a more glorious existence. In the ancient mysteries, we constantly meet with the record of a sad event, a crime which plunges nations into strife and grief, succeeded by joy and exultation.

Astronomically, again, the parallel is perfect, and is in fact only another version of the legend of Osiris. Hiram represents Osiris, i.e. the sun. The assassins place themselves at the west, south, and east doors, that is, the regions illuminated by the sun; they bury the body, and mark the spot with a sprig of acacia. Twelve persons play an important part in the tragedy, viz. the three murderers (fellow-crafts), and nine masters. This number is a plain allusion to the twelve signs of the zodiac, and the three murderers are the three inferior signs of winter, Libra, Scorpio, and Sagittarius. Hiram is slain at the west door, the sun descends in the west. The acacia of Freemasonry is the plant found in all the ancient solar allegories, and symbolising the new vegetation to be anticipated by the sun's resurrection. The acacia being looked upon by the ancients as incorruptible, its twigs were preferred for covering the body of the god-man to the myrtle, laurel, and other plants mentioned in the ancient mysteries. Hiram's body is in a state of decay, having lain fourteen days; the body of Osiris was cut into fourteen pieces (51). But according to other statements, the body was found on the seventh day; this would allude to the resurrection of the sun, which actually takes place in the seventh month after his passage through the inferior signs, that passage which is called his descent into hell. Hiram can only be raised by the lion's grip. It is through the instrumentality of Leo that Osiris is raised; it is when the sun re-enters that sign that he regains his former strength, that his restoration to life takes place. Masons in this degree call themselves the "children of the widow," the sun on descending into his tomb leaving nature of which Masons consider themselves the pupils a widow; but the appellation may also have its origin in the Manichaean sect, whose followers were known as the "sons of the widow" (112).

403. The Raising of Osiris - A painting found on an Egyptian mummy, now in Paris, represents the death and resurrection of Osiris, and the beginning, progress, and end of the inundation of the Nile. The sign of the Lion is transformed into a couch, upon which Osiris is laid out as dead; under the couch are four canopi or jars of various capacities, indicating the state of the Nile at different periods. The first is terminated by the head of Sirius, or the Dog-Star, which gives warning of the approach of the overflow of the river; the second by the head of the Hawk, the symbol of the Etesian wind, which tends to swell the waters; the third by the head of a Heron, the sign of the south wind, which contributes to propel the water into the Mediterranean; and the fourth by that of the Virgin, which indicates that when the sun had passed that sign the inundation would have nearly subsided. To the above is superadded a large Anubis, who with an emphatic gesture, turning towards Isis, who has an empty throne on her head, intimates that the sun, by the aid of the Lion, had cleared the difficult pass of the tropic of Cancer, and was now in the sign of the latter; and although in a state of exhaustion, would soon be in a condition to

proceed on his way to the south. The empty throne is indicative of its being vacated by the supposed death of Osiris. The reason why the hawk represents the north wind is, because about the summer solstice, when the wind blows from north to south, the bird flies with the wind towards the south (Job xxxix. 26). The heron signifies the south wind, because this bird, living on the worms hatched in the mud of the Nile, follows the course of the river down to the sea, just as the south wind does. To know the state of the Nile, and therefore their own personal prospects, the Egyptians watched the birds; hence among other nations, who did not know the principle by which the Egyptians went, arose divination by the flight of birds.[17]

404. The Blazing Star. The representation of a blazing star found in every masonic lodge, and which Masons declare to signify prudence though why a star should have such a meaning they would be at a loss to tell is the star Sirius, the dog-star, mentioned above, the inundation of the Nile occurring when the sun was under the stars of the Lion. Near the stars of the Cancer, though pretty far from the band of the zodiac towards the south, and a few weeks after their rising, the Egyptians saw in the morning one of the most brilliant stars in the whole heavens ascending the horizon. It appeared a little before the rising of the sun; they therefore pitched upon this star as the infallible sign of the sun's passing under the stars of Leo, and the beginning of the inundation. As it thus seemed to be on the watch and give warning, they called it " Barker," "Anubis," " Thot," all meaning the " dog." Its Hebrew name, " Sihor," in Greek became "Seirios," and in Latin "Sirius." It taught the Egyptians the prudence of retiring into the higher grounds; and thus Masons, ignorant of the origin of the symbol, yet give it its original emblematic signification.

---

[17] Hamlet says, "Iam but mad north-north-west; when the wind is southerly I know a hawk from a hand-saw." Thomas Capell, the editor of the Oxford edition of Shakespeare, changes "hand-saw" to "hernshaw," which renders the passage intelligible; for hernshaw is only another name for the heron; and Hamlet, though feigning madness, yet claims sufficient sanity to distinguish a hawk from a hernshaw, when the wind is southerly that is, in the time of the migration of the latter to the north and when the former is not to be seen.

VII

THE HOLY ROYAL ARCH

405. Officers - The members of this degree (founded about the year 1766) are denominated "companions." There are nine officers, the chief of whom (in England) is Zerubbabel, a compound word, meaning "the bright lord, the sun." He rebuilds the temple, and therefore represents the sun risen again. The next officer is Jeshua, the high-priest; the third, Haggai, the prophet. These three compose the grand council. Principals and senior and junior sojourners form the base; Ezra and Nehemiah, senior and junior scribes, one on each side; janitor or tyler without the door. The companions assembled make up the sides of the arch, representing the pillars Jachin and Boaz. In front of the principals stands an altar, inscribed with the names of Solomon, Hiram, king of Tyre, and Hiram Abiff.

406. Ceremonies - On entering the chapter, the companions give the sign of sorrow, in imitation of the ancients mourning for the loss of Osiris. Nine companions must be present at the opening of a royal arch chapter; not more nor less than three are permitted to take this degree at the same time, the two numbers making up the twelve, the number of zodiacal signs. The candidates are prepared by tying a bandage over their eyes, and coiling a rope seven times round the body of each, which unites them together, with three feet of slack rope between them. They then pass under the living arch, which is made by the companions either joining their hands and holding them up, or by holding their rods or swords so as to resemble a Gothic arch. This part of the ceremony used to be attended in some lodges with a deal of tomfoolery and rough horseplay. The companions would drop down on the candidates, who were obliged to support themselves on their hands and knees; and if they went too slowly, it was not unusual for one or

more of the companions to apply a sharp point to their bodies to urge them on. Trials, such as the candidates for initiation into the ancient mysteries had to go through, were also imitated in the royal arch. But few, if any, lodges now practise these tricks, fit only for Christmas pantomimes. The candidates, after taking the oath, declare that they come in order to assist at the rebuilding of Solomon's temple, whereupon they are furnished with pickaxes, shovels, and crowbars, and retire. After a while, during which they are supposed to have been at work and to have made a discovery, they return, and state that on digging for the new foundation they discovered an underground vault, into which one of them was let down and found a scroll, which on examination turns out to be the long-lost book of the law. They set to work again, and discover another vault, and under that a third. The sun having now gained his meridian height, darts his rays to the centre and shines on a white marble pedestal, on which is a plate of gold. On this plate is a double triangle, and within the triangles some words they cannot understand; they therefore take the plate to Zerubbabel. There the whole mystery of Masonry as far as known to Masons is unveiled; what the Masons had long been in search of is found, for the mysterious writing in a triangular form is the longlost sacred word of the Master Mason, which Solomon and King Hiram deposited there, as we have seen in the master's degree (402). This word Jabulon = Jah + Bel + On, Hebrew, Assyrian, and Egyptian names of tha sun, is the logos of Plato and St. John, the omnific word; but the above compound name, intended to bear the same import, is substituted by modern Masons. It is communicated to the candidates in this way: The three principals and each three companions form the triangles, and each of the three takes his left-hand companion by the right-hand wrist, and his right-hand companion by the left-hand wrist, forming two distinct triangles with the hands, and a triangle with their right feet, amounting to a triple triangle, and then pronounce the following words, each taking a line in turn:

> "As we three did agree,
> In peace, love, and unity,

The sacred word to keep,
So we three do agree,
In peace, love, and unity,
The sacred word to search,
Until we three,
Or three such as we, shall agree
This royal arch chapter to close."

The right hands, still joined as a triangle, are raised as high as possible, and the word given at low breath in syllables, so that each companion has to pronounce the whole word. It is not permitted to utter this omnific word above the breath; like the name "Jehovah " or " Oum," it would shake heaven and earth if pronounced aloud. Zerubbabel next makes the new companions acquainted with the five signs used in this degree, and invests them with the badges of Royal Arch Masonry the apron, sash, and jewel. The character on the apron is the triple Tau, one of the most ancient of emblems, and Masons call it the emblem of emblems, "with a depth that reaches to the creation of the world and all that is therein." This triple Tau is a compound figure of three T's, called Tau in Greek. Now this Tau or T is the figure of the old Egyptian Nilometer, used to ascertain the height of the inundation. It was a pole crossed with one or more transverse pieces. As on the inundation depended the subsistence, the life of the inhabitants, the Nilometer became the symbol of life, health, and prosperity, and was thought to have the power of averting evil. It thence became an amulet, and in this manner was introduced among masonic symbols.

407. Passing the Veils - In some chapters the ceremony called "passing the veils" is omitted, but to make the account of Royal Arch Masonry complete I append it here. The candidate is introduced blindfold, his knees bare, and his feet slipshod, with a cable-tow round his waist. The high-priest reads Exod. iii. 1-6, and 13, 14, and the candidate is informed that "I am that I am " is the password from the first to the second veil. He is also shown a bush on fire. He is then led to the second veil, which, on giving the password, he passes, and beholds the

figure of a serpent and Aaron's rod. The high-priest reads Exod. iv. 1-5, and the candidate is told to pick up the rod cast down before him, that the act is the sign of passing the second veil, and that the passwords are " Moses, Aaron, and Eleazar." He then passes the guard of the third veil. The high-priest reads Exod. iv. 6-9, and the candidate is informed that the leprous hand and the pouring out of the water are the signs of the third veil, and that "Holiness to the Lord" are the passwords to the sanctum sanctorum. He is shown the ark of the covenant, the table of shewbread, the burning incense, and the candlestick with seven branches. Then follow long lectures to explain the words and symbols, but their quality may be inferred from the following specimen: " This triangle is also an emblem of geometry. And here we find the most perfect emblem of the science of agriculture; not a partial one like the Basilidean, calculated for one particular clime, but universal; pointed out by a pair of compasses issuing from the centre of the sun, and suspending a globe denoting the earth, and thereby representing the influence of that luminary over the creation, admonishing us to be careful to perform every operation in its proper season, that we lose not the fruits of our labour." What a farmer would say to, or what profit he could derive from, this universal "science of agriculture," or whether he needs the "admonishing " symbol, I am at a loss to imagine. The triple Tau, according to the lecture, means templum Hierosolymce, also clams ad thesaurum, res ipsa pretiosa, and several other things equally true. "But," continues the lecturer, "these are all symbolical definitions of the symbol, which is to be simply solved into an emblem of science in the human mind, and is the most ancient symbol of that kind, the prototype of the Cross, and the first object in every religion or human system of worship. This is the grand secret of Masonry, which passes by symbols from superstition to science." How far all this is from the true meaning of the cross and triple Tau may be seen by reference to 53.

VIII
GRAND MASTER ARCHITECT

408. Ceremonial - In this, the twelfth degree of the ancient Scotch rite, the chapter, or lodge, represents the Temple of Solomon in three compartments. The first to the west, hung with white, is the vestibule. On its northern side is the tomb of Hiram, also white; to the south stands the Brazen Sea. The centre of the lodge, divided from the vestibule by a white, and from the Holy of Holies by a red, curtain represents the interior of the temple. On its floor is the Scotch carpet, showing the three walls round the temple; to the north of the carpet stands the golden table with the shewbread, to the south the candlestick with seven branches. The altar of incense is placed on the carpet itself, and above it hangs the Blazing Star, strongly illuminated. The east is the Holy of Holies. In the centre is an altar, raised on seven steps; the altar represents the ark of the covenant, on which are placed two cherubims, surmounted by the sign of the glory of God, consisting of a transparent disc, having in its centre a triangle, inscribed with 7, 7, 74. The perpetual holy fire burns in a vase on the ark. Eighty-one lights burn on the steps, which, however, are lighted up only when the candidate is to be shown the light of the Holy of Holies. The Master sits at a small table, with a red cloth, and having on this the word of the Order and the vestment of the candidate. The brethren wear an apron embroidered and lined with red. From a sash, worn from the right shoulder to the left hip, the pentagon is suspended, or a gold medal, on both sides of which are engraved the orders of architecture. The master is called " The Most Powerful Grand Architect," the two wardens are called "Ancient Scotch Grand Masters," and the brethren "Perfect Architects."

    The usual questions and answers are put at the opening of the lodge. Here are a few of them:

    "Where does the Most Powerful Grand Architect dwell?"

    "In the east, in the Holy of Holies."

    "Why?"

    "That he, being placed close to the fountain of all light, may point out to the brethren the way by which they may emerge from darkness into light."

"How is this done? "

"By opening the temple; by advice, direction, and examination of the work of the Scotch Architects."

"Give me the password."

"Zididiac, or Zedekiah." Occasionally it is "Rabacim."

"Give me the holy word."

The brethren form a chain to the Grand Master, and whisper the word into each other's ears. We shall presently see what it is.

The questions are continued: "What hour is it?"

"The first hour of the last day of the last year in which Solomon's temple was finished."

The brethren hold up their swords and greet one another by crossing them; then rest them on their left arms, take off their hats, kneel down, and during the prayer that follows make the Grand Scotch sign, i.e. the hand at the forehead. The prayer being over, the brethren rise, put on their hats, and the lodge is declared to be open for the reception of the candidate, who is introduced with a great deal of ceremony, being blindfolded, wearing the master's apron, and slippers on his feet, and whom the Grand Master of Ceremony declares to be a Hiramite, called by the unanimous voice of the Ancient Scotch to become a perfect Architect, to assist in building up the Holy of Holies. He is made to kneel with his right knee on a stool in front of the tomb or coffin, where he is catechised as to his intentions, and all being satisfactory, he is led five times, and then again seven times round the apartment, and finally his eyes are unbandaged, the tomb of Hiram is pointed out to him, as also the letter G in the Blazing Star, which letter stands for "Gnosis," the "inheritance of Perfect Architects." Then ensues a good deal more catechising and lecturing, and finally the new brother has to take the oath, which binds him, however, to nothing more than to secrecy, and the fulfilment of certain moral duties. The members again go through a number of evolutions round or on the carpet; their swords are drawn, held up, crossed, and sheathed again. Then the candidate has his eyes bandaged again; the brethren kneel down, their faces being turned to the Holy of Holies, in which the eighty-one lights are now lighted; the curtain is drawn up, a handful of powder is thrown on the altar of incense, and the bandage taken off the candidate's eyes; the Grand Master makes an edifying moral speech, the brethren flourish their swords, and forming a circle bring them as much as possible in a point over the new brother's head, who is now declared a Perfect Ancient Scotch Architect, touched with the sword on the right and left shoulder, the breast and the back, and the sword is then handed to him by the Grand Master, who concludes with another long speech. As the candidate naturally expects to be let into some kind of secret, he is told that the holy word is "Jehovah," which however is never pronounced out of the Holy of Holies. There is also the word "Gomer," but its meaning is not explained.

Such is an outline of the twelfth degree of the Ancient Scotch rite. It reminds me of what Lessing, the celebrated German author, said after he had been made a Mason. The master having expressed a hope that Lessing had found nothing against the state, religion, and morals in the Order, Lessing replied, " No, I wish I had, for then I should have found at least something! "

IX

GRAND ELECT KNIGHT OF KADOSH

409. The Term Kadosh - This degree, the thirtieth of the ancient and accepted Scotch rite, contains a beautiful astronomical allegory, and is probably derived from Egypt. The term Kadosh means "holy" or "elect." (Every person in the East, preferred to a post of honour, carried a staff, to indicate that he was Kadosh or elect, or that his person was sacred; whence eventually the name came to be applied to the staff itself, and hence the derivation of caduceus, the staff of Mercury, the messenger of the gods.)

410. Reception into the Degree - There are four apartments; the initiation takes place in the fourth. They symbolise the seasons. The first apartment is hung with black, lit up by a solitary lamp of triangular form, and suspended to the vaulted ceiling. It communicates with a kind of cave or closet of reflection, containing symbols of destruction and death. The candidate, after having been left there some time, passes into the second apartment, which is draped with white; two altars occupy the centre; on one is an urn filled with burning spirits of wine, on the other a brazier with live coal, and incense beside it. The candidate now faces the sacrificing priest, who addresses some words of admonition to him, and having burned some incense, directs him to the third apartment. It is hung with blue, and the vaulted ceiling covered with stars. Three yellow tapers light up this room. This is the areopagus. The candidate, having here given the requisite explanation as to the sincerity of his intentions and promises of secrecy, is introduced into the fourth apartment, hung with red. At the east is a throne surmounted by a double eagle, crowned, with outspread wings and holding a sword in his claw. In this room, lighted up with twelve yellow tapers, the chapter takes the title of " senate "; the brethren are called "knights." In this room also stands the mysterious ladder.

411. The Mysterious Ladder - It has seven steps, which symbolise the

sun's progress through the seven signs of the zodiac from Aries to Libra, both inclusive. This the candidate ascends, receiving at every step the explanation of its meaning from a hierophant, who remains invisible to the candidate, just as in the ancient mysteries the initiating priest remained concealed, and as Pythagoras delivered his instructions from behind a veil. When the candidate has ascended the ladder, and is on the last step, the ladder is lowered and he passes over it, because he cannot retire the same way, as the sun does not retrograde. He then reads the words at the bottom of the ladder, Ne plus ultra. The last degree manufactured is always the ne plus ultra, till somebody concocts one still more sublime, which then is the ne plus ultra, till it is superseded by another. What sublimity masonic degrees will yet attain, and where they will stop, no one can tell.

412. The Seven Steps - The name of the first step is Isedakah, which is defined "righteousness," alluding to the sun in the vernal equinox in the month of March, when the days and nights are equal all over the world, and the sun dispenses his favours equally to all.

The second step is Shor-lalan, "white ox" figuratively. This is the only step the definition of which is literally true, which, as it might lead to a clue to the meaning of the mysterious ladder, is thus falsely denominated figurative. Taurus, the bull, is the second sign of the zodiac, into which the sun enters on the 21st April. His entry into this sign is marked by the setting of Orion, who in mythological language is said to be in love with the Pleiades; and by the rising of the latter.

The third step is called Mathok, "sweetness." The third sign is Gemini, into which the sun enters in the pleasant month of May. "Canst thou hinder the sweet influences of the Pleiades, or loose the bands of Orion?" (Job). Now, the Pleiades were denominated by the Romans Vergilice, from their formerly rising when the spring commenced, and their sweet influences blessed the year by the beginning of spring.

The fourth step is Emunah, "truth in disguise." The fourth sign is Cancer, into which the sun enters in June. Egypt at this period is enveloped in clouds and dust, by which means the sun, which figuratively may be called truth, is obscured or disguised.

The fifth step is Hamal saggi, "great labour." The fifth sign is Leo. The great labour and difficulties to which the sun was supposed to be subject in passing this sign have already been alluded to (403).

The sixth step is Sabbal, "burden or patience." The sixth sign through which the sun passes is Virgo, marked by the total disappearance of the celestial Hydra, called the Hydra of Lerna, from whose head spring up the Great Dog and the Crab. Hercules destroys the Hydra of Lerna, but is annoyed by a sea-crab, which bites him in the foot. Whenever Hercules lopped off one of the monster's heads two others sprang up, so that his labour would have been endless, had he not ordered his companion Iolas to sear the blood with fire.

The seventh step is named Gemunah, Binah, Jebunah, "retribution, intelligence, prudence." The seventh sign is Libra, into which the sun enters at the commencement of autumn, indicated by the rising of the celestial Centaur, the same that treated Hercules with hospitality. This constellation is represented in the heavens with a flask full of wine and a thyrsus, ornamented with leaves and grapes, the symbols of the products of the seasons. The sun has now arrived at the autumnal equinox, bringing in his train the fruits of the earth; and recompense is made to the husbandman in proportion to his prudence and intelligence.

The ladder will remind the reader of the ladder of the Indian mysteries; of the ladder seen by Jacob in his dream; the pyramids with seven steps; and the seven caverns of various nations.

Formerly it may be so now in some lodges one of the tests the aspirant to this degree had to undergo was to kill the murderer of Hiram with a dagger, to bring his head to the altar, and drink blood out of a skull. The candidate, being blindfolded, had to place his hand on the beating heart of a sheep, the wool around that part having been shaved off, and, having stabbed the victim, he was freed from the bandage, and was shown a bleeding head, made of wax, which, however, was immediately removed, to prevent his discovering the deception.

X

PRINCE OF ROSE-CROIX

413. Distinct from Eosicrucian, and has various Names - This, the eighteenth degree of the ancient and accepted Scotch rite, is one of the most generally diffused of the higher degrees of Masonry. It is often confounded with the cabalistic and alchemistic sect of the Rosicrucians; but there is a great distinction between the two. The name is derived from the rose and the cross, and has no connection with alchemy; the import of the rose has been given in another place. The origin of the degree is involved in the greatest mystery, as already pointed out. The degree is known by various names, such as "Sovereign Princes of Rose-Croix," " Princes of Rose-Croix de Heroden," i.e. the holy house, i.e. the Temple, and sometimes " Knights of the Eagle and Pelican." It is considered the ne plus ultra of Masonry, which, however, is the case with several other degrees.

414. Officers and Lodges - The presiding officer is called the "Ever Most Perfect Sovereign," and the two wardens are styled "Most Excellent and Perfect Brothers." The degree is conferred by a body called a "Chapter of the Sovereign Princes of Rose-Croix," and in three apartments, the first representing Mount Calvary, the second the site and scene of the Resurrection, and the third Hell. It will thus be seen that it is a purely Christian degree, and therefore not genuine Masonry, but an attempt to christianise Freemasonry. The first apartment is hung with black, and lighted with thirty-three lights upon three candlesticks of eleven branches. Each light is enclosed in a small tin box, and issues its light through a hole of an inch diameter. These lights denote the age of Christ. In three angles of the room, north-east, south-east, and south-west, are three pillars of the height of a man, on the several chapiters of which are inscribed the names of Faith, Hope, and Charity. Every lodge has its picture descriptive of its form, and of the proper place of its officers and emblems. On the east, at the south and north angles, the sun and moon and a sky studded with stars are

painted; the clouds very dark. An eagle is seen beating the air with his wings, as an emblem of the supreme power. Besides other allegorical paintings, there is also one of a cubic stone, sweating blood and water. On the stone is a rose, and the letter J, which means the expiring Word. The space round the picture, representing the square of the lodge, is filled with darkness, to represent what happened at the crucifixion. Below it are all the ancient tools of masonry, with the columns divided and broken into many parts. Lower down is the veil of the temple rent in twain. Before the master is a little table, lighted by three lights, upon which the Gospel, compasses, square, and triangle are placed. All the brethren are clothed in black, with a black scarf from the left shoulder to the right side. An apron, white, bordered with black: on the flap are a skull and cross-bones, between three red roses; on the apron is a globe surmounted by a serpent, and above the letter J. The master and the other officers wear on the neck a wide ribbon of black mohair, from which hangs the jewel, a golden compass, surmounted by a triple crown, with a cross between the legs, its centre being occupied by a fullblown rose; at the foot of the cross is a pelican feeding its young from its breast; on the other side is an eagle with wings displayed. The eagle is the emblem of the sun, the "sun of righteousness"; the pelican, of course, alludes to Christ shedding His blood for the human race; the cross and the rose explain themselves.

415. Reception in the First Apartment - The candidate is clothed in black, decorated with a red ribbon, an apron doubled with the same colour, and a sword and scarf. After much preliminary ceremony, he is introduced into the apartment, and told by the master that the word that is lost and which he seeks cannot be given, because confusion reigns among them, the veil of the temple is rent, darkness covers the earth, the tools are broken, &c.; but that he need not despair, as they will find out the new law, that thereby they may recover the word. He is then told to travel for thirtythree years. The junior warden thereupon conducts him thirty-three times round the lodge, pointing out to him the three columns, telling him their names, Faith, Hope, and Charity, and bidding him remember them, as henceforth they must be his

guides. After a little more talk, he is made to kneel with his right knee upon the Gospel and take the following oath: "I promise by the same obligations I have taken in the former degrees of Masonry never to reveal the secrets of the Knight of the Eagle, under the penalty of being for ever deprived of the true word; that a river of blood and water shall issue continually from my body, and, under the penalty of suffering anguish of soul, of being steeped in vinegar and gall, of having on my head the most piercing thorns, and of dying upon the cross; so help me the Grand Architect of the Universe." The candidate then receives the apron and sash, both symbols of sorrow for the loss of the word. A dialogue ensues, wherein the hope of finding the word is foreshadowed; whereupon the master and brethren proceed to the second apartment, where they exchange their black aprons and sashes to take red ones.

416. Second Apartment - This apartment is hung with tapestry; three chandeliers, with thirty-three lights, but without the boxes, illuminate it. In the east there is a cross surrounded with a glory and a cloud; upon the cross is a rose of paradise, in the middle of which is the letter G. Below are three squares, in which are three circles, having three triangles, to form the summit, which is allegorical of Mount Calvary, upon which the Grand Architect of the Universe expired. Upon this summit is a blazing star with seven rays, and in the middle of it the letter G again. The eagle and pelican also reappear here. Below is the tomb. In the lower part of the square are the compasses, drawingboard, crow, trowel, and square. The cubic stone, hammer, and other tools are also represented.

417. Reception in the Third Apartment - But the second point of reception takes place in a third apartment, which is made as terrifying as possible, to represent the torments of hell. It has seven chandeliers with grey burning flambeaux, whose mouths represent death's-heads and cross-bones. The walls are hung with tapestry, painted with flames and figures of the damned. The candidate, on presenting himself as a searcher of the lost word, has his sash and apron taken from him, as

not humble enough to qualify him for the task, and is covered with a black cloth strewn with dirty ashes, so that he can see nothing, and informed that he will be led to the darkest of places, from which the word must come forth triumphant to the glory and advantage of Masonry. In this condition he is led to a steep descent, up and down which he is directed to travel, after which he is conducted to the door, and has the black cloth removed. Before him stand three figures dressed as devils. He then parades the room three times, without pronouncing a word, in memory of the descent into the dark places, which lasted three days. He is then led to the door of the apartment, covered with black cloth, and told that the horrors through which he has passed are as nothing in comparison with those through which he has yet to pass; therefore he is cautioned to summon all his fortitude. But in reality all the terrible trials are over, for he is presently brought before the master, who asks: "Whence come you? " "From Judeea." " Which way did you come?" "By Nazareth." "Of what tribe are you descended?" "Judah." "Give me the four initials?" "I.N.R.I." " What do these letters signify? " " Jesus of Nazareth, King of the Jews." " Brother, the word is found; let him be restored to light." The junior warden quickly takes off the cloth, and at the signal of the master, all the brethren clap their hands three times and give three huzzas. The candidate is then taught the signs, grips, and password. The master then proceeds to the instruction of the newlymade Knight of the Eagle or Prince Rose-Croix, which amounts to this, that after the erection of Solomon's temple masons began to neglect their labours, that then the cubical stone, the corner-stone, began to sweat blood and water, and was torn from the building and thrown among the ruins of the decaying temple, and the mystic rose sacrificed on a cross. Then masonry was destroyed, the earth covered with darkness, the tools of masonry broken. Then the blazing star disappeared, and the word was lost. But masons having learnt the three words, Faith, Hope, and Charity, and following the new law, masonry was restored, though masons no longer built material edifices, but occupied themselves in spiritual buildings. The mystic rose and blazing star were restored to their former beauty and splendour.

The degree was purely Jesuitical, and its object the restoration of the Stuart family.

XI

THE RITES OF MISRAIM AND MEMPHIS

418. Anomalies of the Rite of Misraim - Another of those diversities, which may be called the constant attendants of the life of vast associations, is the rite of "Misraim," so called from its falsely pretending to trace its origin back to the Egyptian King Menes, or Misraim. What chiefly distinguishes it from other rites, and renders it totally different from masonic institutions, is the supreme power given to the heads, whose irremovability we have seen abolished, in order to open the lodges to the forms of genuine democracy. This rite is essentially autocratic. One man, with the title of "Absolute Sovereign Grand Master," rules the lodges, and is irresponsible an extraordinary anomaly in the bosom of a liberal society to behold a member claiming that very absolute power against which Freemasonry has been fighting for centuries !

419. Organisation - The rite of Misraim was founded by Cagliostro at a time when there was already a question of even further reducing the number of the Scotch rite of thirty-three degrees, practically reduced to five. Then arose the rite of Misraim with ninety degrees, arranged in four sections, viz.: I. Symbolic; 2. Philosophic; 3. Mystical; 4. Cabalistic; which were divided into seventeen classes. The rites are a medley of Scotch rites, Martinism, and Templarism, and the absolute Grand Masters arrogate to themselves the right of governing all masonic lodges throughout the world. The foundations of this system were laid at Milan in 1805, by several Masons who had been refused admission into the Supreme Grand Council. During the first year and for some time after postulants were only admitted as far as the 87th degree; the other three, complementing the system, embraced the unknown superiors. Jews are the chief supporters of this rite. To show its character, details of some of the degrees are here given.

420. History and Constitution - From Milan, the Order spread into

Dalmatia, the Ionian Islands, and the Neapolitan territory, where it produced a total reform in a chapter of Rosicrucians, the "Concordia," established in the Abruzzi. It was not till 1814 that the rite of Misraim was introduced into France, where the pompous denominations of its endless hierarchy met with no slight success. Never had such titles been heard of in Masonry: Supreme Commander of the Stars, Sovereign of Sovereigns, Most High and Most Powerful Knight of the Rainbow, Sovereign Grand Prince Hiram, Sovereign Grand Princes, &c.; these were some of the titles assumed by the members. The trials of initiation were long and difficult, and founded on what is recorded of the Egyptian and Eleusinian mysteries. In the first two sections the founders of the rite seem to have attempted to bring together all the creeds and practices of Scotch Masonry combined with the mysteries of Egypt; and in the last two sections all the chemical and cabalistic knowledge professed by the priests of that country, reserving for the last three degrees the supreme direction of the Order. Attempts were made to introduce it into Belgium, Sweden, and Switzerland, and also into Ireland, and latterly into England; but everywhere it is in a languishing condition. The Grand Orient of France has never recognised the rite as a part of Masonry, though it has three lodges in Paris.

421. Rites and Ceremonies - The Order celebrates two equinoctial festivals, the one called "The Reawakening of Nature," and the other, "The Repose of Nature." In the 69th degree, designated as "Knight of Khanuka, called Hynaroth," particular instructions are given as to man's relation to the Deity, and the cabalistic mediation of the angels. The Supreme Council of the 8th degree has three apartments: the first is draped in black, representing chaos, and lighted up with one light only. The second apartment has three lights, and its walls are hung with green, typifying hope. The third apartment has seventy-two lights, with a transparency showing the word Jehovah over the throne, and another similar one over the entrance door, all symbolising the zodiac and the sun. The sign is raising both hands towards heaven; the grip consists in crossing the hands, and the passwords are: I am We are;

Nature Truth. In the 88th degree the hall of reception is oval, and hung with seagreen. The 89th degree has the password Lux ex tenebris; and the 90th degree holds its meetings in a circular room, and its password is Sophia, or Wisdom; its sacred word is Isis, to which the answer is Osiris. In this rite, altogether modern, we meet with gnostic and cabalistic words and conceits a phenomenon which were impossible did not gnostic ideas permeate all the veins of the masonic body.

422. Rite of Memphis. It is a copy of the rite of Misraim, and was founded at Paris in 1839, and afterwards extended to Brussels and Marseilles. It was composed of ninety-one degrees, arranged in three sections and seven classes. A large volume printed at Paris, with the ambitious title of "The Sanctuary," gives an account of all the sections and their scope. The first section teaches morality, and explains the symbols; the second instructs in physical science, the philosophy of history, and explains the poetical myths of antiquity, its scope being to promote the study of causes and origins. The third and last section exhausts the story of the Order, and is occupied with high philosophy, studying the religious myth at the different epochs of mankind.

XII

MODERN KNIGHTS TEMPLARS

423. Origin - We read that several lords of the Court of Louis XIV., including the Duke de Gramont, the Marquis of Biran, and Count Tallard, formed a secret society, whose object was pleasure. The society increased. Louis XIV., having been made acquainted with its statutes, banished the members of the Order, whose denomination was, "A slight Resurrection of the Templars." In 1705, Philip Duke of Orleans collected the remaining members of the society that had renounced its first scope to cultivate politics. A Jesuit father, Bonanni, a learned rogue, fabricated the famous list of supposititious Grand Masters of the Temple since Molay, beginning with his immediate successor, Larmenius. No imposture was ever sustained with greater sagacity. The document offered all the requisite characteristics of authenticity, and was calculated to deceive the most experienced palseologist. Its object was to connect the new institution with the ancient Templars. To render the deception more perfect, the volume containing the false list was filled with minutes of deliberations at fictitious meetings under false dates. Two members were even sent to Lisbon to obtain, if possible, a document of legitimacy from the " Knights of Christ," an Order founded on the ruins of the Order of the Temple. The deputies, however, were unmasked, and very badly received one had to take refuge in England, the other was transported to Africa, where he died.

424. Revival of the Order - But the society was not discouraged; it grew, and was probably the same that concealed itself before the outbreak of the Revolution under the vulgar name of the Society of the Bull's Head, and whose members were dispersed in 1792. At that period the Duke of CosseBrissac was Grand Master. When on his way to Versailles with other prisoners, there to undergo their trial, he was massacred, and Ledru, his physician, obtained possession of the charter of Larmenius and the MS. statutes of 1705. These documents suggested to him the idea of reviving the Order; Fabre -Palaprat, a

Freemason, was chosen Grand Master. Every effort was made to create a belief in the genuineness of the Order. The brothers Fabre, Arnal, and Leblond hunted up relics. The shops of antiquaries supplied the sword, mitre, and helmet of Molay, and the faithful were shown his bones, withdrawn from the funeral pyre on which he had been burned. As in the Middle Ages, the society exacted that aspirants should be of noble birth; such as were not were ennobled by the society. Fourteen honest citizens of Troyes on one occasion received patents of nobility and convincing coats of arms. During the Revolution the Order was dissolved, but partly restored during the Directorate. After the establishment of the Empire the members re-elected Dr. Fabre de Palaprat; Napoleon favoured the Order, because it promoted community between his new nobility and the members of the old aristocracy. Under the Restoration the liberal tendencies of the Order rendered it suspect, and at the instigation of the Jesuits the Grand Master was repeatedly sent to prison. To restore the Order to its original purpose fighting the infidels the members endeavoured to obtain an island in the Mediterranean; Sir Sidney Smith, later on, wanted to make it the means of suppressing piracy along the African coast.

425. The Leviticon - The society was at first catholic, apostolic, Roman, and rejected Protestants; but Fabre suddenly gave it an opposite tendency. Having acquired a Greek MS. of the fifteenth century, containing the Gospel of St. John, with readings somewhat differing from the received version, preceded by a kind of introduction or commentary, called "Leviticon," he determined, towards 1815, to apply its doctrines to the society governed by him, and thus to transform an association, hitherto quite orthodox, into a schismatic sect. This Leviticon is nothing but the wellknown work with the same title by the Greek monk, Nicephorus. He, having been initiated into the mysteries of the Sufites, who to this day, in the bosom of Mohammedanism preserve the dismal doctrines of the Ishmaelites of the lodge of Cairo (141), attempted to introduce these ideas into Christianity, and for that purpose wrote the "Leviticon," which became

the Bible of a small number of sectaries; but persecution put an end to them. This singular MS. was translated into French in 1822, and printed, with modifications and interpolations, by Palaprat himself. This publication was the cause of a schism in the Order of the Temple. Those knights that adopted its doctrines made them the basis of a new liturgy, which they rendered public in 1833 in a kind of Johannite church called the Temple, and consecrated with great pomp; a society of Ladies of the Temple was also formed at the same time.

426. Ceremonies of Initiation - The lodges in this degree are called encampments, and the officers take their names from those that managed the original institution of the Knights Templars. The penal signs are the chin and beard sign and the saw sign. The grand sign is indicative of the death of Christ on the cross. There is a word, a grip, and passwords, which vary. The knights, who are always addressed as "Sir Knights," wear knightly costume, not omitting the sword. The candidate for installation is "got up" as a pilgrim, with sandals, mantle, staff, cross, scrip, and wallet, a belt or cord round his waist, and in some encampments a burden on his back, which is made to fall off at the sight of the cross. On his approach, an alarm is sounded with a trumpet, and after a deal of pseudo-military parley he is admitted, and a -saw is applied to his forehead by the second captain, whilst all the Sir Knights are under arms. The candidate, being prompted by the master of the ceremonies, declares that he is a weary pilgrim, prepared to devote his life to the service of the poor and sick, and to protect the holy sepulchre. After perambulating the encampment seven times he repeats the oath, having first put away the pilgrim's staff and cross and taken up a sword. In this oath he swears to defend the sepulchre of our Lord Jesus Christ against all Jews, Turks, infidels, heathens, and other opposers of the Gospel. " If ever I wilfully violate this my solemn compact," he continues, " as a Brother Knight Templar, may my skull be sawn asunder with a rough saw, my brains taken out and put in a charger to be consumed by the scorching sun, and my skull in another charger, in commemoration of St. John of Jerusalem, that first faithful soldier and martyr of our Lord and Saviour. Furthermore, may the soul

that once inhabited this skull appear against me in the day of judgment. So help me God." A lighted taper is afterwards put into his hand, and he circumambulates the encampment five times "in solemn meditation"; and then kneeling down is dubbed knight by the grand commander, who says, " I hereby instal you a masonic knight hospitaller of St. John of Jerusalem, Palestine, Rhodes, and Malta, and also a Knight Templar." The grand commander next clothes him with the mantle, and invests him with the apron, sash, and jewel, and presents him with sword and shield. He then teaches him the so-called Mediterranean password and sign. The motto of the Knight Templar is, In hoc signo vinces. In England the encampment of Baldwin, which was established at Bristol by the Templars who returned with Richard I. from Palestine, still continues to hold its regular meetings, and is believed to have preserved the ancient costume and ceremonies of the Order. There is another encampment at Bath, and a third at York, from which three emanated all the other encampments in Great Britain and America. In some of the encampments the following is the concluding part of the ceremony: One of the equerries dressed as a cook, with a white nightcap and apron and a large kitchen knife in his hand, suddenly rushes in, and, kneeling on one knee before the new Sir Knight, says, " Sir Knight, I admonish you to be just, honourable, and faithful to the Order, or I, the cook, will hack your spurs from off your heels with my kitchen knife."

XIII

FREEMASONRY IN ENGLAND AND SCOTLAND

427. Freemasonry in England - The authentic history of Freemasonry, i.e. operative Masonry, in England dates from Athelstan, from whom his brother Edwin obtained a royal charter for the Masons, by which they were empowered to meet annually in a general assembly, and to have the right to regulate their own Order. And, according to this charter, the first Grand Lodge of England met at York in 926, when all the writings and records extant, in Greek, Latin, French, and other languages, were collected; and constitutions and charges in conformity with ancient usages, so far as they could be gathered therefrom, were drawn up and adopted. The Old York Masons were on that account held in especial respect, and Blue or genuine Masonry is still distinguished by the title of the York rite. After the decease of Edwin, Athelstan himself presided over the lodges; and after his death, the Masons in England were governed by Dunstan, Archbishop of Canterbury in 960, and Edward the Confessor in 1041. Down to the present time the grand masters have been persons of royal blood, sometimes the king himself. Till the beginning of the last century, as already stated (390), they were operative masons, and the monuments of their activity are still found all over the land in abbeys, monasteries, cathedrals, hospitals, and other buildings of note. There were, indeed, periods when the Order was persecuted by the State, but these were neither so frequent nor so long as in other countries.

428. Freemasonry in Scotland - Tradition says that on the destruction of the Order of Templars, many of its members took refuge in Scotland, where they incorporated themselves with the Freemasons, under the protection of Robert Bruce, who established the chief seat of the Order at Kilwinning. There is a degree of Prince of Rose-Croix de Heroden, or Herddom, as it is called in French. This Heroden, says an old MS. of the ancient Scotch rite, is a mountain situated in the north-west of Scotland, where the fugitive Knights Templars found a safe

retreat; and the modern Order of Rose-Croix claims the kingdom of Scotland and Abbey of Kilwinning as having once been its chief seat of government. By some writers, however, it is asserted that the word Heredom is simply a corruption of the Latin expression hæredium, signifying "an heritage," and alludes to the castle of St. Germain, the residence of Charles Stuart the Pretender, to further whose restoration the Order of Rose-Croix was invented. The subject is in a state of inextricable confusion, but scarcely worth the trouble of elucidation. King Robert Bruce endeavoured, like other princes before and after him, to secure for himself the supreme direction of those associations, which, though not hostile to the reigning power, could by their organisation become the foci of danger. It is the common opinion that this king reserved for himself and his successors the rank of grand master of the whole Order, and especially of the lodge of Heredom, which was afterwards transferred to Edinburgh.

429. Modern Freemasonry - At the beginning of the last century the operative period of Masonry may be said to have come to an end. In 1716, there being then only four lodges existing in London, a proposition was made and agreed to that the privilege of Masonry should no longer be restricted to operative masons we have seen that it had ere then been broken through (389) but should extend to men of various professions, provided they were regularly initiated into the Order. Thus began the present era of Masonry, retaining the original constitutions, the ancient landmarks, symbols, and ceremonies. The society, proclaiming brotherly love, relief, and truth as their guiding principles, obtained a wider field for their operations, and more freedom in their mode of action. But to what does this action amount? To eating, drinking, and mummery. There is nothing in the history of modern Masonry, in this country at least, that deserves to be recorded. The petty squabbles between Lodges and Orders may help to fill masonic newspapers, but for the world at large they have no interest; and as to any useful knowledge to be propagated by Masons, that is pure delusion. Yet, considering that the Order reckons its members by hundreds of thousands, its pretensions and present condition and

prospects merit some consideration; and it must be admitted that its charities, in England at least, are administered on a somewhat munificent scale. In that respect honour is due to the English craft. And Masons, at all events French Masons, object to their association being called a "Benevolent Society," for when in 1861 M. de Persigny qualified them as such, the Masons protested against it, saying that their charities were the outcome, and not the object, of their meetings. Moreover, their benevolence is not commensurate with their diffusion, and on the Continent is controlled by political considerations; thus the lodge Philadelphia, at Verviers, in 1874, declined to subscribe to the Red Cross Association, because in the Spanish war their succour would be extended to Carlists as well as to the Constitutionals.

XIV

FREEMASONRY IN FRANCE

430. Introduction into France - Freemasonry was introduced into France by the partisans of James and the Pretender, as a possible means of reseating the Stuart family on the English throne. Not satisfied with turning masonic rites to unforeseen and illegitimate uses, new degrees were added to those already existing, such as those of "Irish Master," "Perfect Irish Master," and "Puissant Irish Master," and by promises of the revelation of great secrets, and leading them to believe that Freemasons were the successors of the Knights Templars, the nobility of the kingdom were attracted towards the Order, and liberally supported it with their means and influence. The first lodge established in France was that of Dunkirk (1721), under the title of "Friendship and Fraternity." The second, whose name has not been handed down, was founded in Paris in 1725 by Lord Derwentwater. Other followers of the Pretender established other lodges, of all which Lord Derwentwater was the grand master, until that nobleman lost his life for his devotion to the cause of the Stuarts in 1746.

431. Chevalier Ramsay - The Chevalier Ramsay, also a devoted adherent of the house of Stuart, endeavoured more effectually to carry out the views of his predecessors, and in 1730 attempted in London to lay the basis of a masonic reform, according to which the masonic legend referred to the violent death of Charles I., while Cromwell and his partisans represented the assassins to be condemned in the lodge. He therefore proposed to the Grand Lodge of England to substitute in the place of the first three degrees those of Scotch Mason, Novice, and Knight of the Temple, which he pretended to be the only true and ancient ones, having their administrative centre in the Lodge of St. Andrew at Edinburgh. But the Grand Lodge at once rejected his views, whose objects it perceived. Ramsay went to Paris, where he met with great success. His system gave rise to those higher degrees which have since then been known by the name of the Ancient Scotch rite. Many

of these innovations made up for their want of consistency with masonic traditions by splendour of external decorations and gorgeousness of ceremonies. But the hautes grades of the French, and the philosophic degrees of the Ancient Scotch rite, are not innovations, but illustrations of pure symbolic Masonry.

432. Philosophical Rites - Philosophy indeed began to insinuate itself into Masonry, simplifying the rites and purifying its doctrines. Among the philosophic degrees then introduced, that of the "Knights of the Sun " is noteworthy. Its declared scope was to advocate natural, in opposition to revealed, religion. There is but one light in the lodge, which shines from behind a globe of water, to represent the sun. It has some resemblance to the "Sublime Knight Elected." But, on the other hand, by these innovations systems multiplied, and the Order served as a pretext and defence of institutions having no connection with Masonry. Cabala, magic, conjuration, divination, alchemy, and demonology were taught in the lodges. These abuses led to the establishment of an administrative centre at Arras in 1747. Another was founded at Marseilles in 1751. Three years afterwards the Chevalier de Bonneville founded in Paris a chapter of the high degrees, with the title, afterwards become famous, of the " Chapter of Clermont," and lodged it in a sumptuous palace built by him in a suburb of Paris. The system adopted was to some extent that of Ramsay. Another chapter, in opposition to his, was founded in 1762, with the title of "Council of the Knights of the East." In 1766, the Baron Tschudy founded the Order of the "Blazing Star," in which ideas derived from the Temple and the Jesuits were strangely intermingled.

433. The Duke de Chartres - Freemasonry in France was not without influence on the Revolution. The Duke de Chartres having been elected grand master, all the lodges were united under the Grand Orient; hence the immense influence he afterwards wielded. The mode of his initiation is thus related: Before becoming grand master he was received into the degree of Knight of Kadosh. Five brethren introduced

him into a hall, representing a grotto strewn with human bones, and lighted up with sepulchral lamps. In one of the angles was a lay figure covered with royal insignia. The introducers bade him lie down on the ground like one dead, naming the degrees through which he had already passed, and repeating the former oaths. Afterwards, they extolled the degree into which he was about to be received. Having bidden him to rise, he was made to ascend a high ladder, and to throw himself from the top. Having then armed him with a dagger, they commanded him to strike the crowned figure, and a liquid resembling blood spurted from the wound over his hands and clothes. He was then told to cut off the head of the figure. Finally, he was informed that the bones with which the cave was strewn came from the body of James Molay, Grand Master of the Order of the Temple, and that the man whom he had stabbed was Philip the Fair, King of France. The Grand Orient was established in a mansion formerly belonging to the Jesuits in Paris, and became a revolutionary centre. The share the Grand Orient, the tool of the Duke de Chartres, took in the events of the French Revolution is matter of public history.

XV

THE CHAPTER OF CLERMONT AND THE STRICT OBSERVANCE

434. Jesuitical Influence - Catholic ceremonies, unknown in ancient Freemasonry, were introduced from 1735 to 1740, in the Chapter of Clermont, so called in honour of Louis of Bourbon, Prince of Clermont, at the time grand master of the Order in France. From that time, the influence of the Jesuits on the fraternity made itself more and more felt. The candidate was no longer received in a lodge, but in the city of Jerusalem; not the ideal Jerusalem, but a clerical Jerusalem, typifying Rome. The meetings were called Capitula Canonicorum, and a monkish language and asceticism prevailed therein. In the statutes is seen the hand of James Lainez, the second general of the Jesuits, and the aim at universal empire betrays itself, for at the reception of the sublime knights the last two chapters of the Apocalypse are read to the candidate a glowing picture of that universal monarchy which the Jesuits hoped to establish. The sect spread very rapidly, for when Baron Hund came to Paris in 1742, and was received into the highest Jesuit degrees he found on his return to Germany that those degrees were already established in Saxony and Thuringia, under the government of Marshall, whose labours he undertook to promote.

435. The Strict Observance - From the exertions of these two men arose the "Rite of Strict Observance," so called, because Baron Hund introduced into it a perfectly monkish subordination, and which seemed also for a time intended to favour the tragic hopes of the house of Stuart; for Marshall, having visited Paris in 1741, there entered into close connection with Eamsay and the other adherents of the exiled family. To further this object, Hund mixed up with the rites of Clermont what was known or supposed to be known of the statutes of the Templars, and acting in concert with Marshall, overran Germany with a sect of new Templars, not to be confounded with the Templars that afterwards joined the masonic fraternity. But Hund seems after all

to have rendered no real services to the Stuarts; though when Charles Edward visited Germany, the sectaries received him in the most gallant manner, promising him the most extensive support, and asking of him titles and estates in a kingdom which he had yet to conquer. Thus he was brought to that state of mental intoxication which afterwards led him to make an absurd entry into Rome, preceded by heralds, who proclaimed him king. Hund seems, in the sad story of the Stuarts, to have acted the part of a speculator; and the rite of the Strict Observance, permeated by the Jesuitical leaven, had probably an aim very different from the re-establishment of the proscribed dynasty. It is certain that at one time the power of the New Templars was very great, and prepared the way for the Illuminati.

XVI

THE RELAXED OBSERVANCE

436. Organisation of Relaxed Observance - In 1767, there arose at Vienna a schism of the Strict Observance; the dissentients, who called themselves "Clerks of the Relaxed Observance " the nickname of Relaxed Observance had originally been applied by the members of the Strict Observance, as a term of contempt to all other rites declaring that they alone possessed the secrets of the association, and knew the place where were deposited the splendid treasures of the Templars. They also claimed precedence, not only over the rite of Strict Observance, but also over all Masonry. Their promises and instructions revolved around the philosopher's stone, the government of spirits, and the millennium. To be initiated it was necessary to be a Roman Catholic, and to have passed through all the degrees of the Strict Observance. The members knew only their immediate heads; but Doctor Stark, of Konigsberg, a famous preacher, and Baron Raven, of Mecklenburg, were well-known chiefs of the association.

437. Disputes in German Lodges - Before the establishment of the Strict Observance, various German lodges had already introduced the Templar system; hence disputes of all kinds arose, and a convention was held at Brunswick on 22nd May 1775 to arrange the differences. Dr. Stark presented himself; he was a disciple of Schropfer and of Gugumos, who called himself high- priest, knight, prince, possessor of the philosopher's stone, of the secret to evoke the spirits of the dead, &c. Stark declared to the members of the convention that he was called Archimedes ab aquila fulva, that he was chancellor of the Grand Chapter of Scotland, and had been invited by the brethren of that supreme body to instruct them in the true principles of the Order. But when he was asked to produce his credentials, he refused. The Brunswickers, however, thinking that the brethren of Aberdeen might possess some secrets, sent a deputation thither; but the good folks of Aberdeen knew even less than their German friends, for they knew only

the first three degrees. Stark, though found out, was not to be put down, but wrote a book entitled "The Coping Stone," in which he represented the Strict Observance as hostile to religion, society, and the state.

438. Rite of Zinzendorf - This was not the first attack made on the system of Hund. In 1766, Count Zinzendorf, chief physician in the Prussian army, who had been received into the Strict Observance, was struck from the list of members of the lodge of the Three Globes. In revenge, he founded at Berlin and Potsdam lodges on the Templar system, which, however, he soon abandoned, and composed a new rite, invented by himself, and consisting of seven degrees, which was protected by Frederick the Great. The new Order made fierce and successful war both on the Strict and the Relaxed Observance.

439. African Architects - About 1765, Brother Von Kopper instituted in Prussia, under the auspices of Frederick II., the Order of "African Architects," who occupied themselves with historical researches, mixing up therewith masonry and chivalry. The order was divided into eleven degrees. They erected a vast building, which contained a large library, a museum of natural history, and a chemical laboratory. Until 1786, when it was dissolved, the society awarded every year a gold medal with fifty ducats to the author of the best memoir on the history of Masonry. This was one of the few rational masonic societies. The African Architects did not esteem decorations, aprons, collars, jewels, &c. In their assemblies they read essays, and communicated the results of their researches. At their simple and decorous banquets, instructive and scientific discourses were delivered. While their initiations were gratuitous, they gave liberal assistance to zealous but needy brethren. They published many important works on Freemasonry.

XVII

THE CONGRESS OF WILHELMSBAD

440. Various Congresses - To put an end to the numerous disputes raging among masonic bodies, various congresses were held. In 1778, a congress was convened at Lyons; it lasted a month, but was without result. In 1785, another was held at Paris, but the time was wasted in idle disputes with Cagliostro. The most important was that which assembled at Wilhelmsbad in 1782, under the presidency of the Duke of Brunswick, who was anxious to end the discord reigning among German Freemasons. It was attended by Masons from Europe, America, and Asia. From an approximative estimate, it appears that there were then upwards of three millions of Masons in the different parts of the globe.

441. Discussions at Wilhelmsbad - The statements contained in Dr. Stark's book, " The Coping Stone " (437), concerning the influence of the Jesuits in the masonic body, formed one of the chief topics discussed. Some of the chiefs of the Strict Observance produced considerable confusion by being unable to give information concerning the secrets of the high degrees, which they had professed to know; or to render an account of large sums they had received on behalf of the Order. The main point was to settle whether Masonry was to be considered as a continuation of the Order of the Templars, and whether the secrets of the sect were to be sought for in the modern Templar degrees. After thirty sittings, the answer was in the negative; the chiefs of the Strict Observance were defeated, and the Duke of Brunswick suspended the Order for three years, from which blow it never recovered. The Swedes professed to possess all the secrets; the Duke of Brunswick hastened to Upsala to learn them, but found that the Swedes knew no more than the Germans; whence new dissensions arose between the Masons of the two nations.

442. Result of Convention - The result of the convention of

Wilhelmsbad was the retention of the three symbolical degrees, with the addition of a new degree, that of the "Knights of Beneficence," which was based on the principles enunciated in St. Martin's book, Des Erreurs et de la Verite, and the Tableau Naturel. The foundation of the new Order was attributed to the influence of the Jesuits, because the three initial letters of Chevaliers Bienfaisants, C.H.B., are equal to 3, 8, 2= 13, signifying the letter N, meaning Nostri. Another result was a league between Masonry and the Illuminati and it is still a matter of speculation whether these latter were not behind the Jesuits brought about by the exertions of Spartacus or Weishaupt, who had long ago discerned the influence he could obtain by the co-operation of the Masons, whom he, of course, employed as his unconscious tools. But Jesuitical influence, at that time, was too powerful to be overcome; they sided with, and thus strengthened the influence of, the duke; hence the opposition of Germany to the principles of the French Revolution, which broke out soon after an opposition which was like discharging a rocket against a thunderbolt, but which was carried to its height by the manifesto of the Duke of Brunswick, so loudly praised by courtly historians, and of which the German princes made such good use as to induce the German confederacy to surround France with a fiery line of deluded patriotism. Freemasonry had been made the tool of prince- and priest-craft, though occasionally it turned the tables on the prince, an instance of which is recorded in the next paragraph.

443. Frederick William III. and the Masons - The sudden retreat of the King of Prussia of this name, after having invaded France in 1792, has never been satisfactorily explained. Dr. E. E. Eckert, in his "Magazine of Evidence for the Condemnation of the Masonic Order," writes as follows, quoting from a private letter from M. V __z, of Paris, to Baron von S z, at Vienna, which he qualifies as "thoroughly reliable": "The King of Prussia had crossed our frontiers; he was I believe, at Verdun or Thionville. One evening a confidential attendant gave him the masonic sign, and took him into a subterranean vault, where he left him alone. By the light of the lamps illuminating the room, the king saw his ancestor, Frederick the Great, approaching him. There could be

no mistake as to his voice, dress, gait, features. The spirit reproached the king with his alliance with Austria against France, and commanded him immediately to withdraw therefrom. You know that the king acted accordingly, to the great disgust of his allies, to whom he did not communicate the reasons of his withdrawal. Some years afterwards our celebrated actor Fleury, who acquired such reputation by his performance at the Thédtre Frangais in "The Two Pages", in which piece he represented Frederick the Great to perfection, confessed that he acted the ghost when Frederick William III. was mystified by an appearance, which had been planned by General Dumouriez." Dumouriez was a Freemason.

XVIII

MASONRY AND NAPOLEONISM

444. Masonry protected by Napoleon - "With renewed court frivolities and military pomp, the theatrical spirit of Masonry revived. The institution, so active before and during the Involution, because it was governed by men who rightly understood and worthily represented its principles, during the Empire fell into academic puerilities, servile compliance, and endless squabbles. That period, which masonic writers, attached to the latter and pleased with its apparent splendour, call the most flourishing of French Masonry, in the eyes of independent judges appears as the least important and the least honourable for the masonic order. Napoleon at first intended to suppress Freemasonry, in which the dreaded ideologists might easily find a refuge. The representative system of the Grand Orient clashed with his monarchical principles, and the oligarchy of the Scotch rite aroused his suspicions. The Parisian lodges, however, practised in the art of flattery, prostrated themselves before the First Consul, prostrated themselves before the Emperor, and sued for grace. The suspicions of Napoleon were not dissipated; but he perceived the policy of avoiding violent measures, and of disciplining a body that might turn against The lodges were inundated with the lowest police agents, who rapidly attained the highest degrees, and seized at the very outset the clue of any political intrigue which might be concocted there. Napoleon, after considerable hesitation, declared in favour of the Grand Orient, and the Scotch rite had to assume the second place. A single word Of Napoleon had done more to establish peace between them than all former machinations. The Grand Orient became a court office, and Masonry an army of employe's. The Grand Mastership was offered to Joseph Napoleon, who accepted it though never initiated into Freemasonry, with the consent his brother, who, however, for greater security, insisted on having his trusty arch-chancellor Carnbace"res appointed Grand Master Adjunct, to be in reality the only head of the Order. Gradually all the rites existing in France gave in their adhesion

to the imperial policy, electing Cambace'res as their chief dignitary, so that he eventually possessed more masonic titles than any other man before or after him. In 1805 he was made Grand Master Adjunct of the Grand Orient; in 1806, Sovereign Grand Master of the Supreme Grand Council; in the same year, Grand Master of the rite of Heroden of Kilwinning; in 1807, Supreme Head of the French rite; in the same year, Grand Master of the Philosophic Scotch rite; in 1808, Grand Master of the Order of Christ; in 1809, National Grand Master of the Knights of the Holy City; in the same year, Protector of the High Philosophic Degrees. As every new lodge established in France had to pay the grand master a heavy fee, Masonry yielded to him an annual revenue of two millions of francs.

445. Spread of Freemasonry - But masonic disputes soon again ran high. The arch-chancellor, accustomed and attached to the usages and pomps of courts, secretly gave the preference to the Scotch rite, with its high-sounding titles and gorgeous ceremonies. The Grand Orient carried its complaints even to Napoleon, who grew weary of these paltry farces he who planned grand dramas; and at one time he had determined on abolishing the Order altogether, but Carnbaceres succeeded in arresting his purpose, showing him the dangers that might ensue from its suppression dangers which must have appeared great, since Napoleon, who never hesitated, hesitated then, and allowed another to alter his views. Perhaps he recognised the necessity in French society of a body of men who were free at least in appearance, of a kind of political safety-valve. The French had taken a liking to their lodges, where they found a phantom of independence, and might consider themselves on neutral ground, so that a masonic writer could say: " In the bosom of Masonry there circulates a little of that vital air so necessary to generous minds." The Scotch rite, secretly protected, spread throughout the French departments and foreign countries, and whilst the Grand Orient tried to suppress it, and to prevent innovations, elected a "Director of Rites," the Supreme Grand Council established itself at Milan, and elected Prince Eugene Grand Master of the Grand Orient of Italy. The two highest masonic authorities, which

yet had the same master in Cambace'res, and the same patron in Napoleon, continued to combat each other with as much fury as was shown in the struggle between France and England. But having no public life, no parliamentary debates, no opposition journals, the greater part of the population took refuge in the lodges, and every small town had its own. In 1812, there existed one thousand and eighty-nine lodges, all depending on the Grand Orient; the army had sixty-nine, and the lodge was opened and closed with the cry, Vive l'Empereur!

446. The Clover Leaves - This was an Order founded in Germany about 1808 by John de Witt, called Von Dorring (555), a member of almost every secret society then existing, embracing some of the greatest German statesmen, to further the plans of Napoleon, in the hope that his successes might lead to the mediatisation of all German states, which, with France, were to form but one empire. The name was derived from the fact that three members only were known to one another.

447. Obsequiousness of Freemasonry - Napoleon, unable and unwilling to suppress Freemasonry, employed it in the army, in the newly-occupied territories, and in such as he intended to occupy. Imperial proselytism turned the lodges into schools of Napoleonism. But one section of Masonry, under the shadow of that protection, became the very contrary, anti-Napoleonic; and not all the lodges closed their accustomed labours with the cry of Vive l'Empereur! It is, however, quite certain that Napoleon by means of the masonic society facilitated or secured his conquests. Spain, Germany, and Italy were covered with lodges antechambers, more than any others, of prefectures and military command presided over and governed by soldiers. The highest dignitaries of Masonry at that period were marshals, knights of the Legion of Honour, nobles of ancient descent, senators, councillors, all safe and trusty persons; a state that obeyed the orders of Cambaceres, as he obeyed the orders of Napoleon. Obsequiousness came near to the ridiculous. The half-yearly words of command of the

Grand Orient retrace the history of Napoleonic progress. In 1800, "Science and Peace"; in 1802, after Marengo, "Unity and Success"; in 1804, after the coronation, "Contentment and Greatness"; after the battle of Friedland, "Emperor and Confidence"; after the suppression of the tribune, "Fidelity"; at the birth of the King of Rome, "Posterity and Joy"; at the departure of the army for Russia, "Victory and Return" terrible victory, and unfortunate return !

448. Anti- Napoleonic Freemasonry - Napoleon, we have seen, made a league with Freemasonry to obtain its support. He is also said to have made certain promises to it; but as he failed to keep them, the Masons turned against him, and had a large share in his fall. This, however, is not very probable, and is attributing too much influence to an Order which had only recently recovered itself. Still, the anti-Napoleonic leaven fermented in the Masonic society. Savary, the minister of police, was aware of it in 1810, and wanted to apply to the secret meetings of Freemasons the article of the penal code, forbidding them; but Cambace'res once more saved the institution, which saved neither him nor his patron. Freemasonry, if not by overt acts, at least by its indifference, helped on the downfall of Napoleon. But it was not altogether inactive, for even whilst the Napoleonic star illumined almost alone the political heavens of Europe, a Masonic lodge was formed whose object was the restoration of the Bourbons, whose action may be proved by official documents to have extended through the French army, and led to the seditious movements of 1813.

XIX

FREEMASONRY, THE RESTORATION AND THE SECOND EMPIRE

449. The Society of "France Regenerated" - The Restoration, whose blindness was only equalled by its mediocrity which, unable to create, proposed to itself to destroy what even time respects, the memories and glories of a people could not please Freemasonry much. Hostile to Napoleon in his last years, it could not approve of the conduct of the new government. At all events, the Freemasons held aloof y though cynics might suggest that this was done with a view of exacting better terms. In the meanwhile, a society was formed in Paris, which, assuming masonic forms and the title of " France Regenerated," became an instrument of espionage and revenge in the hands of the new despot. But the very government in whose favour it acted, found it necessary within a year from its foundation silently to suppress it; for it found the rabid zeal of these adherents to be more injurious to its interests than the open opposition of itsavowed enemies.

450. Priestly Opposition to Masonry - The Masonic propaganda, however, was actively carried on. The priests, on their part, considered the moment come for inaugurating an anti-masonic crusade. Under Napoleon the priesthood could not breathe; the court was closed against it, except on grand occasions, when its presence was needed to add outward pomp to imperial successes. As the masters of ceremonies, the priests had ceased in France to be the councillors and confessors of its rulers; but now they reassumed those functions, and the Masons were at once recommended to the hatred of the king and the mistrust of the public. They were represented as abettors of rationalism and regicide; the consequence was, that a great many lodges were closed, though, on the other hand, the rite of Misraim was established in Paris in 1816, whose mother lodge was called the " Rainbow," a presage of serenity and calm, which, however, did not save the society from police persecution. In 1821, this lodge was closed, and not reopened till

1830. Towards the same time was founded the lodge of "Trinosophists." In 1821, the Supreme Grand Council rose to the surface again, and with it the disputes between it and the Grand Orient. To enter into their squabbles would be a sad waste of time, and I therefore pass them over.

451. Political Insignificance of Masonry - The Freemasons are said to have brought about the July revolution of 1830, but proofs are wanting, and I think they may be absolved from that charge. Louis-Philippe, who was placed on the throne by that revolution, took the Order under his protection, and appointed his son, the Duke of Orleans, Grand Master. On the Duke's death, in 1842, his brother, the Duke de Nemours, succeeded him in the dignity. In this latter year, the disputes between the Grand Orient and the Supreme Grand Council were amicably settled. Again we are told that at a masonic congress held at Strasburg the foundations of the revolution of 1848 were laid. It is certain that Cavaignac, Lamartine, Ledru-Rollin, Prudhon, Louis Blanc, Marrast, Vilain, Pyat, and a great number of German republicans, attended that congress, but for this reason it cannot strictly be called a masonic, it was rather a republican, meeting. On the establishment of the Provisional Government after the revolution of 1848, the Freemasons gave in their adhesion to that government; on which occasion some high-flown speeches about liberty, equality, and fraternity were made, and everybody congratulated his neighbour that now the reign of universal brotherhood had begun. But the restoration of the Empire, which followed soon after, showed how idle all this oratory had been, and how the influence of Masonry in the great affairs of the world really is nil.

452. Freemasonry and Napoleon III - Again the Napoleonic air waves around the Grand Orient. The nephew showed himself from the first as hostile to Freemasonry as his uncle had been; but the decree prohibiting the French lodges from occupying themselves with political questions, under pain of the dissolution of the Order, did not appear until the th September 1850. In January 1852, some superior

members of the Order proposed to offer the dignity of Grand Master to Lucien Murat, the President's cousin. The proposal was unanimously agreed to; and on the 19th of the same month the new Grand Master was acknowledged by all the lodges. He held the office till 1861, when he was obliged to resign in consequence of the masonic body having passed a vote of censure upon him for his expressions in favour of the temporal power of the Pope, uttered in the stormy discussion of the French Senate in the month of June of that year. The Grand Orient was again all in confusion. Napoleon III. now interfered, especially as Prince Napoleon was proposed for the office of Grand Master; which excited the jealousy of the Muratists, who published pamphlets of the most vituperative character against their adversaries, who on their side replied with corresponding bitterness. Napoleon imposed silence on the litigants, prohibited attendance at lodges, promised that he himself would appoint a Grand Master, and advised his cousin to undertake a long voyage to the United States. Deprived of the right of electing its own chief, the autonomy of Freemasonry became an illusion, its programme useless, and its mystery a farce. In the meanwhile, the quarrels of the partisans of the different candidates calmed down; Prince Napoleon returned from America; Murat resigned himself to this defeat, as to others, and the Emperor forgot all about Freemasonry. At last, in January 1862, there appeared a decree appointing Marshal Magnan to be Grand Master. A Marshal! The nephew, in this instance, as in many others, had taken a leaf out of his uncle's book.

453. Jesuitical Manoeuvres - Napoleonic Freemasonry, not entirely to lose its peculiar physiognomy, ventured to change its institutions. Jesuitism cast loving eyes on it, and drew it towards itself, as in the days of the Strict Observance. Murat threw out his net, but was removed just when it was most important for the interests of the Jesuits that he should have remained. He proposed to transform the French lodges of which, in 1852, there were 325, whilst in 1861 only 269 could be found into societies of mutual succour, and to abandon or submit the higher masonic sphere of morality and humanity to the

society, which in these last sixty years has already overcome and incorporated the whole Roman clergy, once its rivals, and by oblique paths also many of the conservative sects of other creeds. Murat did not succeed, but others may; and though the Masons say that Jesuitism shall not succeed, yet, how is Freemasonry, that professes to meddle neither with politics nor religion, to counteract the political and religious machinations of the Jesuits? And even if Freemasonry had the same weapons, are there men among the Order able to wield them with the ability and fearlessness that distinguish the followers of Loyola? I fear not.

Besides, the Masons, though they talk loudly of fraternisation and equality, when driven at bay become the stanchest conservatives, wherefore the International at Lyons, in the year 1870, solemnly excommunicated Freemasonry, and in 1880 exacted from every candidate for admission to the society a declaration that he was not a Mason.

XX

FREEMASONRY IN ITALY

454. Whimsical Masonic Societies - We have but few notices of the early state of Freemasonry in Italy. We are told that in 1512 there was founded at Florence a society under the name of "The Trowel," composed of learned and literary men, who indulged in all kinds of whimsical freaks, and who may have served as prototypes to the Order of "The Monks of the Screw," established towards the end of the last century in Ireland. Thus at one time they would meet in the lodge, dressed as masons and labourers, and begin to erect an edifice with trays full of macaroni and cheese, using spices and bonbons for mortar, and rolls and cakes for stones, and building up the whole with all kinds of comestibles. And thus they went on until a pretended rain put an end to their labours. At another time it was Ceres, who, in search of Proserpine, invited the Brethren of the Trowel to accompany her to the infernal regions. They followed her through the mouth of a serpent into a dark room, and on Pluto inviting them to the feast, lights appeared, and the table was seen to be covered with black, whilst the dishes on it were foul and obscene animals, and bones of dead men, served by devils carrying shovels. Finally all this vanished, and a choice banquet followed. This Society of the Trowel was in existence in 1737. The clergy endeavoured to suppress it, and would no doubt have succeeded, but for the accession of Francis, Duke of Tuscany, who had been initiated in Holland, and who set free all the Freemasons that had been incarcerated, and protected the Order. But the remembrance of that persecution is preserved in the rituals, and in the degree of "Magus," the costume is that of the Holy Office, as other degrees commemorate the inquisitors of Portugal and Spain.

455. Illuminati in Italy - The sect of the Illuminati, of whom Count Filippo Strozzi was a warm partisan, soon after spread through Italy, as well as another Order, affiliated with the Illuminati, mystical and alchymistical, and in opposition to the Rosicrucians, called the "

Initiated Brethren of Asia," which had been founded at Vienna. It only accepted candidates who had passed through the first three degrees of the York rite. Like Egyptian Masonry, it worshipped the Tetragrammaton, and combined the deepest and most philosophical ideas with the most curious superstitions.

456. Freemasonry at Naples - In the kingdom of Naples the Masons amounted to many thousands. An edict of Charles III. (1751), and another of Ferdinand IV. (1759), closed the lodges, but in a short time the edicts became a dead letter, and in vain did the minister, Tanucci, hostile to the institution, seek to revive them. The incident of a neophyte dying a few days after his initiation gave a pretext for fresh persecution. The Masons, assembled at a banquet, were arrested; and in vain did Levy, a lawyer, undertake their defence. He was expelled the kingdom; his book in favour of the Order was publicly burnt by the executioner. But Queen Caroline, having dismissed Tanucci, again sanctioned masonic meetings, for which she received the thanks of the Grand Orient of France. It would seem, however, that in a very few years Freemasonry again had to hide its head, for in 1767 we hear of it as a "secret" society, whose existence has just been discovered. The document which records this discovery puts the number of Freemasons at 64,000, which probably is an exaggeration; still, among so excitable a population as that of Southern Italy, secret societies at all times found plenty of proselytes.

457. Details of Document - The document referred to says: At last the great mine of the Freemasons of Naples is discovered, of whom the name, but not the secret, was known. Two circumstances are alleged by which the discovery was brought about: a dying man revealed all to his confessor, that he should inform the king thereof; a knight, who had been kept in great state by the society, having had his pension withheld, betrayed the Grand Master of the Order to the king. This Grand Master was the Duke of San Severe. The king secretly sent a confidential officer with three dragoons to the duke's mansion, with orders to seize him before he had time to speak to any one, and bring

him to the palace. The order was carried out; but a few minutes after a fire broke out in the duke's mansion, destroying his library, the real object being, as is supposed, to burn all writings having reference to Freemasonry. The fire was extinguished, and the house guarded by troops. The duke having been brought before the king, openly declared the objects, systems, seals r government, and possessions of the Order. He was sent back to his palace, and there guarded by troops, lest he should be killed by his former colleagues. Freemasons have also been discovered at Florence, and the Pope and the Emperor have sent thither twenty-four theologians to put a stop to the disorder. The king acts with the greatest mercy towards all implicated, to avoid the great dangers that might ensue from a contrary course. He has also appointed four persons of great standing to use the best means to destroy so abominable a sect; and has given notice to all the other sovereigns of Europe of his discovery, and the abominable maxims of the sect, calling upon them to assist in its suppression, which it will be folly in them to refuse to do. For the Order does not count its members by thousands, but by millions, especially among Jews and Protestants. Their frightful maxims areonly known to the members of the fifth, sixth, and seventh lodges, while those of the first three know nothing, and those of the fourth act without knowing, what they do. They derive their origin from England, and the founder of the sect was that infamous Cromwell, first bishop, and then lover of Anne Boleyn, and then beheaded for his crimes, called in his day "the scourge of rulers." He left the Order an annual income of 10,000 sterling. It is divided into seven lodges: the members of the seventh are called Assessors; of the sixth, Grand Masters; of the fifth, Architects; of the fourth, Executors (here the secret ends); of the third, Ruricori (!); of the second and first, Novices and Proselytes. Their infamous idea is based on the allegory of the temple of Solomon, considered in its first splendour, and then overthrown by the tyranny of the Assyrians, and finally restored thereby to signify the liberty of man after the creation of the world,, the tyranny of the priesthood, kings, and laws, and the reestablishment of that liberty. Then follow twelve maxims in which these opinions and aims are more fully expounded, from which it appears that they were not very different from those of all other republican and advanced politicians.

458. Freemasonry at Venice - The Freemasons were at first tolerated at Venice, but in 1686 the government suddenly took the alarm, and ordered the closing of all lodges, and banished the members; but the decree was very leniently executed, and a lodge of nobles having refused to obey, the magistrates entered it at a time when they knew no one to be there. The furniture, ornaments, and jewels were carried out and publicly burnt or dispersed, but none of the brethren were in any way molested. A lodge was re-established afterwards, which was discovered in 1785, when all its contents were again burnt or otherwise destroyed. From the ritual, which was found among the other effects, it appears that the candidate for initiation was led, his eyes being bandaged, from street to street, or canal to canal, so as to prevent his tracing the locality, to the Rio Marino, where he was first conducted into a room hung with black, and illumined by a single light; there he was clothed in a longgarment like a winding sheet, but black; he put on a cap something like a turban, and his hair was drawn over his face, and in this elegant figure he was placed before a looking-glass, covered with a black curtain, under which were written the words, " If thou hast true courage, and an honest desire to enter into the Order, draw aside the curtain, and learn to know thyself." He might then remove the bandage and look at himself. He was then again blindfolded, and placed in the middle of the room, while thirty or forty members entered and began to fight with swords. This was to try the candidate's courage, who was himself slightly wounded. The bandage was once more removed, and the wound dressed. Then it was replaced, and the candidate taken to a second apartment, hung with black and white, and having in the middle a bed covered with a black cloth, on the centre of which was a white cross, whilst on either side was represented a white skeleton. The candidate was laid on the bed, the bandage being removed, and he was there left with two tapers, the one white, the other yellow. After having been left there for some time, the brethren entered in a boisterous manner, beating discordant drums. The candidate was to show no sign

of trepidation amidst all these elaborate ceremonies; and then the members embraced him as a brother, and gave him the name by which he was henceforth to be known in the society.

459. Abatement under Napoleon - During the reign of Napoleon I., numerous lodges were founded throughout Italy; and it cannot be denied by the greatest friends of the Order, that during that period Freemasonry cut a most pitiful figure. For a society that always boasted of its independence of, and superiority to, all other earthly governments, to forward addresses such as the following to Napoleon, seems something like self-abasement and self-stultification: "Napoleon! thy philosophy guarantees the toleration of our natural and divine religion. We render thee honour worthy of thee for it, and thou shalt find in us nothing but faithful subjects, ever devoted to thy august person!"

460. The Freemasonry of the Present in Italy - Very little need, or can, be said as regards the active proceedings of Italian masonic lodges of the present day, though they have been reconstituted and united under one or two heads. But their programme deserves attention, as pointing out those reforms, needed not only in Italy, but everywhere where Freemasonry exists. The declared object, then, of Italian Freemasonry is, the highest development of universal philanthropy; the independence and unity of single nations, and fraternity among each other; the toleration of every religion, and absolute equality of worship; the moral and material progress of the masses. It moreover declares itself independent of every government, affirming that Italian Freemasonry will not recognise any other sovereign power on earth but right reason and universal conscience. It further declares and this deserves particular attention that Freemasonry is not to consist in a mysterious symbolism, vain ceremonies, or indefinite aspirations, which cover the Order with ridicule. Again, Masonry being universal, essentially human, it does not occupy itself with forms of government, nor with transitory questions, but with such as are permanent and general. In social reforms abstract theories, founded on mystical aspirations, are to be

avoided. The duty of labour being the most essential in civil society, Freemasonry is opposed to idleness. Religious questions are beyond the pale of Freemasonry. Human conscience is in itself inviolable; it has no concern with any positive religion, but represents religion itself in its essence. Devoted to the principle of fraternity, it preaches universal toleration; comprehends in its ritual many of the symbols of various religions, as in its syncretism it chooses the purest truths. Its creed consists in the worship of the Divine, whose highest conception, withdrawn from every priestly speculation, is that of the Great Architect of the Universe; and in faith in humanity, the sole interpreter of the Divine in the world. As to extrinsic modes of worship, Freemasonry neither imposes nor recommends any, leaving to every one his free choice, until the day, perhaps not far distant, when all men will be capable of worshipping the Infinite in spirit and in truth, without intermediaries and outward forms. And whilst man in his secret relations to the Infinite fecundates the religious thought, he in his relations to the Universe fecundates the scientific thought. Science is truth, and the most ancient cultus of Freemasonry.

In determining the relations of the individual to his equals, Freemasonry does not restrict itself to recommending to do unto others what we wish others would do unto us; but inculcates to do good, oppose evil, and not to submit to injustice in whatsoever form it presents itself. Freemasonry looks forward to the day when the iron plates of the Monitor and the Merrimac will be beaten into steam-ploughs; when man, redeemed by liberty and science, shall enjoy the pure pleasures of intelligence; when peace, fertilised by the wealth and strength now devoted to war, shall bring forth, the most beautiful fruit of the tree of life.

461. Reform needed - Greatly, therefore, is the academic puerility of rites to be regretted, which drags back into the past an institution that ought to launch forward into the future. It is self-evident that Freemasonry in this state cannot last, that a reform is necessary; and as De Castro, from whom the above is taken, thinks that it would be an honour to Italy to be the leader in such a reform, it would be an

honour to any country that initiated it. Masonry ought not to be an ambulance, but a vanguard. It is embarrassed by its excessive baggage, its superfluous symbols. Guarding secrets universally known, it cannot entertain secrets of greater account. Believing itself to be the sole depositary of widely-spread truths, it deprives itself and the world of other truths. In this perplexity and alternative of committing suicide or being born anew, what will Masonry decide on?

XXI

CAGLIOSTRO AND EGYPTIAN MASONRY

462. Life of Cagliostro - Joseph Balsamo, the disciple and successor of St. Germain, who pretended at the Court of Louis XV. to have been the contemporary of Charles V., Francis I., and Christ, and to possess the elixir of life and many other secrets, had vaster designs and a loftier ambition than his teacher, and was one of the most active agents of Freemasonry in France and the rest of Europe. He was born at Palermo in 1743, and educated at two convents in that city, where he acquired some chemical knowledge. As a young man, he fell in with an Armenian, or Greek, or Spaniard, called Althotas, a kind of adventurer, who professed to possess the philosopher's stone, with whom he led a roving life for a number of years. What became of Althotas at last is not positively known. Balsamo at last found his way to Rome, where he married the beautiful Lorenza Feliciani, whom he treated so badly, that she escaped from him; but he recovered her, and acquired great influence over her by magnetically operating upon her. There is no doubt that he was a powerful magnetiser. Visiting Germany, he was initiated into Freemasonry, in which he soon began to take a prominent part. He also assumed different titles, such as that of Marquis of Pellegrini, but the one he is best known by is that of Count Cagliostro; and by his astuteness, impudence, and some lucky hits at prophesying, he acquired a European notoriety and made many dupes, including persons of the highest rank, especially in France, where he founded many new masonic lodges. He was the author of a book called " The Rite of Egyptian Masonry," which rite he established first in Courland, and afterwards in Germany, France, and England. After having been banished from France, in consequence of his implication in the affair of the queen's necklace, and driven from England by his creditors, he was induced by his wife, who was weary of her wandering life, and anxious once more to see her relations, to visit Koine, where he was arrested on the charge of attempting to found a masonic lodge, against which a papal bull had recently been promulgated, and thrown

into the Castle of St. Angelo, in 1789. He was condemned to death, but the punishment was commuted to perpetual imprisonment. His wife was shut up in a convent, and died soon after. Having been transferred to the Castle of San Leo, he attempted to strangle the monk sent to confess him, in the hope of escaping in his gown; but the attempt failed, and it is supposed that he died, a prisoner, in 1795.

463. The Egyptian Rite - The Egyptian rite invented by Cagliostro is a mixture of the sacred and profane, of the serious and laughable. Having discovered a MS. of George Cofton, in which was propounded a singular scheme for the reform of Freemasonry in an alchymistic and fantastic sense, Cagliostro founded thereon the bases of his masonic system, taking advantage of human credulity, enriching himself, and at the same time seconding the action of other secret societies. He gave his dupes to understand that the scope of Egyptian Masonry was to conduct men to perfection by means of physical and moral regeneration; asserting that the former was infallible through the prima materia and the philosopher's stone, which assured to man the strength of youth and immortality, and that the second was to be achieved by the discovery of a pentagon that would restore man to his primitive innocence. This rite indeed is a tissue of fatuities it would not be worth while to allude to, did it not offer matter for study to the philosopher and moralist. Cagliostro pretended that the rite had been first founded by Enoch, remodelled by Elias, and finally restored by the Grand Copt. Both men and women were admitted into the lodges, though the ceremonies for each were slightly different, and the lodges for their reception entirely distinct. In the reception of women, among other formalities there was that of breathing into the face of the neophyte, saying, " I breathe upon you this breath to cause to germinate in you and grow in your heart the truth we possess; I breathe it into you to strengthen in you good intentions, and to confirm you in the faith of your brothers and sisters. We constitute you a legitimate daughter of true Egyptian adoption and of this worshipful lodge." One of the lodges was called " Sinai," where the most secret rites were performed; another "Ararat," to symbolise the rest reserved for Masons only. Concerning the pentagon, Cagliostro taught that it would be given to

the masters after forty days of inter course with the seven primitive angels, and that its possessors would enjoy a physical regeneration for 5557 years, after which they would through gentle sleep pass into heaven. The pentagon had as much success with the upper ten thousand of London, Paris, and St. Petersburg, as the philosopher's stone ever enjoyed; and large sums were given for a few grains of the rejuvenating prima materia.

464. Cagliostro's Hydromancy - But beside masonic delusions, Cagliostro made use of the then little understood wonders of magnetism to attract adherents; and as many persons are seduced by the wine-cup, so he made dupes of many by means of the water-bottle, which device, as might be shown, was very ancient, and consisted in divination by hydromancy. A child, generally a little girl, and called the Dove, was made to look into a bottle of water, and see therein events, past, present, and to come; and as Cagliostro was really a man of observation, he made many shrewd guesses as to the future, and sometimes fortune favoured him as in the case of Schropfer (280, 437), one of the leaders of the Illuminati, who refused to join the Egyptian rite; the little girl declared that in less than a month Schropfer would be punished. Now it so happened that within that period Schropfer committed suicide, which of course gave an immense lift to Cagliostro and his bottle. In this respect indeed Cagliostro was a forerunner of our modern spiritualists; and as he did not keep his occult power a secret from all, but freely communicated it, magical practices were thus introduced into the lodges, which brought discredit on the institution. And all this occurred at the period of the Encyclopedists, and on the eve of mighty events !

465. Lodges founded by Cagliostro - He founded the first lodge, gorgeously fitted up, at Paris in a private house, and another one in his own house. A third was founded at Lyons, for which a special grand building was- erected. It was declared the Mother Lodge, and called "Triumphant Wisdom." Its patent ran thus:
" Honour, Wisdom,

Union,
Beneficence, Comfort.

"We Grand Copt, in all eastern and western parts of Europe, Founder and Grand Master of Egyptian Masonry, make known to All, who may read this, that during our stay at Lyons many members of the Lodge of the Orient and Ordinary Rite, which has adopted the distinguishing title of 'Wisdom,' have expressed their ardent wish to place themselves under our rule, to be enlightened in true Masonry. We are pleased to accede to their wish," &c.

Lodges also were founded at Strasburg, a ladies' lodge at The Hague, another at Roveredo, another at Mitau, and a very grand one near Basle, in a sumptuous temple, erected for the purpose. The good citizens of Basle always approached it with feelings of awe, because they imagined Cagliostro destined it to be his tomb.

XXII

ADOPTIVE MASONRY

466. Historical Notice - According to one of the fundamental laws of Masonry and a rule prevailing in the greater mysteries of antiquity women cannot be received into the Order. Women cannot keep secrets, at least so Milton says, through the mouth of Dalila

"Granting, as I do, it was a weakness In me, but incident to all our sex, Curiosity, inquisitive, importune Of secrets; then with like infirmity To publish them; both common female faults."

But we have already seen that Cagliostro admitted women to the Egyptian rite; and when at the beginning of the eighteenth century several associations sprang up in France, which in their external aspect resembled Freemasonry, but did not exclude women, the ladies naturally were loud in their praise of such institutions, so that the masonic brotherhood, seeing it was becoming unpopular, had recourse to the stratagem of establishing "adoptive" lodges of women, so called because every such lodge had finally to be adopted by some regular masonic lodge. The Grand Orient of France framed laws for their government, and the first lodge of adoption was opened in Paris in 1775, in which the Duchess of Bourbon presided, and was initiated as Grand Mistress of the rite. The Revolution checked the progress of this rite, but it was revived in 1805, when the Empress Josephine presided over the "Loge Imperiale d'Adoption des Francs Chevaliers" at Strasburg. Similar lodges spread over Europe, Great Britain excepted; but they soon declined, and are at present confined to the place of their origin.

467. Organisation - The rite consists of the same degrees as those of genuine Masonry. Every sister, being a dignitary, has beside her a masonic brother holding the corresponding rank. Hence the officers are a Grand Master and a Grand Mistress, an Inspector and an Inspectress, a Depositor and a Depositrix, a Conductor and a Conductress. The business of the lodge is conducted by the sisterhood, the brethren only

acting as their assistants; but the Grand Mistress has very little to say or to do, she being only an honorary companion to the Grand Master. The first, or apprentice's, degree is only introductory; in the second, or companion, the scene of the temptation in Eden is emblematically represented; the building of the tower of Babel is the subject of the mistress's degree; and in the fourth, or that of perfect mistress, the officers represent Moses, Aaron, and their wives, and the ceremonies refer to the passage of the Israelites through the wilderness, as a symbol of the passage of men and women through this to another and better life. The lodge-room is tastefully decorated, and divided by curtains into four compartments, each representing one of the four quarters of the globe, the eastern, or farthermost, representing Asia, where there are two splendid thrones, decorated with gold fringe, for the Grand Master and the Grand Mistress. The members sit on each side in straight lines, the sisters in front and the brothers behind them, the latter having swords in their hands. All this pretty playing at Masonry is naturally followed by a banquet, and on many occasions by a ball. At the banquets the members use a symbolical language; thus the lodge-room is called "Eden," the doors "barriers," a glass is called a "lamp," water "white oil," wine "red oil"; to fill your glass is "to trim your lamp," &c.

468. Jesuit Degrees - The Jesuits, qui vont fourrer leur nez partout, soon poked it into Adoptive Masonry for to get hold of the women is to get hold of the better half of mankind and founded new lodges, or modified existing ones of that rite to further their own purposes. Thus it is that a truly monkish asceticism was introduced into some of them, by the Jesuits divided into ten degrees; and we find such passages in the catechism as these: "Are you prepared, sister, to sacrifice life for the good of the catholic, apostolic Roman Church?" The tenth or last degree was called the "Princess of the Crown," and a great portion of the ritual treats of the Queen of Sheba. This rite was established in Saxony in 1779.[18]

---

[18] For another adoptive order, the "Heroine of Jericho," see Miscellaneous Societies, Book XIV., § 701.

XXIII

ANDROGYNOUS MASONRY

469. Origin and Tendency - Gallantry already makes its appearance in Adoptive Masonry; and this gallantry, which for so many ages was the study of France, and was there reduced to an ingenious art, manufactured on its own account rites and degrees that were masonic in name only. Politics were dethroned by amorous intrigues; and the enumerators of great effects sprung from trifling causes might in this chapter of history find proofs of what a superficial and accidental thing politics are, when not governed by motives of high morality, nor watched by the incorruptible national conscience. And Androgynous Masonry did not always confine itself to an interchange of compliments and the pursuit of pleasure; still, as a rule, its lodges for the initiation of males and females defended by some of their advocates as founded on Exod. xxxviii. 8 are a whimsical form of that court life which in France and Italy had its poets and romancers; and which rose to such a degree of impudence and scandal as to outrage the modesty of citizens and popular virtue. It is a page of that history of princely corruption, which the French people at first read of with laughter, then with astonishment, finally with indignation; and which inspired it with those feelings which at last found their vent in the excesses of the great Revolution. Every Revolution is a puritanical movement, and the simple and neglected virtue of the lowly-born avenges itself upon the pompous vices of their superiors.

470. Earliest Androgynous Societies - Some of these were founded in France and elsewhere by an idle, daring, and conquering soldiery. As their type we may take the Order of the "Knights and Ladies of Joy," founded with extraordinary success at Paris in 1696, under the protection of Bacchus and Venus, and whose printed statutes are still in existence; and that of the "Ladies of St. John of Jerusalem," and the "Ladies of St. James of the Sword and Calatrava." They, as it were, served as models to the canonesses, who, till the end of the last century,

brought courtly pomp and mundane pleasures into the very cloisters of France, and compelled austere moralists to excuse it by saying that it was dans le gout de la nation.

471. Other Androgynous Societies - In the Order of the "Companions of Penelope, or the Palladium of Ladies," whose statutes are said to have been drawn up by Fenelon (with how much truth is easily imagined), the trials consist in showing the candidate that work is the palladium of women; whence we may assume the pursuits of this society to have been very different from the equivocal occupations of other Orders. The Order of the "Mopses" owed its origin to a religious scruple. Pope Clement XII. having issued, in 1738, a Bull condemning Freemasonry, Clement Augustus, Duke of Bavaria and Elector of Cologne, instituted, under the above name (derived from the German word Mops, a young mastiff, the symbol of fidelity), what was pretended to be a new society, but what was, in fact, only Freemasonry under another name. Immediately after their establishment the Mopses became an androgynous order, admitting females to all the offices except that of Grand Master, which was for life; but there was a Grand Mistress, elected every six months. Their ceremonies were grotesque. The candidate for admission did not knock, but scratch at the door, and, being purposely kept waiting, barked like a dog. On being admitted into the lodge he had a collar round his neck, to which a chain was attached. He was blindfolded, and led nine times round the room, while the Mopses present made as great a din as possible with sticks, swords, chains, shovels, and dismal bowlings. He was then questioned as to his intentions, and having replied that he desired to become a Mops, was asked by the master whether he was prepared to kiss the most ignoble part of that animal. Of course this raised the candidate's anger; but in spite of his resistance, the model of a dog, made of wax, wood, or some other material, was pushed against his face. Having taken the oath, he had his eyes unbandaged, and was taught the signs, which were all of a ludicrous description. In 1777 there was established in Denmark the androgynous order of the " Society of the Chain," to which belongs the honour of having founded,

and of maintaining at its own expense, the Asylum for the Blind at Copenhagen, the largest and best managed of similar institutions in Europe. The Order of " Perseverance," the date of whose foundation is unknown, but which existed in Paris in 1777, and was supported by the most distinguished persons, had a laudable custom, which might be imitated by other societies, viz., to inscribe in a book, one of which is still extant, the praiseworthy actions of the male and female members of the association. But one of the most deserving masonic androgynous institutions was that of the "Sovereign Chapter of the Scotch Ladies of France," founded in 1810, and divided into lesser and greater mysteries, and whose instructions aimed chiefly at leading the neophyte back to the occupations to which the state of society called him or her. To provide food and work for those wanting either, to afford them advice and help, and save them from the cruel alternative of crime such was the scope of this society, which lasted till the year 1828. The fashion of androgynous lodges was revived in Spain in 1877. From the Chaine cC Union, a masonic publication, we learn that several such lodges were formed about that date, receiving ladies of the highest rank. Thus the Countess Julia A____ , belonging by birth to the Austrian Hungarian nobility, and by her connections to Spain, was initiated into the lodge Fraternitad Iberica on the 14th June 1880; and the Grand Orient of Spain initiated ladies into all the mysteries of masonry, just as if they were men.

472. Various other Androgynous Societies - The Society of the "Wood-store of the Globe and Glory" was founded in 1747 by the Chevalier de Beauchene, a lively boon companion, who was generally to be found at an inn, where for very little money he conferred all the masonic degrees of that time; a man whose worship would have shone by the great tun of Heidelberg, or at the drinking bouts of German students. The Wood-store was supposed to be in a forest, and the meetings, which were much in vogue, took place in a garden outside Paris, called "New France," where assembled lords and clowns, ladies and grisettes, indulging in the easy costumes and manners of the country. Towards the middle of the eighteenth century, there was

established in Brittany the Order of the "Defoliators."

In the Order of "Felicity," instituted in Paris in 1742, and divided into the four degrees of midshipman, captain, chief of a squadron, and vice-admiral, the emblems and terms were nautical: sailors were its founders, and it excited so much attention, that in 1746 a satire, entitled, "The Means of reaching the highest Hank in the Navy without getting Wet," was published against it. Its field of action was the field of love. A Grand Orient was called the offing, the lodge the squadron, and the sisters performed the fictitious voyage to the island of Felicity sous la voile des freres et pilote'es par eux; and the candidate promised "never to receive a foreign ship into her port as long as a ship of the Order was anchored there."

The Order of the " Lovers of Pleasure " was a military institution, a pale revival of the ceremonies of chivalry and the courts of love, improvised in the French camp in Galicia. From the discourse of one of the orators we select the following passage: "Our scope is to embellish our existence, always taking for our guide the words, ' Honour, Joy, and Delicacy.' Our scope, moreover, is to be faithful to our country and the august sovereign who fills the universe with his glorious name, to serve a cause which ought to be grateful to every gentle soul, that of protecting youth and innocence, and of establishing between the ladies and ourselves an eternal alliance, cemented by the purest friendship." This society, it is said, was much favoured by Napoleon I., and hence we may infer that its aim was not purely pleasure; at all events, it is remarkable that a society, having masonic rites, should have given its services to the "august sovereign" who had just withdrawn his support from genuine Freemasonry.

473. Knights and Nymphs of the Rose - This Order was founded in Paris in 1778 by Chaumont, private secretary to Louis-Philippe d'Orleans, to please that prince. The chief lodge was held in one of the famous petites maisons of that epoch. The great lords had lodges in their own houses. The Hierophant, assisted by a deacon called "Sentiment," initiated the men, and the Grand Priestess, assisted by the deaconess called "Discretion," initiated the women. The age of admission for knights was "the age to love," that of ladies "the age to

please and to be loved." Love and mystery were the programme of the Order; the lodge was called the Temple of Love, which was beautifully adorned with garlands of flowers and amorous emblems and devices. The knights wore a crown of myrtle, the nymphs a crown of roses. During the time of initiation a dark lantern, held by the nymph of Discretion, shed a dim light, but afterwards the lodge was illuminated with numerous wax candles. The aspirants, laden with chains, to symbolise the prejudices that kept them prisoners, were asked, "What seek you here?" to which they replied, "Happiness." They were then questioned as to their private opinion and conduct in matters of gallantry, and made twice to traverse the lodge over a path covered with love-knots, whereupon the iron chains were taken off, and garlands of flowers, called "chains of love," substituted. The candidates were then conducted to the altar, where they took the oath of secrecy; and thence to the mysterious groves in the neighbourhood of the Temple of Love, where incense was offered up to Venus and her son. If it was a knight who had been initiated, he exchanged his crown of myrtle for the rose of the last initiated nymph; and if a nymph, she exchanged her rose for the myrtle crown of Brother Sentiment. The horrors of the Revolution scattered these knights and nymphs, who, like thoughtless children, were playing on a volcano.

474. German Order of the Rose - Another order of the Rose was founded in Germany in 1784 by one Francis Matthaus Grossinger, who ennobled himself by assuming the title of Francis Rudolph von Grossing. He was born in 1752 at Komorn, in Hungary; his father was a butcher, his mother the daughter of a tanner. Grossing was a Jesuit, but on the suppression of the Order he led a wandering life, and eventually reached Vienna, where he obtained the protection of the father confessor of the empress, who in 1777 granted him a pension of six hundred florins, which, however, he lost by her death. He then lived by all kinds of swindling, and finally founded a philanthropic order, which, after the name of the supposititious grand mistress, the Lady of Rosenwald, he called the "Order of the Rose." He was very successful at Halle, where he lived, in initiating dupes, on whose contributions he

lived in great style. "When he became too notorious at Halle he transmigrated to Berlin, where he continued his expensive style of living, got into debt, was arrested, but made his escape, after having swindled the Berliners out of twenty thousand dollars.

475. Pretended Objects of the Order - The Order professed to pursue the loftiest philosophic and educational objects. None but men and women endowed with noble souls were to be admitted, and no member was to reveal the name of iny other member, nor what was discussed in the lodges, to outsiders. Masonry was the model for the Order of the Rose, the latter adopting all the good, and rejecting all the bad of the former. The ribbon of the Order consisted of pink silk, both ends terminating in three points; it was marked with a rose, and the name of the member, with the date of his or her reception. Under this was a large seal, displaying a rose, surrounded by a wreath of the same flowers; the ribbon was further adorned with a kind of silhouette, supposed to represent the Lady of Rosenwald, so indistinct and blurred, as to look more like a blot than a portrait. Members also were furnished with a small ticket, giving the explanation of certain terms used by Grossing in his "Rules and Regulations "; thus Freemasons were called "Gamblers "; Jesuits, " Foxes"; Illuminati, "Wasps "; Ghost-seers, "Gnats," &c. The "Rules" were called "A Shell or Case for Thorns "; members, to recognise each other, would say, " Thorns," to which the other would reply, "Forest," after which each would produce his ribbon and ticket. In 1786 the Order counted about one hundred and twenty members, but having no innate vitality, being, in fact, but a company of triflers, many of them withdrew on finding the whole Order but a scheme of Grossing to put money into his pocket, and so it was swept away into the limbus of fashionable follies.

476. Order of Harmony - The Order of the Rose having collapsed, Grossing in 1788 founded, under a fictitious name, the "Order of Harmony." He published a book alleged to be translated from the English, and entitled, "Harmony, or a Scheme for the Better Education of the Female Sex," and wrote in the Preface, " This 'Harmony' is not

to be confounded with that Chdteau en Espagne, with which the founder of the Order of the Rose for some years deluded the ladies of Germany." The Order of Harmony was said to have been founded by Seth, the third son of Adam, to have reckoned among its members Moses and Christ, and to be the refuge of persecuted humanity and innocence. The founder abused princes and priests, proposed the establishment of convents, in which ladies were to take the vows of chastity, obedience, and poverty, but only for a year at a time; a bank was also to be founded in connection with them. And the writer finally proposed that a monument should be erected to the promoter of the Order as a benefactor of mankind! When Grossing was arrested in 1788 at Rotenburg (Prussia), for all kinds of swindling transactions, a number of diplomas were found among his papers, with the names of ladies who were to be admitted to the Order filled in. But the interference of the vulgar police brushed the bloom of romance off the scheme, and the Order of Harmony perished, a still-born babe! Grossing, however, managed to effect his escape, by making his guards drunk; what became of him afterwards is not on record.

477. Masons Daughter - This is an androgynous degree invented in the Western States of America, and given to master masons, their wives, and unmarried sisters and daughters. It refers to circumstances recorded in chapters xi. and xii. of St. John's Gospel. In these women's lodges the banqueting hall is divided into East, West, South, and North sides (the four walls); the grand mistress sits in the East; the temple or lodge is called Eden; the doors are called barriers, the glasses, lamps, the wine is called red oil; to put oil in the lamps is to fill the glasses, to extinguish the lamp is to drink the wine, to "fire!" is to drink. The sign is to place the hands on the breast, so that the right lies on the left, and the two thumbs joining form a triangle. The word is " Eve," repeated five times. Gentlemen are allowed to be present. As the reader will have observed, the degree is an imitation of the Loge Imperiale d'Adoption des FrancsChevaliers, described in 466.

XXIV

SCHISMATIC RITES AND SECTS

478. Schismatic Rites and Sects - The pretended derivation of Freemasonry from the Knights Templars has already been referred to; but Masonry, the system, not the name, existed before the Order of the Temple, and the Templars themselves had masonic rites and degrees three hundred years before their downfall. Those who, however, maintain the above view say that the three assassins symbolise the three betrayers of the Order, and Hiram the Grand Master Molay; and according to the ritual of the Grand Lodge of the Three Globes, a German degree, the lights around the coffin signify the flames of the pile on which Molay was burnt. To the Rosicrucians and to certain German lodges Hiram is Christ, and the three assassins, Judas that betrays, Peter that denies Him, and Thomas that disbelieves His resurrection. The ancient Scotch rite had its origin in other false accounts of the rise of the Order. In the last century schisms without number arose in the masonic body. It would be impossible in a work like this to give particulars of all; we have already done so of several; a few more may be briefly referred to. The Moravian Brothers of the Order of Religious Freemasons, or Order of the "Mustard Seed," was a German rite founded, circa 1712, by Count Zinzendorf, the same who afterwards invented the rite already described in 438. Some authorities assert this Order of the "Mustard-Seed" to have originated in England in 1708, and thence to have spread to Holland and Germany, and to have been adopted by Zinzendorf, circa 1712-14, when he was a student at Halle. The mysteries were founded on the passage in St. Mark iv. 30-32, in which Christ compares the kingdom of heaven to a grain of mustard-seed. The brethren recognised each other by a ring inscribed with the words: "No one of us lives for himself." The jewel was a cross of gold, surmounted by a mustard-plant with the words: "What was it before? Nothing." The members met every year in the chapel of the Castle of Gnadenstadt, and also kept the 15th March and 16th April as holy days. Nearly all the degrees of the Scotch rite are

schismatic. In like manner, all the English and American orders of chivalry, and their conclaves and encampments, are parodies of ancient chivalry.

In 1758, Lacoriie, a dancing-master, and Pirlet, a tailor, invented the degree of the "Council of the Emperors of the East and West," whose members assumed the titles of " Sovereign Prince Masons, Substitutes General of the Royal Art, Grand Superintendents and Officers of the Grand and Sovereign Lodge of St. John of Jerusalem." The ritual consisted of twenty-five degrees, and as it was calculated by its sounding titles and splendour of ritual to flatter the vanity of the frivolous, it was at first very successful; and Lacorne conferred on one of his creatures, a Hebrew, the degree of Inspector, and sent him to America to spread the Order there. In 1797, other Jews added eight new degrees, giving to this agglomeration of thirty-three pompous degrees the title of "Ancient and Accepted Scotch Rite." The Grand Orient of France, seeing its own influence declining, proposed advantageous and honourable terms to the Supreme Grand Council which was at the head of the Scotch rite, and an agreement was come to in 1804. The Grand Orient retaining the first name, received into its bosom the Supreme Grand Council and the rich American symbolism. But the connection did not prosper, and was dissolved in 1805. Again, what is called Mark-Masonry in England is, by some masonic authorities, considered spurious; whilst in Scotland and Ireland it is held to be an essential portion of Freemasonry. These are curious anomalies. About 1869 His Imperial Highness the Prince Rhodocanakis introduced into England the " Order of the Red Cross of Constantino and Rome," which, however, being violently opposed by the Supreme Grand Council of the 33rd, came to an untimely end soon after. The S.G.C. threatened any member of the "Ancient and Accepted" who should dare even to merely visit this new Order with expulsion from the fraternity. And the S.G.C. actually sent a " Sovereign Tribunal " to Manchester to try a brother, who had snapped his fingers at the Council and said he did not care for the " Sovereign." How it all ended is pleasantly related in the pages of Tlie Rectangular, January and April 1871.

479. Farmassoni - There is a Gnostic sect in Russia whom the Eussians identify with the Freemasons, and therefore call "Farmassoni," a corruption of franc-masons. The Farmassoni regard priesthood and ritual as a pagan depravation of the faith and of the true doctrine; they seek, as much as possible, to spiritualise Christianity, and to ground it solely on the Bible and the inward illumination of believers. The earliest traces of them are to be found at the end of the seventeenth century, and their appearance coincides with that of certain German mystics and theosophists in Moscow. The most important of these was a Prussian sub-officer, who was carried to Moscow, having been taken prisoner by the Eussians during the Seven Years' War.

480. The Gormogones - This Order was founded in England in 1724. The names and birthplaces of the members were written in cipher, and the Order was said to have been brought by a Chinese mandarin (a Jesuit missionary?) to England, it being in great repute in China (Eome), and to possess extraordinary secrets. It held a chapter at the Castle Tavern, London, but was dissolved in 1738. It is supposed to have been an attempt of the Jesuits, by the help of masonic ceremonies, to gain converts to Catholicism, and that Earn say, the inventor of the so-called higher degrees, had something to do with it. I have vainly endeavoured to trace the origin and meaning of the term Gormogones. According to one account I have seen it was also called the Order of the Gormones, and was said to have been instituted for the reception of individuals not considered sufficiently advanced for admission to the lodges.

481. The Noachites. or Noachidæ - This Order, founded in the last quarter of the last century, assumed the high-sounding title of "The Fraternity of the Royal Ark Mariners, Mark, Mark Master, Elected of Nine, Unknown, Fifteen, Architect, Excellent and Superexcellent Masons." They professed to be the followers of Noah which no doubt they were in one respect and therefore also called themselves Noachites or Noachidse. Their president, Thomas-Boothby Parkyns,

Lord Eancliffe, bore the title of Grand Noah, and the lodge was called the Eoyal Ark Vessel. The brother mariners in the lodge wore a broad sash, representing a rainbow, with an apron fancifully decorated with an ark. dove, &c. Their principal place of meeting was at the Surrey Tavern, Surrey Street, Strand. They had a poet, Brother Ebenezer Sibley, who was a doctor of medicine and an astrologer to boot, who, like too many masonic poets, wrote indifferent couplets. This Order must not be confounded with the "Noachite or Russian Knight," which is the 21st degree of the Ancient Scotch rite.

482. Argonauts - This Order was founded, for his amusement, by a Freemason, Konrad von Rhetz, residing at Riddagshausen, near Brunswick. He had been the master of a lodge of the Relaxed Observance, but fell out with his brethren, and ceased from visiting any lodge. Near his residence there is a large lake with an island in the centre. On this he built a temple and provided boats to carry visitors to it, where, if they desired it, they were initiated into the new Order. Persons of position and of either sex might claim reception as a matter of right, and many Brunswick Freemasons belonged to it. The Grand Master, or Grand Admiral as he was called, entertained all visitors free of expense, nor was there any charge for initiation. The greeting was " Long live pleasure! "The temple was built in the antique style, though with quaint decorations and a few paintings and engravings. There were also cupboards containing the insignia of the Order. The officers were styled Steersman, Chaplain, and so on; the others were simple Argonauts. The jewel was a silver anchor with green enamel. On the founder's death in 1787 the Order was dissolved; no trace remains of the temple.

483. The Grand Orient and Atheism - In 1877 the Grand Orient abolished in the lodges the acknowledgment of a belief in God, introduced into the ritual in 1854, which has led to a rupture between it and the Grand Lodge of England. The influence of Masonry, both social and political, in France being universal, it is the foundation and support of the war made on the priesthood with a view chiefly to

deprive them of the education of youth. The Spanish and Dutch Grand Lodges approved of the action of the Grand Orient in suppressing the name of God in the ritual of admission. There is no doubt that Continental Masonry aims at the abolition not only of the Roman Catholic Church, but of the human mind's blind surrender to any creed whatever.

484. Ludicrous Degree - The following lodge was actually established about 1717. Some joyous companions, having passed the degree of craft, resolved to form a lodge for themselves. As none of them knew the master's part, they at once invented and adopted a ritual which suited every man's humour. Hence it was ordered that every person during initiation should wear boots, spurs, a sword, and spectacles. The apron was turned upside down. To simplify work of the lodge, they abolished the practice of study in geometry, excepting that form mentioned by Hudibras

"For he, by geometric scale,

Could take the size of pots of ale;

Resolve by sines and tangents straight,

If bread or butter wanted weight."

Some of the members proved that a good knife and fork in the hands of a dexterous brother, over proper materials, rould give greater satisfaction and add more to the rotundity of the lodge than the best scale and compass in Europe; adding that a line, a square, a parallelogram, a rhombus, a rhomboid, a triangle, a trapezium, a circle, a semi-circle, a quadrant, a parabola, a hyperbola, a cube, a parallelepipedon, a prism, a prismoid, a pyramid, a cylinder, a curve, a cylindroid, a sphere, a spheroid, a paraboloid, a cycloid, a paracentric, frustums, segments, sectors, gnomons, pentagons, hexagons, polygons, ellipses, and irregular figures of all sorts, might be drawn and represented upon bread, beef, mutton, ham, fowls, pies, &c., as demonstratively as upon sheets of paper or the tracing-board, and that the use of the globes might be taught and explained as clearly and briefly upon two bottles as upon any twenty-eight inch spheres.

XXV

DIFFUSION OF THE ORDER

485. Freemasonry in Spain and Portugal - In 1726, the Grand Lodge of England granted a patent for the establishment of a lodge at Gibraltar; another was founded in the following year at Madrid, which, declaring itself independent of foreign supervision, established lodges at Cadiz, Barcelona, Valladolid, and other places. The Inquisition, seeing the danger that threatened the Church, persecuted the Order; hence some mystery surrounds the labours of the brotherhood in the Iberian peninsula. But in the troubles which distressed Spain during the Napoleonic wars, the masonic lodges were politically very active. They were suppressed again by Ferdinand VII., and up to the year 1868 were but few in number, and disguised under various names. Since that year they have rapidly increased, and there are now more than 360 lodges in Spain. The Spanish Grand Lodge has 154 lodges under its jurisdiction; the Grand Orient of Spain about 162; the Lusitanian Grand Orient about 40 lodges. There are, moreover, about 40 lodges subject to foreign Grand Lodges. The number of Spanish Masons may amount to 30,000.

In Portugal, the first lodges were founded, not under English, but under French auspices; but English influence soon made itself felt in the establishment of additional lodges, though in great secrecy; which, however, did not save many Freemasons from becoming the victims of the Inquisition.

486. Freemasonry in Russia - In 1731, Freemasonry dared to oppose itself to Russian despotism, which not fearing, and probably despising it, did not molest it. The times were unpropitious. The sanguinary Biren ruled the Empress Anne, whom by means of the amorous fascination he exercised upon her, he easily persuaded to commit all kinds of folly and cruelty; and Masonry, though it knew itself to be

tolerated, yet did not feel secure, and cautiously kept itself in the background. In 1740, England founded a lodge at St. Petersburg, and sent thither a Grand Master. The Order spread in the provinces, and in 1763 the lodge "Clio" was opened at Moscow. Catherine II. wished to know its statutes, perceiving the advantage or injury they might bring to her government as she either promoted or persecuted the association. In the end she determined to protect the Order; and in a country where the court leads opinion, lodges soon became the fashion. But Masonry thus becoming the amusement of a wealthy nobility, it soon lost sight of its primitive objects. In no other country probably did the brotherhood possess such gorgeous temples; but, deprived of the vivifying and invigorating air of liberty, its splendour could not save it from a death of inanition.

487. Freemasonry in Switzerland - English proselytism, always the most active, established a lodge at Geneva in 1737, whose first Grand Master was George Hamilton. Two years afterwards, the foreigners dwelling at Lausanne united and founded the lodge called the "Perfect Union of Foreigners." Lodges were also opened at Berne; but the manoeuvres of the Grand Lodges of the States surrounding Switzerland introduced long and fierce dissensions. In 1765, the Strict Observance founded at Basle the lodge " Liberty," which became the mother-lodge of many others, and, calling itself the " German Helvetic Directory," chose for its chief the celebrated Lavater. Then followed suppressions; but the Order revived, and in 1844 the different territorial Grand Lodges united into one federal Grand Lodge, called "Alpina," which revised the ancient statutes. The Swiss Freemasons intend to erect a grand temple, which perhaps could nowhere find a more fitting site than in a country where four nations of diverse languages and races dwell in perfect liberty.

488. Freemasonry in Sweden and Poland - In 1748, Sweden already had many and flourishing lodges. In 1754 was instituted the Grand Lodge of Sweden, under a patent from the Grand Lodge of Scotland; it afterwards declared its autonomy, which has been recognised by all the

masonic bodies of Europe. In the most ancient Swedish ritual we meet for the first time in Europe with the cry and sign of distress of the sons of Adoniram (383): "To me, the sons of the widow! "

Freemasonry, at first suppressed in Poland, was revived under Stanislaus Augustus, and the auspices of the Grand Orient of France, who established lodges in various towns of that country. These united in 1784 to form a Grand Orient, having its seat at Warsaw.

489. Freemasonry in Holland and Germany - In Holland the Freemasons opened a lodge in 1731, under the warrant of the Grand Lodge of England; it was, however, only what is called a lodge of emergency, having been called to initiate the Duke of Tuscany, afterwards Francis I, Emperor of Germany (454). The first regular lodge was established at The Hague in 1734, which, five years after, took the name of "Mother-lodge." Numerous lodges were opened throughout the country, and also in the Dutch colonies; and the Freemasons founded many schools, with the avowed object of withdrawing instruction from clerical influence.

In Germany lodges were numerous as early as the middle of last century, so that in the present one we have witnessed the centenaries of many of them as, for instance, in 1837, of that of Hamburg; in 1840, of that of Berlin; in 1841, of those of Breslau, Baireuth, Leipzig, and many more.

490. Freemasonry in Turkey, Asia, Africa, and Oceania - The Order also spread into Turkey, where, however, as may be supposed, for a long time it led but a harassed existence. Lodges were established at Constantinople, Smyrna, and Aleppo; and it may be mentioned, as a fact in favour of Freemasonry, that the Turkish Freemasons are in a more advanced state of civilisation than is usual among Orientals generally. They reject polygamy, and at the masonic banquets the women appear unveiled; so that whatever their western sisters may have to say against Masonry, the women of the East certainly are gainers by the introduction of the Order.

The most important masonic lodges of Asia are in India; they are under the jurisdiction of the Grand Lodges of England and Scotland.

Freemasonry was introduced into Africa by the establishment of a lodge at Cape Coast Castle in 1735. There are now lodges at the Cape of Good Hope; in the islands of Mauritius, Madagascar, and St. Helena; and at Algiers, Tunis, Morocco, Cairo, and Alexandria.

Lodges have existed since 1828 at Sydney, Melbourne, Parramatta, and other places; in all, about two hundred.

491. Freemasonry in America - The first lodge established in Canada was at Cape Breton, in the year 1745. Lodges existed from as early a period in the West Indian Islands. On the establishment of the Brazilian empire, a Grand Lodge was initiated; and in 1825, Don Pedro I. was elected its Grand Master. In 1825, the Grand Lodge of Mexico was instituted, where the Liberals and Federalists joined the York rite, whilst the Clerics, Monarchists, and Centralizers adopted the Scotch rite, the two parties carrying on a relentless war. Texas, Venezuela, and the turbulent republics of South America, all had their masonic lodges, which were in many cases political clubs in disguise. Thus the assassination of Garcia Moreno, the President of the Republic of Ecuador, in 1875, was the work of the masonic clubs. The murderer, one Rajo, on being promised his life if he would denounce his accomplices, coolly replied: " It would be useless to save my life; if you spared it, my companions would soon take it; I would rather be shot than stabbed."

The lodges in the territory now forming the United States date as far back as 1729. Until the close of the revolutionary war these were under the jurisdiction of the Grand Lodge of England; but almost every State of the Union now has its own Grand Lodge, independent of all foreign power.

In different parts of the globe there are about 90 Grand Lodges, nearly 12,000 lodges, numbering altogether about 12,500,000 members; of the active members, or such as regularly attend lodges and pay annual subscriptions, there may be half that number.

XXVI

PERSECUTIONS OF FREEMASONRY

492. Causes of Persecution - The secrecy with which the masonic brotherhood has always surrounded its proceedings is no doubt highly grateful to the members, but it has its drawbacks. The outside world, who cannot believe that masonic meetings, which are so jealously guarded against the intrusion of non-Masons, have no other purpose than the rehearsal of a now totally useless and pointless ritual, followed by conviviality, naturally assume that there must be something more behind; and what seems to fear the light is usually supposed to be evil. Hence all governments, as long as they did not know what modern Freemasonry really is, persecuted and endeavoured to suppress it. But as soon as they discovered its real scope and character, they gave it their support, feeling quite convinced that men who could find entertainment in the doings of the lodges, would never, as it is popularly called, set the Thames on fire. One of the first persecutions against Freemasonry arose in Holland in 1734. A crowd of ignorant fanatics, incited thereto by the clergy, broke into a lodge at Amsterdam, and destroyed all its furniture and ornaments; but the town clerk having, at the suggestion of the Order, been initiated, the States-General, upon his report, sanctioned the society, many of the chief persons becoming members. Of course, when lodges were turned into political clubs, and the real business of Masonry was cast aside for something more serious, the matter assumed a very different aspect. The persecutions here to be mentioned will therefore be such only as took place against Freemasonry, legitimately so called.

493. Instances of Persecution - Pope Clement XII., in 1738, issued a decree against the Order, which was followed by a more severe edict next year, the punishment therein awarded for being found guilty of practising Freemasonry being confiscation and death, without hope of

mercy. This was a signal of persecution in the countries connected with Home.

The parliament of Paris, however, refused to register the papal bull; and an apology for the Order was published at Dublin. But Philip V. of Spain declared the galleys for life, or punishment of death with torture to be the doom of Freemasons; a very large number of whom he caused to be arrested and sentenced. Peter Torrubia, Grand Inquisitor of Spain, having first made confession and received absolution, entered the Order for the express purpose of betraying it. He joined in 1751, and made himself acquainted with the entire ramifications of the craft; and in consequence members of ninety-seven lodges were seized and tortured on the rack. Ferdinand VI. declared Freemasonry to be high-treason, and punishable with death. When the French became masters of Spain, Freemasonry was revived and openly practised, the members of the Grand Lodge of Madrid meeting in the hall previously occupied by their arch-enemy the Inquisition. With the return of Ferdinand VII., who re-established the Inquisition, the exterminating process recommenced. In 1814, twenty-five persons suspected of Freemasonry were dragged in chains to confinement; but the subsequent arrests were so numerous, that no correct account is obtainable, nor can the ultimate fate of the accused be recorded. One of the noblest victims of the Spanish Inquisition and the Holy Alliance was Riego, the "Hampden of Spain," who was atrociously murdered by hanging at Madrid in 1823. "Have I got you, you Freemason, you son of the devil! you shall pay for all you have done! "howled the hangman, before strangling him. In 1824, a law was promulgated, commanding all Masons to declare themselves, and deliver up all their papers and documents, under the penalty of being declared traitors. The Minister of War, in the same year, issued a proclamation, outlawing every member of the craft; and in 1827, seven members of a lodge in Granada were executed; while in 1828, the tribunals of the same city condemned the Marquis of Lavrillana and Captain Alvarez to be beheaded for having founded a lodge. In 1848, Masons were no longer executed, but sent to the galleys; as late as the year 1854, members of masonic lodges were seized and imprisoned.

In 1735, several noble Portuguese instituted a lodge at Lisbon, under the Grand Lodge of England, of which George Gordon was Master; but the priests immediately determined on putting it down. One of the best-known victims of the Inquisition was John Coustos, a native of Switzerland, who was arrested in 1743, and thrown into a subterranean dungeon, where he was racked nine times in three months for not revealing the secrets of Masonry. He had, however, to appear in an auto-da-fe, and was sentenced to five years' work as a galley slave; but the British Government claiming him as a subject, he was released before the term of his punishment expired. Thirty-three years passed without anything more being heard of Freemasonry in Portugal; but in 1776, two members of the craft were arrested, and remained upwards of fourteen months in prison. In 1792, Queen Maria I. ordered all Freemasons to be delivered over to the Inquisition; a very few families escaped to New York, where they landed with the words, Asylum quccrimus. Among their American brethren they found not only an asylum, but a new home. The French Empire ushered in better days; but with the restoration of the old regime came the former prejudices and persecutions. In 1818, John VI. promulgated from the Brazils an edict against all secret societies, including Freemasonry; and, again in 1823, a similar though more stringent proclamation appeared in Lisbon. The punishment of death therein awarded was afterwards reduced to fine and transportation to Africa.

In Austria, the papal bulls provoked persecutions and seizures; hence arose the Order of the Mopses (471), which spread through Holland, Belgium, and France. In 1747, thirty Masons were arrested and imprisoned at Vienna. Maria Theresa, having been unable to discover the secrets of the Order, issued a decree to arrest all Masons, but the measure was frustrated by the good sense of the Emperor Joseph II., who was himself a Mason, and therefore knew that the pursuits of the Order were innocent enough. Francis I., at the Diet of Ratisbon in 1794, demanded the suppression of all masonic societies throughout Germany, but Hanover, Brunswick, and Prussia united with the smaller States in refusing their assent.

The history of Freemasonry in Central Italy during the last century and this, as may be supposed, is a mere repetition of sufferings, persecutions, and misfortunes; the members of the craft being continually under punishment, through the intolerance of the priesthood and the interference of the civil power.

But persecution was not confined to Catholic countries. Even in Switzerland, the Masons at one time were persecuted. The Council of Berne, in 1745, passed a law with certain degrees of punishment for members of lodges; which law was renewed in 1782. It is now abrogated. Frederick I., King of Sweden, a very few years after the introduction (1736) of Freemasonry, forbade it under penalty of death. At present the king is at the head of the Swedish craft. The King Frederick Augustus III. of Poland caused, in 1730, enactments to be published, forbidding, under pain of severe punishment, the practice of Freemasonry in his kingdom. In 1757, the Synod of Stirling adopted a resolution debarring all Freemasons from the ordinances of religion. In 1799, Lord Radnor proposed in the English Parliament a bill against secret societies, and especially against Freemasonry; and a similar but equally fruitless attempt against the Order was made in 1814 by Lord Liverpool. The Society is now acknowledged by law; the Prince of Wales is at the head of the craft.

494. Anti-Masonic Publications - One of the earliest English publications against Freemasonry is "The Freemasons; an Hudibrastic Poem" (London, 1723). It is written in the coarsest style of invective, describing the Masons as a drunken set of revellers, practising all kinds of filthy rites. Several works of no literary merit appeared at various intervals between 1726 and 1760, professing to reveal the masonic secrets, but their authors evidently knew nothing of the craft. In 1768, a rabid parson published a sermon, entitled "Masonry, the Way to Hell." It is beneath criticism. Numerous works of a similar tendency, or professing to reveal what Masonry was, thenceforth appeared at short intervals in England, France, Germany, and Italy, such as "Les Plus Secrets Mysteres de la Maçonnerie"; "Le Maschere Strappate" (The Masks torn off); "The Veil Removed, or the Secret of the

Revolutions fostered by Freemasonry "; Robison's " Proofs of a Conspiracy against all the Religions and Governments of Europe carried on in the Secret Meetings of Freemasons, Illuminati, and Reading Societies' a work which must have astonished the Masons not a little, and for which they were no doubt in their hearts very grateful to the author, for he makes the Masons out to be very terrible fellows indeed. The work of the Abbe Barruel is of the same stamp; it is entitled, "Memoires pour servir a l'Histoire du Jacobinisme," and is noteworthy for nothing but absence of critical power and honesty of statement. The Jesuits, though imitating the ritual of the Masons, have naturally always been their enemies, generally secretly, but sometimes openly, as, for instance, through the Italian zappatori (labourers), whose avowed object was the destruction of the Masonic Order. Protestants also have written fiercely against the Order, Lindner's "Mac-Benach" (1818), and Hengstenberg's and Moller's in quite recent years, are samples of such writings.

One of the most voluminous works against Freemasonry is that of Dr. E. E. Eckert, of Dresden. It is in three thick volumes, printed at various places (1852-80). The title is, "Proofs for the Condemnation of Freemasonry as the Starting Point of all Destructive Activity." He sees Masonry everywhere, even in Chinese secret societies! According to Eckert, Freemasons were the originators of the Illuminati and Burschenschaft in Germany, of the Jacobins and Juste Milieu in France, of the Carbonari in Italy, of the Liberals in Spain, and the Giovine Italia! He was expelled from Berlin in consequence of his attacks on highly-placed Masons. The latest work of importance hostile to Masonry is by the late Pere Deschamps, in three large volumes, entitled, "Les Societe's Secretes et la Societe" (Paris and Avignon, 1882-83). The writer, a priest, sees only evil in the fraternity, and, in fact, all evil in the world political, social, moral is due to the occult action of the Masons, whose object is the overthrow of all religion, morality, and justice. In 1873, a German work, entitled, " The Secret Warfare of Freemasonry against Church and State" (an English translation was published in 1875), had brought the same charges against the Society's action on the Continent. And Masonry continues to be the bugbear of the Church. In 1875, Pope Pius IX. fulminated a bull against the Order; in 1884, shortly after the installation of the Prince of Wales as Grand Master Mark-Mason, the Pope issued an encyclical, Httmanum genus, in which he denounced the Order as criminal, impious, revolutionary, and everything bad; towards the end of September of this present year (1896) an anti-masonic congress, convoked by the Church, was held at Trent, and attended by about six hundred priests, presided over by Cardinal Agliardi, armed with the Pope's brief condemning Freemasonry. The whole proceeding was an exact counterpart of the meeting held on the ist February 1762, when " many gentlemen, eminent for their rank and character," including "Pomposo" Johnson, "were, by the invitation of the Rev. Mr. Aldrich, assembled" to inquire into the noises made by the Cock-lane ghost. Sitting with closed doors, the Congress discussed Miss Diana Vaughan, who, in a book published by, or attributed to her, described how at an early age she was initiated into Freemasonry, and that in American lodges she had frequent interviews with Lucifer, and some of his imps. The truth or untruth of this statement was seriously debated by the "learned divines" assembled at Trent! And they left the matter in doubt. The reverend fathers seem to have been particularly shocked at the liberties taken with the devil's personality; yet they must know that the devil has for ages been an object of ridicule, the theme of ribald songs and jokes even in the mystery plays.

Dr. Bataille wrote a book entitled, " The Devil in the Nineteenth Century," which is a specimen of the grossest superstition, which was ridiculed in a reply afterwards published by a Count H. C., and wherein he regrets that a large number of high personages, particularly among the clergy, should have been thus imposed upon. Dr. Bataille in his book referred largely to devil-worship in the East; Count H. C. contradicts most of the doctor's statements.

XXVII

FUTILITY OF MODERN FREEMASONRY

495. Vain Pretensions of Modern Freemasonry - After this necessarily compressed account of Freemasonry, past and present, the question naturally suggests itself -- What is its present use? Are its pretensions not groundless? Is it not an institution which has outlived the object of its foundation? Is not its present existence a delusion and an anachronism? Since all that is said and done in the lodges has for many years been in print, is the holding out of the communication of secrets not a delusion, and the imposition of childish oaths not a farce? The answers to all these questions must be unfavourable to Freemasonry. When Masonry was purely operative, it had its uses; when it became speculative, it was more useful still in its earlier stages, at least on the Continent, and indirectly in this country also; for either by itself, or in conjunction with other societies, such as the Illuminati, it opposed the political despotism, then prevalent all over Europe, and formed an anti-Inquisition to clerical obscurantism and oppression, wherefore it was persecuted by Protestant and Roman Catholic rulers alike. The rapid progress achieved in modern times by humanity and toleration, is undoubtedly due to the tendency which speculative Masonry took in the last, and to its political activity in all countries, except England, in this century. Founded in ages when the possession of religious and scientific knowledge was the privilege of the few, it preserved that knowledge then indeed a small rivulet only from being choked up by the weeds of indifference and superstition; but now that that small rivulet has been overtaken by, and swallowed up in, the boundless, ever-advancing ocean of modern science, which may boldly proclaim its discoveries to the world, a society that professes to keep knowledge for the few is but a retrograde institution. Philo, about 1780, properly defined English Masonry, as it then was, and is to-day: "The lodges indiscriminately receive members, go through ceremonies, play at mysteries without understanding them, eat, drink, and digest well, and now and then bestow alms such are the formal English lodges."

496. Vanity of Masonic Ceremonial - There are thousands of excellent men who have never seen the inside of a lodge, and yet are genuine Freemasons, i.e. liberal-minded and enlightened men, devoted to the study of Nature and the progress of mankind, moral and intellectual; men devoid of all political and religious prejudices, true cosmopolitans. And there are thousands who have passed through every masonic degree, and yet are not Masons; men who take appearances for realities, the means for the end, the ceremonies of the lodge for Freemasonry. But the lodge, with all its symbols, is only the form of the masonic thought. In the present age, however, this form, which was very suitable, nay, necessary, for the time when it was instituted, becomes an anachronism. The affectation of possessing a secret is a childish and mischievous weakness. The objects modern Masons profess to pursue are brotherly love, relief, and truth; surely the pursuit of these objects cannot need any secret rites, traditions, and ceremonies. In spite of the great parade made in masonic publications about the science and learning peculiar to the craft, what discovery of new scientific facts or principles can Masons claim for the Order? Nay, are well-known and long-established truths familiar to them, and made the objects of study in the lodges? Nothing of the kind. That noble character, the Emperor-King Frederick III., who had early in life been initiated, resigned the Grand Mastership when, after patient and diligent inquiry, for which his exalted position gave him exceptional facilities, he, in spite of a secret inclination to the contrary, became satisfied of the unsoundness and vanity of masonic pretensions.

497. Masonry diffuses no Knowledge - We get neither science nor learning from a Mason, as a Mason. The Order, in fact, abjures religious and political discussion in this country, and yet it pretends that to it mankind is indebted for its progress, and that, were it abolished, mental darkness would again overshadow the world. But how is this progress to be effected, if the chronic diseases in the existing religious and political systems of the world are not to be meddled with? As well might an association for the advancement of learning abjure

inquiry into chemical and mechanical problems, and then boast of the benefits it conferred on science! It is Hamlet with the part of Hamlet omitted. If then Masonry wishes to live on, and be something more than a society of Odd Fellows or Druids, more lodges must be formed by educated men and fewer by the mere publicans and other tradesmen that now found lodges to create a market for their goods who might do some good by teaching moral and natural philosophy from a deeper ground than the scholastic and grossly material basis on which all teaching at present is founded, and by rescuing science from the degraded position of handmaiden to mere physical comfort, into which modern materialism has forced it.

498. Decay of Freemasonry - The more I study Freemasonry, the more I am repelled by its pretences. The facility and frequency with which worthless characters are received into the Order; the manner in which all its statutes are disregarded; the dislike with which every brother who insists on reform is looked upon by the rest; the difficulty of expelling obnoxious members; the introduction of many spurious rites, and the deceptiveness of the rites themselves, designed to excite curiosity without ever satisfying it; the puerility of the symbolism; the paltriness of the secret when revealed to the candidate, and his ill-concealed disgust when at last he gets behind the scenes and sees through the rotten canvas that forms so beautiful a landscape in front all these too plainly show that the lodge has banished Freemasonry. And like monasticism or chivalry, it is no longer wanted. Having no political influence, and no political aspirations, or, when it has such aspirations revealing them by insane excesses, such as the citation before masonic tribunals of Napoleon III., the Emperor of Germany, the Crown Prince, the Pope, and Marshal Prim, by French, Italian, and Spanish Masons respectively,and after afarcical sham trial, condemning the accused so cited to which summons of course they paid no attention to death, or in plain English, to assassination, a crime really perpetrated on the person of Marshal Prim; being no longer even a secret society for a society sanctioned by the State, as Freemasonry is, cannot be called a secret society; having no industrial or intellectual rally ingpoint it

must eventually die from sheer inanition. It may prolong its existence by getting rid of all the rites and ceremonies which are neither simple nor grand, nor founded on any authority or symbolic meaning, and by renouncing the silly pretence of secrets, [19] and undertaking to teach what I have sketched in various portions of this work, concerning the origin and meaning of Masonry and its symbols, illustrating its teaching by the ornaments and practice of the lodges. This seems to be the only ground on which Freemasonry could claim to have its lease of existence, as Freemasonry, renewed, for not even the Masonic marriages, introduced by French lodges, will perpetuate its existence. I have before me accounts of two such marriages, performed without the usual ecclesiastic or civil ceremonies, the one in the lodge La France Ma onnique in Paris in 1887, and the other in a lodge at Toulouse, in the same year, as also of two others, celebrated in Paris, in 1882, when M. Elyse'e Reclus, a Freemason, and one of the five well-known Anarchist brothers, gave away two of his daughters to two brothers, at a dinner held in a private house, simply declaring the two couples by that mere declaration to be married. But the ladies do not approve of these hole-and-corner espousals.

499. Masonic Opinions of Masonry - Masons have been very indignant with me for making these statements; but honest members of the craft know, and occasionally admit, that I am right. In 1798 a Mason wrote in the Monthly Magazine, "The landlord (who is always a brother) promotes harmony, as it is called, by providing choice suppers and good liquors, the effects of which are late hours and inebriety; and thus are made up two-thirds of modern lodges." And again: " Hogarth was a member of the fraternity, and actually served the office of Grand Steward in 1735, . . . yet in his picture of; Night,' one of the most conspicuous figures is that of a master of a lodge led home drunk by the tyler." The too facile admission of worthless members is regretted by the same writer, as it is by modern Masons

---

[19] " Un secrete, che sanno tre,
Un secreto mai non è." Italian Proverb.

(e.g. Freemason, 26th June 1875).

Brother John Yarker in his " Notes on the Scientific and Religious Mysteries of Antiquity " (Hogg, I 872), a zealous Mason, says: "As the masonic fraternity is now governed, the craft is fast becoming the paradise of the bon vivant, of the 'charitable' hypocrite, who . . . decorates his breast with the 'charity jewel'; . . . the manufacturer of paltry masonic tinsel; the rascally merchant who swindles in hundreds and even thousands, by appealing to the tender consciences of those few who do regard their O. B.'s, and the Masonic ' Emperors ' and other charlatans, who make power or money out of the aristocratic pretensions which they have tacked on to our institution, ad captandum vulgus" This I think is enough to show that my censures are well founded.

500. Masonic Literature - It is almost absurd to talk of masonic literature; it scarcely exists. Except the works written by Oliver, Mackey, Findel, and Ragon, there is scarcely anything worth reading about Freemasonry, of which a Freemason is the author. The countless lectures by brethren, with a few exceptions, consist of mere truisms and platitudes. Its periodical literature in this country at all events is essentially of the Grub Street kind, consisting of mere trade-circulars, supported by puffing masonic tradesmen and vain officials, who like to have their working in the lodge trumpeted forth in a fashion which occasionally trenches on imbecility, as could readily be shown by extracts from newspaper reports. All attempts permanently to establish masonic periodicals of a higher order have hitherto failed from want of encouragement. The fact is, men of education take very little interest in Masonry, for it has nothing to offer them in an intellectual point of view; because even Masons who have attained to every ne plus ultra of the institution, know little of its origin and meaning.

5ooa. The Quatuor Coronati Lodge - The literary shortcomings of Masonry I have, in the interests of truth, and as an impartial historian been compelled to point out in the previous section, have been recognised by intelligent Masons, and such recognition has, in 1884, led to the foundation of the Quatuor Coronati Lodge.

Members must be possessed of literary or artistic qualifications; to belong to it, therefore, is in itself a distinction, and, as may be supposed, the lodge is composed chiefly of well-known masonic historians and antiquaries, and thus occupies a position totally different from all other masonic lodges. Its objects are the promotion of masonic knowledge, by papers read and discussions thereon in the lodge; by the publication of its transactions, and the reprinting of scarce and valuable works on Freemasonry, such as MSS., e.g. "The Masonic Poem" (circa 1390), the earliest MS. relating to Freemasonry; Matthew Cooke's Harleian and Lansdowne MSS.; or printed works, as e.g., "Anderson's Constitutions" of 1738, or Reproductions of Masonic Certificates. All these have been issued by this lodge in volumes, entitled "Ars Quatuor Coronatorum," well printed, and expensively illustrated. Connected with the lodge is a " Correspondence Circle," whose members reside in all parts of the globe, and form a literary society of Masons, aiming at the progress of the craft. But by progress can only be meant extension of Masonry; the "Transactions" and "Reprints" can add nothing to the knowledge the best-informed members already possess; but the " Reprints," by their aesthetic sumptuousness and the learned comments accompanying them, invest Masonry with a dignity which may attract to it more of the intelligence of mankind than it has hitherto done, and the labours of Quatuor Coronatorum therefore deserve the hearty support of the craft.

BOOK XII

INTERNATIONAL, COMMUNE, AND ANARCHISTS

501. Introductory Remarks - There exists at present in a state of suspended animation an association of working or rather, talking men, pretending to have for its object the uniting in one fraternal bond the workers of all countries, and the advocating of the interests of labour, and those only. Though it protests against being a secret society, it yet indulges in such underhand dealings, insidiously endeavouring to work mischief between employers and employed, and aiming at the subversion of the existing order of things, that it deserves to be denounced with all the societies professedly secret. In this country its influence is scarcely felt, because the English workmen that join it are numerically few: according to the statement of the secretary of the International himself, the society in its most palmy days counted only about 8000 English members and these, with here and there an exception, belonged to the most worthless portion of the working classes. It ever is chiefly the idle and dissipated or unskilled artizan who thinks his position is to be improved by others and not by himself. To hear the interested demagogues and paid agitators of the "International," or of "Unions," the working classes would seem to be exceptionally oppressed, and to labour under disadvantages greater than any that weigh upon other sections of the community. Yet no other class is so much protected by the legislature, and none, except the paupers, pay less towards the general expenses of the country in direct or indirect taxation. The wages a skilled artizan can earn are higher than the remuneration obtainable by thousands of men, who have enjoyed a university education, or sunk money in some professional apprenticeship; whilst he is free from the burden incident to maintaining a certain social status. His hours of labour are such as to leave him plenty of leisure for enjoyment, especially in this country; and as regards extra holidays, he is on the whole pretty liberally dealt with, especially by the large employers of labour, the capitalists, against

whom the street-spouters, who for their own advantage get up public demonstrations, are always inveighing in a manner which would be simply ridiculous, were it not mischievous. But then if they did not constantly attempt to render the workman dissatisfied with his lot, their occupation would be gone. And so, as the doctors who, for want of patients, get up hospitals for the cure of particular diseases, try to persuade every man they come in contact with, that he is suffering from some such disease; so these agitators endeavour to talk the workman into the delusion that he is the most unfortunate and most oppressed individual under the sun. To wish to act for one's self and work out one's own salvation is no doubt very praiseworthy; but workmen ought to bear in mind that they may be the tools of ambitious men in their own class, who look upon and use them as such for their own purposes, men who want to be generals commanding soldiers. But the soldiers of the Unions are not worth much. Those workmen who are not satisfied with adhering to the statutes of the society in order to get rid of troublesome appeals, and to avoid being molested by their comrades, but who fervently embrace its principles and count upon their success, usually are the most idle, the least saving, the least sober. The fanatics of the Unions, those who ought to form their principal strength, are formed, not by the élite t but by the scum of the working classes. The chiefs are not much better. The more intelligent and honest founders of such societies have gradually withdrawn from them in disgust.

502. Socialistic Schemes - Schemes for the regeneration of mankind have been hatched in every age, from Plato and his Republic down to Louis Blanc's Organisation du Travail, and the International. Many communistic movements took place in the sixteenth century, and the brief history of the Anabaptist kingdom of Munster presents striking resemblances with that of the Commune of Paris. Babeuf and the Conspiracy of the Equals remind us of the demagogues who filled Paris with blood and fire. The collegia opificum of Rome, the guilds of France and Germany, the tradescorporations, the compagnonnage all these were the forerunners of modern trade-unions and the

International. The systems of Saint-Simon, Fourier, Cabet, Louis Blanc, and Owen also had their day. In this country no law has been passed against trade-unions, and therefore they flourish here, and have led to deplorable events, such as the Sheffield outrages, which, for diabolical fury, deserve to be placed side by side with the doings of the Commune. The reader will probably remember the fact that men who had belonged to the Sheffield trade-unions, but withdrew from them, were assassinated, their houses blown up, and every imaginable kind of tyranny and persecution practised upon them for the space of some fifteen years. Still, as the majority of the Parisian workmen were innocent of the crimes of the Commune, so the trade-unions were not answerable for the doings of a restricted number of their members. But these trade-unions, dating from about the year 1833, are still to be condemned, because they are the instigators and upholders of strikes, the greatest curse, not on the hated capitalist, but on the poor workman. Now the International was a combination of trade-unions, with the additional poison of Communism diffused throughout its system.

503. History of the International -The first attempt at an international society was made by a small number of German workmen in London, who had been expelled from France in 1839 for taking part in the dmeute in Paris. Its members consisted of Germans, Hungarians, Poles, Danes, and Swedes. Of the few English members, Ernest Jones was one. The society was on friendly terms with the English Socialists, the Chartists, and the London French Democratic Society. Out of that friendship sprang the Society of the Fraternal Democrats, who were in correspondence with a number of democratic societies in Belgium. In November 1847 a German Communist Conference was held in London, at which Dr. Karl Marx was present. In the manifesto then put forth, it was declared that the aim of the Communists was the overthrow of the rule of the capitalists by the acquisition of political power. The practical measures by which this was to be effected were the abolition of private property in land; the centralisation of credit in the hands of the State the leading agitators of course to be the chiefs of

the State by means of a national bank; the centralisation of the means of transport in the hands of the State; national workshops; the reclamation and improvement of land; and the gratuitous education of all the children. But all these fine schemes of amelioration, or rather spoliation, in consequence of the Revolution of February 1848, ended in smoke; and it was not till the year 1859, when the London builders' dispute arose, that new alliances among the working-men were formed. In 1860 a Trade Unionist, Manhood Suffrage, and Vote by Ballot Association was established. As if it had not enough of what might be called legitimate work to do, the association also undertook to agitate in favour of Poland, for which purpose it co-operated with the National League for the Independence of Poland. The London International Exhibition of 1862 induced the French Government to assist many French workmen with means to visit that exhibition; "a visit," said the French press, "which will enable our workmen to study the great works of art and industry, remove the leaven of international discord, and replace national jealousies by fraternal emulation." It is impossible to say how far these French workmen studied the works of art and industry exhibited in 1862, but it is quite certain that the old leaven of international discord, which up to that time had not been very formidable, was speedily replaced by a new leaven of social discord, not so virulent at first, it is true, as it subsequently became in the after-days of the International. Many of the original members of this association, in fact, eventually withdrew from it, as they refused to be identified with its excesses, which had not been planned or foreseen by its founders. On the 5th of August, all the delegates met at a dinner given to them by their English colleagues at Freemasons' Hall, when an address was read which formed, as it were, the foundation-stone of "the International. The Imperial Commission that had enabled the French workmen to visit the London Exhibition had no doubt furnished them with return tickets; but several of the artizans made no use of their second halves, since profitable employment in London was found for them by their English brethren, so that they might form connecting links between the workmen of the two countries. The next year a new meeting was found necessary. There was no longer an

Exhibition, nor subsidies from the Imperial Government to pay travelling expenses. The pretext, however, was found in a demonstration just then made in favour of Poland. Six French delegates having mulcted their mates in contributions towards the pleasant trip, came over, and the democrats of London and Paris were invited to co-operate in the liberation of Poland, and to form an international working-men's alliance. Various meetings were held, and all the stale twaddle concerning Poland and the emancipation of the working classes talked over again. A central committee of working-men of different countries, to have its seat in London truly England is the political and social dunghill of Europe! was appointed, and a collection of course followed, which at the most important meeting realised three guineas. A paltry sum after so much talk! The members of the committee, holding its powers by the resolution of the public meeting held on September 28, 1864, at St. Martin's Hall, then declared the International Working-Men's Association to be established; and congresses were appointed to be held at different times and places, to decide on the measures to be taken to found the working-men's Eldorado. Many societies at first were affiliated, but dissensions soon broke out among them, and many, such as the Italian WorkingMen's Society, withdrew again. In 1866, a meeting or congress was held at Geneva, where it was decided that an inquiry into the condition of the working classes of all countries should be made respecting rate of wages, hours of labour, &c. And this inquiry, which never was made on the part of the International, was to be a preliminary to practical measures no wonder that the association produced nothing practical. At this Geneva Congress resolutions were passed in favour of transferring railways and other means of locomotion to the people, and of destroying the monopoly of the great companies "that subject the working classes to arbitrary laws, assailing both the dignity of man and individual liberty." Resolutions were also passed in favour of direct taxation. How this suggestion would be received by the working-man has very pleasantly been pointed out by Punch or some other comic paper: "Mrs. Brown (loq.) ' Well, Mrs. Jones, my husband says that if they tax him, he will take it out in parish relief.' " The abolition of standing armies and the independence of Poland Poland again were also decided on. Both these points are still decided on, and will probably remain at the same interesting stage of progress a little longer.

504. Objects and Aims of International - To sum up what was proposed at the latter congresses: Quarries, coal and other mines, as well as railways, shall belong to the social collectivity, represented by the State; but by the State regenerated, that will concede them, not, as now, to capitalists, but to associations of workmen. The soil shall be granted to agricultural associations; canals, roads, telegraphs, and forests shall belong collectively to society. Contracts of lease, or letting, shall be converted into contracts of sale; that is to say, capital shall no longer be entitled to claim interest. If I borrow 1000, I shall have paid off the debt in twenty years by an annual payment of 50. Such were the doctrines of this society, whose motto was, La propriety c'est le vol. All these, however, were clothed in very fine words "economic evolution," "social collectivity," " scientific and rational exploitation," " social liquidation," &c. No congress met in 1870, in consequence of the war; but the programme that was to have formed the subject of discussion has been published. The first question was: On the necessity of abolishing the public debt. The third: Concerning practical means for converting landed and funded property into social property. The fifth: Conditions of co-operative production on a national scale. The Belgian Committee proposed as an additional question: Concerning the practical means for constituting agricultural sections in the International. Thus private property was to be abolished, private enterprise destroyed, and the poison of Communism, with which large towns are now infected, to be diffused throughout the country. What would these men have done could they, according to their intention, have met in Paris in 1870? The pertinacity with which the cause of Poland is sought to be identified with the objects of the International has already been alluded to. Poland seems a mine that can never be exhausted. Thousands of rogues and vagabonds of all countries have fattened, are fattening, and will yet fatten on this carcass, as burnt-out tradesmen have been known to flourish on the fire by which they lost

everything!

505. The International in England - In this country, as we have seen, the International had only a limited success. It indeed held public meetings and demonstrations, and led to some insignificant riots, for the occurrence of which our Government of course was very much to blame. There were, indeed, alarmists who were led astray by the "bounce" of the International, and who thus invested it with greater importance than intrinsically attached to it. Thus a Paris paper contained a letter from a London correspondent, which gave an awful picture of the danger threatening this country from the spread of socialistic doctrines. The writer said: "The whole of this vast empire is permeated by secret societies. The International here holds its meetings almost publicly. It is said that the greater number of the dispossessed princes of India, a good number of officers belonging to the army and navy, as well as members of Parliament, and even ministers, are affiliated to it (!). The Government is aware of the infernal plan by which, at a given moment, the public buildings of London are to be exposed to the fate which befell so many in Paris. Boats are already waiting on the Thames to receive the treasures of the Bank of England an easy prey, say the conspirators as soon as the main artery of the Strand shall have been burnt, and the public buildings, the barracks especially, shall have been blown np, as was three years ago the Clerkenwell prison." Perhaps the writer was only joking; and if I thought the leaders of the International possessed any Machiavellian talent, I should say they themselves caused the letter to be written to give the world an exaggerated idea of their power therein imitating the President of the London Republican Club, who boasted of his power of pulling down the monarchy, as that would be the readiest means of attracting fresh members; for the idea of belonging to a powerful and universally diffused brotherhood exercises a great fascination over the minds of only partially educated men, such as form the bulk of the working classes.

506. The International Abroad - Abroad, however, its action was much

more marked. It fomented serious riots in Holland, Belgium, and France; and in the last-named country it especially stimulated Communism, and supported the Paris Commune in all its atrocities, which were spoken of in the most laudatory terms in the then recently published pamphlet, "The Civil War in France" (Truelove, 1871). But even continental workmen have ere this discovered the hollowness of the International. The working engineers of Brussels, instead of receiving during a recent strike fifteen francs weekly, as promised, were paid only six francs; and having imposed upon the masters an augmentation of fifty per cent, on overtime, the masters, in order to avoid this ruinous tariff, had no work performed after the regular hours. The men, finding themselves losers by this rule, enforced on them by the International, sent in their resignations as members of the society, which they described as the " Leprosy of Europe," and the " Company of Millionaires ... on paper." At a conference held in London, the Russian delegate urged that his country especially offered an excellent field for the spread of socialist doctrines, and that the students were quite ripe for revolution. Wherefore it was decided that a special appeal should be addressed to the Russian students and workmen.

507. The International and the Empire - At the time when the International was founded, the French Empire was as yet in all its strength. None of the parties that secretly strove against it seemed to have any chance of success; nor from their political and social characteristics could these parties, though all bent on the overthrow of the empire, coalesce and act as one combined force. The International refused to ally itself to any of them or to meddle with politics, but declared social questions paramount to all political considerations; and to the position thus assumed by the association it was due that the Imperial Government did not molest it, but that the ministers allowed it to develop itself, hoping at the convenient moment to win it over to their interest. These ministers considered themselves very profound politicians, when they had fomented a quarrel between Prussia and Austria; trusting, when these two powers should mutually have

exhausted each other, to seize the Rhenish provinces. They looked upon themselves as small Machiavellis when they permitted the International to grow in order some day to use it against a mutinous bourgeoisie. The Emperor had an opportunity on September 2, at Sedan, and the Empress on September 4, at Paris, to judge of the value of such policy. However, the scheme of the association having been settled in London in 1864, the organisers opened at Paris a bureau- de correspondance, which was neither formally interdicted nor regularly authorised by the Prefect and the Minister. But the constantly-growing power of the International, shown by the strikes of Roubaix, Amiens, Paris, Geneva, &c., after a time compelled the Government either to direct or to destroy it. The Parisian manifesto read at Geneva was stopped at the French frontier; but M. Rouher agreed to admit it into France, if the association would insert some passages thanking the Emperor for what he had done for the working classes a suggestion which was received with derision by the members. In the meantime the old revolutionary party looked with suspicion on the foundation of the International; for, as this last declared that it would not meddle with politics, the others called out, Treason! and thus the two parties were soon in a condition of violent opposition. In 1867, the Congress of Lausanne voted against war, but at the same moment the other fraction of the demagogues, assembled at Geneva, under pretence of forming a congress of peace, declared war to all tyrants and oppressors of the people. However, the two parties, the bourgeois demagogues and the workmen demagogues, eventually united; and thus it came to pass that by virtue of this pact the International took part in two revolutionary manifestations which occurred about six weeks after the one at the tomb of Manin in the cemetery of Montmartre, and the other on the following day on the Boulevard Montmartre, to protest against the French occupation of Rome. The International having thus been carried away to declare war against the Government, the latter determined to prosecute it. The association was declared to be dissolved, and fifteen of the leaders were each fined one hundred francs. The International taking no notice of the decree of dissolution, a second prosecution was instituted, and nine of the accused were condemned to imprisonment for three months. The International now hid itself amidst the multitude of working-men's societies of all descriptions that were either authorised or at least tolerated, and made enormous progress, so that its chiefs at last declared themselves able to do without any extraneous support. The International, said one of the speakers at the Basle Congress (1869), is and must be a state within states; let these go on as suits them, until our state is the strongest. Then, on the ruins of these, we shall erect our own fully prepared, such as it exists in every section. The Volksstimme, the Austrian organ of the society, said: "To us the red flag is the symbol of universal love of mankind. Let our enemies beware lest they transform it against themselves into a flag of terror" To have an organ of its own the International founded the Marseillaise, with Rochefort for its chief, his association therewith having induced certain capitalists to find the necessary funds. Another personage with whom it became connected was General Cluseret (669). Cluseret, as an adventurer, always on the look-out for what might turn up, saw the power such an association as the International might command, and the latter found in him a willing tool. From a letter he addressed from New York to Varlin, on February 17, 1870, it also appears that all the crimes of which he has since then been guilty, were premeditated, and that he had from the first resolved not to perish without involving Paris in his fall. " On that day " (of the downfall of Louis Napoleon), he says, "on that day, we or nothing. On that day Paris must be ours, or Paris must cease to exist." That this feeling was shared by other members of the association may be inferred from the fact that, at the house of one of the affiliated was found a dictionary which formed the key of their secret correspondence. Now, besides the usual words, we find such as nitre-glycerine and picrate of potash; at the house of another, recipes were discovered for the manufacture of nitre-glycerine, and of various other explosive compounds. Some of the recipes were followed by such directions as these "To be thrown in at windows," "To be thrown into gutters," &c. The attempted plebiscite in support of then reforms voted by the Senate, in January 1870, was violently opposed by the International, who declared in favour of a republic. On the occasion of the plot of the Orsini shells, the society, in defending itself against the charge of having had any share in it, declared that it did not war against individual perpetrators of coups d'ttat, but that it was a permanent conspiracy of all the oppressed, which shall exist until all capitalists, priests, and political adventurers shall have disappeared. Such a declaration of war against all men that had any interest in the maintenance of public order, and especially against many men forming the then Imperial Government, naturally induced a third prosecution.

Thirty-eight members were indicted, many of whom we meet again as active members of the Commune. Some were acquitted, others condemned to one year's imprisonment. No one suspected that the names of these obscure workmen, condemned as members of a secret society, would soon be connected with the most horrible disasters of Paris, and that these men, sentenced to such slight punishments, would at the end of a year reappear before a military tribunal, after having for two months and a half filled terrified Paris with pillage, murder, and incendiary fires.

508. The International and the War - The International condemned all war except war against bourgeois, capitalists, monopolists, parasites that is to say, the classes that live not by manual labour, but by intellectual work, or the savings of any kind of labour. It abolished national wars, to replace them by social war. For this reason it so pertinaciously insisted on the abolition of all standing armies, which are of course great obstacles to its own plans. It therefore protested against the Franco-Prussian war, but as this opposition ended in mere talk, it need not further be dilated on. Its only results were to consign some of the most violent opponents to prison; and there is no proof that one single soldier of the regular Prussian army, or even of the Landwehr, deserted or refused to fight, in order to remain faithful to the theories of the society. In France the affiliated of the International were only brave in civil war.

On September 3, 1870, the disaster of Sedan became known at Paris. On the next day, Lyons, Marseilles, Toulouse, and Paris proclaimed the Kepublic. This simultaneous movement was the result of an understanding existing between the leading members of the International in the various parts of France; but that the "Jules Favres and Gambettas," that vermine bouryeoise, as the International called them, should obtain any share of power, was very galling to the demagogues. At Lyons and Marseilles, however, the supreme power fell into the hands of the lowest wretches. The Commune installed at Lyons began its work by raising the red flag that of the International. At Paris the association pretended at first to be most anxious to fight the Prussians. When the battalions were sent to the front, however, it was found that those comprising most Internationals were the most ready " to fall back in good order," or even to flee in great disorder at the first alarm; and General Clement Thomas pointed out this instructive fact to the readers of the Journal Officiel. But when a few Prussian regiments entered Paris, the International, through its central committee, announced that the moment for action was come; and so the members seized the cannons scattered in various parts of the city, and then began that series of excesses, for which the Commune will always enjoy an infamous notoriety.

509. The International and the Commune - One would have supposed that the International would disavow the Communists; but, on the contrary, it approved of their proceedings. Flames were still ascending from the Hotel de Ville, when already numerous sections of the International throughout Europe expressed their admiration of the conduct of the Parisian outcasts.

  At Zurich, at a meeting of the members of the International, it was declared that "the struggle maintained by the Commune of Paris was just and worthy, and that all thinking men ought to join in the contest."

  At Brussels the Belgian section of the International protested against the prosecution of the malefactors of Paris. At Geneva, two days before the entrance of the Versaillais into Paris, an address to the Commune was voted, declaring that it (the Commune) represented "the economic aspirations of the working classes." The German Internationalists were no less positive in their praise of the

Communists: " We are ready to defend the acts of the Commune at all times, and against all comers," said a socialistic paper published at Leipzig. The Italians sent an address to the Commune, ending thus: "To capital which said, Ye shall starve, they replied: We will live by our labour. To despotism they replied: We are free! To the cannons and chassepots of the reactionnaires they opposed their naked breasts. They fell, but fell as heroes! Now the reaction calls them bandits. Shall we permit it? No ! Let us invite our brethren to our homes, and protect them. The principles of the Commune are ours; we accept the responsibility of their acts." The English Internationalists were too few to prove their approbation of the Commune by any public demonstration; but in private they did so very energetically. One of the members even declared that the good time "was really coming." "Soon," said he, "we shall be able to dethrone the Queen of England, turn Buckingham Palace into a workshop, and pull down the York column, as the noble French people has pulled down the Vendome column." (Be it observed here, that as this column chiefly commemorated French victories over the Germans, this act of vandalism has by some authorities been attributed to the influence of Prussian gold liberally distributed to certain patriotic members of the Commune.) But the London section of the International clearly put forth its views on the conduct of the Commune. The pamphlet, "The Civil War in France," published for the council by Truelove, 256 High Holborn, the office of the International, is a continuous panegyric on the Commune, and was at first signed by all the members of the council; but two of them, Lucraft and Odger, afterwards withdrew their names, stating that they had, in the first instance, been appended without their knowledge which appeared to be the fact.

510. Budget of the International - One portion of the organisation of the International, and that the most important for the chiefs, of course! its budget, remains to be noticed. It is scarcely necessary to say that there was a total absence of official accounts; but the following details, referring to France and Belgium, will give some idea as to the way in which funds were raised and applied. Every member on his admission

paid a fee of fifty centimes, for which he received his admission card, which was renewed annually and gratuitously. He had also to pay a minimum annual tax of ten centimes, to go towards the general expenses of the association. Then each federation imposed a special tax for its own expenses. At Lyons and Paris this amounted to ten centimes per month. Thus it appears that the annual tax was very light, amounting only to one franc thirty cents, which was not paying too dear for the honour of belonging to a society that aspired to the government of the world, and commenced by burning it. But this honour could be had at a still cheaper rate; for the Swiss branch charged its members only ten centimes a year. Yet even these small sums seemed difficult to be got in, and the statutes were very severe upon defaulters. But there were taxes to pay to the sections, which raised the yearly contributions to seven or eight francs. Nor was this all. In the various legal prosecutions the society had to undergo there was frequent reference to the caisse federative du sou, though the expression was nowhere exactly defined. So far as has been ascertained it alluded to a voluntary weekly subscription of five centimes, collected in workshops and factories, from workmen who did not belong to the association, but intended to join it, or to support it without joining it. In the statutes of the Parisian branch, Article 9 further said that the council may, if necessary, vote larger sums than the general budget would justify, and proportionately increase the amount of contributions payable by the members. But the most powerful arm of the association, when any particular object was to be attained, such, for instance, as the success of a strike, was subscription. Thus the successful termination of the strike in the building trade of Geneva in 1868, was thought of such importance as to call forth unusual exertions. But the delegate who was sent to London to collect subscriptions from the English workmen met with but slight success; not because these were niggardly, but because, in spite of their avowed hatred of state forms and aristocratic deliberation, they yet so closely imitated both, that the Genevese workmen might have been starved into submission before the English workmen had resolved to succour them, had not the Parisian workmen at once subscribed ten thousand francs. What these annual subscriptions may have amounted to, it is impossible to tell. No doubt the total was very great, considering the large number of members; and yet it was insufficient, in consequence of the strikes that were constantly taking place at all places and times. The journals were full of the fine phrases used by the chiefs of the International concerning the sufferings of the workmen reduced by infamous capitalists to the point of forsaking their work and of leaving the workshops where their misery was turned to account. A confidential letter of Varlin, one of the chiefs of the Paris federation, which was brought into court at the trial of the International on June 22, I 870, at Paris, however, showed that the chiefs did not speak quite so feelingly of these sufferings, when they are not expected to be heard by their dupes: "This strike which we declared closed ten days ago, leaves four hundred workmen on our hands. The day before yesterday they wanted to destroy their former workshops and drive away the mogs that had taken their places. Fortunately we restrained them, but we are greatly bothered by this affair (nous sommes bien embSte's par cette affaire)."

511. Attempt to Revive the International - An International Trades Union Congress was held in London in 1888 for the avowed purpose of reviving the International, which collapsed in 1871, though branches of it, such as the Jurassic Federation of Workmen, the International Brethren, the Council of Dynamite, at whose meetings in Chicago the editor of Freilieit presided, continue to vegetate. But the discussions as to the means of physically and morally raising the working classes as yet remain mere talk. As one of the speakers at the London Congress remarked, "The chief difficulty in the way of the reconstruction of the International lies in the apathy and indifference of the workmen themselves," which shows that the workmen are after all not such fools as agitators think or wish them to be.

512. Anarchists - The fear of hell, the only means known to the churches of all denominations, to keep men from vice, has never been an efficient one for that purpose. In the Middle Ages, which, we are

told, were permeated by deep religious feeling, club-law, persecution of the Jews, and inhuman cruelties indulged in by Church and State were the rule. The latter two have in our days become more civilised, but the masses retain their sting, and men are driven by wretchedness to attempt its removal by the destruction of all existing order. Karl Marx in 1864 first thought of consolidating this principle by a secret society, the International Union of Working-Men. In 1868 the Russian, Michael Bakunin, and the Belgian, Victor Dave, infused into the association the poison of Anarchism, which in 1871 produced the Paris Commune. But disputes arose between the more moderate members, the Social Democrats, and the Anarchists in 1872, who thenceforth formed two distinct camps. The social democrat and bookbinder, John Most (born 1846), joined the Anarchists, and in 1879 founded in London the Freiheit, an Anarchist paper of the most violent character. In 1883 the Anarchists attempted to blow up the German Emperor and those around him at the unveiling of the monument in the Niederwald; the two ringleaders were caught and beheaded, but in 1885 Dr. Rumpf, a high police official, who had been instrumental in securing the conviction of the criminals, was assassinated at Frankfort-on-the-Main; only the least important of the assassins, Julius Lieske, twenty-two years of age, was discovered and beheaded. Most then founded another more secret society of propagandists, to which only the leading members of the association were admitted. When the Freilieit applauded the Phoenix Park murders it was suppressed, but reappeared in Switzerland, and lastly in the United States, to which Most in 1882 emigrated, and the propaganda of Anarchism, whose secret chief seat was at Chicago, made rapid progress in the States, as well as in Europe, and culminated in the dynamite outrages at Chicago, assassinations at Strasburg, Stuttgart, Vienna, and Prague.

In the latter city, early in 1883, a secret council of Anarchists condemned the prefect of the police, who had had some of the assassins arrested, to death; lots were drawn as to who was to do the deed, and it fell on a journeyman glove-maker, named Dressier, who, however, committed suicide to escape becoming a murderer. But before his death he had written a letter to his parents, revealing the existence of the society; the information it gave enabled the police to arrest the most important members. On the 4th July 1883, a shoe manufacturer in one of the most frequented suburban streets of Vienna was set upon in his house by two individuals, who held a sponge saturated with chloroform to his face until he became unconscious, when he was robbed of 782 florins. Some weeks after the crime was traced to an Anarchist association, and seventeen men and two women were arrested, who, after investigation, were found to be members of a secret association, whose aim, according to pamphlets found on them, was to do away with the throne, altar, and moneybags, and to establish a Red Republic. Small associations, it appeared, consisting of from five to nine members each, had been formed among the Radical workmen, each member being bound to establish another such small circle. The trial appears to have broken up the society, though Anarchists in most countries of Europe and other parts of the world remain very active, openly avowing the results they aim at, results in themselves impracticable, and which, if they could be attained, would render the existence of society and of civilisation impossible. The Anarchists, who wish to reform the world, should begin by reforming themselves.

BOOK XIII

POLITICAL SECRET SOCIETIES

"These were days, when my heart was volcanic,
As the scoriae rivers that roll,
As the lavas, that restlessly roll
Their sulphurous currents down Yanik,
In the clime of the boreal pole;
That groan as they roll down Mount Yanik,
In the clime of the ultimate pole."

E. A. FOE.

I

CHINESE SOCIETIES

513. Earliest Secret Chinese Societies - The earliest notice we have of a secret Chinese league is towards the close of the Han dynasty (A.D. 185). Three patriots, having then associated themselves, defended the throne against the " Yellow Cap " rebels, a society numbering among its members the flower of Chinese litterateurs. From that time until the establishment of the present Tartar dynasty (twelfth century), the League showed few signs of vitality. Bat at the beginning of the eighteenth century five monks and seven other persons bound themselves by an oath, which they ratified by mixing blood from the arm of each, and drinking it in common, to overthrow the Tsings, the present Tartar dynasty, and restore the Mings, the dispossessed Chinese dynasty. The name of the society they founded was Pelin-kiao, or the White Lily. The members relied on a prophecy that one of them should be emperor of China. The leaders were Wang-lung and a bonze named Fan-ui. The former made himself master of the town of Shoo-changhien, but was soon driven thence, and eventually captured, and

executed with many of his followers. In 1777 the Pe-lin-kiao again appeared, only to be defeated again; the heads of the' leaders, including those of two women, were cut off and placed in cages for public inspection. In 1800 a sect called the Wonderful Association, and another, called the Tsing-lien-kiao, supposed to be the Pe-lin-kiao under a new name, conspired against the ruling dynasty, but unsuccessfully. Under the reign of the Emperor Kia-King (1799-1820) arose the Th'ien-Hauw-Hoi'h, that is, the family of the Queen of Heaven, spread through Cochin-China, Siam, and Corea, with its headquarters in the southern provinces of the empire. The society on being discovered and, as it was thought, exterminated, arose again under the name of the Great Hung League; Hung literally means flood, and the leaders adopted the name to intimate that their society was to flood the earth. To avoid the appearance of all belonging to one society, they gave different names some borrowed from previously existing sects to the branches they established. Thus they were known as the Triad Society, the Blue Lotus Hall, the Golden Orchid District, and others. These soon attracted the attention of Government, and for some time they were kept in check. About 1826 the chief leader of the League was one Kwang San. It was reported that, to make himself ferocious he once drank gall, taken out of a murdered man's body, mixed with wine. He resided chiefly at the tin-mines of Loocoot, where the brethren then swarmed. The directing power was vested in three persons; the chief, with the title of Koh, i.e. the Elder; the two others took that of Hiong Thi, i.e. Younger Brothers. In the Malacca branches the three chiefs were called Tai-Koh, eldest brother, Ji-Koh, second brother, and San-Koh, third brother. The oath of secrecy was taken by the aspirant kneeling before an image, under two sharp swords. Whilst the oath was being administered the Hiong Thi had also to kneel, the one on the right, the other on the left of the aspirant, and hold over his head the swords in such a fashion as to form a triangle. The oath contained thirty-six articles, of which the following was the most important: "I swear that I shall know neither father nor mother, nor brother nor sister, nor wife nor child, but the brotherhood alone; where the brotherhood leads or pursues, there I shall follow or pursue; its foe shall be my foe." The aspirant, with a knife, then made an incision into his finger, and allowed three drops of blood to fall into a cup of arrack; the three officials did the same thing, and then drank the liquor. In order further to ratify the oath, the newly-sworn member cut off the head of a white cock, which was to intimate that if he proved untrue, his head should be cut off.

514. More recent Societies - In 1850 Tae-ping-wang, the noted revolutionary leader, made a fresh attempt to restore the Ming dynasty, from whom he pretended to be descended. With his defeat and death the League again subsided into obscurity. In the spring of 1863 a quantity of books were accidentally found by the police in the house of a Chinaman, suspected of theft, at Padang (Sumatra), containing the laws, statutes, oaths, mysteries of initiation, catechism, description of flags, symbols, and secret signs of the League, all of which were published in English in a 4to volume at Batavia in 1866. But this discovery showed the League to be still in existence, and about the year 1870 it started into activity again; in Sarawak it assumed such a threatening aspect that the Government made a law decreeing death to every member ipso facto. The disturbances at Singapore in 1872 also were due to the secret societies of the Chinese in the Straits Settlements. On that occasion the Sam- Sings, or "fighting men," were the chief rioters, taking the part of the street hawkers, against whom some severe regulations had been issued. Murder and incendiarism, torturing and maiming, are the usual practices of the League, which again made itself very obnoxious in 1883 and 1885. The section of the " Black Flag," the remnant of the Taepings, as also the "White Lily," were the most active in their demonstrations against the Tsing dynasty. The last police reports from the protected state of Perak, in the Malay Peninsula, say that in 1888 secret societies "caused endless trouble and anxiety," although in 1887 four members of the Ghee Hin Association were sentenced to twenty years' imprisonment for conducting an agency for their society. Half the Chinese in Perak are members of secret societies, tickets being found upon them whenever the police have occasion to search them.

The Straits Times of the 17th September 1889 contained full particulars of the trial of a number of prisoners who were proved to be members of the Ghee Hin or Sam Tian secret society at Sarawak. The six leaders were shot; eleven, being active members, carrying out orders of the leaders, beating, frightening, or murdering non- members, were sentenced to receive six dozen strokes with a rattan, to have their heads shaved, to be imprisoned during the Kajah's pleasure; seven others, against whom no specific charges were made out, were dismissed on swearing to have no further dealings with the society.

Towards the end of the year 1895 a number of Mohammedans rose against the Chinese Government and captured the capital of the province of Kansu; the secret societies in Central China joined the Mohammedan insurgents. Their success, however, was of short duration; in the month of December of the same year the insurrection was crushed, and some fifteen of the leaders were captured and beheaded. Others made their escape. Among these was Sun Yet Sun, or, as he is also called, Sun Wen, a medical man, well known in Hong-Kong. His being made a prisoner in the house of the Chinese Ambassador in London in the month of October 1896, until, at the instance of Lord Salisbury, he was released, is no doubt fresh in the memory of the reader. He asserted that he was kidnapped by the Chinese Ambassador's people, by being induced to walk into the Ambassador's house; but it is a curious circumstance that San Wen, who evidently knew something of London, should not have known where the Chinese Embassy was located, especially after all the excitement caused by Li Hung Chang's visit to the Continent and to England.

In justice to the Taepings and other secret associations in China, it must be stated that the insurrection was and is the war of an oppressed nationality against foreign invaders. The Mantchoos or Tsing dynasty are an alien tribe, ruling over the vast Chinese empire; their government is one of the most despotic the world has ever seen; their laws are so ruthless and unjust, that it would seem they could never be carried out, did not the blood of millions, perishing by every kind of frightful death that the most diabolical cruelty could invent, attest the fact of their being obeyed. Yet British ministers did sanction the enlistment of British officers Bible Gordon being their leader, what a satire! and men in the service of the Mantchoos, whom they further supplied with arms and artillery.

515. Lodges - From the book published at Batavia, and mentioned above, we extract the following information:

The lodge is built in a square, surrounded by walls, which are pierced at the four cardinal points by as many gates; the faces are adorned by triangles, the mystic symbol of union. Within the enclosure is the hall of fidelity and loyalty, where the oaths of membership are taken. Here also stand the altar, and the precious nine-storied pagoda, in which the images of the five monkish founders are enshrined. The lodges, of course, only appear in out-of-theway places, where they are safe from the observation of the Mandarins; in towns and populous neighbourhoods the lodge is dispensed with; the meetings are held at the house of the president. The instruments of the lodge are numerous. First in importance is the diploma; then there are numerous flags; there is th'e " bushel," which contains among other articles the "red staff," with which justice is done to offenders against the laws of the society; the scissors, with which the hair of the neophytes is cut off; a jade foot measure, a balance, an abacus, &c.

516. Government - The supreme government is vested in the grand masters of the five principal lodges, and the affairs of each lodge are administered by a president, a vice-president, one master, two introducers, one fiscal, thirteen councillors, several agents, who are otherwise known as " grass shoes," " iron planks," or " night brethren," and some minor officials, who, as indicative of their rank, wear flowers in their hair.

In times of peace the ranks of the society are filled up by volunteers, but when the League is preparing to take the field, threats and violence are used to secure members. The neophyte, as in Royal Arch Masonry, is introduced to the Hall of Fidelity under the " bridge of swords," formed by the brethren holding up their swords in the form of an arch; he then takes the oath, and has his queue cut off, though this ceremony is dispensed with if he lives amongst Chinese who are faithful to the Tartar rule; his face is washed, and he exchanges his clothes for a long white dress, as a token of purity, and the commencement of a new life. Straw shoes, signs of mourning, are put on his feet. He is then led up to the altar, and offers up nine blades of grass and an incense stick, while an appropriate stanza is repeated between each offering. A red candle is then lighted, and the brethren worship heaven and earth by pledging three cups of wine. This done, the seven-starred lamp, the precious imperial lamp, and the Hung lamp are lighted, and prayer is made to the gods, beseeching them to protect the members. The oath is then read, and each member draws some blood from the middle finger, and drops it into a cup partly filled with wine. Each neophyte having drunk of the mixture, strikes off the head of a white cock, as a sign that so all unfaithful brothers shall perish. Then each new brother receives his diploma, a book containing the oath, law, and secret signs, a pair of daggers, and three Hung medals. The secret signs are numerous, and by means of them a brother can make himself known by the way in which he enters a house, puts down his umbrella, arranges his shoes, holds his hat, takes a cup of tea, and performs a number of other actions.

Henry Pottinger, in a despatch to Lord Aberdeen (1843), perhaps alludes to a secret society, saying: " The song being finished, Ke-Ying, the Chinese commissioner, having taken from his arm a gold bracelet, gave it to me, informing me, at the same time, that he had received it in his tender youth from his father, and that it contained a mysterious legend, and that, by merely showing it, it would in all parts of China assure me a fraternal reception."

517. Seal of the Hung League - Every member of the Hung League is provided with a copy of its seal, which is printed in coloured characters on silk or calico. The original is kept in the custody of the Tai-Koh. Various descriptions of it have been given, and as they differ, it may be presumed that there are more seals than one. But all of them are pentagonal, and inscribed with a multitude of Chinese characters, the

translations given showing no real meaning; the whole is a riddle, which it is scarcely worth while attempting to solve. To give but one sample. In an octagonal space enclosed within the pentagon there are sixteen characters, which, according to the interpreters, signify: "The eldest brother unites to battle-order; every one prepares himself (at the) signal (of the) chief. (The) swollen mountain stream spreads itself (into) canals; ten thousand of years is (he) this day." By many members it is worn as a charm, and great care is taken to conceal its meaning from the uninitiated. As a charm, the seal may be as effective against wounds or death in battle as were the amulets furnished in the fifteenth century by the hangman of Passau, until a soldier had the curiosity to open one, and read, " Coward, defend thyself! "

518. The Ko lao Hui - The secret society which at the present day seems most powerful in China, is that known by the above name. It was at first a purely military association, whose object was mutual protection against the plunder and extortion practised by the civil officials in dealing with the pay and maintenance of the troops. It is believed that the initiation consists in killing a cock and drinking the blood, either by itself, or mixed with wine. It is also believed to use a planch ette, whose movements are attributed to occult influence; gradually persons not connected with the army were admitted; the ticket of membership is a small oblong piece of linen or calico, stamped with a few Chinese characters. The possession of one of these, if discovered, entails immediate execution by the authorities.

The society is anti-foreign and anti-missionary, and is believed to be at the bottom of all the riots against foreigners, and especially against foreign missionaries, which have lately occurred in China. Of course, as long as missionaries, instead of making it their business to convert the heathens at home, will go among people who don't want them, and in China will establish themselves outside Treaty limits, they ought to be prepared to take the risks they voluntarily incur, but whenever attacked, they make the Chinese Government pay them liberally for any inconvenience or loss they may have suffered of course, with the assistance of English gun-boats. In 1891 the Ko lao Hui, which is also anti-dynastic, caused inflammatory placards to be posted up in various parts of the empire, which the authorities immediately tore down, only to be posted up afresh; the society also distributed antimissionary pamphlets, with titles such as this: " The Devil Doctriners ought to be killed," wherein the missionaries are charged with every kind of crime against morals and life; the Eoman Catholics are more severely handled than the Protestants.

In September 1891 it would appear that the society was organising a rising against the Government, and a Mr. C. W. Mason, a British subject, and a fourth-class assistant in the Customs at Shanghai, was implicated in the project, he having been instrumental in introducing arms and dynamite into the country for the use of the conspirators. He was sentenced to nine months' imprisonment with hard labour, and he was further, at the expiration of that period, to find two sureties of $2500 to be of good behaviour, and failing in this he was to be deported from China. This latter happening on his release, he was sent out of the country in September 1892.

In November 1891 a famous Ko lao Hui leader named Chen-kin-Lung fell into the hands of the Chinese Government. He had been staying at an inn with about thirty of his followers. Gagged and bound, he was taken on board a steam-launch kept ready to start, and carried to Shanghai. His examination was conducted with the greatest secrecy by the magistrate and deputies of the Viceroy and the Governor. On his person were found several official documents issued by the Ko lao Hui, and a short dagger with a poisoned blade. He was addressed in the despatches as the " Eighth Great Prince," and was evidently the commander of a strong force. Three examinations were held, but Chen preserved the strictest silence. Torture was employed, but in vain; the only words that could be extracted from him were, "Spare yourselves the trouble and me the pain; be convinced that there are men ready to sacrifice their lives for the good of a cause which will bring happiness to this country for thousands of generations to come." Then more gentle means were employed, but with what result is not known. The Hui League has various offshoots, which being known to be in reality mutual aid societies, are secret societies in name only, and therefore attract but little attention from the Government. One of the largest of these offshoots is the " Golden Lily Hui," which flourishes in the western provinces of China. Its members are divided into four sections, respectively marshalled under the white, the black, the red, and the yellow flag.

That the popular feeling against Christian missionaries in China is very strong cannot be denied, and for the last two f or three years has displayed itself in frequent attacks on their persons and property. Even at the present time such outbreaks are almost regularly reported in the European press. A pretty plain intimation was given to Sir Rutherford Alcock on his bidding adieu to a high Chinese official. "I wish," said that functionary, " now you are going home, you would take away with you your opium, and your Christian missionaries."

A law passed in 1889 in the Straits Settlements for the suppression of Chinese secret societies, according to a report issued in 1892 by the Protector of Chinese in those settlements, has led to the disappearance of those dangerous organisations. But it is admitted that it will take many years for the Triad element to become extinct; the action of the Hung League is merely suspended, and out of it have sprung many minor societies, as offshoots from the parent society, who send gangs of roughs to brothels, coolie-depots, music halls and shops, demanding monthly contributions, under threat of coming in force and interrupting the business of the establishment. The fighting men of these societies are kept in the lodges by the head men on the proceeds of the exactions thus levied. The expulsion of the head men, as the speediest remedy of these evils, has been tried, with as yet only partial success.

II

THE COMUNEROS

519. Introductory Remarks - The downfall of Napoleon, by a pleasant fiction, invented by historians who write history philosophically, that is, chisel and mould history to fit systems drawn from their inner consciousness, is said to have made Europe free. True, the battle of

Waterloo and the Congress of Vienna restored the kings to their thrones, but to say that Europe was thereby made free is false. Instead of one mighty eagle hovering over Europe, the limbs of that ancient Virgin were now torn to pieces by a flock of harpies; instead of one mighty ruler, a host of petty tyrants returned to revel in the delights of a terreur blanche. Religious despotism, by the restoration of the pope, was to be the fit prelude to the political tyranny which followed the "Restoration." But the Napoleonic meteor, in its flight across Europe, had shed some of its light into the dense brains even of the most slavishly loyal German peasant, accustomed to look up to the kingly, princely, or grand-ducal drill-sergeant as his heaven-appointed Landesvater, so that he began to doubt the ruler's divine mission. Hence secret societies in every country whose king had been restored by the Congress of Vienna in Spain, France, Italy, Germany, Austria. Some of those secret societies had been fostered by the princes themselves, as long as their own restoration was the object aimed at; but when the societies and the nations they represented demanded that this restoration should involve constitutional privileges and the rights of free citizens, the " restored " kings turned against their benefactors, and conspired to suppress them. But such is the gratitude of kings. However, turn we to the secret societies formed to undo the evils wrought by Waterloo. I begin with Spain.

520. Earliest Secret Societies in Spain - Even before the French Revolution there existed in Spain secret societies, some averse to monarchical government, others in favour of clerocracy. Among the latter may be mentioned the " Concepcionistas," or "Defenders of the Immaculate Conception" (523), who carried their zeal for Ferdinand VII. and their tenderness for the Church to such a degree as to desire the return of the blessed times of the Holy Inquisition. They also sought to get hold of the management of public affairs, to turn them to their own profit; and the dismal administration of the Bourbons shows that they partly succeeded. Probably from this association arose that of the " Defenders of the Faith," Jesuits in disguise, who in 1820 spread themselves over Spain, taking care of the throne and altar, and still

more of themselves. During the reign of Ferdinand VII. also arose the "Realists," who, to benefit themselves, encouraged the king in his reactionary policy.

521. Freemasonry in Spain, the Forerunner of the Comuneros - After the French invasion of 1809, Freemasonry was openly restored in the Peninsula, and a Grand Orient established at Madrid; but it confined itself to works of popular education and charity, entirely eschewing politics. The fall of Joseph and the Restoration again put an end to these well-meant efforts. In 1816, some of the officers and soldiers, returned from French prisons, joined and formed independent lodges, establishing a Grand Orient at Madrid, very secret, and in correspondence with the few French lodges that meddled with politics. Among the latter is remembered the lodge of the "Sectaries of Zoroaster," which initiated several Spanish officers residing in Paris, among others Captain Quezada, who afterwards favoured the escape of the patriot Mina. The revolution of the island of Leon was the work of restored Spanish Masonry, which had long prepared for it under the direction of Quiroga, Riego, and five members of the Cortes.

522. The Comuneros - After the brief victory, badly-concealed jealousies broke forth; many of the brethren seceded and formed in 1821 a new society, the "Confederation of the Communists" (Comuneros), which name was derived from that memorable epoch of Spanish history when Charles V. attempted to destroy the ancient liberties, and thus provoked the revolution of the Commons in 1520, which was headed by John Padilla, and afterwards by his heroic wife, Maria Pacheco. In the battle of Villalar the Comuneros were defeated and scattered, and the revolution was doomed. The new Comuneros, reviving these memories, declared their intentions, which could not but be agreeable to Young Spain; nearly sixty thousand members joined the society: women could bo initiated, who had their own lodges or torres, or towers, as their meetings were called, and which were presided over by a "Grand Castellan." The scope of the society was to promote by all means in its power the freedom of mankind; to defend in every way

the rights of the Spanish people against the abuses and encroachments of royal and priestly power; and to succour the needy, especially those belonging to the society. Some of the more advanced of the Comuneros were for beheading the king, or exiling him to the Havannah, on the principle that to put a house, whether domestic or national, in order, it was first necessary to get rid of all greedy hangers-on and parasites, and the Spanish throne and the royal family of Spain with them came under the above designations. But the nation thought otherwise. On being initiated the candidate was first led into the "hall of arms," where he was told of the obligations and duties he was about to undertake. His eyes having been bandaged he was conducted to another room, where, after he had declared that he wished to be admitted into the confederation, a member acting as sentinel exclaimed: "Let him advance, I will escort him to the guard-house of the castle." Then there was imitated with great noise the lowering of a drawbridge, and the raising of a portcullis; the candidate was then led into the guard-room, unbandaged, and left alone. The walls were covered with arms and trophies, and with patriotic and martial inscriptions. Being at last admitted into the presence of the governor, the candidate was thus addressed: " You stand now under the shield of our chief Padilla; repeat with all the fervour you are capable of the oath I am about to dictate to you." By this oath, the candidate bound himself to fight for constitutional liberty, and to avenge every wrong done to his country. The new knight then covered himself with the shield of Padilla, the knights present pointed their swords at it, and the governor continued: "The shield of our chief Padilla will cover you from every danger, will save your life and honour; bat if you violate your oath this shield shall be removed, and these swords buried in your breast." Both the Masons and Comuneros sought to gain possession of superior political influence. The former, having more experience, prevailed in the elections and formed the ministry. Hence a contest that agitated the country and injured the cause of liberty. In 1832, the Comuneros endeavoured to overthrow the Freemasons, but unsuccessfully. Still Masons and Comuneros combined to oppose the reactionary party. They also succeeded in suppressing Carbonarism, which had been introduced into Spain by some refugee Italians. These societies, in fact, though professing patriotic views, were nothing but egotistical cliques, bent on their own aggrandisement. How little they were guided by fixed principles is shown by their conduct in Spanish America. In Brazil they placed on the throne Don Pedro, and in Mexico they established a republican form of government, just as it best suited their own private interests. But such is the practice of most patriots.

523. Clerical Societies - But the royal party also formed secret societies. Among these we have mentioned the "Concepcionistas," or "Defenders of the Immaculate Conception," founded in 1823 (see 520 ante), with the sanction, if not at the instigation, of Ferdinand VII. This was followed in 1825 by the "Defenders of the Faith," also previously referred to, and in 1827 by a third, known as the "Destroying Angels." The existence of the last is denied by clerical writers, but that it did exist, and that the Minister Calomarde was its chief, are facts proved beyond dispute. The doings of these clerical secret societies covered the king, a despicable character in every way, with disgrace, and involved the country in constant internecine war and ruin, which are matters belonging to history. But as specially concerning the secret societies of Spain, it should be mentioned that at that period they were split up into four distinct parties: (1) the Aristocratic, who received great support from England; its objects were the restoration of the constitution, and a change of dynasty. (2) The Mineros, whose head was General Mina. They were chiefly military men, closely allied with the Aristocrats, and largely subsidised by England. The American Government, with a view to the conquest of Mexico, also favoured them. Opposed to them were (3) the Republicans, whose designation indicates their object. (4) The Comuneros, who, though also desiring a republican form of government in Spain, opposed the plans of the third party.

III

THE HETAIRIA

524. Origin - The secret society which bore the above Greek name, signifying the "Union of Friends," is, like Carbonarism, one of the few secret associations which attained its objects, because it had a whole people to back it up; a support which the Nihilists, for instance, lack as yet, and hence the present non-success of the latter. The origin of the Hetairia may be traced back to the Greek poet Constantinos Rhigas, who lived in the later half of the last century, and who plotted a Greek insurrection against Turkey, but was by the Austrian Government, in whose territory he was then travelling, basely delivered up to the Porte, and executed at Belgrade in 1798. But the Hetairia he had founded was not destroyed by his death; its principles survived, and a new Hetairia was founded in 1812, on lines somewhat different, however, from those of the old society.

525. The Hetairia of 1812 - In 1812 a society was formed at Athens, which called itself the "Hetairia Philomuse." Since Lord Elgin had carried off whole cargoes of antiques, the need was felt of protecting the Greek treasures of antiquity. The object of the Philomuse, therefore, was to preserve relics of ancient art, to found museums, libraries, and schools. At the same time the members hoped by peaceful means to improve the social and political condition of Greece. They were conservative enough to place their hopes on princes and the Congress of Vienna. Count Capo d'Istria, the private secretary of the Czar, who possessed in the highest degree the confidence of his master, did his best to gain the goodwill of the Congress. The princes and diplomatists, composing it, had then drained the cup of pleasure to the dregs, and it seemed to them a pleasing variation to surround themselves, amidst fetes, balls, and amateur theatricals, with the halo of ancient Hellenistic interests. Ministers, princes, kings, were ready to wear the golden or iron ring, on which the ancient Attic obolus was engraved, the countersign of the Philomuse. The Emperor Alexander,

the Crown Princes of Bavaria and Württemberg, joined the society and subscribed to its funds. But these were not the men or the means to deliver Greece from the Turkish yoke, which had been the object of Rhigas, and of those who thought like him.

526. The Hetairia of 1814 - Hence in 1814 a new Hetairia was founded with purely political objects. It was called the "Hetairia" or "Society of Friends" only, and stood to the Philomuse in the same relation the sword stands to the pen. It was founded at Odessa, where Greek and Russian interests always met, by a little-known merchant, Ikufas, of Arta, and two other obscure men of honour, Athanasius Tsakaloff and the Freemason, E. Xanthos, of Patmos. These men determined to achieve what Europe refused to do to raise the Cross above the Crescent; and in the course of years they succeeded. The fate of Rhigas taught them secrecy. Tsakaloff, who had years before formed a secret league of Greek youths settled in Paris, had some experience as to external forms, and so had Xanthos as a Freemason. The number of grades of their Hetairia was seven Brethren, Apprentices, Priests of Eleusis, Shepherds, Prelates, Initiated, and Supreme Initiated. The latter two grades were invested with a military character, and directly intended for war. The candidates for initiation had to kneel down, at night, in an oratory, and to swear before a painting of the Resurrection, fidelity, constancy, secrecy, and absolute obedience. Little, however, was imparted on admission to a higher degree, the object being mainly to render the initiation more impressive. The brother was told to have his arms ready, and fifty cartridges in his cartridge-box; the Priest, that the object of the Hetairia was the deliverance of Greece: but like all secret societies, this one did not remain untainted from egotism, falsehood, and humbug in general. As the priests were allowed to introduce neophytes, who had to pay them certain amounts of money, the office of priest was much sought after; but it must have appeared strange to many of the candidates, that whilst the priest bade them swear on the Gospel, he at the same time informed them that he initiated them on the strength of the power conferred on him by the High-Priest of Eleusis. The leaders, further, did not hesitate to boast of

a secret understanding with the Court of St. Petersburg, yea, it was intimated that Alexander was the Grand Arch. The Hetairists have been blamed for all this; but it cannot be expected that a revolutionary military league should in all points be faultless, and keep within the rules of civic honesty. Legal means were of no avail; cunning and deceit are the weapons of the oppressed. Politicians have to accommodate themselves to the fancies and prejudices of men.

527. Signs and Passwords - Some of the signs and passwords were common to all the degrees, but others were known to the higher grades only, each of which had its peculiar mysteries. The Brethren saluted by placing the right hand on their friend's breast, and uttering the Albanian word sipsi (pipe), to which the other, if initiated, responded with sarroukia (sandals). The Apprentices pronounced the syllable Lon, and the person addressed, if in the secret, completed the word by uttering the syllable don. In the higher grades the formulas were more complex. The mystical words of the Priests were, "How are you?" and "As well as you are;" and again, "How many have you?" and "As many as you have." If the person accosted had reached the third degree, he understood the mystical sense of the question, and replied, "Sixteen." To be sure of his man the questioner then asked, "Have you no more? " to which his equally cautious friend replied, "Tell me the first, and I will tell you the second." The first then pronounced the first syllable of a Turkish word meaning justice, and the other completed it by uttering the second syllable. The sign of recognition was given by a particular touch of the right hand, and making the joints of the fingers crack, afterwards folding the arms and wiping the eyes. The Prelates pressed the wrist, in shaking hands, with the index finger, reclined the head on the left hand, and pressed the right on the region of the heart. The Prelate addressed responded by rubbing the forehead. If in doubt, the mystical phrases of the Priests of Eleusis were repeated, and if the answers were correctly given, the two repeated alternately the syllables of the mysterious word va-an-va-da.

528. Short Career of Galatis - The sect consisted at first of but few

members. In 1819 the Directory or Grand Arch was composed of the three founders only and four other persons: Galatis, Komizopulos, A. Sekeris, and A. Gazis, with whom afterwards were joined Leventis, Dika'os, Ignatios, and Mavrocordato, and finally, Patsimadis and Alexander Ipsilanti. Galatis early betrayed, and almost ruined, the cause of the Hetairia. Exceedingly vain of his admission to the Grand Arch, he went to St. Petersburg, where he proclaimed himself as the ambassador of the Hellenes, in consequence of which the police arrested him, and an examination of his papers revealed the whole secret of the Hetairia. The Czar, vacillating between his philo-Hellenism and the fear of revolution, was persuaded by Capo d'Istria to set Galatis free, and even to award him compensation in money for his imprisonment. Later on, when Sknfas conceived the bold idea of attacking the enemy in his very capital, and had therefore settled at Constantinople, Galatis excited the suspicion of thinking more of his own advantage than of that of his country; he was always asking for money, and when this was refused him, he uttered threats, whilst alluding to his intimacy with Halet Effendi, the Minister and favourite of Mahmoud. Thereupon the Hetairia decided that he must be removed. Towards the end of 1818 he was ordered on a journey; a few trusted Hetairists were his companions. One day, while he was resting near Hermione, under a tree, a Hetairist suddenly discharged his pistol at him. With the cry, "What have I done to you? " he expired. The murderers, with a strange mingling of ferocity and sentimentality, cut these last words of his into the bark of the tree.

529. Proceedings of the Grand Arch - Skufas had died some months before, but thanks to the stupidity of the Turkish. Government, Constantinople remained the seat of the league. The Grand Arch met at Xantho's house and instituted a systematic propaganda. In all the provinces of Turkey and adjoining states "Ephori" superintendents were appointed, who each had his own treasury, and authority to act in his district for the best of the common cause; only in very important cases he was to refer to the Grand Arch. Gazis undertook preparing the mainland; Greek soldiers, who had just then returned from Russia,

were sent to the Morea and the island of Hydra. But it was essential to gain possession of the most important military point in the Morea, of Mani, usually called Maina, and by means of the patriarch Gregor, who was initiated into the secret of the Hetairia, Petros Mavromichalis, the powerful governor of Maina, was seduced from his allegiance. The emissaries of the Hetairia knew how to reconcile tribes who had for centuries been at feud, and to gain them for their cause, so that in 1820 the Hetairia had secret adherents all over the Peloponnesus, on the Cyclades, Sporades, on the coasts of Asia Minor, the Ionian Islands, and even in Jerusalem. It was now felt to be necessary to appoint a supreme head; the choice lay between Capo d'Istria and Alexander Ipsilanti. The former was a diplomatist, the latter a soldier. Capo d'Istria declined to mix himself up in the matter, at least openly, because his master, the Emperor Alexander, was unwilling to appear as the protector of the Hetairia. Ipsilanti undertook its direction; and as soon as it was known that he had done so, the hopes of the conspirators of the eventual support of Russia rose to fever-heat, and Ipsilanti in 1820 found it advisable to leave St. Petersburg and go to Odessa, to be more in the centre of the movement. But though a soldier, he was no general, and allowed himself to be carried away by the enthusiasm he saw around him. Though contributions in cash came in so slowly that he had to make private loans, he lost none of his confidence. In July he appointed Georgakis commander of the "army of the Danube," and Perrhiivos chief of the "army of Epirotes." He himself intended to enter the Peloponnesus, and to set up at Maina the standard of independence, fancying that the Peloponnesus was a fortified camp, outnumbering in soldiers the Turkish contingents. But he was soon convinced of this error, and he was advised to make his first attempt against the Turkish power in the Danubian principalities; and though other counsellors rejected this proposal, Ipsilanti decided to adopt it, guided by the fact that the treaties between Russia and the Porte forbade the entry of an army into the Principalities, unless with the consent of both parties. Should the Porte, in consequence of the Hetairist rising, send troops to Bucharest, Russia would be bound to support the Greeks.

530. Ipsilanti's Proceedings. - Further hesitation became impossible. A certain Asimakis, a member of the Hetairia, in conjunction with the brother of the murdered Galatis, betrayed to the Turkish police all the details of the conspiracy. Kamarinos, who had been to St. Petersburg, on his return publicly revealed the futility of Russian promises; to silence him the Hetairists had him assassinated. They also endeavoured to take advantage of the quarrel which had broken out between Ali Pasha and the Sultan, whose best troops were then occupied in besieging Janina, Ali Pasha's capital. Ali, being sorely pressed by the Turks, promised the Hetairia his help, their cause being his the overthrow of the Sultan. The Suliotes, also, his ancient enemies, were won over by him, partly in consequence of the bad treatment they received from the Turks, whose side they had at first adopted, and partly because their leaders were initiated into the secret of the Hetairia, in whose success they saw the recovery of their ancient territory, from which Ali had expelled them. In March 1821, Ipsilanti took up his residence at Jassy, whence he issued pompous proclamations to the Greeks, Moldavians, and Wallachians, and also sent a manifesto to the princes and diplomatists, who were then assembled for the settlement of the Neapolitan revolution, inviting Europe, but especially Russia, to favour the cause of Greek independence. But the result of the latter step was fatal to it. Metternich's policy was totally opposed to it; and the Emperor Alexander, who had just proclaimed his antirevolutionary views, as applied to the Italian rising, could not repudiate them when dealing with the Greek question. Knowing nothing of the share his favourite, Capo d'Istria had in it, and of the underhand promises of Russian help the latter had made to the Hetairia, he assured the Emperor Francis, Metternich, and Bernstorff, of his adherence to the Holy Alliance, and his opposition to any revolution, with such zeal and mystical unction, that his listeners were "deeply moved." Ipsilanti's action was utterly reproved; his name was removed from the Russian Army List; the Russian troops on the Pruth were instructed under no pretence to take any part in the disturbances in the Principalities; and the Porte was informed that the Russian Government was a total

stranger to them. Capo d'Istria was compelled to write to his friend, whom he had secretly encouraged, that " he must expect no support, either moral or material, from Russia, which could be no party to the secret undermining of the Turkish Empire by means of secret societies."

531. Ipsilanti's Blunders - Ipsilanti, since his arrival at Jassy, had taken none of the steps which might have insured the success of his enterprise. He did nothing towards centralising the Government, or concentrating his troops. He seemed satisfied with looking upon the Principalities as a Russian depot, and to be waiting for the hand of the Czar to raise him on the Greek throne. As if the victory were already won, he bestowed civil and military appointments on the swarms of relations and flatterers who surrounded him. Chiefs of a few hundred adventurers were grandly called generals; he placed his brothers on the staffs of his imaginary army corps, whilst he neglected and snubbed men who might have greatly advanced the revolution; he favoured worthless creatures, such as Karavias, who, with a band of Arnaut mercenaries, had surprised and cut down the Turkish garrison of Galatz, plundered the town, desecrated the churches, and committed every kind of outrage. Ipsilanti shut his eyes when the rabble of Jassy, on hearing of the horrors committed at Galatz, suddenly attacked the Turks peacefully residing in the former town, and murdered them in cold blood. He further committed a great mistake in imprisoning a rich banker on some frivolous pretence, and only releasing him on his paying a ransom of sixty thousand ducats. This act drove a great many wealthy people to take refuge on Eussian or Austrian territory, and many others to wish for the restoration of Turkish authority, whose oppression was not quite so ominous as that of the newly-arrived " liberators."

532. Progress of the Insurrection - At last Ipsilanti, with an army of two thousand men, whose numbers were everywhere proclaimed to be ten thousand, left Jassy for Bucharest. At Fokshany, on the borders of the two Principalities, he issued another proclamation to the "Dacians," which was as unsuccessful as the former. On the other

hand, his army was here reinforced by the Arnauts of Karavias, and later on by two hundred Greek horsemen, led by Georgakis, one of the most heroic of the Greek patriots. About this time, also, according to the pattern of the Thebans, five hundred youths, belonging to the noblest and richest families, formed themselves into a Sacred Battalion. They were clothed in black, and displayed on their breasts a cross with the words, In this sign you shall conquer." Their hats were decorated with a skull and crossbones! Still, this battalion henceforth distinguished itself above all the other troops of Ipsilanti by discipline and valour. But the chief, instead of affording those youths an opportunity of displaying their zeal, damped it by his delays and slow advance. He did not reach Bucharest before the Qth April. Here the higher clergy and the remaining Boyars declared their adhesion to the cause, in the hope that the leaders of irregular troops who had joined Ipsilanti would do the same, and thus subordinate the anarchical elements of the revolution to the general object. But this hope was only partially fulfilled. Georgakis, indeed, placed himself under Ipsilanti's orders, but other leaders, like Savas and Vladimiresko, were far from following this example. It was even said that the former was secretly working towards the restoration of Turkish supremacy.

533. Ipsilanti s Approaching Fall - In this crisis, Ipsilanti's chief occupation was the erection of a theatre and engaging comedians, whilst he himself was more of a comedian than a general. He daily showed himself in the gorgeous uniform of a Russian general. A numerous staff of officers rushed from morning till night, with aimless activity, through the streets of Bucharest. Wealthy people were visited with arbitrary requisitions; the soldiers of the Hetairia lived, without discipline, at the expense of citizens and peasants; the Sacred Battalion only refrained from these excesses. Under these circumstances arrived the decision from Laybach, and with it the curse of the Church. The Patriarch laid Ipsilanti and the Hetairia under the ban; Sovas and Vladimiresko now openly joined the Rumelian opposition to the Greek cause; the Boyars and the clergy withdrew from it, and from the other classes of the people there had never been any real prospect of

support. Ipsilanti endeavoured to weaken the force of the double blow which had befallen him by asserting that the ban of diplomacy and the Church was a mere form behind which the Czar and the Patriarch wished to conceal their secret sympathy with the Hetairia. He asserted that Capo d'Istria had secretly informed him that the Hetairists were not to lay down their arms before having learnt the issue of the proposals made by Russia to the Turks in favour of the Greeks. In the name of the Greek nation he addressed a number of demands to the C ar and his Ambassador at Constantinople, declaring that he would not relinquish the position he had assumed until these demands were complied with. Minds bolder than his advised him to make his way through Bulgaria to Epirus, to relieve Ali Pasha, closely besieged in Janina, and with the latter's help to set Greece free. But Ipsilanti was not made of the stuff to execute so daring a coup-demain; and when Vladimiresko strongly supported the plan, Ipsilanti felt convinced that he and others intended to lead him into a trap by luring him out of the Principalities. He therefore, instead of moving towards the Danube, on the I 3th April, with his small army, and scarcely any artillery, turned northwards to the Carpathians, distributing his soldiers in so wide a belt that if the Turks had had any forces ready they might easily have exterminated Ipsilanti's army piecemeal. The revolutionary chief intended, should the Turks seriously threaten him, to take refuge on Austrian territory, hoping, through the intercession of the Russian Ambassador at Constantinople, to secure a free passage for himself and his followers. The Russian Government having permitted the advance of Turkish troops into the Principalities to quell the insurrection, Ipsilanti had to be prepared for a speedy encounter. In fact, under the pretence of intending resistance, he ordered intreiichments to be thrown up, and his troops to be exercised in the use of the bayonet, whilst he amused them again with the fable of Russian assistance.

534. Advance of the Turks - In the second week of May the Turks crossed the Danube. The Pasha of Braila undertook the recovery of Galatz, which had been taken by Karavias. The first encounter took place before that town on the I 3th May, on which occasion the

Hetairists, by their bravery, redeemed many of the mistakes committed by their leaders. About seven hundred of the insurgents held three redoubts on the road to Braila; they had two guns. Their position had been so skilfully chosen by their chief, Athanasius of Karpenisi, that it seemed possible to defend it for a long time against a fivefold number of Turks. But the majority of the defenders consisted of rabble sailors taken from the ships in the harbour, and of the robbers and murderers who, under the leadership of Karavias, had rendered themselves infamous, and now felt little inclination to sacrifice themselves for a foreign cause. As soon as the Turks prepared for the attack, the bulk of them fled, leaving it to Athanasius and the few Greeks to engage in the fight. The unequal conflict lasted till night; the redoubts were bravely held by the small number of Greeks; and when darkness came, and the fighting was suspended, the Greeks practised a trick to make their escape. They hung their cloaks outside the redoubts, and the Turks, taking the cloaks for men, fired at them; at the same time the Greeks had loaded their guns in such a way, as to go off one after another as soon as the garrison should have left the redoubts, by which means the attention of the Turks would be diverted from the fugitives. The ruse succeeded; the Greeks escaped, first to a small peninsula at the mouth of the Pruth, and thence to Jassy. The greatest disorder prevailed in that town. Prince Kantakuzeno, to whom Ipsilanti had entrusted its defence, could maintain himself but a few days. In the middle of June, when tho Turkish troops advanced against him, he retreated to Bessarabia, advising Athanasius and the other Greeks to do the same. But these pronounced him a despicable coward; they, they said, were determined to defend the Greek cause to the last, and to die honourably or to conquer. With four hundred men and eight guns they resisted, behind a weak barricade of trees, near Skuleni, for eight days a vastly superior enemy, and by their heroic conduct threw a final halo round the Moldavian insurrection. Athanasius met with the death of a patriot. Nearly a thousand Turks had fallen; three hundred Greeks perished in the fight or in the waters of the Pruth, the remnant took refuge on the opposite bank.

535. Ipsilanti's Difficulties - Moldavia was lost; in the meantime the Pasha of Silistria had entered Bucharest on the 29th May; Ipsilanti, perfectly helpless, was encamped at Tergovist. His troops, even the Sacred Battalion, were thoroughly demoralised; his dissensions with Savas and Vladimiresko continued. The former had readily surrendered Bucharest to the Turks, and had followed Ipsilanti, whom on the first favourable opportunity he intended to take prisoner to give him up to the Turks. Vladimiresko prepared to withdraw to Little Wallachia, there to await the result of his negotiations with the Turks; he had proposed to the Pasha of Silistria to have Ipsilanti and Georgakis assassinated. But his treachery became known to his intended victims; Georgakis suddenly appeared in his camp, took him prisoner in the midst of his officers, and carried him to Tergovist. On being taken before Ipsilanti he protested his innocence, declaring that he had only been trying to draw the Turks into a snare; but Ipsilanti ordered him at once to be shot.

536. Ipsilanti's Fall - Ipsilanti intended to occupy the strategically important village of Dragatschau, but the rapid advance from Bucharest of the Turkish vanguard left him no time to do so. On the 8th June it encountered a Greek division under Anastasius of Argyrokastro; another division, sent for the support of the Greeks from Tergovist, under the command of Dukas, betook themselves to their heels, with their leader at their head, and spread such consternation in the camp at Tergovist, that Ipsilanti's troops, leaving their baggage behind, took to flight. Ipsilanti thereupon with great difficulty made his way to Ribnik, with a view of being near the Austrian frontier, which he intended to cross, if necessary. In spite of the losses he had sustained, he still commanded 7500 men, with four guns. Georgakis considered the opportunity favourable by an attack on Dragatschau, which the Turks had occupied with two thousand men, to raise the sinking courage of his troops. His dispositions were skilfully arranged to surround the enemy, inferior in numbers, and on the 19th June 1821, five thousand insurgents were concentred on the heights surrounding the village, entirely cutting off the retreat of the Turks. Ipsilanti's corps had not

yet arrived. Georgakis sent messenger after messenger to hasten the advance of Ipsilanti, that he might share in the honours of the day. The Turks were aware of their dangerous position. Towards mid-day they attempted a debouch from the village to occupy a height in front of it; but the attempt miscarried, the Greeks would not give way. Thereupon the Turks set fire to the village, in order to effect their retreat under the shelter of tho flames. Karavias, whom Ipsilanti had appointed colonel of the cavalry, considered it a favourable moment to gather cheap laurels; he took the burning of the village as a sign of the flight and defeat of the Turks; envious of Georgakis, he designed to rob him of the honour of this easy victory, and in spite of orders to the contrary, to adventure with his five hundred horsemen on storming the village. He persuaded Nicholas Ipsilanti to support the mad attempt with the Sacred Battalion and his artillery, and, heated with wine, without even communicating with his chief, he led his men across the bridge leading to the village. The Turks at first retreated, as, in fact, they had already commenced a retrograde movement, apprehending a general attack. But when they discovered that Karavias and the Sacred Battalion only were coming against them, they wheeled round and first threw tho cavalry into disorder; the Sacred Battalion, tender youths having but lately assumed arms, could not resist the hardy veteran Spahis. They fell, " like blooming boughs " under the woodcutter's hatchet. Georgakis arrived in time to recover the standard and two guns and rescue the remainder, about one hundred men, of the Sacred Battalion. About thirty of the Arnauts, and twenty of Georgakis' devoted band, were also slain. By this defeat Ipsilanti's last hopo was destroyed. Having taken refuge at Kosia, he negotiated with the Austrian Government for permission to cross the frontier. His safety was in danger from his own people. They talked of handing him over to the Turks and earning the price set on his head. All discipline disappeared. The Hetairists robbed and murdered one another. Among the few men of faith and honour, Georgakis was one of the most prominent. Though he would have preferred Ipsilanti remaining, he assisted his flight. Then he joined his friend Farmakis at Adjile, to continue, faithful to his oath, the struggle for Greece.

537. Ipsilanti's Manifesto - Ipsilanti, true to his system of deceit, continued to spread false reports and letters, stating that the Emperor Francis had declared war against the Porte, that Austrian troops would occupy the Principalities, and that he was going to have an interview with the Imperial governor. But once on Austrian territory, Ipsilanti, who there called himself Alexander Komorenos, was seized and imprisoned in Fort Arad. There he attempted to justify his forsaking his companions in arms by shifting the want of success oft' his shoulders on those of others. In a boastful manifesto he said: " Soldiers! But no, I will not disgrace this honourable name by applying it to you. Cowardly hordes of slaves! your treachery, and the plots you have hatched, compel me to leave you. From this moment every bond between you and me is severed; to me remains the disgrace of having commanded you. You have even robbed me of the glory of dying in battle. Run to the Turks; purchase your slavery with your lives, with the honour of your wives and children."

538. Ipsilanti's Imprisonment and Death - Treaties between Austria and Turkey stipulated that fugitives from either side were only to be received on condition of their being rendered harmless. Consequently, Ipsilanti was compelled to declare in writing, and on his honour, that he would make no attempt at flight. He then was, like a common criminal, taken to the fortress of Munkacs, surrounded by marshes, and obliged to take up his residence in a miserable garret. For years he remained in close confinement, and only when his health began to give way was he permitted to take up his residence in a less unhealthy prison at Theresienstadt, a fortified place of Bohemia. In 1827, at the intercession of the Emperor of Russia, he was set free, but died next year, as it was said, of a broken heart. He had lived to see his followers persecuted and slain, his family ruined, and himself unable to assist, when the people of Greece, more successful than the Hetairists of the Principalities, fought for liberty and their fatherland. Romance has thrown its halo around the prisoner of Munkacs, and the Greeks ended in beholding in him the martyr of Greek freedom.

539. Fate of the Hetairists - The insurrection may be considered to have ended with Ipsilanti's flight; the remnant of his followers now fought for honour only. Readily supported by the people as foolishly as ever supporting their oppressors the Turks made rapid progress in annihilating the remains of Ipsilanti's army. Such Hetairist leaders as surrendered on good faith were mercilessly executed. The traitor Savas, in spite of the zeal he had shown in the Turkish cause, shared the same fate; he was shot at Bucharest, together with his officers and soldiers, and their heads were sent to Constantinople.

540. Georgakis' Death - Georgakis and Farmakis, the bravest and truest leaders of the insurgents, remained. They were determined not to entrust their lives either to Austrian protection or Turkish pity, and therefore again made their way into Moldavia. Georgakis, who was ill, had to be carried on a litter. During the long and painful march the number of his followers was reduced to three hundred and fifty. The peasants everywhere betrayed to the Turks in pursuit every one of his movements, and even before reaching the Moldavian frontier he was surrounded on all sides. Moreover, he was imprudent enough to take refuge in a cul-de-sac, by fortifying the monastery of Sekko, which, with but one outlet, is situate in a deep gorge. However, on the iyth September, he successfully drove back the first attack of the Turkish vanguard, and his confidence increased. He was, moreover, induced by a treacherous letter of the Greek bishop, Romanes, not to allow the treasures of the monastery to fall into Turkish hands, to prolong his stay. This decision proved fatal to the remnant of the Hetairia. On the 20th September, four thousand Turks, led by Roumanian peasants on hitherto unknown paths, made their appearance in the rear of the monastery, traversing the Greek lines of defence, and cutting off the defenders of the monastery, placed at the entrance of the gorge, from their comrades. Farmakis threw himself into the main building of the monastery, while Georgakis, with eleven companions, took refuge in the bell-tower. The Turks set fire to piles of wood close to it. "I shall die in the flames; fly, if you choose, I open you the door!" the

intrepid chief exclaimed; at the same time he threw down the door, flung a firebrand into the powder-stores, and in this way buried the Turks who had forced their way in, and ten of his companions, in the ruins. Only one of the Greeks escaped, as if by a miracle.

541. Farmakis' Death - Farmakis held the monastery for eleven days longer, after which time his ammunition and stores of food were exhausted. On the 4th October he agreed to a favourable capitulation, which the Pasha of Braila and the Austrian Consul (!) guaranteed. The besieged were promised an honourable free marching off with their arms. But in the night, before the conclusion of the treaty, thirty-three of Farmakis' soldiers two hundred altogether made their escape, because they did not trust the Turkish promises. Those who remained had to regret their confidence. On the following day the Turks slaughtered the soldiers; the officers were carried to Silistria, and there executed; Farmakis was sent to Constantinople, where, after having been cruelly racked, he was beheaded.

542. Final Success of the Hetairia - Thus the real Hetairia perished, but its overthrow was not without benefit to the cause; for by the brutalities committed by the Turks who occupied the Principalities, there arose a series of complications between the Cabinets of St. Petersburg and Constantinople, which at last led to an open quarrel. Ipsilanti lived to see the issue of the diplomatic fencing in the beginning of the Russo-Turkish war of 1828 and 1829, when the real Greek people, with genuine means, accomplished to the south of the Balkans what he had vainly attempted with artificial ones in the north. But in this the action of the Hetairia, still existing as a remnant, played only a secondary part, and hence we may here fitly conclude the history of this secret society.

IV THE CARBONARI

543. History of the Association - Like all other associations, the Carbonari, or charcoal-burners, lay claim to a very high antiquity. Some of the less instructed have even professed a descent from Philip of Macedon, the father of Alexander the Great, and have attempted to form a high degree, the Knight of Thebes, founded on this imaginary origin. Others go back only so far as the pontificate of Alexander III., when Germany, to secure herself against rapacious barons, founded guilds and societies for mutual protection, and the charcoal-burners in the vast forests of that country united themselves against robbers and enemies. By words and signs only known to themselves, they afforded each other assistance. The criminal enterprise of Kunz de Kauffungen to carry off the Saxon princes, 8th July 1455, failed through the intervention of a charcoal-burner, though his intervention was more accidental than prearranged. And in 1514 the Duke Ulrich of Wlirtemberg was compelled by them, under threat of death, to abolish certain forest laws, considered as oppressive. Similar societies arose in many mountainous countries, and they surrounded themselves with that mysticism of which we have seen so many examples. Their fidelity to each other and to the society was so great, that it became in Italy a proverbial expression to say, " On the faith of a Carbon aro." At the feasts of the Carbonari, the Grand Master drinks to the health of Francis I., King of France, the pretended founder of the Order, according to the follovving tradition: During the troubles in Scotland in Queen Isabella's time this Isabella is purely mythical many illustrious persons, having escaped from the yoke of tyranny, took refuge in the woods. In order to avoid all suspicion of criminal association, they employed themselves in cutting wood and making charcoal. Under pretence of carrying it for sale, they introduced themselves into the villages, and bearing the name of real Carbonari, they easily met their partisans, and mutually communicated their different plans. They recognised each other by signs, by touch, and by

words, and as there were no habitations in the forest, they constructed huts of an oblong form, with branches of trees. Their lodges (vendite) were subdivided into a number of baracche, each erected by a Good Cousin of some distinction. There dwelt in the forest a hermit of the name of Theobald; he joined them, and favoured their enterprise. He was proclaimed protector of the Carbonari. Now it happened that Francis I., King of France, hunting on the frontiers of his kingdom next to Scotland (sic), or following a wild beast, was parted from his courtiers. He lost himself in the forest, but stumbling on one of the baracche, he was hospitably entertained, and eventually made acquainted with their secret and initiated into the Order. On his return to France he declared himself its protector. The origin of this story is probably to be found in the protection granted by Louis XII. and continued by Francis I. to the Waldenses, who had taken refuge in Dauphine". But neither the Hewers nor the Carbonari ever rose to any importance, or acted any conspicuous part among the secret societies of Europe till the period of the Revolution. As to their influence in and after that event, we shall return to it anon.

The Theobald alluded to in the foregoing tradition, is said to have been descended from the first Counts of Brie and Champagne. Possessed of rank and wealth, his fondness for solitude led him to leave his father's house, and retire with his friend Gautier to a forest in Suabia, where they lived as hermits, working at any chance occupation by which they could maintain themselves, but chiefly by preparing charcoal for the forges. They afterwards made several pilgrimages to holy shrines, and finally settled near Vicenza, where Gautier died. Theobald died in 1066, and was canonised by Pope Alexander III. From his occupation, St. Theobald was adopted as the patron saint of the Carbonari, and is invoked by the Good Cousins in their hymns; and a picture, representing him seated in front of his hut, is usually hung up in the lodge.

544. Real Orifin of the Carboneria - The first traces of a league of charcoal-burners with political objects appear in the twelfth century, probably caused by the severe forest laws then in existence. About that

period also the Fcndeurs (hewers), large corporations with rites similar to those of the Carbonari, existed in the French department of the Jura, where the association was called le Ion cousinage (the good cousinship), which title was also assumed by the Carbonari. Powerful lords, members of the persecuted Order of the Temple, seeing the important services men scattered over so large an extent of country could render, entered into secret treaties with them. It further appears that the Fcndeurs formed the first and the Carbonari the second, or higher, degree of the society collectively called the Carboneria. It is also probable that before the French Revolution the then French Government attempted by means of the society, which then existed at Genoa under the name of the Royal Carboneria, to overthrow the ancient oligarchical government and annex Genoa to France. It is certain that from 1770 to 1790 most of the members of the French chambers belonged to the Order of the Fendeurs, which continued to exist even under Napoleon I. The Carboneria was introduced into Southern Italy by returning Neapolitan exiles, who had been initiated in Germany and Switzerland, and as early as 1807 Salicetti, the Neapolitan minister of police, spoke of a conspiracy instigated by the Carbonari against the French army in the Neapolitan states. But the society was as yet powerless; when, however, the Austrian war broke out in 1809, and French troops had largely to be withdrawn from Italy, the first and head Vendita was formed at Capua, its rules and ordinances being written in English, because the English Government desired to employ the society as a lever for the overthrow of Napoleon. Before, however, proceeding with the history of the Order, we will give particulars of their ritual and ceremonies.

545. The Vendita or Lodge - From the "Code of Carbonarism" we derive the following particulars respecting the lodge: It is a room of wood in the shape of a barn. The pavement must be of brick, in imitation of the mosaic floor of the Masons' lodge, the interior furnished with seats without backs. At the end there must be a block supported by three legs, at which sits the Grand Master; at the two sides there must be two other blocks of the same size, at which sit the

orator and secretary respectively. On the block of the Grand Master there must be the following symbols: a linen cloth, water, salt, a cross, leaves, sticks, fire, earth, a crown of white thorns, a ladder, a ball of thread, and three ribbons, one blue, one red, and one black. There must be an illuminated triangle, with the initial letters of the password of the second rank in the middle. On the left hand there must be a triangle, with the arms of the Vendita painted. On the right three transparent triangles, each with the initial letters of the sacred words of the first rank. The Grand Master, and first and second assistants, who also sit each before a large wooden block, hold hatchets in their hands. The masters sit along the wall of one side of the lodge, the apprentices opposite.

546. Ritual of Initiation -The ritual of Carbonarism, as it was reconstituted at the beginning of the present century, was as follows. In the initiation:

"The Grand Master having opened the lodge, says, First Assistant, where is the first degree conferred?

A. In the hut of a Good Cousin, in the lodge of the Carbonari.

G. M. How is the first degree conferred?

A. A cloth is stretched over a block of wood, on which are arranged the bases, firstly, the cloth itself, water, fire, salt, the crucifix, a dry sprig, a green sprig. At least three Good Cousins must be present for an initiation; the introducer, always accompanied by a master, remains outside the place where are the bases and the Good Cousins. The master who accompanies the introducer strikes three times with his foot and cries: ' Masters, Good Cousins, I need succour.' The Good Cousins stand around the block of wood, against which they strike the cords they wear round the waist and make the sign, carrying the right hand from the left shoulder to the right side, and one of them exclaims, ' I have heard the voice of a Good Cousin who needs help, perhaps he brings wood to feed the furnaces.' The introducer is then brought in. Here the Assistant is silent, and the Grand Master begins again, addressing the new-comer: 'My Good Cousin, whence come you?

I. From the wood.

G. M. Whither go you?

I. Into the Chamber of Honour, to conquer my passions, submit my will, and be instructed in Carbonarism.

G. M. What have you brought from the wood?

I. Wood, leaves, earth.

G. M. Do you bring anything else? , . Yes; faith, hope, and charity.

G. M. Who is he whom you bring hither? . . A man lost in the wood.

G. M. What does he seek?

I. To enter our order. G. M. Introduce him.'

The neophyte is then brought in. The Grand Master puts several questions to him regarding his morals and religion, and then bids him kneel, holding the crucifix, and pronounce the oath: 'I promise and bind myself on my honour not to reveal the secrets of the Good Cousins; not to attack the virtue of their wives or daughters, and to afford all the help in my power to every Good Cousin needing it. So help me God! "

547. First Degree - After some preliminary questioning, the Grand Master addresses the novice thus: " What means the block of wood?

N. Heaven and the roundness of the earth.

G. M. What means the cloth?

N. That which hides itself on being born.

G. M. The water?

N. That which serves to wash and purify from original sin.

G.M. The fire?

N. To show us our highest duties.

G. M. The salt?

N. That we are Christians.

G. M. The crucifix?

N. It reminds us of our redemption.

G. M. What does the thread commemorate?

N. The Mother of God that spun it.

G. M. What means the crown of white thorns?

N. The troubles and struggles of Good Cousins.

G. M. What is the furnace?

N. The school of Good Cousins.

G. M. What means the tree with its roots up in the air?

N. If all the trees were like that, the work of the Good Cousins would not be needed."

The catechism is much longer, but I have given only so much as will suffice to show the kind of instruction imparted in the first degree. Without any explanations following, one would think one was reading the catechism of one of those religions improvised on American soil, which seek by the singularity of form to stir up the imagination. But as in other societies, as that of the Illuminati, the object was not at the first onset to alarm the affiliated; his disposition had first to be tested before the real meaning of the ritual was revealed to him. Still, some of the figures betray themselves, though studiously concealed. The furnace is the collective work at which the Carbonari labour; the sacred fire they keep alive, is the flame of liberty, with which they desire to illumine the world. They did not without design choose coal for their symbol; for coal is the fountain of light and warmth, that purifies the air. The forest represents Italy, the wild wood of Dante, infested with wild beasts that is, foreign oppressors. The tree with the roots in the air is a figure of kingdoms destroyed and thrones overthrown. Catholic mysticism constantly reappears; the highest honours are given to Christ, who was indeed the Good Cousin of all men. Carbonarism did not openly assail religious belief, but made use of it, endeavouring to simplify and reduce it to first principles, as Freemasonry does. The candidate, as in the last-named Order, was supposed to perform journeys through the forest and through fire, to each of which a symbolical meaning was attached; though the true meaning was not told in this degree. In fact, to all who wished to gain an insight into the real objects of Carbonarism, this degree could not suffice. It was necessary to proceed.

548. The Second Degree - The martyrdom of Christ occupies nearly

the whole of the second degree, imparting to the catechism a sad character, calculated to surprise and terrify the candidate. The preceding figures were here invested with new and unexpected meanings, relating to the minutest particulars of the crucifixion of the Good Cousin Jesus; which more and more led the initiated to believe that the unusual and whimsical forms with stupendous artifice served to confound the ideas and suspicions of their enemies, and cause them to lose the traces of the fundamental idea. In the constant recurrence to the martyrdom of Christ we may discern two aims the one essentially educational, to familiarise the Cousin with the idea of sacrifice, even, if necessary, of that of life; the other, chiefly political, intended to gain proselytes among the superstitious, the mystics, the souls loving Christianity, fundamentally good, however, prejudiced, because loving, and who constituted the greater number in a Roman Catholic country like Italy then even more than now. The catechism, as already observed, has reference to the Crucifixion, and the symbols are all explained as representing something pertaining thereto. Thus the furnace signifies the Holy Sepulchre; the rustling of the leaves symbolises the flagellation of the Good Cousin the Grand Master of the Universe; and so on. The candidate for initiation into this degree has to undergo further trials. He represents Christ, whilst the Grand Master takes the name of Pilate, the first councillor that of Caiaphas, the second that of Herod; the Good Cousins generally are called the people. The candidate is led bound from one officer to the other, and finally condemned to be crucified; but he is pardoned on taking a second oath, more binding than the first, consenting to have his body cut in pieces and burnt, as in the former degree. But still the true secret of the Order is not revealed.

549. The Degree of Grand Meet - This degree is only to be conferred with the greatest precautions, secretly, and to Carbonari known for their prudence, zeal, courage, and devotion to the Order. Besides, the candidates, who shall be introduced into a grotto of reception, must be true friends of the liberty of the people, and ready to fight against tyrannical governments, who are the abhorred rulers of ancient and

beautiful Ausonia. The admission of the candidate takes place by voting, and three black balls are sufficient for his rejection. He must be thirty- three years and three months old, the age of Christ on the day of His death. But the religious drama is now followed by one political. The lodge is held in a remote and secret place, only known to the Grand Masters already received into the degree of Grand Elect. The lodge is triangular, truncated at the eastern end. The Grand Master Grand Elect is seated upon a throne. Two guards, from the shape of their swords called flames, are placed at the entrance. The assistants take the name of Sun and Moon respectively. Three lamps, in the shape of sun, moon, and stars, are suspended at the three angles of the grotto or lodge. The catechism here reveals to the candidate that the object of the association is political, and aims at the overthrow of all tyrants, and the establishment of universal liberty, the time for which has arrived. To each prominent member his station and duties in the coming conflict are assigned, and the ceremony is concluded by all present kneeling down, and pointing their swords to their breasts, whilst the Grand Elect pronounces the following formula: " I, a free citizen of Ausonia, swear before the Grand Master of the Universe, and the Grand Elect Good Cousin, to devote my whole life to the triumph of the principles of liberty, equality, and progress, which are the soul of all the secret and public acts of Carbonarism. I promise that, if it be impossible to restore the reign of liberty without a struggle, I will fight to the death. I consent, should I prove false to my oath, to be slain by my Good Cousins Grand Elects; to be fastened to the cross in a lodge, naked, crowned with thorns; to have my belly torn open, the entrails and heart taken out and scattered to the winds. Such are our conditions; swear!" The Good Cousins reply: "We swear." There was something theatrical in all this; but the organisers no doubt looked to the effect it had on the minds of the initiated. If on this ground it could not be defended, then there is little excuse for judicial wigs and clerical gowns, episcopal gaiters, aprons, and shovel-hats, lord mayors' shows, parliamentary procedure, and royal pageants.

550. Degree of Grand Master Grand Elect - This, the highest degree of

Carbonarism, is only accessible to those who have given proofs of great intelligence and resolution. The Good Cousins being assembled in the lodge, the candidate is introduced blindfolded; two members, representing the two thieves, carry a cross, which is firmly planted in the ground. One of the two pretended thieves is then addressed as a traitor to the cause, and condemned to die on the cross. He resigns himself to his fate, as fully deserved, and is tied to the cross with silken cords; and, to delude the candidate, whose eyes are still bandaged, he utters loud groans. The Grand Master pronounces the same doom on the other robber, but he, representing the non-repentant one, exclaims: " I shall undergo my fate, cursing you, and consoling myself with the thought that I shall be avenged, and that strangers shall exterminate you to the last Carbonaro. Know that I have pointed out your retreat to the chiefs of the hostile army, and that within a short time you shall fall into their hands. Do your worst." The Grand Elect then turns to the candidate, and, alluding to the punishment awarded to traitors as done on the present occasion, informs him that he also must be fastened to the cross if he persists in his intention to proceed, and there receive on his body the sacred marks, whereby the Grand Masters Grand Elects of all the lodges are known to each other, and must also pronounce the oath, whereupon the bandage will be removed, he will descend from the cross, and be clothed with the insignia of the Grand Master Grand Elect. He is then firmly tied to the cross, and pricked three times on the right arm, seven times on the left, and three times under the left breast. The cross being erected in the middle of the cave, that the members may see the marks on the body, on a given sign, the bandage being removed, the Cousins stand around the candidate, pointing their swords and daggers at his breast, and threatening him with even a worse death should he turn traitor. They also watch his demeanour, and whether he betrays any fear. Seven toasts in his honour are then drunk, and the Grand Elect explains the real meaning of the symbols, which may not be printed, but is only to be written down, and zealously guarded, the owner promising to burn or swallow it, rather then let it fall into other hands. The Grand Master concludes by speaking in praise of the revolution already initiated, announcing its triumph not only in the peninsula, but everywhere where Italian is spoken, and exclaims: " Very soon the nations weary of tyranny shall celebrate their victory over the tyrants; very soon "... Here the wicked thief exclaims: "Very soon all ye shall perish!" Immediately there is heard outside the grotto the noise of weapons and fighting. One of the doorkeepers announces that the door is on the point of being broken open, and an assault on it is heard directly after. The Good Cousins rush to the door placed behind the crosses, and therefore unseen by the candidate; the noise becomes louder, and there are heard the cries of Austrian soldiers; the Cousins return in great disorder as if overpowered by superior numbers, say a few words of encouragement to the candidate fastened to the cross, and disappear through the floor, which opens beneath them. Cousins, dressed in the hated uniform of the foreigner, enter and marvel at the disappearance of the Carbonari. Perceiving the persons on the crosses, they, on finding them still alive, propose to kill them at once; they charge and prepare to shoot them, when suddenly a number of balls fly into the cave, the soldiers fall down as if struck, and the Cousins re-enter through many openings, which at once close behind them, and shout: " Victory! Death to tyranny! Long live the republic of Ausonia! Long live liberty! Long live the government established by the brave Carbonari! " In an instant the apparently dead soldiers and the two thieves are carried out of the cave; and the candidate having been helped down from the cross, is proclaimed by the Grand Master, who strikes seven blows with his axe, a Grand Master Grand Elect.

551. Signification of the Symbols - Not to interrupt the narrative, the explanation of the meaning of the symbols, given in this last degree, was omitted in the former paragraph, but follows here. It will be seen that it was not without reason that it was prohibited to print it. The cross serves to crucify the tyrant that persecutes us. The crown of thorns is to pierce his head. The thread denotes the cord to lead him to the gibbet; the ladder will aid him to mount. The leaves are nails to pierce his hands and feet. The pickaxe will penetrate his breast, and shed his impure blood. The axe will separate his head from his body.

The salt wilt prevent the corruption of his head, that it may last as a monument of the eternal infamy of despots. The pole will serve to put his head upon. The furnace will burn his body. The shovel will scatter his ashes to the wind. The baracca will serve to prepare new tortures for the tyrant before he is slain. The water will purify us from the vile blood we shall have shed. The linen, will wipe away our stains. The forest is the place where the Good Cousins labour to attain so important a result. These details are extracted from the minutes of the legal proceedings against the conspiracy of the Carbonari.

552. Other Ceremonies and Regulations - The candidate having been received into the highest degree, other Good Cousins entered the cave, proclaiming the victory of the Carbonari and the establishment of the Ausonian republic, whereupon the lodge was closed. The members all bore pseudonyms, by which they were known in the Order. These pseudonyms were entered in one book, whilst another contained their real names; and the two books were always kept concealed in separate places, so that the police, should they find one, should not be able to identify the conspirator. Officers of great importance were the Insinuators, Censors, Scrutators, and Coverers, whose appellations designate their duties. The higher officers were called Great Lights. Some of the affiliated, reserved for the most dangerous enterprises, were styled the Forlorn Hope; others Stabene, or the "Sedentary," who were not advanced beyond the first degree, on account of want of intelligence or courage. Like the Freemasons, the Carbonari had their own almanacs, dating their era from Francis I. They also had their passwords and signs. The decorations in the Apprentice degree were three ribbons black, blue, and red; and in the Master's degree they wore a scarf of the same three colours. The ritual and the ceremonies, as partly detailed above, were probably strictly followed on particularly important occasions only; as to their origin, little is known concerning it most likely they were invented among the Neapolitans. Nor were they always and at all places alike, but the spirit that breathed in them was permanent and universal; and that it was the spirit of liberty and justice can scarcely be denied, especially after the events of the last

decades. The following summary of a manifesto proceeding from the Society of the Carbonari will show this very clearly.

553. The Ausonian Republic - The epoch of the following document, of which, however, an abstract only is here given, is unknown. The open proceedings of Carbonarism give us no clue, because in many respects they deviate from the programme of this sectarian charter; sectarian, inasmuch as the document has all the fulness of a social pact. But to whatever time these statutes belong, they cannot be read without the liveliest interest.

Italy, to which new times shall give a new name, sonorous and pure, Ausonia (the ancient Latin name), must be free from its threefold sea to the highest summit of the Alps. The territory of the republic shall be divided into twentyone provinces, each of which shall send a representative to the National Assembly. Every province shall have its local assembly; all citizens, rich or poor, may aspire to all public charges; the mode of electing judges is strictly laid down; two kings, severally elected for twenty-one years, one of whom is to be called the king of the land, the other of the sea, shall be chosen by the sovereign assembly; all Ausonian citizens are soldiers; all fortresses not required to protect the country against foreigners shall be razed to the ground; new ports are to be constructed along the coasts, and the navy enlarged; Christianity shall be the State religion, but every other creed shall be tolerated; the college of cardinals may reside in the republic during the life of the pope reigning at the time of the promulgation of this charter after his death, the college of cardinals will be abolished; hereditary titles and feudal rights are abolished; hospitals, charitable institutions, colleges, lyceums, primary and secondary schools, shall be largely increased, and properly allocated; punishment of death is inflicted on murderers only, transportation to one of the islands of the republic being substituted for all other punishments; monastic institutions are preserved, but no man can become a monk before the age of forty-five, and no woman a nun before that of forty, and even after having pronounced their vows, they may re-enter their own families. Mendicity is not allowed; the country finds work for able paupers, and succour for invalids. The tombs of great men are placed along the highways; the honour of a statue is awarded by the sovereign assembly. The constitutional pact may be revised every twenty-one years.

554. Most Secret Carlonaro Degree - It was stated in sect. 550 that the Grand Master Grand Elect was the highest Carbonaro degree. But this requires qualification; there was one still higher, called the Seventh, to which few members were admitted. To the Principi Summo Patriarcho alone the real object of Carbonarism was revealed, and that its aims were identical with those of the Illuminati (356). Witt von Dorring (b. 1800), an initiate, tells us in his Autobiography, that the candidate swore destruction to every government, whether despotic or democratic. " The Summo "Maestro," he says, " laughs at the zeal of the common Carbonari, who sacrifice themselves for Italian liberty and independence; to him this is not the object, but a means. I received this degree under the name of Giulio Alessandro Jerimundo Werther Domingone." As there were two modes of initiation, one in open lodge and another by " communication," the supreme chief notifying by a document to the new member his election, which was done in De Witt's case, he never took the oath of secrecy, and thus considered himself at liberty to divulge what had been communicated to him.

555. De Witt, Biographical Notice of - As Jean de Witt was a prominent character in the secret associations of this century, we give a few biographical notes concerning him. Born in 1800 at Altona, he was early placed under the tuition of Pastor Meier of Alsen, who had been a member of the Jacobin club. At the age of seventeen he went to the University of Kiel, and afterwards to that of Jena; in 1818 he joined the Burschenschaft, and was soon after initiated into the sect of the Black Knights, in consequence of which he had to flee to England, where he contributed many articles on German politics and princes full of scandalous details to the Morning Chronicle. Invited by his maternal uncle, the Baron Eckstein, Inspector-General of the Ministry of Police, to come to Paris, he there became acquainted with Count Serre, Minister of Justice, who protected him, whilst De Witt was in close

communication with French and Italian conspirators. In 1821 he was at Geneva as Inspector-General of Swiss and German Carbonari. He was soon after seized in Savoy, and thence taken to Turin, where, however, the Austrian Field-Marshal Bubna, who then commanded all the troops in Upper Italy, and who was a Freemason, treated him with the greatest respect, for as a Freemason De Witt occupied a much higher rank than Bubna; and when the ambassadors of all the Courts at Turin, that of England excepted, insisted on De Witt's extradition to their respective states, he allowed him, on his giving his word of honour to make no attempt at escape, to go to Milan, where he was received with great honour in the house of the Chief of Police, Baron von Gohausen. Bubna had made himself personally answerable to his government for the safe custody of De Witt, and this latter had promised not to escape, though he was allowed to go about almost like a freeman. But when he found that the Austrian authorities intended to begin his trial, he wrote to Bubna that he was determined to make his escape. Orders were sent to watch him closely; but within a week he was in possession of false keys, which fitted all the doors of his prison, and the head gaoler, who had shown himself too zealous in watching him, was transferred to Mantua, and 1200 lire were provided for his journey. He escaped to Genoa, intending thence to sail for Spain, where he was sure of meeting with friends, but finding all vessels bound for that country under close police surveillance, he made his way into Switzerland. Under different names and various disguises he stayed there and in Germany for about a year. All the German Governments offered a large reward for his apprehension, and at last he was seized at Bayreuth, though he had previously been warned that the police were on his traces, a warning which could only have come from highlyplaced officials. And as soon as he was taken some of them waited on him with offers of friendship and protection. But Berlin was then the seat of the Prussian masonic chiefs, and through them De Witt was secretly informed of all the charges which would be brought against him, and the result was that he was acquitted of them all, and restored to liberty, as also was Cousin, a fellow-conspirator and fellowprisoner. Cesare Cantu, the Italian historian, accuses De Witt of having, by his own admission, been thoroughly initiated into all the revolutionary plots in Europe but in order to betray them, and stir up discord among them (see II Conciliatore e i Carbonari, Milano, 1878, p. 164). De Witt's subsequent career seems to lend some support to this charge. In 1828 he married a wealthy lady, and purchased an estate in Upper Silesia, where he was living in 1855, professing highly conservative principles, in fact, to such a degree as to be charged with belonging to the Ultramontanes, in consequence of which he was detested, and frequently attacked, by the democratic party.

556. Carbonaro Charter proposed to England - A charter or project, said to have been proposed by the Carbonari to the English Government in 1813, when the star of Napoleon was fast declining, is to the following effect: Italy shall be free and independent. Its boundaries shall be the three seas and the Alps. Corsica, Sardinia, Sicily, the seven islands, and the islands along the coasts of the Mediterranean, Adriatic, and Ionian Seas shall form an integral portion of the Roman Empire. Rome shall be the capital of the empire. ... As soon as the French shall have evacuated the peninsula, the new emperor shall be elected from among the reigning families of Naples, Piedmont, or England. Illyria shall form a kingdom of itself, and be given to the King of Naples as an indemnity for Sicily. This project in some respects widely differs from the one preceding it, and there is great doubt whether it ever emanated from the Carbonari.

557. Carbonarism and Murat - The excessive number of the affiliated soon disquieted rulers, and especially Murat, King of Naples, whose fears were increased by a letter from Dandolo, Councillor of State, saying: "Sire, Carbonarism is spreading in Italy; free your kingdom from it, if possible, because the sect is opposed to thrones." Maghella, a native of Genoa, who became Minister of Police under Murat, advised that king, on the other hand, to declare openly against Napoleon, and to proclaim the independence of Italy, and for that purpose to favour the Carbonari; but Murat was too irresolute to follow the course thus pointed out, and declared against the Carbonari.

The measures taken by him, however, only increased the activity of the sect and the hopes of the banished Bourbons, who in the neighbouring Sicily watched every turn of affairs that might promise their restoration. Murat proscribed the sect, which induced it to seek the assistance of England, as we have already seen. It also grew into favour with the Bourbons and Lord William Bentinck. The emissaries sent to Palermo, to come to terms with the exiled royal family, returned to Naples with a plan fully arranged, the results of which were soon seen in Calabria and the Abruzzi. The promise of a constitution was the lure with which England whose chief object, however, was the overthrow of Napoleon attracted the sectaries; the Bourbons, constrained by England, promised the Neapolitans a liberal constitution on their being restored to the throne. The Prince of Moliterno suggested to England that the only means of defeating France was to favour Italian unity; and the idea was soon widely promulgated and advocated throughout the country. Murat sent General Manhes against the Carbonari, with orders to exterminate them. Many of the leaders were captured and executed, but the sect, nevertheless, succeeded in effecting a partial and temporary revolution in favour of the Bourbons; which, however, was soon quelled by the energetic measures of Queen Caroline Murat, who was regent during her husband's then absence. About this time, also, dissensions arose among the members of the sect; its leaders, seeing the difficulty of directing the movements of so great a confederacy, conceived the plan of a reform, and executed it with secrecy and promptitude. The members who were retained continued to bear the name of Carbonari, while those who were expelled, according to some accounts, took that of Calderari (Braziers), and an implacable hatred arose between the rival sects. Murat wavered for some time between the two parties, and at last determined on supporting the Carbonari, who were most numerous. But it was too late. They had no confidence in him; and they also knew his desperate circumstances. Murat fell.

558. Trial of Carbonari - An extensive organisation for the union of all secret Carbonaro societies was discovered in 1817 by an attempt,

which was to have been made at Macerata, on the 24th June in that year, to raise the standard of revolt, but which failed through a mere accident the premature firing of two muskets. A great many of the leading Carbonari were apprehended, and conveyed to the Castle of St. Angelo and other prisons in Rome, where they were tried in October 1818 by order of the pope; five of them were sentenced to death, but the pope mitigated their punishment to perpetual confinement in a fortress; three were sentenced to the galleys for life, which punishment was reduced by the pope to ten years. We learn from this Roman trial that the Republican Brother Protectors one of the branches of Carbonarism swore over a phial of poison and a red-hot iron, "never to divulge the secrets of the society, and to submit in case of perjury to the punishment of dying by poison, and having their flesh burnt by the red-hot iron."

559. Carbonarism and the Bourbons - King Ferdinand, having, to recover his crown, favoured the Carbonari, when he thought himself again firmly seated on the throne, and secretly disliking the society, endeavoured to kick down the ladder by which he had mounted. The Carbonari, who had restored not only the king, but order in Calabria and the Abruzzi, and rendered roads and property secure the Carbonari, so highly extolled at one time, that the pope had ordered priests and monks to preach, that making the signs of the Carbonaro would suifice to justify Saint Peter to open the gate of Paradise these same Carbonari were now declared the enemies of God and man. The king refused to keep the promises he had made, and forbade the holding of Carbonari meetings. The Prince of Canosa, who became Minister of Police in 1819, determined to exterminate them. For this purpose he formed the Brigands, who had played a part in the sanguinary scenes of 1799, into a new society, of which he himself became the head, inviting all the old Calderari to join him, on account of their enmity to the Carbonari. He required them to take the following oath: " I, A. B., promise and swear upon the Trinity, upon this cross and upon this steel, the avenging instrument of the perjured, to live and die in the Roman Catholic and Apostolic faith, and to

defend with my blood this religion and the society of True Friendship, the Calderari. I swear never to offend, in honour, life, or property, the children of True Friendship, &c. I swear eternal hatred to all Masonry, and its atrocious protectors, as well as to all Jansenists, Materialists (Molinists?), Economists, and Illuminati. I swear, that if through wickedness or levity I suffer myself to be perjured, I submit to the loss of life, and then to be burnt, &c." But the king having learnt what his Minister had been attempting without his knowledge, deprived him of his office and banished him; and thus his efforts came to nothing. In 1819 took place the rising at Cadiz, by which the King of Spain, Ferdinand VII. , was compelled to give Spain constitutional privileges. This again stirred up the Carbonari; but there was no unanimity in their counsels, and their intrigues only led to many being imprisoned and others banished. An attempt made in 1820 extorted a constitution; the leader was the Abbe Menichini. The influence of the Carbonari increased; lodges were established everywhere. Between 1815 and 1820, in the Neapolitan states alone, more than two hundred thousand members were affiliated, comprising all classes, from the palace to the cottage; it included priests, monks, politicians, soldiers. Giampietro was then chief of the Neapolitan police, who used the most cruel means to suppress the sect; but public discontent was brought to a climax in July 1820, when two officers, Morelli and Silvati, with one hundred and twenty non-commissioned officers and privates, deserted from their regiment at Nola, and, accompanied by the priest Menichini and some leading Carbonari, took the road to Avellino. Lieutenant-Colonel De Concili, also a Carbonaro, who was in command of the troops at Avellino, joined the insurgents. When the news of these events reached Naples, the students of the University, as well as many of the soldiers forming the garrison of the capital, hastened to De Concili's camp. The house of the advocate Colletta became the centre of action at Naples; all the Carbonari prepared to second the action of their brethren. The king, advised to send General Pepe against the insurgents, declined the proposal, because Pe'pe was suspected of being a Liberal. In his stead he sent General Carrascosa, who left Naples on the 4th July; on the 5th he despatched General Nunziante from

Nocera, and General Campana from Salerno, against the insurgents. Carrascosa, unwilling to shed the blood of his countrymen, wished to negotiate. But before he could do so, General Campana had suffered a defeat, and the soldiers of Nunziante raised the standard of the Carbonari, and, joining the troops of De Concili, placed themselves under his command. Carrascosa, with the king's connivance, proposed to bribe the leaders of the insurrection with large sums of money to give up the enterprise and leave the country, but before he had an opportunity of making the attempt, the soldiers remaining in Naples, as well as the population, rose against the king, who found himself entirely forsaken. He was compelled to yield. The Duke of Piccotellis and five other Carbonari presented themselves in the palace and compelled the king to grant them a personal interview, at which they demanded the immediate publication of a Constitution. The king promised one in "perhaps two hours." Piccotellis drawing out his watch held it up to the king's face and said, " It is now one o'clock in the morning; at three o'clock the Constitution must be proclaimed." And he turned his back on the king, and with his attendants left the room. The king granted the Constitution, though with the mental reserve of overthrowing it on the first favourable opportunity. He swore, nevertheless, in the most solemn manner to keep it; the Carbonari leaders were invited to Naples; the king's son, the Duke of Calabria, became a member of the sect, a fatal concession on its part, for now all its secrets, signs, words, and symbols were openly proclaimed; Carbonarism, in fact, was cunningly betrayed by the king and his satellites. Russia, Austria, and Prussia threatened to interfere in Neapolitan affairs in favour of Ferdinand; at a secret meeting of some of the oldest Carbonari it was proposed to shut up the king in the Castle of St. Eleno. Unfortunately this advice was not immediately acted on. The Holy Alliance, to save the king's life, which they knew to be in danger, invited him to join the congress at Laybach, that, in common with the European potentates, he might assist in the settlement of the affairs of his own kingdom. Unwisely the Neapolitan parliament allowed him to depart; yet even on board ship the treacherous despot repeated his assurances of maintaining the

Constitution he had granted his subjects. But on his arrival at Laybach he declared that, in granting the Constitution, he had only yielded to superior force, and that he was determined to return to Naples as an absolute monarch. The pope absolved him from the oath he had taken, and even in a solemn encyclical commanded priests to violate the secret of the confessional whenever wives, mothers, sisters, or daughters had declared relations to belong to the sect of the Carbonari. At the request of Ferdinand himself an Austrian army of 50,000 men, with a Russian army in reserve, marched upon Naples. The king on his way south stopped at Florence, where he decorated the Chapel of the Annunciation with gorgeous gold and silver lamps, and the inscription: " Marice genitrici Dei Ferd. I. Utr. Sic. rex, Don. d.d. anno 1821 ob pristinum imperil decus, ope eius prestantissima recuperatum. (To Mary, the Mother of God, Ferdinand I, King of the Two Sicilies, for the restored splendour of the kingdom, by means of her most valiant help, dedicated these in the year 1821.) Proving once more, if proof were necessary, that " bloodthirsty tyrants are most zealous saints." Every one of the king's immediate attendants had upon him a new cockade bearing the inscription: " Viva Vassoluto potere di Ferdinando I.! "

560. The King's Revenge - General Pepe, who in his youth had for three years been a prisoner in the horrible prison of Marettimo a rock-hewn cistern turned into a dungeon endeavoured to arrest the advance of the foreigner, but his raw militia were ill prepared to meet the disciplined forces of Austria, who defeated Pe'pe' at Rieti, and followed up this victory by marching on the 23rd March into Naples. Then the king glutted his desire for vengeance. All the past treaties with his subjects were considered as void, and all previous acts of pardon annulled. Not a day passed without the sound of the bell tolling for an execution; thousands of the most respected citizens of Naples were condemned to horrible dungeons in the penal islands off Sicily and Naples or the rock-dungeons of San Stefano and Pantelleria, while numbers fled the country as exiles. Morelli and Silvati were hanged for having deserted their standard, and been the prime movers

of the revolution. But the king had entered into a treaty with his people, and sworn to uphold the Constitution he had granted in consequence of the revolution, hence their execution is condemned by logic and justice.

561. Revival of Carbonarism - Carbonarism marks a transition period in the history of secret societies. From secret societies occupied with religion, philosophy, and politics in the abstract, it leads us to the secret societies whose objects are more immediately and practically political. And thus in France, Italy, and other States, it gave rise to numerous and various sects, wherein we find the men of thought and those of action combining for one common object the progress, as they understood it, of human society. Carbonarism, in fact, was revived about the year 1825, and some ten years after combined, or rather coalesced, with the society known as Young Italy, whose aims were identical with those of the Carbonari the expulsion of the foreigner from Italian soil, and the unification of Italy.

The Duke of Modena had for some time coquetted with the Carbonari, in the hope of obtaining through them the sovereignty of the minor duchies, the kingdom of Sardinia and the Lombardo-Venetian states, and had thus encouraged Menotti, the foremost patriot of Central Italy, in counting on his help in driving out the foreigner. When, however, he found that France, on whose co-operation he had relied, would disappoint him, he abandoned the Carbonari and denounced them, but they compelled the Duke to fly to Mantua. They also drove Maria Louisa, the Duchess of Parma, and widow of Napoleon I., into exile. But their triumph lasted only twenty-eight days. At the end of that period the Duke of Modena and the Duchess of Parma were restored by the assistance of Austrian troops, and the Duke caused Menotti to be hanged. From that day the prisons of Modena were filled with Italian patriots. Count Charles Arrivabene said of them, " No words can give an idea of the horrors of the prisons of Modena when I saw them. . . . Excepting the infamous dens of the Papal and Neapolitan states, there is nothing that can be compared with them."

But Carbonarism continued to be at work under the name of Unita Italiana, whose signs and passwords were made public by the prosecution it underwent at Naples in 1850.

562. Carbonarism and the Church - The Carbonari in the Roman States aimed at the overthrow of the papal power, and chose the moment when the pope was expected to die to carry out their scheme. They had collected large forces and provisions at Macerata; but the sudden recovery of the pope put a stop to the enterprise. The leaders were betrayed into the hands of the government, and some of them condemned to death and others to perpetual imprisonment, though the pope afterwards commuted the sentences (558).

563. Carbonarism in Northern Italy - In Lombardy and Venetia also the Carbonari had their lodges, and their object was the expulsion of the foreigner, the Austrian. The most important and influential was the Italian Federation. But here also they failed; and among the victims of the failure were Silvio Pellico, Confalonieri, Castiglia, Torelli, Maroncelli, and many others, who, after having been exposed on the pillory at Milan and other places, were sent to Spielberg and other German fortresses.

564. Carbonarism in France - Carbonarism was introduced into France under the names of Adelphes or Philadelphians, by Joubert and Dugied, who had taken part in revolutionary movements in their own country in 1820, and after having for some time taken refuge in Italy, where they had joined the Carbonari, brought their principles to France on their return from their expatriation. The sect made rapid progress among the French; all the students at the different universities became members, and ventas were established in the army. Lafayette was chosen their chief. Lodges existed at La Rochelle, Poitiers, Niort, Bordeaux, Colmar, Neuf-Brisach, and Belfort, where, in 1821, an unsuccessful attempt was made against the government unsuccessful, because in this, as in other attempts, the government knew beforehand the plans of the conspirators, betrayed to them by false Carbonari.

Risings in other places equally failed; and though the society continued to exist, and had a share in the events of the revolution of 1830, still, considering the number of its members, and the great resources and influence it consequently possessed, it cannot be said to have produced any adequate results.

565. Carbonarism in Germany - Carbonari lodges existed in all parts of Germany, but I will mention one only, because of the excitement its discovery caused at the time. In 1849 the police of Bremen arrested one Hobelmann, who was tutor in the family of a Thuringian nobleman, and who proved to be the chief of a Carbonaro sect calling itself the Todtenbund, or " Society of Death," since its aim was to kill all who should oppose its objects. Its statutes, and a long list of persons condemned to death, were found by the police.

566. Carbonarism in Spain - The sect was introduced into Spain by refugee Italians about 1820, spreading chiefly in Catalonia, without, however, acquiring much influence at first. Their importance dates from the time of the quarrel between the Spanish Freemasons and the Comuneros (1822), when they sided with the former; but when the Freemasons and the Comuneros were reconciled (1823), the Carbonari were opposed by both parties, and lost all influence (522).

567. Giardiniere - As the Freemasons had their Adoptive Lodges, so the Carbonari admitted women, who were collectively called giardiniere, garden-women, each sister taking the name of a flower. Their mission, of course, was to act as lures or spies. But they also fulfilled higher functions; they alleviated the condition of the prisoners of despotism, especially in Italy, where many lady members of the Societd della Misericordia were Giardiniere, and, having free access to the Austrian prisons in Piedmont, supplemented the scanty food allowed to the imprisoned Carbonari by the authorities with liberal additions.

V

MISCELLANEOUS ITALIAN SOCIETIES

568. Guelphic Knights - One of the most important societies that issued, about the year 1816, from the midst of the Carbonari was that of the Guelphic Knights, who were very powerful in all parts of Italy. A report of the Austrian police says: "This society is the most dangerous, on account of its origin and diffusion, and the profound mystery which surrounds it. It is said that this society derives its origin from England or Germany." Its origin, nevertheless, was purely Italian. The councils consisted of six members, who, however, did not know each other, but intercommunicated by means of one person, called the " Visible," because he alone was visible. Every council also had one youth of undoubted faith, called the " Clerk," to communicate with students of universities, and a youth called a " Friend," to influence the people; but neither the Clerk nor the Friend were initiated into the mysteries of the Order. Every council assumed a particular name, such as "Virtue," "Honour," " Loyalty," and met, as if for amusement only, without apparatus or writing of any kind. A supreme council sat at Bologna; there were councils at Florence, Venice, Milan, Naples, &c. They endeavoured to gain adherents, who should be ignorant of the existence of the society, and should yet further its ends. Lucien Bonaparte is said to have been a " great light " among them. Their object was the independence of Italy, to be effected by means of all the secret societies of the country united under the leadership of the Guelphs.

569. Guelphs and Carbonari - The Guelphs in reality formed a high vendita or lodge of the Carbonari, and the chiefs of the Carbonari were also chiefs among the Guelphs; but only those that had distinct offices among the Carbonari could be admitted among the Guelphs. There can be no doubt that the Carbonari, when the sect had become very numerous, partly sheltered themselves under the designation of Guelphs and Adelphi or Independents, by affiliating themselves to these societies.

570. The Latini - This sect existed about 1817. Only those initiated into the higher degrees of Carbonarism could become members. In their oath they declared: "I swear to employ every means in my power to further the happiness of Italy. I swear religiously to keep the secret and fulfil the duties of this society, and never to do aught that could compromise its safety; and that I will only act in obedience to its decisions. If ever I violate this oath, I will submit to whatever punishment the society may inflict, even to death." The most influential vendite were gradually merged in this degree.

571. The Centres - An offshoot of Carbonarism was the society formed in Lombardy, under the designation of the "Centres." Nothing was to be written; and conversation on the affairs of the Order was only to take place between two members at a time, who recognised each other by the words, " Succour to the unfortunate," and by raising the hand three times to the forehead, in sign of grief. The Centres once more revived the hopes of Murat. A rising was to take place under his auspices against the detested Austrians; the ringing of the bells of Milan was to be the signal for the outbreak; and it is said that "Vespers" had been arranged, from which no Austrian was to escape alive. But on the appointed day fear or horror held the hand that was to have given the signal, that of General Fontanelli. Hence, fatal delay and the discovery of the secret. For Bellegarde or Talleyrand sent a certain Viscount SaintAignan among the conspirators, who after having discovered all their plans, betrayed them to Austria, and was never heard of again. Austria seized the ringleaders and instituted proceedings against them, which lasted about three years, and were finally closed by delivering it is not known why, but probably through Carbonaro influence very mild sentences against the conspirators.

572. Italian Litterateurs - This sect, introduced into Palermo in 1823, had neither signs nor distinctive marks. In every town there was a delegate, called the " Radical," who could affiliate unto himself ten others or more, acquiring the name of "decurion," or "centurion." The

initiated were called " sons," who in their turn could affiliate unto themselves ten others, and these could do the same in their turn; so that thus a mighty association was formed. The initiated were called " Brethren Barabbas," Christ representiug the tyrant, and Barabbas the people a singular confusion of ideas, by which the victim slain on the cross for the redemption of human conscience and thought was considered as an example and upholder of tyranny. But it was a symbolism which concealed juster ideas, and more conformable with truth. They recognised each other by means of a ring, and attested their letters by the wellknown initials I. N. R. I. The society was much feared and jealously watched, and helped to fill the prisons. It only ceased when other circumstances called forth other societies.

573. Societies in Calabria and the Abruzzi. These districts, by their natural features and the disposition of their inhabitants, were at all times the favourite resorts of conspirators. We there find the sects of the "European Patriots or White Pilgrims," the " Philadelphians," and the "Decisi," who thence spread into other Italian provinces, with military organisation, arms, and commanders. The first two partly came from France; nor were their operations, as the names intimate, confined to the peninsula. The lodges of the "Decisi" (Decided) were called "Decisions," as the assemblies of the Patriots were called " Squadrons," each from forty to sixty strong, and those of the Philadelphians, "Camps." The Decisi, whose numbers amounted perhaps to forty thousand, held their meetings at night, carefully guarded by sentinels; and their military exercises took place in solitary houses, or suppressed convents. Their object was to fall upon Naples and proclaim a republic; but circumstances were not propitious. Their leader, Giro Annichiarico, a priest, was a man of great resources and vast influence, so that it was necessary to despatch against him General Church, who captured him and had him shot. As Giro was rather a remarkable personage, a brief account of him may not be uninteresting.

574. Giro Annichiarico - This priest was driven from society by his crimes. He was accused of murder, committed in a fit of jealousy, and sentenced to fifteen years of exile, although there is strong reason to

believe that he was innocent. But instead of being permitted to leave the country, according to the sentence, he was for four years kept in prison, whence at last he made his escape, took refuge in the forests, and placed himself at the head of a band of outlaws, and, as his enemies declare, committed all kinds of enormities. At Martano, they say, he penetrated into one of the first houses of the place, and. after having offered violence to its mistress, massacred lier with all her people, and carried off 96,000 ducats. He was in correspondence with all the brigands; and whoever wished to get rid of an enemy, had only to address himself to Giro. On being asked, after his capture, how many persons he had killed with his own hand, he carelessly answered, " Who can remember? Perhaps sixty or seventy." His activity, artifice, and intrepidity were astonishing. He was a first-rate shot and rider; his singular good fortune in extricating himself from the most imminent dangers acquired for him the reputation of a necromancer, upon whom ordinary means of attack had no power. Though a priest himself, and exercising the functions of one when he thought it expedient, he was rather a libertine, and declared his clerical colleagues to be impostors without any faith. He published a paper against the missionaries, who, according to him, disseminated illiberal opinions among the people, and forbade them on pain of death to preach in the villages, "because, instead of the true principles of the Gospel, they taught nothing but fables and impostures." Probably Giro was pretty correct in his estimate of their performances. He could be generous on occasions. One day he surprised General D'Octavio, a Corsican, in the service of Murat who pursued him for a long time with a thousand men walking alone in a garden. Giro discovered himself, remarking, that the life of the general, who was unarmed, was in his hands; "but," said he, " I will pardon you this time, although I shall no longer be so indulgent if you continue to hunt me about." So saying, he leaped over the wall and disappeared. His physiognomy was rather agreeable; he was of middle stature, well made, and very strong. He had a verbose eloquence. Extremely addicted to pleasure, he had mistresses, at the period of his power, in all the towns of the province over which he was continually ranging. When King Ferdinand returned to his states on this side the

Taro, he recalled such as had been exiled for political opinions. Giro attempted to pass for one of these, but a new order of arrest was issued against him. It was then that he placed himself at the head of the Decisi. Many excesses are laid to their charge. A horde of twenty or thirty of them overran the country in disguise, masked as punchinellos. In places where open force could not be employed, the most daring were sent to watch for the moment to execute the sentences of secret death pronounced by the society. It was thus that the justice of the peace of Luogo Rotondo and his wife were killed in their own garden; and that the sectary, Perone, plunged his knife into the bowels of an old man of seventy, and afterwards massacred his wife and servant, having introduced himself into their house under pretence of delivering a letter. As has already been intimated, it was finally found necessary to send an armed force, under the command of General Church, against this band of ruffians. Many of them having been taken, and the rest dispersed, Giro, with only three companions, took refuge in one of the fortified farm-houses near Francavilla, but after a vigorous defence was obliged to surrender. The Council of War, by which he was tried, condemned him to be shot. A missionary offered him the consolations of religion. Ciro answered him with a smile, "Let us leave alone this prating; we are of the same profession; don't let us laugh at one another." On his arrival at the place of execution, Ciro wished to remain standing; he was told to kneel, and did so, presenting his breast. He was then informed that malefactors like himself were shot with their backs to the soldiers; he submitted, at the same time advising a priest, who persisted in remaining near him, to withdraw, so as not to expose himself. Twenty-one balls took effect, four in the head, yet he still breathed and muttered in his throat; the twenty-second put an end to him. This fact was confirmed by all the officers and soldiers present at his death. " As soon as we perceived," said a soldier very gravely, "that he was enchanted, we loaded his own musket with a silver ball, and this destroyed the spell." After the death of the leader, some two hundred and thirty persons were brought to trial; nearly half of them, having been guilty of murder and robbery with violence, were condemned to capital punishment, and their heads exposed near the places of their residence, or in the scene of their crimes.

575. Certificates of the Decisi - To render the account of the Decisi as complete as it need be, I subjoin a copy of one of their patents or certificates:

Tristezza. *Morte.*

Death's Head.				Death's Head.
	S(alentina). D(ecisione). (Salute).	Seal.		

N° V. Grandi Muratori.

L. D. D. G. T.—E. D. T. D. U.[1]

Il Mortale Gaetano Caffieri è un F. D. Numero Quinto, appartenente alla D⁶ del Tonante Giove, sparsa sulla superficie della Terra, per la sua D⁶ avuto il piacere di far parte in questa R. S. D. Noi dunque invitiamo tutte le Società Filantropiche a prestar il loro braccio forte al medesimo ed a soccorerlo ne' suoi bisogni, essendo egli giunto alla D⁶ di acquistare la Libertà o Morte. Oggi li 29 Ottobre 1817.

Pietro Gargaro.   *Il G. M. D. N°. 1.*

. . . .

V°. de Serio 2° Deciso

Gaetano Caffieri
Registratore de' Morti.   Seal.

Cross bones. Terror.				Cross bones. Struggle.

Translation.

The Salentine Decision.
Health!
No. 5, Grand Masons.

The Decision of Jupiter Tonans (the name of the lodge) hopes to make war against the tyrants of the universe, &c.

The mortal Gaetano Caffieri is a Brother Decided, No. 5, belonging to the Decision of Jupiter the Thunderer, spread over the face of the earth, has had the pleasure to belong to this Salentine Republican Decision. We invite, therefore, all Philanthropic Societies to lend their strong arm to the same, and to assist him in his wants, he having come to the decision to obtain liberty or death. Dated this day, the 29th October 1817.

Pietro Gargaro, the Decided Grand Master, No. 1.
Vito de Serio, Second Decided.
Gaetano Caffieri, Registrar of the Dead.

The letters in italics in the original were written in blood. The upper seal represents fasces planted upon a death's head, surmounted by the Phrygian cap, and flanked by hatchets; the lower, thunderbolts casting down royal and imperial crowns and the tiara. The person in whose favour the certificate is issued, figures himself among the signatures with the title of Registrar of the Dead, that is, of those they immolated to their vengeance, of whom they kept a register apart. The four points observable after the signature of Pietro Gargaro indicate his power of passing sentence of death. When the Decisi wrote to any one to extort contributions, if they added these four points, it was known that the person they addressed was condemned to death in case of disobedience. If the points were not added he was threatened with milder punishment. Their colours, yellow, red, and blue, surrounded the patent.[20]

576. The Calderari - This society, alluded to before, is of uncertain origin. Count Orloff, in his work, "Memoirs on the Kingdom of Naples," says they arose in 1813, when the reform of Carbonarism took place. Canosa, on the other hand, in a pamphlet published at Dublin, and entitled, " The Mountain Pipes," says they arose at Palermo, and not at Naples. In the former of these towns there existed different trade companies, which had enjoyed great privileges, until they lost them by the constitution of Lord William Bentinck. The numerous company of braziers (calderari) felt the loss most keenly, and they sent a deputation to the Queen of Naples, assuring her that they were ready to rise in her defence. The flames of the insurrection were communicated to the tanners and other companies, and all the Neapolitan emigrants in Sicily. Lord William Bentinck put the emigrants on board ship and sent them under a neutral flag to Naples, where Murat received them very kindly. But they were not grateful. Immediately on their arrival they entered into the secret societies then conspiring against the French Government, and their original name of Calderari was communicated by them to the conspirators, before then called " Trinitarii." We have seen that on the return of Ferdinand, Prince Canosa favoured the Calderari. He styled them the Calderari of the Counterpoise, because they were to serve as such to Carbonarism. The fate of Canosa and that of the Calderari has already been mentioned (557, 559).

577. The Independents - Though these also aimed at the independence of Italy, yet it appears that they were not disinclined to effect it by means of foreign assistance. The report at that time was that they actually once intended to offer the crown of Italy to the Duke of Wellington; but this is highly improbable, since our Iron Duke was not at all popular in Italy. But it is highly probable that they sought the co-operation of Russia, which, since 1815, maintained many agents in

---

[20] That is : La Decisione di Giove Tonante-Esterminatore dei Tiranni dell' Universo .

Italy with what purpose is not exactly known; the collection of statistical and economical information was the ostensible object, but Austria looked on them with a very suspicious eye, and watched them narrowly. The Independents had close relations with these Russian agents, probably, as it is surmised, with a view of turning Russian influence to account in any outbreak against Austria.

578. The Delphic Priesthood - This was another secret society, having the same political object as the foregoing. The Delphic priest, the patriotic priest, the priest militant, spoke thus: "My mother has the sea for her mantle, high mountains for her sceptre; " and when asked who his mother was, replied: "The lady with the dark tresses, whose gifts are beauty, wisdom, and formerly strength: whose dowry is a nourishing garden, full of flagrant flowers, where bloom the olive and the vine; and who now groans, stabbed to the heart." The Delphics entertained singular hopes, and would invoke the "remedy of the ocean" (American auxiliaries) and the epoch of " cure " (a general European war). They called the partisans of France " pagans," and those of Austria, "monsters"; the Germans they styled "savages." Their place of meeting they designated as the "ship," to foreshadow the future maritime greatness of Italy, and the help they expected from over the sea; their chief was the "pilot."

579. Egyptian Lodges - Immediately after the downfall of Napoleon, societies were formed also in foreign countries to promote Italian independence. The promoters of these were chiefly exiles. Distant Egypt even became the centre of such a propaganda; and under the auspices of Mehernet Ali, who aspired to render himself independent of the Sublime Porte, there was established the Egyptian rite of Cagliostro with many variations, and under the title of the " Secret Egyptian Society." Under masonic forms, the Pacha hoped to further his own views; and especially, to produce political changes in the Ionian Islands and in Italy, he scattered his agents all over the Mediterranean coasts. Being masonic, the society excluded no religion; it retained the two annual festivals, and added a third in memory of

Napoleon, whose portrait was honoured in the lodge. The rites were chiefly those of the ancient and accepted Scotch. Women were admitted, Turks excluded; and in the lodges of Alexandria and Cairo, the Greek and Arab women amounted to more than three hundred. The emissaries, spread over many parts of Europe, corresponded in cipher; but of the operations of the society nothing was ever positively known.

580. American Hunters - The Society of the "American Hunters" was founded at Ravenna, shortly after the prosecutions of Macerata, and the measures taken by the Austrian Government, in 1818, against the Carbonari. Lord Byron is said to have been at its head, having imbibed his love for Italy through the influence of an Italian beauty, the Countess Guiccioli, whose brother had been exiled a few years before. Its ceremonies assimilated it to the "Comuneros" of Spain, and it seems to have had the same aims as the Delphic Priesthood. The saviour was to come from America, and it is asserted that Joseph Bonaparte, the ex- King of Spain, was a member of the society. It is not improbable that the partisans of Napoleon gathered new hopes after the events of 1815. A sonnet, of which the first quatrain is here given, was at that time very popular in Central Italy, and shows the direction of the political wind

" Scandalised by groaning under kings so fell, Filling Europe with dismay in ev'ry part, We are driven to solicit Bonaparte To return from Saint Helena or from hell."

The restored sect made itself the centre of many minor sects, among which were the "Sons of Mars," so called because composed chiefly of military men; of the "Artist Brethren"; " the Defenders of the Country "; the "Friends of Duty;" and others, having the simpler and less compromising forms of Carbonarism. In the sect of the "Sons of Mars," the old Carbonari vendita was called "bivouac"; the apprentice, "volunteer"; the good cousin, "corporal"; the master, "sergeant"; the grand master, "commander"; and the chief dignitaries of Carbonarism still governed, from above and unseen, the thoughts of the sect. Many other sects existed, of which scarcely more than the names are known, the recapitulation of which would only weary the reader.

581. Secret Italian Society in London - London was a great centre of the sectaries. In 1822, a society for liberating Italy from the Austrian yoke was formed in that city, counting among its members many distinguished Italian patriots. Austria took the alarm, and sent spies to discover their plans. These spies represented the operations of the society as very extensive and imminent. An expedition was to sail from the English coasts for Spain, to take on board a large number of adherents, land them on the Italian shores, and spread insurrection everywhere. The English general, Eobert Wilson, was said to be at the head of the expedition; of which, however, nothing was ever heard, and the Austrian Government escaped with the mere fright.

582. Secret Italian Societies in Paris - A society of Italians was formed in Paris, in 1829; and in 1830, French Liberals formed a society under the title of " Cosmopolitans," whose object was to revolutionise all the peoples of the Latin race, and form them into one grand confederacy. La Fayette was at its head, but the man who was the real leader of the movement was totally unknown to the public. Henry Misley seemed occupied only in the sale of the nitre and wheat of his native country, Modena, and afterwards was engaged in the construction of railways in Italy and Spain. But he was the intimate friend of Menotti, and the connecting link between the Italian Carbonari and the revolutionary movement in France. He was also active, from 1850 to 1852, in placing Louis Napoleon at the head of the French nation, co-operating with Lord Palmerston, who, as a Mason, was the great friend and protector of the European revolution, and was the first to recognise Louis Napoleon as Emperor of the French, not hesitating, to further his objects, to falsify despatches which had already received the royal signature. But when Garibaldi, in 1864, visited England, Lord Palmerston co-operated with Victor Emmanuel and Louis Napoleon in restraining the Italian patriot from coming in contact with the revolutionary leaders then in this country, lest he, in conjunction with

them, should plan expeditions, which might have interfered with his (Lord Palmerston's) or the King of Italy's plans. Garibaldi was surrounded with a brilliant suite, and overwhelmed with official fetes. Then Dr. Fergusson declared that Garibaldi's health demanded his immediate return to Italy. His intended visit to Paris was stopped by the Duke of Sutherland taking him in his yacht to the Mediterranean; but Mazzini informed Garibaldi of the scheme to keep him an honoured prisoner, and Garibaldi insisted at Malta on returning at once to Caprera.

583. Mazzini and Young Italy - Joseph Mazzini, who sixty years ago was a prisoner in Fort Savona for revolutionary speeches and writings, may be looked upon as the chief instigator of modern secret societies in Italy having revolutionary tendencies. The independence and unity of their country, with Rome for its capital, of course were the objects of Young Italy. One of the earliest of these societies was that of the Apophasimenes, many of whom Mazzini drew over to his " Young Italy" association.

Here are some of the articles of the " Organisation of Young Italy": I. The society is founded for the indispensable destruction of all the governments of the Peninsula, in order to form one single State with the republican government. 2. Fully aware of the horrible evils of absolute power, and the even worse results of constitutional monarchies, we must aim at establishing a republic, one and indivisible. 30. Those who refuse obedience to the orders of this secret society, or reveal its mysteries, die by the dagger without mercy. 31. The secret tribunal pronounces sentence, and appoints one or two affiliated members for its execution. 32. Who so refuses to perform such duty assigned to him, dies on the spot. 33. If the victim escapes, he shall be pursued, until struck by the avenging hand, were he on the bosom of his mother or in the temple of Christ. 34. Every secret tribunal is competent not only to judge guilty adepts, but to put to death any one it finds it necessary to condemn. (Sig.) Mazzini.

We have seen, in the account of the Mafia (329), that Mazzini constantly recommended the use of the dagger though he took good care to avoid personal danger; and, to give but one instance, that he did not hesitate to employ it, by proxy, was proved in the case of Signer Emiliani, who was assassinated, by Mazzini's order, which is still existing, signed by Mazzini, and countersigned by the secretary La Cecilia, in the streets of Rhodez, a town in the department of the Aveyron, seventy miles from Toulouse. Mazzini had come from Geneva on purpose to sit in judgment on Signer Emiliani, who was accused of having opposed the plans of the Mazzinists.

Committees were established in all parts of the Peninsula; the presses, not only of Italy, but also of Marseilles, London, and Switzerland, were largely employed to disseminate the views of the conspirators; and the police, though they considered themselves well informed, were always at fault. Thus Livio Zambeccari, a leading member, went from Bologna to Naples, thence into Sicily, held interviews with the conspirators, called meetings, and returned to Bologna, whilst the police of Naples and Sicily knew nothing at all about it. General Antonini, under a feigned name, went to Sicily, passed himself off for a daguerreotypist, and lived in great intimacy with many of the officials without being suspected. A Piedmontese officer, who had fought in the Spanish and Portuguese revolutionary wars, arrived at Messina under a Spanish name, with letters of introduction from a Neapolitan general, which enabled him to visit and closely inspect the citadels, this being the object of his journey. Letters from Malta, addressed to the conspirators, were intercepted by the police, but recovered from them before they had read them, by the address and daring of the members of Young Italy. A thousand copies of a revolutionary programme, printed at Marseilles, were smuggled into Italy in a despatch addressed to the Minister Delcaretto. Though occasionally the correspondence fell into the hands of the authorities as, for instance, on the 4th June 1832, the Custom-house officers of Genoa seized on board the steamer Sully, coming from Marseilles, a trunk full of old clothes, addressed to Mazzini's mother, in the false bottom of which were concealed a large number of letters addressed to members of Young Italy, revolutionary proclamations, lists of lodges, and instructions as to the proposed rising. Then the revolutionary correspondence was carried on by means of the official letters addressed to the Minister Santangelo, at Palermo. A wellknown Spanish general, who was one of the conspirators, whose departure and object had been publicly announced in the French papers, went from Marseilles to Naples, and the police were unable to catch him. Italian and other Continental revolutionists in those days, and later on, received much moral support from Lord Palmerston, wherefore it was a saying of Austrian Conservatives

" If the devil has a son,
Surely it's Lord Palmerston."

Panizzi also, a Carbonaro, exiled from Italy, and for many years Chief Librarian of the British Museum, was an ardent supporter of Italian unification.

584. Mazzini, the Evil Genius of Italy - Gregory XVI. died in 1846. The Italians thought this the favourable moment for general action, and the revolutions of Eome, Naples, Palermo, Florence, Milan, Parma, Modena, and Venice followed in quick succession. But they failed, and their failure notably that of the operations of Charles Albert was due to the political intrigues carried on by the Mazzinists, who tampered with the fidelity and discipline of the Sardinian army. Mazzini, in those days, ruined the national cause, and rejoiced in that ruiD, because he was not the leader of the enterprise. Later on, his Roman triumvirate led to the French occupation of Rome, and to the return to that city of Italy's greatest curse, the pope. Many of Garibaldi's noble efforts were thwarted or frustrated by Mazzini's revolutionary fanaticism; and yet such is the mockery of Fate! that selfish demagogue who, to gratify his political crotchets, sent hundreds of misguided youths to a violent death, has a statue in the Palazzo del Municipio at Genoa, an honour which posterity will certainly rescind. Like O'Donovan Rossa, he planned his murderous schemes at a safe distance, taking care never to imperil himself personally, and if danger came near, to run away. In the expedition to Savoy in January 1834, Mazzini at Carra bran dished his rifle to rush to the combat, but was conveniently seized by a fit and

carried across the border in safety. In 1833 Louis Mariotti (a pseudoname), provided with a passport and money by Mazzini, attempted Charles Albert's life; shortly after another man made the same attempt he had a dagger which was proved to have belonged to Mazzini: this hero was one of the first to take flight when Radetzky entered Milan. When in that city he thwarted the endeavours of the royal commissioners to procure men and money, and fed the republican animosities towards the Piedmontese in every part of Italy. The king knew of the Mazzinian manoeuvres, and therefore did not make peace after his defeat, for the republicans would have said he had thrown up the cause of Italy.

585. Assassination of Rossi - This adventurer was born at Carrara, and began his public career as a member of the provisional government of Bologna, when Murat attempted the conquest of Italy. At his master's defeat, he fled into Switzerland, where the Diet entrusted him with the revision of the pact of 1815; in the changes he proposed, radicalism was carried to its utmost limits, and aimed at the overthrow of the Federal Government. With such antecedents, it was but natural that Rossi became a member of Young Italy; though Mazzini placed no faith in him, for he knew that the ci-devant Carbonaro had no fixed political convictions. For this once violent demagogue, having, in the July revolution of 1830, assisted Louis Philippe to ascend the French throne, accepted from him the title of count and peer of France, and was sent as ambassador to Rome. Though he had once belonged to the secret societies of Italy, and by Gregory XVI. been designated as the political renegade, he eventually accepted office under Pius IX., who in 1848, a short time before his flight from Borne, had no one to appeal to, to form a new ministry, but this very adventurer, who did so by keeping three of the portfolios in his own hands, viz., those of Finances, Interior, and Police, whilst the other ministers mutually detested each other; a fact from which Eossi expected to derive additional advantages. His political programme, which excluded all national participation or popular influence, filled Young Italy with rage. At a meeting of Young Italy, held at the Hotel Feder at Turin,

the verdict went forth: Death to the false Carbonaro! By a prearranged scheme the lot to kill Rossi fell on Canino, a leading man of the association, not that it was expected that he would do the deed himself, but his position and wealth were assumed to give him the most ready means of commanding daggers. A Mazzinian society assembled twice a week at the Roman theatre, Capranica. At a meeting of one hundred and sixteen members, it was decided, at the suggestion of Mazzini, that forty should be chosen by lot to protect the assassin. Three others were elected by the same process they were called feratori; one of them was to slay the minister.

The 15th of November 1848, the day fixed upon for the opening of the Roman Chambers, was also that of Rossi's death. He received several warnings, but ridiculed them. Even in going to the Chancellerie, he was addressed by a priest, who whispered to him, " Do not go out; you will be assassinated." "They cannot terrify me," he replied; "the cause of the Pope is the cause of God," which is thought by some to have been a very noble answer, but which was simply ridiculous, because not true, and was, moreover, vile hypocrisy on the part of a man with his antecedents. When Rossi arrived at the Chancellerie, the conspirators were already awaiting him there. One of them, as the minister ascended the staircase, struck him on the side with the hilt of a dagger, and as Rossi turned round to look at his assailant, another assassin plunged his dagger into Rossi's throat. The minister soon after expired in the apartments of Cardinal Gozzoli, to which he had been carried. At that very instant one of the chiefs of Young Italy at Bologna, looking at his watch, said, "A great deed has just been accomplished; we no longer need fear Kossi." The estimation in which llossi was held by the Chamber cannot have been great, for the deputies received the news of his death with considerable sang-froid; and at night a torchlight procession paraded the streets of Rome, carrying aloft the dagger which had done the deed, whilst thousands of voices exclaimed, " Blessed be the hand that struck Eossi! Blessed be the dagger that struck him! " A pamphlet, published at Eome in 1850, contains a letter from Mazzini, in which occur the words: " The assassination of Eossi was necessary and just."

In the first edition I added to the foregoing account the following note:

"P.S. Since writing the above I have met with documents which induce me to suspend my judgment as to who were the real authors of Eossi's assassination. From what I have since learnt it would seem that the clerical party, and not the Carbonari, planned and executed the deed. Persons accused of being implicated in the murder were kept in prison for more than two years without being brought to trial, and then quietly got away. Eossi, shortly before his death, had levied contributions to the extent of four million scudi on clerical property, and was known to plan further schemes to reduce the influence of the Church. But the materials for writing the history of those times are not yet accessible."

More than twenty years after the above was written, now in 1896, the question is as much involved in doubt as ever. True, one Santa Constantini, a radical fanatic, as he was called on his conviction, has been proved to have struck the fatal blow, but as to who instigated him to do the deed, opinions are still divided; the secret has not oozed out. The reasons for attributing the death of Eossi to the Carbonari or the Jesuits are of equal weight on both sides.

The assassination of Eossi and the commotions following it, led, as is well known, to the pope's flight to Gaeta. During his absence from Eome, Mazzini was the virtual ruler of that city, which was during his short reign the scene of the greatest disorders, of robberies, and assassinations. But Eome gained nothing by the restoration of the pope through French arms; the papalians, when once more in power, raged as wildly against the peaceful inhabitants as the Mazzinists had done. The Holy Father personally, and the cardinals and other dignitaries of the Church, caused thousands of the inhabitants of Rome to be cast into noisome dungeons, many of them underground, where they were starved or killed by bad treatment, or after long-delayed trials condemned to the most unjust punishments. I could give numerous instances, did they enter into the scope of this work. The subsequent action of Carbonarism, its renewal of the war against the pope, the collapse of the latter's army, largely composed of Irish loafers, who entered Rome in potato sacks, with a hole for the head and two for the arms, and his final overthrow, are matters of public history.

586. Sicilian Societies - Sicily did not escape the general influence. In 1827 there was formed a secret society in favour of the Greek revolution, the "Friends of Greece," who, however, also occupied themselves with the affairs of Italy. There was also the "Secret Society of the Five," founded ten years before the above, which prepared the insurrection of the Greeks. In Messina was formed the lodge of the "Patriotic Reformers," founded on Carbonarism, which corresponded with lodges at Florence, Milan, and Turin, by means of musical notes. But the Sicilian Carbonari did not confine themselves to political aims: to them was due in a great measure the security of the roads throughout the island, which before their advent had been terribly infested by malefactors of every kind, who almost daily committed outrages against peaceful travellers.

587. The Consistorials - But the conspirators against thrones and the Church were not to have it all their own way; clerical associations were formed to counteract their efforts. The sect of the "Consistorials " aimed at the preservation of feudal and theocratic dominion. The rich and ambitious patricians of Rome and other Italian states belonged to it; Tabot, an ex- Jesuit and Confessor to the Holy Father, was the ruling spirit. It is said that this society proposed to give to the Pope, Tuscany; the island of Elba and the Marches, to the King of Naples; Parma, Piacenza, and a portion of Lombardy, with the title of King, to the Duke of Modena; the rest of Lombardy, Massa Carrara, and Lucca, to the King of Sardinia; and to Russia, which, from jealousy of Austria, favoured these secret designs, either Ancona, or Genoa, or Civita Vecchia, to turn it into their Gibraltar. From documents found in the office of the Austrian governor at Milan, it appears that the Duke of Modena, in 1818, presided at a general meeting of the Consistorials, and that Austria was aware of the existence and intentions of the society.

588. The Roman Catholic Apostolic Congregation - It was formed at the period of the imprisonment of Pius VII. The members recognised each other by a yellow silk ribbon with five knots; the initiated into the lower degrees heard of nothing but acts of piety and charity; the secrets of the society, known to the higher ranks, could only be discussed between two; the lodges were composed of five members; the password was " Eleutheria," i.e. Liberty; and the secret word "Ode," i.e. Independence. This sect arose in France, among the Neo-catholics, led by Lammenais, who already, in the treatise on "Religious Indifference," had shown that fervour which afterwards was to carry him so far. Thence it passed into Lombardy, but met with but little success, and the Austrians succeeded in obtaining the patents which were given to the initiated, two Latin texts divided by this sign:

$$\begin{array}{c|c} C & C \\ \hline A & R \end{array}$$

meaning Congregazione Catholica Apostolica Romana, and their statutes and signs of recognition. Though devoted to the independence of Italy, the Congregation was not factious; for it bound the destinies of nations to the full triumph of the Roman Catholic religion. Narrow in scope, and restricted in numbers, it neither possessed nor, perhaps, claimed powers to subvert the political system.

589. Sanfedisti - This society was founded at the epoch of the suppression of the Jesuits. There existed long before then in the Papal States a society called the "Pacific" or "Holy Union," which was established to defend religion, the privileges and jurisdiction of Rome, and the temporal power of the popes. Now from this society they derived the appellation of the Society of the Holy Faith, or Sanfedisti. The way in which the existence of the society was discovered, was curious. A friend of De Witt (555) during carnival time in 1821, entered a shop in the Contrada di Po at Turin to purchase a costume. He was examining a cassock, when he noticed a pocket in it, containing some papers. He bought it and took it home. The papers gave the

statutes, signs, passwords, &c., of the Sanfedisti. The owner of the cassock, one of the highest initiates, had been struck by apoplexy, and his belongings had been sold. Finding themselves discovered, the Sanfedisti changed the password and sign, making, instead of the former one, an imperceptible cross with the left hand on the left breast. They had been in existence long before 1821; in Franco they conspired against Napoleon, who sent about twenty of them to prison at Modena, whence they were released by Francis IV. The supposed chiefs, after 1815, were the Duke of Modena and Cardinal Consalvi. The first had frequent secret interviews with the cardinals, and even the King of Sardinia was said to be in the plot. Large sums also are said to have been contributed by the chiefs to carry on the war against Austria, which, however, is doubtful. Some attribute to this society the project of dividing Italy into three kingdoms, expelling the Austrians and the King of Naples; others, the intention of dividing it into five, viz., Sardinia, Modena, Lucca, Rome, and Naples; and yet others and these latter probably are most in the right the determination to perpetuate the status quo, or to re-establish servitude in its most odious forms. They also intrigued with Russia, though at certain times they would not have objected to subject all Italy politically to the Austrian eagle, and clerically to the keys of St. Peter. Their machinations at home led to much internal dissension and bloodshed; their chief opponents were the Carbonari. At Faenza the two parties fought against one another under the names of "Cats" and "Dogs." They caused quite as much mischief and bloodshed as any of the bands of brigands that infested the country, and their code was quite as sanguinary as that of any more secular society. They swore with terrible oaths to pursue and slay the impious liberals, even to their children, without showing pity for age or sex. Under the pretence of defending the faith, they indulged in the grossest licentiousness and most revolting atrocity. In the Papal States they were under the direction of the inquisitors and bishops, who, especially under Leo XII., gave them the greatest encouragement; in the kingdom of Naples, under the immediate orders of the police. They spread all over Germany, where Prince HohenlohSchillingsfürst, Bishop of Sardica, protected them. Prince Julius de Polignac was head of the society in France.

VI

NAPOLEONIC AND ANTI-NAPOLEONIC SOCIETIES

590. The Philadelphians - As early as the year 1780 a society of about sixty young men had formed at Besan on a masonic lodge under the above name. Colonel James Joseph Oudet, who, though he served under Napoleon, hated him, and had for some time been looking out for dupes to assist him in bringing back to France the detested Bourbon race, whose secret agent he was, pitched on the members of that lodge, still composed of enthusiastic, but inexperienced, youths, as suitable for his purpose. Having been initiated into nearly every secret society in Europe, Oudet soon invested the Philadelphians with all the machinery of one on a more elaborate scale than they had hitherto thought necessary. According to the approved pattern, every member assumed a pseudonym; Oudet called himself Philopcemen; General Moreau, who, as we shall see, succeeded him as chief of the Order, took the name of Fabius, and so on. Oudet further created a dignity, sovereign, monarchical and absolute, with which, of course, he invested himself, and under which were two degrees: the first, that of Frank Federate, and the second, that of Frank Judge; this second degree comprehended the complement of all the secrets, up to the secret belonging, and known to the supreme chief alone. But to give his adepts something to think and talk about, he told them the establishment of a Sequanese (from Sequana, Seine) republic was his object, whilst he really intended the total overthrow of Napoleon. He introduced the Philadelphian rites into the army, simultaneously into the 9th, 68th, and 69th regiments of the line, into the 20th of dragoons, the 15th of light infantry, and from thence into all the army. Bonaparte heard of the society, and suspected Oudet, who was sent back to his corps, which then occupied the garrison of St. Martin, in the Isle of Hne*. General Moreau took his place, but shortly after had to resign it again to Oudet, he, Moreau, having been implicated in the conspiracy of Pichegru. Before then the conspiracy of Arena to assassinate Bonaparte had been discovered, and a book, seized among

the papers of Arena, and entitled "The Turk and the French Soldier," certainly was written by Oudet. The Philadelphians next attempted to seize Bonaparte while traversing the forests and mountains of the Jura attended by a very small retinue; but the attempt failed, one of the Order having betrayed the plot. Oudet was killed at the battle of Wagram (1809), and with his death the society collapsed.

591. The Rays - During the power of Napoleon, he was opposed by secret societies in Italy, as well as in France. But his fall, which to many seemed a revival of liberty, to others appeared as the ruin of Italy; hence they sought to re-establish his rule, or at least to save Italian nationality from the wreck. The "Rays" were an Anti-Napoleonic society, composed of officials from all parts, brought together by common dangers and the adventures of the field. They had lodges at Milan and Bologna. The Sanfedisti also were an Anti-Napoleonic society (589).

592. Secret League in Tirol - A very powerful association against Napoleon was in the year 1809 formed in Tirol. This country had by the treaty of Presburg (1805) been ceded by Austria to Bavaria. But the Tirolese, strongly attached to their former master, resented the transfer, and when in 1808 a renewal of the war between France and Austria was imminent, secret envoys, among whom was the already famous Andreas Hofer, were sent to Vienna to concert measures for reuniting the Tirol with Austria. But in consequence of the battle of Wagram, and the truce of Znaim, which followed it, Tirol was again surrendered to French troop?. Then the Tirolese, betrayed by Austria, formed a number of secret societies among themselves, to drive out the French. The results of these associations are matters of history; but to show how the secret societies worked, and tested the character and loyalty of some of the leading members, the following incident, communicated by the hero of the adventure, may be mentioned. He had once enjoyed Napoleon's confidence, but having unjustly become suspected by him, he was obliged to take refuge in the most alpine part of the Austrian provinces, in Tirol. There he formed connections with one of the

societies for the overthrow of Napoleon, and went through a simple ceremony of initiation. Two months elapsed after this without his hearing any more of the society, when at last he received a letter asking him to repair to a remote place, where he was to meet a number of brothers assembled. He went, but found no one. He received three more similar summonses, but always with the same result. He received a fifth, and went, but saw no one. He was just retiring, disgusted with the often-repeated deception, when he heard frightful cries, as from a person in distress. He hastened towards the spot whence they proceeded, and found a bleeding body lying on the ground, whilst he saw three horsemen making their escape in the opposite direction, who, however, fired three shots at him, but missing him. He was about to examine the body lying at his feet when a detachment of armed force, attracted by the same cries, darted from the forest; the victim on the ground indicated our hero as his assailant. He was seized, imprisoned, accused by witnesses who declared they had seen him commit the murder for the body of the person attacked had been removed as dead and he was sentenced to be executed the same night, by torchlight. He was led into a courtyard, surrounded by ruinous buildings, full of spectators. He had already ascended the scaffold, when an officer on horseback, and wearing the insignia of the magistracy, appeared, announcing that an edict had gone forth granting a pardon to any man condemned to death for any crime whatever, who could give to justice the words of initiation and signs of recognition of a secret society, which the officer named; it was the one into which the ci-devant officer of Napoleon had recently been received. He was questioned if he knew anything about it; he denied all knowledge of the society, and being pressed, became angry and demanded death. Immediately he was greeted as a brave and faithful brother, for all those present were members of the secret society, and had knowingly co-operated in this rather severe test.

593. Societies in Favour of Napoleon - Many societies in favour of the restoration of Napoleon were formed, such as the "Black Needle," the "Knights of the Sun," "Universal Regeneration," &c. They were

generally composed of the soldiers of the great captain, who were condemned to inactivity, and looked upon the glory of their chief as something in which they had a personal interest. Their aim was to place Napoleon at the head of confederated Italy, under the title of " Emperor of Rome, by the will of the people and the grace of God." The proposal reached him early in the year 1815. Napoleon accepted it like a man who on being shipwrecked perceives a piece of wood that may save him, and which he will cast into the fire when he has reached the land. The effects of these plots are known Napoleon's escape from Elba, and the reign of a hundred days.

According to secret documents, the machinations of the Bouapartists continued even in 1842, the leaders being Peter Bonaparte, Lady Christina Stuart, the daughter of Lucien Bonaparte, the Marchioness Pepoli, the daughter of the Countess Lipona (Caroline Murat), and Count Rasponi. Then appeared the sect of the "Italian Confederates," first called "Platonica," which in 1842 extended into Spain. Another sect, the " Illuminati, Vindicators or Avengers of the People," arose in the Papal States; also those of "Regeneration," of "Italian Independence," of the "Communists," the "Exterminators," &c. Tuscany also had its secret societies that of the "Thirty-one," the "National Knights," the "Revolutionary Club," &c. A "Communistic Society " was formed at Milan; but none of these sects did more than excite a little curiosity for a time. Scarcely anything of their ritual is known.

594. The Illuminati - This society, not to be confounded with an earlier one of the same name (351 et seq.), was founded in France, but meeting with too many obstacles in that country, it spread all over Italy. Its object was to restore the Napoleon family to the French throne, by making MarieLouise regent, until the King of Rome could be set on the throne, and by bringing Napoleon himself from St. Helena, to command the army. The society entered into correspondence with Las Casas, who was to come to Bologna, the chief lodge, and arrange plans; but the scheme, as need scarcely be mentioned, never came to anything.

595. Various other Societies - At Padua a society existed whose members called themselves Sdvaggi, "Savages," because the German democrat, Marr, had said, that man must return to the savage state to accomplish something great. They cut neither their nails nor their hair, cleaned neither their clothes nor boots; the medical students who were members of the sect surreptitiously brought portions of human bodies from the dissecting-rooms of the hospitals to their meetings, over which the initiated performed wild and hideous ceremonies. Not being able to obtain human blood for the purpose, they purchased bullocks' blood in which to drink death to tyrants. One of the members having overgorged himself was found dead in the street. The medical examination of his body led to the discovery of the cause, and by the police inquiry resulting therefrom, to the exposure of the society, their statutes, oaths, and ceremonies.

The members of the Unit a Jtaliana, discovered at Naples in 1850, recognised each other by a gentle rubbing of noses. They swore on a dagger with a triangular blade, with the inscription, "Fraternity Death to Traitors Death to Tyrants," faithfully to observe all the laws of the society, on pain, in case of want of faith, to have their hearts pierced with the dagger. Those who executed the vengeance of the society called themselves the Committee of Execution. In 1849 the grand council of the sect established a "Committee of Stabbers," comitato de pugnalatori. The heads of the society were particular as to whom they admitted into it; the statutes say, "no ex-Jesuits, thieves, coiners, and other infamous persons are to be initiated." The ex-Jesuits are placed in good company truly!

In 1849 a society was discovered at Ancona calling itself the "Company of Death," and many assassinations, many of them committed in broad daylight in the streets of the town, were traced to its members. The "Society of Slayers," Ammazzatori, at Leghorn; the "Infernal Society," at Sinigaglia; the " Company of Assassins," Sicarii, at Faenza; the "Terrorists" of Bologna, were associations of the same stamp. The " Barbers of Mazzini," at Rome, made it their business to "remove" priests who had rendered themselves particularly obnoxious.

Another Bolognese society was that of the "Italian Conspiracy of the Sons of Death," whose object was the liberation of Italy from foreign sway.

596. The Accoltellatori - A secret society, non-political, was discovered, and many of its members brought to trial, at Ravenna, in 1874. Its existence had long been surmised, but the executive did not dare to interfere; some private persons, indeed, tried to bring the assassins to justice, but wherever they succeeded a speedy vengeance was sure to follow. To one shopkeeper who had been particularly active a notice was sent that his life was forfeited, and the same night a placard was posted up upon the shutters of his shop announcing that the establishment was to be sold, as the proprietor was going away. In many cases there were witnesses to the crimes, and yet they dared not interfere nor give evidence. One of the gang at last turned traitor; he gave the explanation of several "mysterious disappearances," and the names of the murderers. The gang had become too numerous, and amongst the number there were members whose fidelity was suspected. It was resolved to sacrifice them. They were watched, set upon and murdered by their fellow-accomplices. This society was known as the Accoltellatori, literally "knifers" cut-throats. It originally consisted of twelve members only, who used to meet in the Cafe Mazzavillani a very appropriate name; mazza means a club or bludgeon, and villano, villainous at Kavenna, where the fate of their victims was decided. The trial ended in most of the members being condemned to penal servitude.

VII

FRENCH SOCIETIES

597. Various Societies after the Restoration. One would think that, according to the "philosophical" historians, no nation ought to have been more content and happy, after being delivered from their tyrant Napoleon, than the French. But, in accordance with what I said in sect. 519, no nation had more reason to be dissatisfied and unhappy through the restoration of a king "by grace of God" and "right divine." Draconian statutes were promulgated by the Chambers, the mere tools of Louis XVIII., which led to the formation of a secret society called the "Associated Patriots," whose chief scenes of operation were in the south of France. But Government had its spies everywhere; many members of the society were arrested and sentenced to various terms of imprisonment. Three leaders, Pleignier, a writing-master, Carbonneau, a leather-cutter, and Tolleron, an engraver, were sentenced to death, led to the place of execution with their faces concealed by black veils, as parricides were formerly executed, and before their heads were cut off, their right hands were severed from their arms for had they not raised them against their father, the king? The conspiracy of the Associated Patriots collapsed. But other societies arose. In 1820 the society of the " Friends of Truth," consisting of medical students and shopmen, was established in Paris, but was soon suppressed by the Government. The leading members made their escape to Italy, and on their return to France founded a Carbonaro society, the leadership of which was given to General Lafayette. It made two attempts to overthrow the Government, one at Belfort, and another at La Rochelle, but both were unsuccessful, and the Carbonaro society was dissolved. The society of the " Shirtless," founded by a Frenchman of the name of Manuel, who invoked Sampson, as the symbol of strength, had but a very short existence. That of the " Spectres meeting in a Tomb," which existed in 1822, and whose object was the overthrow of the Bourbons, also came to a speedy end. The "New Reform of France," and the "Provinces," which were probably founded in 1820, only admitted members already

initiated into Carbonarism, Freemasonry, the European Patriots, or the Greeks in Solitude. A mixture of many sects, they condensed the hatred of many ages and many orders against tyranny, and prescribed the following oath: " I, M. N., promise and swear to be the eternal enemy of tyrants, to entertain undying hatred against them, and, when opportunity offers, to slay them." In their succinct catechism were the following passages: "Who art thou?" "Thy friend." "How knowest thou me?" "By the weight pressing on thy brow, on which I read written in letters of blood, To conquer or die." "What wilt thou?" "Destroy the thrones and raise up gibbets." "By what right?" "By that of nature." "For what purpose?" "To acquire the glorious name of citizen." "And wilt thou risk thy life?" " I value life less than liberty."

Another sect was that of the "New French Liberals," which existed but a short time. It was composed of but few members; they, however, were men of some standing, chiefly such as had occupied high positions under Napoleon. They looked to America for assistance. They wore a small black ribbon attached to their watches, with a gold seal, a piece of coral, and an iron or steel ring. The ribbon symbolised the eternal hatred of the free for oppressors; the coral, their American hopes; the ring, the weapon to destroy their enemies: and the gold seal, abundance of money as a means of success.

After the July revolution in 1830, the students of the Quartier Latin formed the society of "Order and Progress," each student being, in furtherance of these objects, provided with a rifle and fifty cartridges. And if they nevertheless did not distinguish themselves, they afforded the Parisians a new sensation. About three o'clock on the afternoon of the 4th January 1831, the booming of the great bell of Notre Dame was heard, and one of the towers of the cathedral was seen to be on fire. The police, who, though forewarned of the intended attempt, had taken no precautionary measures, speedily made their way into the building, put out the fire, and arrested six individuals, young men, nineteen or twenty years old, and their leader, a M. Considere. The young men were acquitted, Considere was sentenced to five years' imprisonment. And thus ended this farcical insurrection.

Another association, called the " Society of Schools,"

advocated the abolition of the universities and the throwing open of all instruction to the public gratuitously. The "Constitutional Society," directed by a man who had powerfully supported the candidature of the Duke of Orleans, Cauchois-Lemaire, insisted on the suppression of monopolies, the more equal levy of taxes, electoral reform, and the abolition of the dignity of the peerage. The "Friends of the People" was another political society, one section of which, called the "Rights of Man," adopted for its text-book the "Declaration of the Rights of Man" by Robespierre, and drew to itself many minor societies, too numerous, and in most cases too unimportant, to be mentioned. Their efforts ended in the useless insurrection of Lyons on the 13th and 14th April 1834.

598. The Acting Company - But a separate corps of the Rights of Man, selected from among all the members, was formed and called the Acting Company, under the command of Captain Kersausie, a rich nobleman with democratic predilections. On certain days the loungers on the boulevards would notice a crowd of silent promenaders whom an unknown object seemed to draw together. No one understood the matter except the police; the chief of the Acting Company was reviewing his forces. Accompanied by one or two adjutants he would accost the chief of a group, whom he recognised by a sign, hold a short conversation with him, and pass on to another; the police agents would follow, see him enter a carriage, which was kept in waiting, drive up to a house which had a back way out, whence he would gain one of his own for he had several residences, and keep indoors for three or four days.

The Rights of Man society arranged the plot, proposed by Fieschi, to assassinate the king, Louis Philippe, on the 28th July 1835. Delahodde, the police spy, in his Memoirs, says that by the imprudence of one of the conspirators, Boireau, the police obtained a hint of what was intended, but that it was so vague, that it could not be acted on. This is evidently said to screen the police, for on the trial of Fieschi and the other conspirators, it was proved that on the morning of the attempt Boireau had sent a letter doing which was not a mere imprudence to the Prefect of Police, giving full information as to the means to be employed, the individuals engaged in the plot, and the very house in which the infernal machine was placed all which was more than a mere hint but the letter was thrown aside by the Prefect as not worth reading! The failure of the attempt broke up the society of the Rights of Man, but the remnants thereof formed themselves in the same year into a new society, called the " Families," under the leadership of Blanqui and Barbes. Admission to this new society was attended with all the mummery and mystification considered necessary to form an orthodox initiation. Its object, of course, was the overthrow of the monarchical government and the establishment of a republic; but the society having in 1836 been discovered and suppressed, many of its leaders being sent to prisons, the members who remained at liberty reconstituted themselves into a new society, called the " Seasons," into the meeting- place of which the candidate was led blindfolded, and swore death to all kings, aristocrats, and other oppressors of mankind, and to sacrifice his own life, if needful, in the cause. On the 12th May the "Seasons," led by Blanqui and Barbes, rose in insurrection, but were defeated by the Government. Blanqui was sentenced to be transported, and Barb&s condemned to death; the king, however, commuted the sentence of the latter to imprisonment. After a time the "Seasons" were reorganised, and about 1840, Communism first began to be active in Paris, and various attempts were made against the king's life. Considering the number of police spies in the pay of Government, it is surprising that secret societies should have continued to flourish, and should at last have succeeded in overthrowing the throne of Louis Philippe. The spies would get themselves introduced into the secret societies, and then betray them. One of the most notorious of these spies was Lucien Delahodde, who sent his reports to Government under the pseudonym of "Pierre." When, in consequence of the revolution of 1848, "Citizen" Caussidiere became Prefect of Police, and overhauled the secret archives of that department, he found voluminous papers, containing more than a thousand informations, signed " Pierre," proving that the writer had got hold of all the secrets of the " Rights of Man," the "Families" (though strong suspicion rests on Blanqui of having supplied the Minister of the Interior with a secret report on the latter, when under sentence of death), the " Seasons," and sold them to the Government. But who was this Pierre? Unluckily for himself Lucien Delahodde, or Pierre himself, wrote a letter to Caussidiere, asking to be employed in the police. Caussidiere was struck by the writing, compared it with that of the secret reports, and found it to be identical. Delahodde was invited to meet Caussidiere at the Luxembourg, where he was made to confess, and declare in writing, that he was the author of all the reports signed "Pierre." Some members of the provisional government were for shooting him, but he got off with a few months' imprisonment in the Conciergerie. On recovering his liberty Delahodde went to London, where he published a small journal, attacking the Republic and the Republicans.

599. The Communistic societies of the Travailleurs Egalitaires and Communistes Revolutionnaires introduced some of their members into the provisional government that preceded the accession of Louis Napoleon; and their influence even to the present day is too notorious to need specification here. The "Mountaineers," or "Reds of the Mountain," a revival of the name given during the French Revolution to the leaders of the Jacobins, was one of the societies that brought about the events of 1848. According to the Univers of the 2nd February 1852, they swore on a dagger, "I swear by this steel, the symbol of honour, to combat and destroy all political, religious, and social tyrannies." Secret societies continued to play at hide-and-seek after the accession of Louis Napoleon, but were not immediately put down, though he issued the most severe prohibitions against them, and the members who could be apprehended were condemned to transportation to Cayenne or Algiers; they continued to exist for some years after the coup d'etat.

600. Causes of Secret Societies in France - The succession of secret associations against the government of Louis Philippe is not to be wondered at. The king himself was solely bent on the aggrandisement of his own dynasty, either by foreign marriages, or conferring on the

members of his own family every office in the state which could secure the paramount power in directing the destinies of France. The princes had re-established the orgies of the Regency; the court, the ministers, the aristocrats, the inferior functionaries made the public offices and national institutions the objects of shameful corruption; the deputies speculated with their political functions; peers of France patronised gambling in the funds and railway scrip; princes, ministers, ambassadors, and other personages in high positions were constantly making their appearance in the assize courts and found guilty of swindling, forgery, rape, and murder; commercial and manufacturing interests were fearfully depressed, hence the frequent risings of the working classes; hence secret associations to put an end to this rotten condition of society.

VIII

POLISH SOCIETIES

601. Polish Patriotism - It is the fashion to express great sympathy with the Poles and a corresponding degree of indignation against Russia, Austria, and Prussia; the Poles are looked upon as a patriotic race, oppressed by their more powerful neighbours. But all this rests on mere misapprehension and ignorance of facts. The Polish people under their native rulers were abject serfs. The aristocracy were everything, and possessed everything; the people possessed nothing, not even political or civil rights, when these clashed with the whims or interests of the nobles. It is these last whose power has been overthrown it is they who make war on and conspire against Russia, to recover (as is admitted by some of their own writers) their ancient privileges over their own countrymen, who blindly, like most nations, allow themselves to be slaughtered for the benefit of those who only seek again to rivet on the limbs of their dupes the chains which have been broken. It is like the French and Spaniards and Neapolitans fighting against their deliverer Napoleon, to bring back the Bourbon tyrants, and with them the people's political nullity, clerical intolerance, lettres de cachet, and the Inquisition. How John Bull has been gulled by these Polish patriots! Many of them were criminals of all kinds, who succeeded in breaking out of prison, or escaping before they could be captured; and, managing to come over to this country, have here called themselves political fugitives, victims of Russian persecution, and have lived luxuriously on the credulity of Englishmen! Moreover, the documents published by Adolf Beer from the Vienna, and by Max Duncker from the Berlin archives (1874), show that the statement of Frederick the Great, that the partition of Poland was the only way of avoiding a great European war, was perfectly true.

602. Various Revolutionary Sects - One of the first societies formed in Poland to organise the revolutionary forces of the country was that of the "True Poles"; but, consisting of few persons only, it did not last

long. In 1818 another sect arose, that of "National Freemasonry," which borrowed the rites, degrees, and language of Freemasonry, but aimed at national independence. The society was open to persons of all classes, but sought chiefly to enlist soldiers and officials, so as to turn their technical knowledge to account in the day of the struggle. But though numerous, the society lasted only a few years; for disunion arose among the members, and it escaped total dissolution only by transformation. It altered its rites and ceremonies, and henceforth called itself the "Scythers," in remembrance of the revolution of 1794, in which whole regiments, armed with scythes, had gone into battle. They met in 1821 at Warsaw, and drew up a new revolutionary scheme, adopting at the same time the new denomination of "Patriotic Society." In the meanwhile the students of the University of Wilna had formed themselves into a secret society; which, however, was discovered by the Russian Government and dissolved. In 1822 the Patriotic Society combined with the masonic rite of "Modern Templars," founded in Poland by Captain Maiewski; to the three rites of symbolical masonry was added a fourth, in which the initiated swore to do all in his power towards the liberation of his country. These combined societies brought about the insurrection of 1830. In 1834 was established the society of "Young Poland"; one of its most distinguished members and chiefs being Simon Konarski, who had already distinguished himself in the insurrection of 1830. He then made his escape, and in order better to conceal himself learned the art of watchmaking. Having returned to Poland and joined " Young Poland," he was discovered in 1838, and subjected to the torture to extort from him the names of his accomplices. But no revelations could be obtained from him, and he bore his sufferings with such courage that the military governor of Wilna exclaimed, " This is a man of iron! " A Russian officer offered to assist him in escaping, and being detected, was sent to the Caucasian army for life. Konarski was executed in 1839, the people tearing his clothes to pieces to possess a relic of him. The chains he had been loaded with were formed into rings and worn by his admirers. Men like these redeem the sins of many so-called "Polish patriots."

603. Secret National Government - Some time before the outbreak of the Crimean war a secret national government was formed in Poland, of course with the object of organising an insurrection against Russia. Little was known for a long time about their proceedings. Strange stories were circulated of midnight meetings in subterranean passages; of traitors condemned by courts composed of masked and hooded judges, from whose sentence there was no appeal and no escape; of domiciliary visits from which neither the palace nor the hovel was exempt; and of corpses found nightly in the most crowded streets of the city, or on the loneliest wastes of the open country, the dagger which had killed the victim bearing a label stamped with the well-known device of the insurrectionary committee. So perfectly was the secret of the modern Vehmgericht kept that the Russian police were completely baffled in their attempts to discover its members. At that period the Poles were divided into two parties, the "whites" and the "reds"; the former representing the aristocratic, the latter the democratic element of the nation. Each had its own organisation. The whites were mostly in favour of strictly constitutional resistance; the reds were for open rebellion and an immediate appeal to arms. But a union was brought about between the two parties in consequence of the conscription introduced by Russia into Poland in 1863, which set fire to the train of rebellion that had so long been preparing. But Langiewicz, the Polish leader, having been defeated, the movements of the insurgents in the open field were arrested; though the rebellion was prolonged in other ways, chiefly with a view of inducing the Western Powers to interfere in behalf of Poland. But these naturally thought that as the Polish people, the peasantry, had taken very little share in the insurrection, and as Alexander II. had really introduced a series of reforms which materially improved the position of his Polish subjects, there was no justification for the outbreak; and therefore justice was allowed to take its course. Subsequent attempts at insurrection, with a view to re-establish the independence of Poland, were defeated by the action of Italian and other revolutionary sects, because, as Petrucelli della Gatina declared in the Chamber of Deputies at Turin in 1864,

the Poles, being Roman Catholics, would, immediately on their emancipation, throw themselves at the feet of the pope and offer him their swords, blood, and fortunes. These revolutionists are far more astute than our beloved diplomatists.

IX

THE OMLADINA

604. The Panslavists - The desire of the Sclavonic races, comprising Bohemians, Moravians, Silesians, Poles, Croats, Servians, and Dalmatians, to be united into one grand confederation, is of ancient date. It was encouraged by Russia as early as the days of Catherine II. and of Alexander I., who, as well as their successors, hoped to secure for themselves the hegemony in this confederation. But the Sclavonians dreaded the supremacy of Russia, and in the earlier days the Sclavonian writers subject to Austria wished to give the proposed Panslavist movement the appearance more of an intellectual and literary, than of a political and social league. But the European revolution of 1848 infused a purely political tendency into Panslavist ideas, which already in June of the above year led to a Sclavonic-democratic insurrection at Prague, which, however, was speedily put down, Prince Windischgratz bombarding the town during two days. The further progress of the Panslavistic movement is matter of public history; but a society arose out of the Sclavonic races, whose doings have of late been brought into prominence; this society is the Omladina. The exact date of the origin of this society is not at present known; probably it arose at the time when the Italian party of action, led by Mazzini, about 1863, attempted, by assisting the so-called national party of Servia, Montenegro, and Roumania, to cripple Austria in Italy, and so render the recovery of the Venetian territory more easy. Simon Deutsch, a Jew, who had been expelled from Austria for his revolutionary ideas, and afterwards, on the same grounds, from Constantinople, who was the friend of Gambetta, an agent of the International, and of " Young Turkey," was one of the most active members of the society, whose inner organisation was known as the Society Slovanska Liga, the Slav Limetree. This latter, however, did not attract the attention of the authorities till 1876, when its chief, Miletich, a member of the Hungarian Diet, was arrested at Nensalz. But the society continued to

exist, and occasionally gave signs of life, as, for instance, in 1882, when it seriously talked of deposing the Prince of Montenegro, and electing Menotti Garibaldi perpetual president of the federation of the Western Balkans. At last, in January 1894, seventy-seven members of the Omladina, including journalists, printers, clerks, and artisans, mostly very young men, were put on their trial at Prague for being members of a secret society, and guilty of high treason. When the arrests began, one Mrva, better known as Rigoletto di Toscana, was assassinated by Dolezal, who afterwards was seized, and was one of the accused included in the prosecution. This Mrva had been a member of the Omladina, and was said to be a police spy. He made careful notes of all the proceedings of the society, as also of another with which he was connected, and which was called "Subterranean Prague," the object of which was to undermine the houses of rich men, with a view to robbing them. His papers and pocket-books, which after his death fell into the hands of the police, served largely in drawing up the indictment against the Omladina. The result of the trial, ended on the 21st February 1894, was that all the prisoners but two were convicted and sentenced to terms of imprisonment ranging from seven months to eight years. Whether the Omladina is killed or only scotched, remains to be seen; probably it is the latter, for the Panslavic movement it represents is alive, and will some day lead to the solution of the Eastern question. For Panslavism of which the Omladina was tho outcome means Muscovite patriotism, and its war-cry, "Up against the unbelieving Turkish dogs!" finds an echo in all Kussia; and though the Berlin Congress has for a timo checked the progress of Panslavism, yet, as we said above, it is alive.

X

TURKISH SOCIETIES

605. Young Turkey - The vivifying wave of revolutionary ideas which swept over Europe in the first half of this century extended even to Turkey, and, in imitation of its effects in other countries, produced a Young Turkey, as it had produced a Young Germany, a Young Poland, a Young Italy, and so on. Mr. David Urquhart, as violent a Turcophile as he was a Russophobe, attributed to Moustapha Fazyl-Pacha, whom he calls a Turkish "Catiline," the doubtful honour of having been the founder of Young Turkey, whose aims were the abolition of the Koran and of the Sultan's authority, the emancipation, in fact, of Turkey from religious and civil despotism. The society did not make much progress in the earlier half of the century, hence, in 1 867, a new association with the same title, and under the same chief, was formed at Constantinople, Paris, and London. Its objects were the same as those of the first society, with the additional aim of destroying Russian influence in the East by the emancipation of the Christian subjects of the Porte. The members of the directing committee in Paris and London were Zia Bey, A ghia-Eff endi, Count Plater, a Pole, living at Zurich, Kemal Bey, and Simon Deutsch. The chief agent of the committee at Constantinople was M. Bonnal, a French banker at Pera. Moustapha Pacha agreed to contribute annually three hundred thousand francs to the funds of the association. Murad Bey, the brother of the present Sultan, is now the leader of the Young Turkey party, of which Midhat Pacha was a prominent member. Murad Bey attributes to the Sultan himself and the palace camarilla all the evils from which the country is now suffering.

606. Armenian Society - We shall see further on (637) that the Armenians of Russia formed a secret society against that country in 1888; recent events (1896) have prominently brought before Europe the existence in Turkey of Armenian societies. They are organised in the same way as the old venditas of the Carbonari; that is to say, the

committees do not know one another, nor even the central committee from which they receive orders. They number five, and comprise altogether about two hundred members. Each committee has a significant name. They are called Huntchak (Alarm), Frochak (Flag), Abdag (Bellows), Gaizag (Thunderbolt), and Votchintchak (Destruction). The last two are the most recently created. The committees act according to a plan fixed by the occult central committee. Thus the Huntchak organised the demonstration in 1895 at the Porte, while the attack on the Ottoman Bank (1896) devolved on the Frochak committee. There remain three, who will have to act successively. In the following month of October the Armenian revolutionary leaders sent a letter to the French Embassy at Constantinople, threatening further outrages. The latest detailed account of the society, published in December 1896, says: The discovery of seditious papers found in the possession of Armenian conspirators, when arrested in December 1896 at Kara Hissar Charki, reveals all the details of the revolutionary programme, circulated by the leaders of the insurrection, and imposed on their adherents. The programme includes thirty-one draconic rules, to which the members of the numerous Armenian bands have to submit. For instance, each band must be composed of at least seven members, who take an oath that they will submit to torture, and even to death, rather than betray the secrets of the society. By Rule 14 the band is ordered to carry off into the mountains any unjust or cruel Ottoman official, to compel him to reveal any State secret which he may possess, and even to put him to death. Rule 15 authorises the band to attack and plunder the mails and couriers, but it must not assail any person found travelling alone on the roads, unless it is absolutely necessary in the interest of the band to do so. Any member showing cowardice, when fighting, is to be shot at once. The chief is the absolute master of the band, and may punish as he chooses any member with whom he is dissatisfied. Amongst some of the most stringent clauses is one which orders the members to act as spies upon each other, and to report to the chief all the doings and movements of one another. One of the characteristic features of the Armenian revolution is the use of numerous disguises, which enable them to go secretly through towns and circulate arms and seditious literature, pamphlets, and even pictures, with the view of inciting the Armenian population against the Imperial Government. The English agitation of the present day in favour of the Armenians shows the crass ignorance existing in this country as to the true character of that people. If the Armenians were worthy of, or fit for, the liberty they claim, they would do as the Swiss a poor nation, whilst the Armenians are rich did five hundred years ago in fighting Austria they would fight Turkey.

XI

THE UNION OF SAFETY

607. Historical Sketch of Society - Russia has ever been a hotbed of secret societies, but to within very recent times such societies were purely local; the Russian people might revolt against some local oppression, or some subaltern tyrant, but they never rose against the emperor, they never took up arms for a political question. Whatever secret associations were formed in that country, moreover, were formed by the aristocracy, and many of them were of the most innocent nature; it was at one time almost fashionable to belong to such a society, as there are people now who fancy it an honour to be a Freemason. But after the wars of Napoleon, the sectarian spirit spread into Russia. Some of the officers of the Russian army, after their campaigns in Central Europe, on their return to their native country felt their own degradation and the oppression under which they existed, and conceived the desire to free themselves from the same. In 1822 the then government of Russia issued a decree, prohibiting the formation of a new, or the continuance of old, secret societies. The decree embraced the masonic lodges. Every employe of the State was obliged to declare on oath that he belonged to no secret society within or without the empire; or, if he did, had immediately to break off all connection with them, on pain of dismissal. The decree was executed with great rigour; the furniture of the masonic lodges was sold in the open streets, so as to expose the mysteries of masonry to ridicule. When the State began to prohibit secret societies, it was time to form some in right earnest. Alexander Mouravief founded the Union of Safety, whose rites and ceremonies were chiefly masonic frightful oaths, daggers, and poison figuring largely therein. It was composed of three classes Brethren, Men, and Boyards. The chiefs were taken from the last class. The denomination of the last degree shows how much the aristocratic element predominated in the association, which led, in fact, to the formation of a society still more aristocratic, that of the " Russian Knights," which aimed at obtaining for the Russian people a

constitutional charter, and counteracting the secret societies of Poland, whose object was to restore Poland to its ancient state, that is to say, absolutism on the part of the nobles, and abject slavery on the part of the people. The two societies eventually coalesced into one, under the denomination of the " Union for the Public Weal "; but, divided in its counsels, it was dissolved in 1821, and a new society formed under the title of the " Union of the Boyards." The programme of this union at first was to reduce the imperial power to a level with that of the President of the United States, and to form the empire into a federation of provinces. But gradually their views became more advanced; a republic was proposed, and the emperor, Alexander I., was to be put to death. The more moderate and respectable members withdrew from the society, and after a short time it was dissolved, and its papers and documents carefully burnt. The revolutions of Spain, Naples, and Upper Italy led Pestel, a man who had been a member of all the formei secret societies, to form a new one, with the view of turning Russia into a republic; the death of Alexander again formed part of the scheme. But circumstances were not favourable to the conspirators, and the project fell to the ground. Another society, called the North, sprang into existence, of which Pestel again was the leading spirit. In 1824, the " Union of the Boyards " heard of the existence of the Polish Patriotic Society. It was determined to invite their cooperation. The terms were speedily arranged. The Boyards bound themselves to acknowledge the independence of Poland; and the Poles promised to entertain or amuse the Archduke Constantine at Warsaw whilst the devolution was being accomplished in Russia. Both countries were to adopt the republican form of government. This latter condition, however, made by the Poles, displeased the Boyards, who, themselves lusting after power, did not see in a republic the opportunity of obtaining it. The Boyards therefore united themselves with another society, that of the " United Slavonians," founded in 1823 by a lieutenant of artillery, named Borissoff, small in numbers, but daring. As the name implied, it proposed a Slavonian confederation under the names of Russia, Poland, Hungary, Bohemia, Moravia, Dalmatia, and Transylvania. The insurrection was on the point of breaking out; but the Emperor Alexander had already (in June 1823), by the revelations of Sherwood, an Englishman in Russian service, who was ennobled, received some intimation of the plot, but seems to have neglected taking precautions; whilst he was lying ill at Taganrog, Count De Witt brought him further news of the progress of the conspiracy, but the emperor was too near his death for active measures. He died, in fact, a few days after of typhoid fever he had caught in the Crimea. It was rumoured that he died of poison, but such was not the case: the report of Sir James Wylie, who was with him to the last, disproves the rumour. Besides, it is certain that the conspirators were guiltless of the emperor's death, since it took them unprepared and scattered at inconvenient distances over the empire. Immediately on Alexander's death General Diebitsch, commanding at Kieff, ordered Colonel Pestel and about a dozen officers to be arrested. But the conspirators did not therefore give up their plan. They declared Nicholas, who succeeded Alexander, to be a usurper, his elder brother Constantine being the rightful heir to the throne. But Constantine had some years before signed a deed of abdication in favour of his brother, which however was not publicly known; and Alexander I. having died without naming his successor, the conspirators took advantage of this neglect to further their own purposes. But they were not supported by the bulk of the army or the people; still, when it came to taking the oath of fidelity to the new emperor, an insurrection broke out at St. Petersburg, which was only quelled by a cruel and merciless massacre of the rebellious soldiers. Pestel, with many others, was executed, but his equanimity never deserted him, and he died with sealed lips, though torture is said to have been employed to wring confessions from him. Prince Troubetskoi, who had been appointed Dictator by the conspirators, but who at the last moment pusillanimously betrayed them, was nevertheless by the merciless Nicholas I. exiled to Siberia for life, and condemned for fourteen years to work in the mines, and he belonged to a family which had, with the Romanoffs, competed for the throne!

    These secret societies, with another discovered at Moscow in 1838, whose members were some of the highest nobles of the empire, and who were punished by being scattered in the army as private soldiers these secret societies were the precursors of the Nihilists, whose history we have now to tell.

XII

THE NIHILISTS

"There are alarmists who confer upon the issuers of these revolutionary [Nihilistic] tracts the dignified title of a secret society, . . . but the political atmosphere of the country [Russia] ... is no longer so favourable as it used to be to their development."
ATHENAEUM, 29th January 1870.

"A political movement that is perhaps the most mysterious and romantic the world has ever known."
ATHENAEUM, 23rd September 1882.

"Nihilism is the righteous and honourable resistance of a people crushed under an iron foe; Nihilism is evidence of life. . . . Nihilism is crushed humanity's only means of making the oppressor tremble."
WENDELL PHILLIPS
(in speech at Harvard University).

608. Meaning of the term Nihilist - When the first edition of this work was published, but scanty information concerning this society had as yet reached Western Europe. As will be seen by the first quotation above, its scope and importance were at that date not understood; twelve years after, the same publication in eloquent and coming from such an authority significant language paid due honour to it. And indeed since 1870 the Nihilists have made their existence known to the world both by burning words and astounding deeds, which we will record as concisely as possible.

The term " Nihilist " was first used by Turgheneff, the novelist, in his " Fathers and Sons," where one of the characters, Arkadi, describes his friend Bazaroff as a "Nihilist." " A Nihilist " says his interlocutor. " As far as I understand the term, a Nihilist is a man who admits nothing." "Or rather, who respects nothing," is the reply. "A man who bows to no authority, who accepts no principle without examination, however high this principle may stand in the opinions of men." This was Turgheneff's original definition of a Nihilist; at present he means something very different. The term was at first used in a contemptuous sense, but afterwards was accepted from party pride by those against whom it was employed, just as the term of Gueux had in a former age been adopted by the nobility of the Netherlands.

609. Founders of Nihilism - The original Nihilists were not conspirators at all, but formed a literary and philosophical society, which, however, now is quite extinct. It nourished between 1860 and 1870. Its transformation to the actual Nihilism is due, in a great measure, to the Paris Communists and the International, whose proceedings led the youth of Russia to form secret societies, having for their object the propagation of the Liberal ideas which had long before then been preached by Bakunin and Herzen, who may indeed be looked upon as the real fathers of Nihilism, with whom may be joined Cernisceffski, who, in 1863, published his novel, "What is to be Done?" for which he was sentenced to exile in Siberia, but which mightily stirred up the revolutionary spirit of Russia. Herzen, who died in 1869, aimed only at a peaceful transformation of the Russian empire; but Bakunin, who died in 1878, dreamt of its violent overthrow by means of a revolution and fraternisation with other European States equally revolutionised. Even during his lifetime an ultra-Radical party was formed, having for its organ the Onward, founded in 1874 by Lavroff, whose programme was, " The party of action is not to waste its energies on future organisation, but to proceed at once to the work of destruction."

610. Sergei Nechayeff - Another important and influential personage in the early days of Nihilism was Sergei Nechayeif, a self-educated man, and at the time when he first became active as a conspirator, in 1869, a teacher at a school in St. Petersburg. He advocated the overthrow, though not the death, of the Tsar. But the conspiracy was prematurely discovered; Nechayeff had an intimate friend, the student Ivanoff, but ultimately they disagreed in political matters, and Ivanoff,

declaring that his friend was going too far, threatened to leave the secret association. This was looked upon as an act of treason, and on the 21st November 1869 Nechayeff slew Ivanoff in a grotto near the Academy of Agriculture at Moscow. This murder led to the discovery of the society, and eighty-seven members thereof were tried in 1871. Prince Cherkesoff was implicated in this attempt; he had on several occasions supplied the required funds. He was deprived of his rights and privileges, and banished to Siberia for five years. Nechayeff himself escaped to Switzerland, but so great were his powers of organisation and persuasion that the Russian Government set a high price on his head, and finally succeeded in obtaining his extradition from Switzerland, no less than 20,000 francs being paid to the Zurich Prefect of Police, Pfenniger, who facilitated the extradition, which, according to all accounts, was more like an act of kidnapping. The Municipal Council strongly protested, and passed a resolution that even 'common criminals should not be given up to such Governments as those of Russia and Turkey. Nechayeff was sentenced to twenty years' penal servitude in Siberia, but he was too important a person to be trusted out of sight, and so he was confined in the most secure portion of the fortress Peter and Paul. For a time he was kept in chains fastened to a metal rod, so that he could neither lie down, stand up, nor sit with any approach to ease. But even in prison he never lost an opportunity of making converts; he received visits from high officials, nay, the emperor himself " interviewed " him. Of course all these visits were paid with a view of sounding him about the forces and prospects of the revolutionary party, but he remained true to them; and with wonderful self-abnegation preferred remaining in prison to delaying the killing of the Tsar, which delay would have been necessary had his friends undertaken his deliverance. In 1882 the friendly guards around him were arrested, and nothing more was ever heard of Nechayeff beyond the fact that he was cruelly beaten with rods in consequence of a dispute with the inspector of the prison, and died shortly after. Some suppose that he committed suicide, others that he was killed by the effects of the blows. He was keenly lamented by all the Nihilists, for all recognised his ability, his courage, and utter disregard of self.

611. Going among the People - One of the earliest effects of the newly-awakened enthusiasm for social and political freedom was the eagerness with which young men, and women too, went "among the people." The sons and daughters, not only of respectable, but of wealthy and aristocratic, families renounced the comforts and security of home, the love and esteem of their relatives, the advantages of rank and position, to associate with the working classes and the peasantry, dressing, faring, and working like and with them, with the object of instilling into them ideas as to the rights of humanity and citizenship; of expounding to them the principles of Socialism and of the revolution. Thus in the winter of 1872, in a hovel near St. Petersburg, Prince Krapotkine gathered round him a number of working-men; Obuchoff, a rich Cossack, did the same on the banks of the river Don; Leonidas Sciseko, an officer, became a handweaver in one of the St. Petersburg manufactories to carry on the propaganda there; Demetrius Rogaceff, another officer, and a friend of his, went into the province of Tver, as sawyers, to spread their doctrines among the peasants; Sophia Perovskaia, who, like Krapotkine, belonged to the highest aristocracy her father was Governor-General of St. Petersburg took to vaccinating village children; in the secret memoir drawn up in 1875 by order of Count Pahlen, the then Russian Minister of Justice, we also find the names of the daughters of three actual Councillors of State, the daughter of a general, Loschern von Herzfeld, as engaged in this propaganda; and from the same document it appears that as early as the years 1870 and 1871 as many as thirtyseven revolutionary "circles" were in existence in as many provinces, most of which had established schools, factories, workshops, depots of forbidden books, and "flying sheets," for the propagation of revolutionary ideas. But though the propagandists met with some successes among the more educated classes, and received great pecuniary assistance from them thus Germoloff, a student, sacrificed his whole fortune, maintaining several friends at the Agricultural Academy of Moscow; Voinaralski, an ex-Justice of the Peace, gave forty thousand roubles to the propaganda yet among the peasantry their successes were not equal to their energy and

zeal. The Russian peasants, too ignorant to understand their teachers, or too timid to follow their advice, were not to be stirred up to assert the rights belonging to the citizens of any State. Moreover, the young men and women, who went forth as the apostles of revolution, were lacking in experience and caution; hence they attracted the attention of Government, and many were arrested. How many was never known. The propaganda was stamped out with every circumstance of cruelty, the gaols were filled with prisoners, the penal settlements with convicts; half the students at the universities were in durance, and the other half under the ban of the law.

612. Nihilism becomes Aggressive - Nihilism doctrinaire having thus proved a failure, it became Nihilism militant. The Nihilists who had escaped the gallows, imprisonment, or exile, determined that revolutionary agitation was to take the place of a peaceful propaganda. They began by forming themselves into groups in different districts, whose object it was to carry on their agitation among those peasants only whom they knew as cautious and prudent people. The St. Petersburg group was at first, 1876-78, contemptuously called " The Troglodytes," but afterwards, after the paper published by them, "Land and Liberty." There was also a large "group" at Moscow. Most of its members had been students at the Zurich University; it included several girls, one of whom was Bardina, of whom more in the next section. Some of them had entered into sham marriages, which they themselves, in their letters, called farces, and which were performed without any religious ceremony, and were, in most cases, never consummated, their object being simply to render the women independent, and to enable them to obtain passports, and at many a trial it was proved that these women had, in spite of their adventurous lives and intimate association with men, preserved their virtue unimpaired. But the groups, though they held their ground with varying fortunes for several years, remained without results; the immensity of Russia, the vis inertia of the peasantry, and the necessity of acting with the utmost circumspection, rendered these local efforts futile. The leaders at Moscow wrote despairingly. Thus in a letter from

Sdanowitch to the members at Ivanovo, a village of cotton-spinners, we read: "The news from the south are unsatisfactory. . . . We send you books and revolvers. . . . Kill, shoot, work, create riots!" There seems to have been no scarcity of books or money: one member of the association was found in possession of 8545 roubles in cash, a note for noo roubles, and 300 prohibited books, and with another 2450 prohibited books were discovered. The central administration at Moscow, which became necessary when, after the arrests in March 1875, the members went to the provinces, provided books, money, addresses, and false passports; carried on correspondence (in cipher), gave warning of approaching danger and notice of the arrest of brethren, and kept up communication with prisoners. But this Moscow society was discovered in August 1875, and totally extinguished.

613. Sophia Bardina's and other Trials - But Nihilism was not to be suppressed. It continued to gather strength, even among the peasantry, as was shown by the trial of Alexis Ossipoff, who in 1876 was condemned to nine years' penal servitude for having distributed prohibited books. For the same offence Alexandra Boutovskaia, a young girl, was sentenced in the same year to four years' penal servitude.

In March 1877 a new revolutionary society was discovered at Moscow; of fifty prisoners, whose ages ranged from fifteen to twenty-five years, three were condemned to ten years' penal servitude, six to nine years (two of them were young girls), one to five years; the rest were shut up in prisons, or exiled to distant provinces. Sophia Bardina, then aged twenty-three, was one of the prisoners, the daughter of a gentleman; she had on leaving college received a diploma and a gold medal; but to further the Socialistic propaganda, she took a situation as an ordinary work-woman in a factory. Accused of having distributed Liberal pamphlets among the factory hands, she was imprisoned, and kept in close confinement for two years, without being brought to trial; she was included in the trial of the fifty, and sentenced to nine years' penal servitude in Siberia. On being asked what she had to say why sentence should not be passed, she made one of the most splendid speeches ever heard in a court of law. In her peroration, she said, "I am convinced that our country, now asleep, will awake, and its awakening will be terrible. . . . It will no longer allow its rights to be trampled under foot, and its children to be buried alive in the mines of Siberia. . . . Society will shake off its infamous yoke, and avenge us. And this revenge will be terrible. . . . Persecute, assassinate us, judges and executioners, as long as you command material force, we shall resist you with moral force; . . . for we have with us the ideas of liberty and equality, and your bayonets cannot pierce them! "

Then came the monster trial of the one hundred and ninety-three. The whole number of persons implicated in this prosecution originally amounted to seven hundred and seventy. Of the one hundred and ninety-three who were tried, ninety-four were acquitted; thirty-six were exiled to Siberia, and Myschkin, one of the leaders, sentenced to ten years' penal servitude. Seventy prisoners are said to have died before they were brought to trial; the investigations in the trial lasted four years.

At these and other trials which took place in various provinces of Russia, the prisoners conducted themselves with the utmost courage and resolution. The Russian people appreciated their self-sacrificing patriotism. " They are saints!" was the exclamation frequently heard from the lips of even such persons as did not approve of the objects of the accused.

614. The Parti of Terror - The Nihilists continued to put forth manifestoes, in which they distinctly stated their demands. Whilst (justly) accusing the highest officials and dignitaries of dishonourable conduct, avarice, and barbarous brutality, they demanded their removal from the entourage of the emperor, to whom they then intended no harm. It was the court camarilla they were aiming at, and the suppression of the emperor's private chancellery, commonly called "the Third Division." But the more ardent Nihilists were for more drastic measures, and a portion of the party, represented by their organ, Land and Liberty, seceded, and took the name of the "Party of the People," which section was in 1878 divided again, and the seceders called

themselves the " Party of Terror," and were represented by the Will of the People. The party had no definite plans at first; its first overt act was Solovieff's attempt on the life of the emperor (617). And the Government seemed to play into the hands of the Terrorists. It did everything it could to goad the people to desperation: the merest suspicion led to arrest; ten, twelve, fifteen years of hard labour were inflicted for two or three speeches made in private to a few working-men; spies were employed by Government to obtain, by false pretences, admittance to Nihilistic meetings, in order to betray the members. Naturally the Nihilists retaliated by planting their daggers into such traitors as they discovered and could reach. Thus Gorenovitch, originally a member of the propaganda, who had betrayed his companions, was, in September 1876, dangerously wounded, and his face disfigured for life by sulphuric acid; in the same month and year, Tawlejeff was assassinated at Odessa; and in July 1877, Fisogenoff at St. Petersburg.

615. Vera Zassulic - But the signal for the outbreak of the terrorism, which distinguished the latter phases of Nihilism, was given, unintentionally, by the shot fired by the revolver of Vera Zassulic on 24th January 1878. General Trepoff, the chief of the St. Petersburg police, had ordered a political prisoner, Bogolinboff, to be flogged for a slight breach of prison discipline. Vera Zassulic made herself the instrument to punish this offence. Her life had been an apprenticeship for it. She was then twenty-six, and at the age of seventeen she had been arrested and kept in confinement two years, because she had received letters for a revolutionist. She had then passed her first examination as a teacher, and was working at bookbinding. At the end of two years she was released, but in a very few days was seized again, and sent from place to place, and finally placed at Kharkoff, nearly two years under police supervision. At the end of 1875 sne returned to St. Petersburg. Her experiences had prepared her for her deed: she knew what solitary confinement was, and the resentment of Russian society against Trepoff for even persons without revolutionary tendencies called him the Bashi-bazouk of St. Petersburg became in her mind a

conviction that he must be punished, though she had no personal acquaintance either with Bogolinboff or Trepoff. She waited on the latter, presented a paper to him, and while he was reading it, fired her revolver at him, inflicting a dangerous wound, and then allowed herself to be seized, without offering any resistance. Though the attempt was not denied at her trial, the jury pronounced her "Not guilty," and the verdict was unanimously approved as the expression of public opinion in Russia. Men saw in the acquittal a condemnation of the whole system of police, and especially of its chief, General Trepoff. Vera Zassulic was declared to be free; but in the adjoining street her carriage was stopped by the police; a riot ensued, for the people would not allow her to be seized again, and in the commotion Zassulic made her escape, and after a while found refuge in Switzerland. The emperor was furious at her acquittal, went in person to pay a visit of condolence to his vile tool Trepoff whom he made a Councillor of State and then ransacked the whole city in search of Zassulic, to put her in prison again.

616. Officials Killed or Threatened & the Nihilists - The attempt of Zassulic was followed on the 16th August by the more successful one on General Mesentsoff, chief of the third section of police, who had become notorious by being implicated in a trial about a forged will and false bills of exchange. Taking advantage of his irresponsible position, he caused all the witnesses who might have appeared against him to be assassinated. It was known that he starved the prisoners under his charge, subjected them to all kinds of cruelty, loaded the sick with chains, "all by express orders of the emperor." The Nihilists resolved he must die. On 16th August 1878, just as he was leaving a confectioner's shop in St. Michael's Square, two persons fired several shots at him with revolvers. He fell, and his assailants,[21] leaping into a droschky which was waiting for them, made good their escape, and fled in the direction of the Newski Prospect. One of them was a literary

---

[21] Stepniak, after bis death in 1895, was accused by the Eussian press of having been one of them. See section 645.

man, who in 1883 lived in Germany. His name was frequently mentioned in connection with German literature. General Mesentsoff died the same day at five in the afternoon. In a pamphlet entitled Death for Death, which appeared directly after, the writer declared political assassination to be both a just and efficacious means of fighting the Government, which the writer's party would continue to use, unless police persecutions ceased, political accusations were tried before juries, and a full amnesty granted for all previous political offences. But the Government showed no intention of granting any such reforms. Its severity was increased, and trial by jury, in cases of political offences, entirely suspended. Special courts were instituted, guaranteed to pass sentences in accordance with the Tsar's wishes. In September 1878, the St. Petersburg organisation called "Land and Liberty," and consisting of about sixty members, was broken up. A great many were imprisoned, others made their escape, but by the energy of four or five members the society was not only re-established, but was enabled to erect a printing-press, on which their paper, called after the society, was regularly printed. The Tsar having appealed to "Society" to assist him in putting down the revolutionary agitators, the attempts of " Society " to do so led to numerous riots, and in St. Petersburg and Kieff, meetings of students were dispersed by policemen and Cossacks, many of the students being wounded, and some killed. An association of working-men, comprising about two hundred members, whose objects in reality were only Socialistic, was betrayed by the Jewish spy Reinstein, and about fifty of the working-men were imprisoned. Reinstein, however, met his reward by being killed soon after by the Nihilists.

On the 9th February 1879, Prince Alexis Krapotkine, a cousin of the famous agitator, Peter Krapotkine, and Governor of Kharkoff, was shot on returning home from a ball, as a punishment of his inhuman treatment of the prisoners under his charge, which had led the latter to organise " hunger-mutinies " (638), many of them preferring starving themselves to death rather than any longer undergoing the cruelties the governor practised upon them. Goldenberg, their avenger, made good his escape.

On March 12, General Drenteln, the Chief of the Secret Police, was fired at by a Nihilist called Mirski, who managed to escape. The causes of the attempt were: firstly, that Drenteln had caused a prisoner to be hanged for trying to escape; secondly, his general cruelty, which had provoked another "hunger-mutiny"; and lastly, his having sent many Nihilists to prison.

617. First Attempts against the Emperor's Life - Thus we see that the persons aimed at by the Nihilists gradually rose in rank, and the logical conclusion of aiming at the highest, at the Tsar himself, could not be evaded. The idea came to several persons simultaneously. As early as the autumn of 1878 a mine was laid at Nikolaieff, on the Black Sea, to blow up the emperor; but it was discovered by the police, the only one they did discover. About the same time A. Solovieff, who had been a teacher, but who on becoming a Socialist learned the trade of a blacksmith that he might thus place himself into closer connection with the labouring classes, came to St. Petersburg with the intention of killing the emperor. At the same period Goldenberg, still elated with his successful attempt on Prince Krapotkine, also reached the Russian capital with the same object in view the death of the Tsar. Solovieff and Goldenberg entered into communication with some of the chiefs of "Land and Liberty," and eventually Solovieff undertook the task. On the 2nd April 1879, he fired four shots at the emperor as the latter was walking up and down in front of the palace. Solovieff was seized, tried on the 6th June following, of course found guilty, and hanged on the Qth of the same month. At the trial he declared himself a foe of the Government and a foe of the emperor, and at his execution he preserved his composure to the last.

618. Numerous Executions - After Solovieff's attempt a virtual state of siege was established throughout the whole Russian empire, and a police order was issued at St. Petersburg requiring each householder to keep a dvornik, or watchman, day and night at the door of the house to see who went in and out, and that no placards were affixed. In the month of May there were 4700 political prisoners in the Fort

Petropowlovski, who were removed in one night to eastern prisons, to make room for those newly arrested. Eight hundred prisoners, under strong escort, were drafted off from Odessa to Siberia. In the same month the trial took place at Kieff of the persons who, about a year before, had resisted the police sent to arrest them for being in possession of a secret printing-press. Four of the accused were cited as unknown persons, because they refused to give their names and were unknown to the police, but during the trial the names of two of them oozed out. Ludwig Brandtner and one of the unknown, but calling himself Antonoff, were sentenced to be shot. The Governor-General of Kieff, however, ordered them to be hanged. Three others, and Nathalie Arrnfeldt, daughter of a State Councillor, Mary Kovalevski, ranked as a noble, and Ekaterine Sarandovitch, daughter of a civil servant, were condemned to hard labour for fourteen years and ten months. Ekaterine Politzinoy, the daughter of a retired staff-captain, for not informing the police of what she knew of the doings of the other prisoners, was sentenced to four years' hard labour. At another trial, held a day after, two other Nihilists, Osinsky and Sophia von Herzt'eldt, were condemned to be shot.

619. The Moscow Attempt against the Emperor - On the 17th to the 21st June the Nihilists held a congress at Lipezk (province of Tomboff), at which Scheljaboff, a prominent leader, maintained, as we learn from his "Life," written by Tichomiroff, that since the Government officials, such as Todleben at Odessa, and Tschertkov at Kieff, were simply the tools of the Tsar, this latter must be personally punished, which was agreed to by his colleagues. It was decided to blow up the imperial train during the journey of the emperor from the Crimea to St. Petersburg. The mines under the railway line were laid at three different points near Odessa, near Alexandrovsk, and near Moscow. But owing to a change in the emperor's itinerary, the Odessa mine had to be abandoned; in that at Alexandrovsk, the capsule, owing to some defect, did not explode, though the battery was closed at the right moment, and the imperial train passed uninjured over a precipice, to the bottom of which it would have been hurled by the slightest

shock; near Moscow alone the terrorists made at least an attempt. They had purchased a small house close to the railway, and Leo Hartmann, an electrician, Sophia Perovskaia, and others, excavated a passage, commencing in the house and ending under the rails. The work was nearly all done by hand, and owing to the wet weather the passage was always full of water, so that the miners had to work drenched in freezing water, standing in it up to their knees. The attempt to blow up the emperor's carriage was made on the 1st December 1879, but his train, fortunately for him, preceding instead of following the baggage-train, the latter only suffered. When, after the explosion, the cottage was searched some of the apparatus, and even an untouched meal, were found; but the inmates had all disappeared, and were not afterwards apprehended, though many hundreds were sent to prison on the denunciation of Goldenberg (616), who a few days before the Moscow attempt had been seized by the police with a quantity of dynamite in his possession, and who, to benefit himself, as he hoped, betrayed a great number of his fellow-Nihilists. Finding that he did not thereby obtain any alleviation of his own fate, he committed suicide.

620. Various Nihilist Trials - Another great trial of Nihilists took place at Odessa in August. Twenty-eight prisoners were tried, of whom three were sentenced to be hanged. They were Joseph Davidenko, son of a private soldier, and Sergay Tchoobaroff and Dmitri Lizogoob, gentlemen. The latter, who had sacrificed nearly his whole fortune, a large one, to the " cause," and of whom Stepniak gives so moving an account in his " Underground Bussia," justly styling him " The Saint of Nihilism," was betrayed by his steward, Drigo, the Government having promised to give him what still remained of Lizogoob's patrimony, about £4000. The other prisoners were sentenced to various terms of hard labour in the mines, ranging from fifteen to twenty years.

In December another important trial of Nihilists was heard before the Odessa military tribunal. The most prominent prisoner was Victor Maleenka, a gentleman, who was tried for the attempt made three years before to murder Nicholas Gorenovitch, for having betrayed some of his fellow-Nihilists (614). It appeared that Gorenovitch had been enticed to a lonely place in Odessa, where Maleenka felled him with blows on the head, while a companion threw sulphuric acid over what was supposed to be the corpse of Gorenovitch, in order to destroy all traces. But the victim survived, and appeared as a witness at the trial. He presented a horrible appearance: the acid had destroyed his sight and all his features, and even his ears; consequently his head was enveloped in a white cloth, leaving nothing but his chin visible. It may, by the way, be mentioned, that he was then inflicting his awful presence on poor people as a scripture reader, being led about by a devoted sister. Maleenka and two of his fellow-prisoners were sentenced to be hanged.

621. Explosion in the Winter Palace - The failure of the Moscow attempt did not discourage the Nihilists. They now adopted the title of "The Will of the People," and though in January 1880 two of their secret printing-presses were discovered and seized by the police, and numerous arrests were made, they managed to issue on the 26th January a programme, in which they declared that unless the Government granted constitutional rights, the emperor must die. The emperor replied by ordering greater severity and more arrests. Then the Nihilists planned a fresh attempt, more daring than any previous one, to blow up the emperor in his own palace. Its execution was undertaken by Chalturin, the son of a peasant, a very energetic agitator and experienced organiser of workmen's unions. Being also a clever cabinetmaker he easily, under the assumed name of Batyschkoff, obtained a situation in the imperial palace; he ascertained that the emperor's dining-hall was above the cellar in which the carpenters were at work, though between it and the latter there was the guardroom, used by the sentinels of the palace, and his plans were made accordingly. So blind and stupid were the Eussian police that though towards the end of the year 1879 (Chalturin found employment in the palace in the month of October) a plan of the Winter Palace, in which the dining-hall was marked with a cross, was found on a member of the Executive Committee who had been apprehended, in consequence of

which the police made a sudden irruption into the carpenters' quarters nothing was discovered, yet Chaltnrin used a packet of dynamite every night for his pillow! A gendarme, however, was installed in the carpenters' cellars, and a stricter surveillance exercised over all persons entering or leaving the palace. This rendered the introduction of dynamite exceedingly difficult, and greatly delayed the execution of the project.

It may here incidentally be mentioned that what may appear to the reader to have been an exceptionally difficult undertaking, viz., to introduce dynamite into the imperial palace itself, was, after all, very easy. The Winter Palace, till then always a change was made after the attempt had been a refuge for numberless vagabonds, workmen, friends of servants, and others, many without passports, who could not have lived anywhere else in the capital with impunity. It appears there is an old law which gives right of sanctuary, as far as regards the ordinary police, to criminals taking refuge in an imperial palace. When General Gourko searched the Winter Palace, it was found that no fewer than five thousand persons had been living in it, and no one knew the precise duties of half of them. Chalturin gave startling accounts of the disorder pervading the palace, and of the robberies committed by servants. They gave parties of their own, invited scores of friends, who freely went in and out, yea, stayed overnight, whilst the grand staircase remained inaccessible to even highly-placed officials. The servants were such thieves that Chalturin, not to excite their suspicions, was compelled occasionally to take food and other trifles as "perquisites." True, the wages of the upper domestic servants were only fifteen roubles a month.

To resume our narrative. Chalturin suffered terribly from headaches, caused by the poisonous exhalation of the nitroglycerine on which his head rested at night. However, he continued to work on without exciting any suspicion, yea, the gendarme on guard tried to secure the clever workman, who at Christmas had received a gratuity of a hundred roubles, for his son-in-law. At last fifty kilogrammes of dynamite had been introduced; the Executive Committee urged Chalturin to action; and on the 5th February 1880 the explosion took place, Chalturin having had time to leave the palace before it occurred. It pierced the two stone floors, and made a gap ten feet long and six feet wide in the dininghall, in which a grand dinner in honour of the Prince of Bulgaria was laid. Through an accidental delay the imperial family had not yet assembled, and thus escaped total destruction. The explosion killed five men of the palace guard, and injured thirty-five some accounts say fifty-three. Some of the parties implicated in the plot were brought to trial in November 1880, but Chalturin was not captured till early in 1882; he was hanged on the 22nd March of that year, and only then recognised as the cabinetmaker of the Winter Palace. The Executive Committee, in a proclamation, regretted the soldiers who had perished, but expressed its determination to kill the emperor, unless he granted the constitutional reforms asked for. The Tsar, in reply, invested Count Loris-Melikoff with unlimited authority as Dictator. The attempt on the latter's life, made on 3rd March by Hipolyte Joseph Kaladetski, for which he suffered death on the 5th, was not prompted by the Executive Committee, who, on the contrary, expressed their disapproval of it, because Count Melikoff had shown some tendency towards Liberal ideas.

622. Assassination of the Emperor - During the remainder of the year 1880, large numbers of suspected persons were arrested, tried by a secret tribunal, and many of the prisoners condemned to death or transportation to Siberia. In the previous year, 11,448 convicts were despatched eastward, and in the spring of 1880 there were in the prisons at Moscow 2973 prisoners awaiting transportation to Siberia and hard labour in the mines or government factories. But the Nihilistic movement, instead of being killed, acquired fresh strength by these wholesale persecutions; the Tsar, in his blind fury, seemed bent on Mass destruction and it was nearer than he anticipated. The Executive Committee determined that now the emperor must die. Fortyseven volunteers presented themselves to make the attempt on his life. On the 13th March 1881, the Tsar was assassinated. Returning from a military review near St. Petersburg, a bomb was thrown by Ryssakoff, which exploded in the rear of the carriage, injuring several soldiers. The

emperor alighted, and a second bomb, thrown with greater precision, by Ignatius Grinevizki, exploded and shattered both the legs of the emperor below the knees, tore open the lower part of his body, and drove one of his eyes out of its socket. Within one hour and a half the Tsar was dead. Grinevizki was seized, but he was himself so injured that he died shortly after his arrest. He was the son of a small farmer, who with great difficulty for some time managed to keep his family, consisting of eleven persons, but eventually fell into difficulties; his farm was sold, and he became insane. Ignatius, in the greatest poverty, attended several schools. In 1875 he was sent, as the best scholar of his class, to the Technological Institution at St. Petersburg; there he joined the students' unions for Radical purposes, in which, by his activity and address, he soon acquired great influence. In 1879 he would have been satisfied with a moderate constitution, but seeing that there was no prospect of even that small boon, he joined the Terrorists, working with and for them till the great work of his life was assigned to him. The Nihilists ascribe to him the fame of a Brutus, of Harmodius, and Aristogeiton! Return we to the other actors in this historic tragedy.

The signal for throwing the bombs had been given by Jessy Helfmann and Sophia Perovskaia, who were on the watch, waving their handkerchiefs. She and Helfmann were arrested, as also some of the other conspirators, Kibalcie, Micailoff, and Ryssakoff, and, with the exception of Helfmann, who, being four months pregnant, was reprieved, were hanged on the 15th April following. All the prisoners died like heroes; Perovskaia even retained the colour in her cheeks to the last. But the execution was a "butchery." (See Kolnische Zeitung and London Times of i6th April 1881.)

623. The Mine in Garden Street - On the 25th March the revolutionary correspondence found on the prisoners led to the discovery of the conspirators' quarters in Telejewskaia Street, where Timothy Michailoff was arrested. A copy of the proclamation of the new Tsar's ascent to the throne was found on him, on the back of which were marked in pencil three places of the city, with certain hours and days against each. One place thus indicated was a confectioner's

shop at the corner of Garden Street. Just round the corner from this confectioner's in Garden Street was a cheesemonger's shop, kept by one Kobizoff and his wife, whose mysterious disappearance on the day of the assassination led to the discovery of a mine under the street. From subsequent discoveries it* became evident that this mine was not intended to blow up the emperor, but to stop his carriage, and afford others time to assassinate him, after the fashion of the haycart, which stopped General Prim's carriage at Madrid.

624. Constitution said to have been Granted by late Emperor - It was said that the day before his death the emperor had signed a Constitution, and that by their action the Nihilists had deprived their country of the benefits it would have conferred. But what he had signed was merely the appointment of a representative commission to consider whether provincial institutions might not be widened, and the calling together of the zemskij sobor, or communal council, a measure Loris-Melikoff had strongly advised him to adopt, as a means of enlisting the people's co-operation in putting down Nihilism, the minister taking care to remind the emperor that such an assembly would, after all, be only deliberative, and that the final decision would always remain with the crown. The whole scheme was a mere blind to allay public discontent, with no intention on the Tsar's part of relinquishing any portion of his absolute prerogatives. The emperor's death thus did not deprive the Russian of any substantial benefit, but saved them a delusion.

625. The Nihilist Proclamation - Ten days after the Tsar Alexander II. had been put to death, the Executive Committee issued their nobly-conceived and expressed proclamation to his successor, Alexander III., in which, on condition of the emperor granting (1) complete freedom of speech, (2) complete freedom of the press, (3) complete freedom of public meeting, (4) complete freedom of election, and (5) a general amnesty for all political offenders, they declare their party will submit unconditionally to the National Assembly which meets upon the basis of the above conditions. Hundreds of Easter eggs containing this

proclamation were scattered about the streets of Moscow at Easter time. Nay, a rumour was then universally current in St. Petersburg, that the Nihilists had deputed one of their number to wait on the Emperor Alexander and explain to him in unambiguous words what they really wanted. The emperor received him, and after having heard what he had to say, ordered him to be placed in durance in the Fortress Petropowlovski; the police, however, failed to find any clue to his identity. So runs the story, and there is nothing improbable in it, considering the daring self-sacrifice which characterises all the acts of the Nihilists.

626. The Emperor's Reply thereto - The emperor's reply to the Nihilistic proclamation, asking for such constitutional rights as are possessed by every civilised nation, was given in a manifesto, issued on the 11th May, in which the emperor expressed his determination fully to retain and maintain his autocratic privileges. Furthermore, fresh executions were ordered, thousands of his subjects were exiled to Siberia, greater rigour was exercised against the press and every Liberal tendency. Not only did the emperor not grant any reforms, but he even retracted concessions already made, as, for instance, the reduction of the redemption money, whereby nearly four millions of his subjects continued to be kept in virtual serfdom. Ignatieff, the newly-appointed Minister of the Interior, whilst bravely seconding his master in his oppressive measures, tried to open a safety-valve to public dissatisfaction and indignation by fomenting antiJewish riots, the blame of which was laid to the charge of the Nihilists, who, however, published a very spirited reply, showing that it was not their policy to incite the people against the Jews, they being, as was proved at many a trial, and especially those of Southern Russia, great supporters of the Nihilistic movement. But irrespective of this, it was no part of Nihilistic tactics to set one race or religion against another in the empire. Nor did the despoiling of private individuals, such as distinguished the violence against the Jews, enter into their plans. They robbed, they admitted, but only in the interest of the "cause" and of the people. They warned the emperor against listening to pernicious

counsel. But the emperor closed his ears to this advice. Trembling for his life, he shut himself up at Gatshina, to which place he had fled. The day when he was to start, four imperial trains were ostentatiously ready at four different stations in St. Petersburg, with all the official and military attendants, while the emperor fled in a train without attendance, which had been waiting at a siding.

When in June 1881 the Court removed to Peterhoff, the railway between the two places was strictly guarded by troops; for every half verst about one- third of a mile English there was a sentinel with a tent. Besides this, the photographs of all the railway officials were lodged in the Ministry of Ways and Communications, so that any Nihilist, disguised in railway costume, might the more easily be detected.

627. Attempt against General Tcherevin - On November 25, a young man presented himself at the Department of State Police, which was the old third section or secret police under a new name, and asked to see General Tcherevin, the chief director of measures for assuring the safety of the emperor, stating that he had to disclose some business gravely affecting the State. On being ushered into the presence of General Tcherevin, he immediately drew a revolver and fired at the general, but missed him, and was secured. He declared that he was acting as the instrument of others, and for the good of Russia, but named no accomplices. His own name was Sankofsky. As the Eussian Government suppressed as far as possible all allusions to the event and we have no account as to what became of Sankofsky he was probably tried with closed doors, and what was his punishment remains unknown.

628. Trials and other Events in 1882 - Numerous arrests, and trials of persons who had long been in prison, took place in 1882, Of twenty prisoners tried in February, ten, including one woman, were sentenced to be hanged. On 12th June Count Ignatieff, having rendered himself unpopular to the public by his anti-Jewish schemes, and incurred the disfavour of his imperial master by intimating to him that, without the

introduction of the ancient States-General of the Tsars, the government of the country could not be satisfactorily carried on, under the time-honoured fiction of illhealth sent in his resignation. Count Tolstoi, who was known to disapprove of the anti-Semitic policy of Count Ignatieff, was appointed his successor.

Five days after, the Nihilists received a terrible blow. In a house occupied by them on an island in the Neva, there was discovered a great number of bombs and a large quantity of dynamite; but of more importance were the papers found on the Nihilists apprehended at the same time, from which it appeared that they were kept an courant of the Government correspondence in cipher with foreign countries, as far as it referred to themselves, which information they had received from Volkoff, one of the higher officials in the Ministry of Foreign Affairs. In July a secret printing-press of the Nihilists was discovered in the Ministry of Marine; its director committed suicide. Encouraged by the disasters which had befallen the Nihilists, the emperor ventured to return to St. Petersburg, and on the nth of September attended the fete of Alexander Nevsky, the patron-saint of the emperor, but slightly guarded, without evil results; and in the exuberance of his feelings he went so far as to extend his clemency even to the Nihilists, for on October 4 he graciously commuted the sentence of death, passed by a secret tribunal, on two Nihilists for having murdered a police spy, to perpetual labour in the mines and yet the Nihilists were not conciliated! For when, on the 21st November, the emperor and empress paid a visit to St. Petersburg extra precautions were taken on the part of the police and military authorities; all along the route, from the railway-station to the palace, police-officers in sledges and on foot were met with at every half-dozen yards; policemen were posted at regular intervals in the centre of the street, and the bridges over the canals were closely guarded by the marine police. But the emperor maintained his serenity. As the Official Gazette informed its readers: " Towards the end of December the new chief of police, General Grossler, had the honour of exhibiting before his Imperial Majesty several policemen attired in the latest new and last old uniforms of the force. His Majesty carefully examined the difference, consisting mainly in alterations of colours and buttons." He also began to think of his coronation, which was announced to take place at various dates during the current year; but the ceremony was postponed from time to time, and did not finally take place until 27th May 1883.

629. Coronation, and Causes of Nihilistic Inactivity - Great surprise was excited by the peaceful nature of the coronation; but it appeared by the trial (in April 1883) of seventeen Nihilists at Odessa, five of whom were sentenced to death, that the conspirators had made the most extensive preparations for killing the emperor at his coronation, as proposed in 1881 and 1882; but by the vigilance of the police, and the denunciation of spies, their schemes were frustrated, and the terrorists found it impracticable to make the attempt in 1883. As they themselves declared afterwards, they came to the conclusion that such an attempt would damage their interests. They argued that the revolutionary movement in Eussia embraces many persons of moderate views, whose opinions must be taken into consideration; that the people, who came to the coronation would not belong to a class likely to approve of a revolutionary plot. But the Nihilists profited in another way by the coronation. The whole force of the Government, and its most intelligent spies, being concentrated at Moscow, the Nihilists seized this occasion to spread their doctrines and to enrol supporters at St. Petersburg and other large centres, to which may be attributed the great riots which, after the coronation, occurred at St. Petersburg, which were intensified by the fact that none of the expected constitutional reforms were granted. The manifesto issued by the emperor on the coronation day consisted simply of a remission of arrears of taxes; criminals condemned without privation of civil rights had one-third of their terms remitted; exiles to Siberia for life had their sentences commuted to twenty years' penal servitude; those still lying under sentence for the Polish troubles in 1863 were to be set free; but confiscated property was not to be restored. Much more had been expected, and the Burgomaster of Moscow had been bold enough, in his congratulatory address to the emperor, to express those hopes, for which "presumption" he was visited with the emperor's displeasure.

But the disappointment of the people's expectation of an amnesty and a constitution greatly favoured the spread of Nihilistic doctrines. The Nihilists continued to hold secret meetings, issue their papers, flying sheets, and manifestoes. In September 1883 a number of officers were arrested, and a large depot discovered at Charkoff, containing arms of every kind, large quantities of gunpowder, dynamite bombs, and new printing apparatus. It was found that dynamite was being manufactured in Kolpino, close by St. Petersburg. Here 138 naval and 17 artillery officers were arrested and conveyed to the St. Peter and Paul fortress. In Simbirsk an artillery colonel was arrested, who had gained an enormous influence with the peasants, and incited them to revolutionary deeds.

630. Colonel Sudeikin shot by Nihilists - On the 28th December the Nihilists took their revenge by shooting Colonel Sudeikin, the Chief of the Secret Police, in a house to which he had been enticed by the false information of an intended Socialist meeting. They also left a letter stating that the next victims would be Count Tolstoi, Minister of the Interior, and General Grossler, the Chief of the St. Petersburg police. "If ever assassination could be palliated," says the Evening Standard of the 3ist December 1883, "it is in such a case as the present. When men know that sons, or brothers, or wives are being driven to madness or death by prolonged and deliberate cruelty, no Englishman can blame them very greatly if they take vengeance on their tyrants. In a free country, under just laws, assassination of officers for a fancied wrong is altogether unjustifiable and wicked; but under such a regime as exists in Russia, it can hardly be judged in the same way. Men may shudder, but they cannot unreservedly condemn."

631. Attempt against the Emperor at Gatshina - The Nihilists continued to issue journals and proclamations, and to extend their influence among the working classes. Of course they also continued to meet with checks. Early in January 1884 numerous arrests were made among the factory hands at Perm, on the Kama, and many revolutionary documents were found in their possession. Towards the

end of the month of December of the preceding year the emperor had met with what was thought, or at lea t officially represented, to be an accident; while out hunting, his horses took fright, upset the sledge, and the emperor sustained a severe injury to his right shoulder. But in the following January it was rumoured that the accident was really a Nihilist attempt at assassination. It was said that about a fortnight before the murder of Colonel Sudeikin, Jablonski, alias Degaieff, who had sent Sudeikin the letter which led to his death, accompanied by a woman, arrived at the house of the imperial gamekeeper at Gatshina, and producing a letter from Colonel Sudeikin, informed him that the woman was to be received into his house in order to assist the detectives already at Gatshina. The woman remained, and whenever the Tsar went shooting, she attended, disguised as a peasant boy. On the day of the "accident" the woman was not there, but made her appearance next day and reported that the Tsar had met with an accident, one of the gamekeepers having carelessly discharged his gun close to the imperial sledge and frightened the horses. On the day after the assassination of Sudeikin, and when it was known that Jablonski had played the chief part in the tragedy, three detectives arrived at Gatshina and arrested the woman. She was said to be a sister of Streiakoff, who was hanged for complicity in the murder of Alexander II., and there were rumours current afterwards that she had secretly been hanged in one of the casemates of the Petropowlovski Fortress for the attempted murder at Gatshina.

Odessa then became notorious for the frequent murders and attempted assassinations of officers of the gendarmerie by Nihilists. During the summer, Colonel Strielnikoff and Captain Gezhdi were killed; on the 19th of August a determined attempt to kill Captain Katansky, the successor of Strielnikoff, was made by a second Vera Zassulic. The girl, Mary Kaljushnia, who made the attempt, was a merchant's daughter, barely nineteen, and her object, to avenge her brother, who had been sentenced to penal servitude for life in Siberia. She had for some time been under police supervision; she earned a miserable subsistence by giving lessons, maintaining herself on about fourpence a day. Her requests to be allowed to go abroad were persistently refused. On the date above named, she called on Captain Katansky, avowedly with the object of renewing her request, but in the course of conversation she suddenly drew a revolver and fired straight into the officer's face. But the ball only grazed his ear; she was seized before she could fire again, and on the loth September following sentenced to twenty years' hard labour. She was tried by the Odessa Military Tribunal with closed doors. Several political arrests were made about the same time, especially of students and young ladies, one of the latter a doctor of medicine.

632. Trial of the Fourteen - In the month of October a trial took place in St. Petersburg of fourteen Nihilists, including six officers and the celebrated female revolutionist Figner, alias Vera Filipava, who had offered shelter to the regicide Sophia Perovsky, and of another woman, named Volkenstein, who had been implicated in the murder of Prince Krapotkine at Kharkoff in 1879 (616). The tr.bunal was virtually a court-martial with closed doors, ant the greatest secrecy was observed throughout the week for which the trial lasted. The six officers and the two wom.n, Figner and Volkenstein, were condemned to death, and ti\e others sentenced to hard labour in the mines.

633. Reconstruction of the Nihilist Party - After a years silence, the organ published clandestinely in Russia by the Nihilists, the Narodnaia Volia (The Will of the People), reappeared, dated I 2th October I 884, in large 4to. The losses suffered by the party were admitted; their type and printingmachines had fallen into the hands of the police, and some of their chief men were in prison. These losses they attributed to the denunciations of Degaieff, the assassin of Colonel Sudeikin, who had been a leading Nihilist, had turned traitor, but finding the Government not grateful enough, and fearing the vengeance of the Nihilists, had purchased his safety by acting again for the latter and killing Sudeikiu. This latter being killed, and Degaieff rendered harmless, the Committee was able to reconstitute the party. The Will of the People also gave a summary of the principal Nihilistic events during the year, comprising some interesting details concerning the

great development of agrarian Socialism in the south of Russia, facts till then studiously concealed by the Government. The paper further stated that the revolutionary group, which had at one time separated itself from the party of the Will of the People, "The Party of the People" (614) and the revolutionary party of Poland, had coalesced with the Russian Nihilists. Among the other subjects treated, there was an obituary notice of Professor Neoustraieff, who was shot at Irkutsk for striking the governor general of the province. The last pages of the paper were filled with a long list of arrests made, and a paragraph incidentally mentions that M. Larroff never belonged to the Executive Committee, though he is recognised as one of the editors of the review Onwards, published by the Nihilists at Geneva, and as a warm friend of the party.

634. Extension of Nihilism - With such a constant hidden enemy in their very midst, the Government and people of Russia were in a state of chronic alarm. Count Tolstoi, the Minister of the Interior, whilst diligently searching for Nihilists, was also their especial victim. He daily received threatening letters; he scarcely dared stir out of doors, and whenever he did so, the extra precautions that had to be taken involved an outlay of five hundred roubles. And whilst despotism was more violent and resolute than ever, the trials constantly going on showed that Nihilism had extended its influence to the army, and that the military Nihilists did not belong to the lower ranks. Whilst the emperor shut up Nihilists in one fortress, he was a prisoner in another. The official press of Russia about this time (end of 1884) was very sore on the subject of the comments of the English press on Russian affairs, accusing it of basing its opinions about Russia upon the prejudiced writings of expatriated Nihilists, and further charging the English Government with allowing Nihilists to use the very City of London as a place whence to send not only criminal proclamations, but explosive substances, such as dynamite, to Russia. "A family," it was said, "making inquiries about their son, accidentally came across an entire office of Russian Nihilists within the boundaries of the City proper." Of course had the English Government been cognisant of

these proceedings, it would readily have put an end to them.

635. Decline of Nihilism - But Nihilism apparently began to decline. A Nihilist manifesto, published in August 1885, lamented: " Truth compels us to own that the fierce struggle with the Russian Government, and the spirit of national discontent, which gave strength to our party, which was, in fact, its raison d'Stre, has ended in the triumph of absolutism." In the following December a trial took place at Warsaw, at which six persons belonging to the revolutionary association called the Proletariate, including a justice of the police and a captain of Engineers, were sentenced to be hanged; eighteen were condemned to sixteen years' hard labour in the mines, two to ten years and eight months' penal servitude, and two others to transportation to Siberia for life. Early in January 1886 the police discovered a Nihilist rendezvous opposite the Annitchkine Palace, at St. Petersburg. A number of explosive bombs and a printing-press were seized, and several arrests were made. In April it was reported that a Nihilist conspiracy, directed against the life of the emperor, had been discovered at a place near Novo Tcherkask, the capital of the Don Cossacks, to which the emperor was expected to make a visit. Early in December some five hundred students attempted to celebrate the anniversary of a certain Bogolinboff, a once popular poet; but the police interfered, and a number of arrests were made, including many lady students, eighteen of whom were sent off from St. Petersburg by an administrative order, without the least notion whither they were to be taken, or what was to become of them.

Such are the scanty notices we have of Nihilism in 1886.

636. Nihilistic Proceedings in 1887 - In 1887 the Nihilists displayed greater activity. In February another conspiracy was discovered, but the details were not allowed to transpire. All that became known was that a young prince, a cadet in one of the military schools, attempted to commit suicide by shooting himself, the reason alleged being his complicity in some plot which he thought had been discovered. An inquiry into the matter in one or two of the military and naval schools

resulted in the arrest of a large number of young men, as well as of two or three naval officers.

On Sunday, the 13th March, the anniversary of the assassination of Alexander II., a determined attempt to kill his successor was made. The Russian police had previous information that such an attempt would be made, from Berlin, London, and Bucharest. On Saturday night a couple of men in a restaurant on the Nevsky attracted the attention of the detectives, who followed and watched them all night. Next day the police were able to watch the posting of six individuals, including three students, at three different parts of the route to be followed by the Tsar. They carried bombs in the shape of books, of a bag, an opera-glass, and a roll of music. As soon as they had apparently taken their positions they were pounced upon by the police and secured. Altogether fifteen persons were arrested, twelve men and three women, one of the latter being the landlady of the house at Paulo vna, on the Finnish railway, where the bomb manufactory was discovered a day or two after the attempt of the 13th. Nine of the twelve men were students, and the other three were two Polish nobles from Wilna and an apothecary's assistant. Seven of the accused were condemned to be hanged, and the other eight to various terms of imprisonment with hard labour, from twenty years downwards. It was reported at the time that each prisoner was found to have a small bottle containing a most active poison suspended round the neck, next to the bare skin. In case of failure, or refusal at the last moment to accomplish the task, secret agents of the party, who were on the watch all the time, were to strike the chest of the faint-hearted or unsuccessful conspirator, thus smashing the bottle and causing the poison to enter the wound made by the broken glass. The Nihilists seem not to have been discouraged by the last failure, for on the 6th April next a fresh attempt on the emperor's life appears to have been made, though particulars, beyond those of the seizure of several suspected persons, were not allowed to transpire. But it was reported from Odessa that in the month of the same year (1887) 482 officers of the army arrived in that town under a strong military escort. They were accused of participation in the last attempt on the Tsar's life, and were to be transported to Eastern Asia.

In June the trial of twenty-one Nihilists, accused of various revolutionary acts in the years 1883 and 1884, took place at St. Petersburg. The prisoners included the sons of college councillors, priests, superior officers, a Don Cossack, tradesmen, peasants, and two women, one of them a staff-captain's daughter. Fifteen were condemned to death, but on the Court's recommendation, eight death sentences were mitigated to from four to fifteen years' hard labour, and subsequently the emperor for once reprieved the remaining seven, five of whom were to undergo hard labour in Siberia for life, and the others from eighteen to twenty years each.

Another blow was sustained by the Nihilists at the end of November, when the police discovered laboratories for the manufacture of dynamite in the Vassili, Ostrou, and Peski quarters of St. Petersburg. No wonder that they began to utter cries of despair towards the end of the year 1887. "Liberalism," they said, in one of their publications, "has not eradicated the feeling of loyalty in society. . . . Even the 'intelligent Liberals' have rejected the invitation to establish free printing offices, ... or even to serve the revolutionary press abroad by sending it articles for publication." The Messenger of the Will of the People, which was the official exponent of the party during the year, ceased to appear "for want of intellectual and material aid from Russia." "Little is to be expected," the Nihilists said elsewhere,"from the present generation of Russians. . . . Russian society, with its dulness, emptiness, and ignorance, is to blame. . . . Most of the so-called cultured classes belong to that category of passengers who are made to travel in cattle-trucks. . . . Russian society has become a flock of sheep, driven by the whip and the shepherds' dogs."

637. Nihilism in 1888 - Little or nothing was heard of Nihilism in that year. There was indeed a rumour in January that a new Nihilist conspiracy against the life of the Tsar had been discovered at St. Petersburg, and that many officers and others had been arrested; but it went no further than a rumour. Extensive police precautions were

adopted at St. Petersburg early in March, in anticipation of Nihilist manifestations on March 13, the anniversary of the death of the late Tsar; but the day went by without disturbances of any kind. The accident which occurred to the Tsar's train in November 1888 is very generally supposed to have been the result of a Nihilist plot. But the unchangeable despotic character of the Russian Government was again exemplified during the year by its anti-Semitic policy at two extremities of European Russia. Some two thousand Jews received notice to quit Odessa, and the expulsion laws against the persecuted Hebrews were also enforced in Finland. The Finnish Diet having refused to adopt the Russian view of the case, the Government determined upon enforcing the law as it exists in Russia; all the Jews to leave within a year, with the exception of those who had served in the army. According to the emperor's own statement, this wholesale expulsion of the Jews was due to the fact that Jews have been mixed up with all Nihilistic plots.

In December 1888 the papers reported the discovery by the Russian Government of a ramification of secret societies among the young and educated Armenians, upon the model of the "Young Italy" societies, as they were constituted in 1848. The object of the Armenian societies is revolution against Russian rule, and the establishment of Armenian union and independence.

638. Slaughter of Siberian Exiles, and Hunger-Strikes - Towards the end of the year 1889, the civilised world was horrified by the account of the slaughter of a number of exiles at Yakutsk, on their way to the extreme east of Siberia, near the shore of the Polar Sea. These exiles were not criminals, but exiled by "administrative order," that is to say, they had not been tried and convicted by any tribunal: Government, not the Law, arbitrarily had ordered them to Siberia as suspects. Simply for asking to take with them sufficient food and clothing for the terrible journey still before them, they were declared to have resisted the authorities, and a number of them shot down; a woman, Sophie Gourewitch, was ripped open by bayonets; the vice-governor himself twice fired at the exiles. Not satisfied with this butchery, the surviving

exiles were tried by court-martial; three were sentenced to death, and many others to long terms of penal servitude in the mines. Early in 1890, still more horrifying details of hunger-strikes among the exiles reached Europe, and of the means adopted by the Russian Government to repress them. One lady, Madame Sihida, was dragged out of bed, where she lay ill, and received one hundred blows. She died in two days from the effects. Many of her companions in misery took poison; so did many of the male prisoners. This occurred at Kara, in Eastern Siberia. In fact, the condition of Russian prisons, especially of those where political prisoners are confined, is too horrible to be described in these pages; the moral and physical suffering wantonly inflicted on the victims of a Tsarish cruelty is without a parallel in the history of absolutism. The Tsar cannot be absolved from personal responsibility in the matter: to say that he was not aware of the cruelties practised in his name, is saying in as many words that his neglect of inquiring into them encouraged them; but he must know them; they had been frequently communicated to Alexander III., notably in a long letter written in March 1890 by Madame Tshebrikova, a lady of position, and not in any way connected with the Nihilists; but for writing it she was arrested, and sent to Penza, in the Caucasus, and placed under strict police surveillance.

639. Occurrences in 1890 - The Russian students having in recent times shown decidedly Liberal tendencies, Government endeavoured to repress them, which led to repeated riots and endless arrests, as many as five hundred and fifty students, who had protested against the new and oppressive statutes promulgated by the authorities, being arrested at Moscow in March 1890. In April all the police stations and prisons of St. Petersburg were full of arrested students; the ringleaders, mostly young men belonging to good families, were eventually sent as private soldiers into the disciplinary battalions near Orenburg.

In May, fourteen Russians were arrested in Paris, which has always been a favourite place of residence with Nihilists, Colonel Sokoloff, who was expelled from France, Krukoff, a printer, and Prince Krapotkine being among their chiefs. The prisoners above mentioned were proved to have been in possession of bombs, many of which had been manufactured in Switzerland. There were two women among the accused; they were acquitted, the men were sentenced to three years' imprisonment.

In November in the same year the Russian General Seliverskoff was found in his room in a Paris hotel, shot in the head; he died on the following day without having recovered consciousness. He had been a Russian spy on the Nihilists.

In the same month five Nihilists were tried at St. Petersburg, one of them being a woman, Sophie Gunzburg, who was arrested in Russia, in possession of bombs and revolutionary proclamations. Four of the prisoners were condemned to death. Another trial took place about the same time, and as in the first-mentioned trial the principal figure was a woman, so in this second trial the chief personage was a young girl, Olga Ivanovsky, niece of Privy Councillor Idinsky, director of a department of the Holy Synod. As the names of high ecclesiastical functionaries were concerned in the affair, the authorities shrouded it in more than the usual secrecy, so that no details have reached the outer world.

640. Occurrences from 1891 to Present Date - The Nihilists appear to have been rather, but not quite, inactive during these later years. In May 1891 a secret printingpress was discovered and seized at St. Petersburg. In November of the same year a far-reaching political conspiracy was discovered at Moscow, and some sixty persons, belonging to the nobility, the literary profession, and the upper middle class, were arrested. In December a great number of arrests were made, some of the accused being found to be in possession of plans and details of the imperial palaces. In 1892 a number of Nihilists were arrested at Moscow, for an alleged conspiracy to kill the Tsar on his return journey from the Crimea. An anonymous letter had warned the authorities that the attempt was to be made at a small railway station. The line was examined, and a bomb discovered under each line of rails. In spite of these failures, the Nihilistic agitation was actively carried on. The revolutionists endeavoured to stir up the lower classes against the

Tsar by telling them that, though he pretended to supply the masses with food during the famine, he allowed his subordinates to rob the people. The insinuation, however, had but little success with the Russian people of the lower class, brought up in slavish adoration of the emperor, who can do no wrong. In the month of December, Major-General Droszgovski was assassinated at Tashkend, in Russian Turkestan. He had been acting as president of a court-martial for the trial of a number of Nihilists, most of whom were sentenced to various terms of imprisonment. To avenge them their friends killed the president.

In May 1893 the decapitated body of a Russian student was discovered in a forest, near Plussa Station, on the Warsaw railway. The deceased was supposed to have been a member of a secret society, and to have been killed to prevent his revealing its secrets. Two young men were arrested for the crime, and immediately hanged. A widespread Nihilistic conspiracy against the life of the Tsar was discovered (in September 1893) at Moscow, in consequence of which eighty-five university students, eight professors, and five ladies belonging to the aristocracy, were arrested.

Early in 1894 the Government Commission appointed to inquire into the condition of Siberian prisons issued its report, in which instances without number were recorded of merciless floggings, lopping off of arms and fingers by sabre cuts, of cannibalism under stress of famine. During the whole of 1892 there was an almost continuous string of convoys of corpses from Onor, the prison on the island of Saghalien, to Rykovskaya, the residence of the authorities, and most of the bodies were terribly mutilated. In 1893, if any one of a band of convicts failed in his work, he was at once put on half rations, then on third rations; and when he could work no more, the inspector finished him with a revolver bullet. What wonder, then, that in November 1894 three secret printing-presses, in full working order, with a great quantity of Nihilistic literature, were discovered at Kieff, at Kharkoff, and at Nicolaieff respectively? The press at Kharkoff -was being worked by the students of the university in that city. Upwards of eighty persons were arrested. In September 1895, it was reported that a widespread Nihilistic plot against the life of the Tsar and the imperial family had been discovered by the Russian police. Some of the leaders were quietly arrested, while dynamite bombs, arms, and piles of revolutionary pamphlets were seized daring a number of domiciliary visits at Moscow. In March of the year 1896 six officers of the garrison of Kieff, including a colonel, were arrested for participating in a Nihilist conspiracy. According to the Central News, in October 1896 the Russian Custom-house officers confiscated on the Silesian frontier a quantity of light canes destined for sale to the upper classes, and containing in their hollow interior thousands of Nihilist proclamations, printed on tissue paper. The Nihilists, evidently, are still at work. There is a Nihilist club, composed chiefly of Jews, in London, who publish a paper, similar in character to Most's Freiheit (512) in Yiddish, and printed with Hebrew type.

641. Nihilistic Finances - The number of active Nihilists never amounted to more than a few dozen men and women; they may have had twelve or thirteen hundred supporters, who assisted the leaders by distributing their books, pamphlets, dec., concealing them when pursued by the police or otherwise in danger, assisting them to escape from prison, assisting them with money, &c.; though those who sympathised with the Nihilists, without, however, taking any active part in the propaganda, may be assumed to have been perhaps one hundred thousand. Whence did the Nihilists obtain the means for executing their schemes? for creating a literature, purchasing materials, travelling, carrying out terroristic measures, supporting and delivering prisoners?

In 1869 Nechayeff had obtained from Herzen the revolutionary fund collected in Switzerland, and amounting to more than;iooo; the members of the society, of course, gave their contributions; Lizogoob sacrificed his fortune of about 200,000 roubles to the "cause"; the Justice of the Peace Voinaralski gave 40,000 roubles; a Dr. Weimar, a very active Nihilist, supplied large sums; rich people, who sympathised with Nihilism, but would not compromise themselves, contributed money either anonymously, or ostensibly for charitable purposes. Besides these voluntary contributions, the Nihilists obtained compulsory ones by threatening timorous rich men, or such as were known to have enriched themselves at the expense of the State, that unless they assisted the Nihilistic cause, they would be condemned to death by the Executive Committee. The Nihilists also occasionally helped themselves to the Government cash; in 1879 they robbed the State bank of Kharkoff by means of a subterranean passage, and carried off one million and a half of roubles. But their outgoings were considerable; the Moscow mine and the other two attempts made at the same time, for instance, cost nearly 4000, and consequently the Nihilists were often hard pressed for money. The most extravagant reports were circulated at times as to their financial resources; thus the Cologne Gazette in April 1879 declared the Nihilistic propaganda to count as many as 19,000 members, and to be possessed of a fund amounting to two millions of roubles. The Nihilists accomplished their objects with a tenth of that amount. In fact, in 1881 they were driven to imitate the device of Peter's Pence and the Red Cross. In January 1882 they founded the association of the Red Cross, and made appeals in the Will of the People for contributions. This appeal was published by Lavroff in the Paris paper I? Intransigeant, which led to his expulsion from France. However, according to the Will of the People and other Nihilistic publications, 53,000 roubles were received in 1881. But the figures dealing with Nihilistic finances can never be anything but approximate. They received contributions from French, Swiss, German, English, Italian, and Austrian sympathisers, a fact showing the international unity of the Revolutionists, and the extensive foreign connections of the Russian Nihilists.

642. The Secret Press - The revolutionary party early felt the necessity of propagating their opinions by the press, hence in the earliest stages of the movement, as far back as the year 1860, secret printing-presses were set up; and all the various organisations established afterwards, attempted to have their own presses; but the difficulty of maintaining secrecy was too great; one after the other they were discovered and

seized. At last, in 1876, Stephanovitch, a leading spirit among the Nihilists, succeeded in establishing a secret printing-press at Kieff. He lived in one house, and had the press at another. A friend of his who lodged with him was arrested; he sent a note to Stephanovitch to warn him; but the messenger handed the note to the police, which led to the arrest of Stephanovitch. His sole object now was to save the printing apparatus. A woman and her husband presented themselves before the landlord of the house where the printing office was, and producing the key of the rooms, the woman told the landlord that she was Stephanovitch's sister, who had given it her, and given her and her husband permission to occupy the rooms till his return. The landlord had no suspicion, and made no objection. The pair secretly removed all the printing apparatus and left the house. Soon after the police made their appearance; they had made a house to house visitation at Kieff in search of the printing office, and the few types and proofs they found here and there left in corners, satisfied them that they had come too late. The printing apparatus was carried to Odessa, but what became of it there, is not known.

A clever and enterprising Jew, Aaron Zundelevic, a native of Wilna, in 1877 managed to smuggle into St. Petersburg all the necessary apparatus for a printing office, which could print works of some size. He learned the compositor's art, and taught it to four other persons. For four years the police discovered nothing, until treachery and an accident came to their aid. Not only the members of the organisation "Land and Liberty," which maintained the office, but even the editors and contributors of the journal printed there, did not know where it was. It was occupied by four persons. Mary Kriloff, who acted as mistress of the house, was a woman of about forty-five. She had been implicated in various conspiracies. A pretty, fair girl passed as the servant of Madame Kriloff. Intercourse with the outer world was maintained by a young man of aristocratic, but silent, manners. He was the son of a general, and nephew of a senator, and was supposed to hold a ministerial appointment, but his portfolio contained only MSS. and proofs of the prohibited paper. The other compositor, Lubkin, was only known by the nickname of the "bird," given to him on account of his voice. He was only twenty-three years of age; consumption was written on his face; having no passport, he was compelled always to remain indoors. When after four hours' desperate resistance the printing office of "Land and Liberty" fell into the hands of the military, he shot himself.

The apparatus, as a rule, was extremely simple; a few cases of various kinds of type, a small cylinder of a kind of gelatinous substance, a large cylinder covered with cloth, which served as the press, a few jars of printing ink, a few brushes and sponges. Everything was so arranged that in a quarter of an hour it could be concealed in a large cupboard. To allay any suspicion the dvornik could conceive, they made him enter the rooms under various pre tences, having first removed every vestige of the printing operation.

We have seen in preceding paragraphs how the capture by the police of one printing-press speedily led to the setting up of another; and that the number scattered all over Kussia must have been great is evident from the number which were discovered, and from which the multitude of those undiscovered may be inferred. And their publications were scattered all over the country. Handbills and placards seemed to grow out of the earth. The army was deluged with them, the labourer found them in his pocket, the emperor on his writing-table. Nihilists wandered all over Kussia, leaving them in thousands at every halting-place. Jessy Helfmann was a travelling postoffice; her pockets were always full of proclamations, newspapers, handbills, and tickets for concerts and balls for the benefit of prisoners, or of the secret press.

643. Nihilistic Measures of Safety - When Nihilism began to assume terroristic features, and the vigilance of the police consequently became more strict, and arrests were of daily occurrence, the Nihilists had to adopt various means for their self-protection. A primary condition was the possession of a passport, for in Eussia every one above the peasantry must be registered, and have a passport. Many young men matriculated as students, not with a view of attending university lectures, but to obtain the card of legitimation. Non-students at first paid high prices for passports, but eventually took to manufacturing them. Every

society established its own passport office, forging seals and signatures. One of these offices, furnished with every necessary appliance, was discovered by the police at Moscow in 1882. "Illegal" men, that is to say, those who lived with a false passport, or one lent by a friend, of course did not go by their true names, and their correspondence was taken care of by friends. The Nihilist had to lead a very regular life, not to excite the suspicions of the dcornik. Their larger meetings took place in "conspiracy-quarters," which were carefully selected. The windows must be so placed that signals can easily be displayed or changed. The walls of the room must not be too thin, and the doors close accurately, so that sounds may not reach the outside. There must be a landing outside, to command the staircase, so that in case of a surprise a few resolute men can resist a troop of gendarmes, until all compromising papers and other objects are removed.

The conspiracy-quarters generally were regular arsenals; at the storming of the office of the Will of the, People, every one of the five Nihilists was armed with two revolvers; the dozen gendarmes were afraid to advance, and soldiers had to be sent for; from eighty to a hundred shots were fired on that occasion. When to some of the Nihilists all these precautions became irksome, and they consequently neglected them, Alexander Michailoff, to whom they therefore gave the nickname of dvornik, severely censured them; he would follow his associates in the street, to see if they behaved with caution, or he would suddenly stop one, and ask him to read a signboard, and if he found him shortsighted, insist on his wearing glasses. He insisted on their dressing respectably, and would often himself find the means for their doing so. He himself lived like the Red Indian on the war-path. He endeavoured to know all the spies, to beware of them; he had a list of about three hundred passages through houses and courtyards, and by his intimate knowledge of places of concealment, saved many a companion from arrest. The Nihilists frequently change their lodgings, and keep them secret. Then they rely also for their safety on the Ukrivaheli, or Concealers, who forma large class in every position, beginning with the aristocracy and the upper middle class, and reaching even down to the police, who, sharing the revolutionary ideas, make use of their social or official position to shelter the combatants by concealing, whenever necessary, both objects and men. Strange causes sometimes led to the most unlikely people becoming "Concealers," Thus a Madame Horn, a Danish lady, seventy years of age, became one. She had married a Russian, who held some small appointment in the police. When the Princess Dagmar became the wife of the hereditary Prince of Russia, Madame Horn wished the Danish ambassador to obtain for her husband some appointment in the establishment of the new archduchess. The ambassador was rude enough to laugh at her. This turned her in favour of the Nihilists, who she hoped would punish the ambassador. She began by taking care of the Nihilists' forbidden books, attended to their correspondence, and eventually concealing the conspirators themselves. Thanks to her age, her prudence, presence of mind, she escaped all suspicion. Her husband, whom she ruled absolutely, had to furnish her with all the police intelligence he could gather.

644. The Nihilists in Prison - In spite of all their precautionary measures, many of the Nihilists, as we have seen, fell into the hands of the police. The historian, unfortunately, has no impartial reports to rely on as to their treatment in prison; only once, during the ministry of Count Loris-Melikoff, Kussian papers were allowed to partly reveal the secrets of Russian imprisonment and Siberian exile, which virtually confirmed all the "underground" literature had asserted, and these revelations are horrifying. They show up the imperfection and cruelty of Russian state institutions, the brutality and irresponsible arbitrariness of Russian officials. We find that the accused are kept in prison and what prisons! for two or three years before being brought to trial, and for what crime? simply for having given away a Socialistic pamphlet. We find women in large numbers undressed in the presence of, or even by, the gendarmes themselves, and searched by them, to the accompaniment of coarse jokes. We are told how prisoners were tortured, how nervous prisoners were disturbed in their sleep, to entice them in their state of excitement to make confessions. Condemned prisoners were treated with the same refined cruelty. There is a large

prison at Novobfelgorod, near Kharkoff, whence the prisoners addressed in 1878 that is, before the attempts on the emperor's life an appeal to Russian society, from which we will quote a few facts. In a dark cell, whose window is partly smeared over with dark paint, lay Plotnikoff, on boards only thinly covered with felt, without covering or pillow, terribly weakened by years of solitary confinement. One day he rose from his boards and began reciting the words of a favourite poet. Suddenly his gaoler rushed in. "How dare you speak loud here! " he cried; " perfect silence must reign here. I shall have you put in irons." The prisoner vainly pleaded that his legal term for being in irons had expired, and that he was ill. The irons were again fastened on him.

Alexandroff, another prisoner, heard some peasants singing in the distance; their song found an echo in his heart, and he sang the melody. He had ceased for some time when the guard entered his cell. " Who has allowed you to sing?" he said; "I will give you a reminder," and with his fist struck him in the face. Even common criminals are better treated. They are allowed to sit together, two or three in one cell. Seriikoff was put into the career for not saluting a gaoler standing a little way off. The career is a cage totally dark, and so small, that a prisoner has to remain in it in a stooping position. It is behind the privy, whence the soil is but seldom removed.

The prisoners in the fortress Petropaulovski are no better off. Their cells are dark, cold, and damp; the windows being darkened with paint, lights have to be burnt nearly all day. Their food consists of watery soup and porridge for dinner, and a piece of bread morning and evening. The stoves are heated only once every three days, hence the walls are wet, and the floors literally full of puddles. The prisoners are allowed to take exercise every other day, but for a quarter of an hour only. They have no other distraction. When Subkoffski once made cubes of bread to study stereometry, they were taken away from him. "Prisoners are not allowed amusements," he was told. No wonder that disease, insanity, attempts at suicide, and deaths are of daily occurrence. Hunger-mutinies were another consequence of this treatment. A very serious one occurred at Odessa in December 1882. It arose in this way. A prisoner asked for invalid's food, but the prison doctor replied,

"You are a workman; invalid's food costs seventy kopecks; you will do without it." Another prisoner, a student, asked for some medicine for a diseased bone in his hand. The same doctor replied, "Suck your hand, you have plenty of time." When this prisoner shortly after wanted to consult another surgeon, the prison doctor replied, "You want no doctor, but a hangman." The final circumstance which brought about the mutiny was the order of the gaoler to confine a prisoner who was consumptive, and had asked for a hammock, in the career. Then the prisoners sent for the head of the police, but he only abused them. Then the hunger-mutiny broke out. The prisoners refused to take their food, but the governor of the prison ordered those who could not be persuaded to eat to be kept alive by means of injections.

The horrors of transportation to Siberia have often been described. We need not repeat the fearful tale. But we may state that these horrors are intensified for political prisoners, whilst common criminals are allowed to soften them if they have means. Thus Yokhankeff, the wellknown forger, who was tried at St. Petersburg in 1879 or embezzling thousands, instead of having to make his way partly on foot and partly by rail, was allowed to travel with every comfort, accompanied by a female, and to put up at the best hotels en route.

The Russian Government, even under Alexander II., became ashamed, it seems, of the many trials, and resorted, to avoid this public scandal, to removing suspected persons by what is called the administrative process, an extra judicial procedure under which hundreds of persons were dragged away from their homes and families without trial of any kind, no one knowing what became of them. We may, however, surmise that many were sent to Siberia, since in 1880 further prison accommodation had to be constructed in Eastern Siberia in consequence of the great influx of political prisoners.

What I have stated as to the treatment of prisoners is but what is based on authentic documents. Had I quoted from the "underground" press, I should be accused of exaggeration; but taking the above statements only, does such conduct become a civilised government?

645. Nihilist Emigrants - It is difficult to estimate their number. Many of them conceal themselves to escape the Russian spies scattered all over the Continent, and not to involve the countries affording them an asylum in diplomatic difficulties. There may be about one hundred exiles in Switzerland; there are said to be about seventy in Paris, and perhaps fifty in London; but these numbers can only be approximate, and from the nature of circumstances, must always be changing. Some of these fugitives date from the earliest stages of the revolutionary movement before 1863, as, for instance, M. Elpidin, the bookseller, at Geneva. Others, like Lavroff, were involved in the conspiracies of 1866 and 1869. Others belong to the Socialistic propaganda, like Prince Krapotkine. Others, again, were members of the "Land and Liberty" or "Black Division" parties. After 1878 there was a large addition to the emigration.

But few of these exiles have been able to save any portion of their property. Before engaging in the movement some sold their estates, others leased them to their relations, and allowed them to be burdened with debts, so that in the end but little remains to be confiscated by the Government. Most, even those who receive assistance from home, are compelled to rely on their own exertions. Some give lessons in music, in Eussian, in science; others write for Eussian and foreign newspapers. Others, again (about twenty), are employed in the three Russian printing-offices at Geneva; and perhaps the same number practise the trades of locksmiths, carpenters, and shoemakers, which they once learned for the purposes of the propaganda. Many, unable to work, their mental and physical powers having been broken by long incarceration, are supported by the contributions of the party. To suppose, as it often has been supposed, that the Nihilistic movement in Bussia is directed by these emigrants, is a mistake. The telegraph cannot be employed by them, and correspondence is too slow and unsafe. Whatever has to be done in Russia, must be decided on and carried out by the members residing there. The exile ceases to take any active part in the revolution at home, though he may indirectly influence it by his literary efforts, as, for instance, Krapotkine and Stepniak have done to a large extent. The death of this latter, so well known by his brilliant and authoritative work, La Russia Sotterranea, caused great sorrow to all true lovers of Russia. He was accidentally killed on the 23rd December 1895, when crossing the railway near Chiswick, by being caught by the engine of a train, knocked down, and fearfully mutilated.

Stepniak's real name was Serge Michaelovitch Kravchinsky. After his death the St. Petersburg press asserted that it was he who assassinated Adjutant-General Mesentsoff (616), the chief of the political police, by stabbing him with a dagger. But this was never proved.

According to Dalziel, six officers of the garrison of Kieff, including a colonel, were arrested in March 1896 for participation in a Nihilist plot; whence it would appear that Nihilism is not dead yet, nor is it likely to die until it has attained its aim; and the present emperor does not seem likely to voluntarily satisfy it.

646. Nihilistic Literature - The bibliography of Nihilism is already an extensive one. Among the most important newspapers and periodicals we have:

1. The Bell (Kolokol), edited by Herzen and Bakunin, from 1st July 1857 to 1869. London and Geneva. After Herzen's death it was revived for a short time in 1870; six numbers in 4to appeared.

2. Flying Sheets. Heidelberg, 1862. 78 pp. 8vo.

3. Free Word. Berlin, 1862. 590 pp. 8vo.

4. Liberty. 1863. Two numbers, the organ of the party " Land and Liberty."

5. The Underground Word, by M. Elpidin. Geneva, 1866. Two pamphlets.

6. Cause of the People, by Bakunin and Elpidin. 1868 and 1869. Nine pamphlets.

7. Onwards, a review in nine volumes. 1873-77. Two thousand copies.

8. Onwards, a fortnightly publication of three thousand copies in large 4to. 1875 and 1876. Published in London.

9. The Tocsin. Monthly. 1875 to 1881.

10. General Cause. Monthly. Geneva.

11. The Commune, nine numbers of which appeared at Geneva in 1878.

12. Land and Liberty. 1878 and 1879.

13. Will of the People, the organ of the Terroristic Executive Committee. 1879.

14. Black Division. 1880-81.

15. Free Word.

Of books we have:

1. The Filled and the Hungry, published by the Anarchists at Geneva.

2. The Terroristic Struggle, N. Morosoff. London, 1880.

3. Terrorism and Routine, W. Tarnoffski. London, 1880.

4. Biographies of Perofskaia, Scheljabow, and others. Geneva, 1882.

5. Le Nihilisme en Eussie, S. Podolinski. Paris, 1879.

6. La Russia Sotterranea, by Stepuiak. Milan, 1882. An English translation appeared in London, 1883.

7. Buried Alive; Keport concerning the Prisoners in the Peter and Paul Citadel at St. Petersburg. 1878.

8. Almanack of the Will of the People. Geneva, 1883.

I have given the more important periodical publications and books only; besides these, there are published by Nihilists numerous flying sheets, proclamations, addresses, reports of trials, &c.

647. Trials of Nihilists - The following list is taken from the "Almanack of the Will of the People":

| Date. | Number of Trials. | Number of Accused. | Sentences. |||||||
			Executions.	Penal Servitude.	Exile.	Imprisonment.	Interned.	Other Punishments.	Acquitted.
1871	2	88	...	4	3	27	...	...	54
1872	1	1	...	1	...	...	...	1...	...
1874	1	13	...	5	...	...	3	...	5
1875	2	7	...	5	...	...	...	2	...
1876	5	12	...	6	1	2	3	...	...
1877	11	303	...	29	67	20	71	12	104
1878	8	30	1	5	7	2	4	1	10
1879	22	166	16	66	19	6	4	28	27
1880	21	130	5	48	20	11	4	29	13
1881	11	34	6	10	10	...	6	1	1
1882	10	37	3	30	1	...	...	2	1

Subsequent Trials Collected from other Sources.

| Date. | Number of Trials. | Number of Accused. | Sentences. |||||||
			Executions.	Penal Servitude.	Exile.	Imprisonment.	Interned.	Other Punishments.	Acquitted.
1883	...	155	...	...	...	...	...	...	...
1884	...	15	...	10	...	...	...	...	...
1885	...	6	...	...	2	...	...	...	...
1886	...	...	...	...	...	...	18	...	...
1887	2	36	14	22	...	...	...	...	...

The above sentences are those pronounced by the tribunals; but many of the accused were, in reality, punished more severely than is apparent. Those who were acquitted were, as a rule, placed under police supervision, imprisoned, or banished to no one could tell where. The table, moreover, does not show those who were never tried, but dealt with administratively, as it is mildly termed: they died in prison, or were hanged without trial. This has frequently been the case since 1883, whence it is impossible to give the numbers with the same fulness as before that date. How many victims were so quickly "removed," it will probably be impossible ever to ascertain.

XIII

GERMAN SOCIETIES

648. The Mosel Club - In 1737 there was a carpenter named Vogt, living at Weimar, who, being a native of Traubach, on the Mosel, was, according to the custom of craftsmen, called " the Moseler." He established a tavern, which was largely patronised by students, who, in time, formed a club, which called itself the Mosel Club, and in 1762 became a secret political club, whose object was to raise Prussia to the ruling power of Germany, to effect which the members even pledged themselves to send Frederick II., who was a Freemason, armed assistance. In 1771 a more secret league was formed within the Mosel Club, consisting chiefly of Alsatians and Badois, and calling itself the "Order of Friendship." None was received into it who was not a member of the Mosel Club. The sign was a peculiar pressure of the hand, and touching the face. The members wore a cross attached to a yellow ribbon. After the year 1783 the candidate had to swear fidelity to the Order over four swords, laid crosswise on a table, on which four candles were burning. The words were: " If I become unfaithful to my oath, my brethren shall be justified to use these swords against me." Lodges were established at Jena, Giessen, Erfurt, Gottingen, Marburg, and Erlangen. The students defied the statutes of the universities, which in 1779 led to a judicial inquiry and the abolition of the Order, which, however, was quickly re-formed under the new name of the "Black Order"; at Halle it assumed that of the "Unionists." But in the course of a few years the Order became extinct. Still Germany continued till the middle of this century to be a hotbed of secret societies, in which the students of its many universities were the chief actors. Between the years 1819 and 1842 such associations were especially numerous; legal investigations on the part of the different governments proved in the latter year the existence of thirty-two of them. How much the members of such societies loved the rulers " restored " to them, appears from the fact that "Young Germany" amused itself on the king's (of Prussia) birthday with shooting at his

portrait. Their statutes were very severe against treason, or even mere indiscretion. A Dr. Breidenstein wrote to Mazzini in June 1834 that one Strohmayer, a member of the society, had been sentenced to death, not that he was a traitor, but his indiscretion was to be feared. Sixteen months after, on the morning of 4th November 1835, a milkman found the body of the student Louis Lessing, pierced with forty-nine dagger wounds, in the lonely Sihl valley, near Zurich. Though the legal investigation did not positively prove it, yet it was the general opinion that Lessing had acted as spy on the "German Youth" society, and been sentenced to death by them.

Still, what those obscure students aimed at is now an accomplished fact; and the prediction of Carl Julius Weber in his " Democritos " (published in 1832), that Prussia, united with the smaller German states, would be the dictator of Europe, a reality. But a sad reality for Europe, since it has

"Thrust back this age of sound industriousness To that of military savageness! "

Yes, Germany seems to be retrograding to the days of Hildebrand; for has not Bismarck gone to Canossa, in spite of his assertion he would not do so? and has not the mighty emperor-king knelt to the Pope?

649. German Feeling against Napoleon - Napoleon, whilst he could in Germany form a court composed of kings and princes obedient to his slightest nod, also found implacable and incorruptible individualities, who swore undying hatred to him who ruled half the world. Still, those who opposed the French emperor had no determined plan, and were misled by fallacious hopes; and the leaders, always clever in taking advantage of the popular forces, threw the more daring ones in front like a vanguard, whose destruction is predetermined, in order to fill up the chasm that separates the main body from victory.

650. Formation and Scope of Tugendbund - Two of the men who were the first, or amongst the first, to meditate the downfall of the conqueror before whom all German governments had fallen prostrate,

were Count Stadion, the soul of Austrian politics, and Baron Stein,[22] a native of Nassau, who possessed great influence at the Prussian Court. The latter, devoted to monarchical institutions, but also to the independence of his country, groaned when he saw the Prussian Government degraded in the eyes of Europe, and undertook to avenge its humiliation by founding in 1812 the secret society of the "Union of Virtue" (Tugendbund), whose first domiciles were at Konigsberg and Breslau. Napoleon's police discovered the plot; and Prussia, to satisfy France, had to banish Stein and two other noblemen, the Prince de Wittgenstein and Count Hardenberg, who had joined him in it. But the Union was not dissolved; it only concealed itself more strictly than before in the masonic brotherhood. During Stem's banishment, also, the cause was taken up by Jahn, Professor at the Berlin College, who, knowing the beneficial influence of bodily exercise, in 1811 founded a gymnasium, the first of the kind in Germany, which was frequented by the flower of the youth of Berlin, and the members of which were known as Turner, an appellation which is now familiar even to Englishmen. These Turner seemed naturally called upon to enter into the Union of Virtue; and Jahn thought the moment fast approaching when the rising against the oppressor was to take place. Among his coadjutors were the poet Arndt; the enthusiastic Schill, who with 400 hussars expected in 1809 to rouse Westphalia and overthrow Jerome Bonaparte; Doremberg, the La Rochejaquelein of Germany, and several others. Stein, in the meanwhile, continued at the court of St. Petersburg the work on account of which he had been exiled. The Russian Court made much of Stein, as a man who might be useful on certain occasions. He was especially protected by the mother of the emperor, in whom he had enkindled the same hatred he himself entertained against France. He kept up his friendship with the Berlin patricians, and had his agents in the court of Prussia, who procured him and Jahn adherents of note, such as General Bliicher. Still there was at the Prussian Court a party opposed to the Tugendbund, whose

---

[22] The original MS. of the great reorganisation projects for the Prussian State, 1807, was found in 1881, in the gartenhaus of the Stein family, at GrossKochberg, Saalfeld, in Thuringia.

chiefs were General Bulow and Schuckmann, who preferred peace to the dignity of their country, and possibly to royal and serene drill-sergeants who, though no friends to Napoleon, were indifferent to the public welfare. A party quite favourable to the Union of Virtue was that headed by Baron Nostitz, who formed the society of the " Knights of the Queen of Prussia," to defend and avenge that princess, who considered herself to have been calumniated by Napoleon. This party was anxious to wipe away the disgrace of the battle of Jena, so injurious to the fate, and still more to the honour, of Prussia; and therefore it naturally made common cause with the Tugendbund, which aimed at the same object, the expulsion of the French.

651. Divisions among Members of Tugendbund - The bases of the organisation of the Tugendbund had been laid in 1807 at the assembly at Konigsberg, where some of the most noted patriots were present Stein, Stadion, Bliicher, Jahn. The association deliberated on the means of reviving the energy and courage of the people, arranging the insurrectionary scheme, and succouring the citizens injured by foreign occupation. Still there was not sufficient unanimity in the counsels of the association, and an Austrian party began to be formed, which proposed the re-establishment of the German Empire, with the Archduke Charles at its head; but the opposition to this scheme came from the side from which it was least to be expected, from the Archduke himself. Some proposed a northern and a southern state; but the many small courts and provincial interests strongly opposed this proposal. Others wanted a republic, which, however, met with very little favour.

652. Activity of the Tugendbund - One of the first acts of the Union of Virtue was to send auxiliary corps to assist the Russians in the campaign of 1813. Prussia having, by the course of events, been compelled to abandon its temporising policy, Greisenau, Scharnhorst, and Grollmann embraced the military plan of the Tugendbund. A levy en masse was ordered. The conduct of these patriots is matter of history. But, like other nations, they fought against Napoleon to

impose on their country a more tyrannical government than that of the foreigner had ever been. They fought as men only fight for a great cause, and those who died fancied they saw the dawn of German freedom. But those who survived saw how much they were deceived. The Tugendbund, betrayed in its expectations, was dissolved; but its members increased the ranks of other societies already existing, or about to be formed. The " Black Knights," founded in 1815, and so called because they wore black clothes, said to be the old German costume, headed by Jahn, continued to exist after the war, as did "The Knights of the Queen of Prussia." Dr. Lang placed himself at the head of the "Concordists," a sect founded in imitation of similar societies already existing in the German universities. A more important association was that of the "German Union " (DeutscherBund), founded in 1810, whose object was the promotion of representative institutions in the various German states, which Union comprised within itself the more secret one of the "Unconditionals " (Die Unbedingteri), whose object was the promotion of Liberal ideas, even without the concurrence of the nation. The Westphalian Government was the first to discover the existence of this society. Its seal was a lion reposing beside the tree of liberty, surmounted by the Phrygian cap. All these societies were in correspondence with each other, and peacefully divided the territory among themselves; whilst the German Union, true to its name, knew no other limits than those of the German confederation. Dr. Jahn was active in Prussia, Dr. Lang in the north, and Baron Nostitz in the south. This latter, by means of a famous actress of Prague, Madame Erode, won over a Hessian prince, who did not disdain the office of grand master.

653. Hostility of Governments against Tugendbund - After the downfall of Napoleon the German Government, though not venturing openly to attack the Tugendbund, yet sought to suppress it. They assailed it in pamphlets written by men secretly in the pay of Prussia. One of these, Councillor Schmalz, so libelled it as to draw forth indignant replies from Niebuhr and Schleiermacher. What the Germans could least forgive was the scurrilous manner in which Schmalz had calumniated Arndt, the "holy." Schmalz had to fight several duels, and even the favour of the Court of Prussia could not protect him from personal outrages. The king

then thought it fit to interfere. He published an ordinance, in which he commanded the dispute to cease; admitted that he had favoured the "literary" society known as the Tugendbund during the days when the country had need of its assistance, but declared that in times of peace secret societies could not be beneficial, but might do a great deal of harm, and therefore forbade their continuance. The action of the Government, however, did not suppress the secret societies, though it compelled them to change their names. The Tugendbuud was revived, in 1818, in the Bursclienschaft, or associations of students of the universities, where they introduced gymnastics and martial exercises. These associations had been projected as early as the year 1810, as appears from Jalm's papers. Their central committee was in Prussia; and sub-committees existed at Halle, Leipzig, Jena, Gottingen, Erlangen, Wiirzburg, Heidelberg, Tubingen, and Freiburg. Germany was divided into ten circles, and there were two kinds of assemblies, preparatory and secret. This secret section was that of the Black Knights, mentioned in the preceding paragraph. The liberation and independence of Germany so, Waterloo had not effected these objects? was the subject discussed in the latter; and Russia being considered as the greatest opponent of their patriotic aspirations, the members directed their operations especially against Russian influences. It was the hatred against Russia that put the dagger into the hand of Charles Louis Sand, the student of Jena, who stabbed Kotzebue (9th March 1819), who had written against the German societies, of which there was a considerable number. This murder led to a stricter surveillance of the universities on the part of governments, and secret societies were rigorously prohibited under stern penalties; the Prussian Government, especially, being most severe, and prosecuting some of the most distinguished professors for their political opinions. The Bursclienschaft was broken up, and its objects frustrated, to be revived in 1830; the insurrectionary attempt made by some of the students at Frankfort on the 3rd April 1833, the object of which was the overthrow of the despotic, in order to establish a constitutional, government, led to the prosecution of many members of the Burschcnschaft, and to the suppression at least nominally and apparently of all their secret societies.

XIV

THE BABIS

654. Bab, the Founder - His name for Bab is a title was Ali Mohammed, and he is said to have been a Seyyid, or descendant of the family of the Prophet. He was born in 1819 at Shiraz, where his father was a merchant. Ali at first engaged in trade himself, but in 1840 he began to preach his new doctrine, declaring himself to be the Bab,[23] i.e. Door of Truth, the Mahdi. In 1843 ne made the pilgrimage to Mecca, but on his return was arrested by order of the Shah, and from 1844 to 1849 kept in semicaptivity at Ispahan and Tauris, at which latter place he was sentenced to be shot. He was suspended by cords from the walls of the citadel, and a dozen soldiers were ordered to fire at him. When the smoke from their discharges was dispelled the Bab had disappeared a cleverly-managed manoeuvre to establish a miracle. But he was soon after reapprehended, and again condemned to death. The details of his execution are not known; it is reported that he was shot. His long captivity and mysterious death were favourable to the spreading of his doctrine, as also the fact that during his life he was subject to occasional fits of frenzy, and in the East and sometimes in the West a madman is considered to be inspired. And the Bab, like all prophets, did not disdain availing himself of mundane means to propagate his new doctrines; he was greatly assisted therein by the eloquence, combined with marvellous personal beauty, of Kurratu'l Ayn, a young lady of good family, who early embraced Babism, and suffered martyrdom for it (655). The Bab was examined as to his teaching in 1848 by Nasreddin, then Crown Prince of Persia, afterwards Shah, and a number of Mullahs, the result of which inquiry was that he was sentenced to the bastinado, in consequence of which it is said he recanted and revoked all his claims; but as we have none but Mussulman historians his enemies to rely on, as the examination was

---

[23] Bab in Arabic and Chaldean means door, gate, or court; hence we have Babylon, the court of Bel; Babel-Mandeb, the gate of sorrow, probably so called on account of its dangerous navigation and rocky environs.

held with closed doors, we may doubt this statement.

655. Progress of Babism - The Bab's teaching had not only theological, but also political aims. Persian rulers have always been conservative,. but Babism was reformatory, and the common people readily embraced it, as it seemed favourable to the breaking down of the despotic powers exercised by provincial governors, by whom the country was fearfully oppressed. When, therefore, the Babis considered themselves strong enough they seized Mazanderan, about fourteen miles south-east of Barfurush; but the Shah's troops having cut off all supplies, they had to surrender, and were all slain. This was in 1847. I n 1848, on the accession of the late Shah a thousand Babis rose against him; they, however, were defeated by Mehdi Kouli Mirza, uncle of the new Shah, and the three hundred survivors who surrendered cruelly slaughtered, though they had been promised their lives. Moulla Mohammed Ali, a Bab leader, in 1849 converted seven thousand of the twelve thousand inhabitants of Zanjau, seized the town, and drove the governor from the citadel; eighteen thousand royal soldiers were sent against him, and more than eight thousand of the combatants killed, and tho surviving Babis had to surrender, and were put to death with horrible tortures. In 1850 a follower of Bab, ambitious rather than fanatical, Sayid Yahya Darabi, preached Babism at Niriz, and gathered round him two thousand followers, with whose help he hoped to hold the town. But the Shah's troops attacked him; he was assassinated by being strangled with his own girdle; the starved-out Babis had to yield, and were all cruelly butchered. In 1852 some Babis attempted to murder the Shah; the inquiry following thereon proved that at Ispahan and in all the great towns of Persia there was a vast association of Babis and Loutis, whose object was the overthrow of the reigning dynasty. All convicted of Babism were seized, and executed openly or in secret; terrible scenes were enacted by the Shah's orders in many towns of Persia during a reign of terror, which lasted nearly two years. The Shah's anger at the attempt, but especially his alarm, was so great, that to test the loyalty of his subjects he devised the "devilish scheme," as one writer calls it, of making all classes of society share in the revenge he took on the Babis.

Thus the man who had fired the shot which wounded the king was killed by the farrashes literally, the carpet-spreaders, but officially, the lictors of Eastern rulers. They first tortured him by the insertion of lighted candles in incisions made in his body. When the candles were burnt down to the flesh, the fire was for some time fed by that. In the end he was sawn in two. The Master of the Horse and the attendants of the royal stables showed their loyalty by nailing red-hot horse-shoes to the feet of the victim handed over to them, and finally " broke up his head and body with clubs and nails." Another Babi had his eyes plucked out by the artillerymen, and was then blown from a gun. Another Babi was killed by the merchants and shopkeepers of Teheran, every one of whom inflicted a wound on him until he died. Vambe'ry, in his "Wanderings and Experiences in Persia," mentions one Kasim of Niriz, who was shod with red-hot horse-shoes, had burning candles inserted in his body, all his teeth torn out, and was eventually killed by having his skull smashed in with a club. These are but a few specimens of the cruelties inflicted by order of the amiable gentleman who, on his visits to this country, was so loudly cheered by the assembled crowds. Among the victims of that persecution was Kurratu'l 'Ayn (the Consolation of Eyes), a beautiful and accomplished woman, who professed and preached Babism. The manner of her death is uncertain; some say she was burnt, others that she was strangled. Dr. Polak, who actually witnessed her execution, in his "Persia, the Land and Its Inhabitants," simply says, "I was a witness to the execution of Kurratu'l 'Ayn, which was performed by the Minister of War and his adjutants; the beautiful woman underwent her slow death with superhuman fortitude." He gives no details as to the manner of it. In spite of this persecution, or rather, in consequence of it, Babism spread with astonishing rapidity throughout Persia, even penetrating into India. Not only the lower classes, but persons of education and wealth have joined the sect. The only portion of the Persian population not affected by its doctrines appear to be the Nuseiriyeh and the Christians.

656. Babi Doctrine - It is contained in the Biyyan, the "Expositor,"

attributed to the Bab himself, and consisting of three parts written at different periods. It is to a great extent rhapsodical, frequently unintelligible. It abounds with mysticism, degenerate Platonism, beliefs borrowed from the Guebres, vestiges of Magism, and in many places displays the influence of a transformed Christianity and French philosophy of the last century, propagated as far as Persia through masonic lodges, though they were never tolerated in Persia. We shall see further on how one recently established came to grief. The Babi Koran inculcates, among other superstitions, the wearing of amulets, men in the form of a star, women in that of a circle; the cornelian is particularly recommended to be put on the fingers of the dead, all which implies a return to Aramean Paganism. The book maintains the divinity of the Bab; he and his disciples are incarnations of superior powers; forty days after death they reappear in other forms. "God," says the Biyyan, "created the world by His Will; the Will was expressed in words, but words are composed of letters; letters, therefore, possess divine properties." In giving their numerical value to the letters forming the words expressing God, they always produce the same total, viz. 19. Hence the ecclesiastical system of the Babis; their colleges are always composed of 19 priests; the year is divided into 19 months, of 19 days each; the fast of the Ramadan lasts 19 instead of 30 days. During his life Ali Mohammed chose eighteen disciples, called "Letters of the Living," who, together with himself, the "Point" (the Point of Revelation, or "First Point," from which all are created, and unto which all return), constituted the sacred hierarchy of nineteen, called the " First Unity." Now, Mirza Yahya held the fourth place in this hierarchy, and on the death of the " Point," which occurred, as already stated, in 1849, and the first two "Letters," rose to be chief of the sect; but Beha, whose proper name is Mirza Huseyn Ali of Nur, was also included in this unity, and he asserted that he was the one by whom God shall, as Bab had prophesied, make His final revelation; for, be it observed, the Babi Koran, which at present consists of eleven parts only, shall, when complete, contain nineteen, and when that revelation is made, Babism will be finished, and with it will come the end of this present world; for, according to the belief of his followers, the Bab was the forerunner of Saheb-ez-Zeman, the Lord of Ages, who resides in the air, and will not be seen till the day of resurrection.[24] In consequence of the claim of Beha the sect was split up into two divisions, the Behais and the followers of Mirza Yahya Subh-i-Ezel (the Morning of Eternity), and after him called Ezelis. The majority of the sect are Behais, and the exiled chief Yahya lives at Famagusta, in Cyprus, where Mr. Browne, the translator of the work "A Traveller's Narrative," visited him in 1890, as he also visited Beha, at Acre, shortly after. The Babis are so far in advance of their Eastern brethren that they wish to raise the status of woman, maintaining that she is entitled to the same civil rights as man; and one of their first endeavours to attain that end is that of abolishing the veil. Various charges, as against all new sects, are made against them; they are accused of being communists, of allowing nine husbands to a woman, of drinking wine, and of other unlawful practices; but proofs are wanting. It is said that they have special modes of salutation, and wear a ring of peculiar form, by which they recognise one another. They arrange their hair in a characteristic manner, and, as a rule, are clothed in white, all which practices, on the part of people who have to conceal their opinions, appears very strange to outsiders. The Bab forbade the use of tobacco, but the prohibition was withdrawn by Beha. Though only half a century old, the sect already possesses a mass of controversial writings on points of faith for in all ages men have disputed most on what they understood least. The Babis may yet become a great power in the East; in the meantime they afford us an excellent opportunity of watching within our own day the genesis and development of a new religious creed, in which vast power and authority is conferred on the priests, greatly overshadowing that of the king himself, unless he is a member of the sect, which, in fact, if the creed becomes paramount, he must be to preserve his dignity; for, according to the teaching of the founder, he who is not a Babi has no right to any possession, has no civil status. To enhance the influence of the priests, divine service is to be performed

---

[24] I find this mentioned by one writer only, Professor de Filippi, in his "Viaggio in Persia nel 1862," published in the Italian periodical Politecnico, vol. xxii. p. 252, where there is a lengthy account of the Babis.

with the utmost pomp; the temples are to be adorned with the costliest productions of nature and art.

But it is certain the doctrines of the Babis suit neither the Sunnites nor the Shiites,[25] the latter of whom are the dominant religious party in Persia, and who particularly objected to the Bab's claim of being the promised Mahdi, whose advent was to be ushered in by prodigious signs, which, however, were not witnessed in the Bab's case. The latter also was opposed by the new Sheykhi school. Early in this century Sheykh Ahmad of Ahsa preached a new doctrine, considered heterodox by true believers; still he found many adherents, and on his death, about the year 1827, was succeeded by his disciple Haji Seyyid Kazim of Resht. He died in 1844, prophesying the coming of one greater than himself. Then Mirza Ali Mahammad, who came in contact with some disciples of the deceased Seyyid Kazim, saw his opportunity, and proclaimed himself the Bab; the old Sheykhi party strongly supported him. But some of the followers of Seyyid Kazim did not accept the new prophet, and became, as the new Sheykhi party, his most violent persecutors. The Bab consequently called the leader of the latter party the "Quintessence of Hell-fire," whilst he, in his turn, wrote a treatise against the Bab, entitled, "The Crushing of Falsehood." From such mutual courtesies the transition to mutual recrimination and accusation of objectionable teaching and practice is easy, and consequently quite usual, and therefore not to be too readily believed.

657. Recent History of Babism - The fearful reprisals the late Shah in 1852 took on the sect of the Babis, whatever may be thought of their moral aspect, appear to have had the desired political effect. From that day till the recent assassination of the Shah, the outcome of old grievances, and of an uncalled-for renewal of a fierce persecution, they have committed no overt act of hostility against the Persian Government or people, though their number and strength are now double what they were in 1852. But this has not softened the feeling of

---

[25] According to the doctrine of the Sunnites, the Imamate, or viceregency of the prophet, is a matter to be determined by the choice and election of his followers; according to the Shiites, it is a matter altogether spiritual, having nothing to do with popular choice or approval.

the Shah or of the Mullahs against them. This was clearly shown in 1863. In that year a Persian who had travelled in Europe suggested to the Shah the establishment of a masonic lodge, with himself as the grand master, whereby he would have a moral guarantee of the fidelity of his subjects, since all persons of importance and influence would no doubt become members, and masonic oaths cannot be broken. The Shah granted permission, without, however, being initiated himself; a lodge, called the Feramoush-Khanek, the "House of Oblivion" since on leaving the lodge the member was supposed to forget all he had seen in it was speedily opened, and the Shah urged all his courtiers to join it. He then questioned them as to what they had seen in it, but their answers were unsatisfactory; they had listened to some moral discourse, drunk tea, and smoked. The Shah could not understand that the terrible mysteries of Freemasonry, of which he had heard so much, could amount to no more than this; he therefore surmised that a great deal was withheld from him, and became dissatisfied. This dissatisfaction was taken advantage of by some of his friends who disliked the innovation, and they suggested to him that the lodge was probably the home of the grossest debauchery, and, finally, that it was a meetingplace of Babis. Debauchery the Shah might have winked at, but Babism could not be tolerated. The lodge was immediately ordered to be closed, and the author of its establishment banished from Persia. In quite recent times the Babis have undergone grievous persecutions. In 1888 Seyyid Hasan and Seyyid Huseyn were put to death by order of the then Shah's eldest son, Prince Zillu's Sultan, for refusing to abjure Babism. When dead their bodies were dragged by the feet through the street and bazaars of Ispahan, and cast out of the gate beyond the city walls. In the month of October of the same year Aga Mirza Ashraf of Abade was murdered for his religion, and the Mullas mutilated the poor body in the most savage manner. In 1890 the Babi inhabitants of a district called Seh-deh were attacked by a mob, and seven or eight of them killed, and their bodies burnt with oil. But it appears that on various occasions the Shah restrained the fanaticism of would-be persecutors of the Babis; it did not, however, save him from the vengeance sworn against him by the sect for former persecutions.

On the 1st May 1896 Nasreddin Shah, the Defender of the Faith, was shot in the mosque of Shah Abdul Azim, near Teheran, and died immediately after he was brought back to the city. The assassin, who was at once arrested, was Mirza Mahomed Eeza of Kirman, a follower of Jemal-ed-din, who was exiled for an attempt at dethroning the Shah in 1891. After Jemal's departure Mahomed Reza was imprisoned; after some time he was set free, but continuing to speak against the Persian Government, he was again imprisoned, but some time after obtained his release, and even a pension from the Shah. He confessed that he was chosen to kill the Shah, and that he bought a revolver for the purpose, but had to wait two months for a favourable opportunity. His execution, some months after the deed has it inspired the Babis with sufficient dread to deter them from similar attempts in the future?

XV

IRISH SOCIETIES

658. The White-Boys - Ireland, helpless against misery and superstition, misled by hatred against her conquerors, the rulers of England, formed sects to fight not so much the evil, as the supposed authors of the evil. The first secret society of Ireland, recorded in public documents, dates from 1761, in which year the situation of the peasants, always bad, had become unbearable. They were deprived of the right of free pasture, and the proprietors, in seven cases out of nine not Irish landlords, but Englishmen by blood and sympathy, began to enclose the commons. Fiscal oppression also became very great. Reduced to despair, the conspirators had recourse to reprisals, and to make these with more security, formed the secret society of the "White- Boys," so called, because in the hope of disguising themselves, they wore over their clothes a white shirt, like the Camisards of the Cevennes. They also called themselves "Levellers," because their object was to level to the ground the fences of the detested enclosures. In November 1761 they spread through Munster, committing all kinds of excesses during the next four-and-twenty years.

659. Right-Boys and Oak-Boys - In 1787 the above society disappeared to make room for the "Right-Boys," who by legal means aimed at obtaining the reduction of imposts, higher wages, the abolition of degrading personal services, and the erection of a Roman Catholic church for every Protestant church in the island. Though the society was guilty of some reprehensible acts against Protestant pastors, it yet, as a rule, remained within the limits of legal opposition. The vicious administration introduced into Ireland after the rising of 1788, the burden of which was chiefly felt by the Roman Catholics, could not but prove injurious to the Protestants also. The inhabitants, whether Catholic or Protestant, were subject to objectionable personal service hence petitions rejected by the haughty rulers, tumults quenched in blood, whole populations conquered by fear, but not subdued, and

ready to break forth into insurrection when it was least expected. Therefore the Protestants also formed societies for their security, taking for their emblem the oakleaf, whence they were known as the "Oak-Boys." Their chief object was to lessen the power and imposts of the clergy. Established in 1764, the society made rapid progress, especially in the province of Ulster, where it had been founded. Unable to obtain legally what it aimed at, it had recourse to arms, but was defeated by the royal troops of England, and dissolved.

660. Hearts-of-Steel, Threshers, Brealc-of-Day-Boys, Defenders, United Irishmen, Ribbonmen - Many tenants of the Marquis of Donegal having about eight years after been ejected from their farms, because the marquis, wanting to raise £100,000, let their holdings to Belfast merchants, they, the tenants, formed themselves into a society called "Hearts-of-Steel," thereby to indicate the perseverance with which they intended to pursue their revenge against those who had succeeded them on the land, by murdering them, burning their farms, and destroying their harvests. They were not suppressed till 1773, when thousands of the affiliated fled to America, where they entered the ranks of the revolted colonists. The legislative union of Ireland with England in 1800 did not at first benefit the former country much. New secret societies were formed, the most important of which was that of the "Threshers," whose primary object was the reduction of the exorbitant dues claimed by the clergy of both persuasions, and sometimes their conduct showed both generous impulses and grim humour. Thus a priest in the county of Longford had charged a poor woman double fees for a christening, on account of there being twins. The Threshers soon paid him a visit, and compelled him to pay a sum of money, with which a cow was purchased, and sent home to the cabin of the poor woman. This was in 1807.

Government called out the whole yeomanry force to oppose these societies, but without much success. Political and religious animosities were further sources of conspiracy. Two societies of almost the same nature were formed about 1785. The first was composed of Protestants, the " Break of-Day-Boys," who at dawn committed all sorts of excesses against the wretched Roman Catholics, burning their huts, and destroying their agricultural implements and produce. The Roman Catholics in return formed themselves into a society of "Defenders," and from defence, as was natural, proceeded to aggression. During the revolt of 1798 the Defenders combined with the " United Irishmen," who had initiated the movement. The United Irish were defeated, and their leader, Lord Edward Fitzgerald, having been betrayed by Francis Higgins, originally a pot-boy, and afterwards proprietor of the Freeman's Journal, was taken and condemned to death; but he died of his wounds before the time fixed for his execution. The society of the United Irish, however, was not dispersed. Its members still continued to hold secret meetings, and to reappear in the political arena under the denomination of "Ribbonrnen," so named because they recognised each other by certain ribbons. The Ribbonman's oath, which only became known in 1895, was as follows: "In the presence of Almighty God and this my brother, I do swear that I will suffer my right hand to be cut off my body and laid at the gaol door before I will waylay or betray a brother. That I will persevere, and will not spare from the cradle to the crutch or the crutch to the cradle, that I will not pity the groans or moans of infancy or old age, but that I will wade knee-deep in Orangemen's blood, and do as King James did."

661. St. Patrick Boys - These seem to have issued from the ranks of the Ribbonmen. Their statutes were discovered and published in 1833. Their oath was: "I swear to have my right hand cut off, or to be nailed to the door of the prison at Armagh, rather than deceive or betray a brother; to persevere in the cause to which I deliberately devote myself; to pardon neither sex nor age, should it be in the way of my vengeance against the Orangemen." The brethren recognised each other by dialogues. "Here is a fine day!" "A finer one is to come." "The road is very bad." "It shall be repaired." "What with?" "With the bones of Protestants." "What is your profession of faith?" "The discomfiture of the Philistines." "How long is your stick?" "Long enough to reach my enemies." "To what trunk does the wood belong?" "To a French

trunk that blooms in America, and whose leaves shall shelter the sons of Erin." Their aim was chiefly the redress of agrarian and social grievances.

662. The Orangemen - This society, against which the St. Patrick Boys swore such terrible vengeance, was a Protestant society. Many farms, taken from Roman Catholics, having fallen into the hands of Protestants, these latter were, as we have seen (660), exposed to the attacks of the former. The Protestants in self-defence formed themselves into a society, taking the name of "Orangemen," to indicate their Protestant character and principles. Their first regular meeting was held on the 2ist September 1795, at the obscure village of Loughgall, which was attended by deputies of the Breakof- Day-Boys (660), and constituted into a grand lodge, authorised to found minor lodges. At first the society had only one degree: Orangeman. Afterwards, in I 796, the Purple degree was added; after that, the Mark Man's degree and the Heroine of Jericho (see 701) were added, but eventually discarded. The oath varied but little from that of the entered Apprentice Mason, for Thomas Wilson, the founder of the Order, was a Freemason. The password was Migdol (the name of the place where the Israelites encamped before they passed through the Red Sea Exod. xiv. 2); the main password was Shibboleth. The pass sign was made by lifting the hat with the right hand, three fingers on the brim, then putting the three fingers on the crown, and pressing the hat down; then darting off the hand to the front, with the thumb and little finger together. This sign having been discovered, it was changed to exhibiting the right hand with three fingers on the thigh or knee, or marking the figure three with the finger on the knee. This was the half sign; the full sign was by placing the first three fingers of each hand upon the crown of the hat, raising the elbows as high as possible, and then dropping the hand perpendicularly by the side. This sign was said to be emblematical of the lintels and side-posts of the doors, on which the blood of the passover lamb was sprinkled. The distress word of a brother Orangeman was, "Who is on my side? who?" (2 Kings ix. 32). The grand hailing sign was made by standing with both hands resting

on the hips. In the Purple degree the member was asked, "What is your number?" "Two and a half." The grand main word was, "Red Walls" (the Red Sea). The password was Gideon, given in syllables. The society spread over the whole island, and also into England, and especially into the manufacturing districts. A grand lodge was established at Manchester, which was afterwards transferred to London, and its grand master was no less a person than the Duke of York. At the death of that prince, which occurred in 1821, the Duke of Cumberland, afterwards King of Hanover, succeeded him both of them men to have the interests of religion confided to them! In 1835 the Irish statutes, having been revised, were made public. The society bound its members over to defend the royal family, so long as it remained faithful to Protestant principles. In the former statutes there were obligations also to abjure the supremacy of the Court of Rome and the dogma of transnbstantiation; and although in the modern statutes these were omitted, others of the same tendency were substituted, the society declaring that its object was the preservation of the religion established by law, the Protestant succession of the crown, and the protection of the lives and property of the affiliated. To concede something to the spirit of the age, it proclaimed itself theoretically the friend of religious toleration; but facts have shown this, as in most similar cases, to be a mere illusion. From England the sect spread into Scotland, the Colonies, Upper and Lower Canada, where it reckoned 12,000 members; and into the army, with some fifty lodges. In the United States the society has latterly been showing its toleration! Its political action is well known; it endeavours to influence parliamentary elections, supporting the Whigs. The efforts of the British House of Commons to suppress it have hitherto been ineffectual.

That the custom of indulging in disgraceful mummeries at the ceremony of initiation into this Order has not gone out of fashion, is proved by an action brought in January 1897, in the Middlesex (Massachusetts) Superior Court by one Frank Preble against the officers of a lodge, he having at his initiation been repeatedly struck, when blindfolded, with a rattan, hoisted on a step-ladder, and thrown into a sheet, from which he was several times tossed into the air. Afterwards a red-hot iron was brought to his breast, and he was severely burnt. The jury disagreed, but the outside world will not disagree as to the character of such proceedings.

Other Irish societies, having for their chief object the redress of agrarian and religious grievances, were the "Corders," in East and West Meath; the "Shanavests" and "Caravats" in Tipperary, Kilkenny, Cork, and Limerick; the Whitefeet and Blackfeet, and others, which need not be more fully particularised.

663. Molly Maguires - This Irish sect was the successor of the White-Boys, the Hearts of Oak, and other societies, and carried on its operations chiefly in the West of Ireland. It afterwards spread to America, where it committed great outrages, especially in the Far West. Thus in 1870 the Molly Maguires became very formidable in Utah, where no Englishman was safe from their murderous attacks, and the officers of the law were unable, or unwilling, to bring the criminals to justice. This led to the formation of a counter society, consisting of Englishmen, who united themselves into the Order of the Sons of St. George, who were so successful as to cause many of the murderers to be apprehended and executed, and ultimately the Molly Maguires were totally suppressed. The Order of St. George, however, continued to exist, and still exists, as a flourishing benefit society; it has lodges in Salt Lake City, Ogden, and other towns in Utah. The name of Molly Maguires was afterwards adopted by a secret society of miners in the Pennsylvanian anthracite districts; with the name of their Irish prototypes they assumed their habits, the consequence of which was that in 1890 ten or twelve members of the society were hanged, and the society was entirely broken up.

664. Ancient Order of Hibernians - This Order is widely diffused throughout the United States, where it numbers about 6000 lodges. It is divided into two degrees, in the first of which, counting most members, no oath is exacted, and no secrets are communicated. But the second consists of the initiated, bound together by terrible oaths, and

who receive their passwords from a central committee, called the Board of Erin, who meet either in England, Scotland, or Ireland, and every three months send emissaries to New York with a new password. Their avowed object is the protection of Irishmen in America they receive only Roman Catholics into the society but they are accused of having given great encouragement and assistance to the Molly Maguires, above spoken of, and also of having greatly swelled the ranks of the Fenians. The bulk, however, of the Hibernians ignore the criminal objects of their chiefs; hence the toleration they enjoy in the States, a toleration they undoubtedly deserve, for they have recently (November 1896) nobly distinguished themselves by providing; 10,000 for the endowment of a chair of Celtic in the Roman Catholic University of New York.

665. Origin and Organisation of Fenianism - The founders of Fenianism were two of the Irish exiles of 1848, Colonel John O'Mahoney and Michael Doheny, the latter one of the most talented and dangerous members of the Young Ireland party, and a fervent admirer of John Mitchel. O'Mahoney belonged to one of the oldest families in Munster, but becoming implicated in Smith O'Brien's machinations and failure, he made his escape to France, and thence to America, where, in conjunction with Doheny and General Corcoran, he set the Fenian Brotherhood afloat. It was at first a semisecret association; its meetings were secret, and though its chief officers were publicly known as such, the operations of the Brotherhood were hidden from the public view. It rapidly increased in numbers, spreading through every State of the American Union, through Canada, and the British provinces. But in November 1 863 the Fenian organisation assumed a new character. A grand national convention of delegates met at Chicago, and avowed the object of the Brotherhood, namely, the separation of Ireland from England, and the establishment of an Irish republic, the same changes being first to be effected in Canada. Another grand convention was held in 1864 at Cincinnati, the delegates at which represented some 250,000 members, each of which members was called upon for a contribution of five dollars, and this

call, it is said, was promptly responded to. Indeed, the reader will presently see that the leaders of the movement were never short of money, whatever the dupes were. One of the resolutions passed at Cincinnati was that "the next convention should be held on Irish soil." About the same time a Fenian Sisterhood was established, and the ladies were not inactive; for in two months from their associating they returned upwards of 200,000 sterling to the Fenian exchequer for the purpose of purchasing arms and other war material. At that period the Fenians confidently relied on the assistance of the American Government. The New York press rather favoured this notion. In Ireland the Brotherhood never attained to the dimensions it reached in the United States, and without the assistance of the latter could do nothing. Still the Irish, as well as the American Fenian, association had its chiefs, officers, both civil and military, its common fund and financial agencies, its secret oaths, passwords, and emblems, its laws and penalties, its concealed stores of arms, its nightly drills, its correspondents and agents, its journals, and even its popular songs and ballads. But traitors soon set to work to destroy the organisation from within. Thus the Head Centre O'Mahoney, who was in receipt of an official salary of 2000 dollars, is thus spoken of in the Official Report of the Investigating Committee of the Fenian Brotherhood of America (1866):

"After a careful examination of the affairs of the Brotherhood, your Committee finds in almost every instance the cause of Ireland made subservient to individual gain; men who were lauded as patriots sought every opportunity to plunder the treasury of the Brotherhood, but legalised their attacks by securing the endorsement of John O'Mahoney. ... In John O'Mahoney's integrity the confidence of the Brotherhood was boundless, and the betrayal of that confidence, whether through incapacity or premeditation, is not a question for us to determine.... Sufficient that he has proved recreant to the trust.... Never in the history of the Irish people did they repose so much confidence in their leaders; never before were they so basely deceived and treacherously dealt with. In fact, the Moffat mansion (the headquarters of the American Fenians) was not only an almshouse for pauper officials and hungry adventurers, but a general telegraph office for the Canadian authorities and Sir Frederick Bruce, the British Minister at Washington. These paid patriots and professional martyrs, not satisfied with emptying our treasury, connived at posting the English authorities in advance of our movements."

From this report it further appears that in 1866 there was in the Fenian treasury in the States a sum of 185,000 dollars; that the expenses of the Moffat mansion and the parasites who flocked thither in three months amounted to 104,000 dollars; and that Stephens, the Irish Head Centre, in the same space of time received from America, in money sent to Paris, the sum of upwards of 106,000 dollars, though John O'Mahoney in many of his letters expressed the greatest mistrust of Stephens. He no doubt looked upon the latter as the more clever and daring rogue, who materially diminished his own share of the spoil. Stephens's career in Ireland is sufficiently well known, and there is scarcely any doubt that whilst he was leading his miserable associates to their ruin, he acted as spy upon them, and that there existed some understanding between him and the English authorities. How else can we explain his living for nearly two months in the neighbourhood of Dublin, in a house magnificently furnished, whilst he took no precautions to conceal himself, and yet escaped the vigilance of the police for so long a time? His conduct when at last apprehended, his bravado in the police court and final escape from prison, his traversing the streets of Dublin, sailing for Scotland, travelling through London to France without once being molested all point to the same conclusion. The only other person of note among the Fenians was John Mitchel, who had been implicated in the troubles of 1848, was transported, escaped, and made his way to the United States. During the civil war which raged in that country he was a supporter of the Southern cause, was taken prisoner by the North, but liberated by the President at the request of the Fenians in America.

The Fenian agitation also spread into England. Meetings were held in various towns, especially at Liverpool, where men of considerable means were found to support the Fenian objects and organisations; and on one occasion as much as £200 was collected in a few minutes in the room where a meeting was held. But disputes about the money thus collected were ever arising. The man who acted as treasurer to the Liverpool Centre, when accused of plundering his brethren, snapped his fingers at them, and declared that if they bothered him about the money he would give evidence against them and have the whole lot hanged. The Fenians, to raise money, issued bonds to be redeemed by the future Irish Republic, of one of which the following is a facsimile:

Harp.	£1	Goddess of Liberty.	£1	Shamrock.
\multicolumn{5}{c}{Ninety days after the establishment of **THE IRISH REPUBLIC**}
\multicolumn{3}{l}{Redeemable by _____}	\multicolumn{2}{l}{Board of Finance.}
Sunburst.				

666. Origin of Name - Irish tradition says that the Fenians were an ancient militia employed on home service for protecting the coasts from invasion. Each of the four provinces had its band, that of Leinster, to which Fionn and his family belonged, being at the head of the others. This Fionn is the Fin gal of MacPherson, and the leaders of the movement no doubt saw an advantage in connecting their party with the historical and traditionary glories of Ireland. But the Fenians were not confined to Erin. The name was invented for the society by O'Mahoney, but the Irish never adopted it; they called their association the Irish Republican Brotherhood, or briefly, the I. R. B. Fenianism was officially restricted to the American branch of the movement.

667. Fenian Litany - From the Patriotic Litany of Saint Lawrence O'Toole, published for the use of the Fenian Brotherhood, the following extract may suffice:

" Call to thine aid, most liberty-loving O'Toole, those Christian auxiliaries of power and glory the soul-inspiring cannon, the meek and faithful musket, the pious rifle, and the conscience-examining pike, which, tempered by a martyr's faith, a Fenian's hope, and a rebel's charity, will triumph over the devil, and restore to us our own in our own land for ever. Amen.

O'Toole, hear us.
From English civilisation,
From British law and order,
From Anglo-Saxon cant and freedom,
From the hest of the English Queen,
From Rule Britannia,
From the cloven hoof,
From the necessity of annual rebellion,
From billeted soldiery,
From a pious church establishment,
} *O'Toole, deliver us!*

Fenianism to be stamped out like the cattle plague!

We will prove them false prophets, O'Toole.

Ireland reduced to obedience,
Ireland loyal to the crown,
Ireland pacified with concessions,
Ireland to recruit the British army,
Ireland not united in effort,
} *It is a falsehood, O'Toole.*

Ireland never again to be dragged at the tail of any other nation!

Proclaim it on high, O'Toole.

668. Events from 1865 to 1871 - In speaking of Stephens, it was mentioned that he was a spy on the Fenians, but he was not the only informer that betrayed his confederates to the English Government; which latter, in consequence of "information thus received," made its first descent on the Brotherhood in 1865, at the office of the Irish People, and captured some of the leading Fenians. Shortly after, it seized Stephens, who, however, was allowed to make his escape from Richmond Prison, where he had been confined, in the night of November 24 of the above year. Further arrests took place in other parts of Ireland, and also at Liverpool, Manchester, and other English towns. The prisoners were indicted for treason-felony, and sentenced

to various degrees of punishment. Various raids into Canada, and the attempt on Chester Castle, all ending in failure, next showed that Fenianism was still alive. But it was more prominently again brought before the public by the attack at Manchester, in September 1867, on the police van conveying two leaders of the Fenian conspiracy, Kelly and Deasey, to the city prison, who were enabled to make their escape, whilst Sergeant Brett was shot dead by William O'Meara Allen, who was hanged for the deed. A still more atrocious and fatal Fenian attempt was that made on the Clerkenwell House of Detention, with a view of liberating two Fenian prisoners, Burke and Casey, when a great length of the outer wall of the prison was blown up by gunpowder, which also destroyed a whole row of houses opposite, killed several persons, and wounded and maimed a great number. On that occasion again Government had received information of the intended attempt by traitors in the camp, but strangely enough failed to take proper precautionary measures. On December 24, 1867, the Fenians made an attack on the Martello Tower at Fota, near Queenstown, Co. Cork, and carried off a quantity of arms and ammunition; and their latest exploit, in 1871, was another Canadian raid, when they crossed the border at Pembina, and seized the Canadian Custom-House and Hudson's Bay post. They were, however, attacked and dispersed by American troops, and General O'Neil was made prisoner. This raid, the object of which was to secure a base of action, and also to receive from the American Government a recognition of belligerency, was carried out totally independently of the new Irish Fenian confederation, of which O'Donovan Rossa was the moving spirit; and the Irish papers therefore pooh-poohed the account of this fiasco altogether, or merely gave the telegrams, denying that the enterprise had any connection with Fenianism. About this time it seemed as if the Fenian Brotherhood was breaking up; O'Donovau Rossa retired from the "Directory" of the confederation, and went into the wine trade. The Fenians themselves denounced the notorious Stephens, who reappeared in America, as a "traitor" and government informer; and though the acquittal of Kelly for the murder of head-constable Talbot seemed to point to a strong sympathy surviving amongst the Irish people with Fenianism, the jury perhaps could give no other verdict than the one they arrived at, the prosecution having been altogether mismanaged by the Government.

669. The Soi-disant General Cluseret - Another personage had in the meantime become connected with the Fenians, a soi-disant General Cluseret, who had been a captain in the French army, but had been compelled to quit it in consequence of some irregularity in the regimental funds, of which Cluseret had kept the books and the cash. He afterwards served with Garibaldi in Sicily, and Fremont in the United States, after which he bestowed on himself the rank of General. He came to Europe with the mission of reporting to the Fenians of New York on English arsenals, magazines, and ports of entry. In an article published by him in Fraser in 1872, entitled, "My Connection with Fenianism," he tells the world that he offered to command the Fenians if 10,000 men could be raised, but the money to do so was not forthcoming. He asserted that he had communications with the Reform League, whose members favoured his designs; but he failed, as he says, because he had a knot of self-seekers and ignorant intriguers to deal with; "and traitors," he might have added, for it is certain that the intended attack on Chester Castle failed because the English Government had had early notice of the plot. A rising Cluseret attempted to head in Ireland came to grief, and the general speedily made his escape to France, where he became mixed up with the Commune (507).

670. Phoenix Park Murders, and Consequences - Fenianism for a time was quiescent, but about 1880 the Land League was established, and by its agents, the "Moonlighters," entered on a course of outrages, chiefly against farmers for paying rent, which has not yet ceased, though their leader, D. Connell, and a number of his followers were apprehended early in 1882. This year was farther distinguished in the annals of crime by the murder of Lord F. Cavendish, the Chief Secretary for Ireland, and Mr. Thomas Burke, the Under- Secretary, in Phoenix Park, Dublin; but the assassins were not apprehended until January 1883, one of the guilty parties, James Carey, having turned

informer. He received a pardon, and was sent out of the country, but shortly after shot by O'Donnell, who was executed for this murder. The law, of course, cannot sanction the slaying of an informer, but public sentiment says, "Served him right," especially in this case, as Carey was as deeply implicated in the Phoenix Park murders as any of the other criminals. The trial of these led to the disclosure of an organisation known as the "Irish Invincibles," whose chief was P. J. Tynan, who passed under the sobriquet of Number One, and which organisation was the instigator and executor of the Phoenix Park and of many other murders, including, for instance, the massacre of the Maamtrasna family.

671. Dynamite Outrages - In this year (1882) the Fenians began the use of dynamite; a large quantity of this material was discovered, together with a quantity of arms, concealed in a vault in the town of Cork; later on the Fenians attempted the storing up of dynamite and arms in London and other English towns; a considerable number of rifles and large quantities of ammunition were seized in a house at Islington in July 1882; dynamite was sent to this country from America, but its introduction being difficult, the Fenians attempted to manufacture it here; a laboratory, stocked with large quantities of the raw and finished material, was discovered at Ladywood, near Birmingham, in April 1883. Still, the explosive and infernal machines continued to be smuggled into this country, and attempts were made to blow up public buildings in London and elsewhere, the attempts, however, doing, fortunately in most cases, but little harm. One of the most serious was the one made at Glasgow early in 1883. In a manifesto issued in April 1884 by the Fenian brotherhood, signed by Patrick Joyce, secretary, the Fenians call this " inaugurating scientific warfare," and declare their intention to persevere until they have attained their object, the freedom of Ireland. In December 1884 an attempt to blow up London Bridge with dynamite had no other result but to blow up the two men who made the attempt; the chief instigators of all these attempts were two American organisations; the first was that of O'Donovan Eossa, the second that of the association

called the Clan-na-Gael. Rossa had agents in Cork, London, and Glasgow; but two of the most important, Fetherstone (whose real name is Kennedy) and Dalton, were apprehended, and sentenced to penal servitude for life. Since then the party of Rossa has been powerless. An unsuccessful attempt on O'Donovan Rossa's life was made early in 1885 by an English lady, a Mrs. Dudley. Within a fortnight after an advertisement appeared in O'Donovan's paper, offering a reward of ten thousand dollars for the body of the Prince of Wales, dead or alive. And yet, but a few months ago (1896), this would-be assassin, or instigator of assassination, was permitted to walk about in England, in perfect freedom, and even to enter the Houses of Parliament! The Clan-na-Gael is a more serious affair; originally it was a purely patriotic scheme for the removal of British power over Ireland; it did not advocate the slaughter of innocent people by the indiscriminate use of dynamite. But eventually a certain violent faction obtained control, and gained possession of the large funds of the Clan, the bulk of which they absorbed for their own enrichment. Dr. Cronin, who could have proved this, was murdered. The branches of the Clan-na-Gael extend over the whole of the United States. Its heads are three in number: Alexander Sullivan, of Chicago; General Michael Kerwin, of New York; and Colonel Michael Boland, of the same city. Sullivan was a great friend of Patrick Egan, the treasurer of the Land League. One of the agents of the Clan-na-Gael was John Daly, who intended to blow up the House of Commons by throwing a dynamite bomb on the table of the House from the Strangers' Gallery. He was arrested at Chester in April 1884, and sentenced to penal servitude for life. The attempts on the House of Commons, and the explosions at the Tower and Victoria Railway Station, were also the work of the Clan-na-Gael, twenty-five members of which have been condemned to penal servitude, two-thirds of them for life. John S. Walsh, residing in Paris, and the Ford family in America, are also known as dangerous agents of the association. The dynamiters were not quite so active after the capture and conviction of so many of their party, but confined themselves to occasional and comparatively insignificant attempts, but murder was rife in Ireland. These events, however, are now, thanks to the Report of the Judges of the Parnell Commission, so easily accessible to every reader, that they need not be specified here.

672. The National League - This is scarcely an association, though generally considered such. It is not an Irish production, but created in a foreign land, and directed by foreign agents, whose designs are unknown. The people have given their allegiance to it because of the large bribes it offered to their cupidity, and the fear it inspired. The secret societies give the League their assistance, without which it would be powerless. But the real heads who direct the operations of the rank and file keep carefully out of the way; but whilst the rank and file know they have nothing to fear from the people, who will not give them up, they know that any one of their own body may at any time betray them by turning informer. The Invincibles held their own for a long time, but once the police got hold of them, informers appeared in every direction. This shows, according to Ross of -- Bladensburg, in Murray's Magazine, December 1887, from which I quote, that the Irish have no real faith in their own cause; that they are not, like the Nihilists, honest patriots, prepared to suffer in a cause they consider just, but a people led astray by a band of selfish agitators, whose machinations -are pleasantly exposed in the following passages, with which I will endeavour to give an enlivening finish to this necessarily dry account of the Fenian movement up to 1888.

673. Comic Aspects of Fenianism - In "The New Gospel of Peace according to St. Benjamin," an American publication of the year 1867, the author says: " About those days there arose certain men, Padhees, calling themselves Phainyans, who conspired together to wrest the isle of Ouldairin from the queen of the land of Jonbool. Now it was from the isle of Ouldairin that the Padhees came into the land of Unculpsalm. . . . Although the Padhees never had established government or administered laws in Ouldairin, they diligently sought instead thereof to have shyndees therein, first with the men who sought to establish a government for them; but if not with them, then with each other. . . . Now the Padhees in the land of Unculpsalm said one to

another, Are we not in the land of Unculpsalm, where the power of Jonbool cannot touch us, and we are many and receive money; let us therefore conspire to make a great shyndee in the isle of Ouldairin. . . . And they took a large upper room and they placed men at the outside of the outer door, clad in raiment of green and gold, and having drawn swords in their hands. For they said, How shall men know that we are conspiring secretly, unless we set a guard over ourselves? And they chose a chief man to rule them, and they called him the Hid-Sinter, which, being interpreted, is the top-middle; for, in the tongue of the Padhees, hid is top, and sinter is middle. . . . And it came to pass that after many days the Hid-Sinter sent out tax-gatherers, and they went among the Padhees, and chiefly among the Bidhees throughout the city of Gotham, and the other cities in the land of Unculpsalm, and they gathered tribute, . . . and the sum thereof was great, even hundreds of thousands of pieces of silver. Then the Hid-Sinter and his chief officers took unto themselves a great house and spacious in the city of Gotham, . . . and fared sumptuously therein, and poured out drink-offerings night and day unto the isle of Ouldairin. And they set up a government therein, which they called the government of Ouldairin, and chose unto themselves certain lawgivers, which they called the Sinnit. . . . Now it came to pass when certain of the Padhees, Phainyans, saw that the Hid-Sinter and his chief officers . . . fared sumptuously every day, . . . and lived as if all their kinsfolk were dying day by day, and there was a ouaic without end, that their souls were moved with envy, and they said each within his own heart, Why should I not live in a great house and fare sumptuously? But unto each other and unto the world they said: Behold, the HidSinter and his officers do not govern Ouldairn righteously, and they waste the substance of the people. Let us therefore declare their government to be at an end, and let us set up a new government, with a new Hid-Sinter, and a new Sinnit, even ourselves. And they did so. And they declared that the first Hid-Sinter was no longer Hid-Sinter, but that their Hid-Sinter was the real Hid-Sinter, . . . and moreover they especially declared that tribute-money should no more be paid to the first Hid-Sinter, but unto theirs. But the first Hid-Sinter and his officers would not be set at nought, . . . and so it came to pass that there were three governments for the isle of Ouldairn; one in the land of Jonbool, and two in the city of Gotham in the land of Unculpsalm. But when the Phanyans gathered unto themselves men, Padhees, in the island of Ouldairin, who went about there in the night-time, with swords and with spears and with staves, the governors sent there by the queen of Jonbool took those men and cast some of them into prison, and banished others into a far country," &c.

674. Events from 1888 to 1896 - The revelations made in 1888 and 1890 before the "Special Commission," have rendered the history of the Fenian conspiracy quite familiar up to that date. Of subsequent events the following are noteworthy. On the 22d October 1890 the Convention of the Fenian brotherhood in America was held at New Jersey, when it was resolved to make it an open association de facto, it was already so after the disclosures before the Commission the council only being bound by oath, and that the object should be to form naval and military volunteer forces to aid the United States in the event of war with any foreign State. At a convention held at New York in July 1891, it was again argued that the only organisation now advisable was one with a military basis. The Clan-na-Gael continued to hold abortive meetings; outrages of every kind, including murder, were rife in Ireland up to 1892, since which time Ireland is supposed to be pacified, though the frequently repeated dynamite outrages in England, and the revival of Fenianism in America, would lead to a very different conclusion. As to this revival, the Irish Convention, commonly called "the physical force convention," met in September 1895 at Chicago, and resolved on the formation of a permanent organisation for the recovery, by arms, of Irish independence. Among the delegates there were more than one thousand present were O'Donovan Rossa and Tynan (No. 1), and the chairman, Mr. John Finerty, ex-member of Congress.

   In August 1896 a Belfast paper stated that, owing to the discovery of a secret society of Ribbonmen in Armagh, special detective duty had been ordered by the constabulary authorities at

Dublin Castle.

And yet, in spite of all this, Government has recently released some of the most atrocious dynamiters, originally and justly sentenced to lifelong penal servitude!

In September 1896, the notorious Patrick Tynan, known under the name of No. I, and who was implicated in the Phoenix Park murders, was arrested at Boulogne; but the demand of the British Government for his extradition was refused by that of France, on the grounds that sufficient evidence identifying him with No. I had not been produced; that even if such identification were established, there was not sufficient proof to identify Tynan as one of the men who participated in the murder of Mr. Burke; and, lastly, that his case was covered by "prescription," which in France is acquired after ten years, an extension to twenty years being allowed only after a trial at which the accused had been present. But Tynan had effected his escape after the murders. And so he was set at liberty by the French Government, though it was shown that he had been in frequent communication whilst at Boulogne with English dynamiters, plotting against England at that very time. Of course the French acted on the strict letter of the Code Napoleon and of the Extradition Treaty between the two countries; but when the law and the treaty afford such loopholes to the vilest of criminals, it is high time both were revised. On his release from the French prison, Tynan wrote a long letter to his wife why should it be published? in which he expresses his admiration of Russian civilisation (!), and thanks God for tempering the wind to the shorn lamb (!). Beware of a murderer who gives vent to such language; he is more dangerous than the one who is violent and brutal in his speech.

675. Most Recent Revelations - One of the dynamiters whom Tynan had been in close and recent communication with was Edward J. Ivory, alias Bell, an American, who had been apprehended on British territory, and was charged at the Bow Street Police Court, on the 13th November 1896, with conspiring with others to cause dynamite explosions within the United Kingdom. He was committed for trial, but when that took place at the Old Bailey, in January 1897, the prosecution, in

spite of the fact that the prisoner's movements gave room for very grave suspicions, suddenly collapsed on a purely technical point, and Ivory was, by the judge's direction, pronounced "Not guilty" by the jury, and of course immediately discharged. Were it necessary to vindicate the impartiality of English justice, and its tender regard for the interests and claims of a person accused, the issue of this trial would afford a very striking and honourable instance of both. How far the interests of justice, the maintenance of law, and the dignity of the country are served by such verdicts, is altogether a different question, the answer to which cannot be satisfactory.

BOOK XIV

MISCELLANEOUS SOCIETIES

676. ABC Friends, The - A society whose avowed scope was the education of children, its real object the liberty of man. They called themselves members of the ABC, letters which in French are pronounced abaisst; but the abased that were to be raised were the people. The members were few, but select. They had two lodges in Paris during the Restoration. Victor Hugo has introduced the society in *Les Misérables*, part iii. book iv.

677. Abelites - A Christian sect, existing in the neighbourhood of Hippo, in North Africa, in the fourth century. The members married, but abstained from conjugal intercourse, because, as they maintained, Abel had lived thus, since no children of his are mentioned. To maintain the sect, they adopted children, male and female.

A sect having the same name existed in the middle of the last century, who professed to imitate Abel in all his virtues. They had secret signs, symbols, passwords, and rites of initiation. Their principal meetings were held at Greifswald, near Stralsund, at which they amused themselves with moral and literary debating.

678. Academy of the Ancients - It was founded at Warsaw by Colonel Toux de Salverte, in imitation of a similar society, and with the same name, founded in Rome towards the beginning of the sixteenth century. The object of its secret meetings was the cultivation of the occult sciences.

679. Almusseri -This is an association similar to that of " Belly Paaro," found among the negroes of Senegambia and other parts of the African continent. The rites of initiation bear some resemblance to the Orphic and Cabiric rituals. In the heart of an extensive forest there rises a temple, access to which is forbidden to the profane. The receptions take place once a year. The candidate feigns to die. At the appointed

hour the initiated surround the aspirant and chant funereal songs; whereupon he is carried to the temple, placed on a moderately hot plate of copper, and anointed with the oil of the palm a tree which the Egyptians dedicated to the sun, as they ascribed to it three hundred and sixty-five properties. In this position he remains forty days this number, too, constantly recurs in antiquity his relations visiting him to renew the anointing, after which period he is greeted with joyful songs and conducted home. He is supposed to have received a new soul, and enjoys great consideration and authority among his tribe.

680. Anonymous Society - This society, which existed for some time in Germany, with a grand master resident in Spain, occupied itself with alchymy.

681. Anti-Masonic Party - In 1826 a journalist, William Morgan, who had been admitted to the highest masonic degrees, published at New York a book revealing all their secrets. The Freemasons carried him off in a boat, and he was never afterwards seen again. His friends accused the Masons of having assassinated him. The latter asserted that he had drowned himself in Lake Ontario, and produced a corpse, which, however, was proved to be that of one Monroe. Judiciary inquiries led to no result. Most of the officers, it is said, were themselves Masons. The indignation caused by the crime and its non-punishment led to the formation, in the State of New York, of an Anti-Masonic party, whose object was to exclude from the public service all members of the masonic fraternity. But the society soon degenerated into an electioneering engine. About fifty years after the occurrence, Thurlow Weed published, from personal knowledge, precise information as to Morgan's assassination by the Freemasons. His grave was discovered in 1881 at Pembroke, in the county of Batavia, State of New York, and in the grave also was found a paper, bearing on it the name of a Freemason called John Brown, whom, at the time, public rumour made one of the assassins of Morgan. To this latter a statue was erected at Batavia in 1882. Certain American travellers, indeed, asserted having, years after, met Morgan at Smyrna, where he taught English; but their

assertions were supported by no proofs.

682. Anti-Masons. This was a society founded in Ireland, in County Down, in 1811, and composed of Roman Catholics, whose object was the expulsion of all Freemasons, of whatever creed they might be.

683. Apocalypse, Knights of the - This secret society was formed in Italy in 1693, to defend the Church against the expected Antichrist. Augustine Gabrino, the son of a merchant of Brescia, was its founder. On Palm-Sunday, when the choir in St. Peter's was intoning the words, Quis est iste Rex Gloriae? Gabrino, carrying a sword in his hand, rushed among the choristers, exclaiming, Ego sum Rex Gloriae. He did the same in the church of San Salvatore, whereupon he was shut up in a madhouse. The society, however, continued to flourish until a woodcarver, who had been initiated, denounced it to the Inquisition, which imprisoned the knights. Most of them, though only traders and operatives, always carried a sword, even when at work, and wore on the breast a star with seven rays and an appendage, symbolising the sword seen by St. John in the Apocalypse. The society was accused of having political aims. It is a fact that the founder called himself Monarch of the Holy Trinity, which is not extraordinary in a madman, and wanted to introduce polygamy, for which he ought to be a favourite with the Mormons.

684. Areoiti - This is a society of Tahitian origin, and has members throughout that archipelago. They have their own genealogy, hierarchy, and traditions. They call themselves the descendants of the god Oro-Tetifa, and are divided into seven (some say into twelve) degrees, distinguished by the modes of tattooing allowed to them. The society forms an institution similar to that of the Egyptian priests; but laymen also may be admitted. The chiefs at once attain to the highest degrees, but the common people must obtain their initiation through many trials. Members enjoy great consideration and many privileges. They are considered as the depositaries of knowledge, and as mediators between God and man, and are feared as the ministers of the taboo, a

kind of excommunication they can pronounce, like the ancient hierophants of Greece or the court of Home. Though the ceremonies are disgusting and immoral, there is a foundation of noble ideas concealed under them; so that we may assume the present rites to be corruptions of a formerly purer ceremonial. The meaning that underlies the dogmas of the initiation is the generative power of nature. The legend of the solar god also here plays an important part, and regulates the festivals; and a funereal ceremony, reminding us of that of the mysteries of antiquity, is performed at the winter solstice. Throughout Polynesia, moreover, there exists a belief in a supreme deity, Taaroa, Tongola, or Tangaroa, of whom a cosmogonic hymn, known to the initiated, says: "He was; he was called Taaroa; he called, but no one answered; he, the only ens, transformed himself into the universe; he is the light, the germ, the foundation; he, the incorruptible; he is great, who created the universe, the great universe."

685. Avengers, or Vendicatori - A secret society formed about 1186 in Sicily, to avenge public wrongs, on the principles of the Vehm and Beati Paoli. At length Adiorolphus of Ponte Corvo, grand master of the sect, was hanged by order of King William II. the Norman, and many of the sectaries were branded with a hot iron.

686. Belly Paaro - Among the negroes of Guinea there are mysteries called "Belly Paaro," which are celebrated several times in the course of a century. The aspirant, having laid aside all clothing, and every precious metal, is led into a large wood, where the old men that preside at the initiation give him a new name, whilst he recites verses in honour of the god Belly, joins in lively dances, and receives much theological and mystical instruction. The neophyte passes five years in absolute isolation, and woe to any woman that dares to approach the sacred wood! After this novitiate the aspirant has a cabin assigned to him, and is initiated into the most secret doctrines of the sect. Issuing thence, he dresses differently from the others, his body being adorned with feathers, and his neck showing the scars of the initiatory incisions.

687. Californian Society. Several Northern Californian tribes have secret societies, which meet in a lodge set apart, or in a sweat-house, and engage in mummeries of various kinds, all to frighten their women. The men pretend to converse with the devil, and make their meeting-place shake and ring again with yells and whoops. In some instances one of their number, disguised as the master-fiend himself, issues from the lodge, and rushes like a madman through the village, doing his best to frighten contumacious women and children out of their senses. This has been the custom from time immemorial, and the women are still gulled by it.

688. Cambridge Secret Society - In 1886 a number of young men formed the "Companions of St. John" secret society, under the leadership of the Rev. Ernest John Heriz-Smith, M.A., Fellow of Pembroke College. In 1896 it was supposed to number upwards of one thousand members. The primary and avowed object was to inculcate High Church principles and confession; its real object to be a member of a secret society. They took an oath; the candidate had his hands tied, knelt at a table, had his eyes bandaged, and took a vow to obey the head of the society in all things, and never to mention anything relating to the society except to a member. If he disobeyed he was sent to his room, and tied to a table leg. They wore for some time a badge with the letters L and D (Love and Duty); afterwards they wore it concealed under their clothes, whence the members were named "Belly-banders." Whether this society still exists, or whether ridicule has killed it, we cannot say.

689. Charlotteriburg, Order of - This was one of the numerous branches grafted on the trunk of the Union of Virtue.

690. Church Masons - This is a masonic rite, founded in this country during this century, with the scarcely credible object of re-establishing the ancient masonic trade-unions.

691. Cougourde, The - An association of Liberals at the time of the

restoration of the Bourbons in France. It arose at Aix, in Provence, and thence spread to various parts of France. Its existence was ephemeral. Cougourde is French for the calabash gourd.

692. Druids, Modern. This society, the members of which pretend to be the successors of the ancient Druids, was founded in London in 1781. They adopted masonic rites, and spread to America and Australia. Their lodges are called groves; in the United States they have thirteen grand groves, and ninety-two groves, twenty-four of which are English, and the remainder German. The number of degrees are three, but there are also grand arch chapters. The transactions of the German groves are printed, but those of the English kept strictly secret. In 1872 the Order was introduced from America into Germany. The Order is simply a benefit society.

693. Duk-Duk - A secret association on the islands of New Pomerania, originally New Britain, whose hideously masked or chalk-painted members execute justice, and collect fines. In carrying out punishment they are allowed to set houses on fire or kill people. They recognise one another by secret signs, and at their festivals the presence of an uninitiated person entails his death. Similar societies exist in Western Africa (see 723).

694. Egbo Society - An association said to exist among some of the tribes inhabiting the regions of the Congo. Egbo, or Ekpe, is supposed to be a mysterious person, who lives in the jungle, from which he has to be brought, and whither he must be taken back by the initiates alone after any great state ceremonial. Egbo is the evil genius, or Satan. His worship is termed Obeeyahism, the worship of Obi, or the Devil. Ob, or Obi, is the old Egyptian name for the spirit of evil, and devil-worship is practised by many barbarous tribes, as, for instance, by the Coroados and the Tupayas, in the impenetrable forests between the rivers Prado and Doce in Brazil, the Abipones of Paraguay, the Bachapins, a Caffre tribe, the negroes on the Gold Coast, and firmly believed in by the negroes of the West Indies, they being descended

from the slaves formerly imported from Africa.

In the ju-ju houses of the Egbo society are wooden statues, to which great veneration is paid, since by their means the society practise divination. Certain festivals are held during the year, when the members wear black wooden masks with horns, which it is death for any woman to see. There are three degrees in the Egbo society; the highest is said to confer such influence that from £1000 to £1500 are paid for attaining it.

695. Fraticelli - A sect who were said to have practised the custom of self-restraint under the most trying circumstances of disciplinary carnal temptation. They were found chiefly in Lombardy; and Pope Clement V. preached a crusade against them, and had them extirpated by fire and sword, hunger and cold. But they were guilty of a much higher crime than the one for which they were ostensibly, persecuted; they had denounced the tyranny of the popes, and the abuses of priestly power and wealth, which of course deserved nothing less than extermination by fire and sword!

696. Goats, The - About the year 1770 the territory of Limburg was the theatre of strange proceedings. Churches were sacked, castles burnt down, and robberies were committed everywhere. The country people were trying to shake off the yoke feudalism had imposed on them. During the night, and in the solitude of the landes, the most daring assembled and marched forth to perpetrate these devastations. Then terror spread everywhere, and the cry was heard, "The Goats are coming!" They were thus called, because they wore masks in imitation of goats' faces over their own. On such nights the slave became the master, and abandoned himself with fierce delight to avenging the wrongs he had suffered during the day. In the morning all disappeared, returning to their daily labour, whilst the castles and mansions set on fire in the night were sending their lurid flames up to the sky. The greater the number of malcontents, the greater the number of Goats, who at last became so numerous that they would undertake simultaneous expeditions in different directions in one night. They

were said to be in league with the devil, who, in the form of a goat, was believed to transport them from one place to another. The initiation into this sect was performed in the following manner: In a small chapel situate in a dense wood, a lamp was lighted during a dark and stormy night. The candidate was introduced into the chapel by two godfathers, and had to run round the interior of the building three times on all-fours. After having plentifully drunk of a strong fermented liquor, he was put astride on a wooden goat hung on pivots. The goat was then swung round, faster and faster, so that the man, by the strong drink and the motion, soon became giddy, and sometimes almost raving mad; when at last he was taken down, he was easily induced to believe that he had been riding through space on the devil's crupper. From that moment he was sold, body and soul, to the society of Goats, which, for nearly twenty years, filled Limburg with terror. In vain the authorities arrested a number of suspected persons; in vain, in all the communes, in all the villages, gibbet and cord were in constant request. From 1772 to 1774 alone the tribunal of Foquemont had condemned four hundred Goats to be hanged or quartered. The society was not exterminated till about the year 1780.

697. Grand Army of the Republic - A secret society founded after the Civil War in the Northern States of America, to afford assistance to indigent veterans and their families. The Order is a purely military one; its chief is called the Commandant-General, the central authority the National Camp, and subordinate sections are styled Posts. In 1887 the society counted 370,000 members.

698. Green Island - A society formed at Vienna in 1855. The language used at their meetings was a parody on the knightly style as it was supposed to have been; its object was merely amusement. The society reckoned many literary men of note among its members. Whence it took its name is not clear, but it appears to have been a revival of the Order of Knights founded in 1771. See infra, under " Knights, Order of."

699. Hamgari - A secret society, dating from 1848, among Germans in North America. They pretended to be descended from an ancient German order of knighthood, and possess about two hundred lodges, with 16,000 members. The diffusion of the German language is one of their chief objects. But why surround themselves with the mist of secrecy but from a childish love for mysterymongering?

700. Hemp-smokers, African - At Kashia-Calemba, the capital of the natives of Bashilange-Baluba, in Africa (lat. 3° 6', long. 21° 24'), a sacred fire is always kept up in the central square by old people, appointed for the purpose, who also have to cultivate and prepare for smoking the chiamba (Cannabis indica); it is known in Zanzibar as Changi or Chang. It is smoked privately, and also ceremonially as a token of friendship, and is also administered to accused persons as a species of ordeal. As the symbol of friendship, it is considered as a religious rite, known as "Lubuku," practised by an organisation, of which the king is ex officio the head; a social organisation only indirectly of political importance. Its rules, signs, and working are secret; its aims and objects unknown to outsiders; its initiatory rites have never been witnessed by an uninitiated person, much less by any European. Certain external evidences of its inward nature are however sufficiently obvious to all who care to investigate the subject. Chiamba-smoking has a most disastrous effect on both the health and wealth of its devotees. A dark inference of its true nature may be drawn from the lax, and indeed promiscuous, intercourse between the sexes. Another indication of its licentiousness is afforded by the customs observed at the marriages of its male members, and repealed for three successive nights, in which all decency is outraged in the most revolting and most public way imaginable. The initiatory rites are performed generally by the king, or by Meta Sankolla, the present king's sister, on an islet in the Lulua, an affluent of the Sankoro Eiver, a short distance above Luluaburg, a European station on the top of a hill 400 feet above the river. The public smoking is begun by the chief or senior man present placing the prepared weed in the "Kinsu dhiamba," or pipe, and after smoking a little himself, passing it on to the man next to him. The pipe

consists of a small clay bowl, inserted in the larger end of a hollow gourd, the smaller end of which has a large aperture, against which the smoker places his mouth and inhales the smoke in great gulps, till his brain is affected, and he becomes for a time a raving madman.

701. Heroine of Jericho - This degree is conferred, in America, exclusively on Royal Arch Masons, their wives and widows. Its ritual is founded on the story of Rahab, in the second chapter of the Book of Joshua. The first sign is in imitation of the scarlet line which Rahab let down from the window to assist the spies to make their escape. It is made by holding a handkerchief between the lips and allowing it to hang down. The grand hailing sign of distress is given by raising the right hand and arm, holding the handkerchief between the thumb and forefinger, so that it falls perpendicularly. The word is given by the male heroine (not the candidate's husband) placing his hand on her shoulder and saying, "My Life," to which the candidate replies, "For yours." The male then says, "If ye utter not," to which the candidate answers, "This our business." The word Eahab is then whispered in the lady's ear. The latter swears never to reveal this grand secret. She is told that Eahab was the founder of the Order, but it was most probably invented by those who were concerned in the murder of William Morgan (681), who, by swearing their female relatives to conceal whatever criminal act perpetrated by Masons might come to their knowledge, hoped to protect themselves.

702. Human Leopards - A black secret society in the country near Sierra Leone, who indulge in cannibalism, buying young boys, feeding them up, and then killing, baking, and eating them. They also attack travellers, and, if possible, kill them for the same purpose. Three members of the society were hanged in the Imperi country, a British colony, on the 5th August 1895, for this crime. Dressed in leopard skins, they used to secrete themselves in the bush near a village and kill a passer-by, to be eaten at a cannibal feast. One of those three men had been a Sunday-school teacher at Sierra Leone. His conversion to Christianity had evidently not been very profound. Cannibalism is as

prevalent on the east coast of Africa as on the west, but in the former, where the natives eat father and mother and any other relations as soon as they grow old, it has a sort of sacramental meaning, the fundamental idea being that the eater imbibes the properties of the person eaten. At the meeting of the British Association in September 1896, Mr. Scott Elliott read a paper on the Human Leopards.

703. Hunters, The - In 1837, after the first Canadian insurrection, a society under the above title was formed, whose object was to bring about a second insurrection. The United States supported them. MacLeod, one of the insurgents of Upper Canada, came to St. Albans, the centre of the society's operations, and was initiated into all the degrees, which he afterwards promulgated through Upper Canada. There were four degrees the Hunter, the Racket, the Beaver, and the Eagle. This last was the title of the chief, corresponding with our rank of colonel; the Beaver was a captain, commanding six Rackets, every Racket consisting of nine men; the company of the Beaver consisted of seventy affiliates or Hunters. Every aspirant had to be introduced by three Hunters to a Beaver, and his admission was preceded by fear-inspiring trials and terrible oaths. Though the society lasted two years only, it distinguished itself by brave actions in the field; many of its members died on the scaffold.

704. Hustanawer - The natives of Virginia gave this name to the initiation they conferred on their own priests, and to the novitiate those not belonging to the priesthood had to pass through. The candidate's body was anointed with fat, and he was led before the assembly of priests, who held in their hands green twigs. Sacred dances and funereal shouts alternated. Five youths led the aspirant through a double file of men armed with canes to the foot of a certain tree, covering his person with their bodies, and receiving in his stead the blows aimed at him. In the meantime the mother prepared a funeral pyre for the simulated sacrifice, and wept her son as dead. Then the tree was cut down, and its boughs lopped off and formed into a crown for the brows of the candidate, who during a protracted retirement,

and by means of a powerful narcotic called visocean, was thrown into a state of somnambulism. Thence he issued among his tribe again and was looked upon as a new man, possessing higher powers and higher knowledge than the non-initiated.

705. Indian (North American) Societies - Nearly all the Indian tribes who once roamed over the vast plains of North America had their secret societies and sacred mysteries, but as the different tribes borrowed from one another religious ceremonies and symbols, there was great similarity between them all, though here and there characteristic signs or tokens distinguished the separate tribes. Dancing with all of them was a form of worship from the aborigines of Hispaniola to those of Alaska, as, in fact, it was with all savage nations, whether African, American, or Polynesian. The Red Indian tribes all had their medicine-huts and men, their kivas, council-rooms, or whatever name they gave to what were really their religions houses. Most tribes kept up a sacred fire, which was extinguished once a year, and then relighted. The sacred dogmas and rites of the Indians of the Gulf States bore so close a resemblance to those of the ancient Jews, that it was long seriously contended by ethnologists and historians that they were the Lost Tribes! The Cherokees, Delawares, and Chippewas kept records on sticks, six inches in length, and tied up in bundles, which were covered with devices and symbols, which were called Kepnewin when in common use, and Keknowin when connected with the mysteries of worship. The most remarkable record was that contained in the Walum-Olum, or red score; it contains the creation myth and the story of the migrations of the tribes, represented in pictorial language. Such pictographs are owned by every tribe. The Ojibwas have produced some very elaborate ones, showing the inside of the medicine-lodge filled with the presence of the Great Spirit, a candidate for admission standing therein, crowned with feathers, and holding in his hand an otter-skin pouch; the tree with the root that supplies the medicine; the goods offered as a fee for admission; an Indian walking in the sky, a drum, raven, crow, and so on. The Iroquois mysteries were elaborate, but are not well known; but it

appears they were instituted to console Manabozko for the disappearance of Chibiabos, who afterwards was made ruler of the dead the parallel in this case to Persephone is as curious as is the similarity of the instrument used in the Kurnai initiation to the Greek popBos (72). The Iroquois were originally made up of five different tribes, which afterwards were increased to seven, and their national organisation was based, not on affinity, but on an artificial and arbitrary brotherhood, having signs and countersigns resembling those of modern secret societies. The secret associations of the Dakotas were more numerous and more marked than those of the Iroquois, but some of them were mere social societies, while others were simply religious. Miss Alice Fletcher, who has lived among them, and the Rev. J. O. Dorsey, testify to the number of societies among them, but to their secrets they were not admitted. Mr. Frank Gushing was, in 1883, initiated into the secret societies of the Zunis; Dr. Washington Matthews has given us descriptions of the sacred ceremonies of the Navajos, and Captain E. G. Bourke of the snake-dance of the Moquis. Dr. Franz Boos has described the customs of the Alaskans, and shown that there are many societies among them, some of which require that a person should be born into them to be a member. In 1890 the Sioux ghost-dance attracted much attention. But what of all these Indian mysteries which in recent years have been endowed with a factitious interest and importance? They may have a special attraction for the comparative ethnologist; to the general reader they merely convey the conviction that from China to Peru, and from the Arctic to the Antarctic Pole, man is everywhere ruled by the same instincts, fears, and aspirations, which reveal themselves in the same customs, beliefs, and religious rites.

706. Invisibles, The - We know not how much or how little of truth there is in the accounts, very meagre indeed, of this society, supposed to have existed in Italy in the last century, and to have advocated, in nocturnal assemblies, atheism and suicide.

707. Jehu, Society of - This society was formed in France during the

Revolution, to avenge its excesses by still greater violence. It was first established at Lyons. It took its, name from that king who was consecrated by Elisha to I punish the sins of the house of Ahab, and to slay all the i priests of Baal; that is to say, the relations, friends, and agents of the Terrorists. Ignorant people called them the Society of Jesus, though this name scarcely suited them, since they spread terror and bloodshed throughout France. The society disappeared under the Consulate and the Empire, but reappeared in 1814-15 under the new name of "Knights of Maria Theresa," or "of the Sun," and by them Bordeaux was betrayed into the hands of the English, and the assassins of the Mayor of Toulouse at Bordeaux, of General Ramel at Toulouse, and of Marshal Brune at Avignon, were members of this society.

708. Karpokratians - A religious society founded by Karpokrates, who lived in the time of the Emperor Adrian at Alexandria. He taught that the soul must rise above the superstition of popular creeds and the laws of society, by which inferior spirits enchain man, and by contemplation unite with the Monas or highest deity. To his son Epiphanes a temple was erected after his death on the island of Cephalonia. The sect, in spite of its moral worthlessness, continued to exist to the sixth century; the members recognised each other by gently tickling the palm of the hand they shook with the points of their fingers.

709. Klobbergoll - Associations on the Micronesian Islands, living together in houses apart, and bound to accompany their chiefs on their war expeditions, and perform certain services for them. There are on these islands also female clubs, the members of which attend at festivities given to foreign guests, and render them various services.

710. Knights, the Order of - A satirical order to ridicule medieval knighthood, founded curiously enough by Frederick von Gone, a Knight of the Strict Observance, who himself believed in the descent of the Freemasons from the Knights Templars. It was instituted at Wetzlar in 1771. The members assumed knightly names; thus Gothe, who belonged to it, was Gotz von Berlichingen. They held the "Four

Children of Haimon " to be symbolical, and Gothe wrote a commentary thereon. The Order was divided into four degrees in sarcastic derision of the higher degrees of spurious masonry, called, (1) Transition, (2) Transition's Transition, (3) Transition's Transition to Transition, (4) Transition's Transition to Transition of Transition. The initiated only could fathom the deep meaning of these designations!

711. Know-Nothings - This was an anti-foreign and nopopery party, formed in 1852 in the United States of America, and acting chiefly through secret societies, in order to decide the Presidential election. In 1856 it had almost become extinct, but came to life again in 1888, having reestablished secret lodges throughout the country, but being especially strong in New York and California. It then held large meetings for the purpose of renominating for the presidential post Major Hewitt, who maintained that all immigrants ought to live in the States twenty-one years before they could vote. They were, however, defeated, General Harrison being elected.

712. Ku-KLux-Klan - A secret organisation under this name spread with amazing rapidity over the Southern States of the American Union soon after the close of the war. The white people of the South were alarmed, not so much by the threatened confiscation of their property by the Federal Government, as by the nearer and more present dangers to life and property, virtue and honour, arising from the social anarchy around them. The negroes, after the Confederate surrender, were disorderly. Many of them would not settle down to labour on any terms, but roamed about with arms in their hands and hunger in their bellies, whilst the governing power was only thinking of every device of suffrage and reconstruction by which the freedmen might be strengthened, and made, under Northern dictation, the ruling power in the country. Agitators came down among the towns and plantations; and organising a Union league, held midnight meetings with the negroes in the woods, and went about uttering sentiments which were anti-social and destructive. Crimes and outrages increased; the law was

all but powerless, and the new governments in the South, supposing them to have been most willing, were certainly unable to repress disorder. A real terror reigned for a time among the white people; and under these circumstances the Ku-Klux started into existence, and executed the Lynch-law, which alone seems effective in disordered states of society. The members wore a dress made of black calico, and called a " shroud." The stuff was sent round to private houses, with a request that it should be made into a garment; and fair fingers sewed it up, and had it ready for the secret messenger when he returned and gave his preconcerted tap at the door. The women and young girls had faith in the honour of the "Klan," and on its will and ability to protect them. The Ku-Klux, when out on their missions, also wore a high tapering hat, with a black veil over the face. The secret of the membership was kept with remarkable fidelity; and in no instance, it is said, has a member of the Ku-Klux been successfully arraigned and punished, though the Federal Government passed a special Act against the society, and two proclamations were issued under this Act by President Grant as late as October 1871, and the habeas corpus Act suspended in nine counties of South Carolina. When the members had a long ride at night, they made requisitions at farmhouses for horses, which were generally returned on a night following without injury. If a company of Federal soldiers, stationed in a small town, talked loudly as to what they would do with the Ku-Klux, the men in shrouds paraded in the evening before the guard-house in numbers so overwhelming as at once reduced the little garrison to silence. The overt acts of the Ku-Klux consisted for the most part in disarming dangerous negroes, inflicting Lynch-law on notorious offenders, and above all, in creating one feeling of terror as a counterpoise to another. The thefts by the negroes were a subject of prevailing complaint in many parts of the South. A band of men in the Ku-Klux costume one night came to the door of Allan Creich, a grocer of Williamson's Creek, seized and dragged him some distance, when they despatched and threw him into the Creek, where his body was found. The assassins then proceeded to the house of Allan's brother, but not finding him at home, they elicited from his little child where he was staying. Hereupon they immediately proceeded to the house named; and having encountered the man they sought, they dealt with him as they had dealt with his brother Allan. It appears that Allan had long been blamed for buying goods and produce stolen by the negroes, and had often been warned to desist, but without avail. The institution, like all of a similar nature, though the necessity for its existence has ceased to a great extent, yet survives in a more degenerate form, having passed into the hands of utter scoundrels, with no good motive, and with foul passions of revenge or plunder, or lust of dread and mysterious power alone in their hearts. Thus in November 1883 seven members of the society, the ringleaders being men of considerable property, were found guilty at the United States Court, Atalanta, Georgia, of having cruelly beaten and fired on some negroes for having voted in favour of an opposition candidate of the Yarborough party in the Congressional election. They were sentenced to various terms of imprisonment.

713. Kurnai Initiation - The Kurnai, an Australian tribe, performed rites of initiation into manhood, somewhat similar to those of the O-Kee-Pa (725), as did also all the Tasmanian tribes. But details are not known; the nature of the rites is only inferred from the fact that all young men examined by Europeans were found to be deeply scarified on the shoulders, thighs, and muscles of the breast. The Kurnai mysteries are chiefly referred to here because of the curious parallel they offer in the use of an instrument resembling the ρόμβος, which was one of the sacred objects in the Eleusinian mysteries (72). The Kurnai call the instrument the turndun; it is a flat piece of wood, fastened by one end to a thong, for whirling it round, and producing a roaring noise, to warn off the women. For a woman to see it, or a man to show it her, was, by native law, death to both. It is not unknown in England; we call it a whizzer or bullroarer. A similar instrument is used by the Kafirs of South Africa, where it is used for just its two principal Australian purposes, namely, for rain-making, and in connection with the rites of initiation to warn the women off. The bullroarer was also in use in New Zealand. In Australia it is known by the names of witarna and muyumkar.

714. Liberty, Knights of - A sect formed in 1820 in France against the government of the Bourbons. Its independent existence was brief, as it was soon merged in that of the Carbonari.

715. Lion, Knights of the - This was one of the transformations assumed in Germany in the last century by Masonic Templars.

716. Lion, The Sleeping - This was a society formed in Paris in 1816, with the object of restoring Napoleon to the throne of France. The existing government suppressed it.

717. Zudlam's Cave - A comic society, formed at Vienna in 1818, and so named after a somewhat unsuccessful play of Oehlenschlager. The members were called bodies; candidates, shadows. The latter underwent a farcical examination, and if found very ignorant, were accepted. Many literary men belonged to it; but though their professed object was only amusement, the society was in 1826 suppressed by the police of Vienna.

718. Mad Councillors - This comical order was founded in 1809 by a Doctor Ehrmann of Frankfort-on-the-Main. Diplomas, conceived in a ludicrous style, written in Latin, and bearing a large seal, were granted to the members. Jean Paul, Arndt, Goethe, Inland, had such diplomas; ladies also received them. On the granting of the hundredth, in 1820, the joke was dropped.

719. Magi, Order of the - Is supposed to have existed in Italy in the last century, as a modification of the Rosicrucians. Its members are said to have worn the costume of Inquisitors.

720. Mahdrdjas - This is an Indian sect of priests. It appears abundantly from the works of recognised authority written by Maharajas, and from existing popular belief in the Vallabhacharya sect, that Vallabhacharya is believed to have been an incarnation of the god

Krishna, and that the Maharajas, as descendants of Vallabhacharya, have claimed and received from their followers the like character of incarnations of that god by hereditary succession. The ceremonies of the worship paid to Krishna through these priests are all of the most licentious character. The love and subserviency due to a Supreme Being are here materialised and transferred to those who claim to be the living incarnations of the god. Hence the priests exercise an unlimited influence over their female votaries, who consider it a great honour to acquire the temporary regard of the voluptuous Maharajas, the belief in whose pretensions is allowed to interfere, almost vitally, with the domestic relations of husband and wife. The Maharaja libel case, tried in 1862 in the Supreme Court of Bombay, proved that the wealthiest and largest of the Hindoo mercantile communities of Central and Western India worshipped as a god a depraved priest, compared with whom an ancient satyr was an angel. Indeed, on becoming followers of that god, they make to his priest the offering of tan, man, and dhan, or body, mind, and property; and so far does their folly extend, that they will greedily drink the water in which he has bathed. There are about seventy or eighty of the Maharajas in different parts of India. They have a mark on the forehead, consisting of two red perpendicular lines, meeting in a semicircle at the root of the nose, and having a round spot of red between them. Though not a secret society, strictly speaking, still, as their doings were to some extent kept secret, and their worst features, though proved by legal evidence, denied by the persons implicated, I have thought it right to give it a place here.

721. Mano Negra - This association, the Black Hand, in the south of Spain, is agrarian and Socialistic, and its origin dates back to the year 1835. It was formed in consequence of the agricultural labourers having been deprived of their communal rights, the lands on which they had formerly had the privilege to cut timber and pasture their cattle having been sold, in most instances, far below their value, to the sharp village lawyers, nicknamed caciques, who resemble in their practices the gombeen men of Cork, though these latter do not possess the political influence of the former. The caciques, though they bought

the land, in many instances had not capital enough to cultivate it, hence the agricultural labourer was left to starve, a condition which led to many agrarian disturbances. The members of the society were bound by oath to punish their oppressors by steel, fire, or poison; incendiarism was rife. The association was strictly secret; to reveal its doings by treachery or imprudence meant death to the offender. The society had a complete organisation, with its chiefs, its centres, its funds, its secret tribunals, inflicting death and other penalties on their own members, and on landlords and usurers, such as the caciques. The members, to escape detection, often changed their names; they corresponded by cipher, and had a code of precautions, in which every contingency was provided against. From 1880 to 1883 the society was particularly active, especially in Andalusia, which induced the Spanish Government to take the most severe repressive measures against it. Many trials of members took place in 1883. The rising was a purely Spanish one; it was absolute hunger which drove the Spanish peasant into the hands of native agitators. Foreign anarchists endeavoured to utilise the movement, but had little influence on it.

722. Melanesian Societies - The groups of islands stretching in a semicircle from off the eastern coast of Australia to New Caledonia, including New Guinea, the Solomon Islands, the New Hebrides, New Caledonia, and also the Fiji Islands, all abound with secret societies, which, however, have nothing formidable in them, since all their secrets are known; the people join, but laugh at them; their lodges are their clubs, chiefly devoted to feasting; strangers are admitted to them as to inns; they exclude women, though on the Fiji Islands there are societies which admit them. Young men are expected to be initiated; those who are not, do not take a position of full social equality with those who are members. When the ceremonies and doctrines were as yet mysteries, outsiders thought that the initiated entered into association with the ghosts of the dead, a delusion strengthened by the strange and unearthly noises heard at times in and around the lodges, and the hideously-disguised figures, supposed to be ghosts, which appeared to the "dogs outside." Now it is known that the ghosts are merely

members, wearing strangely-decorated hats made of bark and painted, which hats cover the whole head and rest on the shoulders, while the mummers are dressed in long cloaks, made of leaves, and shaped in fantastic designs. It is also known that the noises which used to frighten the natives are produced by a flat smooth stone, on which the butt-end of a fan of palm is rubbed, the vibration of which produces the extraordinary sound. At the ceremony of initiation the usual pretence of imparting secret knowledge is gone through on a par with that imparted in some societies nearer home, and, as with the latter, it is all a question of fees, though in some societies there is also some rougher ceremony to be submitted to; thus in that called welu, the neophyte has to lie down on his face in a hole in the ground, cut exactly to his shape, and lighted cocoanut fronds are cast upon his back. He cannot move, and dare not cry; the scars remain on his back as marks of membership. The neophyte, when initiated, remains goto, that is, secluded for a number of days in some societies for one hundred days during which time he has to attend to the oven and do the dirty work of the lodge. Learning the dances, which the initiated on certain festivals perform in public, as particularly pleasing to their gods, seems to be the principal item of the instruction received in the sanctuary. The number of societies, as already stated, is very large, and they are known by various names. The New Britain Society is called Duk-Duk (693); that of Florida, Matambala; that of the Banks Islands, Tamate; that of the Northern New Hebrides, Qatu; that of Fiji, Nanga. The ghosts supposed to be present are called duka; in Florida the consultation of the ghosts is known as paluduka. The lodge is called Salagoro; it is usually situate in some retreat near the village, in the midst of lofty trees, and must not be approached by women; masked figures guard the path to it, which is marked by bright orange-coloured fruits stuck on reeds, and the customary soloi taboo marks, forbidding entrance. The members of different societies are distinguished by particular badges, consisting of leaves or flowers, and to wear such a badge without membership is a punishable offence.

723. Munibo-Jumbo - We have seen (687) that there is a Californian

society, whose object it is to keep their women in due subjection. Among the Mundingoes, a tribe above the sources of the river Gambia, a somewhat similar association exists. Whenever the men have any dispute with the women, an image, eight or nine feet high, made of the bark of trees, dressed in a long coat, -crowned with a wisp of straw, and called a Mumbo-Jumbo, or Mamma Jambah, is sent for. A member of the society conceals himself under the coat and acts as judge. Of course his decisions are almost always in favour of the men. When the women hear him coming they run away and hide themselves, but he sends for them, makes them sit down, and afterwards either sing or dance, as he pleases. Those who refuse to come are brought by force, and he whips them. Whoso is admitted into the society has to swear in the most solemn manner never to divulge the secret to any woman, nor to any one not initiated. To preserve the secret inviolable, no boys under sixteen years of age are admitted. About 1727 the King of Jagra, having a very inquisitive wife, disclosed to her the secret of his membership, and the secrets connected therewith. She, being a gossip, talked about it; the result was, that she and the king were killed by the members of the association.

Obcah, see Egbo Society.

724. Odd Fellows - This Order was founded in England about the middle of the last century. The initiatory rites then were of the usual terrifying character we have seen practised in the ancient mysteries, accompanied by all the theatrical display intended to overawe the candidate, who had to take the oath of secrecy. The Order has its signs, grips, words, and passwords; one word was Fides, which was uttered letter by letter; one sign was made by placing the right hand on the left breast, and at the same time pronouncing the words, "Upon my honour." Another sign was made by taking hold of the lower part of the left ear with the thumb and forefinger of the right hand. What the signs, grips, and passwords now are, it is impossible to tell, since these, as the only secrets of the Order, are kept strictly secret. Every half-year a new password is communicated to the lodges. In 1819 the Order was

introduced into the United States. There, are three degrees: the White, Blue, and Scarlet; there is also a female degree, called Rebecca, and High Degrees are conferred in "Camps." The Odd Fellows in the lodges wear white aprons, edged with the colours of their degree; in the camps they wear black aprons similarly trimmed. Since the American prosecutions of the Freemasons, which also affected the Odd Fellows, the oath of secrecy is no longer demanded (see 741).

725. O-Kee-Pa - A religious rite, commemorative of the Flood, which was practised by the Mandans, a now extinct tribe of Red Indians. The celebration was annual, and its object threefold, viz.: (1) to keep in remembrance the subsiding of the waters; (2) to dance the bull-dance, to insure a plentiful supply of buffaloes (though the reader will see in it an allusion to the bull of the zodiac, the vernal equinox); and (3) to test the courage and power of endurance of the young men who, during the past year, had arrived at the age of manhood, by great bodily privations and tortures. Part of the latter were inflicted in the secrecy of the " Medicinehut," outside of which stood the Big Canoe, or Mandan Ark, which only the "Mystery-Men" were allowed to touch or look into. The tortures, as witnessed by Catlin, consisted in forcing sticks of wood under the dorsal or pectoral muscles of the victim, and then suspending him by these sticks from the top of the hut, and turning him round until he fainted, when he was taken down and allowed to recover consciousness; whereupon he was driven forth among the multitude assembled without, who chased him round the village, treading on the cords attached to the bits of wood sticking in his flesh, until these latter fell out by tearing the flesh to pieces. Like the ancient mysteries, the O-Kee-Pa ended with drunken and vicious orgies. The Sioux at Rosebud Agency, in Dakota, still practise the same barbarous rites, but in a milder form.

726. Pantheists - An association, existing in the last century in this country and in Germany; Bolingbroke, Hume, and other celebrities belonged to it. Its object was the discussion of the maxims contained in Toland's "Pantheisticon." John Toland was born in Ireland about

1670, and was a Deistical writer, who anticipated, two centuries ago, the "higher criticism " of the present day in his "Christianity not Mysterious." His writings attracted much attention here and in Germany, which country he repeatedly visited. As his teaching was considered atheistical, its followers had to study it secretly. The members of the association met at the periods of the solstices and of the equinoxes, and the profane, and even the servants, were rigorously excluded from the meetings.

727. Patriotic Order Sons of America - This Order was organised in Philadelphia in 1847. It suspended operations during the Civil War, but at its conclusion it was reorganised, and now counts over 200,000 members. The aims and objects of the Order are the teaching of American principles; born Americans only are admitted. Its lodges are called camps. It is a benefit society, and, like all similar associations, has no secrets, but simply endeavours, by certain symbols and signs of recognition, to impress on their members their principles and brotherhood.

Pednosophers, see Tobaccological Society.

728. Phi-Beta-Kappa - The Bavarian Illuminati according to some accounts, spread to America. Students of universities only are admitted to the Order. The password is φιλοσοφια βιου κυβερυητης, philosophy is the guide or rule of life. The three letters forming the initials of the Greek sentence were chosen as the name of the society, whose object is to make philosophy, and not religion, the guiding principle of man's actions. The Order was introduced into the United States about the year 1776. It had its secret signs and grips, which, however, were all made public, when about the year 1830 the society ceased from being a secret one: the sign was given by placing the two forefingers of the right hand so as to cover the left corner of the mouth, and then drawing it across the chin. The grip was like the common shaking of hands, only not interlocking the thumbs, and at the same time gently pressing the wrists. The jewel or medal, always of

silver or gold, and provided at the candidate's expense, is suspended by a pink or blue ribbon. On it are the letters Ph, B, and K, six stars, and a hand. The stars denote the number of colleges where the institution exists. On the reverse is S. P. for Societas Philosophise, and the date December 5, 1776, which indicates the time of the introduction of the Order into the States.

729. Pilgrims - A society whose existence was discovered at Lyons in 1825, through the arrest of one of the brethren, a Prussian shoemaker, on whom was found the printed catechism of the society. Though the Pilgrims aimed above all at religious reform, yet their catechism was modelled on that of the Freemasons.

730. Police, Secret - Whilst revolutionaries and disaffected subjects formed secret associations for the overthrow of their rulers, the latter had recourse to counter-associations, or the Secret Police. In France it was very active in the early part of the last century, but chiefly as the pander to the debaucheries of the Court. For political purposes women of loose morals were employed by preference. Thus a famous procuress, whose boudoirs were haunted by diplomatists, a Madam Fillon, discovered and frustrated the conspiracy of Cellamare, the Spanish ambassador in 1718 at the court of the Eegent (Philippe d'Orleans, who governed France during the minority of Louis XV.), which was directed against the reigning family, in favour of the Duke of Maine. The ambassador was obliged to leave France. From the clironique scandaleuse of those times it is evident that the police were always closely connected with the ladies of easy virtue, whom they employed as their agents. Towards the end of the eighteenth century the police were secretly employed in preventing the propagation of philosophical works, called bad books. The Revolution abolished this secret police as immoral and illegal; but it was, as a political engine, re-established under the Directory, to which the expelled royal family opposed a counter-police, which, however, was discovered in the month of May 1800. Napoleon, to protect himself against the various conspiracies hatched against him, relied greatly on the secret police he

had established; but there is no doubt that the mad proceedings of Savary, Duke of Rovigo, Napoleon's last chief of police, hastened the downfall of the Empire. Under Louis Philippe again the secret police had plenty of work to do, in consequence of the many secret societies, whose machinations we have already described (597).

In Prussia also the secret police was very active from 1848 to the Franco-Prussian war, during which its chief duty was to protect the King of Prussia, his allied princes, and Bismarck against the attempts at assassination which were then so rife. How the secret police had plenty of occupation in Russia, where it was known as the "Third Division," we have seen in the account of the Nihilists. In this country a secret police has never been tolerated; it is opposed to the sentiment of the people, who always connect it with agents provocateurs.

We have seen (693) that a kind of secret police exists in New Pomerania and Western Africa.

731. Portuguese Societies - During the early part of this century various secret societies with political objects were formed in Portugal, but as they never attained to any importance or permanence, it will be sufficient to mention the names of three of them: the Septembrists, Chartists, and Miguellists, the latter founded in favour of Don Miguel, who for a time occupied the throne of Portugal.

732. Purrah, The - Between the river of Sierra Leone and Cape Monte, there exist five nations of Foulahs-Sousous, who form among themselves a kind of federative republic. Each colony has its particular magistrates and local government; but they are subject to an institution which they call Purrdh. It is an association of warriors, which from its effects is very similar to the secret tribunal formerly existing in Germany, and known by the name of the Holy Vehm (206); and on account of its rites and mysteries closely resembles the ancient initiations. Each of the five colonies has its own peculiar Purrah, consisting of twenty-five members; and from each of these particular tribunals are taken five persons, who form the Grand Purrah or supreme tribunal.

To be admitted to a district Purrah the candidate must be at least thirty years of age; to be a member of the Grand Purrah, he must be fifty years old. All his relations belonging to the Purrah become security for the candidate's conduct, and bind themselves by oath to sacrifice him, if he flinch during the ceremony, or if, after having been admitted, he betray the mysteries and tenets of the association.

In each district comprised in the institution of the Purrah there is a sacred wood whither the candidate is conducted, and where he is confined for several months in a solitary and contracted habitation, and neither speaks nor quits the dwelling assigned to him. If he attempt to penetrate into the forest which surrounds him, he is instantly slain. After several months' preparation the candidate is admitted to the trial, the last proofs of which are said to be terrible. All the elements are employed to ascertain his resolution and courage; lions and leopards, in some degree chained, are made use of; during the time of the proof the sacred woods resound with dreadful howlings; conflagrations appear in the night, seeming to indicate general destruction; while at other times fire is seen to pervade these mysterious woods in all directions. Every one whose curiosity excites him to profane these sacred parts is sacrificed without mercy.

When the candidate has undergone all the degrees of probation, he is permitted to be initiated, an oath being previously exacted from him that he will keep all the secrets, and execute without demur all the decrees of the Purrah of his tribe, or of the Grand and Sovereign Purrah.

Any member turning traitor or rebel is devoted to death, and sometimes assassinated in the midst of his family. At a moment when a guilty person least expects it, a warrior appears before him, masked and armed, who says: "The Sovereign Purrah decrees thy death." On these words every person present shrinks back, no one makes the least resistance, and the victim is killed. The common Purrah of a tribe takes cognisance of the crimes committed within its jurisdiction, tries the criminals, and executes their sentences; and also appeases the quarrels that arise among powerful families.

It is only on extraordinary occasions that the Grand Purrah

assembles for the trial of those who betray the mysteries and secrets of the Order, or rebel against its dictates; and it is this assembly which generally puts an end to the wars that sometimes break out between two or more tribes. From the moment when the Grand Purrah has assembled for the purpose of terminating a war, till it has decided on the subject, every warrior of the belligerent parties is forbidden to shed a drop of blood under pain of death. The deliberations of the Purrah generally last a month, after which the guilty tribe is condemned to be pillaged during four days. The warriors who execute the sentence are taken from the neutral cantons; and they disguise themselves with frightful masks, are armed with poniards, and carry lighted torches. They arrive at the doomed villages before break of day, kill all the inhabitants that cannot make their escape, and carry off whatever property of value they can find. The plunder is divided into two parts; one part being allotted to the tribe against which the aggression has been committed, whilst the other part goes to the Grand Purrah, which distributes it among the warriors who executed the sentence.

When the family of the tribes under the command of the Purrah becomes too powerful and excites alarm, the Grand Purrah assembles to deliberate on the subject, and almost always condemns it to sudden and unexpected pillage; which is executed by night, and always by warriors masked and disguised.

The terror and alarm which this confederation excites amongst the inhabitants of the countries where it is established, and even in the neighbouring territories, are very great. The negroes of the bay of Sierra Leone never speak of it without reserve and apprehension; for they believe that all the members of the confederation are sorcerers, and that they have communication with the devil. The Purrah has an interest in propagating these prejudices, by means of which it exercises an authority that no person dares to dispute. The number of members is supposed to be about 6000, and they recognise each other by certain words and signs.

733. Pythias, Knights of - This Order was instituted shortly after the American Civil War in 1864 at Washington, whence it soon spread

through the United States. Its professed object was the inculcation of lessons of friendship, based on the ancient story of Damon and Pythias. It calls itself a secret organisation, but in reality is only an ordinary benefit society, though it may have a secret object, since it has within itself a "uniform rank," which in its character is essentially military. The drill has been so revised as to bring it into perfect harmony with the tactics of the United States army; the judges at the competitive drills of the order are officers of the United States army. This "uniform rank" counts upwards of 30,000 members.

734. Rebeccaites - A society formed in Wales about 1843, for the abolition of toll-bars. Like the Irish White-Boys the members dressed in white, and went about at night pulling down the toll-gates. Government suppressed them. The supposed chief of the society was called Eebecca, a name derived from the rather clever application of the passage in Genesis xxiv. 60, "And they blessed Eebekah, and said unto her . . . Let thy seed possess the gate of those which hate thee."

735. Redemption, Order of - A secret and chivalrous society, which in its organisation copied the order of the Knights of Malta. Its scope is scarcely known, and it never went beyond the walls of Marseilles, where it was founded by a Sicilian exile.

736. Red Men - In 1812, during the war between England and the United States, some patriotic Americans founded a society with the above title. They took its symbolism from Indian life: the lodges were called tribes; the meeting-places, wigwams; the meetings, council fires, and so on. On festive occasions the members appeared in Indian costume. A great many Germans, settled in America, joined the society, but being looked down upon by the thoroughbred Yankees, the Germans seceded and founded an order of their own, and called it the "Independent Order of Red Men." In both societies there are three degrees the English has its Hunters, Soldiers, and Captains; the German is divided into the Blacks, Blues, and Greens. There are higher degrees conferred in "camps." The two societies count about forty thousand

members. After the cessation of the war with England (1814) the societies lost their political character, and became mere benefit societies, which they now are.

737. Regeneration, Society of Universal - It was composed of the patriots of various countries who had taken refuge in Switzerland between 1815 and 1820. But though their aims were very comprehensive, they ended in talk, of which professed patriots always have a liberal supply on hand.

738. Saltpetrers - The county of Hauenstein, in the Duchy of Baden, forms a triangle, the base of which is the Rhine from Sackingen to Waldshut. In the last century the abbot of the rich monastery of St. Blasius, which may be said to form the apex of the triangle, exacted bond-service against the Hauensteiners. This they resented; a secret league was the result. From its leader, Fridolin Albiez, a dealer in saltpetre, it took the name of Saltpetrers. The abbot, supported by Austria in 1755, finally compelled them to submit, though the sect was revived at the beginning of this century to oppose reformatory tendencies in church and school. Mutual concessions in 1840 put an end to the strife and to the society. In Tirol the Manharters, so called after their leader, Manhart, had the same object in view resistance to Reformation principles and were successful in attaining them, they being warmly supported by the Pope.

739. Sikh Fanatics - The Sikhs - Sikh means a disciple, or devoted follower first came into notice in 1510 as a religious sect. Their prophet was Nanuk. Two centuries afterwards Guru Govindu developed a more military spirit; he added the sword to their holy book, the "Granth." From 1798 to 1839 the Sikhs were at the zenith of their power. Their distinguishing marks were a blue dress, because Bala Ram, the brother of Krishna, is always represented as wearing a blue dress, with long hair and beard; every man had to carry steel on his person in some form. The ordinary Sikh now dresses in pure white. All the sect were bound in a holy brotherhood called the Khalsa (meaning

the saved or liberated), wherein all social distinctions were abolished.

The fierce fanatical Akalis were soldier-priests, a sombre brotherhood of military devotees, chiefly employed about their great temple at Amritsar (meaning the fountain of immortality). They initiate converts, which is done by ordering the neophyte to wear blue clothes, by being presented with five weapons a sword, a firelock, a bow and arrow, and a pike. He is further enjoined to abstain from intercourse with certain schismatic sects, and to practise certain virtues. As, according to tradition, Govindu, when at the point of death, exclaimed, "Wherever five Sikhs are assembled, there I shall be present," five Sikhs are necessary to perform the rite of initiation. The Sikhs may eat flesh, except that of the cow, which is a sacred animal to them as well as to the Hindus.

The phase of Sikh fanaticism which revealed its existence in 1872 by the Kooka murders may be traced to the following sources: The movement was started a good many years since by one Earn Singh, a Sikh, whose headquarters were fixed at the village of Bainee, in the Loodhiana district. His teaching is said to have aimed at reforming the ritual rather than the creed of his countrymen. His followers, moreover, seem to have borrowed a hint or two from the dancing dervishes of Islam. At their meetings they worked themselves into a sort of religious frenzy, which relieved itself by unearthly howlings; and hence they were generally known as the "Shouters." Men and women of the new sect joined together in a sort of wild war-dance, yelling out certain forms of words, and stripping off all their clothing, as they whirled more and more rapidly round. Ram Singh himself had served in the old Sikh army, and one of his first moves was to get a number of his emissaries enlisted into the army of the Maharajah of Cashmere. That ruler, it is said, would have taken a whole regiment of Kookas into his pay; but for some reason or another this scheme fell to the ground. Possibly he took fright at the political influence which his new recruits might come in time to wield against him or his English allies. Ram Singh's followers, however, multiplied apace; and out of their number he chose his lieutenants, whose preaching in time swelled the total of converts to something like 100,000. Of these soubahs, or lieutenants, some twenty were distributed about the Punjab. The great bulk of their converts consisted of artisans and people of yet lower caste, who, having nothing to lose, indulged in wild dreams of future gain. Their leader's power over them appears to have been very great. They obeyed his orders as cheerfully as the Assassins of yore obeyed the Old Man of the Mountain. If he had a message to send to one of his lieutenants, however far away, a letter was entrusted to one of his disciples, who ran full speed to the next station, and handed it to another, who forthwith left his own work, and hastened in like manner to deliver the letter to a third. In order to clinch his power over his followers, Ram Singh contrived to interpolate his own name in a passage of the "Granth" the Sikh Bible which foretells the advent of another Guru, prophet or teacher. But, whatever the teachings of this new religious leader, there is reason to think that his ultimate aim was to restore the Sikhs to their old supremacy in the Punjab by means of a religious revival; and he stirred up the religious fervour of his followers by impressing on them that their war was a war against the slayer of the sacred cow, which to their European conquerors of course is not sacred, and has ceased to be so to many natives of India. But the insurrection was quickly suppressed. The whole band, which never numbered three hundred, was literally hunted down, and the ringleaders blown from guns. This may appear severe punishment; but it is to be borne in mind that though the number of insurgents who were taken with arms in their hands was only small, they had behind them a body of nearly 100,000 followers, bound together by one common fanaticism, who had to be taught by very prompt and severe action that our power in India is not to be assailed with impunity.

The Sikhs are divided into numerous sects, the most important being the Govind Sinhi community, comprehending the political association of the Sikh nation generally. The Sikh sect, as a religious and secret one, is rapidly diminishing.

740. Silver Circle, Knights of the - A secret organisation formed in the Rocky Mountains in 1893 against the suspension of silver coinage. The Knights threatened, in case the Sherman Law should be repealed, to

compel Colorado to leave the American Union and unite with the republic of Mexico, which is a silver coinage country. The western states were at that time honeycombed with secret societies deliberating the question of secession. Many of these societies were armed organisations, and were, it is said, in the habit of holding moonlight meetings for purposes of drill. The members had secret signs and passwords to recognise one another in public. But the repeal of the Sherman Act in August 1893 crushed their hopes, and caused the collapse of the society.

741. Sonderbare Gesellen - German societies, formed on the model of the English Odd Fellows, whose name they took, and of which the above is a literal translation. They now call themselves Freie Gesellen (Free Brethren), or Helfende Brüder (Helping Brethren). But, unlike their English prototypes, who have no other secrets than their signs, grips, and passwords, the German Gesellen are closely connected with Freemasonry, which, as we have seen, is not so colourless abroad as it is here, and they proclaim themselves an institution for the deliverance of nations from priests, superstition, and fanaticism. The Order was introduced into Germany in 1870, and gradually into Switzerland, France, Holland, Mexico, Peru, Chili, Sweden, Spain, and even some Polynesian islands, so that now it counts upwards of fifty grand lodges and nearly eight thousand lodges, exclusive of English ones (724).

742. Sopkisiens. "The Sacred Order of the Sophisiens," or Followers of Wisdom, was founded by some French generals engaged in the expedition to Egypt (1798-99), and was to a certain extent secret. But some of its pursuits oozed out, and were to be found in a book, partly in MS. and partly printed, the title of which is "Melanges relatifs a L'ordre sacre des Sophisiens, etabli dans les Pyramides de la Republique frangaise," in 4to. (See No. 494 in the catalogue of Lerouge.) Where is the book now?

743. Star of Bethlehem - This Order claims a very ancient origin, having, it is alleged, been founded during the first century of the

Christian era. In the thirteenth century it was an order of monks called Bethlehemites, closely identified with the Church of the Nativity built by the Empress Helena in the year 330, in the centre of which is the grotto of the Nativity, where a star is inlaid in the marble floor in commemoration of the star which shone over Bethlehem. The Order was introduced into England in 1257, and soon became a benevolent order, and members were called Knights of the Star of Bethlehem. Women were admitted to membership in 1408. In 1681 it was introduced into America by Giles Cory, of ye City of London, but fanaticism soon drove it out of that continent, for in September 1694 the grand commander was cruelly put to death "for holding meetings in ye dead hours of ye night." It was reintroduced into New York in 1869 by A. Gross of Newcastle-on-Tyne. In 1884 the members dropped the title of Knights, and the original name of Order of the Star of Bethlehem was reassumed.

744. Thirteen, The - To Balzac's fertile imagination we are indebted for the book entitled Les Treize, the fictitious story of a society of thirteen persons who during the First Empire bound themselves by fearful oaths, arid for objects the author dare no more reveal than the names of the members, mutually to support one another. The work consists of three tales, the first being the most interesting for us, since it pretends to record the stormy career of Ferragus, one of the associates, and chief of the Devorants spoken of in the French Workmen's Unions (369). A society of thirteen (not secret) has recently been founded in London, in imitation, I assume, of a society formed in 1857 at Bordeaux for the same purpose as the London one, namely, by force of example to extirpate the superstition regarding the number thirteen, of which very few persons know the origin. In the ancient Indian pack of cards, consisting of seventy-eight cards, of which the first twenty-two have special names, the designation of card XIII. is " Death," and hence all the evil influences ascribed to that number !

745. Tobaccological Society - When in 531 Theodora from a ballet

girl had become the wife of the Emperor Justinian I., she wished to be surrounded by philosophers, especially the expounders of Pythagoras. But for once the philosophers stood on their dignity, and declined imperial patronage. This led to their persecution, and the closing of their schools and academies; they were not allowed to hold meetings. But Pythagoreans must meet, hence they met in secret, first in a ruined temple of Ceres on the banks of the Ilissus, and afterwards in an octagonal temple, built by one of them, at the foot of Mount Hymettus. They called themselves Pednosophers, which in a philologically incorrect manner they interpreted as meaning "Children of Wisdom." For their symbol they adopted the anemone, which flower was said to have sprung from the blood of Adonis, wounded by a wild boar so philosophy arose afresh from philosophy persecuted by superstition. At first women and children were admitted, but they were told part only of the secret, whatever it was. The sign was crossing the arms on the breast, so that the index finger touched the lips. The sacred word was theus-theos, "Hope in God." The chief of the Order was known to but a few members by his real name; to the rest he passed under a pseudonym. There were different degrees in the Order, which perpetuated itself until 1672 in various countries, England included. In this year Charles II. prohibited all secret societies, and the Pednosophers changed their name to Tobaccologers, and adopted the tobacco plant as their emblem, its red flower suggesting to them philosophy persecuted by Justinian and others. At their meetings they discussed chiefly academical subjects; in fact, modern academies owe to them their origin. Many men of note belonged to the Order, which was divided into four degrees the glamour of secrecy must be kept up to the last! The members in the lodge wore a triangular apron. Towards the end of the last century the Order declined in this country, and its papers, its records, and mysteries eventually fell into the hands of the French Marquis d'Etanduere, who left them to his son, at whose death they were examined by a M. Doussin, to whom he had left them; and this M. Doussin thereupon reconstituted the society at Poitiers in 1806, where it continued till about the year 1848. The tobacco plant, its culture and manufacture, were the subjects of symbolical instructions, and for the real names of the towns where lodges existed, the names of localities famous for fine sorts of tobacco were substituted. Persons known to belong to the society popularly went by the designation of snufftakers.

746. Turf, Society of the - When the failure of the Carbonaro conspiracy, and especially its non-success in its attempt on Macerata (562), led to the temporary suppression of the Carbanaro society, the youths of Italy, who had hoped to distinguish themselves by fighting and driving the Austrian out of Italy, felt sorely disappointed. The more rational ones submitted to the inevitable, and returned to peaceful occupations. But the more hot-headed and restless members of the society sought outlets for their exuberant spirits in forming associations of various kinds, and sometimes of the most objectionable character. Such a one was the Compagnia delta Teppa, or Turf Society, which arose at Milan in 1818. [26]

Two derivations of the name of the society are given.

The members of the society wore plush hats, and it was a regulation that this plush was to be cut as short and as smooth as turf. The other, and more probable, origin of the name is the fact that the members held their meetings at first on the lawns of beautiful turf in the Piazza CastelLo at Milan. Their pursuits may be described as a revival of Mohocking; they bound themselves to beat every man they met in the streets after dark, which practice, however, was chiefly resorted to against men having handsome wives, whom members of the society wished forcibly, or with consent, to disgust with their husbands or abduct from their homes; and a certain amount of ridicule attaching to the infliction of such a beating, the victims in most cases made no public complaint. Of course, in many cases it was the Turfists who got

---

[26] The account which follows is taken chiefly from the Cento Anni of Rovani, who relied, in his turn, on the statement of one Milesi, a member of the Turf Society. There is also a report of the police, which finally suppressed the society, but this report is inaccessible to the public. In the Ambrosinian Library at Milan there is a MS. in several volumes, written by Prebendary Mantovani, giving the history of the Teppa, but this information reached the author too late to be utilised here. As, however, Milesi refers to that MS., he probably incorporated in his own account its most important details, so that we may safely conclude that in Rovani's work we have all that is known about the Teppa.

the worst of the encounter. The Austrian police shut its eyes to all these proceedings, of which, through its spies, it was fully cognisant, on the principle that it was better these young men should vent their overflow of spirits, their physical and mental energies, on such follies, and even on criminal exploits, than employ them in political schemes and pursuits, which would be certain to be directed against Austrian rule and rulers. The society might have subsisted longer than it did had it not grown foolhardy by long impunity. What at last compelled the police to interfere was as follows:

There lived in the Via Pennacchiari a dwarf known by the nickname of Gasgiott, who earned his living by artificial flower making. He was of a violent and quarrelsome temper, but thought himself a great favourite with the women; none of them, he fancied, could withstand him. One night, as some members of the Teppa happened to be in the Via Pennacchiari, a girl complained to one of them, Milesi (the author of the MS. consulted by Rovani?), a man of athletic proportions, that Gasgiott had grossly insulted her. Milesi bestowed on the dwarf a sound thrashing, and carrying him to an inn, where Baron Bontempo, the chief of the Teppa, was waiting for him, suggested shutting up the dwarf, with scanty food, for some time in the country to "cool his blood," which was done. But one idea suggests another: the capture of one dwarf led to a regular hunt after the species, and in a short time about a dozen of them were shut up in a mansion belonging to Baron Bontempo, called Simonetta, and situate outside the walls of Milan. Then another thought suggested itself to the members of the Teppa.

Among the fine pretences with which they sought to justify their questionable proceedings was the allegation that it was their duty to redress wrongs of which the law took no cognisance. Now, they argued, there are every year hundreds of men, young men, just entering life, and married men with families, ruined through the wiles and the extravagance of designing women, whom the law cannot touch for the injuries they have inflicted on their victims. Many women, notorious for such conduct, some of them ladies of position, and connected with aristocratic families, were then living at Milan. It struck the Turfists they would be suitable companions for the imprisoned dwarfs. The idea was carried out. About ten ladies were by treachery or force brought to Simonetta, and there shut up with the dwarfs. The orgy that ensued, says Eovani, could only be described by the pen of an Aretino. But it is easy to understand that a number of ladies, so entrapped, would not quietly submit to such abduction or the advances of the dwarfs. The authors of the mischief were only too glad to release them on the very next day, and the dwarfs also. As all the prisoners had been brought to the mansion by roundabout ways, and in close carriages, and were taken away in the same manner, they had no clue to the position of their prison; but a scheme like this could not be carried out without a good many persons being let into the secret; the ladies who had been carried off cried aloud for vengeance, and many young men, belonging to respectable families, who had joined the society from curiosity, or, as they fancied, to increase their own importance, seeing the dangerous practices in which they had involved themselves, were ready to give information. The police could no longer shut its eyes and pretend ignorance, and so one morning, in the year 1821, more than sixty members of the society were arrested, and, for want of more suitable accommodation, at first imprisoned in the convent of St. Mark, whence some were sent to Szegedin and Komorn, or drafted into the army. Many others were arrested afterwards; some of the members made their escape, having been warned beforehand. Thus the society collapsed, between three and four years after its foundation.

The members recognised one another by the one saluting the other with both hands joined, whereupon the other put his right hand to his side, as if going to place it on the hilt of his sword. There were only two degrees, that of captain and that of simple brother; the former was bound to initiate four new members. General meetings were always held in the same place, special ones in different localities, which were constantly changed. The society was, moreover, divided into two grand centres, the centre of Nobles and that of Commoners.

747. Utopia - A society founded at Prague in the fifties, and which had

such success that in 1885 it reckoned eightyfive lodges in Germany, Austria, Hungary, Switzerland, and other countries. A council of the league was held at Leipzig in 1876, and another at Prague in 1883. The president of every lodge is called Uhu (screech-owl); at manifestations of joy they cry "Aha! " and at transgressions against the laws of Utopia, "Oho! " The members are divided into three degrees: Squires, Younkers, and Knights; guests are called Pilgrims. The German name of the society is Allschlaraffia; Schlaraffenland in German means the "land of milk and honey," the land of Cocagne, where roast-pigeons fly into your mouth when you open it, and roasted pigs run about the streets with knife and fork in their backs. From the name, the character of the society may be inferred.

748. Waliabees - This sect, the members of which attracted considerable attention in 1871, on account of their suspected connection with the murders of Chief-Justice Norman at Calcutta, and of Lord Mayo in 1872, has the following origin: About 1740 a Mohammedan reformer appeared at Nejd. named Abdu'l Wahab, and conquered great part of Arabia from the Turks. He died in 1787, having founded a sect known as the Wahabees. The word Wahab signifies a Bestower of Blessings, and is one of the epithets of God, and Abdul Wahab means the servant of the All Bountiful. The Wahabees took Mecca and Medina, and almost expelled the Turk from the land of the Prophet. But in 1818 the power of these fierce reformers their doctrine being a kind of Islam Socinianism, allowing no title to adoration to Mohammed waned in Arabia, to reappear in India under a new leader, one Saiyid Ahmad, who had been a godless trooper in the plundering bands of Amir Khan, the first Nawab of Tonk. But in 1816 he went to Delhi to study law, and his fervid imagination drank in greedily the new subject. He became absorbed in meditation, which degenerated into epileptic trances, in which he saw visions. In three years he left Delhi as a new prophet, and journeying to Patna and Calcutta, was surrounded by admiring crowds, who hung upon his accents, and received with ecstasy the divine lesson to slay the infidel, and drive the armies of the foreigner from India. In 1823 he passed

through Bombay to Eohilkhand, and having there raised an army of the faithful, he crossed the land of the Five Rivers, and settled like a thundercloud on the mountains to the northeast of Peshawur. Since then the rebel camp thus founded has been fed from the head centre at Patna with bands of fanatics, and money raised by taxing the faithful. To account for such success, the reader will have to bear in mind that in Mohammedan countries a doctor of civil law, such as Saiyid Ahmad was, may hold the issues of peace or war in his hands, for with Mohammedans the law and the gospel go together, and the Koran represents both. Akbar, the greatest Mohammedan monarch, was nearly hurled from the height of his power by a decision of the Jaunpur lawyers, declaring that rebellion against him was lawful. And the Wahabee doctrine is, that war must be made on all who are not of their faith, and especially against the British Government, as the great oppressor of the Mohammedan world. Twenty sanguinary campaigns against this rebel host, aided by the surrounding Afghan tribes, have failed to dislodge them; and they remain to encourage any invader of India, any enemy of the English, to whom they would undoubtedly afford immense assistance. Though the general impression in England and India seems to be that the murder of Mr. Norman is not to be attributed to a Wahabee plot, yet so little is known of the constitution, numerical strength, and aims of the secret societies of India, that an overweening confidence in the loyalty of the alien masses as the Times curiously enough terms them on the part of the English residents in India, is greatly to be condemned, for there still exists an active propaganda of fanatic Wahabees at great Mussulman centres; and though the vast Mussulman community throughout India look on the fanatics with dislike or indifference, yet they need careful lookingafter by Government ("Cyclopaedia of India," by Surgeon General Edward Balfour. Three vols. London, 1885).

A few lines higher up we referred to secret societies of India; from among these we may specially mention the Mina robber settlement at Shahjahanpur, which town formed part of the possessions of the Rohilla Patans, whose dominion was overthrown by the British in 1774. The Minas are the descendants of Rohilla chiefs, and the district they occupy being the centre of a small tract of land, entirely surrounded by independent native states, affords them refuge and ready means of escape when pressed by the British police. And they are doubtless fostered and protected by the minor chiefs and head-men of native states, who share the spoil. They are supposed to form a corporation somewhat similar to the Garduna (306-311). It has been suggested that the Minas, possessing a splendid physique and animal courage, the very qualities needed for such a purpose, should be utilised in frontier and border forces, as the Mazbis, a similar marauding tribe, were utilised and reclaimed.

www.ingramcontent.com/pod-product-compliance
Lightning Source LLC
Chambersburg PA
CBHW072018240426
43667CB00043B/1461